A HISTORY OF JAPAN
VOLUME III / PART 2

A HISTORY OF JAPAN

VOLUME III

The Tokugawa Epoch
1652-1868

PART 2

JAMES MURDOCH

Revised and Edited by
JOSEPH H. LONGFORD

Foreword and Selected Bibliography by
JOHN L. MISH
Chief, Oriental Division, New York Public Library

FREDERICK UNGAR PUBLISHING CO.
NEW YORK

Printed in the United States of America

Library of Congress Catalog Card No. 64-15695

CONTENTS

PART 2

APPENDICES

A HISTORY OF JAPAN
VOLUME III / PART 2

CHAPTER X

IYESHIGE AND IYEHARU (1744–86)

TO Yoshimune,[1] the eighth Tokugawa Shōgun, must be accorded the distinction of having demonstrated the real capacity of paternal government when it is at its best. When, however, everything depends upon the personal character and abilities of the head of the national household, the principle of primogeniture is attended with the gravest of risks as was now to be shown in the most conclusive manner. In Iyeshige, the ninth Shogun, it appears to be impossible to recognize one single moral feature of his illustrious sire. The contrast between Yoshimune and Iyeshige was even greater than that between Yorimoto and Yoriiye, for the roystering Yoriiye's vices were those of a robust man, and he had, at least, the traditional Minamoto aptitude for manly martial exercises. What Iyeshige really was may be gathered from Titsingh's account of him, an account whose general correctness is only too substantially corroborated by all the contemporary Japanese evidence.

Three Branch Families ", each of the three being vested on their foundation with a revenue of 100,000 *koku*. All this was in imitation of what had been done by Iyeyasu when he created the *Go san-ke*. " The Three Houses " of Kii, Mito, and Owari, the heads of the powerful and wealthy fiefs of those names, conferred by Iyeyasu on his three younger sons, from whose families an heir to the Shōgunate was to be selected in case of failure of the direct line. The *Sankyō* were a second reserve for Tokugawa heirs in case of failure of both direct and Sanke lines. Mito took his title from his castled town in the province of Hitachi ; the other two from the provinces in which were their castled towns of Wakayama (Kii) and Nagoya (Owari). All three took precedence of all other Daimyōs of every degree, and of course had very large revenues. Iyeyasu's direct line came to an end with Iyetsugu, the seventh Shōgun, who died childless, and the next seven Shōguns, from Yoshimune downwards, were all members of the House of Kii. The fifteenth and last Shōgun, Yoshinobu (1866–8), was of the House of Mito, his immediate predecessor having also died childless at an early age. Both the *Go san-ke* and the *Go Sankyō* are to be distinguished from the *Go Sekke*, " The Five Regent Families " of the Imperial Court, Konoe, Kujō, Nijō, Ichijo, and Takatsukasa, from among whom the " Kuambaku " or Regent during the minority of an Emperor was always chosen. They were all of Fujiwara descent and the highest nobles in the Empire. The three *Sankyō* and the five *Sekke* are repeatedly mentioned throughout history and all these families enjoy high rank in the modern peerage.

[1] Titsingh gives the following description of his last illness and death :—

" In the month of June, 1751, he had for the second time a paralytic seizure, and so rapid was its progress that, in the following month, prayers were ordered to be put up in all the great temples for his recovery and the physicians were specially charged to neglect no means for restoring him to health ; but all their efforts were fruitless, and he expired on the 20th of the same month (12th July, 1751) to the great regret of the whole Empire. The mourning was general. Women and children, the high and the low wept for him as for a father."—J. H. L.

" On the death of Yoshimune in 1751, Iyeshige became sole master of the Empire, and governed without control. An inordinate passion for women and strong liquors had already impaired his health. In his youth, and while still heir-apparent, he had indulged these propensities to such an extent that his father severely reprimanded him on the subject ; and with a view to divert him from his bad inclinations he had frequently made him pass six or seven days together at the country house of Suga-no-goten, where he had no other amusement than hawking. After the death of his father, being released from the only curb that restrained him, he again plunged into the same excess, and spent whole nights, either with women or in drinking *saké*, so that his health declined from day to day. His speech became affected, he could no longer make himself understood but by signs, and he was obliged to issue his orders through Idzumo-no-Kami. He was soon obliged to keep his apartments on account of a weakness of the urinary organs. On stated occasions the Shōgun is obliged to go to the Temples of Uyeno, Zōzōji and Momiji-yama to offer up his prayers before the tablets consecrated to his predecessors. It was not without difficulty that Iyeshige was able to perform this duty . . . In 1755, returning from the Temple of Uyeno in his palanquin, he had scarcely reached the gin-seng warehouse which is close to it when he felt a natural call, which he could not defer till his arrival at the palace, and which compelled him to order his people to take him back to the Temple, a circumstance heretofore unexampled. The architects were immediately commanded to erect three resting-places for the Prince on each of the two roads to the Temples of Uyeno and Zōzōji ; but this precaution was useless, as the increasing infirmities of the Shōgun confined him ever afterwards to the palace."

On the very face of it, it will be plain that Yoshimune could not possibly have found a more incompetent successor than this *fainéant* sensualist, Iyeshige. " A cypher ! A mere figure-head ! " the reader may be tempted to exclaim, but this would be to misconceive the true bearings of the situation very seriously indeed. The Shōgunate as an institution was now vastly different from what it had been five centuries before in the Kamakura epoch. Then, in truth, the office of Shōgun was ornamental, and its successive occupants, high-born Fujiwaras or Imperial Princes, could be, and were, treated as so many bedizened puppets ; at any time their nominal subordinates, the Hōjō Regents, could afford to seize their persons, and pack them off to Kyōto, like so many bales of damaged merchandise, without the slightest compunction and with the utmost impunity. So far, under the Tokugawas, no subordinate had been able to enact the role of a Hōjō Regent. Apart from Iyetsugu, who died in his infancy (1716), Iyetsuna (1651–80) was the only one of the Tokugawa Shōgun who had not in the last resort ruled the empire in reality as well as in name. During the last decade of his sway, the Tairō Sakai became all-powerful but, on the death of Iyetsuna, the aspiring Tairō met with such short shrift from Iyetsuna's successor, Tsunayoshi, that the lesson was not likely to be forgotten nor Sakai's ambitious attempt imitated. Tsunayoshi's will was really law in the empire when he chose to exert it, as in the case, to take one illustration, of his insensate " Life-Protecting Statutes " which continued to be enforced for more than a score of years. His immediate successor, Iyenobu, was a man of no great originality, it is true, but it was he and not Arai or the Rōjū who governed Japan from 1709 to 1716, and during the twenty-nine succeeding years, between 1716 and 1745, Yoshimune was not merely the master of Japan, but the first servant of the State.

The result of this was that the Shōgun's great office was regarded with profound respect mingled with awe ; the prestige of the Shōgunate as the great operative institution of the age never stood higher than it did during the first six years of Iyeshige's administration while Yoshimune still survived. Even when Yoshimune had passed away (1751) no high official would dream of taking a step of any consequence without the Shōgun's assent. Every one knew that a word, nay, a stutter, from the stammering Iyeshige would be sufficient to strip him of office, rank, revenue, and domains, while a mere hint to commit the " Happy Dispatch " could not be gainsaid, if it chanced to be dropped. For presuming to tender a memorial of advice, Iyeshige's own brother was ordered to confine himself to his own mansion. Yoshimune's most trusted Councillor, Matsudaira Norimura, after the Shōgun himself the ablest statesman of the time, had once suggested to Yoshimune the advisability of disinheriting Iyeshige. This fact, perhaps reached the new Shōgun's ear, but, apart from it His Highness bore Norimura a special grudge for having induced Yoshimune to relegate him to the Suga villa when his excesses had gone too far. At all events, one of the first things Iyeshige did was to dismiss this great statesman and, within a year from his accession, all his father's Great Councillors, with the exception of Hotta, Sagami no Kami, had met with the same fate. Hotta was a man of ability, it must be admitted ; as Commandant of Ōsaka he earned a great reputation as a judge and administrator, and as regards mere intellectual ability, his contemporaries classed him with Matsudaira Norimura and Ōoka Tadasuke, but the course of events was soon to prove that he was of inferior moral fibre. He had shown himself very eager to stand well with the heir apparent ; perhaps he divined that Matsudaira Norimura's career would be a brief one under the new Shōgun, and that he could then aspire to a chief place in the Great Council. Immediately after the death of Yoshimune, Hotta discharged all the old Shōgun's personal attendants :—

" To prevent a tumult he gave to those who have been in the service twenty years 50 *kobans* (£70), and thirty to such as had served ten years, that, as he said, they might be enabled to support their wives and families. The old Shōgun had given them a place to live in, but Hotta turned them out, and each was obliged to hire a small apartment. They consulted together as to what should be done, and drew up a petition which they presented to the High Priest of Uyeno, begging to be employed by the reigning Shōgun, as they had been by his father. The High Priest promised to lay it before the councillors of state, which he did, without effect. Among these poor creatures was a man named Nakashima Shimbei, who went every day for three years to entreat the Priest to procure his reappointment, but his efforts proved unsuccessful owing to the malice of Hotta. Hotta's cruelty to so many servants of the old Shōgun whom he turned without cause out of their places, rendered him an object of public hatred."

Hotta was quite well aware that the new Shōgun had no liking for any of his father's friends or favourites and it was by time-serving devices like the foregoing that he continued to maintain his position in the Rōjū down to his death in 1761. Besides Hotta, the only man of ability in the Great Council was Matsudaira Takemoto, Ukon Shōgen.[1] In 1747, he had been promoted to the Rōjū at the instance of Yoshimune, although " every one exclaimed against the danger of conferring such important functions on a person of his years ". He did not fail, however, to justify the old Shōgun's belief in him. He possessed energy equal to his intelligence. His extreme indulgence to his inferiors won their affection, and gained him universally the character of an excellent master. The old Shōgun, before he died, whispered in his ear, so as not to be heard by any other person, that he was to direct alone all the affairs of the State. Under a Shōgun like Yoshimune, Matsudaira Takemoto would have had a great and beneficent career of public usefulness. Under a later Kamakura Shōgun, or under a Shōgun like Iyetsuna, he might also have accomplished a great deal, but as has just been insisted upon, Iyeshige, though grossly incompetent, could not be regarded as a cypher or treated as a puppet. To do anything

---

[1] " Ukon Shōgen," officer of the Bodyguard of the Right, i.e. the second company of the Household Guards.—J. H. L.

of consequence without his sanction would rouse his wrath, and to
incur his ill-will meant dismissal from office, if not absolute ruin.
Now, Iyeshige was often so ill, so drunk, or so befuddled that he
could not meet his Councillors at all. When he did meet them
subsequently, they were in mortal terror for frequently they could
not make out what he said, or rather what he was trying to say.
Almost everything had to be interpreted by one of his personal
attendants, who could understand his language of grunts and
stutters and signs. Titsingh seems to have been correctly informed
about this peculiar situation when he says :—

"Ōoka, Idzumo no Kami, one of the bodyguard of the young
Shōgun, Iyeshige, rose from day to day higher in his favour. The
Councillors of State, both ordinary and extraordinary, applied to him
to submit their petitions to the Shōgun, and the placemen, from the
highest to the lowest, paid court to him. Whoever was desirous of
obtaining an employment, or being removed to a better one, had
recourse to him and offered him presents. Matsudaira Takemoto was
the only one who was above calling on him ; nay, he did not send him
the tail of a fish. ' He is but one of the bodyguard,' said he, ' while we
are officers of distinction ; let others do as they think proper ; I, for
my part am resolved not to degrade myself.' Thus there was always
some coolness between them ; Matsudaira gave himself no concern
on that account, but continued to perform the duties of his post with
zeal and intelligence."

The Ōoka Tadamitsu, Idzumo no Kami, here alluded to, came
of the same stock as the famous City Magistrate but he belonged
to a cadet branch of the family. In his youth, he had been attached
to the person of the heir apparent, and in this difficult position he
succeeded in winning the goodwill of Iyeshige and the confidence
of Yoshimune alike, while he was also extremely popular with all
with whom he came in contact. Indulgent and ever ready to excuse
the faults of others, he followed in all points the example of Yoshimune's most trusted Sobayōnin, Kannō, Ogasawara, and Shibuya.
It was not till the death of the old Shōgun that his real character
became apparent. In the very year of Yoshimune's death he was
made a Daimyō ; in 1754, he entered the Junior Council, and two
years later he was formally appointed Sobayōnin. During the nine
years of Iyeshige's own personal rule (1751–60) Ōoka was the most
powerful figure at the Shōgun's court, and at the date of his death
in 1760, he was one of the wealthiest men in Japan. The fortune
he amassed was not a very cleanly earned one, in fact it was mainly
the results of " presents ", or in plain language, bribery and

corruption.   In the art of dissimulation both Ōoka Tadamitsu and
Hotta must have been tolerably proficient, for Yoshimune was a
wonderfully keen judge of character.   Present-giving has always
been not merely a recognized but an indispensable feature in
Japanese social intercourse, and to the unsophisticated, outside
barbarian, its etiquette is often a very puzzling matter.   It has
been said with reason that in no country of the world do " *les petits
cadeaux qui entretiennent l'amitié* " play a more charming part
than in Japan.   On the other hand, the Japanese, no less than the
Greeks of old, are often most to be dreaded when " bearing gifts ".
To draw the exact line between genuine tokens of disinterested
goodwill and attempts at bribery and corruption is now and then
a truly difficult business.   Iyenobu found it advisable to repress
lavish present-giving, and in this he was followed by Yoshimune.
Now, on the contrary, the Daimyō were officially informed that,
henceforth, their gifts should be of a really substantial nature, and
certain of them who were somewhat slow to accept the hint, presently
found themselves saddled with the onus of repairing Temples, and
executing similar public works in Yedo.

These presents, or their alternatives, of course, tended to impose
a strain upon the finances of the fiefs, and the clan tax-collectors
had to become somewhat rigorous in their methods.   Under the
old Shōgun, Daimyō found that the surest way to court favour lay
in the efficient and benevolent administration of their domains ;
now it was becoming plain that it was the tax-product of their fiefs,
and not the methods by which it was obtained that was of prime
importance.   Within ten years from the death of Yoshimune the
administration in some of the outside lands had become scandalous.
In Kanamori's little fief of Gujō in Mino, for example, the farmers
had been driven to riot and insurrection, and at last, after many
vain attempts, were able to bring their grievances before the Great
Council in Yedo, in 1759.   Meanwhile, their lord had become involved
in a series of lawsuits about some shrine lands on his domain, and
these had been before the Hyōjōsho for some time.   The investigation that now took place disclosed that wholesale bribery had been
going on in the High Court of Justice itself.   One of the Great
Council, a Junior Councillor, a Finance Magistrate, a Censor, the
local Gundai in Mino, were all cashiered or otherwise punished,
while Kanamori was stripped of his fief, two of his Karō executed,
and several others of the fief councillors deported to the islands of

Idzu. In this special case, Matsudaira Takemoto appears to have been able to assert himself to good purpose, but he must have been painfully conscious that to stem the tide of maladministration and corruption which had now set in would be hopeless so long as his efforts were paralysed by the incompetence of the Shōgun. The wonder is that he did not abandon the attempt to do so, and vacate his office in sheer hopelessness and disgust. Long before this he must have found his position a lonely one, for all Yoshimune's illustrious officers had already left or been removed from the scene. In 1748, Ōoka Tadasuke retired. From 1737 onwards, the pivot on which the whole local administration turned was the great Finance Magistrate, Kamio, Wakasa no kami. He died in 1753, and his later colleagues and successors were not of *his* kind. Most of them knew only too well that Ōoka Tadamitsu, Idzumo no Kami was a very amiable, pleasant-spoken gentleman, with a little weakness for presents, and that it was far more important to keep the Shōgun's keeper in good humour than it was to ensure the strict discharge of their official duties by the *Gundai* and *Daikwan*, as Kamio had done. And so, through the whole civil service, the dry-rot of favouritism, fraud, and corruption spread from the top downwards with appalling rapidity.

Every one of the three dozen Gundai or Daikwan on the Bakufu Home Domains, besides being a lawyer, was supposed to be a man of more than ordinary practical common sense, a passable judge of character, and an expert accountant. Every one of them could appreciate the change in the moral atmosphere of Yedo officialdom since the deaths of Yoshimune and Kamio, and in the altered circumstances of the time many of them had no difficulty in arriving at the conclusion that, so far from being the best policy, honesty was the scurviest kind of policy that could be imagined, it was becoming a mere luxury, and a very expensive and unfashionable one at that. Hence, honesty presently vanished ; there was no longer a pestilent " Complaint-Box " to be feared—if people were so misguided to put anything into it, the Shōgun would not be in a condition to read it, and Ōoka, Idzumo no Kami was a very amiable, good-natured, pleasant-spoken gentleman with a little weakness for presents. So presents he should have, as should also the new Finance Magistrates, to their dear hearts' content. Within five years from the death of Yoshimune, Gundai and Daikwan had convinced themselves by practical experience that, provided they retained the goodwill of Ōoka and their superiors in Yedo, they could do pretty much as they chose in the wide tracts of country committed to their tender mercies. The prosperity prevalent among the Bakufu agriculturalists made it tolerably easy for them to find the wherewithal to placate the higher bureaucrats at first. The whole Bakufu domain was now assessed at a little over 4,000,000 koku, but in good years the total of the crops raised in it went far beyond that figure.[1]

Each of the forty local officers would thus administer a domain assessed at about 100,000 koku on the average. The legitimate tax-product to be forwarded to Yedo or sold in Ōsaka or stored in the local granaries, as the case might be, would amount to about 40,000 koku, and would come from perhaps a hundred different villages. Under Yoshimune, the annual levy was fixed at a permanent figure, as we have seen. We now hear of instances of Daikwan reverting to the old mitori system on their own responsibility. This enabled them to vary the annual tax on the produce of any plot of land at their own arbitrary will; if the revenue officer delayed to appear to make the appraisement, the crop might be ruined, for it could not be reaped until it had been appraised. The farmer found it to his advantage to conciliate the local officials betimes, and, if he did so, his tax would be reduced in proportion to the value of his thankofferings. Newly reclaimed land was usually exempt from taxation for a certain term. In the case of much of the soil reclaimed in Yoshimune's time, that term was now reaching its limit. Here again, much might be accomplished by judicious thank-offerings. Again, there were repartitions of the gross taxation of the Intendancy among the various villages within its circuit, and among the various households in single villages. In connexion with this we meet with a good many of the abuses which made the levy of the taille in contemporary France so vexatious. There were boundary disputes between villages, quarrels between households, suits between temples and shrines and their incumbents and parishioners. Altogether there was plenty of opportunity for fishing in troubled waters, if the Daikwan and his subordinates were minded to do so.

---

[1] In 1838 this assessment stood at 3,281,578 koku. For details of the Gundai and Daikwan districts, see Journal of American Oriental Society, vol. xxxi, pt. ii, p. 157. Dr. Asakawa's series of papers in that Journal are of great interest and high value.

In addition to all this, the Daikwan began not merely to increase the old taxes but in some instances to impose new ones on their own responsibility, and the *corvée* work, that had always been a prominent feature in Japanese rural administration, developed into a terrible engine for the punishment of villages that made themselves offensive. The net result was that the Bakufu lands were presently seething with discontent. What especially aggravated the situation was that the change for the worse in local administration was so extraordinarily sudden. In Yoshimune's time, we do indeed meet with two mentions of agrarian outbreaks, one in the Yamagata and the other in the Sendai fief, but neither of these was in the Bakufu domains. There had been few, if any, *Monso* (Gate-Complaints) even.[1]

A Daikwan, who by his exactions furnished reasonable grounds for a *Monso*, would have been summarily dismissed in Yoshimune's time. Now Monso became quite frequent; they had ceased to have any great terror for the local officials, for in case rumours of them did get transmitted to Yedo, they could easily be glossed over or explained away. The peasants, finding *Monso* of little avail, soon had recourse to still more desperate expedients in certain quarters. One section of the widely scattered home domain lay far away in central Hyūga in Kyūshū, and the remoteness and isolation of the situation probably emboldened the Daikwan to play the petty tyrant with even more than the measure of truculence that had now become common. Here, by 1759, the peasants had been fleeced to the skin, and even their skins seemed to be threatened. So, to save them, some of the bolder spirits among them resolved to make a supreme effort. A great crowd abandoned their holdings and marched over the border into the lands of the Daimyō of Takanabe, and purposed to settle there. This did have the effect of at last bringing the officials to their senses. While they were considering what steps should be taken to retrieve the immediate situation, the remaining farmers on the estate rose in a seething

---

[1] Punishment of farmers who make complaint to the Lord with menaces and then desert the village :—

"For the ringleaders, death ; for the *nanushi*, banishment from the province for a long period ; for the *kumi-gashira*, banishment from the village with forfeiture of land ; for the village itself, a fine based on the amount of its assessment. However, the punishment may, according to circumstances, be reduced one or two degrees if the lord has been guilty of injustice, and especially is severe punishment to be avoided if the farmers are not in arrears for their taxes." *Kujikata Osadamegaki* II. Art. 28 (1741).

mob under mat-flags and with pointed bamboos for spears drove
the Daikwan and his posse of two-sworded constables out of the
Government buildings which were then wrecked and plundered.
It was only when troops were obtained from the neighbouring
Daimyō of Nobeoka and Sadowara that the outbreak was quelled
and order restored.   It was but eight years since the death of
Yoshimune, and yet here was more than matter enough to make
the good old Shōgun turn in his tomb.

Repeated incidents of this description were of the worst augury
for the near future. Extortion, fraud, chicanery, official corruption
in every form soon utterly disgusted and disheartened the peasant.
Of what use was it, he asked himself, to drudge and moil, if all the
results of any extra exertion on his part were to be at once pounced
upon by the tax-collectors and his fellow harpies ? Those farmers
who could do so, absconded ; those who had to stay on made
a point of exerting themselves as little as possible. In many places,
one-half of the population was trying to support itself by gambling
or the exercise of its bucolic wits. Naturally enough the bounteous
harvests of Yoshimune's times became a thing of the past ; the
yields of cultivated fields tended to diminish and great stretches of
fine land to go out of cultivation. This meant a diminution of the
tax-rice, of course ; and to make up for the deficiency the revenue
officers put an extra turn of the screw upon anything that was
taxable. Rice was no longer stored annually in the local granaries
according to the terms of Yoshimune's legislation, and presently
to make up the cargoes of tax-rice that had to be dispatched to
Yedo and Ōsaka, the local storehouses were depleted. Even so,
the Bakufu revenue began to shrink, and the granaries on the banks
of the Sumida had to be emptied to meet current expenses. In an
over-populated empire of some 30,000,000 souls, the pinch of
hunger was sometimes felt, even in ordinary seasons. What was
likely to happen in the event of a series of unpropitious years and
natural calamities, such as had been experienced towards the end
of Tsunayoshi's administration ? There was a dearth in 1749, and
again in 1757, but few of the administrative officials seem to have
worried greatly over the difficulties of the situation or the general
drift of affairs. Doubtless a man of Matsudaira Takemoto's moral
and intellectual calibre must have pondered deeply over the
impending menace, but while Iyeshige was Shōgun he could do
little to avert it. The only ray of hope was that Iyeshige could not

possibly live for long ; he must soon pay the penalty for his long career of unbridled debauchery acting on a physique that had always been delicate. These anticipations were realized and he died in 1761 at the age of 55 years, but already in the previous year he had made way for the tenth Shōgun by resigning his office to his son, Iyeharu, who thus became Shōgun at the age of 23 years. On the very day when he was invested by Imperial patent about half the city of Yedo was burned down, a natural bonfire to celebrate the joyful event.

Matsudaira Takemoto had now plausible reasons for hoping that his talents might at last become of some real positive service to the empire. One of his colleagues, a mere nonentity, had just died, and another one was transferred for service with the retired Shōgun in the Nishi Maru. In 1761, the able but unscrupulous and time-serving Hotta, Sagami no Kami, died about the same time as the ex-Shōgun Iyeshige, and of the new Councillors appointed to fill the vacancies in the Rōjū, one Akimoto, Tajima no Kami, was a man after Matsudaira's own heart, intrepid, energetic, sturdily honest, a sworn foe to favouritism and venality. At the time, men of such a breed were sorely needed indeed. But, after all, it was the character of the new Shōgun that was the real key to the situation, and there were ample grounds for expecting great things from him. As a boy he had been the chief solace of his grandfather's heart, his great sheet-anchor of hope for the future. As a child he had been winsome and quick-witted ; in fact, some of the anecdotes recorded of him indicate that people regarded him as a sort of infant prodigy. But, as in only too many cases of precocity, his index of mental expansion was a small one, and the limits of development were not difficult to reach. This may have been partly the result of his unfavourable environment as he grew up ; possibly, if he had had the benefits of Yoshimune's training for some years longer, he might have become an infinitely abler man than he proved to be. Until the death of Yoshimune his education had not been neglected. His tutor, Narushima, laid much stress upon Japanese history, and Iyeharu was uncommonly well-acquainted with the exploits of the great figures in the national pantheon, while he was carefully instructed in the orthodox theories of administration. Unlike his father, he was no physical sluggard ; on the contrary, he was proficient in all the martial accomplishments of the samurai, and was one of the best shots of his time, whether with the bow, or the musket.

He began his régime with an effort to make the Hyōjōsho once more what it had been in the times of his grandfather. At his accession he discovered that it was seriously in arrear with the suits before it, and he at once instructed the bench to have them all cleared off within six months, and to make it a rule that no case in future should be allowed to drag on for a longer term unless for some very special reason. Shortly afterwards, the whole Hyōjōsho bench were instructed to revise Yoshimune's code, and to append to its various articles any modifications that experience had shown to be necessary or advisable. This work was not finally accomplished until 1767, when the *Kajōruiten* received the Shōgun's sanction. Iyeshige had troubled himself as little about the military training of the samurai as Tsunayoshi had done, and in this field it seemed that Yoshimune's work had ultimately proved of no avail. Iyeharu now showed himself inclined to take it vigorously in hand. In front of Iyeyasu's shrine in Uyeno he instituted exhibitions of horse-archery, and many of the Samurai again became assiduous in their practice at the butts. Unfortunately, the new Shōgun did not insist upon these functions being carried out with the simplicity that characterized them in the Kamakura age, as his grandfather had done. On the contrary, they were always held with great pomp and circumstance, and so were eagerly welcomed by the frivolous, fashionable society of Yedo as occasions for making display of its taste in dress and personal adornment. At this date, too, a great craze for temple-going and sermons was prevalent, and its inspiring motive was neither piety nor devotion, but a mere love of display. To devotees of this description the horse-archery functions at Uyeno came as a veritable godsend, and the drapers and tailors and haberdashers of Yedo profited immensely. One outcome of all this was to plunge many of the samurai still more deeply into the slough of financial distress. We have seen that, by 1736, the crops had become so abundant that it was necessary to resort to a debasement of the coinage, and various other devices in order to bolster up the price of rice in the interests of those who drew rice rations from the Bakufu and clan granaries. The immediate result of this was to drive up the price of commodities generally. After the death of Yoshimune the harvests began to dwindle, and now, owing to the scandals that disgraced the local administration, almost everywhere they had shrunk so far that they were insufficient to supply immediate demands, while the storage of surplus rice had become an impossibility. Naturally, rice now went up tremendously, apart from any question of a debasement of the coinage, but the samurai, as a class, did not profit much by this state of things, for the deficiency in the annual crops made it necessary to reduce their stipends. On the other hand, most of them were so entangled in the mad whirl of fashionable life that it was impossible for them to "reduce their standards of luxury and display", for any such course would have exposed them to the contempt of their associates. Greed and vanity, whether singly or in combination, must unfortunately be counted among the most common and most powerful determinants of human action in every country under the sun, and none among the sinful sons of men have been greater slaves to vanity than the average Japanese, especially the average samurai. He was supposed to be greedy of nothing save honour, but his very respect for what he regarded as the claims of honour, the approbation of small-souled people as vain and giddy as himself, now made him intensely greedy of money in spite of all traditions.

The point of supreme importance was to attract the favourable notice of the Shōgun, or of those who had access to his ear. Not only in the case of archery festivals, but in everything else, Iyeharu gave indications that he was exceedingly fond of magnificence and sumptuous display. Hence, to those who aspired to shine in the fashionable life of the time—and there were few who did not—money became a matter of the utmost consequence. Those in positions of influence—or supposed positions of influence—acquired it easily enough, " presents " came streaming in upon them. On the other hand, most of those who paid them court were in a vastly different situation, they were nearly all living beyond their steadily diminishing incomes. Some were over head and ears in debt to the *fuda-sashi*, with their stipends mortgaged for several years to come. Others, still more unfortunate, fell into the clutches of some member or other of the guild of blind Shampooers (*Zatō*),[1] whose tender mercies towards their debtors were those of the wicked. Duns were to be met with in the porch of every second or third Hatamoto house in Banchō, while many of the clan samurai

---

[1] Zatō is the general term for blind men who follow the occupations of shampooers or street musicians, both of which classes alike perambulate the streets. The blind shampooers have always been the most merciless and exacting of usurers.—J. H. L.

had to be careful about the quality of their callers. The young Shōgun was exceedingly popular not merely with the samurai but with the citizens as well, for his personal tastes were good for trade. Yet Iyeharu was the reverse of affable; on the contrary, it was exceedingly difficult, if not absolutely impossible, for even the higher officials to approach him. As he grew up he began to evince a marked dislike for new and unfamiliar faces, and presently the only people he cared to see were his own personal attendants, whom he trusted implicitly, and the ladies of the Court. Not that he was either a profligate or a physical sluggard like his father, for he spent a good deal of his time in the healthy open air, hawking and hunting, and, at first, he interested himself in what his Great Councillors and other officers were doing though he was not at all anxious to meet them personally. During his régime there was a certain amount of legislation—sumptuary laws among others—and some of the measures submitted for the Shōgun's sanction seemed to be excellent, but it most unfortunately proved that they were rarely seriously enforced; like the great horse-archery functions of Uyeno they were mainly for purposes of show. They were almost invariably placed before His Highness not by the Rōjū or its monthly president but by his personal attendants, who were his media of communication with the great executive officers. One consequence of this was that the traditions of Iyeshige were continued. The real rulers of Japan were still the Sobayōnin.

In Iyeshige's time the all-powerful favourite, Ōoka Tadamitsu, took care to attach his son, Tadayoshi, to the person of the heir apparent, and now, on the deaths of Iyeshige and the senior Ōoka, the sons of the two continued the relations that had subsisted between their fathers. However, the young Ōoka had to share the confidence of Iyeharu with a colleague, a certain Tanuma Mototsugu. Tanuma (born in 1719) was the son of one of the Kishū samurai who accompanied Yoshimune to Yedo. In the old Shōgun's time he held an officer's commission in the *Koshō-gumi*, but does not seem to have been regarded with any very marked degree of favour. Under Iyeshige he found means of ingratiating himself with Ōoka Tadayoshi, and the latter, discerning in him a serviceable tool, contrived to place him near the person of Iyeharu. A few years after the latter's accession young Ōoka died, and henceforth, down to Iyeharu's death in 1786, Tanuma continued to be his master's right hand man in everything. In Iyeshige's last years he was

raised to Daimyō rank, and assigned a seat on the Hyōjōsho bench.
A few months later he was transferred to a new fief of 20,000 *koku*,
and under Iyeharu he was formally appointed Sobayōnin.   In
this man—if we are to trust the native historians—we meet with
an extreme instance of one of the worst types of Japanese character.
Towards his superiors, or those whom he had any reason to court
or fear, insinuating and smooth-spoken, and in case of need, fawning,
cringing, and servile; to those below him, or to such as he had no
reason to dread, or who did not choose to propitiate him duly,
insufferably haughty and outrageously insolent.   And withal, an
exceedingly able man; no great scholar, or rather no scholar at all,
so far as the Chinese classics went, but exceedingly well-read in
the great book of human nature, and especially well acquainted
with its most unclean pages.

Before many years passed Tanuma had almost every one of
the officials quailing before him.   One morning, in 1767, he met the
Rōjū, Akimoto, Tajima no Kami, in the great corridor of the
palace, and according to the established etiquette he should have
saluted his superior in the official hierarchy by placing his hands
upon his knees and bending forward.   So powerful had he lately
become that he could even venture to slight the Rōjū, and he was
on the point of passing Akimoto by without any notice when the
latter sharply called him to account and exacted the proper
salute from him.   A few weeks later Akimoto found it advisable
to tender his resignation and retire into private life.   Two years
afterwards, Tanuma was appointed Acting-Councillor, while in 1772
he was installed as a regular member of the Rōjū.   In the Great
Council he occupied the lowest seat, but he was far more powerful
than all his colleagues combined, who soon appreciated the wisdom
of thwarting him in nothing.   On the contrary, official salvation
consisted in divining and anticipating his wishes.   One of his wishes
was easy enough to divine, but to satisfy it or rather to satiate it,
was a very different matter.   Ōoka Tadamitsu had a pronounced
weakness for " presents ", but Tanuma's appetite for them was
ravening and unappeasable.   It might have been supposed that
the increased revenue of his new fief of Sagara in the province of
Tōtōmi (assessed at 57,000 *koku*), which Ieharu bestowed on him
at an early stage in their relations as lord and vassal, would have
been ample to maintain his state, but even its revenues were no
more than a trickling rivulet among the huge streams of wealth
that poured in upon him from many quarters.

Some of this wealth Tanuma had to disburse ; it was of great consequence for him to be on the best of terms with the ladies of the Palace, and although flattery there might do much, it was not injudicious to reinforce it by more solid and substantial tokens of esteem. One of Yoshimune's first cares was to curb all extravagance in the Great Interior of the Palace, and to place everything there on a footing of economy and simplicity. Under his grandson, as great a proportion of the minishing annual revenues of the Bakufu were absorbed by the Great Interior as had been the case in the wasteful times of Tsunayoshi. Iyeharu's harem was perhaps fully as costly as the *Parc aux Cerfs* of Louis XV on the other side of the globe, although Iyeharu was not a profligate like Tsunayoshi or His Most Christian Majesty of France ; it was simply that he had a profound, ingrained dislike for anything that approached rusticity or simplicity, and a consuming passion for what the Japanese call *Kwabi*,[1] pomp, parade, splendour, and magnificence. Accordingly, Tanuma knew better than to allow the official auditors to make any stir or trouble about the innumerable financial irregularities that were to be found in the portentously increasing household accounts of His Highness; nay, rather than have his numerous friends among the fair dames of the court clamouring about any stint of supplies, he would satisfy them out of his own means from time to time, as he was perfectly well able to do without feeling the slightest pinch of inconvenience. When his chief *yashiki* was confiscated at his fall in 1786, it was found to be glutted with what might have been the accumulated spoil of a great captured treasure-house, while a huge surplus of valuables, which could find no room in the recesses and store-houses of the *yashiki*, overflowed into a row of accessory buildings. Nearly all this immense hoard of treasure had been contributed by office-seekers, either such as aimed at being gazetted to posts for the first time, or such as hoped for promotion. Without Tanuma's sanction or aid, access to the world of office, or advancement to its more lucrative and influential posts, was equally impossible. The old posts were fairly numerous, and many new ones were created, but, even so the official loaves and fishes could not be made to satisfy everyone, for the hungry applicants were legion. Many handsome presents from people who could but ill-afford to make them, brought the tenderers nothing, not

---

[1] In its primary meaning Kwabi signifies " beautiful as flowers in bloom ".
—J. H. L.

even an expression of thanks, yet whoever aspired to anything must needs cast his bread upon the waters. Again, those who actually did obtain something durst not be ungrateful or unmindful, they could be dismissed with far greater ease than they had been appointed. If tolerably regular in their tribute, their tenure of office was secure in spite of all but the most serious shortcomings. What would have been regarded as outrageous scandals in Yoshimune's time were now nothing more than mere peccadilloes to be passed over with a smile. Public decency indeed became of little consequence when Tanuma was at the summit of his power.

About that time a certain Mikami, Mino no Kami, was promoted to the Colonelcy of the Nishi Maru Shoimban (Inner Company of Life Guards) and a week or so later he gave a banquet to celebrate the occasion in his mansion in Banchō. Among the guests were at least half-a-dozen who added the title *Kami* to their names, as lords of their several fiefs. Some years before this, the Geisha (singing-girls) had made their first appearance, and now at the great banquets held every night in some Yedo mansion they, as well as the Taiko-mochi or buffoons from the Yoshiwara, were in great request. On this occasion the host had engaged the services of some of those most in vogue. Before the evening was far advanced every one was tipsy, and Geisha, buffoons, and guests all alike began to pelt each other with the viands. The dinner tables and service were smashed, the interior of the mansion wrecked, and after a number of indescribable pranks the aristocratic host and all his guests poured out in an uproarious rout and proceeded to finish the hideous orgy in the Yoshiwara.[1] On the next day there was an important Palace function, and the new Colonel of the Inner Life Guards and his guests were still too drunk to be able to appear at their posts of duty. This was an offence punishable with at least the entire confiscation of all the offenders' property; while "evil moral reputation" involved deportation to an island, or perhaps an order to commit *hara-kiri*. Had such a scandal been possible in Yoshimune's day the extreme penalty would probably have been inflicted. As it was, the offence was too glaringly gross and flagrant to be passed over, but all that was done was to relieve the offenders of their commissions. For a few years this special outburst in Mikami's Banchō mansion continued to be spoken of

---

[1] For a similar episode in contemporary Paris see Taine's *L'ancien Régime*, bk. ii, ch. ii, at end.

as the greatest and wildest orgy of the time but, in sober truth, there was no lack of similar functions, equally unrestrained and riotous, and if the Colonel and his guests had been able to appear on duty on the following morning the incident would have brought him *éclat* rather than punishment. In the penultimate decade of the eighteenth century, Yedo banquets were characterized by even a deeper measure of sumptuous dissipation than any of the "little suppers" in contemporary Versailles or Paris, and while no less extravagant, they descended to lower depths of licence and to the worst forms of depravity. Gambling was also as common and involved at high stakes in Yedo as in Paris, and the austere characteristics of the samurai in the days of Kiyomasa and Yoshi-mune seemed to be replaced by those of profligate and self-indulgent roués, eager to acquire money, which it was formerly the samurais' proud boast to despise, by any means, for the gratification of their vices. It has been stated that, in addition to the samurai proper, the various *yashiki* in Yedo were thronged with crowds of menials drawn from the Kwantō and the neighbouring lands. They were generally hired by the year. At the end of their term of employment (although many remained in the capital) they were supposed to return to their native villages and there resume their original avocations. It is not hard to conceive what the moral effects of their return to the country must have been upon the social economy of the village communities to which they belonged. These were now generally seething with an only too justifiable spirit of unrest and discontent, inasmuch as the extortions, exactions, chicanery, and insolence of the local administrative chiefs and their petty minions made it very hard to earn a livelihood by honest labour alone. These menials returned from Yedo had, as a Japanese author alleges, acquired the speculative point of view, and the extravagant habits that ruled there. They thus carried about them a certain restless and flippant air, and the half-exhausted inhabitants of the village contained elements most susceptible to this sort of influence. Soon every part of the country came to feel a longing for easy money and an easy life. From the end of the seventeenth century the supply of applicants, even for menial service in the warrior's or merchant's household, was growing scarce. In order to remedy this difficulty the authorities, who in the earlier years had taken great pains to forbid sales of persons and to limit the terms of personal service, were now obliged to modify the law to a considerable extent. Every

district, if not every village, contained landless persons who would
live rather by speculation, trading on popular superstitions,
gambling, fraud, or robbery, than by any form of honest labour.
Gambling had become so generally prevalent throughout the
provinces of Shimōsa, Kōdzuke, and Shimotsuke by 1767 that
the taxes were mostly in arrear, agriculture neglected, and large
tracts of arable land gone, or going, out of cultivation. The village
usurer, who was not infrequently a gambler, and often in collusion
with the petty officials, held scores of his neighbours in his clutches.
Even in the good times of Yoshimune, a contemporary expert
asserted that a debt of 5 *ryō* (£7) would ruin an average farmer
in five years. Now the rates of interest exacted were much higher
than they were in 1720, for the risks were far greater. Not a few
of the hopeless, broken men took to the high road, and whole
provinces, especially around Yedo, were presently infested with
gangs of the most desperate class of brigands.

In the great south-western fiefs, such as Satsuma, Higo, Chōshū,
Tosa, and in Mayeda's wide Kanazawa domain, matters were not
quite so bad. On the contrary, in some of them, in Higo especially,
much administrative work of a high degree of honesty and efficiency
was actually being done at the time. In other fiefs the state of
things was about as desperate as it was in the Bakufu domains.
So much is clearly apparent in the case of the Uyesugi fief of
Yonezawa before the new chieftain Harunori entered upon his
famous reforms about 1770. It has already been mentioned that
the Uyesugi chieftain had incurred ill-favour with the Yedo
authorities for failing to protect or to avenge his natural father,
Kira Yoshinaka, assassinated by the Forty-seven Rōnin in 1703,
the Hyōjōsho having actually gone so far as to recommend the
confiscation of his domains. In 1753, the clan incurred the displeasure of Iyeshige or his favourites—possibly it had not fulfilled
legitimate expectations in the matter of " presents "—and found
itself saddled with the task of repairing the main building of the
Tō-ei-zan Temple in Uyeno. The cost of this work made a serious
inroad upon the finances of Yonezawa, and it appeared to be the
intention of the Bakufu to ruin the clan entirely, as Uyesugi,
having completed the first task, was next ordered to re-erect the
grand entrance to the fane. It was only by inducing the Daimyō
of Owari to intervene that the *corvée* was transferred to another
clan, the Ogasawara of Kokura. As it was, the Uyesugi fief was

so terribly crippled that its position seemed to be well-nigh hopeless.
Its 750 square miles of territory lay away from the sea in the far
north of the Main Island, ringed in with rugged, inhospitable
mountain-ranges.   In fertility and natural resources its valleys
ranked very low and they were buried deeply in snow for five
months in each year.   It was sparsely peopled, according to the
Japanese standard, for it supported only about 100,000 souls.
" Supported " is scarcely the word to use, for, at this time, the
penury and destitution that prevailed within the Yonezawa domains
almost beggared description.   Whoever could do so absconded,
and those who could not only remained to rot and die.   The exactions
of the tax-collector were ruthless ; the debts of the clan amounted
to a fabulous sum while we are assured that at times samurai
and officials could not raise so much as five gold pieces among them
by their united efforts.   To crown all, the last of the Uyesugi seemed
on the point of passing away, leaving no posterity behind him but
a crazed, half-witted, delicate girl.   It was with no small difficulty
that a husband could be procured for her for personally, of course,
she had no attractions to tempt any suitor, while the terrible
conditions of the ancestral domains made her of but scant consideration as an heiress in the marriage market.   It was finally
arranged that a younger son of the Akizuki family, who held a
27,000 *koku* fief in Hyūga, should wed her and assume the heavy
responsibilities of Chief of the Uyesugi house.   When it is stated
that the new chief, Uyesugi Harunori, was a mere boy of sixteen
when he assumed the position, it would scarcely seem that the
dismal prospects of the clan had been sensibly improved.   The
cynical fashionable society of Yedo must have been vastly amused
at what might well be regarded as the precocious and impracticable
manifestation of his ambitions that was soon made by what they
regarded as a verdant youth.   On the very day of his instalment
as chief of the Uyesugi clan he sent in the following vow to the Great
God of Kasuga, his tutelary deity throughout his life :—

I. The exercises, literary and military, such as I have prescribed
to myself, shall I prosecute without negligence.

II. To be a father and a mother to my people shall be my first and
chief endeavour.

III. The words that follow shall I never forget, day or night :—
> " No extravagance, no danger.
> Give in charity, but waste not."

IV. Inconsistency between words and acts, injustice in rewarding and punishing, unfaithfulness and indecency—from these I shall diligently guard myself.

The above shall I strictly observe in future, and in case of my neglect of the same, let the punishment of heaven overtake me at once, and the family fortunes be for ever ruined.

It was not till two years after this (in 1769) that the youthful chief fared forth from Yedo to assume charge of his mountain-ringed domain in the wilds of the far north. When he crossed the Yonezawa frontier, the succession of sights that met his eyes was lamentable in the extreme. It was heart-breaking. Away towards the foot-hills a sour, sullen, sombre, expanse of bleak, wind-swept moors and wastes ; alongside the high road wretched huts, and here and there clusters of hovels where villages should be. Wherever any-thing human was met, there were fluttering rags, shivering nakedness, filth, misery, destitution, and utter degradation. Towards the end of the first day's weary and depressing journey, his attendants observed the young lord diligently blowing through the stem of his tobacco pipe at the tiny charcoal fire in the brazier in his palanquin. "We can serve your Lordship with a good fire," said one of his suite. "Not now," was the reply, "I am now learning a great lesson. What it is I will tell you by-and-by." When they put up at an hotel for the night, the attendants were summoned together. Said the Chief :—

"As despair took hold of me as I witnessed my people's miseries, my attention was caught by the tiny charcoal fire before me that was just on the point of going out. I built it up, and by blowing at it gently and patiently, I succeeded in resuscitating it. 'May I not be able in the same way to resuscitate the land and the people under my care ?' This I said to myself, and hope revived within me."

The object-lesson and the parable were approved and most effective instruments of instruction in old Japan. To save the clan from imminent dissolution the crushing burden of debts had to be at least lightened. The stipends of the retainers were at once cut down by half, but in this case not charity but economy had to begin at home. The chief's household budget had hitherto stood at 1,050 *ryō*, it was now reduced to 209 *ryō*. Forty-one out of the fifty female servants were discharged ; Uyesugi himself would wear nothing but cotton clothing, and have only three courses of the plainest food at a meal. All this was nothing more than a mere detail in his scheme of administration. His fundamental maxims here were, (1) To have no waste places in his domains, and (2) to have no idlers among his people :—

" His samurai he turned into farmers, and recovered thousands of acres from desolation and the wilderness in that way. He ordered lacquer-trees to be extensively planted. Every samurai family was required to plant fifteen nurslings in its yard, and every other family five, and every temple twenty within its enclosure. For every tree planted over the required number a bounty of 20 *mon* was given, and for every one that died and was not replaced, a fine of the same amount was exacted. Over one million nurslings of this valuable tree were thus planted within his territory in a very short period—a matter of very great consequence to posterity A million more of the paper-mulberry were planted in places which allowed no cultivation. But Uyesugi's chief aim was to make his domain a great silk-producing district. For this purpose, funds were required which his impoverished treasury could not supply. He therefore still further reduced his household budget from 209 to 159 *ryō*, and used the money thus saved to promote the silk industry. The few thousand mulberry stocks he began with soon propagated themselves, and in course of years his whole domain had no space left for more. ' The Yonezawa district to-day and its splendid silk-produce testify to the patience and benevolence of its ancient chief. The Yonezawa brand ranks highest in the market.' When public welfare was at last assured (all the clan debts had been paid off by 1785, in sixteen years) Uyesugi could think of no impossibility, for he had patience to make up for any lack of means. So it was that the poorest of the Daimyō projected and completed two of the most stupendous engineering works ever undertaken in Old Japan. One was the conduct of water for a distance of twenty-eight miles over viaducts and long and high embankments, all of which are masterpieces of hydraulic engineering. The other was the turning of the course of a large stream through a tunnel, 1,200 feet of which was through solid granite. The latter work took twenty years. Among Uyesugi's vassals was a certain Kuroi, a slow speechless man, passing as a good-for-nothing. The chief discovered in him a mathematician of rare ability. With his rude instruments he made careful surveys of the ground, and planned out the two works which to his contemporaries appeared like madness. He completed the first and died while engaged on the second. The work was nevertheless continued according to his plan, and twenty years after its commencement the tunnel was bored through from both ends, the outlet section meeting the intake section four feet *below* the level of the latter—a wonder of accuracy in calculation when the transit and the theodolite were unknown instruments in the land. Deserts began to bloom, and plenty flowed in abundance into Uyesugi's territory, Yonezawa alone of all northern provinces, knows of no drought to this very day.

" Uyesugi furthermore imported improved breeds of stock, stocked ponds and streams with eels and carp, brought in miners and weavers from other provinces, removed all toll-houses and commercial restrictions, and endeavoured in every way to develop the resources of the fief. These measures, with his extermination of idlers from among his people, and their conversion into useful workers, brought about such changes that the once poorest district in the land became a type of productivity towards the close of Uyesugi's life, and has continued to be so ever since."

So much as regards some of the mere material results of Uyesugi Harunori's administration, an administration on which he entered it must not be forgotten when he was an inexperienced youth of eighteen or nineteen years. Still more important is it to consider the discipline and methods by which these results were achieved.[1]

Uchimura continues his story :—

" No good government is possible without right men in right places, and such men Uyesugi would have, though the hereditary nature of the feudal government was against his democratic idea of ' a man according to his abilities '. Out of his impoverished treasury he paid men of abilities very liberally, and placed them over his people in three distinct capacities, First there were the governor and his sub-officers, ' fathers and mothers ' of the people. To these one of his injunctions was as follows :—

" ' The child has no knowledge of its own ; but she who mothers it understands its needs and ministers thereto, because she does it from her sincerity. Sincerity begets love, and love begets knowledge. Only be sincere and nothing is unattainable. As is the mother to the child, so must the officer be to his people. *If only the heart that loves the people lies in you, you need not lament the lack of wisdom in you.*'

" The second class of officers were itinerant preachers, who were to teach the people in morals and ceremonies, ' of filial piety, of compassion towards widows and orphans, of matters of marriage, of decency in clothing, of food, and ways of eating, of funeral services, of house repairs, etc. The *whole* territory was divided into twelve districts (dioceses) for this purpose, each with a presiding teacher (lay-bishop) over it. These bishops were to meet twice a year for mutual conference, and to make occasional reports to the Chief of the progress of their works among the people. The third class were policemen of the strictest kind. They were to detect the people's vices and crimes, and to punish them severely for their offences. Mercy they were to show to none, and every nook of villages and towns was to be carefully scrutinized. It was a diocese's shame to furnish offenders and every preacher took upon himself responsibilities for troubles his district gave to the police.

" The three functions together worked admirably. His general administrative policies went through the governor and his subsidiaries. But our Lord says ' To rule a people that is not taught is costly and ineffectual '. And such teaching was furnished by the lay-bishops to give ' life and warm circulation to the whole '. Teaching without discipline is ineffectual. Hence the strictest police system to make the teaching more effectual and the mercy shown more conspicuous. The youth of nineteen must have had no little insight into human nature to have enabled him to frame such a system of governing mankind.

" The new machinery was in operation for five years without meeting with molestation from any quarter. Order began to show itself, and hopes revived of the possible resuscitation of the despaired-of society.

---

[1] The extracts already indicated are from *Japan and the Japanese*, by Uchimura Kanzō, a little book of very high merit. The literature on Uyesugi Harunori and his tutor Hosoi runs to many thousands of pages. Possibly Mr. Ikeda's *Life*, published in 1906, will be found most serviceable by those more deeply interested in Uyesugi.

Then came the trial. One day seven of the highest dignitaries of the district approached the young chief with their grievances, and tried to wrest from him words for the immediate abrogation of the new system of government. The chief is silent. He would have his *people* judge him, and if *they* object to the new administration, it and he would willingly yield up its and his places to the better and abler. So he called a general council of his subjects at once. Armoured and sword-girt they gather in thousands in the Castle and wait for the business. Meanwhile our Lord resorts to the temple of the great god of Kasuga to pray for a peaceful issue to the trouble. Then he meets his beloved subjects, and asks them if, in their opinions, his administration is against Heaven's will. The governor and his associates say ' No '. The police, one and all, say ' No '. Captains and sergeants say ' No '. Different mouths with one voice say ' No '. Our Lord is satisfied. His mind is made up. He calls the seven before him and passes sentence upon them. Half of the fiefs of five of them were confiscated and the five were ' shut up within their gates for ever '. Two of them, the head conspirators, were dealt with according to the code of the samurai. They were permitted to perform *hara-kiri*, bowel-cutting, a dignified method of self-destruction. Conservatives and grumblers thus disposed of, good began to flow in in abundance.

" One beautiful feature of the oriental knowledge is that it has never treated economy apart from morality. Wealth with their philosophers is always the effect of virtue, and the two bear the relation to each other of the fruit to the tree. You manure the tree, and the fruit will surely come, without your effort. You manure ' Love to the people ', and wealth will be a necessary outcome. ' Therefore the wise man thinketh of the tree, and he hath the fruit. The small man thinketh of the fruit, and he hath it not.' Such was the Confucianism indoctrinated into Uyesugi's mind by his worthy teacher, Hosoi. Herein, therefore, lies the grandeur of all of Uyesugi's industrial reforms, that his chief aim was to make *virtuous* people out of his subjects. The hedonistic view of happiness was repugnant to him. Wealth was to be had that all might be made ' decorous people ' thereby, for said the ancient sage ' Decorum is known only when life's necessaries are had '. Remarkably free from the conventionalities of his time, he aimed at leading his heaven-entrusted people into the ' ways of man ', binding alike on the Daimyō and the tiller of the soil. Thus by one man's sincerity was chaos turned to order, and the earth was made to give out what it hid from the eyes of the unfaithful. It is yet to be seen how much sincerity can make out of this planet."

The hard-working, abstemious man enjoyed continuous health for three score years and ten. Most of his early hopes were realized. He saw his fief firmly established, his people well supplied, and his whole domain abundantly replenished. The clan, that had not been able to raise five pieces of gold by their united efforts, could now raise 10,000 at a moment's notice. The end of such a man could not be anything but peace. On 19th March, 1822, he breathed his last :—

" The people wept as if they had lost their good grandfather. The lamentations of all classes no pen can describe. On the day of his funeral tens of thousands of mourners filled the wayside. Hands clasped and heads all bowed, deep wailings went up from them all, and even mountains, rivers, and plants joined in the universal sorrow."

That an inexperienced youth of eighteen should have been able to devise such a wide-reaching and salutary project of reform as Uyesugi Harunori actually carried through in the teeth of difficulties that might have daunted even an Iyeyasu, is surely not the least astonishing circumstance in Uchimura's wonderful tale. It is true that this youth had not been reared as an elder son and heir to the fief; if he had been so reared, he never could have achieved a tithe of what he did. The intelligent reader will have no difficulty in surmising that at first, at least, there must have been some great *Kuromaku* or prompter behind him. We have seen what Arai did for the sixth Shōgun, Iyenobu. But Arai would probably have failed in Yonezawa in 1769; he would have concentrated too much attention upon such matters as " a reform of the ceremonies ", to the neglect of the far more insistent and vital problem of finding the wherewithal to pay off the crushing load of clan indebtedness and to fill the bellies of the starving tatterdemalion vassals and peasants. In the hands of Hayashi Dōshun, young Uyesugi might have become a prodigy of learning, but Hayashi could never have fired his soul and inspired him to the achievement of the real man's work he accomplished in his day and generation. With Ogyu Sorai for his early preceptor, Uyesugi might indeed have developed into a great politician. Sorai was perhaps the very best intellect among the Confucianists of Japan ; the clearest, the most vigorous, the most original thinker of them all, but his cardinal tenet was that every member of the " damned race " is shapen in sin and conceived in iniquity, and his chief, if not his sole agent of reform, would have been the policeman. Until the advent of the " blessed millennium ", the " damned race " will doubtless always stand in need of a modicum of the policeman, or the " fear o' Hell " or of the hangman, or of some other visible or imaginary penalty, but to get their best out of the sinful sons of men by mere coercion and terrorism is impossible. At this crisis in Yonezawa it was in getting the very best of which he was capable out of every one of his subjects that Uyesugi discerned the sole hope of salvation. To effect this, some-

thing more was necessary than the " Honesty-is-the-best-policy "
doctrine. Nakae Tōju's " Do right for the mere sake of doing right ",
transcendental and impracticable as it might appear, was really the
only practical kind of creed for the work-a-day exigencies of the
situation.   From his early boyhood, Uyesugi Harunori was in the
hands of Hosoi Heishū who continued instilling the bracing tenets
of oriental transcendentalism into him early and late.   Hosoi
accompanied his young lord to Yonezawa, and remained with him
there till his death in 1801. Hosoi, it was, who was the prompter
of the boy chieftain's grand projects of reform.

Three or four centuries before, the Uyesugi family were great
patrons of learning.   The Ashikaga Gakkō—Xavier frequently
refers to it as the University of Bandoue, and thought of getting
missionaries installed in some of its chairs—owed much to their
munificence.   In their great Echigo domain, one of the first, if not
indeed the very first of the modern clan schools, was organized in
Hideyoshi's time, but since the removal of the clan to Yonezawa,
there had been no local college for the samurai.   Now, even before
the debts of the clan were entirely liquidated, Uyesugi established
the Kōjō Kwan, and installed Hosoi as its Provost :—

" The magnitude and equipment of the school were out of all
proportion to the finances of the clan.   It provided many free scholar-
ships to enable the worthy poor to obtain a high-class education.   For
nearly a century after its establishment, the Yonezawa school continued
to be a type and example to the whole country. Later on, a medical
department was opened.   At the time when the European medical art
was looked upon with fear and suspicion, Uyesugi caused several of his
subjects to be trained in the new system by Dr. Sugita, of great celebrity
as the first Japanese physician after the Dutch method.   Once convinced
of its superiority over Chinese medicine, he spared no expense to get all
the medical apparatus he possibly could, and placed it in his school to
be freely used in instruction and practice.   Thus, fifty years before
Perry's squadron appeared in the Bay of Yedo Western medicine was
in general use in one of the mountain districts of north Japan."

The modern Japanese are frequently twitted with their low
and lax notions of commercial morality, while, during two centuries
of seclusion, records and edicts alike tend to show that the men of
Nippon were then as inveterate smugglers as any contemporary
Cornishmen. Kuranari, a contemporary writer, describes how it
stood with Uyesugi's subjects in these respects :—

" In Yonezawa is what they call the Label-market. Away from the
habitations of men, by the side of public roads, sandals, shoes, fruit,
and other commodities are exposed for sale with their prices labelled

upon them and their owners all absent. People go there, leave the
prices as marked, take the goods, and pass on ; and nobody ever thinks
of stealing anything from these markets. The dominion has no custom-
houses or any such obstructions to free commerce on its borders and yet
no smuggling is ever attempted."

It is a sad and cheerless business to have to leave this little
nook of Paradise Regained in the most forbidding circumstances
in the snowy and sequestered wilds of the far north, and return
to the foul cesspool of the Yedo bureaucracy and the Bakufu lands.
The open and unabashed traffic in offices of public trust has already
been adverted to. By this time the Courts of Justice had become
as the farm-yard of Augeas. Probably they were in as evil a case
as those of Kamakura were just before the fall of the Hōjō. The
only wise thing for an honest man to do was to keep out of them at
any cost, for unless " offerings " were duly tendered to Tanuma
or his favourites, the litigant with the best case in the world would
assuredly find himself cast and probably ruined. And this, too,
in spite of the fact that the Shōgun Iyeharu began his administration
by admonishing and reforming the Hyōjōsho bench and
endeavouring to restore judicial purity and efficiency to the same
high standard which characterized it in his grandfather's time.
Naturally enough, the local administration of justice by the *Gundai*
and *Daikwan* took its colour from that of the central Supreme Court.

The petty local tyrants, however, discovered that it was after all
possible to push things too far. The Hyūga *émeute* of 1759, has
already been mentioned. Five years later, in 1764, the population
of a whole county at the base of the Chichibu range in Musashi,
driven to desperation by the exactions of the officials, abandoned
their homes, and formed an entrenched camp, where they proposed
to defy the authorities till their grievances were redressed and a
guarantee received for proper treatment in the future. Circulars
were dispatched to the villages in the neighbouring provinces, and
received a prompt response. The Daikwan, as in the Hyūga case,
had to appeal to the local Daimyō for troops, and in storming the
farmers' rude fortifications several hundred men are said to have
fallen. The captured peasants were forwarded to Yedo, where they
filled the Temma gaol, and prison accommodation had to be provided
for them in Asakusa and Shinagawa, where they were packed so
closely together that they are said to have died in scores. Some
thirty or forty of their ringleaders were executed, and the others
were presently returned to their villages. From this date, almost

every year was marked by the promulgation of edicts prohibiting
" forcible petitioning " and rioting, but still the agrarian riots went
on in one quarter or another. The odd thing to find is that meanwhile the penalties for these offences were not increased, but
reduced. This would seem to indicate that the authorities recognized
that the peasants' grievances were serious, and that they were
afraid to push things to extremities. In truth, as the result of
these outbreaks, the Kwantō Daikwan became very cautious and
circumspect, for the Bakufu was now reprimanding them for the
progressive diminution in the annual tax-yield forwarded to Yedo.
Prices, already high, still kept rising. Once more the truth of
Gresham's generalization manifested itself, only the most inferior
of the various kinds of coin then supposed to be in circulation were
current to any extent. The Finance Magistrates thought to find
a remedy for inflated prices in extensive new issues from the
mint, but the supply of copper was insufficient, and speculators
began to reap a rich harvest as mining prospectors. These
" Yamashi " [1] (Mountain-teachers), as they were called, would
report the existence of a copper-mine in the territories of a Daimyō,
and the Bakufu would forthwith incorporate that special district
in the Tokugawa household domain. Some of these adventurers
were not slow to indicate other ways and means of replenishing
the Yedo exchequer. One suggested to Tanuma that there were
" possibilities " in the Chinese trade of Nagasaki. Its great staple
was sea-weed and similar marine produce. At that time, the
supply came from the great northern island of Yezo, and was
furnished almost entirely by the Matsumae family. A " Yamashi "
was now dispatched to Yezo to investigate the actual and pot ntial
profits of the traffic, and, a little later, the Bakufu deprived
Matsumae of his chief source of revenue, and declared the Yezo-
Nagasaki trade a government monopoly. The officials sent to
conduct it almost at once began to cheat and maltreat the Ainu,
and a series of Ainu riots had to be put down with the help of the
Matsumae Samurai (1784).

Two other " Yamashi " pointed out that a considerable revenue
might be obtained from the silk-produce of Shimotsuke and
Kōdzuke. The story is a long and intricate one, but the main
incidents were the erection of silk inspecting offices throughout the

---

[1] *Yamashi*, in commercial parlance signifies an unscrupulous speculator, an
adventurer or promoter of bubble companies.

two provinces, the exaction of high fees for the services of the officials, and the confiscation of all silk found in the Yedo market without the official stamp upon it. At last the population rose, burned the inspector's houses, and drove the authorities to their wits' ends. Here again it was felt that it might not be advisable to push things to extremities, for Tanuma was too deeply involved in the affair.

The Bakufu was now to discover that it had been gaily dancing on the deadly brink of a precipice for years. Apart from some great fires in Yedo, and a few typhoons and floods in the provinces, it had so far had to deal with no great succession of natural calamities such as had marked the earliest years of the century. But this happy immunity was now destined to end just at the very time when the long-continued maladministration had made it utterly hopeless for officialdom to cope with them. The angry gods now began a seven years' reign of wrath. Although its actual results were nothing but the merest foretaste of what was to follow, the initial calamity was at once terribly sensational, and sufficiently destructive. It began in the summer of 1783 :—

" On 27th July, at eight o'clock in the morning, there arose in Shinano a very strong east wind, accompanied with a dull noise like that of an earthquake, which increased daily, and foreboded the most disastrous consequences. On 1st August, there was a tremendous noise accompanied by earthquake shocks, the walls of the houses cracked and seemed ready to tumble ; each successive shock was more violent, till the flames burst forth with a terrific uproar from the summit of Asama-yama, followed by a tremendous eruption of sand and stones. Though it was broad day, everything was enveloped in profound darkness, through which the flames alone threw at times a lurid light. Till the 4th of August the mountain never ceased to cast up sand and stones.

" The large village of Sakamoto and several others situated at the base of the volcano were soon reduced to ashes by the ignited matter which it projected, and by the flames which burst forth from the earth. The inhabitants fled ; but the chasms everywhere formed by the yawn-ing of the ground prevented their escape, and in a moment a great number of persons were swallowed up or consumed by the flames ; violent shocks continued to be felt till the 5th, and were perceptible to the distance of twenty or thirty leagues ; enormous stones and clouds of sand were carried by the wind blast towards the east and north.

" The water of the Yoko and Karuizawa streams boiled ; the course of the Tone-gawa, the largest river in Japan, was obstructed and the boiling water inundated the adjacent country, doing incredible mischief. The bears, hyænas (sic) fled from the mountains and flocked to the neighbouring villages, where they devoured the inhabitants or mangled them in a horrible way."

The foregoing contemporary account, supplied to Titsingh,

harmonizes wonderfully well with the generality of the vernacular accounts I have had to read through. In a later report, transmitted to Titsingh, the following details are noteworthy :—

"On 4th August, about one o'clock several rivers became dry ; at two a thick vapour was seen at Azuma over the Tone-gawa, the black muddy water of which boiled up violently. An immense quantity of red-hot stones floating on the surface gave it the appearance of a torrent of fire. . . . On the 5th at ten in the morning, a torrent of sulphur, mixed with rocks, large stones and mud, rushing from the mountain, precipitated itself into the Azuma-gawa and swelled it so prodigiously that it overflowed, carried away houses and laid waste the whole country. The number of persons who perished was immense . . . At Karuizawa there fell such a prodigious quantity of red-hot stones that all the inhabitants perished in the flames with the exception of the chief magistrate ; the exact number of the dead is not known . . . On the 6th about one o'clock large trees and timbers of houses began to be seen floating in the river of Yedo, which was soon afterwards completely covered with mangled carcasses of men and beasts . . . In Shinano the devastation extended over a tract of thirty leagues. [Here follows a list of villages overwhelmed.] Many other villages, besides these here named either partly disappeared or were swept away. It was impossible to determine the number of the dead, and the devastation was incalculable." [1]

---

[1] This was a season of considerable seismic activity in Japan. In 1780, the volcano on Vries Island, outside the entrance to Yedo Bay, covered a great part of the surface of the island with about 20 feet of ashes and scoriæ. In the year before, the peak of Mitake in Sakurajima in the Bay opposite the city of Kagoshima burst into action, and about 140 of the islanders perished.

The most costly in human life of all these calamities was the series of cataclysms that overwhelmed the castle-town of Shimabara in 1793. On 25th February, the whole summit of Mount Onsen fell in, and the chasm was so deep that it was impossible to hear the noise made in falling by the stones thrown into it. Torrents of boiling water gushed from all parts, and the vapour which rose from it resembled a thick smoke. On 17th March, there was an eruption about half-a-league from the summit. The flame ascended to a great height ; the lava spread with rapidity at the foot of the mountain, and in a few days the whole country for miles round was in flames . . . The fire was not like ordinary fire, it was sparkling and of a reddish colour, interrupted from time to time by brown blazes. On 1st April, at ten in the evening, a tremendous earthquake was felt throughout Kyūshū, but particularly in the Shimabara peninsula . . . Fortunately the mischief was not so great as had been feared. The mountain meanwhile continued burning, and the lava spread obliquely towards the castle ; but being stopped in its course by a great number of rocks, it turned slowly to the north. On 10th May, when everybody was at dinner, a fresh shock was felt which lasted upwards of an hour and a half, and became more and more violent ; threatening all round with instant destruction. Several houses beyond the castle were presently ingulfed with their inhabitants. Prodigious rocks falling from the mountain overthrew and crushed everything in their way. A tremendous noise resembling loud and repeated discharges of artillery was heard underground and in the air ; at length when the danger was supposed to be over, a horrible eruption of Mayeyama took place. The many lovely pine-clad islets, which render the bay of Shimabara a scene of surpassing beauty, are said to have been formed of fragments of the mountain hurled into the sea by this explosion. The greatest part of it was exploded into the air, fell into the sea, and by its fall raised the water to such a height as to inundate both the town and country. At the same time, an enormous quantity of water issuing from the clefts of the mountain, met the sea-water in the streets and produced whirlpools which in some places washed away the very foundations

The actual and immediate loss of life has been variously estimated; the *Tokugawa Jikki* puts it at 20,000; other accounts carry it to as much as 35,000, while the domestic animals that perished are said to have been " incalculable ". But the immediate loss of life, although no doubt it may impress the unreflective reader most, was perhaps less serious than other results of the eruption. It put most of the soil in Kōzuke, Kai, and Suruga feet deep under ashes. All that year's crop was utterly ruined ; in many of these districts there was scarcely a *koku* of revenue for the lord, and almost nothing for the cultivator left. The natural consequence was that thousands died of famine before the devastated soil could be cleared and resown. Huge tracts of the empire, as remote from the scene of the eruption of Asama as the Home Provinces on the one hand and Ōshu and Dewa on the other, were in not much better case in this year of 1783–4. Even in the preceding year there was a partial failure of the crops in the Go-Kinai. The Government granaries here had been denuded of the stores accumulated in them in the eighth Shōgun's time many years before, while in the far north, outside of Uyesugi's fief of Yonezawa there was perhaps not one single domain with any reserve of cereals to draw upon in case of famine or any similar emergency. What now happened in Ōshu and Dewa is terrible beyond belief, so terrible indeed that the ghoulish details given in the note-books of several travellers in the afflicted districts seem more like the obsessions of a hideous nightmare than anything else. However, if anyone is to be credited, surely the Regent of the empire is to be so ; and this is what he recounts :—

---

of the houses, so as not to leave a vestige of habitations. The castle alone remained uninjured, because the water could not penetrate its strong massive walls ; several houses near it were so completely destroyed that not one stone was left upon another. Men and beasts were drowned by the flood. Some were found suspended from the trees, others standing upright, others kneeling, and others again on their heads in the mud ; and the streets were strewed with dead bodies. Out of all those who fled for refuge in the castle, a very small number effected their escape, and all these had received more or less injury. The cries of those who were still alive beneath the ruins pierced the heart. At length fifty criminals were sent from the castle to extricate the miserable wretches still living, and to inter the dead . . . The tubs which are used in Japan instead of coffins, were uncovered in the cemeteries, or broken, the large stones laid over them being carried away by the torrent . . . A great number of vessels, which lay at anchor in the neighbourhood, went to the bottom ; and an incredible multitude of carcasses of men and beasts, and other wrecks, were brought down by the current, so that ships could scarcely force a passage through them. The wretchedness that everywhere prevailed was inexpressible, and filled the beholder with horror. The number of those known to have perished exceeded 53,000 ; and it is impossible to describe the consternation produced by the catastrophe. The number of dead bodies floating upon the river was incalculable."

" The famine of the third year of Temmei (1783) was particularly severe in the northern part of the country. A trustworthy man, who had travelled in this district told me that in a village which had previously contained 800 houses there were only 30 left, the inhabitants of the rest all having died. Having entered a village in which the houses seemed to be larger and more numerous than usual, he proposed to rest there for the night. He soon discovered, however, that not a single house was inhabited, but in all the houses he saw bones and skulls scattered about the floor. As he went on he saw innumerable bones and skulls by the roadside. He met a man leading a pack-horse on the road, who said that he could survive without eating the flesh of human beings as he was supported by a rich uncle. In some places even those who abandoned themselves to eating human flesh could not find food enough to live. Great numbers starved to death. The price paid for a dog was 500 *mon*, sometimes even as high as 800 *mon*, a rat 50 *mon*. A rare work of art found no purchasers and could not be exchanged for a *go* of rice. If a person died he was of course eaten by the survivors. Those who died of starvation, however, could not be eaten, because their flesh decayed so soon. Some people, therefore, killed those who were certain to starve and put the flesh into brine so as to keep it for a long time. Among other people there was a farmer who went to his neighbour and said, ' My wife and one of my sons have already died from want of food. My remaining son is certain to die within a few days, so I wish to kill him while his flesh is still eatable, but being his father, I do not dare to raise the sword against him, so I beg you to kill the boy for me.' The neighbour agreed to do this, but stipulated that he should get a part of the flesh as a reward for his service. This was agreed to and the neighbour at once killed the boy. As soon as the deed was done, the farmer, who stood by, struck his neighbour with a sword and killed him, saying that he ' was very glad to avenge his son and at the same time have double the quantity of food '. These are a few of the terrible stories told of the great famine of Temmei. ' In these times,' says our author, ' stealing and incendiarism were not considered wrong and went unpunished.' "

In 1785 there was a drought in the Home Provinces, and the crops there failed again. In the following year, there were terrible floods in the Kwantō ; the embankments of the Tone-gawa gave way in many places, and all the wide plain traversed by the river was ravaged and ruined for that year utterly. Large sections of Yedo were under water and many of the people were drowned. Elsewhere, especially in the north, there was no rain at all, and the crops withered utterly. According to Bakin,[1] a contemporary writer :—

---

[1] Bakin (1767-1848) is Japan's most famous novelist, and though his works are not altogether favourably criticized by Dr. Aston, the most competent of European critics, who gives a full description of Bakin's life and works in his *History of Japanese Literature*, he merits a high place among the best known writers of fiction of the world. The first extract in the text is from the works of Shirakawa Rakuo, who was not Regent but Minister of Finance under Iyenari.

" Next year (1787) the price of rice rose higher than before. The price had been double the normal rate, but it soon advanced till it was three and four fold. Barley, wheat, and millet rose proportionately. Some rice dealers refused to sell at any price. What made matters worse was that rice dealers, both wholesale and retail, for the sake of making larger profits, had bought up all the rice, especially from the Samurai class. In many cases rice merchants over-reached themselves and stored the rice until it was worm-eaten. The people noticed the avarice of these speculators and forestallers, and petitions were sent in to the Government to force the dealers to sell their rice and not to store it. In May the *machi-bugyō* (city governors) answered the petitioners, saying that they had examined the rice dealers and found that there was no rice to sell. Instead, the governors told them to use beans, peas, wheat, and millet. This advice did not satisfy the people, and they began to abuse their rulers. This was the beginning of a series of riots. At the same time the rice dealers formed a union not to sell more than a certain amount (from 100 to 200 *mon*) to each person daily. Even this amount was sold only at certain fixed hours in the day, gener- ally very early in the morning, so that men and women, young and old, who feared to be too late, gathered together in crowds in front of the rice shops, and shouted and quarrelled in their struggle to get their *quantum* of rice. After a time, however, the rice dealers refused to sell any rice at all, but, it is said, concealed it in their godowns. From this time there was really nothing left for the poorer classes to eat except a kind of sea-weed. Some rich men, such as Mitsui and Mitsukoshi, wisely put boiled potatoes in front of their stores, and allowed apprentices under fifteen years of age, who ran errands for their masters, to eat as much as they pleased. In this way the consumption of rice was economized. But most people were in a wretched half-starving condi- tion. Cattle and horses lay dead by the wayside. By June, I saw dogs eating grass.

" On the night of the 20th June a crowd of people (whence they came was never known) destroyed the house of a rice dealer in Kojimachi. This was the first act of destruction. After this, mobs collected every- where, and by the 24th, all the houses and godowns of the rice dealers of Yedo were destroyed. Not a single rich man who sold or hoarded rice escaped. Besides the rice dealers, the sellers of *saké* (wine) and *mochi* (rice-bread) were attacked. On the 25th the work of destruction extended to the rice dealers of Shinagawa, Kawasaki, and Kanagawa. The mobs usually consisted of from 50 to 100 men. At first they carried on their work of destruction by night, or very early in the morning. Most shopkeepers lit a candle in their shops to show that they were not rice dealers ; the other shops were generally torn down and looted. Finally, however, the rioters became bolder and carried on the work of destruction by day. Sounds of crashing, shouts, and clamour, were heard a long way off. ' I saw,' says Bakin, ' the shop of a rice-dealer, called Mansaku, in Demma-cho, attacked by the mob. They cut open the bags of rice and scattered the grain on the street. Chests and boxes

and both extracts in their English form are quoted from Professor Garrett Droppers' paper on " The Population of Japan in the Tokugawa Period ", which has already been referred to. —J. H. L.

they broke to pieces and threw the contents out of the shop. Respectable women and children of the poorer class mingled with beggars and pickpockets and put the rice in their sleeves and bags. No one attempted to stop them or drive them away. The dealers were utterly helpless and did nothing to stop them. At last the Government sent officers to quell the rioting, but they did not succeed in arresting anyone. At the head of one of the most notorious mobs, was a young apprentice 15 or 16 years of age, who was so active that people were frightened at his mere appearance, and thought that he must be a kind of hobgoblin, called *tengu*. As for the rest, no one knew who they were. The Government finally gave orders that anyone might seize a rioter or even kill him if necessary. So every shopkeeper armed himself with a long bamboo spear in order to drive off the mob. But in reality the measure proved futile. As soon as the mob came, the shopkeeper stood shivering at his own door helplessly watching them destroy his shop in his very presence. The same condition of affairs existed in Kyōto, Ōsaka, and the surrounding districts, so that it seemed as if the rioters acted in concert on some secret understanding. This, however, was not the case. In all these cities the houses and godowns of rice-dealers fell a prey to the fury of the mobs, until finally there was nothing left for them to destroy. Thus after about a month of this lawlessness the rioting came to an end.

"In the autumn of the year 1787, the Government imported rice into Yedo from all parts of the country and offered it for sale as cheaply as possible. Moreover, the new crop of wheat and barley was harvested and helped to relieve the famine. A considerable quantity of worm-eaten rice which had been stored by speculators in out-of-the-way places also was sold about this time. Yet in spite of all these favourable circumstances, the price of rice remained for a long time double the ordinary price."

The results of this state of affairs are apparent in the census returns. In 1780, the non-Samurai population stood at 26,010,000 ; in 1786, it had gone down to 25,086,466 ; while in 1792, by which time there must have been a slight measure of recovery since the last year of distress (1789–90), it was no more than 24,891,441. "This is the lowest figure recorded in any census of the Tokugawa period, and is a fitting culmination to an era, noted in the history of Japan, as a time of starvation and misery." Thus, in the course of these seven lean years something between a million and a million and a quarter of victims must have succumbed to the horrors of famine and the resulting or accompanying diseases. This exceeds by almost a full half the total that perished on the battlefields of the most deadly European struggle of the century. During the Seven Years' War, waged on three continents and on as many oceans, no more than 850,000 combatants are reckoned to have perished. During the two centuries of seclusion Japan was spared from the horrors

of war, it is true. Yet the closed State, especially with the population pressing hard upon the limits of subsistence, is not exempt
from peculiar risks of its own.[1]

What makes the tale of these seven inexpressibly disastrous
years so extremely sad is that most of the misery could have been
averted. That such was the case is abundantly clear from the
record of the Yonezawa fief. The wretched condition of this bleak
and inhospitable tract in 1769 has already been set forth. Yet
before the advent of the years of famine Uyesugi had the granaries
of his clan full to repletion. Many of his subjects doubtless felt the
pinch of hunger somewhat severely before the worst was over, but
none actually died of starvation it is said. Now what was possible
in the forbidding circumstances of Yonezawa was surely equally
feasible in more favourably situated domains. What might actually

---

[1] It may be interesting to draw a comparison between this famine—the famine
of Temmei as it is termed, Temmei being the *nengo* of the period in which it occurred
—and that which occurred in Ireland, sixty years later, during the years 1846-9.
That of Temmei lasted continuously in its full force from 1783 to 1787 or, according
to Professor Droppers, less severely from 1781 to 1788. There were other great
calamities during the same period, especially the disastrous erruption of the
volcanic mountain, Asama, which caused the deaths of 35,000 people. According
to the figures in the text, between 1,000,000 and a 1,250,000 people died
from famine or diseases that naturally followed famine, while the population
between 1780 and 1792, five years after the famine, had decreased by 1,119,000.
During these years Japan was not only prevented by her national policy of isolation
from obtaining the food that was available in cheap abundance from abroad, but
even within her own boundaries, where the ruin of the crops was not universal,
the different fiefs resembled, to some degree, the national in their local policy
of seclusion, and those not affected by the scarcity selfishly retained for their own
use the food that might have been shared with others. In Ireland, the great famine
lasted from 1846 to 1849, and did not come entirely to an end till 1851. Warning
had been given of its approach, and as Ireland was open to all the world and all
the world knew of its calamity when it came, full provision could have been made
to meet it and to relieve it. Abundance of food was even produced in Ireland itself,
but in the view of the English Government which ruled Ireland at the time, the
legitimate course of trade could not be interfered with, and the food was exported
to provide the funds necessary for the payment of their rack-rents to absentee
landlords. According to Earl Grey : " If the landlords, as a body, had done their
duty to the population under them, the existing state of society would never have
been such as it was." As it was, the resultant horrors were terrible enough, though
not so ghastly as in Japan. " Many people were glad to live on a single meal of
cabbage a day ; many feasted on the dead bodies of horses, asses, and dogs ; there
is at least one horrible story of a mother eating the limbs of her dead child ; seaweed,
diseased cattle, and diseased potatoes were greedily devoured." This was in 1846.
Matters were worse in 1847, and continued till 1849, in which there was a return
to the greater ghastliness and more multitudinous horrors of 1847. The mortality
from famine in five years was officially recorded at 985,366. This was in a population in round numbers, of 8,000,000, as compared with 30,000,000 in Japan.
Emigration took away 1,180,000 people, of whom 200,668, enfeebled by hunger and
disease, died on the voyages or on their arrivals at their destinations. " The holds
of the emigrant ships, crowded and filthy, carrying double the legal number of
passengers, ill fed and imperfectly clothed, with no doctor on board, were like the
Black Hole of Calcutta." In 1841, the population of Ireland was 8,175,000.
Ten years later it had fallen to 6,552,000, though the Irish, as a prolific people,
easily rival the Japanese. (These particulars are taken from *The Parnell Movement*,
by Mr. T. P. O'Connor, M.P.)

be done to retrieve the disaster by determination and energy, even where no due preparations had been made to meet it, was demonstrated in the not very remote fief of Shirakawa. Young Matsudaira Sadanobu, the future Regent of the empire, succeeded to the headship of this clan in the very midst of the awful famine of 1784. That very year he had to face a loss of seventy per cent. or eighty per cent. of the usual revenue, while his peasants were on the point of starvation. He at once started the repair of the Abukuma-gawa embankments as relief-works, imported cereals, dried fish, and other kinds of cheap food, and had the satisfaction of finding the death-roll on his estates a mere fraction of what it was in the neighbouring daimyoates.

As for the Bakufu, down to 1786, it did little or nothing. In that year it issued the so-called " Thrice Advantageous Decree ". In the midst of its beautiful platitudes one clause of this document ordered the rich merchants of Ōsaka to advance funds to the Daimyō, and the Daimyō were ordered to borrow from the merchants. The Bakufu was going to appropriate one-seventh of the interest paid. The traders openly said that this would deprive them of capital which was absolutely necessary for the prosecution of their businesses, and that if so deprived of it they would be driven to close their establishments. But their real secret ground of reluctance to sacrifice themselves for the country was that they could not trust the Government. The decree was merely another device, they held, to help Tanuma to fill his already richly plenished coffers and warehouses. So little or nothing came of this Threefold Advantageous Decree, for it could not be enforced. At last, however, in 1787, the problem of famine relief was attacked resolutely by the Bakufu. And with good faith, too, for in 1786 there had been a sweeping change in the personnel of the administration. Iyeharu, the tenth Shōgun, had passed away, and Tanuma had fallen.[1]

---

[1] Iyeharu died on the 30th September, 1786, at the age of 47 years, after a reign of twenty-four years. He is accredited with having had six children, two sons and two daughters, and two adopted children. the latter furnishing an instance of the curious results of adoption in Japan, where adopted are not only vested with all the legal rights of natural-born children, and are subject to all their liabilities of absolute subjection, but seem to receive and return all the affection that may be expected from, or by, the latter. Of Iyeharu's own children, one daughter and one son died in childhood. The surviving daughter married the great feudatory of Owari, and the son was the young prince whose early death is described below. The adopted son succeeded to the Shōgunate as Iyenari, the eleventh Shōgun, and the adopted daughter married Prince Kujo, one of the " Go sekke ", the five Regent Houses, of the Imperial Court at Kyōto.

CHAPTER XI

IYENARI'S MINORITY (1786–93)

OF Iyeharu's two sons, one died in childhood. The other, born in 1763, was formally named heir apparent in his third year. As he grew up, he gave abundant promise of capacity ; and in addition to this he had the great gift of endearing himself to all classes of his future subjects. Accordingly, on his premature death in 1779, the nation went into voluntary mourning for him, as they had done for Iyenobu in 1712.[1]

Titsingh asserts that the young prince died of a spitting of blood, occasioned by falling with his horse (one imported by the Dutch) down a precipice while hunting. Presently, it began to be whispered that Iyemoto had really been poisoned by one of his attendants in the hunting field (at Shinagawa), at the instigation of Tanuma. Tanuma possibly looked forward to the accession of Iyemoto with a good deal of apprehension, but that he really prompted such an atrocious crime as rumour now laid to his charge is scarcely probable. The Shōgun, soon after this sad event, determined to adopt a member of one of the Sankyō houses as a son, and so provide for the succession in case of his own sudden demise. It was not from Tayasu, the senior, but from Hitotsubashi, the second of the three families, that the heir was selected. One reason for this was that Tanuma's younger brother was seneschal in the Hitotsubashi mansion, where he was all-powerful. Thus, the accession of a new Shōgun taken from that family would not be likely to threaten the power of Tanuma and his camarilla in any way. So, in 1781, Hitotsubashi Harunari's eldest son, Iyenari, was adopted by Iyeharu and duly installed in the Nishi-maru as heir apparent to the Shōgunate.

---

[1] Some Japanese writers assert that Iyemoto was the first and only Tokugawa prince for whom the nation went into voluntary mourning, but Arai Hakuseki claimed this distinction for Iyenobu, sixty-seven years earlier. Other authors maintain that it was Yoshimune who introduced sugar-cane cultivation into Japan although we find Iyenobu asserting that the Japanese were able to grow sugar-cane themselves. The distinction of being the pioneer in anything, no matter how trivial, is eagerly coveted by some Japanese, and the historian must always be on his guard against accepting the validity of these claims without exhaustive investigation.

Two years later, in 1783, Tanuma's son, Mototomo, Yamashiro no Kami, was assigned a seat in the Junior Council. His tenure of office was, however, brief. On 13th May, 1784, he was assassinated as the Tairō, Hotta, was exactly a century before. This incident has been very fully dealt with by Titsingh, and yet his accounts leave the reader in a state of uncertainty and doubt, for there are not a few statements in them that seem to be at serious variance with each other :—

"Though many Japanese of the highest distinction and intimately acquainted with matters of government still consider Japan as the first empire in the world, and care but little for what passes out of it, yet such persons are denominated by the most enlightened *I no uchi kaeru*, or 'frogs in a well', a metaphorical expression which signifies when they look up, they can see no more of the sky than what the small circumference of the well allows them to see. [The frog in the well knows not the great ocean.] The eyes of the better informed had long been fixed on Tanuma, the son of the Counsellor of State, a young man of uncommon merit, and of enterprising mind. They flattered themselves that when he should succeed his father he would, as they expressed it, widen the road. After his appointment, he and his father incurred the hatred of the grandees of the court by introducing various innovations that were censured by the latter as detrimental to the welfare of the empire. He was assassinated on 13th May, 1784, by Sano Masakoto, as related in my *Annals of Japan*. *His crime put an end to all hopes of seeing Japan opened to foreigners, and its inhabitants visiting other countries.* Nothing more, however, would be required for the success of such a project than one man of truly enlightened and imposing character. At present after mature reflection on all that is past, they are convinced that the secret artifices and intrigues of the priests of Shaka were the real cause of the troubles which for many years disturbed the peace of the empire."

While this view of the general situation is not necessarily totally at fault, I have so far found nothing going to confirm its correctness in the native records of the time. On the other hand, the long and circumstantial account given of Tanuma's assassination in Titsingh's *Annals of Japan*, tallies very well indeed with the purport of what we meet with in these records.

Tanuma's assassin, an officer in the Shimban-gumi, or "New Company of Life Guards" held an estate at Sano, not far from where the Tōkaidō Railway to-day descends the slope from Gotemba, at the base of Fuji-san, to Numadzu. Tanuma had requested him to exchange it for another, but as it had been held by the family for generations, Sano declined to do so. A little later he was deprived of it. Tanuma had also refused to return a genealogical chart which Sano lent him and he had insulted Sano in the hunting field. Thus the assassin had ample grounds for harbouring resentment on his own personal account, but Japanese writers contend that he was also prompted by public and patriotic motives, although they are not so explicit on this point as Titsingh.

" From all the circumstances attending the murder, it is to be presumed that several persons of the highest distinction were privy to, and encouraged, it ; and the general hatred which the two counsellors of State had drawn upon themselves serves to confirm the opinion. It is even asserted that the original intention was to kill the father to prevent the reforms which he and his son, who were in the highest favour with the Shōgun and his family, were successively introducing into the different departments of the State, and by which they had incurred great odium. But it was considered that, as the father was old, death would naturally soon put a stop to his projects, whereas the son, who was in the prime of life, would have time to carry into effect all the innova- tions they had planned and that, moreover, it would be impossible to inflict a severer blow on the father than by snatching from him his son. The death of the latter was, in consequence, determined on."

The assassin was indeed permitted to die by his own hand ; but the function was carried out in the *agariya* or gaol, with a prison official and not a personal friend of the culprit's as " second " :—

" His wife, a lady of exquisite beauty, and only 22 years of age, when informed of his death, commended his conduct, and plunged a dagger into her throat with a courage equal to that of her husband. Tanuma's corpse was privately interred in the night. The hatred and indignation of the people were so violent that they threw stones from all sides at the coffin and those who accompanied it. Sano, on the contrary, became an object of public veneration. He was considered as a victim, who had devoted himself for his country. His grave, on which a stone was erected as a mark of honour, is visited by all persons of distinction, and by the military who repair thither to offer up prayers and thanksgiving for the service which he rendered to the State." [1]

The elder Tanuma soon began to realize that his position

---

[1] The sentiment which does honour to the memory of political assassins, still survives in Japan. The spirits of the Forty-seven Rōnin are steadfastly worshipped, notwithstanding the commercial materialism that has largely replaced the all-sacrificing devotion of feudalism, but a more modern instance is that of Viscount Mori, Minister of Education and at one time Envoy in London, who was assassinated by a youth named Nishino Buntaro on the very day in February, 1889, on which all the nation was joyfully celebrating the promulgation of the new Constitution. The assassin was cut down on the spot but, from the paper found on him, it appeared that the reason for his act was that Viscount Mori had dese- crated the Imperial Shrine at Ise by touching a curtain with his walking stick. The grave, not of the murdered minister, but of the fanatical assassin was for years afterwards, and may be so still, never without fresh flowers, and it was the object of such frequent pilgrimages and prayers, that, at last, the Government decreed that the practice of honouring dead criminals should cease.—J. H. L.

was becoming critical. The Shōgun's death was not likely to be long deferred, and during the minority of his successor (Iyenari) attempts to overthrow him were certain. His chief hope lay in getting the prospective Shōgun's father, Hitotsubashi Harunori, chosen as Regent. The crisis actually came in September, 1786, when Iyeharu's days were seen to be numbered. Tanuma had two of his own physicians taken into the Shōgun's service, but their services were futile, and Iyeharu died on 12th September. Tanuma tried to conceal his death till he could perfect his arrangements, but the Go-san-ké were keenly on the alert. They met in the Owari *yashiki* and promptly concerted their measures. On 18th September, when Tanuma proceeded to the Castle, he was met by a Sobayōnin who " advised " him to return to his *yashiki* and send in his resignation. Tanuma at once saw that the bolt had fallen in spite of all his precautions. Shortly afterwards, his brother (a Sobayōnin) and two Finance Magistrates, the leading figures in his camarilla, were stripped of their offices.

The Go-san-ké at first pressed Tayasu's second son, the lord of Matsuyama in Iyo, to assume the office of Tairō. As he was on good terms with Tanuma, and was aware that one of his first duties would be to degrade him, the lord of Matsuyama positively refused to enter the Great Council. The Go-san-ké then fell back upon his younger brother, Matsudaira Sadanobu, Lord of Shirakawa, who had been adopted into the Matsudaira Hisamitsu house a few years before. He was now made President of the Rōjū and, in the following year, when Iyenari received his patent as Shōgun, he was promoted to the great office of Hosa or Regent. In December, 1786, the Go-san-ké went so far as to deprive Tanuma of 20,000 *koku* of his revenue and his chief *yashiki* in Yedo, and to order him into seclusion. In the following year, his castle was demolished, and his fief confiscated, and in 1788, he died a poor, dishonoured, and broken man. How far we have got the exact truth about him it is impossible to say ; his enemies had triumphed and could do what they pleased, and to tamper with the records in those days was considered no mortal sin, even by those of the most tender conscience. Why Titsingh's estimate of Tanuma is so greatly at variance with the one usually accepted in Japan has, of course, to be accounted for. Probably it was inspired by Kuze, Tango no Kami, one of the Governors of Nagasaki, who had served for long under the fallen statesman.

Although he had not yet reached his thirtieth year, the newly appointed Regent, Matsudaira Sadanobu, had already won great reputation as an administrator. The measures he had adopted to combat the famine in his own fief of Shirakawa in 1784 have already been referred to. In many respects he appears to have adopted Uyesugi Harunori's administration as a model. Some problems, however, he solved in his own way :—

" When he first went down to Shirakawa he found that there were more men than women ; that it was difficult for poor men to marry ; that the population was yearly decreasing, and that the cultivated land was gradually becoming desolated. In order to remedy this state of affairs, he arranged that old people above ninety should be pensioned, that pregnant women be registered, that a mother having more than five children be rewarded with rice. At the same time he sent commissioners to Echigo to collect poor women, who were brought to Shirakawa and married to bachelors, assigned land and houses, and instructed in farming and weaving. In this way he put a stop to the old vice ; population began to increase, and many new lands were opened. Sadanobu also encouraged the planting of young trees, so that within a few years a traveller entering his domain was delighted by seeing green all around him as far as the eye could reach."

The occurrence of famine, or any similar calamity was often seized upon by feudal lords as a pretext for curtailing the stipends of the samurai. Sadanobu contented himself with retrenching his own expenses, and only resorted to a reduction of his vassals' incomes when such a step could not possibly be avoided. One of the very first things he did as Regent was to express his high admiration for Uyesugi Harunori and his work, and to recommend the administration of the Yonezawa fief as a model to the other Daimyō. His own work as Regent touched almost every sphere of the national and social economy. Yet extensive as it was, it is possible to deal with it succinctly enough. He began by announcing that it was his prime intention to revert to the institutions of Kyōhō (1716–35) that is to say, to the régime of his grandfather, the illustrious Yoshimune. In 1790, orders were again issued that all the feudatories should store 100 *koku* of rice in the clan granaries for every 10,000 raised on their estates. In the Bakufu domains no new taxes were to be imposed, but the coinage was to be reformed, and frugality strictly enforced. Even in the matter of dress it was his grandfather that Sadanobu took as a model. He repaired to the Castle in the cheapest and simplest of raiment, and his gaily-attired colleagues were promptly shamed into drawing up a self-denying ordinance prohibiting the wearing of costly apparel, and the giving or receiving of presents. A Daimyō, who fancied that Sadanobu was really a hypocrite at bottom, sent him a gift worth 100 *ryō*. The Regent at once acknowledged the mark of affection and devotion by sending him a return gift of the value of 150 *ryō*. The hint was a gentle one, but it was enough ; when the incident became generally known, Sadanobu ceased to be troubled by the tender of any " thank-offerings " for favours to come. Among other things, the Regent insisted on looking very closely into the Shōgun's household budget. The stern measure he had just meted out to the grizzly-haired favourite of the Court Ladies (Tanuma) had incensed them greatly ; when they saw that sacrilegious hands were to be laid upon what was to them as the very ark of the covenant, the commotion was intense. The court dames refused to discharge their duties any longer. One of them, a certain Lady Ōzaki, one of Tanuma's chief agents, was then dismissed, and thereupon the rest of them tendered their resignations. To smooth over this matter took much time and trouble and, down to the end of his administration. Sadanóbu's " dearest " foes were those of the Great Interior.

The Regent was fortunate in finding able men of his own cast of mind and temper willing to serve under him. Matsudaira Nobuaki in the Rōjū ; the two Junior Councillors, Honda and Hotta ; the Sobayōnin, Kanō ; the Finance Magistrate, Negishi, and the City Magistrate, Ishikawa, all entered into his plans and projects of reform with the greatest enthusiasm and determination. The administration of justice by the Hyōjōsho again became pure, prompt, and efficient ; in the country districts, the Gundai and Daikwan were held to strict account, the corrupt and inefficient among them being cashiered, and capable and honest men appointed in their places. Naturally to restore to the cultivator the measure of prosperity he had enjoyed in Yoshimune's time was an uphill, if not a hopeless, task as the maladministration of the previous forty years had greatly demoralized the agrarian prole-tariat. It sounds ludicrous to be assured that habits of luxury had spread among peasant communities where the ordinary standard of living was so terribly low according to all modern European notions. But a whole crowd of Japanese writers well acquainted with the actual conditions of the time are at once unanimous and emphatic in this seemingly absurd contention :—

The artificial dead peace, together with the debased currency of the period, had continually tended to breed luxury among the toiling population of the village, and furthermore luxury did often so operate as to reduce the productive capacity of the peasant family. "Formerly," says a writer of the Sendai fief in 1790, "when a farmer could bring up two, three, four, or five sons, all the younger sons were hired out to other farmers as soon as they were old enough, saved their wages and married, or were adopted into families. There was everywhere an abundant supply of cheap labour for the fields. The farmers could also keep horses which yielded manure. The productive power of the soil was large and rice was plentiful. The peasants could likewise afford to have daughters. Marriage was inexpensive, the population increased at the normal rate and the Heavenly Law was fulfilled. But now (1790) marriages cost the man 30 *kwan*, and the woman's family almost 40. It being increasingly hard to maintain a household, the average peasant has now seldom more than three children, and the poorer tenant only one child. Labour gets scarce and dear, having risen from 5 or 6 to 10 *kwan*, and still rising every year. Horses get fewer, and manure more difficult to procure. It being often impossible to take care of one's own holding, it is rented to anyone willing to till it, but who is naturally inclined to neglect the land that is not his own. In recent years most land has yielded on the average only 15 to 16 *koku* per *chō*, instead of the former average of 20 *koku*."

This was the condition of affairs in Sendai, where the administration was distinctly good. In the Bakufu lands matters were infinitely worse at this date. To devise and apply effective remedies for the ingrained evils of the previous generation of maladministration would, of course, be the work of years. Yet by well-considered and vigorous measures, sumptuary laws among them, the Regent did not a little to revive the drooping fortunes of agriculture in the Tokugawa household estates. But the great source and sink of corruption was Yedo, the belly of the empire. All through the Tokugawa epoch we are continually hearing of the increasing prosperity of Yedo; indeed, writers are just as unanimous and emphatic about this phenomenon as they are about the impoverishment and decay of the rural districts. Yoshimune, as we have seen, early discerned a menace in this state of affairs, and by relaxing the Sankin Kōtai regulations for a time, and by other measures endeavoured to send the superfluous floating population of the metropolis back to the land. In Ōoka's early days, the non-*yashiki* population was reduced to 501,000. In 1787, it was found that it stood at 1,367,840 souls. In this human hive, of course, it was not all luxury and magnificence. The picture of the extremes of wealth and want meeting there described by Siebold, just half-a-century later, would have been perfectly applicable to the Yedo of Iyenari's earliest years. And of the magnificence that prevailed a great deal was utterly unsubstantial and factitious. By this time, thousands of Hatamoto and samurai families had hopelessly outrun their means, and were plunged in a bottomless quagmire of indebtedness. Yet appearances had to be kept up, and a gay and gallant show abroad maintained, although the family rice-pot at home was all but empty. So desperate was the general financial situation that the Regent became convinced that the knot could not possibly be untied ; the only thing to do was to cut it summarily. Under the Ashikaga Shōguns, *Toku-sei* or "Acts[1] of Benevolent Administration", otherwise a cancellation of samurai indebtedness, were resorted to on perhaps half-a-score or a dozen of occasions. A similar drastic remedy was now applied. Sadanobu ordered that all Hatamoto debts of more than six years' standing should be nullified, and that those incurred within that term should be paid off in instalments at reduced interest. Furthermore, the maximum rate of interest was henceforth to be no more than one per cent. monthly. The following extract from Professor Mikami's Biography of the Regent is instructive :—

" Sadanobu was very eager to purify society of its licentious and dissolute habits. Many years of peace had led the young Hatamoto into idle and profligate courses. The old spirit of the Samurai, which placed honour above everything, was well-nigh a thing of the past. Greed took possession of the Samurai, so that we find in the new Buké-Shohatto of 1787 the following additional clause. ' In negotiations for adoption or marriage, no reference must be made to money or property.' As a matter of fact, people could not marry unless they were well off, and in consequence many fell into dissolute habits. In days of old when Samurai assembled, the talk used to turn upon personal prowess and warfare ; it now ran upon fair women, and many young Hatamoto were constant *habitués* of the Yoshiwara.[2]

" Sadanobu made a hard endeavour to reform these young men, and to stem the profligacy of the time. On the one hand he rewarded filial sons, virtuous wives and faithful servants, and, on the other, reprimanded and punished dissolute samurai, and harassed the keepers

---

[1] The expedient of the " Tokusei " was first used under the administration of Sadatoki, the seventh of the Hōjō Regents (1284–1300). He issued a law in 1297, which interdicted the pledging of their property by samurai, forbade all legal processes for the recovery of interest, and cancelled all mortgages. The experiment was repeated many times under the Ashikaga (by Yoshimasa alone thirteen times) for the relief of the samurai from the results of dissipation and extravagance. Under the Hōjō, it was intended to relieve distress caused by the expenses of the repulse of the Mongols. The literal meaning of *Tokusei* it may be said, is "Virtuous Government ".—J. H. L.

[2] This is an almost verbatim repetition of the phraseology to be met with in several Genroku and Hō-ei (1688–1709) documents, referring to the dissoluteness of these year-periods. The new clause that Professor Mikami says was now inserted in the *Buké Shohatto* does not appear in those of 1787. It is to be found in those of Iyenobu drafted by Arai Hakuseki.

of brothels and women of easy virtue, especially the *Geisha*. In 1789, he proscribed the establishment of new brothels, took rigorous measures to suppress unlicensed prostitution, and prohibited mixed bathing in the bath-houses of the city."

The conventional and time-honoured theory, of course, was that a samurai's soul should be above all considerations of money or filthy lucre. But, even, as early as the latter half of the seventeenth century, the language used in certain clauses of Mitsukuni of Mito's famous Instructions to his vassals is conclusive that theory and practice were vastly different matters. Under Tsunayoshi and again under Iyeshige and Iyeharu, we have seen that jobbery and bribery were notorious and rampant. Now the bribe-takers and many of the bribe-tenderers were samurai. Again, in Tanuma's time, public offices were sold and almost everyone was acquainted with the fact. And those who profited by this most illegal and nefarious traffic were samurai. The difference between the traffic in offices in Japan and in contemporary France were two. In France, the traffic was perfectly legal, and commoners might purchase offices and so become nobles. In Japan, the traffic was decidedly illegal, and commoners could not purchase office directly and so become samurai. In Arai's time we have met with an instance of a rich merchant trying to mate his daughter with a poor samurai and ultimately succeeding in doing so. By this date (1787) it had become not only usual for rich commoners to marry their daughters to samurai, but to get their sons adopted into samurai families. In truth, what the Russian Golownin was told about a quarter of a century later is fairly accurate :—

" Merchants are not privileged to bear arms ; but though their profession is not respected their wealth is ; for in Japan, as in Europe, riches supply the want of talents and dignity, and attain privileges and honourable appointments. The Japanese told us that their officers of state, and men of rank, behave outwardly with great haughtiness to merchants, but in private, are very familiar with the wealthy of that class, and are often under great obligations to them. We had with us for some time a young officer who was the son of a rich merchant, and who, as the Japanese said, owed his rank not to his own merit, but to his father's gold, thus, though the laws do not favour the mercantile profession, yet its wealth raises it, for even in Japan, where the laws are so rigorously enforced, they are often outweighed by the influence of gold."

The average Japanese samurai was not avaricious by nature but he was often vain, and far too fond of display, and far too eager for distinction. This led him into an expensive and ostentatious style of living ; and the consequence was that, in spite of all the fine-spun, high-sounding theories of Bushidō, money came to be of supreme importance to him. He often became not so very scrupulous as to the means and methods of acquiring it, and, worse than that, he was forced to become a hypocrite, with sounding phrases about honour on his lips and the worship of Mammon in his heart of hearts. In the remote country fiefs things, happily, were often vastly different, but there can be but little question that the true old samurai spirit of Katō Kiyomasa's age was well-nigh extinct in the Yedo of 1786. Long before this, as has been asserted in a previous chapter, the *Rusui* or resident Karō in the Daimyō's *yashiki*, who represented their lord in Yedo during their alternate years of absence on their fiefs, had made themselves notorious by their ostentatious extravagance and debauchery. The Regent now deemed it well to give them a hint to mend their ways. When they showed a disposition to treat the admonition as a joke, Sadanobu spoke in much plainer and sharper terms, and during the succeeding years the *Rusui* felt constrained to behave with some regard for decorum. But by the end of the century they were once more at their old time-honoured pranks undisturbed.

From first to last there was a tremendous amount of sumptuary legislation during the Tokugawa régime. During Iyetsuna's minority the Bakufu councillors, no less than clan officials, were especially active in this direction. Again, under Iyenobu and Yoshimune, we hear much of " Economy Decrees " (*Kenyaku-rei*), and under these two Shōguns, who could at least claim the merit of personally practising what they made their ministers preach, these regulations were really enforced. Under Tsunayoshi and again under Iyeshige and Iyeharu, we also meet with frequent mention of *Kenyaku-rei*. But these were merely part of the great game of keeping up appearances that then went on everywhere. All these Shōguns were lovers of the sumptuous and magnificent, and their subjects, no doubt, keenly appreciating the humour of Satan gravely reproving sin, paid no heed to the *Kenyaku-rei* whatever. In the course of the two centuries we are dealing with in this volume the Bakufu had intermittent spasms of virtue. Under the Regency of Matsudaira Sadanobu (1786–93) the authorities were assailed by one of them, and although the attack was of no long continuance, it was exceedingly acute while it lasted.

The females of the non-samurai classes were forbidden to

embroider their garments ; no gold hair-pins or similar costly ornaments were to be used, neither were tobacco-pipes nor pouches to be ornamented with precious metals. The manufacture of expensive sweetmeats was interdicted ; gold and silver foil were not to be used on toys, and even the dimensions of dolls were to be curtailed ; in short it was war to the knife upon everything that savoured of Vanity Fair. A few of the articles in these decrees of Sadanobu's were new, but most of them were merely repetitions of some of his grandfather's sumptuary regulations. Fifty years or so later on, we shall find Yedo suffering from a still more intense spasm of official virtue, the outward symptoms of the malady being to all intents and purposes identical with those of the period immediately before us.

Much had been done for the municipal organization of Yedo in Yoshimune's time. Sadanobu now carried his grandfather's work in this sphere a step further. In 1790, he called for a detailed statement of municipal finance for the preceding quinquennium. On ascertaining the average annual budget, he reduced it some-what and of the amount thus economized he ordered ten per cent. to be allotted for extraordinary expenses, twenty per cent. to be refunded to the landowners, and the remaining seventy per cent. to be accumulated as a city fund. This fund, to which a government subsidy was twice added, was entrusted to the management of the aldermen (*machi-doshiyori*) and was utilized to cope with unexpected disasters and emergencies.

On the whole, the Regent's six years' term of administration was highly beneficial to the empire at large, but it might very well have been more so, if Matsudaira Sadanobu had been a man of his grandfather's calibre. That he fell a good many inches short of Yoshimune's intellectual stature becomes clear when we turn to a consideration of the mistakes he committed. In two instances, at least, he showed a lack of judgment and in one a lack of principle where the eighth Shōgun would not have been found tripping. The first of these brought him into serious collision with the Imperial Court, and ultimately led to his retirement. In connexion with it, it may be well to review the relations of Kyōto with Yedo since the death of Iyenobu.

Under the fifth and sixth Shōguns, these relations were exceedingly harmonious and cordial, as we have said. Indeed, it had been arranged that Iyenobu's son, the seventh Shōgun,

Iyetsugu, should wed an Imperial Princess when he became of age, and that in future the Shōgun's consort should be of Imperial stock. The premature death of Iyetsugu in 1716 interfered with this project, indeed, it was not till a century and a half later that it was realized, and it was then adopted mainly as a means of propping up the failing and tottering fortunes of the Tokugawa Shōgunate. Upon Yoshimune's accession (1716) the intercourse between Yedo and the Imperial Court became much less intimate than it had been under his three predecessors. One of the eighth Shōgun's great aims was to revive the military spirit among his vassals, to restore the old traditions of simplicity and frugality, and to check all empty pomp and display that might lead the Daimyō and Hatamoto into frivolity and effeminacy. The appearance of missions from the Imperial Court in Yedo had become exceedingly frequent since 1680, and the Imperial envoys always had to be sumptuously entertained and fêted. A continuance of this state of things would have interfered seriously with Yoshimune's cherished projects, so he courteously gave it to be understood in Kyōto that henceforth Imperial envoys need not be sent to Yedo except on what were practically statutory occasions. It is obvious that he really intended no slight to the Court of Kyōto by this intimation, and that he was far from wishing to wound the *amour propre* of the courtiers in any way. Yet the intimation gave serious offence. Towards the end of his life, Yoshimune established two of his sons with high rank and titles as heads of houses that might supply a successor to the Shōgunate in the event of the main line failing ; and, later on, yet another similar house was created. This appeared an imitation of the Four Imperial Princely Houses that could furnish an occupant to the throne in case of the Emperor dying childless, and the Kyōto nobles were not slow to murmur about the overweening presumption of the Bakufu in this affair. Yet, in most matters, Yoshimune showed himself most respectful towards the Imperial household. Tsunayoshi began the task of investigating the sites of the old *misasagi* or burial mounds and tombs of the Emperors and putting them in a state of decency and repair. This work was carried on and completed by Yoshimune, although his successors neglected it scandalousy. Means for the proper celebration of the great court functions, such as the *Dai-jō-e*,[1] were liberally

---

[1] The Dai-jō-e (called also the Daijōsai) is the ceremony of offering rice at the coronation of an Emperor to the spirits of the Imperial ancestors.—J. H. L.

supplied, while the revenues of the Sovereign and the courtiers were always promptly paid in full.

Notwithstanding, the courtiers were far from being as well off as they were two generations before. Then they earned large incomes as instructors in certain kinds of esoteric lore of which they held a virtual hereditary monopoly. This monopoly had gone. In astronomy, in history, even in Japanese antiquities and ancient literature, they were now outclassed by a crowd of outsiders, while in Chinese philosophy they were mere amateurs as compared with the great lights of the Teishu and the rival schools that had arisen. In fact, instead of sitting in the seat of the teacher, we now find them figuring as docile and appreciative pupils. Even a century before, we have seen them acknowledging the superiority of Kumazawa Banzan, and it was on account of his growing influence among the Court Nobles that Kumazawa's philosophical discussions were brought to such an abrupt termination by the Bakufu. Now, just 100 afterwards, there was a repetition of the Kumazawa Banzan incident. A certain Takenouchi Shikibu from Echigo had settled in Kyōto to study medicine. His object was merely to obtain a means of support; his main interests being Chinese philosophy and Shintōism. It is in him that Yamazaki Anzai and the principles he taught at last appear as an active militant force. Takenouchi had studied the old Shintō doctrines under Tamaki Isai, one of their earlier expounders, and he had also been deeply impressed with the *Seigen Igen* and other writings of Asami Keisai,[1] one of Yamazaki's most distinguished pupils, and a most uncompromising advocate of the " Divine Right of Kings ". Presently Takenouchi began to give courses of lectures. In these the old and threadbare platitudes about " Loyalty " duly appeared, but the question was asked, " Loyalty to whom ? " His discourses on the *Kojiki* and *Nihongi* and the early history of Japan and Japanese Institutions supplied an answer to the query, which, of course, was a most inconvenient and soul-perturbing one to the Bakufu officials in the Castle of Nijō. In 1755 or 1756, the lecturer was denounced to these authorities but, as the result of the investigation then ordered, he was found to have been misrepresented. This may have emboldened him ; at all events in 1757 no less a personage than the

---

[1] I cannot identify either this author or his work, and neither are mentioned in Dr. Aston's *History of Literature*. It is impossible to translate the title of the work without having the ideographs in which it is written, but it may signify *The Dignity of an Oath*, though this is little better than guesswork.—J. H. L.
See *Dictionnaire d'Histoire et de Géographie du Japon*, par E. Papinot, M.A.

Kwampaku himself again called the Shoshidai's attention to Taken-ouchi's activities. By this time he had acquired a numerous and influential following among the Court Nobles, and it was probably the unrestrained expression of virulent Anti-Bakufu sentiments which had become common among the courtiers that excited the Kwampaku's anxiety about the possible consequences. This time, Takenouchi was put under ward ; and seventeen of his titled pupils were degraded and stripped of their offices and emoluments. Some authorities assert that Takenouchi was then punished for teaching his pupils military science and for secretly procuring a store of arms, but all the authentic evidence is against any such contention. His chief offence was his bold assertion of the Emperor's right to rule Japan, his doctrine that the loyalty of every Japanese was due not so much to his immediate over-lord or to the Shōgun as to the august descendant of the Sun-Goddess. In 1758, Takenouchi was released, but he was ordered to withdraw from Kyōto. After eight or nine years, chiefly spent in Ise, he appeared in Yedo, and there became entangled in one of the most mysterious complications of the century, the alleged plot of Yamagata Dai-ni and his confederates.

Yamagata (1725–68) had been a Bakufu police-officer in Kai, but was discharged for killing a man in a quarrel. He then went to Yedo, and there established himself as a *Gungakusha* (Military Lecturer) and in time acquired a large clientele of pupils. There were many public abuses rife at the time, and Yamagata was not slow to assail them whenever he found a sympathetic audience. Ultimately it was resolved that active measures should be taken to effect a reform, although what the conspirators really aimed at is difficult to make out. We are told that their intention was to begin by burning down the capital with " fire-works ". That would have been no difficult thing to do, for half of Yedo was burned down every decade or so without any question of " fire-works " at all. The incendiarism of Yedo was indeed one of the items in the programme of the Great Rōnin Conspiracy of 1651, but it was nothing more than a detail in a wide-ramifying, well-thought-out, general plan of opera-tions. What was to be accomplished by the concerted action of 3,000 to 4,000 resolute men at widely separated points of the empire, while Yedo was in flames and immediately afterwards, was the all-important feature in the great attempt of 1651. Here we can discern nothing whatsoever in the shape of a general plan of action ; the whole volume was to consist of a few haphazard chapters of accident which the city police alone could have very well brought to a summary conclusion at any time. It it questionable if even as many as fifty men were seriously committed to this wild and fantastic adventure, and of those actually engaged in it a large number could in no wise be depended on. Several turned informers, three at least, retainers of the Rōjū Abé, the former Shoshidai of Kyōto, were plainly nothing but *agents provocateurs*. The leading spirit really seems to have been a certain Fujü Umon, who had been in the service of, or at least had connexions with, a prominent court noble. Fujü pointed out that among the conspirators there was no name of sufficient weight to figure as a head for such a great enterprise, and he was commissioned to inveigle some of the Kyōto *Kugé* into the plot. Takatsukasa appears to have been informed of it, at all events, at the last meeting of the plotters, we hear of an enigmatical poem of his being read and construed as encouragement and sanction for proceeding with the business. Meanwhile, the Rōjū Abé had become cognizant of what was going on, and now one of his colleagues was also approached by an informer. In 1766, the Bakufu suddenly pounced upon thirty-four of the band and put them in prison where they remained for about a year, but no more than twenty-two of the thirty-four arrested received any further punishment, and most of these who did were merely expelled from Yedo, or banished to the islands of Idzu. One of them was ordered to commit *hara-kiri*; Yamagata and Fujü were decapitated, and Fujü's head exposed on the public pillory at Shinagawa. One small Daimyō, Oda, a descendant of the great Nobunaga, was so far compromised in this affair that he was stripped of his fief and confined to his own city mansion.

Takenouchi, sentenced to banishment, died on his way to Hachijō. It was he that the conspirators had used as their intermediary with Kyōto:—

"Takenouchi who had gained many friends at the court of the Dairi during his long residence in Kyōto, observed that Okamoto, a physician of Kyōto, was as well as himself an intimate friend of Tokudaiji, a servant of the Dairi, a man of great bravery and abilities, who had often declared in their hearing that *he was ashamed of living in such a mean way with the Dairi, while the Shōgun, nay, even the princes, lived in greater splendour than the Dairi himself, and that if he had sufficient strength he would overthrow the government.* They in consequence directed Okamoto to communicate their design to him in hopes that if he entered into it, they would obtain a written permission from the Dairi."

This passage taken from Titsingh is really of consequence, for it gives us a glimpse of the earliest germination of the seed that was to spring up and attain its full fruition in the Restoration of Meiji just a century afterwards.

The somewhat subterranean Imperialistic movement thus initiated by Takenouchi was carried on during the next generation by two rather noted successors. In 1765, Takayama Masayuki, then eighteen years of age, arrived in Kyōto to prosecute his studies. He presently obtained the favour and protection of the Dainagon, Nakayama, an ardent Imperialist, and one of the ablest of the court nobles, who directed his protégé's attention to the ancient history of the empire. On the Bridge of Sanjō, the young man knelt down, facing towards the Imperial Palace, and publicly venerated the Emperor from afar. Then he started forth on a crusade to rouse in the people of the empire at large the long-dormant sense of respect and duty towards the line of the Sun-Goddess. His end was a very strange one ; in 1793, he committed *hara-kiri* at Kurume in Chikugo " afflicted at the state of the country, and offering himself up as a victim to the Imperial cause ". By this time, Gamō Kumpei, then twenty-five years of age, had entered upon a similar mission, and was scouring the country deploring that " the tombs of the Emperors were in ruins and that their authority was unrecognized and contemned ". In their day and generation, Takayama and Gamō were regarded as mere eccentrics (*kijin*), and their utterances were the voices of men crying in the wilderness. Such episodes were nevertheless of sinister and menacing portent to the fortunes of the Bakufu. It must be frankly admitted that Tokudaiji and his fellow-nobles had ample grounds for resentment on the score of the niggardly pittances doled out to them by the Bakufu, and the squalid meanness of the establishments to which most of them were reduced. The annual rice-allowances for the Imperial nobles (between 120,000 and 130,000 *koku*) were the product of certain definite lands, and under Yoshimune these lands had usually produced the crop necessary for the full payment of these allowances. Under Iyeshige and Iyeharu the Imperial estates were as badly managed as the Bakufu domain generally, and there were besides occasional droughts and floods and typhoons in the Go-Kinai. These lands thus came to show a serious deficit. It had been customary to make up such a deficiency, or at least a part of it, from the Bakufu rice-granaries in Fushimi, but ultimately the officials began to raise difficulties in the way of this practice. About 1774, the Court protested ; an investigation into accounts and account-books followed, and a wholesale system of fraud, swindling, and peculation was disclosed. Some of the stewards and their subordinates in the employment of the Palace and of the nobles were decapitated, and others were banished, while certain of the offending Bakufu officials were dealt with drastically. In 1788, matters appear to have again become nearly as unsatisfactory as they were in 1774 ; at all events we then find Kobori, the hereditary magistrate of Fushimi, summarily cashiered and stripped of his 10,000 *koku* fief at Komuro in Ōmi. This was the work of the Regent, Matsudaira Sadanobu, who had visited Kyōto about that time in connexion with the work of the re-erection of the Imperial Palace then in progress. In spite of the terrible famine that had to be fought in northern Japan, this task had to be taken vigorously in hand, for the Palace was reduced to ashes in common with the whole ancient capital in the Great Fire on 8th–12th March, 1788.[1] The Bakufu at once issued orders for the rebuilding of the Imperial Palace and that of the ex-Empress, the expenses being levied from the various clans. The Regent himself superintended the work, and was careful to see to it that the new structures should be much more magnificent than those just burned down. While the contractors were at work he appeared in Kyōto and was granted audience with the Emperor and the ex-Empress, and when their Majesties proceeded to occupy the new Palaces, towards the end of 1790, they were greatly pleased with the buildings, and conferred rewards upon the Shōgun and the Regent. It seemed as if the cordial relations of Tsunayoshi and Iyenobu's times between the Imperial and the Yedo courts were on the point of being restored. Yet, within a year, the Regent had come into sharp and bitter conflict with the Emperor and his ministers. To understand the point at issue, it becomes necessary to devote some little study to the Imperial genealogical table.

---

[1] From one of his Japanese correspondents, Titsingh got a very detailed account of this great conflagration in which 2,630 lives were lost and 183,000, or, as some other accounts say, 191,000, dwellings were consumed. If we allow an average of five for each household, the citizen population of Kyōto would then have amounted to 915,000 or 945,000 souls. In Siebold's time (1826) it stood at 780,000 in 117,000 houses, an average of nearly seven inhabitants for each. If the figures for 1788 are correct, Kyōto must have been considerably more extensive then than it was when Siebold passed through it.

The following table shows the descent of the Emperor Kōmei (1847–67) the 121st Emperor of the line from the Emperor Higashi-Yama (1687–1709) the 113th Emperor.

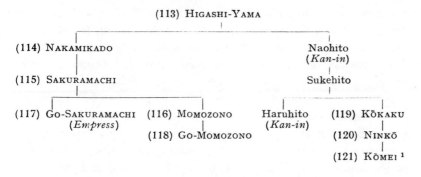

It will be seen that the line of Higashi-Yama's son, Nakamikado, failed with the 118th sovereign, Momozono II, who died in 1779. The grandson of Higashi-Yama's younger son, Naohito, then ascended the throne as Kōkaku Tennō. His father, Prince Sukehito, who was then alive, never having reigned. The youthful sovereign, who was only ten years of age at his accession, was very anxious to have his father treated as an ex-Emperor. In the early Hei-an age, it was the custom for a new Emperor to offer the title of Dajō-Tennō (otherwise Dajō-kō or Jōkō) [2] to his abdicated predecessor, but the custom, like so many others, was abandoned during the troubles of Ōnin (1467–77), and was only resumed in 1736. On two occasions, once in the early thirteenth and once in the fifteenth century, this title of Dajō-Tennō had been bestowed by Emperors on fathers who had never reigned. There was therefore undoubtedly good precedent for the step the Emperor Kōkaku now wished to take and it was the unquestionable prerogative of the sovereign at his own discretion to grant titles and to confer Court rank. Yorimoto, the founder of the Shōgunate, had never called this into question for a moment, all that he insisted on was that none of his *own vassals* should be granted Court rank or office without his

---

[1] For the dates of the reigns, etc., of these sovereigns, *vide* Appendix. The numbers here prefixed to each sovereign's name, are for the reason explained in the appendix, one in advance of those formally recognized by the Japanese as correct.—J. H. L.

[2] Dajō is synonymous with Daijo—great Government—as in Daijōkwan—supreme council of the Empire—Dajō-Tennō literally signifies "Great Government Emperor".—J. H. L.

assent or recommendation. This limitation applied only to the original grant; with their subsequent promotion in the Court hierarchy he did not presume to interfere. For a sovereign of Japan to have to appeal to the Bakufu for its sanction to the new measure now contemplated by Kōkaku Tennō was surely a great derogation from the Imperial dignity. Yet, in 1789, the sanction of the Bakufu for the measure in question was actually solicited. No immediate official reply was given, but the Regent wrote a private letter to his kinsman, Takatsukasa, giving him to understand that he could not approve of the Imperial wish. For some considerable time the matter remained dormant but, in 1791, the young Emperor (then in his twentieth year) had the courage to attempt to force the situation. He convoked all the great officers of his court, laid the circumstances before them, and requested them to advise him as to what course should be pursued. With only a few dissentient voices they urged that the Bakufu should be pressed to return a definite official answer forthwith. The Regent again endeavoured to evade the issue. However, Kyōto became so insistent that the issue could not be evaded any longer and the Imperial Court was at last informed that it was a very serious matter to confer the title of Dajō-Tennō upon one who had never occupied the throne, and that such a title could not be so lightly handled. The discontent, which had been simmering among the Court nobles, now burst into a violent explosion and relations between Yedo and Kyōto became a good deal more than strained. Finally, however, the ex-Empress Sakuramachi II expressed the opinion that the sovereign would be acting more dutifully towards his father if he abandoned the project rather than raise troubles by pressing it. This view of the situation at last commended itself to the Emperor ; the Bakufu on its part offered to contribute 2,000 bales of rice to the support of Prince Sukehito's establishment, and the incident was supposed to be closed. Before this settlement was reached, however, two Court nobles, Lords Nakayama and Hōki-machi, had been summoned to Yedo to account for their conduct in connexion with the affair. Sharp words had then passed between them and the Regent, and Nakayama had been punished with 100, and his colleagues with 50 days' confinement, each in his own mansion. Later on, they were deprived of their offices, while the Bakufu did not scruple to vent its ill-will upon other prominent supporters of the Imperial project.

The truth would seem to be that the Regent's visit to Kyōto, in 1788, ostensibly for an inspection of the work of re-erecting the burned palaces was really for the purpose of making himself acquainted with the actual trend of opinion among the Court nobles, and that he returned to Yedo far from satisfied.　The strong Imperialist, anti-Bakufu sentiment, awakened by Takenouchi a generation before, had not been extinguished; indeed, it seemed to be spreading.　At that very time Takenouchi's work had been taken up and was being vigorously prosecuted by Takayama. Sadanobu's attitude in this Imperial title affair seems to have been determined by the resolve to overawe the Court nobles, and to give the Imperialistic movement a set-back, if not an absolute check.　If such indeed was the secret mainspring of his action on this occasion, the event merely serves to demonstrate his mediocrity in the sphere of political manœuvring.　If he had been minded to bring matters to a decisive issue on some one point or other and on that crush the Court nobles in open conflict, he could scarcely have selected his battle-ground with less adroitness and perspicacity. On constitutional grounds he was hopelessly in the wrong, and he was sure to be overborne in any reasoned argument over the point at issue.　Then the question united the Court nobles in one common cause, while the Hōjō policy towards them had almost invariably been " Divide et impera ".　Furthermore, this matter now furnished the Court with a distinct and easily understood grievance; it was the best of platforms for the discourses of perfervid Imperialist partisans like Takayama and Gamō.

Some of the Kugé at this time were men of ability, notably that Lord Nakayama who had been selected to argue the Imperial-Title case at Yedo.　What threatened, however, to make reawakened Imperialistic sentiment an active and formidable force was its advocacy by plebeian literati, who had taken umbrage at the neglect with which their class had latterly been treated in Yedo. How highly considered a personage the Chinese lecturer (*jusha*) was in the days of Tsunayoshi and Iyenobu has already been described.　Under Yoshimune, whose mind was of an eminently practical cast, real scholarship was far from being slighted, but little respect was shown for the mere platitudinous pedantry into which Japanese Confucianism then threatened to degenerate.　Original minds like Ogyu Sorai still met with respectful treatment, but such minds were comparatively few in the later days of the eighth

Shōgun. All the changes, radical or immaterial, that could be
rung on the leading concepts and propositions of the various
schools of Chinese philosophy had been rung by this time, and for
any real positive advance fresh sources of knowledge had to be
tapped. Hence, Yoshimune's encouragement of old Japanese
studies, of astronomy, of medical science ; hence, his interest in
Dutch learning and his fondness for modern Chinese books. Apart
from Dazai Shuntai, there was perhaps not a single Chinese scholar
of first-class rank in Yedo at the death of Yoshimune. Under
Iyeshige, not even the slightest encouragement was extended to
Chinese scholarship by the Bakufu, while in Iyeharu's time the Court
lecturers often found themselves treated with ridicule, covert,
generally, but now and then open and downright. Hayashi Nobuyoshi's *Seidō* was burned in the great conflagration of 1772. One
feature of the economy then professedly practised by the Bakufu
was to close as many public buildings as possible, and of those
burned or otherwise destroyed from time to time to rebuild only
those which were absolutely necessary. The authorities acting on
this principle refused to rebuild the Seidō, whereupon Hayashi
protested strongly. When his protest came before the Rōjū,
Tanuma looked at the paper and remarked, " The Seidō ? The
Seidō ? What is worshipped there, a *kami* or a *hotoke* ? " A Finance
Magistrate gravely informed him that it " was neither a *kami* nor
a *hotoke*, but a Chinaman, named Confucius, who lived more than
2,000 years before, and who wrote a book called *Rongo*, which
seemed to be rather famous ". Not a single one present at the
sitting so much as smiled. No doubt Tanuma's crass ignorance
was merely feigned ; and his colleagues probably fancied they would
best curry favour with him by entering into his humour of thus
mocking the scholars and their cult. Later on, we hear of bands of
gay young Hatamoto life-guardsmen scandalizing the Court lecturers
by stopping them as they passed to inquire whether Madame
Confucius was good-looking or not ! No wonder then, that scholars
had shaken the dust of Yedo off their sandals as a testimony against
the insolence and contumely with which they were being treated
in the Shōgun's capital. In Kyōto, the Court nobles had but scanty
fare to offer them, but to be appreciated by the highest in rank and
the bluest-blooded in the empire was soothing to that *amour propre*
which had been so badly ruffled in Yedo. Hence, many of the ablest
literati of the time had set their faces towards Kyōto, where they

presently began to find the conditions of existence not so very straitened after all. It had been usual for the outside clans to send the most promising students in their schools to Yedo to finish their education in Hayashi's Seidō. Now, with Yedo a sink of moral corruption, the Seidō in a hopeless state of inefficiency, and the Court lecturers treated as so many learned buffoons, the more intelligent Daimyō began to think twice before dispatching the best intellects in their clans to be debauched and demoralized in the Shōgun's Gomorrah, and Kyōto became the great resort of the graduates of the clan colleges bent on a further prosecution of their studies. As regards higher educational facilities, even Ōsaka, that great city of shop-keepers, was far ahead of Yedo, and the school of Nakae Sekizen was by no means the only great one in the city that was now thronged with country students, although it was the chief. In addition to this, some of the clans, Chōshū, Higo, Hizen, Yonezawa, for example, had men of high reputation and ability on the staffs of their colleges, while some of the small obscure fiefs in the north of Shikoku were hives of *Kangakusha*.

The Regent was shrewd enough to appreciate the dangers that lurked in this situation, and his visit to the west in 1788 doubtless impressed him with the necessity of taking some measures of reform. The Seidō must be restored and reorganized, and its old prestige revived. Its then head, Hayashi Nobuyoshi, was childless, and it was therefore arranged that he should adopt the second son of the Daimyō of Iwamura in Mino, who had a great reputation as a scholar, and entrust the fortunes of the Seidō to him. Shortly before this, Shibano, Okada and other scholars had been invited to settle in Yedo, and they, as well as Bitō, were now appointed to chairs in the Seidō under Jussai, as the new Hayashi was called. The Seidō, now a purely government institution, speedily regained a measure of its old prestige in spite of the fact that it was reorganized as a mere "cramming-school". The intellectual viands provided in its halls cannot have been very satisfying to the honest and disinterested searcher after truth and knowledge. The only fare provided being the orthodox Teishu gospel. The commentaries chosen as textbooks were carefully selected, and no lecturer was allowed to criticize or supplement their contents in any way. On the part of the students, everything was to be accepted unhesitatingly, without question or argument or discussion. It was a most heinous crime to cavil at any *ex cathedra* utterance ;

the expression of any doubts or dissent was sure to lead to the expulsion of the daring offender. A greater travesty of education could scarcely be imagined, if the two great aims of every teacher should really be to stimulate intelligence and to help to build up character. The Procrustean regulations enforced in the Gakumonjo[1] (as the Seidō was called from 1797) with Draconic rigour were expressly intended to stifle all individual intellectual initiative, while their effect on the formation of character was to put a premium on hypocrisy. Imagine Nakae Tōju being invited to occupy a chair in the renovated University of Yedo! On occasion Nakae could make use of emphatic and straight-flung language, and his reply to such a hypothetical invitation would be highly entertaining reading. It goes without saying that few men of any real force of character would be found on Hayashi's staff of professors, while any intellectually able man in the faculty must have been painfully conscious of the falsity of the position he occupied. Such indeed was the case with the famous Satō Issai (1772–1859), who really belonged to the school of Ōyōmei.[2]

Under Tanuma, as we have seen, the civil service had become thoroughly demoralized, and appointments to its offices a mere matter of money. The Regent had at once put a stop to this, and during his very first year he succeeded in thoroughly purging and purifying the service. In the reforms he instituted the old system of examinations was resuscitated and amended, and it was to this circumstance mainly that the Seidō owed the great measure of consideration in which it was presently held by the Hatamoto. These gay young roysterers could no longer venture to amuse themselves by quizzing the grave and solemn Court lecturers with impudent queries about the looks of Madame Confucius. On the contrary, they suddenly found themselves under the iron heel of the new Hayashi and his Professors. Hayashi Jussai was of a masterful character, and a martinet in discipline, with a strong

---

[1] Gakumonjo means simply a school-house or any building devoted to study. Seido, in its primary sense, means a temple dedicated to Confucius, and this sense was extended to the building in which the study of his works was carried on.—J. H. L.

[2] "It was only for considerations of worldly interest that Satō did not proclaim himself to be a thorough-going follower of Ōyōmei's system. Like the Bishop of Gloucester in the days of Charles I, of whom it is said that he required £1,500 a year to prevent him from declaring his conversion to Roman Catholicism, so Satō was a Shushi philosopher simply because he was at the head of a Shushi school. He lacked the courage of his opinions, and it was not until after his death that his real opinions were found expressed in unequivocal language." *T.A.S.J.*, vol. xxxiv, pt. iv, p. 60.

inclination to magnify the importance of his office and position. In 1795, he induced the Bakufu to issue an edict declaring that henceforth only those who subscribed to the Teishu body of doctrine (as expounded in the Seidō of course) should be eligible as candidates for government positions ! This " Prohibition of Heresies " as it was called, was soon enforced in the outside fiefs, and the great clan schools became as narrow, rigid, and hide-bound in their curricula and regulations as the Seidō itself. As was only to be expected, this " Prohibition of Heresies" called forth a great storm of protest from the adherents of the Ōyōmei and Kogaku schools, but it was quite ineffective, and " heretical" professors had presently to choose between conformity or resignation of their positions.

As has just been said, it was Hayashi Jussai who prompted this measure. Two years before it was issued the Regent had demitted his office. Yet it was enforced with Sadanobu's full approval, and Japanese writers are nearly unanimous in the view that it was really Sadanobu who was responsible for it. In this matter at least, he did not follow in his grandfather's steps, for we have seen Yoshimune making it a point to treat all schools of thought with respect and extending his favours impartially to all who seemed in any way to merit them. Sincerity was a quality on which Yoshimune had set great store ; his grandson while professing to value sincerity, made no scruple about putting a great premium on hyprocrisy. Sexual immorality is not lightly to be condoned, and for his efforts to cope with this vice, then so prevalent in Yedo, Sadanobu is entitled to respect, but to suppress brothels and street-walkers on the one hand and, on the other, to convert the best men into intellectual prostitutes, is surely a case of straining at a gnat and swallowing a camel. At the date of its promulgation, the " Prohibition of Heresies " might perhaps have been regarded as not merely a harmless but even as a salutary measure. Its enforcement, however, was ultimately destined to prove terribly disastrous to the fortunes of the Tokugawa Shōgunate. For the next two generations the ablest intellects among the youth of the outside clans continued to smart and wince under the tyranny of the lifeless tread-mill system of instruction imposed upon them with an ever-growing irritation, a more and more over-mastering tendency to revolt. Among the protagonists in the movement that led to the overthrow of the Bakufu, some of the ablest drew their force and

inspiration from the "Heresies" of the Ōyōmei school. The
Regent's action in the Imperial-Title case had furnished the Court
nobles with a real and easily comprehended grievance and knit them
into a common bond of hostility to the Bakufu. The effect of the
Prohibition of Heresies was to excite a deep measure of sullen and
rootęd resentment in the successive leaders and moulders of popular
opinion among the clan samurai. In 1795, it was a case of sowing
the wind; two generations later the whirlwind had to be duly
reaped by the Bakufu.

In these two affairs it was the Regent's political acumen that was
at fault. In a third matter, his treatment of the distinguished
scholar Rin Shi-hei, Matsudaira Sadanobu appears to great moral
disadvantage. This Sendai scholar had made three visits to Nagasaki
and had there learned a great deal from the Dutchmen about the
march of political events in the west. In the expansion of the
Muscovite empire he discerned a great future menace to Japan, and
in his *Sangoku Tsūran*,[1] published in 1786, he endeavoured to arouse
his countrymen to a sense of the peril. As if to lend point to his
contentions, in that very year a Russian man-of-war appeared on
the Yedo coast. In 1788, Rin Shi-hei had an interview with the
court noble Nakayama (whom we have just seen in conflict with
the Regent) and, in the following year, with the Regent, to whom
he then expounded his views at length. Meanwhile, since 1777,
he had been at work on his *Kaikoku Heidan*,[2] in which he dealt
with the question of the coast defence of the empire. In 1792, this
book was published at Sendai. The reward for his fifteen year's
hard work on this treatise was a scurvy one indeed. At the beginning
of 1793 he was arrested by orders of the Bakufu and conveyed
under escort to Yedo, where he was presently condemned to
imprisonment in his brother's house in Sendai on the ground that :—

"With a view of acquiring a reputation he had written strange and
absurd stories about the risk of forei gn invasion based on mere hearsay
or groundless conjecture, that he had agitated the people, and that he
had described points of strategic importance and-inserted maps in his
books."

---

[1] Sangoku Tsūran, a study of three countries.—J. H. L.
[2] Kaikoku Heidan—war talks on the coastal provinces. Rin Shi-hei is
better known as Hayashi Shihei, Rin being the sinico-Japanese equivalent of
Hayashi. In his great work, he pointed out that the marine policy of Japan, which
forbade the building of large ships, left her coasts, on which there were no defences,
helpless against naval attacks by foreigners. Not only was he imprisoned till
his death, but the blocks of his book were broken up.—J. H. L.

Six months later on he died in confinement.   Now follows the strange thing.   In that very year the Regent issued orders to the sea-board clans to strengthen their defences, and about the same time he proceeded on a tour of inspection along the Idzu, Sagami, Awa, and Kadzusa coast !   His biographer says :—

" Many people laughed at his precautions, but the course of subsequent events was to demonstrate that he was uncommonly far-sighted."

Now to acquire a knowledge of a man's original views, to imprison their author, and then to acquire a reputation for foresight by acting upon these views, does not strike one as being a masterpiece of plain dealing or honesty.   In fact, it may be fairly said to have been quite the reverse.   This was almost the last of Matsudaira Sadanobu's official acts as Regent.   In that year (1793) he suddenly sent in his resignation, and it was accepted.   Although he had been strongly supported by the Go-san-ké and the Rōjū, there had always been a strong cabal working against him in the youthful Shōgun's immediate entourage.   The Shōgun's own father, Hitotsubashi Harunari, had expected to be made Regent as Tanuma intended he should be.   When Harunari tried to establish an ascendency over his son, Sadanobu interfered, and his interference occasioned some painful scenes between the boy Shōgun and the Regent.   The Ladies of the Court also cherished a bitter resentment against him, and their continual carping at last began to influence Iyenari, who had now attained his twentieth year and wished to assume the personal discharge of the functions of his office.   But the chief cause of the Regent's retirement was to be sought elsewhere ; his action in the Imperial-Title affair had raised up a band of formidable enemies against him.

In the six years of his Regency, Matsudaira Sadanobu repeated the work of his grandfather in a measure.   Between 1670 and 1709, the clock of state and local administration had run down, and Yoshimune had wound it up and set it going once more.   Between 1751 and 1786, it again ran down, and Sadanobu did his best to retrieve the situation.   The history of the next sixty years is to a great extent an account of a third running down of the administrative timepiece, and the strenuous but abortive attempt of Mizuno Tadakuni, Echizen no Kami, to repeat the work of Matsudaira Sadanobu.

CHAPTER XII

IYENARI (1793–1841)

THE eleventh Tokugawa Shōgun, Iyenari, was destined to have a longer tenure of office than any other occupant of the Shōgunal dais. The last Shōgun of the Kamakura period had been a puppet for five-and-twenty years;[1] in the Ashikaga age, Yoshimitsu, the third Shōgun of that house was titular Shōgun from 1368 to 1395, and wielded authority for thirteen years more after his nominal retirement. Three Tokugawa Shōguns—Iyetsuna, Tsunayoshi, and Yoshimune—occupied the main castle of Yedo for nine-and-twenty years each, while the last spent six years more in the Nishi Maru as ex-Shōgun. From his accession in 1786, down to his retirement in 1837, Iyenari was titular Shōgun for a full half-century. It is true that for the first six or seven years of this period, down to 1793, he was under tutelage. On the other hand, although he made way for his son, Iyeyoshi, and removed to the Nishi Maru in 1837, it was really by him that the Shōgunal power was exercised until his death in 1841. Thus, his personal rule lasted for the unprecedentedly long term of eight-and-forty years.

Like his immediate predecessor, Iyeharu, Iyenari had enjoyed a great reputation for cleverness and ability in his youth. It need scarcely be said, however, that the standard by which the youthful abilities of a prospective Shōgun were measured was not necessarily a very high one. What is plain is that Iyenari, while a better man than Iyetsuna or Iyeshige, was neither a statesman nor a great worker. In the age of Iyeyasu he would have been a nonentity; if the eldest son of Iyeyasu, he would probably have been summarily set aside in favour of the second-rate, yet safe, sagacious and plodding Hidetada. As Hidetada's successor he would probably have wrecked the Tokugawa Shōgunate, while, if in the position of Yoshimune in 1716, he would have placed the fortunes of his

---

[1] The six Shōguns of the Kamakura period were all, though either of the noble Fujiwara lineage or of the Imperial family, helpless puppets under the domination of the Hōjō regents, and the only difference between the last and his five predecessors was that he held his phantom dignity longer than any other.—J. H. L.

house in the direst jeopardy.   To accomplish the work of the eighth
Shōgun he would have been utterly impotent ; he would probably
never have attempted to accomplish it, even if he had had the
prescience to discern the crying and urgent need for it.   The
splendour, the magnificence, the luxury of the Genroku and Hō-ei
periods (1688–1709) would have been so irresistible in their appeal,
that their traditions would infallibly have been continued.   Apart
from this, even if desirous of reform as Yoshimune was, Iyenari's
limited capacity would have been sadly unequal to any such task.
Intellectually, he was a mediocrity ; physically, while not exactly
an invalid, he was far from robust.   He was subject to epileptic
fits ; but, apart from this infirmity, he had not the bodily stamina
that enabled the great Yoshimune to "toil as terribly" as the
very best of the Hōjō ever did.

It would, however, be a serious misconception to regard Iyenari
as a puppet.   Any one venturesome enough to persist in thwarting
him did so at the peril of his fortunes.   The Regent, Matsudaira
Sadanobu, did impose his will upon Iyenari in various matters,
notably in preventing the Shōgun's father, Hitotsubashi Harunari,
from taking up his quarters in the Nishi Maru ; and the Sobayōnin,
Matsudaira Nobuaki, did remonstrate with the youthful ruler more
than once in very frank language, but it was before Iyenari assumed
the personal direction of affairs.   After 1793, we do indeed meet
with instances of opposition to the Shōgunal will, and sometimes
the opposition appeared to be effectual, but in the end Iyenari
contrived to have his own way, and those who may have been
inclined to remonstrate, finding such a course highly detrimental
to their own prospects, prudently refrained from doing so.   On the
other hand, scarcely one of the fifteen Tokugawa Shōguns could
be characterized as an autocrat pure and simple.   The nearest
approach to an autocratic régime was in the days of Iyemitsu,
who, as has been said, filled nearly all the great offices of State with
"new men", very much as Louis XIV did in the latter half of the
same century.   Yet, although of autocratic temper, the third Shōgun
was not capricious. Once provided with proper tools for the execution
of his purposes he rarely, if ever, discarded them, and although
he made no scruple about amending, he rarely presumed to ride
rough-shod over the established laws of the land.   Tsunayoshi,
again, was of a somewhat autocratic temper, but he seldom thought
fit to change the personnel of the Great Council, and of the higher

departments of the civil service. He merely ignored the Rōjū, and
acted through his Sobayōnin, Makino, Yanagisawa, and Matsudaira
Terusada. He was indeed able to impose his pernicious and foolish
Life-Protecting Statutes upon the empire, but, on the other hand,
although desirous to spare the lives of the Forty-seven Rōnin,
he did not dare to suspend the law even in a case where popular
sympathy was so markedly on the side of the culprits. One of
Yoshimune's great merits had been that he had confirmed the
claims of established law and usage so far as they were not unsuitable
to the peculiar circumstances of his age. In truth, during the period
with which we are now dealing, the nearest approach to arbitrary
autocracy was under the Tairō Sakai, (1672–80), and afterwards
under Tanuma.

On several occasions, between 1652 and 1853, we meet with
instances of the operation of more or less effective external checks
upon the power of the Shōgun. In Iyetsuna's time, we find the
Go-san-ké exercising an important influence in various matters of
high State policy. They had seats in the Council convoked to decide
what answer should be returned to Koxinga's appeal for Japanese
intervention in the affairs of China. Under Tsunayoshi, the only
Daimyō who presumed to protest against the Life-Protecting
Statutes, was Mitsukuni of Mito. Before this it had been owing to
Go-san-ké support that Hotta was enabled to frustrate Sakai's plans
in 1680. At the death of Iyeharu and accession of Iyenari in 1786,
these three great branches of the Tokugawa house asserted themselves to good purpose in two matters of vital moment. As we
have just seen, they proved strong enough to break the yoke of
the hitherto all-powerful Tanuma, to upset his project of making
the young Shōgun's father (Hitotsubashi Harunari) Regent, and to
instal a nominee of their own in that great office. At all times, they
had the prerogative of expressing their views on matters of high
policy, and of remonstrating whenever the occasion seemed to
justify remonstrances. During the early years of Iyenari's rule, the
Go-san-ké had still to be reckoned with. Later on, two of Iyenari's
own sons were adopted either as heads or prospective heads of the
Owari and Kishū families, and any opposition from these two great
houses was therefore no longer to be feared. On the death of the
eighth lord of Mito without children in 1829, an attempt was made
to set aside his younger brother, Nariaki, and to deal with Mito as
Owari and Kishū had been dealt with. But the intrigue—for such

it really was—failed. One outcome of this incident was that the Mito house presently became antagonistic to the Shōgunate and ultimately contributed greatly to its subsequent overthrow. Besides, the Go-san-ké the Daimyō, who met in the Tamari Hall of the Castle, had the privilege of freely expressing their opinions on the government and its policy. The first *Tamari-tsumé* was the son of Hoshina of Aidzu, who was Regent during the minority of the fourth Shōgun. At this date, the Daimyō who met in the Tamari-no-ma were Hoshina of Aidzu, Ii of Hikone, and Matsudaira of Takamatsu. In 1793, this Council was greatly strengthened by the inclusion of Matsudaira Sadanobu, who was appointed a member of it upon laying down the Regency.[1]

In addition to the influence he exercised as a *Tamari-tsumè*, Sadanobu could act through his friends and former subordinates who still remained in the Rōjū. Of these, Honda (attached to the Nishi Maru) held office till 1798 ; Matsudaira Nobuaki till he was dismissed in 1803, and Toda till 1806. Down to the end of the century, the Great Councillors succeeded in imposing their will upon the Shōgun in not a few matters but, after that date, there was a steady decline of their authority, and by 1841 they were quite as powerless as they had been under the fifth Shōgun, Tsunayoshi. It was not because there were no good or capable men among them, for Matsudaira Nobuaki (reappointed in 1806) Ōkubo Tadazane (1818–37), and Mizuno Tadakuni were all men of respectable ability, the last indeed a man of very considerable ability and of great force of character. The real reason was that Iyenari had recourse not to the Great Council but to favourites of his own for advice. It was the influence of the Shōgunal seraglio that was now dominant in Japan.

Even during the first ten years of Iyenari's personal rule the Rōjū, though powerful, had an uphill battle to fight. The Shōgun's father, Hitotsubashi Harunari, had been baulked by the Regent in his intention to instal himself in the Nishi Maru. On Sadanobu's resignation (1793), he was at last able to compass his purpose. Over his son he exercised a strong and, on the whole, pernicious influence and, down to his death in 1826, he continued to interfere in the

---

[1] Sakai of Himeji was added later on. As for Sadanobu, it should be said that after his retirement from office, he was transferred from Shirakawa to Kuwana in Ise (the original fief of the Hisamitsū Matsudaira house) in 1823, that he became *inkyo* in 1826, and died in 1829. His time was mainly devoted to the administration of his own fief which he raised to a high degree of prosperity.

administration, often thwarting the best-considered projects of the constitutional councillors. Matsudaira Nobuaki and his colleagues were really serious in their intentions to carry on and complete the reforms instituted by the Regent. Hence, year after year, we meet with notices of sumptuary legislation and measures aimed at the gross moral corruption of the times, but Japanese writers are correct in their contention that, in the long run, such measures were merely dead-letters. Doubtless, they might be vigorously enforced when promulgated, but the ardour of the executive officers soon cooled, and within a few months matters would be much as they had been before. When this came to the knowledge of the Rōjū, there would be a repetition of the ordinances, another spasm of activity on the part of the officials, and then an outburst of extravagance in some new direction. The minor officials soon grasped the fact that power was slipping from the hands of the Rōjū, and that a judicious measure of conformity to the tastes of the occupants of the Nishi Maru might ultimately inure to their advantage. The Shōgun's father was a man of the age of Tanuma (in fact Tanuma's brother had been his chief *karō*) and had but little liking for what he considered to be the Puritanical fads of the erstwhile Regent. Through his efforts Mizuno Tadamoto and a good many others of the old Tanuma coterie were restored to favour and office, not a few of them being attached to his own court ; and life in the Nishi Maru was rapidly becoming as gay and festive and magnificent as it was in the Shōgun's palace before the fall of Tanuma. Thus, the high moral principles and the Draconian sumptuary legislation of the Rōjū tended to become matter for open ridicule among the courtiers, and the knowledge that this was so, did much to temper the zeal of the smaller official with discretion. Before the death of Hitotsubashi Harunari in 1826, corruption, wastefulness, and extravagance had become nearly as pronounced as they had been in Tanuma's time, and during the subsequent decade and a half matters certainly did not improve. The influence emanating from the harem was almost as pernicious as that of the Nishi Maru. Iyenari had wedded in 1789, his consort being a daughter of Konoye Tsunehiro. But she was merely an adopted daughter of Konoye, for she was born in Kagoshima, the third daughter of Shimadzu Higehide, that long-lived Daimyō of Satsuma, whom we meet with in the narrative of Siebold as well as in the pages of Titsingh. This alliance naturally tended to bring the Shōgun into intimate relations with the court nobles as well as with the great feudal house of Shimadzu. One son of Shigehide had been adopted by the Kuroda family of Chikuzen and yet another as the head of the Okudaira family of Nakatsu; in 1826, we find the eighty-four year old ex-Prince of Satsuma going with the Prince of Nakatsu to Ōmori to welcome Siebold, then on his way to Yedo. The Okudaira and Kuroda houses thus also came to acquire a considerable influence at the Shōgun's court, as did others of the numerous relatives and friends of the Shōgun's legitimate consort. At all events, we sometimes find them ignoring the regulations of the Rōjū in at least certain minor matters. The Shōgun, however, was no believer in monogamy as an institution. What the exact tale of his concubines amounted to it is difficult to say, but that they must have been fairly numerous becomes apparent from the fact that only a few of them presented him with as many as two children, and that he was ultimately credited with the paternity of no fewer than fifty-one. It is true that a good many of these cost little more than the expenses of an infant funeral, and that many others died before the age of puberty. Even so, nearly a score remained to be provided for. The practice of creating new appanages for the Shōgun's younger sons was definitely abandoned in the time of Yoshimune, and to add to the number of the Go-sankyō was deemed inadvisable. Accordingly adoption was resorted to as the easiest measure of relief. Two sons were adopted as prospective heads of the Kishū and Owari families; another was disposed of to the house of Echizen, and three or four others to as many Fudai Daimyō. Daughters were married to the Lords of Kaga, Hizen, Mito, Owari, Echizen, and various other feudatories. Naturally this affinity with the Shōgun greatly raised the prestige and importance of these special houses, and relieved them from the dread of the Rōjū, in which their ancestors had stood for several generations. Naturally, also, they became recipients of special marks of the Shōgun's favour; their court rank was raised, and they were allowed certain privileges in the use of crests, saddle furniture, and various items in the paraphernalia of feudal pomp and State generally reserved for scions of the ruling house. Not to be hopelessly eclipsed by these favourites of fortune the other feudatories resorted to bribery on a lavish scale to secure equivalent privileges. It was in the sale of offices that Tanuma and his gang had found one of the chief sources of their ill-gotten wealth ; now it was in the traffic of marks of distinction, the privilege to make use of certain trappings of pomp and parade that the Palace favourites found their most lucrative returns.   During the last twenty years of Iyenari's régime, the pomp and splendour of the feudal processions were such as Yedo had never witnessed before.   It may indeed be questioned if they had ever been equalled in Kyōto in the very hey-day of the old capital's magnificence under the third Ashikaga Shōgun, Yoshimitsu.

Not only between the Daimyō themselves and their *Karō* and superior vassals, but between the lower samurai of the various clans there was the keenest rivalry in the matter of making a gay and gallant show on the way from the *yashiki*, up through the Castle gates and on to the Shōgun's palace.   Naturally enough, the Hatamoto, the Shōgun's own devoted vassals could not allow themselves to be outvied in taste, in style, in the graces and splendour of personal adornment, by mere country samurai, and the social and economic results of all this display may be inferred easily enough.   In the first place, if need be, and there generally was the most pressing need, money was freely borrowed.   Most of the Daimyō were deeply in debt to the great merchants and bankers of Ōsaka or their agents in Yedo ; their retainers were often at the mercy of the blind moneylender, as the Hatamoto were at that of the *Fuda-sashi*.   The creditor class, of course, tended to become wealthier and wealthier. Again, the extravagance of the hitherto unheard-of feudal pomp that now prevailed, the wastefulness and luxury of *yashiki* and Castle life, stimulated trade and industry—especially the artistic artisan crafts—into abnormal activity.   Yedo and the other great cities were now raised to the very acme of their material prosperity. With plenty of money to spend, their citizens lived right royally ; and brothel-keepers, tea-house and fashionable restaurant-owners, *geisha*, mountebanks, actors, and all the other parasites of society, generally as numerous and varied in the Shōgun's capital at that and some other periods of its history as they were in Paris under the third empire or in London in the years preceding the great War, now reaped a golden harvest.   Where the money now tended to go, if not always to remain, is not hard to perceive.   Neither is it hard to find an answer to the question where it came from.   The sole and only resource of the feudatory, when hard pressed, to keep afloat in the maelstrom of empty and costly frivolity in Yedo and to effect a partial composition with his banker from time to time, was to levy fresh taxes upon the already over-burdened peasantry of his domains, sweating and toiling in his rice swamps from early morn to dewy eve.

How much the great Yoshimune effected for the agriculturist has already been set forth. At no time in the history of the empire was the Japanese peasant so prosperous as he was between 1720 and 1751, in spite of the famine of 1735, and the deficient harvest of 1749. Under Yoshimune's two successors the *dégringolade* had been swift and terrible. During his brief Regency of six or seven years, Matsudaira Sadanobu exerted himself strenuously to retrieve the situation, but apart from his own fief, where he indeed accomplished marvels, and the Bakufu domain, where his efforts were only beginning to bear fruit at the date of his resignation, he really did not succeed in ameliorating the lot of the Japanese peasant at large. He officially commended Uyesugi for his excellent work in Yonezawa, and he sharply reprimanded Hachisuka of Awa for his flagrant excesses. The Regent undoubtedly had good intentions in abundance, but the gap between aspiration and achievement was not to be bridged by anything less than the terrible toil of a quarter of a century at least. The fact is that, from the close of the eighteenth century, the wretched state of the Japanese peasant became more and more miserable. The burden of taxation continued to augment : the main tax on land, mostly paid in rice, but occasionally commuted, or partially commuted into money, had long been so heavy that there was no possibility of increasing it. In addition, however, to the land tax, there were secondary customary imposts, special taxes on subsidiary products, and on occupations, and corvées. As for the corvées, they belonged to two different categories. In the first place, the peasants had to render certain gratuitous services to their lord, repairing the roof of his dwelling and out-houses, attending to his fences and drains, cutting and supplying his firewood and many others. In the second, they had to construct or repair roads, bridges, reservoirs, and other public works. The corvées were levied either on the holding in land, or on the adult peasantry, and were often commuted for money. Some payment had originally been made for them, and the expenses for extraordinary public works, as, for example, after a flood or an earthquake or a volcanic eruption (such as Fuji in 1707 and Asama in 1783) were supposed to be disbursed by the authorities, but the tendency was towards the exaction of unpaid labour, and towards the end of the eighteenth century this tendency became more and more pronounced. In 1616, in Satake's fief of Akita, the corvée had been 236 days' labour for every 100 *koku* of assessed revenue per annum. In 1799, the 200,000 peasants on the Mito fief of 350,000 *koku* had to furnish 2,000,000 days' labour between them. In 1845, in the Sendai fief, the corvée, instead of being 236 days' labour per 100 *koku* as it had been in Akita in 1616, was fixed at 6,000 such units per 100 *koku*![1]

It is not infrequently asserted that one great cause for the augmentation of the peasant's burdens was the increasing costs of the administration. Such a proposition is a disputable one, at least. At this date, the various bureaux were certainly over-staffed and the ship of State generally over-manned, but it had been so from the beginning of the régime. It was partly the outcome of the jealousy and suspicion that permeated the whole structure of Tokugawa administration where almost every man was a spy upon his neighbour and was in his own turn, under his neighbour's surveillance. Under Iyenari, there was no very marked increase either in the number of administrative officials or in the current expenses of the actual administrative machine. Neither the Great Council nor the Junior Council nor any of the three great magistracies cost more than before. As regards the outside offices, we indeed find that, from about 1815 onwards, an extra allowance of 10,000 *koku* per annum was granted to the Kyōto *Shoshidai*, and an equal amount to the commandant of Ōsaka Castle. This was really in the nature of a secret service fund. Iyenari determined to conciliate the Imperial family and the Court nobles so bitterly estranged by the Regent's action in the Imperial-Title affair, and, for this purpose so much money had been found necessary that one *Shoshidai* after another had vacated his post in seriously embarrassed circumstances. As it had now become the settled routine for the Ōsaka Commandant to be promoted to *Shoshidai*, an annual allowance of 10,000 *koku* was allotted to him also to enable him to enter upon office in Nijō Castle with ample funds in hand.

The Russian menace had got seriously upon the nerves of the authorities in consequence of Muscovite activity in the Northern

---

[1] As regards the customary dues, and the general state of affairs among the farming population, it will be advantageous to consult Dr. Asakawa's *Notes on Village Government in Japan after* A.D. 1600, in the *Journal of the American Oriental Society*. The amount of honest work that these short papers entailed must have been immense.

seas ; and official after official was dispatched to Yezo to investigate and report on the position. Even as early as 1800, we find Ino Chūkei setting forth to make a survey and a map of the island, but at his own expense. In 1802, the Bakufu deprived the Matsumaye family of the administration of Eastern Yezo and installed a Governor (*Bugyō*) of its own at Hakodate. His stipend was no more than 1,500 bales of rice, and the expenses of his staff could not have been very heavy ; in truth, the appropriated territory must have more than defrayed the costs of its administration. In 1808, we hear of as many as 2,000 samurai being dispatched to garrison Yezo, but as they were drawn from the two clans of Aidzu (1,550 men) and Sendai (400 men) there was no drain upon the Bakufu treasury in connexion with them. Close to Yedo, there had been a slight increase of expense in connexion with the port of Uraga at the entrance to the Bay, a Governor and staff having been installed there to deal with the inspection of the papers of the Ōsaka freighters. Now, in 1819, in consequence perhaps of Captain Gordon's [1] visit to Yedo in his 65-ton brig in the preceding year, an extra Governor was appointed. The expense was, however, insignificant, the post not being very high in the official hierarchy. In Yedo, we find the stipend of Hayashi, Daigaku no Kami, raised to 3,000 koku, while the regular professors in the reorganized University were now paid by the Bakufu. All these items, with a number of still smaller ones, did not amount to any considerable total ; indeed, it is questionable whether the expenses of genuine state administration were augmented by as much as 50,000 *koku* during the period with which we are now dealing. Bribery was rampant and notorious, it is true, and the average official relied more upon his opportunities than upon his stipend for support. Doubtless the bribe that went into the official's pocket had to be wrung from the tiller of the soil in the last resort, but bribes and the legitimate expenses of the administration are different things.

What was really extravagantly costly at this time was the Shōgun's domestic establishment. As soon as the Regent and his colleague had been removed from the control of the household Budget, the expenses went up with a bound, and, since that date,

---

[1] Captain Gordon was an English naval officer who entered Yedo Bay in a small brig in June, 1818, and asked permission to trade. He was subjected to all the restrictions imposed on the Dutch at Nagasaki, and the permission was refused, but otherwise he was courteously treated. See Hildreth's *Japan as it Was and Is*, chap. xiv.—J. H. L.

they had been ever mounting and mounting. In 1838, the year after Iyenari became *inkyo*, the Nishi Maru was burned to the ground, and the ex-Shōgun then had to return to the main palace. He was accompanied by 350 Court ladies and 250 female attendants.[1]

It was on these and their relatives that money was now spent more lavishly then it had been before. In Yoshimune's time, when the Bakufu lands were assessed at 4,080,000 *koku*, the revenue was no greater than it now (1838) was when the assessed yield had shrunk to 3,281,000 *koku*. A larger proportion of the taxes had come to be paid in money, and the money receipts were about 50 per cent. greater than they had been a century before. Yoshimune's household had been managed with the strictest economy, and had consumed only a small percentage of the gross annual revenue. With Iyenari, the case was vastly different, and waste, profusion, extravagance, and empty ostentation held high carnival in the Yedo seraglio. In Yoshimune's time, the granaries had been filled to their roofs with cereals intended to cope with a possible series of lean years. The demands of the " Great Interior " now made any such thing an impossibility. Some writers have treated Iyenari as a Tokugawa analogue of the third Ashikaga Shōgun, the magnificent Yoshi-mitsu (1368–95) but, on scanning the matter a little closely, the superficiality of the analogy soon becomes apparent. With all his faults and shortcomings, and they were many, Yoshimitsu could, and did, work hard when there was any pressing necessity for him to do so ; he unquestionably possessed the reserve of staying power which is indispensable for success as a statesman. It would be gross flattery to describe the eleventh Tokugawa Shōgun as a worker. Yoshimune probably accomplished as much strenuous toil in a month—or even in a week perhaps—as Iyenari did in a year. We hear of Iyenari summoning the Bench of Magistrates to the Fuki-age gardens to discuss and decide cases in his presence, but this was only on very rare occasions, and the proceedings were merely formal, if not actually farcical. When we recall Yoshi-mune's untiring and assiduous efforts to render the administration of justice pure and efficient, and the many hours of lonely toil he spent over the contents of the " Complaint-Boxes ", we must be pardoned the smile provoked by Iyenari's cheap posturing and posing as a Solomon. And yet Iyenari is often bracketed with Yoshimune as having done much to retrieve the fortunes of the

---

[1] See Ikeda's *Ō oku no Jōchū* (Ladies of the Tokugawa Harem).

Tokugawa Shōgunate; and the years of Kwansei (1789–1800) are often coupled with those of Kyōhō (1716–35). But the reforms of Kwansei were not constructive as were unquestionably those of Kyōhō, they were mostly of the nature of palliatives that never got near the root of the matter at all. Besides, the reforms of Kwansei, such as they were, were no work of Iyenari's. They were effected by the Regent, Matsudaira Sadanobu; and all that Iyenari subsequently did, during his eight-and-forty years of personal rule, was to undo them, or to allow them to be undone.

The points of real analogy between Iyenari and the great Ashikaga Shōgun, Yoshimitsu, are three in number. In the first place, both had a profound liking for magnificence, splendour, and costly display. In the second, Yoshimitsu had been socially intimate with his great feudatories, and, as we have just seen, the unusually close relations between Iyenari and some of the great feudal houses led to a marked decline of the power and prestige of the Rōjū. In the third place, there are points of similarity in the respective attitudes of Yoshimitsu and Iyenari towards the Imperial House and the Court nobles.

In the early years of Iyenari's régime, the relations between the Bakufu and the Court were rather peculiar. Iyenari himself had married the adopted daughter of Konoye Tsunehiro, and the Go-san-ké were also connected with others of the Go-sekké by marriage. This ought naturally to have led to a certain degree of intimacy between the Court and the house of Tokugawa. But Matsudaira Sadanobu's action in the Imperial-Title affair had estranged the Court and the Court nobles. In the course he had then followed he dissatisfied the Go-san-ké, to whom he had originally owed his appointment, while he had been strenuously opposed by the Shōgun's father, Hitotsubashi Harunari. On the resignation of the Regent in 1793, the Bakufu officials in Kyōto found themselves in a very difficult situation. They had taken their tone from the Regent, and had latterly conducted themselves with a certain measure of overbearing arrogance towards the Court nobles. Now this had to be modified, they felt, for the relations of affinity between the Go-sekké on the one hand, and the Shōgun and the Go-san-ké on the other, might very well provide a medium for preferring complaints against them that might possibly be attended with serious consequences. Accordingly, they had recourse to lavish bribery to still the tongues of their Courtly critics. So lavish indeed had this present-giving latterly become that, as has been said, every successive *Shoshidai* now vacated his post in serious financial difficulties and, although the office was often an immediate stepping-stone to a place in the Rōjū, it had come to be but little coveted. In 1804, a certain Mizuno Tadashige, Dewa no Kami, learned that it was intended to make him Ōsaka Commandant. This meant that, in the ordinary routine of promotion, he would by-and-by find himself installed in Nijō Castle with all the responsibilities of *Shoshidai* upon his shoulders. He at once hurried off to his patron, the Shōgun's father, pointed out to him the difficulties of the *Shoshidai's* position and begged to be appointed to a home post, if he really was to be promoted. Accordingly, instead of being sent to Ōsaka, he was thereupon made a Junior Councillor (*Wakado-shiyori*) with the special duty of superintending the affairs of the interior of the Shōgun's palace (*okugakari*).

His duties now brought him much in contact with the Shōgun ; and as he was not deficient in ability, he soon got to know His Highness perfectly. He was not a Mizuno by birth but, after chopping and changing from one family to another, he was now the prospective head of one branch of the Mizuno stock. At this time, it should be remarked, the Mizunos were as numerous and prominent and as confusing to the historian as the Hondas were in Iyeyasu's later days, for during the earlier decades of the nineteenth century, half-a-dozen Mizunos at least appear more or less conspicuously in the Tokugawa records. The rise of the Mizuno house was owing to its connexion with Tanuma, and still more, with Tanuma's friend, the Shōgun's father, Hitotsubashi Harunari. Several Mizuno dames also were influential in the harem, and the influence of the harem at this date was in certain respects quite as great as that of the Rōjū. Now, Mizuno Tadashige, Dewa no Kami, was a man who knew how to profit by his opportunities. He soon made himself nearly as indispensable to Iyenari's personal comfort as Ōoka had been to Iyeshige's, though his rise of official position was steady rather than swift. In 1812, he was attached as adjutant (Sobayōnin) to the person of the heir apparent Iyeyoshi in the Nishi Maru. In 1817 he became Honorary Rōjū, while in 1818, he was made an ordinary member of the Great Council. During the next seventeen years, down to his death in 1835, he was perhaps the most influential man in the empire. For fully thirty years he must be regarded as a real force in the social and political world of his day ; and during this time he had the satisfaction of seeing the relations between Yedo and Kyōto gradually placed on the footing of cordiality and harmony that had characterized them between 1680 and 1716.

In the Tokugawa age official intercourse between the Shōgun and his sovereign was carried on in a rather circuitous fashion. The Shōgun communicated his will to the Rōjū ; the Rōjū transmitted the communication to the *Shoshidai* in Kyōto ; the latter then sent one or other of the two Tensō with the message to the Kwampaku, by whom it was finally laid before the Emperor. The Emperor's reply passed through an equal number of hands (or mouths) before it reached the Shōgun ; only instead of the Tensō, the Gisō were employed to transmit the return dispatch (or message) to the *Shoshidai*. The number of the Gisō varied from three to five ; all were of comparatively high rank, selected from among the Dainagon, Chūnagon or Sangi, who were of course all court nobles. At this period, Mizuno seems to have been in constant communication with the *Shoshidai*, and to have often acted independently of and without the knowledge of, the Great Councillors. In so doing he was undoubtedly undermining the power of the Rōjū, which was also being sapped at the same time by the unwonted measure of consideration accorded by the Shōgun to the great feudatories who had become connected with him by marriage or adoption. His plainly expressed approval of the bribery then resorted to at Kyōto is also censurable. In 1815, when Sakai, the *Shoshidai*, joined the Rōjū in Yedo, he was head-over-ears in debt to certain Ōsaka millionaires, and was being lampooned in street songs in Kyōto for his inability to discharge his obligations. It was at this time that, owing to Sakai's complaints and Mizuno's representations, the extra annual allowance of 10,000 *koku* was accorded to the two great outside officials, the *Shoshidai* of Kyōto and the commandant of Ōsaka Castle. Shortly after this the two hundredth anniversary of the death of Iyeyasu came round and, in connexion with the attendant ceremonies, a special Imperial mission was sent from Kyōto to Yedo. It had again become customary at this time to treat Imperial envoys to Yedo with as much consideration and distinction as had been bestowed upon them during Tsunayoshi's Shōgunate, and to shower valuable gifts upon them. On this occasion, special and extraordinary efforts were put forth to please the Imperial representatives, and they must have returned to

Kyōto highly charmed and delighted with their experiences in
the Kwantō. In 1817, the great festival of the Iwashimizu shrine,
which used to be graced by the presence of the Sovereign and his
Court, was restored in all its ancient splendour at the expense of
the Bakufu. About the same time the Emperor, Kōtaku, abdicated,
and the new palace then erected for him gave the ex-sovereign
the keenest delight. During the last two reigns, there had been
no celebration of the Dai-jō-e; this great function was now revived
with surpassing magnificence. In 1824, when the ex-Emperor
proceeded in state to the Shūgakuji, the *Shoshidai* was charged
with the duty of escorting him with the full garrison of Nijō and
all the officials under him; and this became an annual function
for which the Bakufu provided the funds. The coronation ceremony
of the new sovereign, Ninkō, was also celebrated with unwonted
brilliance, likewise at the expense of the Shōgun. Nothing, in short,
was left undone by Iyenari to conciliate the goodwill of both the
Emperor and his Court at Kyōto.

The Imperial Court on its part, was not slow to evince its high
appreciation of the unwonted attentions thus lavished upon it.
In 1817, Iyenari was made Udaijin (Minister of the Right), a little
later, Sadaijin (Minister of the Left), while, in 1827, upon attaining
his fortieth year of tenure of office as Shōgun he was advanced to
the supreme dignity of Chancellor of the Empire (Dajōdaijin).[1]
It is true that Hidetada, as well as Iyeyasu, had been recipients
of the same great title but, in their cases, it was conferred upon
them only after they had made way for a successor in the Shōgun's
office. Of all the fifteen Tokugawa Shōguns, Iyenari was the
first as well as the last to combine the offices of Chancellor of the
empire and Shōgun in his person at the same time. Taira Kiyomori
had indeed been Dajōdaijin; but there was no permanent Shōgunate
in his day. In the whole course of Japanese history the third
Ashikaga Shōgun, Yoshimitsu, is the only instance of a member
of the military house occupying the peculiarly distinctive position
that Iyenari now held. In the person of the eleventh Shōgun,
the House of Tokugawa had seemingly attained the very zenith
of its splendour, but in sober truth, it may well be questioned
whether any of the fourteen successors of Iyeyasu did so much
towards bringing the fabric of Tokugawa greatness crashing to

---

[1] Dajodaijin and Daizodaijin are synonymous.—J. H. L.

the ground as the Magnificent Iyenari. It was upon the efficiency of the administrative machinery installed by Iyeyasu and supplemented by Iyemitsu that the fortunes of the Shōgunate mainly depended in the last resort. By more than one previous Shōgun, the Great Council of the Bakufu had been treated with but scant respect, but by no previous Shōgun had the prestige of the Rōjū been wounded as it was in the early decades of the nineteenth century by Iyenari.

Intercourse between the Shōgun and the sovereign's Court had become amicable and intimate, and—what was especially damaging to the Rōjū—direct. The courtiers of Kyōto were ceasing to tremble at the mere idea of incurring the displeasure of the Yedo Councillors, now that there was easy access to the ear of the Shōgun, who could make or mar each and all of the Councillors at his own good pleasure. A similar remark applies to the great feudatories, with whom the Shōgun had formed ties of affinity. In certain respects, the difference in the measure of authority wielded and the degree of respect enjoyed by Iyenari's Councillors and Iyemitsu's " New Men ", two centuries before, almost amounted to a contrast. It is often asserted that such a state of affairs was merely the natural result of the mental and moral inferiority of the men of the time, but against this facile explanation, several considerations may be urged. Under Iyenari's long administration there never was any lack of men of respectable talents. Now and again, in such cases as some of the Matsudairas, of Ōkubo, of Mizuno Tadakuni, of Abé Masahiro, we meet with men who might have been able to hold their own in the Great Council even in the early years of Iyetsuna, but during Iyetsuna's minority a Great Councillor did not need to be anxious about his position ; under Iyenari the ever-present consciousness of the risk of dismissal must have done much to paralyse all energy and initiative whether individual or collective. The case of Mizuno Tadakuni, Echizen no Kami, will be found instructive. He was perhaps the ablest man of his time, which covered the last years of Iyenari's and the first half of Iyeyoshi's régime. He entered the Great Council in 1834, the year in which the Shōgun's favourite, Mizuno Tadashige, ended his long career. Shortly afterwards Iyenari decided to imitate the first two and the eighth Shōguns, and make way for a successor in the person of his son, Iyeyoshi. This was a step that involved a great deal of expense, and it was mainly by handsome financial assistance from Shimadzu of Satsuma and some of the other feudatories, related by marriage or adoption to the Shōgunal house, that the Nishi Maru (Western Enceinte) was renovated properly to serve as a palace for the retired (inkyo) Shōgun. In 1837, Iyeyoshi was duly invested with the Imperial Patent, and his father and his huge household removed to the Nishi Maru. In the following year the renovated Nishi Maru was reduced to ashes, and the re-erection of the structure from the bare foundations had to be undertaken. With the finances in disorder, and the empire just escaping from the pinch of one of the greatest famines recorded in its history, this was a task that was not likely to be undertaken gladly by anyone, especially as the structure was to be re-erected on a much more magnificent scale. However, Mizuno Tadakuni did not seek to shirk the responsibility when he was nominated General Superintendent of the enterprise. To procure the needed funds he began by levying a tax of two per cent. upon the revenues of some forty of the feudatories, among whom were Kishū, Owari, and Kaga, and it was proposed to impose a heavy contribution upon the Hatamoto and petty castle officials, most, if not all, of whom were hopelessly in debt, so that the prospect of a new burthen of taxation created an intensely bitter feeling among them. Thereupon, Mizuno dropped the project, and appealed to the goodwill of the Daimyō. Mito and Satsuma responded with liberal contributions, both of money and material; their example was followed by others, and presently the smaller Tokugawa vassals began to send in petitions praying to be allowed to tender specific sums. Mizuno's adroit management won him Iyenari's regard and goodwill. The ex-Shōgun presently entrusted him with the work of making alterations in the interior. This brought Mizuno into contact with some petty authorities with divergent aims, and he was denounced to Iyenari by some of those he had unwittingly offended. He was now in imminent danger of disgrace, and he was only able to save himself by conciliating a small official, who had the ex-Shōgun's ear, with a bribe of 500 or 600 ryō. The ablest member of the Great Council was at the mercy of the domestics of the ex-Shōgun, and constrained to bribe a petty underling to make peace for him and save him from ruin.

In connexion with this episode Mizuno discovered that bribery had been systematized and elaborated into a great business enterprise. Narushima, the compiler of the *Tokugawa Jikki*, was then at work in the Castle, and he had mastered the methods of the palace harpies. This knowledge he now placed at the disposal of Mizuno. Shortly afterwards (1841) Iyenari died, whereupon Mizuno addressed himself to the task of cleaning out this Tokugawa analogue to the Stables of Augeas, and several hundreds of the palace officials or menials were duly punished for their misdeeds. As at the death of Tsunayoshi, so now something of an ecclesiastical scandal had to be dealt with. One of Iyenari's favourite mistresses was a devout adherent of the Nichiren sect of Buddhists, and she had succeeded in persuading the ex-Shōgun to make a profession of that special creed, and he heaped temporal and mundane favours upon its priesthood, both in Yedo and the vicinity. The Tokugawa house had from old been adherents of the Jōdo sect, and this defection of the ex-Shōgun (together with its very practical consequences) excited a strong feeling among the monks of Zōjōji. They had always had the *entrée* of the Palace, and most of the palace Ladies went to them for ghostly counsel. They thus had ample opportunity to intrigue and to counter-mine, and they now exerted themselves might and main to baffle the insidious attempts of the Nichiren Sectaries to oust them from the Shōgunal favour and patronage which they had enjoyed without interruption from the days of Iyeyasu. At the death of Iyenari, the two palaces in Yedo Castle were divided into two great religious factions, that is, so far as the Ladies of the " Great Interiors " were concerned. As Mizuno, Lord of Echizen, Abé Masahiro, the Temple Magistrate, and most of their coadjutators all belonged to the Jōdo sect, it was perhaps no great matter for wonder that the interloping Nichiren monks and their supporters should now find themselves not only reft of all influence and favour, but even, in certain cases, severely punished for what was now characterized as arrogant presumption and chicanery. The Ladies of the Great Interior were soon to prove Mizuno's most dire and dangerous foes ; it was most fortunate for him at this juncture, perhaps, that their religious animosities threw them into great opposing camps, and so made general united action against the reformer's innovations impossible for a season.

For years the absolute necessity for drastic reforms had been apparent to a few thinking men. That the body politic had once more become seriously distempered was indisputable, symptoms of the gravest significance were to be detected in almost every rank of society by the eye of the discerning, although the governing class in general and the bourgeoisie in Yedo and the other great cities of the empire were perfectly contented both with themselves and with the general political and economic situation of the empire. However, in 1837, there came an incident sufficient to rouse the discerning to some sense of the dangers into which the nation had been drifting for a full generation or more.

It will be remembered that there had been a seven years' famine in the penultimate decade of the eighteenth century. Now, after a series of normal harvests, the country was again called upon to face a succession of six lean years. The cause of the dearth varied from year to year, and from place to place. At one time it was excessive cold, at another a long continued drought, in one section of the country a plague of noxious insects, elsewhere typhoons, floods, or frosts. Again the starving people perished in tens of thousands hopelessly and helplessly in many districts. In the large cities— in Yedo especially—the authorities did make an effort to relieve the absolutely destitute, but the results could not be described as satisfactory. The agents employed in this work often proved to be entirely unsuitable for it. They showed themselves to be at once callous, greedy, and dishonest, and thought it no shame to find in their office of mercy a means of enriching themselves. If the Yedo famine relief work was inefficient and unsatisfactory, in Ōsaka, the situation was nothing short of a great open public scandal. As has been said, Ōsaka was the great distributing centre for Tokugawa Japan. In this great mart there were at all times stocks not merely of rice but of almost every kind of perishable commodities, and to fight the famine on one spot should have been comparatively easy, in spite of the fact that, at one time, the failure of the crops in the Home Provinces had been complete, and the streets of the city congested with throngs of starving peasants who had been driven from their little holdings in the country by sheer hunger. The holders of these stocks of rice and other necessaries of life were merchants whose gospel it was that the trader's business was to make as great a profit as he could on all occasions, so that when famine was stalking abroad, there was nothing unreasonable in his refusing to part with his stores for anything less than famine prices. From what we are told about the merchants of old Japan, we gather the unwilling impression that they were often terribly cold-blooded and heartless, callously indifferent to every considera-

tion except their own financial gains or losses. We are told by the
annalist that in Ōsaka at this time

" The authorities acted in the most shameful manner towards
the helpless and destitute people. The rich merchants also, by bribing
the officials, took advantage of the general distress and bought up
all the rice and other necessaries and sold them only at outrageous
prices, thus making capital out of the general misery and filling their
own pockets at the expense of the starving thousands. Instead of
doing anything for their assistance they added to their own luxury
and spent their ill-gotten gains in every kind of degraded pleasure."

What made it comparatively easy for the merchants to corner
the market, not merely in rice, but in almost every staple of commerce
was the peculiar system of Guilds Merchant which had grown up
in the course of the previous six generations. It must be understood,
however, that Guilds had been a feature of Japanese industrial
and commercial life ages before the Tokugawa supremacy began.
In the thirteenth century the Hōjō Regents had limited the number
of traders that might ply their vocations in the city of Kamakura,
and they either were organized, or organized themselves into
corporations, whose members had to submit to regulations devised
to check unprofessional practices and to promote the general welfare
of the body corporate. Into this body corporate admission had to
be purchased by a new member, and that could only be done when
a vacancy occurred, either by forfeiture or by death without heirs.
Thus, membership in any of these corporations came to have a
monetary value, and in certain circumstances it might really be a
very valuable asset.

In the Tokugawa age the fundamental principle remained
unchanged. The main difference between the Guild system of
Kamakura and of Yedo days was that resulting from political,
social, and economic developments. In the thirteenth century,
there were no more than two considerable cities in Japan—Kyōto
and Kamakura—and between these there was scarcely any exchange
of commodities. In Kamakura, life was simple, and wants were
few ; and hence the merchant Guilds were generally composed of
pedlars or retail dealers, while outside of Kamakura and Kyōto,
most of the country districts were self-supporting, subsisting
on their own products, and purchasing almost nothing from elsewhere. This was still the case throughout the greater portion of
rural Japan in Tokugawa days, although of course, the Daimyō

and their more considerable vassals would naturally expend part
of their revenues in the castle-towns of their fiefs, and so occasion
the rise of commercial communities in quarters where such communities were unknown in Kamakura days. Here, doubtless, there
would be something of the nature of guilds among the traders as
well as among the artisans, but the political and social circumstances
of the age and the environment made it impossible for these local
corporations to attain any great measure of development or to
acquire any considerable measure of power and influence. On the
lands composing the Tokugawa domains, the situation was vastly
different. Scattered as they were over the face of the empire from
Hyūga to Yezo these lands formed by far the largest domain in
Japan. And—what was most important of all in the present
connexion—they contained an urban population of some 3,000,000
or 4,000,000 souls. Instead of the two great cities of Kamakura
days, there were now five so-called " Imperial " towns. Two of
these, it is true, were not very populous ; but in spite of that they
were of no little consequence. Sakai was in a sense merely a suburb
of Ōsaka, but it was the seat of the copper-smelting establishments
which supplied the Dutch with their chief staple of export. Nagasaki
was the sole seat of foreign trade and, notwithstanding its comparative insignificance, it contributed more to the Bakufu treasury
than all the other so-called " Imperial " cities together. Kyōto,
the ancient capital, was now the great manufacturing and industrial
centre of Japan ; Ōsaka was the great distributing centre ; and
Yedo, the capital, to the support of which it was the duty of all
other districts to contribute. Not only were these five great cities
in intimate tradal relations with each other but, as has been said,
the great bulk of the inter-clan commercial transactions had to pass
through the hands of Ōsaka firms. Here, it will be seen, there was
ample scope for the development of commerce on the grand scale ;
in short, the situation demanded an elaborate and complex system
of organization, of combination, and of specialization. That the
Japanese traders were not slow to rise to the height of the possibilities opened up to them by the passing of the great commercial
marts of the empire into the sole control of the Tokugawa Shōgunate
the English merchants then in Japan very soon discovered to their
cost and vexation. On 19th March, 1620, Cocks wrote :—

" That which chiefly spoiled the Japon trade is a company of ruch
usurers whoe have gotten all the trade of Japon into their owne handes
. . . which maketh me altogether aweary of Japon."

In this " company of ruch usurers " we have an early example
of a Tokugawa " guild merchant ". A certain number of firms
domiciled in the Shōgunal cities have organized themselves into a
corporation for the purpose of obtaining complete control over the
chief staples of foreign trade, and have succeeded in obtaining
the approval of the authorities. Later on, when the Dutch got
penned up in Deshima, this corporation came to have the monopoly
of all the wares that arrived in Dutch ships. It was only by being
formally admitted into the corporation that any other Japanese
firm could get permission to participate in this particular trade, and
to obtain admission it was necessary to purchase the rights of
some member who wished to retire from it. Thus, membership
of the guild was something analogous to a share in a modern joint-
stock company. As has just been said, it came to be a valuable
asset which could be sold (although not without the approval of
the other members of the guild) or pledged, and was not infrequently
deposited as security when it became necessary or advisable to
negotiate a loan. This special corporation was subject to strict
governmental supervision in certain respects as both the Bakufu
Treasury and the municipality of Nagasaki exacted a fixed annual
revenue from the Deshima trade, but, apart from this liability, the
guild prosecuted its operations in its own fashion through officers
elected or appointed by itself. The prime objects were to restrain
any outsiders from poaching in its own special preserves, to regulate
all prices, and if not to eliminate competition entirely, at all events
to restrict it to certain simple well-defined and openly recognized
channels.

In the purely domestic trade of the Shōgunal towns, a system
of analogous guilds rapidly tended to establish itself in almost
every line of trade, with this difference, that for a considerable
time there was no direct Government interference, inasmuch as the
Government had no thoughts of deriving any revenue from the internal
commerce of the empire. In a society where the family and not
the individual was the unit, something like a mild caste system
easily grew up in commerce no less than in handicrafts. Once a
household had established itself as purveyors of any special com-
modity, the tendency was for son to succeed father in the special
occupation for generation after generation. Any neighbour venturing
to set up a new rival establishment would naturally be regarded
as an interloper and those already in possession of the field

would organize themselves into what were practically guilds to protect themselves against any such unwelcome competition. In so doing, they could count upon the tacit approval of the constituted authorities, for the Tokugawa government was anxious to secure worthy representatives in each branch of trade, and was not averse to seeing all trades becoming hereditary in old established households. The trade guilds were thus in the main a natural growth of custom, and in a measure the great bulwark of custom against the inroads of competition.

It was in Ōsaka that the guild system showed its earliest and most powerful development. Here, the old established firms were long able to restrict the number of houses entitled to do business in any special line of commodities merely by those methods of moral suasion to which Japanese society was so extremely sensitive and so readily responsive in the good old days of feudalism. It would be hard to mention a single item of commerce that was not entirely manipulated by one of those spontaneous growths for the mutual protection of all who made their livelihood by dealing in it. In the middle of the eighteenth century there were about 100 guilds, great and small, in Ōsaka. Some of these included several hundred establishments; the bathhouse *Kumi* counted as many as 2,004 members; the wholesale rice dealers' *Kumi* 1,351 members; the vintners', 1,707; the pawnbrokers', 613, and the druggists', 273. The others were much smaller in number; there were no more than fifty-two money-changers; fifty booksellers; forty wholesale greengrocers, and only nine wholesale oil merchants.

For many years, the guilds appear to have been dominated by a combination of the most powerful among them, including the trades concerned with the great staples of commerce, cotton, dry goods, ironware, paper, oil, drugs, matting, earthenware, lacquered ware, and wine. This was known as the "ten *Kumi*" of Ōsaka, and towards the end of the seventeenth century a similar combination was formed in Yedo, though the guilds in the capital were far from being as powerful as they were in Ōsaka; in fact their components were, in a majority of cases, either originally or actually mere branches of great Ōsaka houses, and they never exceeded sixty-eight in number. Among the most important of them were the wholesalers; the rice-brokers (*fuda-sashi*) for dealing with the rice-stipends of the Hatamoto, and the castle officials; the bathhouses, and the hairdressers. In Yedo, the artisan-guilds were not without importance, while there were corporations of Government merchants and of contractors for river-cleaning, garden-making, aqueduct repairing, road-making, and bridge-building. Besides these, there were guilds for merchandise-boats, passenger-boats, water-boats, and even mud-scows. Many of these Yedo *Kumi* were merely local and not of very much intrinsic significance, but apart from the powerful fishmongers' corporation, most of the Yedo guilds concerned with the great staples of life were greatly dependent upon, if not actually controlled by, the similar confraternities in Ōsaka, a circumstance that presently gave umbrage to the Bakufu authorities.

In the first half of the Tokugawa régime, the guilds pursued the even tenor of their way without either provoking or inviting Government interference. In 1659 the authorities did take upon themselves to determine the personnel of the pedlars' guild. Eight years before they had given some attention to the bath-houses of Yedo, but the grounds of interference were ethical and political rather than economic. The Bakufu councillors, at this date, were attempting to grapple with the prevalence of sexual immorality, and they were also in grave anxiety about the Rōnin who might readily utilize the bath-houses as rendezvous. In the upper stories of these bath-houses vices were practised which the authorities could not hope to control without enlisting the services of the bath-house keepers by means of the licence system. As Yedo grew in dimensions, these licences increased in value, so that pawnbrokers readily accepted them in pledge for loans. Almanac-makers were also in time subjected to the licence system, their numbers being limited to eighty-one. From the early part of the seventeenth century there were money-changers both in Ōsaka and Yedo. In 1660 those in Ōsaka organized themselves into a corporation, but it was not till 1718 that the Yedo men were incorporated. This was done at the instance of the authorities who furnished 600 of them with licences, and at the same time prohibited unlicensed persons from pursuing the avocation. In 1725 the Government also sanctioned a rice-exchange at Dojima in Ōsaka. Four years later a similar rice-exchange was organized in Yedo but it lasted only a few years. On the other hand the Yedo *fuda-sashi* guild, which was also regulated, if not instituted by the authorities in 1724, continued in existence down to the fall of the Tokugawa Shōgunate. With these and perhaps a few other minor exceptions the guilds continued to be virtually self-constituted and autonomous down to the latter half of the eighteenth century. The volume of trade had then increased to such proportions that the guilds found themselves no longer able to control the enterprise of interlopers, and so application was then made for Government recognition and sanction of the monopoly which the guilds claimed to be entitled to by old-established use and wont. This period (1764–86) was the age of the Tanumas, when bribery, more or less in evidence at all times, was especially rampant and notorious. Thus, the guilds had no great difficulty in obtaining their demands, and thenceforward each guild was accustomed to pay an annual " thank-offering ", and to supplement it with presents of the staples in which it dealt. A quarter of a century after this, the authorities were openly in receipt of as much as £20,000 per annum as " thank-offerings " from the guilds of Yedo, and the perquisites of the officials from the guilds as a whole must have been of no inconsiderable value.

At this time, the whole trade of the five Tokugawa cities had passed into the hands of what were virtually trusts, that is to say, into the control of associations of merchants engaged in the same branch of commerce and pledged to observe certain rules in the conduct of their business, and to adhere to fixed rates. No member of a confederation was now allowed to dispose of his licence except to a near relative, and if any interloper ventured to engage in the business of any licensed confederation he made himself subject to condign punishment. In spite of the limit imposed upon the transfer of these certificates of membership, these documents were varied in value from £80 to £6,400, and so, of course, counted as a very valuable security when a loan had to be contracted. These monopolistic traders gradually acquired immense wealth and fell into the most luxurious habits. We hear stories of some of them spending £5 upon the first bonito of the season, and more than twice that sum on the first fruit of the egg-plant ; while the luxurious sumptuousness of their private establishments, as it became more and more pronounced, naturally excited the envy and cupidity of the less-favoured members of the community. It especially offended the aristocrats and the two-sworded men, many of whom were almost permanently under heavy financial obligations to these plebeian merchant princes. This feeling had been steadily growing since the beginning of the nineteenth century, and in the thirties of that century when the whole empire was being pinched and emaciated by a seemingly interminable famine, the indifference and callousness of the rich mercantile class provoked the most bitter resentment among those to whom the claims of compassion and humanity still counted for something.

It was in Ōsaka that this resentment found its clearest and most forcible expression. In the course of the great dearth half-a-century before there had been serious rice riots in Yedo and elsewhere, and the rich merchants were probably aware that these might now be repeated. A mere outbreak of mob violence was, however, not so very formidable a matter ; the constituted authorities might safely be counted upon to deal effectually with any such contingency. A peasant revolt under peasant leaders could never go very far or continue very long, although it might do some considerable damage to property. On the other hand, the case might be very different if two-sworded men were the organizers and leaders of the outbreak. Now, for the first time in Tokugawa history since the siege of Shimabara, exactly two centuries before, we find samurai actually making common cause with the afflicted and down-trodden plebeians ; and the result was a commotion far more serious than any that had occurred since that time.[1]

The protagonist in this great Ōsaka *émeute* of 1837 was not merely a two-sworded man but an ex-Government official. Ōshio Heihachirō was the son of an Inspector of Police attached to the City Magistrate of Ōsaka. In his fourteenth year, Heihachirō was placed under the care of Hayashi, Daigaku no Kami, in the Seidō, and after a distinguished course of five years there, he received an appointment as instructor in that institution. Shortly after, his father died, and Heihachirō was summoned to Ōsaka, where he succeeded to his father's office and emoluments. As Police-Inspector, Ōshio had certain limited judicial functions to perform, and his honesty and uprightness in the discharge of his duties won him the regard of the people, as well as of Takaye, the City Magistrate of Ōsaka. The latter was recalled to Yedo in course of time, and his successor, Atobe, proved to be corrupt and heartless. Ōshio, finding the situation hopeless, presently resigned and devoted himself to the education of a number of disciples he had gradually gathered around him.

---

[1] Yui no Shosetsu's conspiracy in 1651, would have been a much graver affair, if it had not been detected while still in the bud.

In a previous chapter, some allusion was made to the " reforms " introduced into the University of Yedo in the last decade of the eighteenth century. No one was now allowed to enter the University who failed to conform with the rigid orthodoxy of the Teishu philosophy which had been adopted as the official doctrine of the bureaucracy. It was upon this doctrine that Ōshio had been reared, but he had really little sympathy with the dry, narrow, conventional formalism which characterized that creed and its professors. So strong became his dislike for the exaggerated importance placed upon mere external mechanical propriety that at last he threw the Teishu system overboard, a thing which many a promising young official no doubt wished to do, but one which very few indeed had the courage to do, for it meant the sacrifice of all prospects of a career. In the rival Ōyōmei school—now branded as heretical— stress was laid upon the worth of generous impulses and the prompt- ings of a pure conscience ; and in this, the philosophy of Nakae Tōju's latter days, Ōshio found both a spiritual refuge and a source of inspiration. " Do right for the sake of doing right " was the main spirit of the doctrine that he impressed upon the ardent followers who now gathered around him to learn wisdom and— fencing.

As the famine got worse and worse, and the authorities did nothing, Ōshio memorialized the City Magistrate, Atobe, praying earnestly that steps should be taken to relieve the terrible distress that was getting more and more intense every day. His petition was ignored. Then he gave free rein to his indignation and hotly denounced the callous selfishness of the officials and the merchant princes. He furthermore sold off all his property and spent the proceeds in relief work. All he could do was, of course, no better than a drop in the ocean ; its only value lay in furnishing a model for imitation, but he had no imitators.

Then, as 1836 had been a terrible year, and 1837 promised no improvement, he became desperate and resolved to have recourse to desperate means. In consultation with his followers, old friends among the police, some young samurai, and—what was most significant of all—a few Rōnin, he sketched out a plan for over- throwing the officials and " depriving the merchants of their inhuman gains ". A manifesto entitled the " Punishment from Heaven " was distributed in Ōsaka and the neighbouring districts, copies being affixed to the pillars of all the temples and shrines.

The language used was as simple and plain as possible, and parts of it were very significant.

"The officers have no respect for *the will of the Emperor*, and act in utter violation of the laws established by the Tokugawa Shōgunate."

The 25th of March was the day selected for the outbreak. On that day the two Magistrates were to inspect the wards of the city, and after the inspection they were to take their recreation in the house of a police inspector, situated just in front of Ōshio's own abode. Ōshio called together his party of police, samurai, Rōnin, students, and the more wealthy farmers in the neighbourhood; their plan was to kill the Magistrates in the house opposite, seize the castle, and then compel the capitalists to distribute their property among the suffering people. Two police inspectors in the plot were to burn the Magistracy by way of a diversion. However, on the preceding day, a constable who doubted the success of the enterprise revealed the whole plot to Atobe, the Magistrate, and the two inspectors who were to set the Magistracy on fire were sent for. One of them died fighting, the other escaped and ran off to Ōshio to inform him that they had been betrayed. The only thing that now remained was to sally forth, do all that could be done, and die gallantly. Ōshio thereupon fired his own house, while his men set the torch to great mansions in various parts of the city, calling upon the destitute to take whatever they pleased. The Castle authorities sent out all their troops and desperate fighting ensued, Oshio's party being ultimately overborne by sheer weight of numbers. But they had succeeded in reducing a great part of the city to ashes, over 18,000 houses, 1,100 "godowns" and five bridges being burned in the course of the two days' conflagration. Ōshio made good his escape to Yoshino, but on returning to Ōsaka the house in which he found refuge was discovered and surrounded by officers of the law, whereupon he set fire to the building and committed suicide with time-honoured samurai orthodoxy.[1]

It was significant that Ōshio was not slow to find imitators. Shortly afterwards there was a similar outbreak in Echigo, and in the following year another in Mikawa. To find samurai and

---

[1] Oshio was "accompanied in death" by his son, who, as the father was only forty-five years of age, must have been little more than a youth. As is usual in such cases, he left a memorial condemning the corruption and neglect of the officials and their indifference alike to the welfare of the sovereign and the nation.

Rōnin heading revolts against the Tokugawa authorities was extremely ominous in the light of subsequent events. These events took place sixteen years before the appearance of Perry and his "black ships" at Uraga. Another sixteen short years were to pass, and then the stately fabric of Tokugawa autocracy and splendour was destined to fall in ruins to the ground, the chief agents in its destruction being not so much great feudatories and their old high-placed hereditary *Karō*, as discontented, ambitious, two-sworded men of the feudal rank and file among whom some of the most enterprising and the most dangerous were Rōnin.

Upon the old Shōgun Iyenari, who had attained the age of sixty-four years, and was then preparing to demit his office after having held it for fifty-one years, it is questionable whether this great Ōsaka *émeute* produced any serious impression, but one of the Great Council seems undoubtedly to have taken the matter to heart, if we are to judge by subsequent developments. Mizuno Tadakuni, Echizen no Kami, had then been a member of the Rōjū for three or four years. Under Iyenari there was no scope for initiative, and to enter upon the scheme of reform on which he had evidently been brooding for some time was impossible, so long as the old ex-Shōgun continued to direct or rather to misdirect affairs. With Iyenari's demise in 1841, the situation became greatly changed, and Mizuno at last found himself in a position where he could venture to act with a fairly free and firm hand. The new Shōgun, Iyeyoshi (1837–53) was little better than a nonentity, though, having been born in 1782, he was already forty-five years of age when his father made way for him. During the four years of his titular rule he had not evinced the slightest inclination to form any judgment or to exert any will of his own, and after he became the actual, as well as the nominal head of the Bakufu system (1841), he continued to be almost equally lethargic. Whoever among his ministers and courtiers could secure his ear and his confidence could safely count upon being allowed a free hand in the discharge of his duties without risk of check from the Shōgun. In 1841, Mizuno's reputation for ability stood exceedingly high; and Iyeyoshi was glad to leave all matters of policy in his charge. Mizuno had, however, been taking measures to provide himself with more than Shōgunal countenance if not support.

In revolving his projects of reform he had naturally made a close study of Matsudaira Sadanobu's efforts and methods between

1786 and 1793. Sadanobu had been a nominee and representative of the Go-san-ké—the noble houses of Kishū, Owari, and Mito— and it was mainly owing to their sympathy and support that he had been able to maintain his position and achieve the measure of reform he succeeded in effecting. Now, however, it was vain for Mizuno to expect any aid from Kishū and Owari, for sons of Iyenari had been adopted as heads of these two great houses. With Mito the case was very different. In 1829, the eighth Daimyō of Mito died without leaving any offspring of his own, and his legitimate successor was his brother Nariaki, then twenty-nine years of age. Nariaki was already known as an able, strong-willed man, and the hereditary clan councillors, who had allowed the fief to drift into disorder and demoralization, were by no means eager to see a chief at the head of affairs who would be likely to take his position and his duties seriously. Accordingly, when the Shōgun (Iyenari) through his favourite, Mizuno Tadashige (*not* Tadakuni) attempted to impose another of his sons upon Mito (as he had already done in the case of Kishū and Owari) the responsible councillors of the fief showed themselves complacent and compliant enough. The project was, however, extremely distasteful to some of the Mitō samurai, and the leaders of this faction—Kawase, Aizawa, and Fujita Tōko—were ultimately able to secure the succession for the legitimate heir, Nariaki, and naturally one of his first steps upon his accession was to replace the old clan councillors with the men who had so loyally supported him. This episode was the origin of a bitter internecine clan feud which, after smouldering and simmering for nearly forty years, at last broke out into a bloody and disastrous local civil war. The new Mito councillors were not slow in inaugurating drastic reforms, though they were mainly of a con-servative nature. They aimed at tightening the reins of administra-tion, restoring the ancient discipline, and reverting to the good old days of the second Mito prince, the famous Mitsukuni. Their spirit differed greatly from that presently abroad in the neighbouring little fief of Sakura, where a ready welcome was being accorded to Dutch learning, and to a body of new ideas which were vehemently scouted by the scholars and politicians of Mito, who were intensely nationalistic and even Chauvinistic. It was upon the glories of the past, and not the pregnant possibilities and promise of the future, that their attention was fixed. Interest in the ancient history of Japan and in Shintō had for long been intense in their fief, and although at this date, the Teishu philosophy was supposed to be the orthodox official philosophy in Mito as elsewhere, the Mito scholars had developed, or were developing, a pragmatic eclecticism of their own. The leading man in the intellectual life of the clan was now Fujita Tōko, who was a curious blend of the littérateur, the philosopher, the teacher, and the practical statesman. He counted as a force far beyond the narrow confines of his own clan, and several of the men, who subsequently figured as protagonists in the great revolution of 1868, were eager to profit by his acquaintance and his instruction.

Shortly after Ōshio's *émeute* in Ōsaka, Fujita had directed his attention to the general conditions of trade and commerce, and had come to the reasoned conviction that the guilds, with their virtual monopolies, were highly detrimental to the economic interests of the empire at large. One special point in his argument was that since Ōsaka was the controlling centre of the guilds the system exposed the Yedo market to all the vicissitudes of the great distributing emporium, where commercial crises and fluctuations were becoming more and more frequent. The pamphlet in which these views were propounded was not without its influence, and Fujita's views were generally endorsed and adopted by his lord, Nariaki, who was on intimate terms with Mizuno, Echizen no Kami, the most influential member of the Great Council. The latter now took drastic action with respect to the guilds and by a series of edicts issued in the course of 1841–2 he practically exterminated them. The terms *kumiai* (guild), *toiya* (wholesaler), *nakama* (partner), and other characteristics of the system, were to be used no longer ; the payment of yearly " thank-money " (*myōga-kin*) and of all other guild burdens was abolished ; no merchant must henceforth confine himself to wholesale trade ; forestalling was strictly forbidden, and retail selling was in no case to be stopped. Finally, all present prices were to be reduced twenty per cent. and a schedule of the reductions was to be set out in front of every shop for official inspection. Lord Mizuno had excellent intentions, but he had no very deep knowledge of economics, and the Seidō men, to whom he generally resorted for enlightenment, were not much better informed. In a year or two commercial prosperity was found to have departed from Yedo. With the loss of their shares, many merchants were ruined, while mutual confidence disappeared, and the volume of transactions shrank to a small

part of what it had been.   The effect on producers and on prices
soon became disastrous, and within a few years, the city elders
were found petitioning the Government for the re-establishment
of the old order.   In 1851 the guilds were actually re-established
with their old regulations, modified by certain new provisos.   All
newcomers were henceforth to be freely admitted as members,
unless special exigencies, approved by the Government, made
restrictions advisable.   Henceforth, there was to be no limitation
of shares ;   share-certificates were no longer allowed, and yearly
fees no longer exacted by the authorities.

Any modern economist who makes a special study of this
episode in the commercial history of Japan will do well to bear
in mind that the effects of the abolition of the guild system were
complicated by other features of the great and sweeping reform
attempted by Mizuno, in which indeed the guilds were one item
only.   In addressing himself to this effect, Mizuno had assured
himself of the support of the powerful Nariaki of Mito, whose
drastic reforms within his own fief made the Mito administration
famous throughout the length and breadth of the empire.   He also
took further measures to strengthen his position.   To have possession
of the Shōgun's ear was all-important, accordingly Hori, a relative
and a trusted confidant of Mizuno, was now made *Sobayōnin* or
Adjutant to His Highness.   Furthermore, fresh blood was introduced
into the Great Council itself.   Hotta, Daimyō of Sakura, who later
on was to negotiate the American treaty with Townsend Harris,
was raised from the Junior Council to the Rōjū, while a place in
the Rōjū was also found for Sanada, the Lord of Matsushiro in
Shinano.   Sanada was a Tozama, or outside Daimyō, although it
is to be noted that he ranked henceforth as a Fudai.   He was, by
birth, the second son of the Regent, Matsūdaira Sadanobu.   He
attracted Mizuno's attention by his firmness of character, while
he was also remarkable for his advanced opinions, opinions which
he mainly drew from his retainer, Sakuma Shōzan, a strong
advocate of the reopening of Japan to foreign intercourse.   Hotta
was at that time, or was shortly to become, a great admirer of
Western science ;   at all events, from 1844 onwards he did everything he possibly could to promote the study of Dutch among his
retainers, and to derive all the practical benefits he could from
European science and culture.

In the lower branches of the administration Mizuno exerted

himself to find what he considered to be the right men for the
various posts, but he was not very fortunate ; indeed, one special
appointment of his was peculiarly unfortunate. For the execution
of his reform measures the City Magistrates of Yedo were all-
important functionaries and one of these was soon found to be
lacking in zeal. The man that after a short time replaced him
erred in his excess of zeal, and by his Draconic severity he did
much to bring his patron Mizuno into that public odium which
ultimately led to his fall. Torii was an able man in his way,[1] but
there were grave defects in his character. He was a hide-bound
pedant, a Pharisee of the Pharisees among the orthodox Teishu
philosophers ; the bitter foe of all heresy whether in the form of
the Ōyōmei school or of Dutch learning. In addition, he was utterly
unscrupulous, and so malignant that he acquired the nickname of
" the Viper ".

In 1841, instructions were issued to the officials that the
administration was thenceforth to be conducted on the models of
Kyōhō (1716–35), and Kwansei (1789–1800), which meant that
an effort was to be made to imitate the reforms of the eighth
Shōgun, Yoshimune, and of the Regent, Matsudaira Sadanobu.
A cursory glance at a catalogue of Mizuno's " Reforms " is, however,
enough for us to perceive that the reconstructive spirit which
animated Yoshimune's work had never been grasped at all, and
that even Matsudaira Sadanobu's " Reform " had been imitated
more in its details than in its essentials. The Regent had taken
the samurai vigorously in hand. Yoshimune had made his influence
felt by the Daimyō as well as by every other class in the land,
mainly by moral suasion and the force of personal example. Mizuno
was always careful not to offend those in high places ; and now it
was commoners, and especially the townsmen of Yedo, who
experienced the rigour of his reforming hand. The houses and
villas of some worthy citizens, whose style of living was too luxurious,
were demolished and the owners banished from Yedo, the famous
actor, Ichikawa Danjurō, being among the culprits. Theatres
were put under strict regulations, most of the story-telling halls
were closed ; tea-houses and archery booths were also closed, and
their female inmates sent to the Yoshiwara ; women were forbidden
to take lessons on the *samisen* or to learn *Jōruri*. Professional

---

[1] Several of his legal decisions will be found in Wigmore's *Materials for the
Study of Private Law in Old Japan, T.A.S.J.*, vol. xx, supplement, pt. iii.

female hairdressers lost their licences, and every woman had to dress her own hair. Merchants and their dependents were allowed no dress that was not made of one of the three regulation materials, spun silk, cotton, or hemp. The use of *habutaye*, crêpe, satin, or imported silk (including imitations) for sashes, collars, or fringes for sleeves was strictly prohibited. Hairpins, combs, and cakes all received official attention, while novels and decorated sign boards were among the scores of things that were now prohibited.[1] As for farmers, they were forbidden to appear in Yedo, while all those then in the city were ordered back to their respective districts and punished severely when they failed to obey the order. Such are a few examples of Mizuno's legislation at this time. In Yedo, Torii and his minions enforced the various ordinances with the sternest rigour ; cases of people, even women, dressed above the standard being stripped naked in the streets were not infrequent. The constables on the other hand, often found a source of revenue in the regulations. It soon became known that they were receiving bribes and extorting blackmail, and this fact helped to swell the outcry that began to make itself heard against the Reform and its authors. Presently, the citizens were clamouring that trade was being utterly disorganized and brought to a standstill and that the prosperity of Yedo was being wantonly ruined. As time went on, Mizuno's colleagues endeavoured to convince him that his measures were being enforced with too great severity, and that many of them were ill-advised. At the beginning of 1843, one of his colleagues, Inouye Masaharu, was dismissed from the Rōjū, and, in the October of the same year, the resignation was accepted of Mizuno's former right-hand man, Hotta, who had been remonstrating rather strongly with his chief and former friend. A month afterwards, Mizuno himself was dismissed, while all his followers, including Torii, were at the same time summarily stripped of their offices.

The Court ladies had joined in the clamour against the reforms, and they were formidable adversaries.[2] Mizuno had, however,

---

[1] It was at this date the Tamenaga Shunsui, the author of the *Iroha-bunko*, was imprisoned, not for that work, but for the pornographic strain in several of his other books.

[2] An interesting story is quoted by Dr. Greene in the appendix to his essay on Takano Chōei. The Shōgun was fond of flavouring his stewed fish with ginger sprouts. One day, the fish came on without the accustomed flavour, and on the Shōgun asking the reason, he was told that Mizuno had forbidden the cultivation of ginger, as he regarded it as a luxury. The Shōgun then said that he remembered having a conversation with Mizuno on the general topic of luxuries, and had given his assent to their prohibition, but he had no idea that he would deprive the people of ginger sprouts.

come into conflict with many besides the Court ladies, over various matters of policy before his fall. Inundations in the Kwantō had made extensive riparian works necessary, and when Mizuno urged the local Daimyō to take them in hand, they insisted that the expenses should be defrayed by the Bakufu. The projected visit of the Shōgun to Nikkō entailed great expense, and Sanada urged that the visit should be postponed to allow funds to be spent on the coast defences. On this question Mizuno was on bad terms with one of his chief supporters. The money was ultimately found, but it was only obtained by a further debasement of the coinage, an expedient to which Mizuno had already had recourse on more than one occasion to make good the annual deficit in the Bakufu treasury. What was most serious of all was that Mizuno had now lost the backing of Lord Nariaki of Mito, while his efforts to retain it had brought him into collision with his fellow-councillors and even with many among his own followers. Nariaki was a fervid exponent of *kinnō*, of devotion to the Imperial House, and Mizuno fancied the surest way of retaining Nariaki's goodwill was by showing unusual attention to the Court in Kyōto. Among other marks of regard, he established a school for the Court nobles to be supported by Bakufu funds. Twenty years later, this institution became of consequence when the empire was convulsed with the cry of " *Sonnō Joi* " ! In spite of all this, Mizuno came into collision with Lord Nariaki on the question of foreign intercourse. Nariaki was aware of the weakness of the national defences, and was constantly impressing on the Bakufu the necessity of casting cannon and building modern men-of-war. He strongly advocated the repeal of the old law which two centuries before had strangled Japanese maritime enterprise, but he was at the same time strongly opposed to the small school of thinkers who advocated an indulgent treatment of foreigners. He firmly believed that the Expulsion Decree of 1825 should be enforced in all its rigour, and it was over the question of modifying its severity that he and Mizuno became estranged. Fuller details about this subject will be given in a following chapter: here it will suffice to say that when Mizuno did presume to modify the Expulsion Decree in 1842, his old friendship with Nariaki came to an end.

In less than a year after his fall, Mizuno was again back in office, while Lord Nariaki had been ordered to make way for his son as head of the Mito fief, and to confine himself to his Komagome

mansion in Yedo. This, however, was no work of Mizuno. Doi, who
had succeeded him in November, 1843, had long looked askance
at Lord Nariaki's reforms and his *kinnō* doctrines, while he looked
with suspicion upon his projects for building men-of-war and casting
ordnance.   Early in 1844 Nariaki had caused the bells of many
Buddhist monasteries in his fief to be melted to provide material
for his cannon-founders, and the Buddhist priests, supported by
the strong opposition party in Mito, had been able to bring influence
to bear upon the Shōgun and his ministers. Nariaki was removed
from the headship of his house ; the progressive Councillors,
Fujita Tōko and his colleagues, were ordered into confinement, and
representatives of the opposition called to office in the clan. As
these men were all of mediocre capacity, the Mito fief soon began to
drift back into the conditions of 1829 when Lord Nariaki initiated
his reforms. Although thus removed from direct control over his
own fief, Nariaki was a power still to be seriously considered.
Many of the other great feudatories expressed a lively sympathy
with him and the views he advocated, and the ascendancy he was
gaining among these nobles now became stronger than ever.
Although in confinement, he was still one of the most influential
men in the empire, a fact that the astute Abé Masahiro, presently
to be head of the Rōjū, was not slow to appreciate.

Abé Masahiro, when only twenty-five years of age, entered the
Great Council upon Mizuno's fall in 1843. His chief, Doi, did not
last long. The castle was destroyed by fire in 1844, the Shōgun
barely escaping with his life, while there were many casualties
among the ladies of the Great Interior. Doi had to face the onerous
task of reconstruction, and in this he failed signally. Abé Masahiro
could then easily have become head of the Rōjū, but he recommended
the recall of Mizuno to that position. Besides the reconstruction
of the Castle, there was yet another very serious problem to be
dealt with, and Abé preferred not to be saddled with the chief
responsibility. The King of Holland had sent his famous letter
to the Shōgun, the reply to this had to be considered, while the
whole position with respect to foreign relations called for the most
careful and profound deliberation. In this field, Mizuno had already
made some considerable innovations ; and he was known to have
definite and well-considered views on the subject. Hence the chief
reasons for his recall. His term of office was a brief one on this
occasion. In March, 1845, he was suddenly dismissed, banished

to a poor fief at Yamagata in northern Japan, and ordered to confine himself to his own house. This was the end of his career. His second and final fall was owing to no immediate offence of his own, but to the misconduct of some of his former subordinates, for which he was held to be indirectly responsible. About this time there was a bitter dispute between two rival claimants for the headship of the Gōtō family, in which the superintendence of the mint had been vested since the days of Iyeyasu, and in connexion with this case there were many surprising and unsavoury revelations. It became apparent that Torii, the former City Magistrate, had been grossly unjust in some of his decisions, and that in more than one instance he had been a judicial murderer. He was now ordered to be confined for life in the ward of the Daimyō of Marugame. (He was only released in 1866, and survived till 1874.) Mizuno's return to the Rōjū had caused a great panic among the officials. Rumours of impending dismissals on a wholesale scale were afloat, and when it was known that Torii was exerting himself to get back into official life his adversaries joyously availed themselves of the disclosures in connexion with the Gōtō case to push the matter home, and so make a summary end of him and his patron, Mizuno.

Mizuno Tadakuni is now only remembered on account of the extravagances in his futile attempts at reform. It is quite possible to exaggerate the importance of the economic factor in history, although, indeed, it is often the dominant one, and in most cases a very weighty one. Yoshimune clearly grasped the fact that any moral amendment must be preceded and accompanied by wide-reaching constructive economic measures. He was unwearied in his efforts to stimulate production and increase the wealth of the nation in every possible way, and as regards the distribution of that wealth, he tried to persuade the privileged and administrative class that justice demanded that the hard-working producer—especially the farmer—should be ensured a fair share of the produce of his toil. Behind Mizuno's reforms we search in vain for any such fundamental principles. Yoshimune was unwearied in his quest for the right men to aid him in carrying out his projects ; Mizuno, on the other hand, was singularly unfortunate in the selection of his subordinate officers. His ideas of reform have not inaptly been likened to the notion of curing a distempered constitution by cutting off the heads of the most prominent pimples appearing on the face and the surface of the body. At the very time he was turning Yedo topsy-turvy with his so-called Reforms, the mantle of Yoshimune had fallen upon a real reformer, who in his humble sphere was truly working wonders. In previous chapters a good deal has been said about Nakae Tōju, Yoshimune, the great Shōgun, and Uyesugi Harunari, the Lord of Yonezawa. In these three men and in Ninomiya Sontoku we see Tokugawa Japan at its very best.[1]

It is impossible to go into the details of Ninomiya's work here. Only it may be said that Ninomiya was a mere self-educated peasant born (1787) and brought up in the most grinding poverty, and that to the end of his days he was lord of no domain, but at best a trusted servant of others. His early work was on Ōkubo's fief of Odawara, which he extricated from a very hopeless position. Then he was in the service of the Soma family, which he made one of the wealthiest feudal houses of the time. His career came to an end in the employ of the Bakufu, which sent him to effect a reform in the Nikkō district in the very year (1853) the " black ships " came to Uraga. Three years afterwards, he died in harness at Imaichi in the seventieth year of his age. The moral and economic work accomplished by this extraordinary man was really marvellous, and its results persist to this very day for, even in the highest official circles in the empire, there is a powerful school of thinkers who are strenuous advocates of " Ninomiya principles " while, in several sections of Japan, Ninomiya's credit associations still play an important part in the social and economic life of the people. Ninomiya Sontoku was in every way a far greater and finer man than Mizuno Tadakuni.

The pressing question of a reply to the Dutch king's dispatch seemed to have been almost settled when Mizuno was removed from the political stage. Abé Masahiro, Ise no Kami, assumed the chief place in the Great Council. For the next twelve years, Abé will continue to be the most prominent figure in the administration policy of Japan. Young, vigorous, able, versatile, and supple, he

---

[1] For Ninomiya, see Mr. Uchimura's *Japan and the Japanese* ; the Rev. R. C. Armstrong, " Ninomiya Sontoku " in *T.A.S.J.*, vol. xxxvii, pt. ii ; Professor Droppers, " A Japanese Credit Association," and Professor Longford, " Notes on Ninomiya Sontoku," both in *T.A.S.J.*, vol. xxii, pt. i. Professor Droppers gives a good bibliography in *A Japanese Credit Association, T.A.S.J.*, vol. xxii, pt. i. The last has a good bibliography, the most important item in which, Tomita's *Hōtoku-ki*, has recently been translated by Mr. T. Yoshimoto.

was the proper man to pilot the ship of State through the unwonted storms to which it was presently to be exposed, but there was one serious defect in his character. He was too prone to shirk the burden of responsibility in difficult crises, and to transfer it to other shoulders. And this defect had not a little to do with the collapse of the Bakufu within little more than a decade from his death in 1857.

CHAPTER XIII

A LLUSION has already been made to the circumstance that by a strange irony of fate one of the factors that contributed to the ultimate overthrow of the Tokugawa power was that very school of Chinese philosophy which had been sedulously encouraged and fostered by Iyeyasu and elevated to something analogous to the position of an Established Church for the military caste by his later successors. Here, in the words of the Japanese adage, was a veritable case of one " getting one's hand bitten by a pet dog ". It is to be remarked, however, that if Chinese philosophy had continued to retain undisputed possession of the intellectual field, it is not very probable that its exponents would have been so ready to turn their pens against a Government that had done so much for it. For nearly 100 years, however, there had been fierce strife between the Kangakusha (or Chinese scholars) and the Wagakusha, whose speciality was native Japanese learning ; and by the beginning of the nineteenth century the Wagakusha had made such headway that several of their doctrines were either explicitly or tacitly admitted and adopted by the followers of the orthodox Teishu philosophy. One of the most important of these was the divinity of the Mikado and his undoubted right and title to claim the unquestioning obedience of all within the seas of the empire. With the Chinese philosophers, loyalty still, as before, counted as the greatest and most imperative of all the virtues, but now, under the influence of the teachings of the Wagakusha, several of the orthodox philosophers began to consider the question as to the precise direction in which that loyalty should be directed in the case of a clash of claims upon it. For the time being, with Yedo indisputably in the ascendant, the question was merely an academical one ; but should Kyōto choose to assert itself, it would at once be swept into the vortex of practical politics, and on the precise answer returned to it, much—in fact, everything—would depend. So much Ogyu Sorai seems to have perceived nearly a century and a half before the problem began to press for solution.

It is somewhat strange to find that Matsudaira Sadanobu, the Shōgun's Prime Minister (1787–93) was not alive to the danger for, in his time, the revival of pure Shintō had gone so far that no great prescience or acuteness was necessary to perceive in it something more than a mere potential menace to the fortunes of the Bakufu. And yet, when in 1795 he proscribed all the heterodox schools of Chinese philosophy, instead of laying a heavy hand upon the Shintōists as well, he even went out of his way to patronize and encourage them, although indications of the effect of their propaganda must have been patent everywhere.   In 1781–2, some of his Japanese friends insisted to Titsingh, Head of the Dutch Factory in Deshima, that Europeans were mistaken in applying the term " Emperor " to the Shōgun, the " Dairi " being the only legal Emperor, and the Shōgun but an officer to whom the " Dairi " had entrusted the administration.   In spite of the " stationary " civilization of the Tokugawa régime, things in Japan had been moving since the days of Nobunaga, of the Taikō and of Iyeyasu— for in those times it does not appear that any Japanese insisted, either to the Jesuits or to the Philippine missionaries, or to the English or the Dutch, that the " Dairi " was the true and the only " Emperor " of Japan.   In this fact, if known, a really far-seeing Minister would have discerned a dire menace to the Tokugawa sway, but Matsudaira Sadanobu, although much extolled by some writers for his sagacity, does not seem to have had any large measure of the constructive imagination characteristic of the true statesman.

The story of the revival of Chinese learning in Japan under Iyeyasu has been told in a former chapter. For nearly a century after the institution of the Tokugawa Shōgunate the study of this learning engrossed the attention of the national intellect. Towards the close of the seventeenth century, however, in certain quarters a consciousness arose that Japan in the past had had a literature of her own and that her literature was not altogether unworthy of study. This feeling was especially strong in Mitō, where the Daimyō was spending about a fifth of the revenues of the fief upon the production of his great historical and antiquarian works. These works were indeed written in Chinese, or rather in Japanese-Chinese ; but, dealing exclusively with the early fortunes and developments of the empire as they did, it is not difficult to understand how it came to pass that Mitsukuni's interest in Japanese scholarship was roused, and a certain Shimokabe was entrusted by him with the task of editing and writing a commentary on the *Manyōshū* (or "Collection of one Thousand Leaves"), the oldest of the numerous anthologies of Japanese poetry. This was a compilation of the later eighth or earlier ninth century, and to the Japanese of Mitsukuni's time it was no more intelligible than Caedmon's Paraphrase was to Dryden's contemporaries. In the course of six or eight centuries there had been almost as great (if not, indeed, greater) changes in the language of Japan than there had been in that of England in the same period,—changes in vocabulary, in accidence, and in syntax alike.

Antecedent to the introduction of Chinese literature into the country, the Japanese appear to have had no system of writing of their own, and the oldest Japanese literary work that has come down to us was expressed in Chinese characters. This work was the *Kojiki*, or Records of Ancient Events, compiled in A.D. 712, which sets forth the early traditions of the Japanese, beginning with the myths which constitute the basis of Shintō, and bringing its story down to A.D. 628. Although it was all written in Chinese characters yet the bulk of the text is Japanese phonetically expressed in the same script. Eight years after its compilation the *Kojiki* was followed (720) by another work covering the same ground as the *Kojiki* and bringing the history down as far as A.D. 697. This work, the *Nihongi*, was not merely written in Chinese characters but in the Chinese language, and from this time onwards Chinese in Japan was employed almost exclusively in the composition of histories and of serious works generally to an even greater extent than was Latin for these purposes in contemporary Europe. Not-withstanding all this, the eighth, ninth, and tenth centuries, during which Chinese was emphatically the language of the learned in Japan, were the golden age of pure Japanese classical literature. Towards the end of the period, about A.D. 1000, the Court-lady Murasaki-no-Shikibu in Japan actually succeeded in doing what Richardson and Fielding only accomplished in England a little more than a century and a half ago. Her *Genji Monogatari* (Narrative of Genji) is a true novel realistic in the best sense of the word—that is, in so far as " we see depicted real men and women, especially women, as they are, in their everyday lives and surroundings, their sentiments and passions, their faults and weaknesses ". About the quality of the work, and about the claim of certain Japanese critics that it deserves to be ranked with the masterpieces of European fiction, there may be some room for discussion, but about its proportions there can be no dispute whatsoever. For these proportions are extremely bounteous ; it is in fifty-four books, and in one well-known edition there are no fewer than 4,234 pages. However, with its qualities or with its proportions we have little to do here. What is to our purpose—which is to indicate the origin and progress of the revival of interest in old Japanese literature and old Japanese institutions which ultimately contributed in no small measure to the fall of the Shōgunate—is the following extract from Mr. Aston :—

" The *Genji* is not intrinsically a very difficult work, and no doubt the author's contemporaries found it quite easy to understand. But since then the language, institutions, and manners, and customs of Japan have changed so much as greatly to obscure the meaning not only to European students but to the Japanese themselves. Piles of commentary by native editors have been accumulated over it, and their interpretations are often so blundering and inadequate that Motoori found it necessary to devote to its elucidation a critical work in nine volumes, mostly taken up with correcting the errors of his predecessors."

This *Genji Monogatari* of the Court-lady was preceded by other so-called *Monogatari* or Narratives, all, however, stories of no great length, and of a romantic character far removed from the realities of daily life. These were also all written in Japanese, not in Chinese as the professedly serious works of the time were ; and besides the *Monogatari* were diaries, travels, and miscellanies, among which last the *Makura Zōshi* of Murasaki's fellow Court-lady, Sei Shōnagon, holds the place of honour. In all this body of literature, neither political theories, nor history, nor systems of religion, nor philosophy, were touched, much less seriously dealt with and, apart from literature of this kind and the *Kojiki* already alluded to, the only Japanese prose of the epoch of any importance was the *Genjishiki*, or " Institutes of the Period Genji " (901–923), the two first volumes of which contained " minute directions for the celebration of the Shintō rites of worship, including the Norito or liturgies used on these occasions, which were now for the first time, so far as we know, committed to writing, although in existence for centuries previously.

Furthermore, as things go in Japan, the *corpus poetarum Japonicorum* for these two or three centuries was a considerable one. For, as has been already hinted, while the prose of Japan is the prose of Brobdignag, her poetry is that of the Land of

Lilliput. A standard novel in fifty-four volumes and 4,234 pages ;
an ordinary " poem " in thirty-one syllables dispersed in five
lines ! The two great and famous anthologies of this time are
composed entirely of these five-line flights or—dashes. In the
Kokinshu, the later of these collections compiled about A.D. 922,
there are over 1,100 pieces, and in all these there are only
five *Naga-uta*, or " Long Poems ". When it is stated that
" Locksley Hall " would be a very long " Long Poem " in Japanese,
it will be readily admitted that whatever may have been the
offences of Japanese prose writers on the score of prolixity, Japanese
bards have always evinced an unfaltering trust in the maxim that
" brevity is the soul of wit ".

The earlier of the two anthologies is that *Manyōshū*, or
" Collection of a Thousand Leaves ", to which reference has already
been made. It is much more extensive than the *Kokinshu*, for it
includes as many as 4,000 " poems ". But the difference between
the two anthologies is not one of bulk merely. In the course of the
100 odd years that lie between the dates of their compilation
a most important innovation in the art of writing had been made
in Japan. The poets of the *Manyōshū* expressed themselves by
the employment of Chinese characters, using them phonetically.
This system was open to two objections. " A Chinese character
is a complicated contrivance, consisting of numerous strokes, and
as a complete character was required for each syllable of the poly-
syllabic Japanese words, an intolerable cumbersomeness was the
result. The second objection was that a Japanese syllable might
be represented by any one of several Chinese characters. Several
hundreds were actually in use to write the forty-seven syllables of
which the language consists. It was no easy matter to remember so
many either in reading or in writing. To meet those difficulties the
Japanese did two things ; they restricted themselves to a limited
number of characters for use as phonetic signs, and they wrote
these in an abbreviated or cursive form. There are two varieties
of the script thus produced, which are known as the *Katakana* and
Hiragana. No exact date can be assigned for their introduction,
but for the present purpose it is sufficient to know that both had
come into use by the end of the ninth century "—that is, in the
interval between the compilation of the *Manyōshū* and of the
Kokinshū. This consideration serves to explain how much easier
it was for later students of early Japanese to understand the

Kokinshū (Poems Ancient and Modern) than it was for them to make out the *Manyōshū*, and how it was that the publication of commentaries on the *Manyōshū* became so extensive during the literary renaissance of the Tokugawa age.[1] Thus, all things considered, among them the perverse ingenuity of Fujiwara-no-Sadaiye (thirteenth century A.D.) in the matter of the *Gosho-kana*, alluded to in the footnote, it will easily be understood why it was a harder task for the scholars of the times of Mitsukuni of Mitō (1622–1700) to grapple with the riddles of the *Manyōshū* than it was for Dryden's contemporaries to deal with the text of *Beowulf*. Hence, there is no necessity to have recourse to sheer criminal laziness as an explanation of the laggard progress made by Shimokabe in the execution of the task entrusted to him by the Daimyō of Mitō. Meanwhile, the fame of Keichū (1640–1701), a Buddhist priest, but the son of a *samurai*, who since 1662, had been travelling over Central Japan prosecuting his studies, especially that of Japanese poetry, reached Mitsukuni's ears, and Keichū was promptly invited by him to settle in Yedo and there complete Shimokabe's work. This invitation and subsequent ones were declined, but Mitsukuni sent one of his own retainers to study under Keichū, and the priest then set to work and soon completed a commentary of twenty volumes on the *Manyōshū*, and dedicated it to Mitsukuni. About the same time Kitamura, another scholar,

---

[1] Writes Mr. Otsuki: "After letters were introduced, composition came into use, and by means of these letters (i.e. Chinese characters) the various meanings of words were explained; but in these (Japanese) writings the foreign style of composition had to be adhered to. When Chinese learning had made much progress in Japan, the native literature was made to imitate it, and even Government enactments were in accordance with Chinese style. Nevertheless, the colloquial language could not be changed, so that although the Chinese style was used for the written language, the spoken language remained as it always had been. Even at the present day the written and spoken languages are different from each other. Before the Japanese Middle Ages the orthoepic differences between direct and indirect sounds, or pure and impure, were distinctly observed. *On this account, that which was written coincided exactly with that which was spoken.* As Chinese learning became more extensively followed, this ancient precision was gradually lost. Still, during the periods Kwampei (A.D. 889–97) and Yenchō (A.D. 923–30) the priest Shōjū and Minamoto-no-Shitagō each published a dictionary, in both of which the definition of the words was very clear, and the spelling in the Japanese alphabet-sounds was particularly good, so that up to this time the deterioration had not been very considerable. *After this there were few who studied the correct accents, and none who corrected the faulty pronunciations.* Fujiwara-no-Sadaiye, following the profession of poet, established a system of his own for the employment of the Japanese alphabet-sounds, which not only differed from that in ancient use, but also impugned the correctness of ancient books on this subject. *This false system called the 'Goshokana' was used for four hundred and fifty years without its errors being discovered by anyone.*"

edited and annotated the *Makura Zoshi, the Genji Monogatari,* and other *Monogatari* (narratives) of the tenth and eleventh centuries.

To the government of the time all this seemed not merely harmless but even praiseworthy and laudable. It was Iyeyasu's policy to induce the Kyōto Court nobles to devote their attention to poetical studies and poetical exercises, and now, the greater their absorption in the craze for recovering and writing in the " true ancient style ", the less time would they have to occupy themselves with contemporary affairs and—with intrigue. So long as this antiquarian craze was a purely literary and poetical one, the argument was perfectly sound and perfectly rational. But, by the middle of the eighteenth century the leaders of the movement were beginning to assert that the mere composition of Tanka in the " true ancient style " was the smallest of the interests to be attended to. And before the end of the century the dragon's teeth of militant political Shintōism had been effectually sown.

In this revival of pure Shintō the Japanese regard Kada Adzumamaro (1669–1736), a son of the warden of the Shintō temple of Inari, near Kyōto, as the pioneer. He differed from Keichū mainly in devoting less attention to poetry and more to antiquarianism—to the oldest national records, to old laws, and to the chronicles of the noble families—while he almost marks a new departure in sounding the first note of that hostility against Chinese learning which was to become a dominant passion with his successors. Somewhere about 1730, he was commissioned by the Yedo authorities to revise and edit the ancient texts, and on returning to Kyōto the Tokugawa authorities are said to have actually given a favourable response to the memorial he presented to them urging the establishment of a school for the study of the Japanese language and literature. In this document he protested most vigorously against the utter neglect of Japanese learning for Chinese, which up to that time (1735) had been almost universal. However, his death in 1736, interfered with the project.

Some two years before his death, Kada had received a certain Mabuchi, then a man of thirty-six or thirty-seven years, among his pupils. During the latter half of his life Mabuchi (1697–1769) gave a wonderful development and impulse to the main ideas he had received from his teacher. With him the chief aim was to illustrate the early and the prehistoric ages and, inasmuch as the accounts of these had been strongly tainted and vitiated by an admixture of Chinese notions in their transmission, Mabuchi's insistence upon the necessity of the mind of the student being perfectly emancipated from Chinese influences, and his hostility to the predominance of Chinese studies in Japan, were even more pronounced than those of Kada had been. He studied poetry assiduously, and indeed he composed no small amount, but with him all this was merely a means to the supreme end, of thoroughly mastering the old language in order to deal with the documents illustrating the history and development of the empire before it became "contaminated" by intercourse with China. "Contaminated" is a strange word to use ; yet that that was precisely what Mabuchi meant is abundantly clear from scores of passages in his works. The following citations from Sir E. Satow's Monograph on the *Revival of Pure Shintō* may suffice to indicate how very strong Mabuchi's anti-Chinese bias really was :—

"In ancient time, when men's dispositions were straightforward, a complicated system of morals was unnecessary. It would naturally happen that bad acts might occasionally be committed, but the straightforwardness of men's dispositions would prevent the evil from being concealed and growing in extent. So that in those days it was unnecessary to have a doctrine of right and wrong. But the Chinese being bad at heart, in spite of the teaching which they got, were only good on the outside, and their bad acts became of such magnitude that society was thrown into disorder. The Japanese, being straightforward, could do without teaching."

Possibly enough the Tokugawa authorities would allow all this to pass with approval, and such of them as had a sense of humour with a certain amount of amusement, for the 8,000,000 gods of the old pantheon had evidently bestowed upon the arch-champion of their cult a "gude conceit o' himsel'" and eke of his ancestors in no stinted measure. Yet as a sober matter of fact, before the lapse of 100 years the development and the extension of this national or tribal "gude conceit o' oorsells" was to cause the Tokugawa administration much trouble and embarrassment—was, in short, to contribute in serious measure to its overthrow and ruin. For Mabuchi must bear no small measure of the responsibility for that ferocious and fanatical hatred of foreigners and all things foreign which occasioned so much of trouble in the land between 1853 and 1868. However, as in Mabuchi's time Japan was really a hermit nation, with no intercourse with the outside world, and apparently free from all risk of having the equilibrium of its internal economy either upset or changed by the impact of external powers or forces, the Tokugawa councillors may very well have considered it perfectly safe to give this nationalistic and anti-Chinese propaganda the fullest scope. But what about the following ?—

"Mabuchi argues that 'while the Chinese for ages past have had a succession of different dynasties to rule over them, Japan has been faithful to one uninterrupted line of Sovereigns. Every Chinese dynasty was founded upon rebellion and parricide. Sometimes a powerful ruler was able to transmit his authority to his son and grandson, but they in their turn were inevitably deposed and murdered, and the country was in a perpetual state of civil war. A philosophy which produced such effects must be founded on a false system.

"'When Confucianism was first introduced into Japan, the simple-minded natives, deceived by its plausible appearance, accepted it with eagerness, and allowed it to spread its influence everywhere. The consequence was the civil war which broke out immediately after the death of Tenji Tennō in 671 between that Emperor's brother and son, which only came to an end in 672 by the suicide of the latter. In the eighth century the Chinese costume and etiquette were adopted by the Court. This foreign pomp and splendour covered the rapid depravation of men's hearts, and created a wide gulf between the Mikado and his people. So long as the Sovereign maintains a simple style of living, the people are contented with their own hard lot. Their wants are few, and they are easily ruled. But if the Sovereign has a magnificent palace, gorgeous clothing, and crowds of finely-dressed women to wait on him, the sight of these things must cause in others a desire to possess themselves of the same luxuries ; or, if they are not strong enough to take them by force, it excites their envy. If the Mikado had continued to live in a house roofed with shingles, and whose walls were of mud, to wear hempen clothes, and to carry his sword in a scabbard wound round with the tendrils of some creeping plant, and to go to the chase carrying his bow and arrows, as was the ancient custom, the present state of things would never have come about. But since the introduction of Chinese manners, the Sovereign, while occupying a highly dignified place, has been degraded to the intellectual level of a woman. The power fell into the hands of servants, and although they never actually assumed the title, they were Sovereigns in fact, while the Mikado became an utter nullity.'"

Why the ever-suspicious Tokugawa censorate, with, as a certain writer has put it, "its eagle eye swift to smell out offences and heresies," failed to suppress this passage and the whole *Koku-i-kō* in which it appears, belongs to that category of questions which it is easier to ask than to answer. Possibly its officers fancied that there was no necessity to watch or to doubt the loyalty and fidelity of a scholar who by express invitation had entered the service of a scion of the house of Tokugawa, for from 1746 to 1760, Mabuchi was patronized by Tayasu Munetaka, the son of the previous, and the brother of the then ruling, Shōgun, and the founder of one of the three Go-sankyō families.   Likely enough the censors failed to perceive that the term *Koku-gaku*, or " national learning " was on the point of expanding its scope far beyond the poetastering in " the true ancient style " with which it had till then been held to be synonymous.   Most of the numerous pupils that flocked to Mabuchi doubtless wished to acquire nothing from him except the profficiency in the art of rounding or capping a stanza, the display of which at proper times and seasons frequently lifted needy and obscure courtiers to place and power.   But among them were some who went further than this.

"By a fortunate coincidence, the study of pure Shintō could not be successfully prosecuted at first hand without a previous acquaintance with ancient forms of the language, and the result was a natural tendency towards a combined devotion to the two subjects, which is explanatory of the wide meaning of *Koku-gaku*, 'national learning,' sometimes erroneously used to signify the study of poetry alone."

However, be the explanation what it may, the fact remains that the Bakufu censorship interfered neither with Mabuchi nor with his still more illustrious successor, Moto-ori, the great body of whose work was instinct with latent political tendency highly menacing to the domination of Yedo.   Moto-ori (1730–1801) who was a physician at Matsuzaka in Ise, had only one interview with Mabuchi.   This was in 1761, when Mabuchi was sixty-four and Moto-ori about thirty years of age.   The conversation on this occasion was a remarkable one.   The younger man,

"spoke of his project of writing a commentary on the *Kojiki*. Mabuchi replied that he also had wished to explain the sacred writings but in order to do this it was first necessary to get rid of the effects of Chinese philosophy, and discover the genuine beliefs of antiquity.   The first step towards their elucidation was to recover the ancient language, which could only be done by studying the *Manyōshū*.   This preliminary task he had himself accomplished, and he urged Moto-ori, who was yet young, to apply himself diligently to the study of the *Kojiki*."

The outcome of this advice was that for some thirty-four years Moto-ori was engaged on his monumental *Kojiki-den*—a work pregnant with dire disaster to the Tokugawa supremacy.   This, an edition of the *Kojiki*, with an elaborate commentary, was commenced in 1764, its first part completed in 1786, the second in 1792, and the last in 1796.   The printing of it, however, which was undertaken in 1789, was not finished until 1822, a score of years after the death of the author. It runs to forty-four large volumes of clear print, two of which are devoted to prolegomena, three to indexes arranged chronologically, while one contains a tract on Cosmogony by Hatori, one of Moto-ori's pupils.

Before the scope of this work can be appreciated, it becomes necessary to have some notion of at least the general character and the outlines of that *Kojiki*, to which the briefest of reference has been made early in this chapter (p. 469). A highly competent authority has pronounced it to be a very poor production, whether considered as literature or as a record of facts ; as history, being much inferior to the contemporary *Nihongi*, written in Chinese. It must be borne in mind that although Moto-ori made full use of the *Nihongi* (and its continuations), yet his attitude towards it was exceedingly hostile. For not only was it written in Chinese but it was strongly infected with pestilential nonautochthonous notions, with vain and vile imaginings fabricated in, and imported from, China. And Chinese imaginings or Chinese philosophy or Chinese anything else at once sufficed to excite the spleen of Moto-ori who, whatever his shortcomings, was certainly entitled to have the merit of being a " good " hater imputed to him for righteousness. So much at least may reasonably be inferred from numerous passages analogous in tenor to the following :—

" In China all good and bad fortune of men, all order and disorder in the State—everything, in short, which happens in this world— is ascribed to the action of *Ten* (Heaven). Using such terms as the Way of *Ten*, and the Principle of *Ten*, they regard it as a thing to be honoured and feared above all. China, however, is a country where the true way generally has not been handed down. There they do not know that all things are the doings of the gods, and therefore resort rashly to such innovations. Now Heaven is nothing more than the region where the gods of Heaven dwell. It is a thing destitute of sense, and it is unreasonable to talk of its " command " and the like. To fear and honour *Ten*, and not fear and honour the gods, is like yielding an idle honour and awe to the Imperial Palace, and showing no reverence or honour to its Sovereign. Foreign countries, however, not having attained to the knowledge that everything is the doing of the gods, may be pardoned for believing this doctrine of the Way of *Ten*, or the Principle of *Ten*. But what is to be thought of those who, in this Imperial country, where a knowledge of the true way has been handed down, do not take the trouble to examine it, but, simply accepting the erroneous doctrines of foreign lands, imagine that which they call *Ten* is a thing of peerless excellence, and in all matters can talk of nothing but its principle ? Take, again, their pedantic and wearisome *Taiki* (the Great Limit), *Muki* (the Limitless), *Yin* and *Yang* (Positive and Negative Principles of Nature), *Ch'ien* and *K'un* (Celestial and Terrestrial Principles), *Pakwa* (Eight Diagrams of the Book of Changes), and *Wu-hing* (Five Elements), which are pure inventions of the Chinese, and for which there is really no sound reason. What consummate folly it is for those who would interpret our sacred books to rely implicitly on principles of this kind. In recent times even those who try to divest themselves of Chinese prejudices in their interpretations fail to understand the falseness of their doctrines of *Ten*, and of the Positive and Negative Powers of Nature, and do not succeed in bursting the barrier because they do not put thoroughly away from them their Chinese notions, nor resolutely rouse themselves from their deluding dreams. Moreover, the refusal of some to identify Amaterasu-no-Ohomi Kami (the Sun Goddess) as the Sun of Heaven is owing to their being steeped in Chinese narrow-minded reasonings, and so become blind to the wondrous and profound principle of the true way."

As Mr. Aston has truly said, there is food for reflection in the fact that it was possible for a man of high intelligence and vast learning like Moto-ori, not unacquainted with the philosophy and religions of India and China, to accept these childish fables as the basis of his belief. When, however, Mr. Aston goes on to make his confession of faith in Moto-ori's absolute sincerity, he need not be surprised [1] if the cynically sceptic refuse to follow him. Many anecdotes go to indicate that, in common with not a few of his countrymen, Moto-ori suffered shrewdly from " that last infirmity of noble minds "—the lust for fame. A keen, shrewd man, as he undoubtedly was, could have perceived that to garner any specially lasting meed of reputation as an expounder of Chinese philosophy would be no easy task in those days. In Japan, Chinese scholars were fully as plentiful as Doctors of Philosophy are in the Germany of to-day. During the previous century and a half every nook and cranny of Chinese philosophy had been explored, almost every Chinese commentary of note had been translated and adapted, and not seldom given forth in Japan as original work. To achieve any real originality in speculative work the Japanese intellect had been impotent. So much possibly Moto-ori observed ; at all events, there is the strongest of reason to believe that he quickly recognized that his own strength did not lie in the direction of handling philosophical abstractions. He made a merit of confessing that he did not understand what the Sung schoolmen meant by their *Taiki*, their *Yin*, and their *Yang*, and the similar figments of their imaginations. Moto-ori's mental bent was all towards the concrete and the matter-of-fact and as a consequence he found himself

---

[1] Mr. Aston died long before this was written.

strongly fascinated by the old "national learning", where everything was at once beautifully concrete, and if not exactly matter-
of-fact, certainly matter-of-fact-like. That "national learning"
he could master successfully and thoroughly, and inasmuch as not
much beyond the pioneer work had been done by his predecessors
Keichū, Kada and Mabuchi, a wide field for investigation and
research here lay virgin and unexplored. Here, indeed, "originality"
could be shown, and laurels reaped even from a plain straightforward
non-contentious exposition of his discoveries. But if, in addition
to this, the results he reached could be utilized as ammunition for
a vigorous and swingeing polemic against that Chinese philosophy
which now held the Japanese intellect in thraldom, the crop of bays
would be all the thicker and all the more enduring. By assiduous
yet judicious sounding of the tribal drum, he could hope not
unreasonably to swell the proportions of his audience—mayhap
of his disciples and followers, for it could not prove unpleasant to
many of his compatriots to be assured and to have it demonstrated
to them that after all "*they* were the people". The natural
tendency of the Japanese mind, in common with the human mind
generally, is to believe too readily and to believe too much, and this
tendency is far from being at its weakest when the propositions or
theories people are requested to accept as truths are pleasantly
flattering to their importance and dignity and national vanity.
Of all this the shrewd Moto-ori was no doubt perfectly well aware ;
certainly there is no reason to suppose that he was ignorant of the
Japanese proverb to the effect that "it is the quality of faith
that is important, were its object only the head of a sardine ".

In spite of all this it must be candidly confessed that not a little
can be advanced in support of Mr. Aston's contention that Moto-
ori was really a sincere believer in that Shintō faith he professed,
revived, and propagated so indefatigably. He was born and bred
and spent most of his long life at Matsuzaka, only a few miles from
Yamada in Ise, with its famous shrines (the most revered and
sacrosanct in the empire) sacred from remote antiquity to the
worship of the Sun Goddess, the ancestress of the Imperial line of
Japan. Here in his boyhood he must have seen not merely thousands
but millions of pilgrims pass the door of his widowed mother's house
on their way to the holy places. It is more than probable that, as
Mr. Aston suggests, the influence of this environment upon his
mental bent and his career was considerable. It would tend to

awake and develop his patriotism, and intensity of patriotism not
infrequently makes the patriot violently anti-foreign. This consideration might go a considerable way to account for Moto-ori's
violent and virulent antipathy to Chinese philosophy and to
everything Chinese. But Mr. Aston will have it that there was a
greater and a deeper cause at work :—

" As already stated, the Chinese nation has a strong bias against
the conception of the power which rules the universe as a personal being.
The *Ten* (Heaven) of Confucius and Mencius and the *Tâo* (Way) of
Laotze, not to speak of the *Taiki* and other metaphysical conceptions
of the Sung schoolmen, all fall short of this idea. The main bent
of the Japanese mind is in the same direction. But there is evidence
in both countries of a contrary current of thought. Here, too, there
are men born with a craving which refuses to be satisfied with abstractions in the place of a personal God (or gods) to whom they can look
up as the Creator and Ruler of the Universe, and as exercising a
providential care over mankind. Moto-ori was one of these . . . But
whatever be the case with philosophical notions, no man can evolve
a god from his own inner consciousness. He must accept the god
or gods which he finds already acknowledged, whether by his own or
by other people's fathers. Moto-ori's intensely patriotic temper compelled him to seek at home for the satisfaction of his inborn religious
instincts. He naturally turned to Shintō. But in his time Shintō had
fallen on evil days. It had suffered grievously from the encroachments
of Buddhism. Buddhist priests had assumed the guardianship of the
great majority of the shrines of the native cult, and had adulterated
its ceremonies and doctrines with much that was alien. The native
gods were not abolished—they had still some hold on the popular
mind ; but they were degraded to temporary manifestations of Buddha.
As one of Moto-ori's pupils said, they were made domestics in the
Buddhist household.

" This state of things was a great relief to Moto-ori. It drove him
back from the present to the old unadulterated Shintō taught in the
Kojiki, Nihongi, and *Norito.* Here he found the satisfaction to his
mind and heart which he had failed to find elsewhere. Himself
convinced of the excellence of the old national religion, he made it the
business of his life to propagate it among his fellow-countrymen, and
to denounce the abominable depravity of those who neglected it in
favour of sophistical heresies imported from abroad."

Now at first blush this line of argument in support of the
sincerity of Moto-ori in his belief in the faith he championed would
seem to be a cogent one. But it may be questioned whether its
cogency is not really less than its plausibility. The weakness in it
lies in the circumstance that while the Buddhists had appropriated
Shintō gods and shrines and revenues the Chinese philosophers
had not intruded any of their number into the Shintō priesthood,
nor had they interfered with the Shintō shrines either pecuniarily

or in any other way. Yet it was not against the Buddhist corrupters and despoilers but against the inoffensive Chinese scholars that the full bitterness of Moto-ori's virulent polemic was directed. So much, indeed, appears from Mr. Aston's next paragraph :—

" Hence arose a controversy which is not without interest to ourselves as an episode in the unending conflict between science and religion. Both parties to the struggle fought under serious difficulties. Not only could the *Kangakusha* (Chinese scholars) offer nothing to satisfy the heart-need of a personal deity, but they were sorely hampered by the imperfections of their philosophy, and by a belief in divination, ghosts, and spiritual beings, which they did not perceive to be inconsistent with it. Moto-ori and his followers, on the other hand, were weighted by an antiquated mythology, which presented many glaring absurdities even when viewed in the dim light of Chinese philosophy. The *Wagakusha* (Japanese scholars) were also embarrassed by the absence from Shintō of anything like a code or morals. They were therefore driven to deny the necessity of anything of the kind, or to put forward, as derived from Shintō, a system of ethical teaching which was really borrowed from China."

A little further on, Mr. Aston admits that " towards Buddhism Moto-ori's antagonism is less pronounced—that he acknowledges elements of good in it ". Yet the writer might not unreasonably maintain that this assertion, so far from invalidating his contention, actually lends it no slight measure of substantial support. For so far from flouting—or still worse ignoring—the autochthonous gods of Japan, Buddhism had annexed the whole pantheon as avatars of its deities and saints. Nay, more, its priestly ingenuity had been found equal to the task of devising new national gods—Hachiman and Kompira, for instance—in addition to the 8,000,000 of aboriginal Shintō deities. However, as the fact remains that if the Shintō gods had been reduced to the position of domestics in the Buddhist household, it might have been expected that Buddhism, and not the philosophy of the Sung schoolmen, would have had to bear the main brunt of Moto-ori's onslaughts. But then, Buddhism was not contemptuously aggressive, and certainly could not offend Moto-ori's native pride and patriotic susceptibilities in the wantonly outrageous fashion some of the *Kangakusha* did. Ogyu Sorai (1666–1728), for example, had maintained that China was the centre of civilization, the only enlightened country and the only one producing sages, he himself and his countrymen being merely Eastern barbarians. Furthermore, Sorai had actually gone so far as to recommend that the Mikado, the lineal descendant of the Sun Goddess, should be stripped of his prerogative of bestowing titles upon his subjects. In his fierce resentment against all this Moto-ori was undoubtedly sincere, and Satow is probably perfectly correct in his surmise that,

" The violence of his prejudices in favour of everything native and antique is probably due to a reaction against Chinese ideas and forms of expression, which at the time he thought and wrote bade fair to extinguish every trace of Japanese nationality."

The ancient records and the old myths had, when not entirely contemptuously ignored, been handled in no gentle manner by certain of the *Kangakusha*. In 1716, Arai Hakuseki had penned a treatise in which they were all subjected to the clear, cold and unkind judgment of reason, and therein the Sun Goddess is euhemerised into a mere mortal, while Takama-no-Hara (" The Plain of Heaven ") is made out to be the place where her very mundane capital stood. Others, perhaps, of smaller note and name than Arai had perpetrated similar offences of a hue no less deep than his. Indeed, it comes not so much as a surprise as a shock to most men of this Imperialistic era of Meiji to find how little credence was reposed either in the ancient myths in general or in the theory of the divine descent of the Mikado in particular in eighteenth-century Japan before Moto-ori began his thirty years' polemic in their support. His propaganda really seriously began in 1771, with the publication of his tract *Naobi-no-Mitama* (" Spirit of Straightening ") which was afterwards incorporated in the Kojiki-den. That tract, in which, among other doctrines of a somewhat extraordinary nature, that are now implicitly accepted, that of the divinity of the Mikado was emphatically asserted, elicited a response from a certain Ichikawa who writes in the following very outspoken terms :—

" The Japanese word *kami* (god) was simply a title of honour, but in consequence of its having been used to translate the Chinese character *shin* (*shen*), a meaning has come to be attached to it which it did not originally possess. *The ancestors of the Mikados were not gods, but men, and were no doubt worthy to be reverenced for their virtues ; but their acts were not miraculous nor supernatural. If the ancestors of living men were not human beings, they are more likely to have been birds or beasts than gods.*"

In connexion with this controversy with Ichikawa—for such it became by the publication of Moto-ori's *Kuzuhana* (1780) in reply to him—one circumstance must be adverted to inasmuch as it had some bearing on the question of Moto-ori's sincerity of belief in the doctrines he championed. Ichikawa had roundly asserted that,

" The stories told us about early ages must have been invented by the Mikados. The name of Amaterasu (the Sun-Goddess) is probably a posthumous title conferred at a later period. If the Sun-Goddess (Amaterasu) is the real Sun in heaven, it must have been quite dark before she was born ; and yet it is stated that before she was born there were trees and plants, clothing, weapons, boats, and buildings. If all these things existed before her birth, it seems probable that both Sun and Moon preceded that event. It is curious that stars are not mentioned in the *Jin-dai-no-maki.* To say that the Sun was born in Japan is a fiction which was probably invented by the earlier Mikados in order to support the assertion that this country is the root, and all other countries only branches. The gods in heaven make no difference between different races of mankind who are formed into separate nations by seas and mountain ranges which divide them off from each other, and the sun shines equally over all."

" To this Moto-ori made a neither very ingenious nor ingenuous answer.

" In reply to the argument that if Amaterasu and the sun be identical, there must have been perpetual night before she was born, which is inconsistent with the fact of trees and plants being in existence before her birth, and that therefore the Sun must have been previously hanging in the sky, *he reiterates the statement that the goddess and the sun are one and the same.* For although she will continue to shine as long as heaven and earth endure, *she was born in Japan, and her descendants to this day rule over the empire.* The difficulty of reconciling the statements that the world was plunged into darkness when she retired into the cavern, and that darkness did not exist before she was born, is one that would strike even a child's intelligence. The critic need not make so much fuss about this point as if it were entirely a new discovery of his own (!). *The very inconsistency is the proof of the authenticity of the record, for who would have gone out of his way to invent a story apparently so ridiculous and incredible.*"

Nor is this glaring case of *Credo quia absurdum est* the only one of the kind in Moto-ori. Witness the following extract from Mr. Aston :—

" Moto-ori's religion is frankly anthropomorphic, as indeed it could hardly fail to be if he attached any credence to the statements in the *Kojiki.* He says in so many words that the Shintō deities had hands and legs. When pressed with the obvious inconsistencies which are involved in this belief, Moto-ori has nothing better to say than they are ' a proof of the authenticity of the record, for who would have gone out of his way to invent a story so ridiculous and improbable, if it were not true (*Credo quia impossibile*) ? The acts of the gods are not to be explained by ordinary principles. Man's intelligence is limited, and there are many things which transcend it '."

Now all those European scholars who are intimately acquainted with Moto-ori's writings are at one in attributing to him great ability as a controversialist and a high amount of the logical faculty. If they are correct in this, what is to be thought of the "sincerity" of the foregoing and of other similar passages ? The founders or would-be-founders of new religions, or the would-be revivers of exploded cults, who have constituted a much more numerous tribe than is generally supposed, on occasion have begun by duping themselves. But more frequently from the first they have been fully conscious of the large measure of truth in the Japanese proverb already quoted, and fully aware that if the absurd be propounded as the mysterious, and insisted upon boldly enough and frequently enough, they will be pretty sure to attract disciples whose sincerity of belief will be unimpeachable. Hence, when Mr. Aston supports his contention for Moto-ori's own sincerity by remarking that "he had a large and zealous body of followers drawn from the highest and most enlightened classes of his fellow-country-men", the argument is perhaps not so weighty as it seems. It is to be noted, however, that all Moto-ori's prodigious erudition and all his immense energy (it was equal to the production of no fewer than fifty-five distinct works in more than 180 volumes during the spare hours of an extensive medical practice) were *not* devoted to the resuscitation of pure Shintō so as to make it the rule of life in his time. Any such intention he expressly disclaimed ; perhaps because he was shrewd enough to perceive that it was really hopeless to "call back the deities of the old pantheon to the Hades to which the neglect of the nation had consigned them". (Presently we shall find that the enthusiasm of his disciple Hirata was moderated by none of his teacher's common-sense appreciation of the practical and the possible in the direction in which, and the extent to which, "pure" Shintō could be exploited.) His professed object was merely to present the age of the gods in its real form.

"All that comes to pass in the world whether good or bad in its nature, is the act of the gods, and men have generally little influence over the course of events. To insist on practising the ancient ' way of the gods ', in opposition to the customs of the present age, would be rebellion against that ' way ' and equivalent to trying to excel it. *If men in their daily practice obey the laws made from time to time by the authorities, and act in accordance with general custom, they are practising Shintō.*"

It was perhaps in a certain measure, on the score of diplomatic utterances like this, that Moto-ori not merely contrived to escape

the inconvenient attentions of the censorship, but even to attract
the favourable regard of the Tokugawa authorities. But he was
also careful to avow his loyalty to the Shōgunate, and he was so
much thought of by the Tokugawa Daimyō of Kii, on whose fief
he was born, that he was invited by that Prince to draw up a
memorandum on the methods by which a fief should be administered
(1787), while in 1795 he was actually invested with office in the
principality of Kishū. When he resigned this position in the last
year of his life, he accepted an invitation to deliver lectures in
Kyōto. Here he had crowded audiences, while the Princes of the
Blood and many of the Court nobles sought instruction from him
in matters relating to the " age of the gods " and the early history
of Japan.

In spite of all his professed loyalty to the Bakufu, there can be
little question that this work of the last months of Moto-ori's life
contributed considerably to its ultimate overthrow. During the
decade and a half preceding the fateful year of 1868, the great cry
of the patriots who effected the Revolution was " Sonnō Jō-i ",
" Honour the Emperor and Expel the Foreign Barbarians." Now
this cry was a compendious and practical summing up of the
logical results of Moto-ori's teaching. In all likelihood Satow is not
far astray in his supposition that the ruling passion with Moto-ori
was hatred of those Chinese influences so dominant in Japan in his
time. To assail these with effect it was advisable, if not indeed
necessary, to make it clear that not China, but Japan, was the
centre not merely of civilization but of the universe, and in the
cosmogony of the ancient records which Moto-ori adopted and
utilized for this purpose the position of the Sun-Goddess (Amaterasu)
was a pivotal one.

" Japan is the country which gave birth to the Goddess of the Sun,
Amaterasu O-ho-mi-kami, which fact proves its superiority over all
other countries. The goddess, having endowed her grandson Ninigi-
no-Mikoto with the three sacred treasures, proclaimed him Sovereign
of Japan for ever and ever. His descendants shall continue to rule
it as long as the heavens and the earth endure " . . . " To the end of
time each Mikado is the goddess's son. His mind is in perfect harmony
of thought and feeling with hers. He does not seek out new inventions,
but rules in accordance with precedents which date from the age of the
gods, and if he is ever in doubt he has resort to divination, which reveals
to him the mind of the great goddess . . . The eternal endurance of
the dynasty of the Mikados is a complete proof that the way called
' Kami-no-michi ', or Shintō (Way of the Gods) infinitely surpasses the
systems of all other countries."

Possibly it was mainly to lend support to the tenet that Japan ranks far above all other countries that he insisted so strongly upon his central " truths " that the Sun-Goddess, who was identical with the Sun in heaven,[1] was born in Japan, and that the successive Mikados were her divine descendants. In one passage at least he goes so far as to assert that for these reasons no other nation is entitled to equality with her, and *that all are bound to do homage to the Japanese Sovereign and to pay tribute to him*. Elsewhere, in repudiating all indebtedness to Lâo-tsze, he writes :—

" It has been asked whether Shintō is not the same as the Taōism of Lâo-tsze. Lâo-tsze hated the vain conceits of the Chinese scholars and honoured naturalness, from which a resemblance may be argued ; but *as he was born in a dirty country not under the special protection of the Sun-Goddess*, he had only heard the theories of the succession of so-called Holy-Men, and what he believed to be naturalness was simply what they called natural. He did not know that the gods (i.e. of Japan) are the authors of every human action, and this ignorance constituted a cause of radical difference."

Yet, although it may have been chiefly to prove Japan's national superiority that these " central truths " were urged, it ought to have needed no great sagacity to perceive that they could be applied to other purposes. Passages like the following were certainly suggestive :—

" The ' Holy Men ' of China were merely successful rebels. The Mikado is the Sovereign appointed by the pair of deities, Izanagi and Izanami, who created this country. The Sun-Goddess never said ' Disobey the Mikado if he be bad ',[2] and therefore, whether he be good or bad, no one attempts to deprive him of his authority. He is the immovable ruler who must endure to the end of time, as long as the sun and moon continue to shine. In ancient language the Mikado was called a god, and that is his real character. Duty therefore consists in obeying him implicitly without questioning his acts. During the Middle Ages such men as Hōjō Yoshitoki, Hōkō Yasutoki, Ashikaga Takauji and others violated this duty (*michi*) and took up arms against him. Their disobedience to the Mikado is attributable to the influence of Chinese learning."

---

[1] " What doubt can there be that O-ho-mi-kami (the Sun-Goddess) is the great ancestress of the Mikados and that she is no other than the Sun of Heaven which illumines the world ? These things are in their nature infinite, not to be measured, and mysterious."

[2] This is evidently levelled at Mencius's refusal of any claim of a right divine to a sovereign who failed to exercise his rule for the good of the people. " The people are the most important element in a nation ; the altars to the spirits of land and grain are the second ; the sovereign is the lightest." " The monarch whose rule is injurious to the people, and who is deaf to remonstrance and counsel should be dethroned."

Now to the casual reader this might seem merely one of Moto-ori's innumerable splenetic onslaughts upon " Chinese learning ", against which, indeed, it was explicitly levelled. But the suspicious or the discerning might well have been forgiven for entertaining the fancy that what was really important here was what was to be read between the lines. For the implicit attack was something vastly different from the explicit assault on " Chinese learning ", which might have been used here as a mere stalking-horse or scapegoat. Suppose Moto-ori to have addressed this or similar passages to his Kyōto audiences, what would have been the natural effect ? Resentment might indeed have been roused against " Chinese learning " ; but the full strength of his hearers' indignation would not have been spent on it, but have been directed against the feudal chiefs who had presumed to raise impious and sacrilegious hands against not the " Lord's annointed " but against the Lord himself— for Moto-ori had told them that " in ancient language the Mikado was called a god, and that is his real character ". Now although the publication of histories of the Tokugawa times had been forbidden by the Yedo censorship, the Court nobles who flocked to hear Moto-ori were far from ignorant of how the Mikados had been treated by Iyeyasu and his descendants. They must have remembered perfectly well that Go-Yojō had been compelled (1611) to abdicate at the age of 41 ; Go-Mizuo (1630) at the age of 35, although he lived to 85 ; the Empress Myōshō at that of 21, although she lived to 74 ; and Reigen (1687) at 34, although he survived to 79. Even in the very year (1801) when Moto-ori was delivering his lectures in Kyōto, Go-Sakuramachi, Empress in her own right from 1763 to 1771, was then alive and hale. All this the Princes of the Blood and the Court nobles must have discussed exhaustively in the intervals between their attendances in Moto-ori's lecture-room. Although making loud and glib and frequent avowal of his loyalty to the Tokugawa Shōgunate, Moto-ori in paragraphs like the foregoing was, without even once mentioning it, by implication merely, dealing it the death-strokes of doom.

How extremely Chauvinistic Moto-ori's patriotism was might be gleaned from certain of the extracts just quoted from his writings. But inasmuch as he was in no small measure responsible for the fanatical hatred of foreigners displayed by a considerable section of his countrymen after the (forced) resumption of foreign intercourse in 1853, it may be well to give further instances of his

virulence. Our purpose will perhaps be best served by a reproduc-
tion of Satow's summary of the *Gio-jin Gaigen*, a gentle title which
is translated as " Indignant Words about Ruling the Barbarians ".
It takes the form of a review of the relations between Japan and
other countries from the earliest period down to the time of Iyeyasu,
not touching, however, upon the early European intercourse of the
sixteenth and seventeenth centuries, probably because Christianity
was a forbidden question.

" That on the earliest occasion when the Mikado exchanged letters
and envoys with the Chinese Sovereign the first step should have been
taken by the former is a source of deep annoyance to Moto-ori. This
deplorable event occurred in the year 707 under the Empress Suiko,
when an envoy was sent to China to fetch a Buddhist sûtra which
Shōtoku Taishi remembered to have possessed during a previous state
of existence, when he was studying the sacred mysteries in that country.
It is true that the Chinese histories contain notices of tribute-bearers
from Japan much earlier than this date ; but these envoys, whatever
may have been their character, certainly were not commissioned by the
sovereign. As for their paying tribute, the statement is due to the
inordinate vanity of the Chinese, who fancy themselves superior to all
surrounding nations, whereas they are no better than barbarians themselves and are bound to acknowledge the supremacy of Japan (!).
One of the Chinese histories has an account of the mission sent by
Suiko, and gives what purports to be a letter from that Empress, in
which appears the famous phrase, ' The Tenshi (Son of Heaven) of the
place where the Sun rises send a letter to the Tenshi of the place where
the Sun sets '. If the Empress Suiko really sent such a letter she treated
the Chinese sovereign with far too much civility, and if she had addressed
him with some such phrase as ' The Heavenly Emperor notifies the
King of Go (Wu) ', he ought to have been filled with gratitude, instead
of which he is represented by the Chinese historiographer as having
been offended at being treated as an equal. But the truth is that
Suiko wanted to get something from him, and therefore condescended
to flatter his vanity (!)."

Uninterrupted intercourse seems to have continued between
the two Courts for about two centuries, and then to have ceased
during a period of about thirty years.

" It was unworthy of Japan to enter into relations with a base
barbarian State, whatever might be the benefits which she expected
to obtain. It resulted in too many cases in the shipwreck of the vessels
and the profitless death of the envoys by drowning. Had the Chinese
ruler paid due reverence to the Mikado as a being infinitely superior
to himself the objection might have been less."

After the tenth century the Mikados appear to have ceased
sending envoys to China, and Moto-ori remarks that,

" so long as Japan wanted anything from China she overlooked the insolent pretensions of the Chinese sovereigns, but now, being no longer in a position to gain by the interchange of courtesies, she rejected all further overtures of friendship ! "

And so the long tirade runs on. Satow has well observed that the most remarkable thing about it was that Japan was indebted to China for all the arts and sciences that make life better than nonentity, for a complete system of government and laws, and even for the very art of writing which enabled the writer to record his arrogant and spiteful feelings. Of all this Moto-ori, whose erudition was immense, must have been perfectly well aware. What, then, in this matter at least, is to be said about his sincerity ? Furthermore, the naïve fashion in which he hints that it is semi-excusable to flatter another's vanity in order to get something from him, or to submit to insolent Chinese pretensions so long as something was wanted from China, is certainly worthy of note. Moto-ori, Hirata, and Shintōists generally are never weary of expatiating upon the superiority of *Yamato-damashii*, the true Japanese spirit. It may well be asked how far this diatribe of Moto-ori's is to be regarded as a practical exposition of it, and how far it lends support to the contention that the natives of the " Country of the Gods " are possessed of " a naturally perfect and true disposition ".

Yet with all his shortcomings, it must be frankly recognized that this country doctor, whose speciality was infantile diseases, did not fall much short—if, indeed, he fell short at all—of being a great man. In his writings and in his teaching we find a chief source of that *Sonnō-Jō-i* movement which within three-score years and ten from the date of his death was to sweep the Shōgunate and feudalism into endless night. It is not indeed given to many of the sons of men who have to eke out an impecunious existence as a medical practitioner of children to count as a first-class political force in one of the most populous empires of the world for a round 100 years. And from the beginning of Moto-ori's nationalistic and Chauvinistic propaganda in 1771, down to the overthrow of feudalism just a century later, his influence, latent perhaps, was in all probability nearly as great as that of any other man of these three generations. Besides, for the men that came after him he created a new literary dialect, and we are told that his *wabun*, or Japanese composition, continues to exercise a perceptible influence in some departments of contemporary literature. In his hands Japanese, as distinct from Sinico-Japanese, became full, flowing, picturesque and expressive. The only fault that can be urged against it is its prolixity. That, as Mr. Aston points out :—

" is partly inseparable from his purism, which leads him to reject many useful and thoroughly naturalized Chinese words in favour of Japanese forms of expression, however circuitous, and is partly owing to an inveterate habit which he has of repeating himself, especially when an opportunity offers of denouncing Chinese proclivities or of magnifying Shintō."

To his Japanese readers, however, all this would hardly count as a drawback. The rapid headway made by the fundamental ideas he inculcated is in no small degree to be ascribed to his consummate merits as a stylist. On occasion he could write in the simplest and homeliest of fashions ; witness his *Tama Kushige* (Precious Casket), the memorandum he penned at the request of the Daimyō of Kishu—a work, by the way, which goes to indicate that Moto-ori could have administered a fief with no inconsiderable ability.

As has been observed, Moto-ori had too firm a grasp upon the actualities and possibilities of his times to expend his energies in a vain endeavour to resuscitate pure Shintō so as to make it the rule of life. In this matter his successor, Hirata, showed himself Moto-ori's inferior in discretion, as he did in style and in everything else except application, erudition, and the quantity of work he produced. Yet withal, this Hirata was a remarkable man ; all the more remarkable as he came from Northern Japan, which has at all times been singularly unproductive of literary talent. Born at Kubota in Dewa in the year of the Declaration of American Independence (1776) he migrated to Yedo in 1795, and, becoming acquainted with Moto-ori's writings in 1801, he formally enrolled himself as one of his pupils two months before the old man's death. In 1804, he himself began to take pupils, and altogether, we are told, 553 students received their training from him. In the previous year he had embarked on that long career of authorship which was to result in the publication of more than 100 distinct works, besides a great mass of manuscript which has never been put into print. Although he was no great master of style like Moto-ori—in fact, the native History of Literature dismisses him in a few contemptuous sentences—his writings were considerably read in his time, and certain of them did indeed exercise no small influence. But it is questionable whether those of them on which he set the greatest store were much appreciated by his public. His strenuous attempts to evolve a living, practical cult from the *Kojiki*, the *Nihongi*, and kindred ancient records had to rest satisfied with the virtue of having made the effort as their most substantial reward. To the student of comparative religion his ingenious efforts to co-ordinate the old myths into a work-a-day faith for the nation are doubtless interesting enough, but inasmuch as we are dealing merely with forces that have either promoted or retarded or influenced in one way or other the political and social development of Japan, the *Tama-no-Mi-hashira*, with its diagrams, and many similar works must be passed over in silence. What is really of consequence is the development or modification of Moto-ori's political and ethnical teachings received from the hands of Hirata, and the part the younger man played in contributing to bring latter-day *Wagakusha* (Japanese scholars) and *Kangakusha* (Chinese scholars) into line on a common basis of hostility to white-faced foreigners from the West.

In this connexion his *Summary of the Ancient Way* is important. Of its ten sections one explains why Japan is " the country of the gods " ; the following one, how it is certain beyond a doubt that every Japanese is a descendant of the gods ; another treats of the uninterrupted continuance of the Imperial line from the beginning of the world, together with proofs of the superiority of Japan over all countries in the world, both materially and morally ; while yet another inculcates the truth that the Japanese, being natives of " the country of the gods ", are born with a naturally perfect and true disposition, which from the most ancient times has been called *Yamato-damashii* or *Yamato-gokoro* (the " spirit " or " heart " of Yamato, i.e. of Japan). All this no doubt was very flattering to the tribal conceit of Hirata's readers. The following remarks from one of these sections, if not exactly humorous, are at all events amusing :—

" It is most lamentable that so much ignorance should prevail as to the evidences of the two fundamental doctrines that Japan is the country of the gods, and her inhabitants the descendants of the gods. Between the Japanese people and the Chinese, Hindoos, Russians, Dutch, Siamese, Cambodians, and other nations of the world, there is a difference of kind rather than of degree. *It was not out of vainglory that the inhabitants of this country called it the land of the gods.* The gods who created all countries belonged, without exception, to the Divine Age and were all born in Japan, so that Japan is their native country, and all the world acknowledges the appropriateness of the title. The Koreans were the first to become acquainted with this truth, and from them it was gradually diffused through the globe, and accepted by everyone."

The following from a cosmological exposition that differs somewhat from that of Moto-ori would indicate that, however much Hirata might differ from him in his account of the Creation, he was thoroughly at one with him in holding national modesty to be but a scurvy virtue at best :—

" As it was Japan which lay directly opposite to the sun when it had sprouted upwards and separated from the earth, it is quite clear that Japan lies on the summit of the globe. It is equally evident that all other countries were formed at a much later period by the spontaneous consolidation of the foam of the sea and the collection of mud in various localities, when Izanagi and Izanami brought together the eight islands of Japan, and separated the land from the water. Foreign countries were of course produced by the power of the creator gods, but they were not begotten by Izanagi and Izanami, nor did they give birth to the Goddess of the Sun, *which is the cause of their inferiority*. The traditions about the origin of the world which are preserved in foreign countries are naturally incorrect, just as the accounts of an event which has happened at the capital become distorted when they travel to a province, and it finally comes to be believed the province was the actual scene of the event. The fact is patent that the Mikado is the true Son of Heaven, who is entitled to reign over the four seas and the ten thousand countries."

And elsewhere he calmly and complacently assures us that :—

" from the divine descent of the Japanese people proceeds their immeasurable superiority to the natives of other countries in courage and intelligence ! "

His Chauvinism was, however, much less virulent and aggressive than that of Moto-ori's, and it was also expressed in much less violent and offensive language. Furthermore, the younger man's horizon was much wider. When the latter thought of foreigners he thought only of the sons of Han. Hirata took other Asiatic peoples into account, while he has also a good deal to say about the Dutch and the Russians. The existence of these latter had been forced upon his attention in a somewhat startling and unpleasant fashion. The ambassador Resanoff, resenting his rebuff at Nagasaki, had subsequently dispatched two small vessels under Davidoff and Chwostoff to plunder the Japanese settlements in Saghalin and Iterup (1806–7), and of this expedition Hirata gives an account in his *Chishima Shira-nami* (White Waves of the Kuriles) which was intended also to be a manual of the way to " restrain barbarians " and of maritime defence. As regards the Dutch, we meet with many references to them in his works. For example, in his *Summary of the Ancient Way* (1811), already alluded to, he praises them warmly for their achievements in natural science, according to them a much higher place among philosophers than he does to the Chinese, whom, however, he dismisses as empty visionaries. It is from the Hollanders that he adopts the theory of the revolution of the earth, and he candidly acknowledges his indebtedness to them in the account he gives of the formation of the earth and its division into five continents. He mentions Kämpfer, and actually sets forth a summary of his so-styled *History of Japan*. In Aston's *Japanese Literature*, will be found a translation of an amusing altercation (before 1805) he had with a rationalistic acquaintance raised in connexion with the machine invented by the Hollanders called " electer ". All this, of course, furnishes so much testimony to that development and diffusion of Dutch studies since the days of Thunberg (1775–6), which we deal with in another chapter.

As regards the alien cults in Japan—as regards Chinese philosophy, at all events—Moto-ori's attitude had been that of Cato towards the Punic capital—*Delenda est Carthago*. Hirata, on the other hand, was anxious to proceed to no such extremities. Buddhism and Chinese philosophy alike were to be captured and tamed and subjected to the yoke as beasts of burden in the service of Shintō. It is true that two of Hirata's works are devoted to the ridicule of popular Buddhism,[1] but when asked whether a pious Shintō believer was to worship Buddha, Hirata replied in the affirmative, on the ground that Shaka was also a *kami* (Shintō god). That such was really the case was proved by the Buddhist miracles which had been worked in Japan as in other countries ; and further-more, as everything which took place in the world was ordered by the *kami*, Buddhism must be in accordance with their will. Hitherto the *kami* had been domestics in the Buddhist household ; Hirata would rectify matters by inverting the relative position of master and drudge.

---

[1] " They are racy and entertaining diatribes, but, it must be added, are disgraced by scurrilous abuse quite unworthy of the would-be founder of a new form of religion."—Aston.

Towards Chinese philosophy, or at least towards Confucianism, his attitude was no less diplomatic. One of his earliest books, the *Kishin Shinran* [1] is intended to prove that the Sung schoolmen, whose system was then dominant in Japan, had misunderstood the teachings of Confucius with regard to supernatural beings, and to show by quotations from the Analects and elsewhere that he had believed in their actual existence. Furthermore, Hirata was keen enough to understand that a religion which is without a moral code cannot hope to become the universal rule of conduct. Accordingly, instead of devising one of his own, he calmly proceeded to pilfer one from those very Chinese against whom Moto-ori had railed for thirty years in eighty-five distinct works and 180 volumes. Thus he writes :—

" Devotion to the memory of ancestors is the mainspring of all virtue. No one who discharges his duty to them will ever be disrespectful to the gods, or to his living parents. Such a man will also be faithful to his prince, loyal to his friends, and kind and gentle with his wife and children. For the essence of this devotion *is in truth filial piety.* These truths are confirmed by the books of the Chinese, who say that the ' loyal subject issues from the gate of the pious son ', and again, ' filial piety is the basis of all good actions.' "

Hirata perceived that Chinese learning had too strong a hold upon the intellect of the nation to be driven thence with a pitchfork, as Moto-ori would have driven it if he could have but had his way. Besides the Confucianist university in Yedo and the great private schools in Kyōto and Ōsaka, most of the great fiefs had each their seminary, where the mental pabulum supplied was almost entirely Chinese. From the day he began to read to the day when he quitted school or college, the average *samurai* youth at the beginning of the nineteenth century was occupied with Chinese classics, Chinese commentaries, and Chinese histories. To supplant Chinese commentaries and Chinese philosophy in the schools by purely native Japanese studies and by Shintō Hirata knew to be hopeless. The best that could be done was to endeavour to insinuate them gradually. Chinese learning could not be crushed ; the only thing then, that remained to be done was to conciliate it, and, to use a somewhat vulgar phrase, to steal its thunder.

This astutely conciliatory attitude of Hirata's, although perhaps effecting not very much for the acceptance of his theological

---

[1] *New Treatise on the Gods* (1805). It is in this work that the " electer " machine incident is given.

system, contributed not a little towards bringing Shintōists and certain of the *Kangakusha* into line on what were soon to be two matters of cardinal practical importance. The thesis of the divine descent of the Japanese and their consequent superiority to all other peoples in courage and intelligence was one that could not be very offensive to the most hidebound Confucianists in Japan—especially when it was made out, or attempted to be made out, that there was nothing in the writings of the sage that was really inconsistent with this doctrine so productive of comforting self-complacency. By a good many of the young samurai fresh from school it was adopted enthusiastically ; and in 1853 we shall find even Hayashi, the head of the Confucianist University in Yedo, winding up an interview with Commodore Perry with a panegyric, if not on the superiority of the Japanese in courage and intelligence, at all events on the pre-eminence of Japan over all other nations in virtue and humanity. The spirit of the age had indeed changed since the times when Ogyu Sorai had spoken of himself as an " Eastern barbarian ". Although Hirata's Chauvinism was neither so intense nor so openly pronounced as that of Moto-ori, yet he did quite as much as the elder scholar to stimulate and diffuse that inordinate national self-conceit which expressed itself in the cry of *Jō-i* (" expel the barbarians ") during the years preceding the Revolution of 1868. Nowhere during these years was the contempt for, and hatred of, the Western barbarians greater than among the Court nobles of Kyōto. Now, during the whole of the Tokugawa regime, Kyōto had been the great seat of the prosecution of native Japanese studies in distinction to that of Chinese learning. Allusion has already been made to the enthusiastic reception Moto-ori met with there in 1801, and to the not inconsiderable practical results of his visit. In 1822, Hirata had been requested by the Abbot of Uyeno, a Prince of the Blood, to present him with copies of his chief work on Shintō ; and in the following year he went up to Kyōto and received the patronage of some of the Court nobles who brought his writings to the notice of the retired Emperor Kōkaku. It is safe to assume that in Kyōto the seed Hirata sowed fell upon no unfruitful soil.

In another direction his adoption—" lifting " is really the right word—of a moral code from the *Kangakusha* contributed its quota to ulterior developments of still greater consequence. In the chapter on Chinese Philosophy it was pointed out that the only change made by the Japanese when they accepted the moral teachings of the Sung schoolmen—which was really that of Confucius—was to remove filial piety from the first to the second place in their "Table of Moral Precedence", and to assign the most commanding position in it to loyalty. It was also remarked that loyalty meant not so much the reverent submission due by all his subjects to the Mikado, although in theory that was not lost sight of, as of the Daimyōs to the Shōgun, and, in a still higher degree, of men of the two-sworded class to their immediate chiefs. Now, while Hirata insisted on the high claims of this virtue, the whole general tendency of his writings and teaching was, at least by implication, to raise the question whether in a conflict of duties, this loyalty was to be directed not so much towards one's immediate chief or even the Shōgun himself as towards the chief and superior of all, the Mikado, who "was the true Son of Heaven, entitled to reign over the four seas and the ten thousand countries". How quickly this question passed from the mere theoretical to the stern sphere of practice will be recognized when we recall the fact that within less than a score of years after the death of Hirata (1843), not scores but hundreds of samurai were withdrawing themselves from the service of their chiefs, giving up all their emoluments and becoming homeless *rōnin* (Wave-men) in order that their duty might be undivided towards the Son of Heaven alone.

It certainly might appear strange that the Shōgunate allowed this propaganda, so inimical to its existence, to go on without curb or check. As a matter of fact, although too late in the day, it did awake to the danger. In 1836 it suppressed a work of Hirata's, just then published, which had drawn forth warm praises from the Mikado and the *Kwanbaku*, and four years later (1840) it banished the author to his native town of Kubota, which he had not seen since the day he had surreptitiously left it with a single *ryō* in his pocket five-and-forty years before. But Hirata had already done his work; nothing now could neutralize forty years' assiduous propagation of his views both in print and in lectures to successive scores of pupils.

However, important as the influence of Hirata, and still more so that of Moto-ori, upon subsequent political developments undoubtedly was, we must be carefully on our guard against over-estimating. Although it counted for a good deal in precipitating the Revolution of 1868, it was far from being the only force at work.

CHAPTER XIV

FOREIGN INTERCOURSE

(1721–1853)

" The ancient writers justly compare the minerals to the bones, and the other revenues of a country to the blood, the flesh, the skin, and the hair which make up the human body. The things with which taxes are paid consist in rice and other cereals, in hemp, in cloth, and in different utensils. These are renewed like the blood, the flesh, the skin, and the hair, while the minerals do not reproduce themselves, as a bone once removed from the body, does not grow again."

SUCH is Arai Hakuseki's exposition of a view that had become a firmly held article of economic belief among the statesmen and publicists of his age. The eighth Shōgun, Yoshimune, was far from being an unreserved admirer of Arai, and, on his accession to power, he reversed Arai's policy on more matters than one. But he was in thorough agreement with Arai's views on the value of foreign trade and on the expediency, nay, the necessity, of checking the efflux of precious metals, and of copper, from the empire. When he became Shōgun in 1716 there had been no drain of silver for more than thirty years. The Dutch had been prohibited from exporting the white metal in 1668 ; and the Chinese in 1685. The latter had never taken gold away and the Hollanders were furnished with their gold at such an exorbitant profit to the Japanese that the few *Koban* the Company now exported were taken sorely against the grain. Although a maximum of 25,000 piculs had been set upon their annual export of copper in 1685, an extra export had sometimes been connived at, and in 1698 the lading amounted to 29,397 piculs. In 1715 the maximum was reduced to 15,000 piculs. In 1721 it was still further lowered to 10,000 piculs. The state of affairs must have been very puzzling to the Dutchmen ; but it is very easy for us to understand it. The treatment accorded the annual mission to Yedo was now far better than it had been in Kämpfer's time. There were no more of the undignified variety shows the envoys had to furnish to the Shōgun ; on the contrary the mission was treated with courtesy and respect. Yoshimune had been shown some Dutch books with engravings, and he had conceived a high opinion of Dutch civilization. In 1721 he abolished the old law of 1630, forbidding the translation of European works, and he encouraged his officers to learn as much from the Dutch as they could.

When he reduced the annual export of copper first to 10,000, and later on to 5,000 piculs in 1743, the Hollanders fancied that he was trying to drive them out of the empire. Their complete withdrawal from Japan was the last thing the Shōgun desired, but he did not want them to deplete the country of its ores; and so he kept tendering them various Japanese products in lieu of copper, products, however, which the Dutch declared they could turn to no advantage. He had early grasped the fact that the empire, with all emigration forbidden by law, was face to face with a dire population question. The measures he took to deal with that have been set forth in a previous chapter. Naturally, the effect of some of these must have been felt by the Dutch and Chinese traders. For one thing, the Shōgun was trying to grow sugar and ginseng and to produce as many other foreign commodities as he could in Japan. For another, the spirit of simplicity, sobriety, and economy, he tried to inculcate among officials and feudal potentates had a tendency to reduce the demand for the objects of luxury and the curiosities on which Dutch and Chinese alike had hitherto made extravagant profits. As a matter of fact, the Chinese were more seriously affected by the new limitations than were the Dutch. The seventy Chinese junks were reduced first to twenty, and then to half that number, while the Chinese were also greatly stinted in their allowance of copper.

When, however, in 1743, the Japanese authorities notified the Dutch that henceforth one ship per annum would be enough to take away their reduced quantum of copper, they found that for once their zeal had outrun their discretion. This step on their part was met by Imhoff, the Governor-General at Batavia, with a courteously worded intimation, that if the proposed regulations were enforced, the Factory of Deshima would be abandoned forthwith, and thereupon the Japanese not only receded from their ground but promised some new concessions. The result was that from 1745, for the next ten years onwards, the average annual profits of the Company advanced to nearly 680,000 guilders (£56,500), and that, too, in spite of the fact that, meanwhile (1750), the export of gold had been totally prohibited. It is true that this restriction did not affect the public trade of the Company in any way, for, having to purchase the new light *koban* at 68 *mas*, any exchange operations in gold would have been disastrous. But the Company's servants, who still enjoyed their right of private trade, contrived to acquire these coins at their current value in Japan and made a considerable profit by getting them smuggled out of the country. The Company was none too well served by its Deshima agents, who knew no Japanese, took no interest in what was going on around them, and generally conducted themselves in a fashion that did little to win for them the respect of those Japanese who were really desirous of knowing something about the civilization of Holland. As a rule, they had no interests beyond their ledgers, their guilders, and the schnapps ; and, being not incorrectly estimated by the Japanese as dollar-grinders, pure and simple, they were regarded by the best of them with a good deal of not undeserved contempt.[1] In 1755 the Director again thought fit to complain about scanty profits, and to prefer new requests, and went so far as once more to threaten the abandonment of the Deshima Factory. This time, to his unpleasant surprise, he was curtly told that the Dutch were at liberty either to go or to stay, as they listed. They stayed ; and the Japanese raised the tax on copper till the Japan trade began to bring the Company more loss than profit. However, the Hollanders kept on complaining—among other things, of the cost of the annual mission to Yedo, and succeeded in finding means to throw a good deal of the expenses in connexion with it upon the Nagasaki Treasury. In 1764, it was proposed to them that they should go on the embassy on alternate years only, but the local agents, who obtained considerable perquisites from the journey, declined this offer. These agents, with their private trade and their smuggling, still continued to eke out a fairly comfortable material existence, and in their interest as much as

---

[1] Two incidents may help us to appreciate the mental calibre of some of these worthy gentlemen. At Batavia, Thunberg tells us that Feith, with whom he had gone on the embassy to Yedo in 1776, on being asked at table what the name of the ruling Shōgun was, had to confess that he did not know. And yet Feith had been in Japan fourteen years and had headed the mission to the Shōgun's Court no fewer than five times. The amount of intelligent interest he took in his general surroundings was evidently not very great. On the other hand, the interest the Deshima agents took in their guilders was exceedingly keen. In 1765, the Shōgun expressed a wish to obtain a pair of Persian horses. They were later offered as a present, were gladly accepted, and the Dutch got a return present of copper worth some 45,000 guilders. Later on another pair of horses were asked for and delivered. The Shōgun's favourite son—the Dutch call him the Crown Prince—was killed by a fall from one of these horses, and the father was so frantic that he poniarded the unhappy man that brought the news to him. And the directors of the Company, notwithstanding, kept on repeatedly asking for a return present for the horses !

anything else, perhaps, the Deshima establishment was still maintained.   About 1771 or 1772 one of those unforeseen accidents
that will now and then happen to dislocate the most cleverly
planned and sharpest schemes, occurred.   In one or other of these
years, one of the annual vessels from Batavia, disabled in a typhoon,
was abandoned by her crew, who, in their haste neglected the
standing order of the Company in such cases to set her on fire.
She did not sink but some few days after she drifted to the coast of
Japan, and was towed into the harbour of Nagasaki.   On board
this derelict the Japanese found a number of chests—all marked
with the names of the Dutch functionaries to whom they belonged
or were consigned—crammed full to their lids with contraband
goods.   Hitherto it had been usual for the captains of the ships
and the director of the Factory to pass at pleasure to and from the
ships without being searched, but this discovery made the astute
Japanese (to use a vulgar locution) " smell a rat "—and a fat one,
too.   In reality, the captains had profited by their immunity from
the general search to dress themselves out, for the express purpose
of smuggling, in a gorgeous blue silk, silver-laced coat, cut very
large and bounteously, and in this mandarin apparel they were
wont to make three trips a day to and fro from Deshima, generally
so loaded down with goods that they had to be supported by a
sailor under each arm.   The Japanese, on seeing the nature of the
contents of the chests discovered on the derelict, came to the
conclusion that it might be just as well to bring all and sundry,
captains and director not excepted, under the scope of the search
regulations.   This resolution—a very natural one in the circumstances—gave rise to much impotent gnashing of the teeth among
the highly respectable Dutch smugglers, and to one exceedingly
comical incident at least.   In 1775, Carl Thunberg, the great
Swedish scientist, arrived in Japan, and the captain of the vessel
that brought him had not heard of the new regulations.   The worthy
skipper had rigged himself in the usual capacious blue silk, silver-
laced mandarin style but, much to his disappointment, the Japanese
officers who boarded the vessel brought orders that he should dress
like the rest ; that he and the director should also be searched when
they landed, and that the skipper should either stop on board, or,
if he landed, should remain on shore, being allowed to visit the
ship only twice during her stay.   " It was droll enough," says
Thunberg, " to see the astonishment the sudden reduction

in the size of our bulky captain excited in the major part of the
ignorant Japanese, who before had always imagined that all our
captains were actually as fat and lusty as they appeared to be."

The Japanese, put upon their mettle by the discoveries they
had made in the Dutch derelict of 1771 or 1772, were now very
strict in the discharge of their Custom-house duties. The examination of the clothes and persons of all who passed to and from the
ship was so strict that not even the very smallest of contraband
articles could be landed. The large chests were turned upside down,
and their sides, tops, and bottoms sounded to see if they were not—
like so many promises—hollow. Beds were ripped open and the
feathers turned over, as if the Dutch had not been proverbia
for their cleanliness. Iron spikes were thrust into the butter-tubs
and preserve-jars ; a square hole was cut in the Gouda cheeses,
and they were mangled by a thick pointed wire being thrust through
their interiors in every direction. Even some of the innocent but
addled eggs laid by the Javanese hens in Batavia were broken,
to make sure that they did not harbour contraband valuables.
From Thunberg the Swedish scholar and gentleman, we get some
hints of the why and wherefore of the contempt showered upon the
vulgar and grasping Dutch traders by the more refined Japanese
clients.

" Formerly the Dutch took the liberty to correct with blows the
Japanese coolies employed on board the ship ; but in his time this was
absolutely prohibited. The respect of the Japanese for the Dutch was,
he writes, not a little diminished from their observing "in how unfriendly
and unmannerly a style they usually behave to each other, and the
brutal treatment which the sailors under their command frequently
experience from them, together with the oaths, curses, and blows with
which the poor fellows are assailed by them."

Nor does the account he gives of the life in Deshima tend to
induce us to rate the intellectual and moral characteristics of the
dozen or thirteen permanent prisoners then resident in it very
highly.

" A European that remains here is in a manner dead and buried
in an obscure corner of the globe. He hears no news of any kind ;
nothing relative to war or other misfortunes and evils that plague and
infest mankind ; and neither the rumours of inland or foreign concerns
delight or molest his ear. The soul possesses here one faculty only,
which is the judgment (if, indeed, it be at all times in possession of that).
The will is totally debilitated, and even dead, because to a European
there is no other will than that of the Japanese, by which he must
exactly square his conduct. The European way of living is, in other

respects, the same as in other parts of India, luxurious and irregular. Hence, just as at Batavia, we pay a visit every evening to the chief, after having walked several times up and down the two streets. These evening visits generally last from six o'clock till ten, and sometimes even eleven or twelve at night, and constitute a very disagreeable way of life, fit only for such as have no other way of spending their time than droning over a pipe of tobacco and a bottle. Through the incapacity in some, and indolence in others, the Dutch possessed no Japanese vocabulary, and all the knowledge they had of the language did not go beyond the names of a few familiar articles."

In spite of all the troubles they had had with the Japanese, Thunberg found the Dutch on their embassy to Yedo were now better treated than they had been in Kämpfer's time. In 1691–2, only the director had been allowed to use a *norimon* (palanquin), the doctor and the secretary being compelled to go on horseback. Now all the Europeans in the party were promoted to the dignity of being carried in palanquins. Again, at the Court itself, the old tomfoolery of a variety show before the Shōgun and his Court was dispensed with; the Shōgun in lieu of this merely coming *incognito* to the ante-chamber to have a nearer view of the Hollanders and their dress. It appears also that in receiving the ambassador, who as usual made his obeisance in the Japanese fashion, the Shōgun and the heir apparent stood, instead of as usual sitting, "in the most interior part of the room." Altogether, on this occasion, the mission had little to complain of in the cordiality and courtesy of its reception. Indeed, it would seem that about this date an influential Liberal party, in favour of extended foreign intercourse, was forming, and if the Dutch directors had really been men of tact and ability, they might easily have reaped solid advantages from the new development. However, the man able to gauge the political situation and to profit by it did not appear until Titsingh arrived in Deshima in August, 1779.

For once at least, the Company now had an agent in Japan who was very much more than a mere man of business. A good man of business Titsingh undoubtedly was; but in addition he was a scholar and a diplomatist, and, if we are to accept Siebold's estimate of him, a statesman. Very courteous, but at the same time very frank and very firm, he at once made a most favourable impression upon the ablest men among the better-class Japanese, as one who respected himself as well as them, and so when he refused to submit to personal search, as former directors had done, on the ground that it was inconsistent with his dignity, the authorities, so far from

insisting or arguing the matter with him, not only at once yielded
the point, but from that date onwards treated him with the most
marked courtesy.   In a very short time, he found himself not
merely on a friendly but on an intimate footing with them.   This
he achieved in a very simple way.   He kept profit-making in its
proper place—which was the background—and promoted his
advantage and that of his employers by displaying a real and
unfeigned interest in the institutions, the sociology, and the history
of the people among whom his lot was not unhappily cast for the
time being.   In a remarkable passage, whose general correctness
is marred by one unfortunate statement, however, Siebold, without
referring to Titsingh or mentioning him by name, explains the why
and wherefore of the astonishing success the latter achieved in
Japan.

" The Japanese," writes Siebold, " is an enthusiast for his Father-
land, and proud of the great deeds of his ancestors ; the educated as
well as the ordinary man has an unlimited devotion to the ancient
dynasty of the Mikados, and is deeply attached to the old civilization,
the ancient customs and usages.   Accordingly the stranger within the
gates recommends himself in no common degree, if he flatters the
nationality of the Japanese, if he holds their religion, their customs and
their usages in honour, and lends a willing ear to the recital of their
ancient Sagas, and the eulogies of their deified heroes.   Of this weak
side of the Japanese the old Netherlanders were perfectly well aware,
and knew very well how to profit by it.   It was also by this simple
means that the tradal advantages accorded in modern times were
acquired by Herrn Doeff and J. C. Blomhoff."

The unfortunate assertion in this passage is that the " old
Netherlanders " were fully aware of this amiable and far from
contemptible " weak side " of the Japanese.   The only " old "
servants of the Dutch East India Company who appear to have
been aware of it were Caron, Kämpfer, and Thunberg.   Not one of
these was a Netherlander.   Caron was born of French parents in
Holland ; and the obtuse materialism of the Dutch traders constrained him to leave their employment with disgust, and to take
service under Colbert.   Kämpfer was a German, and although
he knew this amiable weak side of the Japanese, he, according to
his own account, relied much more upon a " submissive behaviour ",
bribery and—the bottle ! [1]   Thunberg was a Swede, and although

---

[1] In recounting the means he took to acquire the assistance of the Japanese in
his botanical studies, Kämpfer writes :   " But I must confess, likewise, that at
the beginning of our journey I took what pains and tried what means I could to
procure the friendship and assistance of my fellow-travellers, obliging some with

he was also aware of this " weak side " of the Japanese, he obtained his liberty to botanize in the environs of Nagasaki chiefly by playing upon the sponging proclivities of the petty Japanese officials.[1] But Titsingh's own mental ability and moral backbone made any recourse to bribery or the bottle with the lower ranks of officialdom entirely unnecessary. Quick to take their cue from the attitude of their superiors, as soon as they perceived that these superiors were treating the new director as what he undoubtedly was—a gentleman—they were not slow to become very polite towards him. Nay, not merely polite, but exceedingly helpful. Titsingh was an assiduous book-hunter ; and in procuring him the works he wanted they were very ready to assist, while the interpreters aided him to fathom their meaning in a fashion that evoked his heartiest commendation. Five of these knew enough Dutch to be highly serviceable, and of these he writes :—

" Far from finding them suspicious and reluctant, as Europeans are usually pleased to represent these persons, in order to palliate their own indolence, they manifested, on the contrary, an eagerness to procure for me every practicable information, to consult in various matters beyond their capacity the best informed individuals among the magistrates and clergy, and to furnish me with books which might serve as a guide to my labours."

Titsingh made many friends in Yedo, whither he went as envoy in 1780 and 1782. Usually it was the physician of the party who, on account of his superior scientific attainments, was the centre of attraction to the scholars of the capital. It must have therefore been somewhat of a surprise to the Japanese to find in the head of the mission a man of extensive learning and of rare mental ability. Accordingly, with the real intellectual society of Yedo Titsingh at once became exceedingly popular, and with several of the friends he made here—Kuchiki, Daimyō of Fukuchiyama in Tamba, among others—he maintained a regular correspondence not merely while in Deshima but for years after he had left Japan. As has been said, for some dozen years or so previous to this, as regards

---

a submissive humble conduct and ready assistance as to physic and physical advice, others with secret rewards for the very meanest favours and services." Again, in dealing with the search for contraband or prohibited goods of exports in the houses of Dutch before embarking from Deshima, he remarks : " Upon my own departure, although my things *for good reasons* were visited but slightly, *and over a bottle*, yet they seized upon an old Japanese razor and a few other things, just because they happened to see them."

[1] Every one of his half-day excursions cost him some £4 or £5 in providing a feast for the useless parasites that invariably attached themselves to him.

extended foreign intercourse, a spirit of liberalism had been in the air. In 1769, Matsudaira, Settsu-no-Kami, a member of the Junior Council (*Wakadoshiyori*), had actually gone so far as to propose the construction of ships and junks suitable for long over-sea voyages, and Titsingh asserts that it was only his premature death that prevented the abolition of the restrictions upon Japanese ship-building and foreign trade. Still, in spite of the death of its leader, the liberal party was fairly strong. Says Titsingh :—

" Though many Japanese of the highest distinction, and intimately acquainted with matters of government, still consider Japan as the first empire of the world, and care but little for what passes out of it, yet such persons are denominated by the more enlightened *Ido-no-Kawadzu*—that is, ' Frogs in a Well '—a metaphorical expression which signifies that when they look up they can see no more of the sky than what the small circumference of the well allows them to perceive."[1]

At this date Tanuma, the Chief Councillor, was all-powerful in Yedo, and, as has been remarked elsewhere, has been limned by contemporary pamphleteers and chroniclers in the blackest of colours. His son had lately been appointed a member of the Junior Council, and if we are to believe Titsingh, this appointment caused the Conservatives extreme chagrin, for the Liberals made no secret of their hope that when the young man succeeded his father he would " widen the road ". As it was, the innovations he introduced roused the hatred of the " Frog-in-the-Well " Court grandees, and the result was the assassination of the younger Tanuma in the palace itself by one of those political fanatics who have done so much to besmirch the pages of Japanese history (13th May, 1784).

The death of Tanuma, like that of Matsudaira, Settsu-no-Kami, proved fatal to a project which might well have modified the subsequent history of the empire. In 1783 Tango-no-Kami, Governor of Nagasaki, probably acting on Tanuma's instructions, had requested Titsingh to bring carpenters from Batavia to instruct the Japanese in building more substantial vessels for the transport of copper from Ōsaka to Nagasaki. The ostensible reason for this was the frequent loss of junks and their cargoes on the trip ; but it may be surmised that what really lay at the bottom of the affair was an intention of proceeding cautiously to the realization of

---

[1] Old Japanese proverb, " *I no kwazu daikai wo shirazu*," A frog in a well knows nothing of the great Ocean.

Matsudaira's project of 1769.[1] Skilled carpenters were scarce at
Batavia, and could not be sent from there, so Titsingh proposed to
carry a number of Japanese with him when he returned to be
instructed in the Batavian dockyards. The prohibition against
any native leaving the country made this course impossible, and
thereupon Titsingh promised to have a model ship built at Batavia,
and conveyed to Nagasaki. The promise was faithfully kept, but
the assassination of Tanuma and the croaking of the " Frogs-in-the-
Well ", who were now regaining the ascendency, made the model
ship of scant service, and indeed put an end to all hopes that had
been formed of a modification in the exclusive policy of the
Japanese.

It might have been expected that during his three visits to
Japan, Titsingh would have found means to improve the conditions
of the Deshima trade. He did find means to do so very easily.
In 1782, in consequence of the war between Great Britain and the
Netherlands, no ships appeared from Batavia ; and the director
took advantage of the fact to stipulate for a considerable advance
in the prices of the Dutch imports for the next fifteen years.

Before half that term had elapsed, however, the Dutch trade
in Deshima was in a more desperate position than it had ever been
in before. In the first place, beginning with 1783, there was a
succession of five terrible famines, which reduced the population
of the empire by a good deal more than 1,000,000 souls. In such a
situation the authorities were averse to seeing money squandered
upon the articles of luxury—or at least not of necessity—which
constituted the bulk of the Dutch imports ; while, wedded as they
were to a strong belief in an extreme form of that mercantile theory
of political economy (of which, perhaps, they had never heard),
they deemed it no advantage to a suffering country to be depleted

---

[1] Ōsaka, or rather Sakai, was the seat of Japanese copper-smelting. A merchant
of Ōsaka, Sumitomo by name, was taught by a Portuguese named Haku-sui
about 1590, how to separate silver from lead or copper, even when it occurs in a
small quantity only. Sumitomo introduced the new process in his metallurgical
works, rose in wealth and power, and received an Imperial patent for the purifica-
tion of copper and the separation of silver from lead and copper. In 1691, when
Kämpfer was in Japan, the Sumitomos acquired the mine of Besshi in Shikoku,
which even to-day is the chief source of wealth of that great mercantile house.
In Kämpfer's time most of the copper came from Kii, Echigo, and Suruga. " That
of Suruga is charged with a considerable quantity of gold, which the Japanese at
present (1691–2) separate and refine much better than they did formerly, which
occasions great complaints among the refiners and Brahmines upon the coast of
Coromandel. All the copper is brought to Sakai, one of the five Imperial towns,
where it is refined and cast into small cylinders about a span and a half long and
a finger thick."

of its metallic resources. Then, again, the Conservatives had meanwhile been rapidly regaining power in the Yedo councils, and when,
with the appointment of Matsudaira Sadanobu as Regent during
the minority of the new Shōgun Iyenari, the elder Tanuma was
driven from office in 1786, the last hope of the Liberals vanished.
Shintōism, thanks to Moto-ori's efforts, was now making strong
headway, and, according to its teaching, the autochthonous Japanese,
the offspring of gods, only degraded and disgraced themselves by
a maintenance of intercourse with outer barbarians, from whom
they could derive neither temporary nor temporal benefit. Last
of all, the factors, who came after Titsingh's final departure in
1784, seem to have been fitted rather for bagmen than for the
cultured representatives of a great territorial power, treated in
Japan on the footing of Daimyō. The old complaints about taels
and guilders, and small profits, and great expenses, and all the
rest of a petty shopkeeper's grievances were again revived, and the
Conservatives of Yedo, with their open contempt for the mere
trader and his money bags, were in no mood to listen to all these
dismal rigmaroles about percentages and expenses and losses.
In 1789 the Dutch actually discontinued their annual presents to
the Governors and officials of Nagasaki, and complained bitterly
about the expenses of the embassy to Yedo. In the following year
they were informed that although the presents had to be forwarded
annually as before, an embassy would henceforth be received only
once every four years, and that from that date not 10,000 but only
6,000 piculs of copper (5,300 for the Company, and 700 for the
Director) were to be exported annually, and only one, not two,
Dutch ships allowed to come to Nagasaki every autumn. At the
same time, however, in lieu of copper some new articles of export
were offered, but the Dutch took no advantage of the concession.
They continued their complaints to the Governor of Nagasaki, and
these unexpected conditions led to the discovery (1792) that the
interpreters had failed to communicate to them the exact purport
of the contemptuous reply returned to their representations two
years before. For this offence the chief interpreter had to pay
dearly, and the passage he had suppressed in the instructions
issued in reply to the requests of the Hollanders was now imparted
to them in all its curt severity.

" If the Netherlanders press in future for any greater increase
in the export of copper, then not only shall their demand be refused ;

but the goods they have brought for it shall be burned, and trade with Japan entirely forbidden to them."

The Netherlanders had cried " Wolf " too often already with regard to the threat of abandoning Deshima ; the Conservative Yedo Cabinet under the influence of the pragmatic and ultra-nationalistic Regent, Matsudaira Sadanobu, now gave them clearly to understand that such a threat would not so much be regarded with equanimity as resented as a piece of presumptuous impertinence seeing that the presence of the Hollanders in Deshima was now not so much an advantage to the empire as a nuisance that had to be tolerated in consequence of the ill-judged promise of the deified Iyeyasu made to them nearly two centuries before.

The Chinese, who had ever been envious of that privilege of sending an embassy to Court which the Dutch regarded as a burden, now seized this opportunity to petition for the favour once more. The petition was refused ; but the petitioners were graciously allowed to export more than twice the amount of copper assigned to the Dutch—13,000 piculs.

Meanwhile in Europe and elsewhere the Hollanders had had to face a succession of calamities. The war with England in 1780–3 had almost ruined their foreign commerce for the time being, and one Article in the Treaty of Peace had assured the British full freedom of trade with the Dutch India possessions. In 1787 the internal dissensions of the Netherlands had to be allayed by Prussian armed intervention, and the United Provinces had then to enter into a reluctant and compulsory alliance with Great Britain as well as with Prussia. In 1794–5, the French cavalry occupied Amsterdam, and advancing across the ice, captured the whole Dutch fleet then at the Texel. The next six years, down to the Peace of Amiens in 1801, witnessed a Constitution-mongering and a kaleidoscopic succession of governments that did far more damage to the country than did the loss of its fleet at the battle of Camperdown in 1797. The great Dutch East India Company had paid no dividend since 1782, and in 1798 it was finally dissolved.[1] The effects of this ultimately made themselves felt as far distant as Deshima, on the other side of the world. Dutch vessels were no longer available to maintain its communications with Batavia, and

---

[1] During the 198 years of its existence it had paid 3,600½ per cent. in dividends, an annual average of 18 per cent.

foreign ships had to be chartered. This circumstance is interesting
from the fact that it led to the first appearance of the American
flag in Japanese waters—in 1797, fourteen years after the
acknowledgment of American independence, and fifty-six years
before Perry's appearance at Uraga. The arrival of the first of
these American vessels—the *Eliza*, Captain Stewart (who, however,
was an Englishman who passed himself off as an American), created
a great sensation among the Nagasaki officials. The interpreters
at once perceived that the crew did not speak Dutch, but English ;
and it was with the greatest difficulty that they were made to
understand that although the men spoke English, they were not
" the English ", but belonged to another nation ; and, what was
still more vital, that they had nothing to do with the trade, but were
merely hired to bring the goods in order to save them from capture.
Hemmy, the head of the Factory, had succeeded in getting this
explanation accepted by the Yedo Court, when next year disquieting
incidents occurred. He had then gone on the second of the quadriennial embassies, and had been well received, when he died suddenly
at Kakegawa on his return journey—having poisoned himself, as
was generally thought. Then it was reported that the authorities
discovered a project for establishing tradal relations between the
Dutch and the Daimyō of Satsuma. The Japanese compromised
in the affair were severely punished, but although " there were
sharp speeches against the Dutch " they did not suffer. Rather,
indeed, the reverse ; for after an *ōmetsuke* (censor) had come down
from Yedo to visit Nagasaki and Deshima, the copper exports were
increased, while Hemmy's family received a considerable present
from the Shōgun, and the Governors of Nagasaki exerted themselves
to make the Dutch mission to Yedo an annual one, as it had been
before.

The *Eliza* came again to Japan in 1798, and in 1799, 1800, 1801,
1802, and 1803, the annual vessels were also American ; while, in
1806 there came under the Dutch flag an American and a Bremener ;
in 1807 an American and a Dane, and in 1809, another American.
From that year, down to 1817, there was no Dutch trade done at
Deshima. In 1801 the Japanese began to complain about these
American vessels, the Governor of Nagasaki going so far as to remark
that " if the Company for any reason whatsoever was no longer in
a position to carry on its trade with Japan itself, then all reason
for the stay of the Hollanders in Japan disappeared ". To the Dutch-

men this seemed a mere pretext for dispensing with their Company, for they had heard that the authorities were at the same time negotiating with the Chinese for a full supply of those European and Indian products which constituted their own staples of import. Indeed, the supply of these commodities brought by the Cantonese junks was very considerable, for the Chinese could obtain these articles from the English East India Company's factory in Canton in exchange for tea on very advantageous terms. In England at this time the development of the factory system was proceeding apace, and in the supplies furnished to establishments like that at Canton the Dutch had seen such a menace that Titsingh had been sent to Peking in 1794 expressly to counterwork Macartney's mission there. However, it is likely that the Japanese were perfectly sincere in their complaints. They saw in these non-Dutch vessels an insidious attempt on the part of Europeans to break down the barriers of seclusion they had maintained for more than a century and a half. Shortly before this there had been several open attempts to obtain that end. In 1791, the *Argonaut*, an English vessel employed in the north-west American fur industry, arrived on the west coast of Japan, and attempted to trade there ; in 1795-7, Captain Broughton touched at several points in Saghalien, then Japanese territory, and Japanese officers were dispatched from Yezo to restrict his communications and to send him away as speedily as possible.

All these attempts were still fresh in the memory of the Japanese when in 1800, Captain Stewart, who had brought the Dutch goods to Japan in an American ship in 1797, and 1798, now appeared in an American brig with a cargo of his own, and endeavoured to open up commercial relations with the empire, not on account of the Dutch, but of himself.[1] In 1803, Stewart in company with Torrey

---

[1] The *Eliza*, laden with camphor and copper, struck on a hidden rock as she was leaving Nagasaki for Batavia in 1798 and sank. All attempts to raise her were abortive till a Japanese fisherman achieved the task in a very ingenious yet very simple way. For this achievement he was made a *Samurai* by his lord the Daimyō of Saga. (This is interesting as going to indicate that in certain of the fiefs a plebeian of merit could occasionally elevate himself in the social scale.) When repaired and reloaded, the *Eliza* set sail again, only to be dismasted in a storm, and while she was refitting at Nagasaki the ship of 1799 came in. Stewart did not wait for her company but sailed in the *Eliza*, in which he never reached Batavia. Next year, according to one account, " he reappeared at Nagasaki, representing himself as having been shipwrecked with the loss of everything " ; but as having found a friend at Manila who had enabled him to buy and lade the brig in which he had now come back, for the purpose, as he said, of discharging

reappeared with two vessels flying American colours, but really as the envoys of Calcutta merchants eager to open up a trade with Japan. He was supplied with water and fuel gratuitously, but was told to carry his rich cargoes of Indian and Chinese goods elsewhere.

Thus, the Japanese may very well have entertained a suspicion that in employing foreign ships to bring their cargoes to Deshima the Hollanders were really in collusion with other Western Powers in an attempt to force Japan open to the trade of the world. The attitude taken up by the Dutch towards Stewart in 1803 tended, however, to dispel this suspicion, and next year the appearance of a ship of Dutch nationality confirmed the impression that the Hollanders were really not playing false. In 1805 the annual ship was also a Dutchman, and this was perhaps fortunate, for the Dutch had been once more compromised by the appearance of other European claimants for intercourse with the hermit empire.

The first accredited envoy from any European Court to Japan, since the repulse of the mission from Lisbon in 1647, appeared at Nagasaki in 1804, on board the first European man-of-war that ever cast anchor in a Japanese harbour. Both envoy and ship had come from St. Petersburg—or rather from Kronstadt.

To understand the purport and importance of this mission, it becomes necessary to cast a brief glance at the Russian advance to and on the Pacific. The Muscovites first reached the Great Ocean by water when the Cossack Dejneff made his extraordinary voyage from the river Kolyma through Behring Strait to Anadyr in 1648. This route was never followed again till modern times, and for generations the only communications between Russia and the Pacific were overland. As a matter of fact the Russians had reached the Sea of Okhotsk in 1639, nine years before Dejneff's wonderful expedition. In 1649, the town of Okhotsk was founded, and it was long the sole Russian base in Far Eastern seas. It was here that Behring's ships were put together and fitted out mainly with materials sent overland from Europe ; and, for long afterwards, all the Russian ships that sailed the Pacific came from the slips of

---

out of the sale of her cargo his debt due to the Factory for the advances made for the repairs of his lost vessel. Director Waardenaar, however, saw, or thought he saw, in this proceeding a scheme for gaining a commercial footing at Nagasaki independent of the regular trade from Batavia. He caused the goods to be sold and applied to the discharge of Stewart's debt ; but he declined to furnish any return cargo for the brig, and he arrested Stewart and sent him a prisoner to Batavia ; whence, however, soon after his arrival there, he made his escape.

Okhotsk. Kamchatka was occupied about 1700, and a second Far Eastern base was ultimately established at Petropavlovsk. The Kurile Islands soon attracted the attention of the Russians; in 1713 the Cossack Kosierewski made his way as far south as Kunashir. Twenty-three years later, in 1736, the Japanese annals record the appearance of a Danish ship on the Nambu coast. This vessel was no Dane, but she was commanded by the Dane, Spagenberg, then in the Russian service. Forty years later, in 1777, Potonchew was surveying the seas to the north of Japan, ten years before the appearance of La Perouse in the same waters.

Long before this the Russians had come into contact with stray Japanese castaways who were stranded on the coast of the continent from time to time. We hear of a Japanese crew being hospitably treated by them as early as 1690; and we know of several such incidents in the course of the next century. In 1778 some Russians appeared at Nemuro in quest of trade, but were informed, after a year's delay, that all the foreign trade of Japan was limited to Nagasaki. In 1782, a junk from Ise was wrecked among the Aleutian Islands, and her rescued crew were sent to Irkutsk where they learned Russian. A few years later, Catherine II of Russia thought of opening up relations with Japan and in 1792 she instructed the Governor of Siberia to send the Irkutsk Japanese home, and to dispatch an envoy along with them, not as from her, but as from himself. Lieutenant Laxman was selected for the mission; he sailed from Okhotsk in the autumn of 1792 and passed the winter at Nemuro in Yezo. Next spring he proceeded to Hakodate, whence he went by land to Matsumaye. Here, after communicating with Yedo, the authorities handed him a document to the effect :—

" That although it was ordained by the laws of Japan that any foreigners landing upon the coast, except at Nagasaki, should be seized and perpetually imprisoned ; yet, considering the ignorance of the Russians, and their having brought back the shipwrecked Japanese, they might be permitted to depart on condition of never approaching, under any pretence, any part of the coast except Nagasaki. As to the Japanese, brought back, the Government was much obliged to the Russians, who, however, were at liberty to leave them or take them away again as they pleased, it being a law of Japan that such persons ceased to be Japanese, and became the subjects of that Government into whose hands destiny cast them. With respect to commercial negotiations, those could only take place at Nagasaki ; and a paper was sent authorizing a Russian vessel to enter that port for that purpose ; but as the

Christian religion was not allowed in Japan, any persons admitted into Nagasaki must carefully abstain from it." [1]

The Japanese seem to have expected the speedy arrival of a Russian mission at Nagasaki ; at all events the sea-board Daimyō were notified that the appearance of Russian vessels off their coasts might be looked for. But none came ; and all excitement about the Muscovites would probably have died down but for the circumstance that the Bakufu at least learned that a Russian settlement of some eighty men had been established on the island of Urup in 1795. At this time, the Japanese used to send parties to trade with the Ainu in the neighbouring island of Iterup in summer, but they had there no permanent establishment. In 1786 the Bakufu sent a commission to explore Yezo, with the interior of which, and with even a great part of the coast-line, the authorities were still unacquainted. In the following years commissioners continued to be dispatched on similar missions, and all through the closing years of the century the Shōgun's officers were very active in Yezo, in Saghalin, and in the southernmost of the Kuriles, the Russian settlement in Urup being regarded as a serious menace. The settlers had diminished to fourteen, and, by forbidding the Ainu to have any dealings with them, the Japanese tried hard to starve them out. Meanwhile they had put the greater part of Matsumaye fief under direct Bakufu control; had garrisoned posts in Yezo and in Iterup with levies from Tsugaru and Nambu ; had surveyed and charted a direct sea-route from Nemuro to Yedo, and had dispatched the famous mathematician, Ino Chūkei, to make a map of Yezo and its dependencies. In 1800, Takadaya Kahei, a merchant of Hyōgo, built a vessel of 1,500 *koku* burthen, and with her opened up communication between Iterup, Hakodate, and Yedo. We hear of this craft hoisting the *Hi no maru* or Sun-flag of Japan—and we learn a good deal about this Takadaya Kahei from foreign sources, for in 1812 he was captured by the Russians, and he appears as Tachatay-Kachi in the narratives of Golownin and Rikord. Altogether this little outpost of the Russian Fur Company on Urup occasioned the Japanese a large amount of

---

[1] It ought, perhaps, to be said that Laxman although instructed by Catherine II to proceed on his mission, was ostensibly the representative of the Governor of Irkutsk. In this city, Catherine II had introduced into the Navigation School a Professorship of Japanese, the chair being filled by occupants selected from Japanese shipwrecked from time to time on the coast of Siberia. It was from the Japanese Professor in Irkutsk (a member of the Greek Church) that Klaproth (1806) acquired his knowledge of the language.

worry and anxiety. At last on 27th September, 1804, the Governor of this Fur Company sailed into Nagasaki harbour in a Russian man-of-war as envoy from Alexander I to the " Emperor " of Japan.

" When Shelikov, the Siberian fur-trader and merchant, visited St. Petersburg in 1788, Rezánov, then a young man of twenty-four, met the great colonizer by chance and immediately became interested in his plan to obtain a monopoly of the fur-trade in the islands and territories added by the Golikov-Shelikov Company to Russia, a monopoly which would not only increase vastly the wealth of the stock-holders, but prevent the wholesale slaughter of sables, seals, otters, and foxes by small traders and foreigners. Rezánov became a partner in the Company, and developed an astonishing capacity for business and hard work. When Shelikov died in 1795, having obtained from Catherine only a moiety of the power and privileges he had solicited, his new partner's ambitions had far outrun his own. The two leading companies had been amalgamated, several others had been drawn in, ships and factories had been built and protected by forts, but it remained for Rezánov to father the first great Trust put into operation on American soil. For this a charter was necessary."

The charter was at last obtained in 1799, after great difficulties had been overcome.

" Rezánov was now the guardian of a Company granted, for a period of twenty years, full and exclusive privileges in hunting, trading, building, and in all new discoveries over the vast region beginning from 55 degrees north, and including the long chain of islands between Kamchatka and Alaska, and the archipelago between Kamchatka and Japan. Alaska contained over 500,000 square miles, and there were numberless other islands besides those included in the archipelagos, all of them the haunts of the richest fur-bearing animals in the world.

The Emperor Paul was murdered in 1801. Alexander, young, ardent, ambitious, ascended the throne, and the most brilliant and energetic member of his Court had no difficulty in persuading him to fit out an expedition to circumnavigate the globe, and include a diplomatic mission to Japan. In 1803, the *Nadesha* and the *Neva* put out of the harbour of Kronstadt, and, after a voyage of fourteen months, hazardous and uncomfortable, but scientifically valuable (during which Rezánov kept a diary that is preserved in the St. Petersburg Academy of Science), the ships separated, and the one bearing the Ambassador entered with pomp and pride the waters of Japan." [1]

The " pomp and pride " had but little success on this occasion. Difficulties at once began when the *Nadesha* was boarded by the Japanese officials, accompanied by Doeff, the chief of the Deshima factory. The officers insisted on treating the Russian warship

---

[1] See Miss Atherton's essay on Rezánov in the *North American Review* for May, 1909. The great man from Kyōto she there speaks of was really a rather humble official from Yedo, Toyama, a *metsuke* or censor.

as they did the Dutch merchant-men, and ordered her armament
to be sent ashore. Rezánov ultimately agreed to give up his
powder, and no more; he also brusquely refused the prostrations
which the Governor's underlings demanded as representatives of
the " Emperor ". After these questions had been referred to Yedo,
the *Nadesha* was at last assigned an anchorage, the Dutch ships
being removed to another and a distant berth. After the first
evening, the only communication between the Dutch and the
Russians were clandestine, connived at by the interpreters, and it
was only after Rezánov had become seriously ill that he was
allowed to land, after permission had been obtained from Yedo.
Finally, about seventy days after his arrival, a storehouse was
constructed for the envoy on a small island, so closely hedged in
with bamboos that nothing within it could be seen. The guard of
seven marines who landed with him were permitted to carry muskets,
but they were allowed no powder, and the *Nadesha* was constantly
surrounded by guard-boats during the whole of her stay. After
a detention of nearly six months, Rezánov was informed that a
representative of the " Emperor " had arrived in Nagasaki, and
that he would be received in audience on the following day. It
took a long time to settle all the details of the prospective interview.
Rezánov was given to understand that he must prostrate himself
before this functionary.

" He declined to do so in the name of the Emperor of all the Russias
but, after more parleys, he consented, there being no chairs in the hall
of audience, to sit on his heels for a few minutes."

Next day he was taken ashore in the Prince of Hizen's barge,
and carried to the Governor's house in Doeff's palanquin, which
had been borrowed for the occasion. But all his suite had to walk;
all doors and windows were closed, the street gates fastened, and
the inhabitants told to keep out of sight. At the first interview
nothing was done.[1]

---

[1] To quote Miss Atherton: " If Rezánov looked anything like the full length
painting of him lost in the fire of San Francisco, which had been brought down from
Sitka after the purchase of Alaska by the United States, he must have been a
superb figure in his full Ambassador's costume—red sash, cocked hat, and orders
blazing on his breast. He had a tall, straight, commanding figure; a long, pale
face, smoothly shaven; a finely cut nose; a firm, rather large mouth; eyes
humorous and brilliant under heavy lids, and light hair which he wore short and
unpowdered. At any other Court but that of Japan he would have been the most
imposing figure in the diplomatic corps; but what impression can a man make
sitting on his heels ? "

On the following day a flat refusal was given to all the Russian requests, while all the presents were returned. The refusal to receive the envoy or his presents was placed on the ground that if they were received, it would be necessary to send a return mission with equal presents. To this not only was the poverty of Japan an obstacle but also the strict law in force for 170 years past against any Japanese going abroad. It was also stated that Japan had no great wants, and little use for foreign productions, of which the Dutch and Chinese brought all that was required, and that any considerable trade could only be established by means of intercourse between Japanese and foreigners, which the laws strictly forbade.

To the proud-spirited and magnificent envoy of the Tsar, this rebuff was mortifying in the extreme, and it also touched him very nearly as Governor of the Great Russian Fur Company. When he reached Okhotsk he found commissions from both the Tsar and the Company to remain in the new dominions and reform all abuses. Travelling slowly among the islands he established measures to protect the fur-bearing animals from marauding foreigners and dishonest employees, punishing, banishing, rewarding. The farther he travelled, the more he appreciated the fact that without a constant supply of foodstuffs, which the treaty with Japan would have insured, the Company would perish. He spent the winter of 1805-6 at New Archangel (Sitka) in Alaska, evolving plans for bringing the whole of the Pacific slope under the Russian flag.[1]

In pursuance of this grandiose project he visited San Francisco in the following spring, and in October he set out for St. Petersburg to obtain Imperial sanction and assistance. Meanwhile the wound inflicted on his amour-propre by the Japanese had been rankling. At Sitka he built a small vessel for operations against them and, when he reached Okhotsk, this vessel and another he had bought from an American captain were dispatched to wrest Saghalin from the Japanese, and to ravage Yezo and the Kuriles.

---

[1] On 15th February, 1806, he wrote to Zapinsky : "I think I may say that at the Columbia we could attract a population from various parts, and in the course of ten years we should be strong enough to make use of any favourable turn in European politics to include the coast of California among the Russian possessions. The Spaniards are very weak in these countries, and if, in 1798, when war was declared by Spain, our Company had had a force corresponding to its proportions, it would have been very easy to seize California from 34 degrees to Santa Barbara and to appropriate this territory for ever, since the geographical position of Mexico would have prevented her from sending any assistance overland." It is tolerably safe to assume that it was only Rezánov's premature death (at Krasnoiarsk in March, 1807) that prevented the whole Pacific sea-board of North America from becoming and remaining Russian territory.

Chowstoff and Davidoff, the commanders of the two vessels, had little more than sixty men under their orders; yet this insignificant expedition proved sufficient to keep the whole of the north of Japan in a state of panic and turmoil for two years.[1] In 1806 the two ships burned the Japanese settlement at Kushunkotan, carrying off all the stores, seven or eight Ainu and one Japanese prisoner. Next spring, they captured the two Japanese forts in Iterup, appeared off Hakodate when they captured a war-junk, and then turned their attention to Saghalin again, plundering some junks they found in Soya Strait. In these earliest hostilities between Muscovites and Japanese, the " Soul of Yamato " so much lauded by Moto-ori and Hirata did not show to any conspicuous advantage; in truth the episode showed only too clearly that there was " something rotten in the state of Denmark ", at least in the northern territory of Tokugawa Japan.

In the following year (1808) there was an equally significant incident at Nagasaki in the south.[2]

Of the incident in question we have an account by Doeff, President of the Factory, and another by one Tokuyemon, a sort of aide-de-camp to the Governor, and both accounts are at one as representing the cowardice and incompetence of the officials—the Governor excepted—when called upon to face a surprising emergency. The Japanese account (of which a précis has been made by Mr. Aston) is especially instructive. After telling us how when, late in September, hopes of the arrival of the annual Dutch ship had been abandoned, notice was given of the appearance of a " white sail " on the horizon, the Japanese account, as summarized by Mr. Aston, proceeds :—

" The news caused a joyful excitement among all classes in Nagasaki. There were few of the townspeople who had not some share in the profitable monopoly of foreign trade enjoyed by that city, and although our manuscript is silent on the subject, we may be sure the Japanese

---

[1] For details see Aston, " Russian Descents in Saghalin and Iterup " : *T.A.S.J.*, vol. i, pt. 1.

[2] The Russians meanwhile made a practical attempt to open a trade at Nagasaki. " In 1807 the *Eclipse*, of Boston, chartered at Canton by the Russian-American Company for Kamtchatka and the north-west coast of America, entered the harbour of Nagasaki, under Russian colours, and was towed to the anchorage by an immense number of boats. A Dutchman went on board and advised the captain to haul down his colours, as the Japanese were much displeased with Russia." She was not allowed to trade, but received a gratuitous supply of provisions, and on the third day was towed out of the haven by about 100 boats.

officials had also good reason for satisfaction at the news. Of course the joy was greatest in the Dutch settlement of Deshima. After more than a year without news of Europe, without letters from friends and relations, and deprived of many a little comfort which the land of their exile could not supply, the delight of the Dutch residents may be easily imagined. The ship approached rapidly, and was already visible in the distance off the entrance to the harbour, when the interpreter who had been sent to convey the news to the Dutchmen arrived in Deshima. He reported on his return that the Kapitan (Doeff) had taken him aside, and, after expressing the joy which he and his countrymen felt at the arrival of the ship, had added : ‘ There are, however, some suspicious circumstances. It is very improbable that she should have delayed her departure from Batavia until so late in the season. If she had left at the usual time, and were only arriving now, she must have met with an accident and lost one or two of her masts. But the ship approaching is not deeply laden. She sails well on the wind, and her masts and rigging are in excellent order. She may be a ship of some other country, and it would be disloyal of me if I did not warn you to take every precaution.’ ”

As a matter of fact, although flying the Dutch colours, it was no Dutch merchantman, but a crack ship of the English navy, one of the frigates known as the “ Saucy Channel Four ”, that was coming racing toward the fiord. The *Phaeton*, commanded by Captain Pellew, had left England eight months before, and on arriving in Bengal, Pellew, hearing that two Dutch ships were going to Nagasaki that year, had at once set out to capture them.[1] When the Japanese with the two Dutch clerks who had gone to board the vessel, approached her, a boat was lowered, and its crew seized the Dutchmen while the Japanese sculled back in the greatest trepidation. When these unlucky officials who had thus allowed the clerks to be carried off from under their very noses returned to Government House, and were admitted into the Governor’s presence, they made at once a pitiable and a comical appearance. With deep-drawn sighs and chattering teeth, they told how, “ all of a sudden fifteen men with pistols and naked swords had sprung out of the bottom of the foreign boat, captured the ‘ Redhairs ’, and carried them off in the twinkling of an eye. The crew of this boat were like so many fierce tigers. They were so nimble in their movements, and looked so terrible, that it seemed in no wise possible to approach them. They nevertheless pursued them, and were about to put them to the sword, when they reflected that such a course would

---

[1] Great Britain and Holland were then at war, for Holland at that date was practically an appanage of France, Napoleon’s brother, Louis, having been installed as King of the country in 1806.

cause the Governor great anxiety, and might give rise to serious trouble (!). They therefore resolved to come back and report what had happened."

The Governor, Matsudaira, Dzusho-no-kami, whom the crisis, according to Dr. Aston's description, shows to have been a brave and gallant man, rated the poltroons in scathing terms, and to Doeff, who just then rushed in, he broke out with fury in his face, " Be quiet, Kapitan ; I shall take care that your people are restored." But he soon learned to his consternation that at the harbour guard-house, where 1,000 men ought to have been stationed, there were only sixty or seventy, and these uncommanded. As has been stated in the first volume, the Daimyōs of Saga (Nabeshima) and of Chikuzen (Kuroda) had been made responsible for the defence of Nagasaki harbour but, as for generations no foreign foe had appeared there, their councillors had not unnaturally come to regard the task as a mere empty piece of formal routine. The Governor at once informed the responsible military officers that immediate measures must be taken to recover the Dutchmen and to burn and sink the ship, as the Spaniard had been destroyed nineteen years before,[1] and that combustibles and fire-ships should be provided and a scheme of action drawn up on paper and submitted for his consideration. Next day, however, the Commander-in-Chief, on being asked how the plan for burning the ship was progressing, made answer that he personally knew nothing about it, but would instruct his lieutenants to furnish a written report on the matter. At the same time, an officer, ordered to the batteries on a visit of inspection, candidly replied that he had no inclination to perform the duty of inspector, and that, besides, he had no clothes suitable for such a service. The Governor, determined to act with the few men of his own he could collect, got ready arms in the principal hall, told the head cook to look after the commissariat, and repeated his urgent messages to the Daimyō's officers, from whom, however, came only excuses and remonstrances in reply. One man forced himself into the Governor's presence and besought His Excellency to think of his mother ! These are only a few of the instances of the general incapacity and cowardice that may be culled from

---

[1] His Excellency was weaker in his history than in his spirit. No Spanish ship had been burned and sunk at Nagasaki either ninety or 190 years before. What he most probably was referring to was the *Madre de Dios* incident of 1610.

Tokuyemon's narrative—a cowardice so general, indeed, that the Governor's physician said that *everybody* was sick—that their loins were out of joint from fright, and that he would like to have the chance of prescribing for them. However, if we are to believe Doeff, not only the Governor himself, but his secretary also, acted with courage and determination ; it being with the greatest difficulty that Doeff dissuaded the latter from proceeding on board the *Phaeton* to demand the delivery of the Dutchmen, and, failing to obtain that, to stab first the captain and then himself.

It presently appeared that the Dutchmen had been seized merely to serve as interpreters and hostages to ensure the delivery of needed supplies of wood, water, and provisions. On these being sent off, one of the Dutchmen came back with a letter from Pellew asking for beef and vegetables, and threatening to fire the Japanese and Chinese junks in the harbour in the case of a refusal. The Governor still meant to fight, but the supplies were sent off in the Dutch barge, and His Excellency, seeing that all prospect of burning the *Phaeton* was hopeless, made up his mind to order her to depart at once. Some anxiety was felt lest she might not obey this order, as beef had not been sent, but about two in the afternoon, " a gentle breeze having sprung up, the ship swung round, and, setting three sails, went off like an arrow."

" Meanwhile troops had begun to pour into Nagasaki from the neighbouring provinces, and much zeal was displayed in keeping a strict watch on the departing ship from the shore, and from boats which were sent out to observe her motions. The military officers *now* reported by letter that, in accordance with the instructions received on the previous day, preparations had been made at Fukahori to burn the foreign ship, that fire-junks had been prepared, and that they had been on the point of reporting that everything was in readiness to carry out the plan without fail, when the message came ordering them to desist from the attempt."

With all this, it is surprising to find Seibold, eighteen years later (1826), in dealing with the elaborate secret measures of Japanese harbour defence, asserting that he knew from trustworthy sources that if Pellew had ventured further into the harbour he certainly would not have escaped. As far as can be seen from Tokuyemon's account of the episode, so long as she did not actually ground, the frigate could have done pretty much as she liked anywhere in the harbour without the least risk to herself. The elaborate precautions for harbour protection, Siebold writes, were all adopted after, and almost entirely on account of this *Phaeton* incident and of the Russian descendants in the North in the preceding year. After the English ship was out of sight a fleet of eighty Chikuzen war-junks did indeed enter the harbour, but it was undoubtedly fortunate for themselves that they found her gone. Her artillery would have made very short work of them ; for the old Tokugawa regulations, preventing the construction of fighting ships of more than 500 *koku* (50 tons) burthen, were still in force, and a few score of crazy Lilliputian craft of this description could have effected but little against one of the crack frigates of the British navy.

It is indeed regrettable to find that this episode cost the life of the only man who had behaved like an intrepid and gallant gentle-man in the crisis. On the night of the departure of the warship, Tokuyemon, after leaving the Governor, had returned to his own quarters.

" I think," he writes, " it must have been midnight when Tanabe came rushing in by the front entrance, weeping and exclaiming, ' Haven't you heard that His Excellency has committed suicide.? ' I sprang up, not knowing east from west or what I was doing. I then ran to the Governor's apartments ; and, just beyond the sitting-room, in front of the guardian god and close under the hedge, I found that he had spread a carpet, seated on which he had made a long narrow wound below his navel, and had then thrust the dagger through his throat up to the hilt. It was a magnificent *hara-kiri* ! The spirit had already departed. Watanabe tried to pull out the dagger, but it was fast clutched in the dead man's hand. What a pitiable sight ! Alas ! the day on which it pleased Heaven to allow so brave a gentleman to perish !."

Several of the military officers who had misbehaved on this occasion were afterwards condemned to commit *hara-kiri*, while the Daimyō of Saga, though resident in Yedo at the time of the *Phaeton's* appearance in Nagasaki, was imprisoned in his own *yashiki* for a space of 100 days, and required to pay an annual pension to the son of the dead Governor.

From Japanese sources we know that the Dutch had long been describing the English in the blackest of colours, dwelling especially upon all the enormities they had committed and were committing in Hindostan. This episode of the *Phaeton* did much to confirm the belief of the Tokugawa officials in the truth of the Dutch accounts. At the same time, the Hollanders seem to have exerted themselves to excite the suspicion of the Japanese against the Russians. In the fifth chapter of Golownin's narrative will be found some strange evidence in support of this charge.   The interpreter, Murakami, informed Golownin that the " Dutch had represented that Russia and England, then united against France and her allies, had determined to extend their power towards the East ; that England, acting by sea, and Russia by land, and reciprocally supporting each other, had for their ultimate object to divide China and Japan between them ".   Golownin asserts that when at Portsmouth in 1807, he incidentally obtained evidence from captured letters of the secretary of the Council at Batavia that Rezánov's mission had miscarried mainly on account of the manœuvres of the Dutch and their interpreters at Nagasaki.   Siebold must have been well acquainted with this passage.   In accounting for Rezánov's failure he even quotes some sentences from Golownin's *Narrative* which had been suppressed by the censor.[1]   As regards the Russians, however, the Bakufu authorities were considerably reassured when they obtained a declaration from the Governor of Siberia that Chowstoff's and Davidoff's depredations had never been sanctioned by the Russian Government, and that the Imperial Government disapproved of, and profoundly regretted, the events of 1806–7. This statement was obtained in a rather remarkable way.

Captain Golownin, in the warship *Diana*, had been dispatched on a cruise to survey the coasts of Yezo and chart the seas around the Kuriles, and landing on Kunashir with some eight or nine of his ship's company, he was seized by the Japanese in the summer of 1811.   He was sent to Hakodate, and from there to Matsumaye, where he was kept for about two years.   It was only when Captain Rikord (who was sent to rescue him) was able to furnish the Japanese authorities with the assurance alluded to that the Russian captives were released.   By this time captors and prisoners had learned to appreciate each other's good qualities ; at all events, in the formal address of farewell from the officials to Golownin, the following sentence occurs :—

" During your long residence here, such an intimacy has arisen between us, that we cannot help regretting the necessity of our separation." [2]

---

[1] Siebold, *Nippon*, vol. ii, pp. 164–5.   For Dutch double-dealing towards a projected Danish expedition to Japan in 1637, see Nachod, p. 256.   Rezánov afterwards blamed the Dutch for his failure ; and Langsdorff and Krusenstern both adopt the same view.   Siebold's loyalty to his employers, it may be remarked, was far greater than Kämpfer's ; indeed it now and then seems to betray him into special pleading on their behalf.

[2] Golownin's *Narrative* and Rikord's *Account* are interesting documents well worth a careful perusal.

The last paragraph in the document handed to Rikord by the Japanese Commissioners is worthy of remark, for it put an end to all intercourse between Russia and Japan for forty years—until Admiral Count Putiatin appeared at Nagasaki in 1853. The paragraph in question runs as follows :—

"Our countrymen wish to carry on no commerce with foreign lands, for we know no want of necessary things. Though foreigners are permitted to trade at Nagasaki, even to that harbour only those are admitted with whom we have for a long time maintained relations, and *we do not trade with them for the sake of gain, but for other important objects.* From the repeated solicitations which you have hitherto made to us, you evidently imagine that the customs of our country resemble those of your own ; but you are very wrong in thinking so. In future, therefore, it will be better to say no more about commercial intercourse."

In Golownin's *Narrative*, the real good-heartedness of the Japanese towards their captives becomes apparent in dozens of passages. At this time their attitude towards the Dutch in Deshima seems to have been considerate and generous, and to have fully deserved the panegyric it has elicited from Siebold.[1] At this time the Deshima trade had ceased entirely, and from 1809 to 1817 no Dutch vessel appeared in Nagasaki roadstead. The Hollanders could make no more presents either to the Shōgun or to the Governor and officials of Nagasaki, or to anyone else. The resources of the Factory were thoroughly exhausted, and its staff was reduced to the direst straits. In such circumstances the conduct of the Japanese did them honour, for the sympathy they extended to the Dutch was a truly practical one, and highly admirable. In 1813, however, there was one rather lively interlude in the dull monotony of these eight years, during which the Dutchmen in Deshima knew nothing of what was happening in the great outside world. Batavia had fallen into English hands on 8th August, 1811, and, until the treaty of 1814, Java was a British possession. Sir Stamford Raffles, its energetic Governor, turned his attention to Deshima and determined to get control of the Factory and of the Dutch trade with Japan. To quote Hildreth's summary of the incident :—

"Great was the delight of Doeff when, in the spring of 1813, two vessels appeared in the offing of Nagasaki, displaying the Dutch flag, and making the private signals agreed upon in 1809. A letter was brought on shore, announcing the arrival from Batavia of Heer Waardenaar (Doeff's predecessor as Director) to act as warehouse master, of Heer Cassa to succeed Doeff as Director, and of three assistants or

---

[1] Siebold, *Nippon*, vol. ii, p. 166.

clerks. A Japanese officer and one of the Dutch clerks were sent on board. The Japanese speedily returned, saying he recognized Waardenaar, who had declined, however, to deliver his papers except to Doeff personally, and that all the officers spoke English, whence he concluded that the ships must be chartered Americans. Doeff went on board, and was received by Waardenaar with such evident embarrassment that Doeff declined to open the package of papers he presented, except in Deshima, whither he was accompanied by Waardenaar. This package being opened was found to contain a paper signed ' Raffles, Lieutenant Governor of Java and its Dependencies' appointing Waardenaar and a Dr. Ainslie commissioners to Japan. In reply to his question, ' Who is Raffles ? ' Doeff learned that Holland had been annexed to France, and Java occupied by the English. Doeff patriotically refused to believe in the annexation of Holland to France, and in spite of all the efforts of Waardenaar to shake him, he declined obedience to an order coming from a colony in hostile occupation. His mind thus made up, Doeff called in the Japanese interpreters, and communicated to them the true state of the case. Alarmed for their own safety, they made to Waardenaar frightful representations of the probable massacre of the crews, and burning of the vessels, should the secret go any further, especially considering the hostile feelings towards the English excited by the proceedings of the *Phaeton* in 1808 ; and finally the commissioners were persuaded to enter into an arrangement by which Doeff was to remain as director and to dispose of the cargoes as usual, first paying out of the proceeds the debt (160,000 gulden) which, since 1807, the factory had been obliged to contract for its sustenance. Ainslie was also to remain as a factory physician, but passing as an American."

By this venture the English lost about 28,000 dollars. The elephant they brought as a present for the Shōgun was declined on the ground of the difficulty of transporting it to Yedo.[1]

" In 1814, a single ship was sent from Batavia with Heer Cassa again on board. He brought tidings of the insurrection in Europe against France, and relied upon the probable speedy restoration of Java to Holland as an argument for inducing Doeff to submit

---

[1] It is astonishing to find how quickly intelligence was transmitted in Japan even in those days. While the vessels were still in Nagasaki, Golownin was in Matsumaye ready to leave for Hakodate. One day Takahashi and Uyehara casually told him that two large Dutch ships laden with East India goods had arrived at Nagasaki from Batavia. " They gave us a minute description of these vessels, telling us their length, breadth, depth, burthen in tons, the number of the crew on board each, and to what nation each individual belonged. One of these vessels must have been very large, since it was upwards of 100 feet in length and had more than 100 men on board. An elephant which the Dutch had brought from the Island of Sumatra, as a present for the Japanese Emperor, was described with the greatest minuteness imaginable. No circumstance was omitted, the place of his nativity, his age, length, height, thickness, the food he was accustomed to consume, and how many times in the course of the day, and in what portions he was supplied with the different articles, were all carefully noted. A native of Sumatra, who was the keeper of the elephant, was described with corresponding precision." All this reminds us of Arai Hakuseki's meticulous details about Father Sidotti.

temporarily to the English—an object which Sir Stamford Raffles had very much at heart. When Doeff refused, Cassa resorted to intrigue. He gained over two of the interpreters, through whom he endeavoured to induce at Yedo a refusal to allow Doeff (whose term of office had already been so unusually protracted) to remain any longer as director. Doeff, however, got wind of this intrigue, frightened the two interpreters by threatening to tell the whole story to the Governor of Nagasaki, and finally carried the day. He paid, however, rather dearly for his obstinacy as Raffles sent no more ships, and Director Doeff was obliged to pass three years more without either goods or news, cooped up and kept on short allowance in his little island, with the satisfaction, however, that there, if nowhere else in the world, the flag of Holland still continued to wave."

In 1813, J. Cock Blomhoff, Doeff's assistant, had returned with the English vessels to Batavia. As he refused to forward Raffles's projects he was sent to England as a prisoner. On regaining his liberty he went home, and furnished the Dutch authorities with full information about the state of affairs in Japan ; and, in 1817, he reappeared in Nagasaki to relieve Doeff and take charge of the Dutch-Japan trade, now a monopoly of the Netherlands-India Government. Along with Blomhoff came several ladies, among them Mrs. Blomhoff with her infant child. This threw the Japanese officials into great consternation, and although Mrs. Blomhoff was ultimately allowed to land, she had to go back to Batavia with the returning ships. Probably the precedent of 1662 had been forgotten by both Japanese and Dutchmen. In 1818, and again in 1822, the new director proceeded to Yedo, where he met with an extremely cordial reception, and became exceedingly popular. On the last occasion he was able to obtain an increase to 11,000 piculs in the annual allowance of copper for export, at which figure it stood till 1828, when the diminished returns of the mines occasioned a reduction to 7,000 piculs. Inasmuch as one ship was sufficient for this lading, and as the Dutch obtained the copper at half the rate the Chinese paid for it (25 taels, which was in turn five taels under the current price in Japan), the reduction did not affect their profits materially, especially as their charges for presents and factory maintenance were considerably lessened at the same time. Camphor continued to be the only other considerable item among the exports, the average value of which, from 1820 to 1826, was 339,000 gulden, a little more than one-third of what it had been in Kämpfer's days, and one-ninth of what it had been in 1671. In the early 'forties there was a considerable drop in the value of imports.

In 1840, cloth and woollen goods were sold to the value of 111,786 gulden, but during the next six years the average annual sales only amounted to about 68,000 gulden. Mizuno, Echizen no Kami's drastic campaign against luxury in Yedo was evidently not without its effect upon the foreign trade of the empire.

Chinese competition in the supply of European wares, chiefly obtained through the English factory in Canton, was meanwhile giving the Dutch increasing trouble. No more than a dozen junks were now permitted entry, but the value of the maximum return freights that were allowed them might reach 900,000 taels, five or six times as much as the average value of the Dutch lading between 1820 and 1826. As much as 360,000 taels of this went in the form of copper ; the remainder had to be taken in marine produce and miscellaneous Japanese wares. The Chinese still, as in Kämpfer's time, found the stress of weather a very convenient excuse, and the people of the Satsuma sea-board still kept up their reputation as adepts in the art of smuggling. Others besides the Chinese would appear to have had illicit dealings with the men of Satsuma. Great quantities of Satsuma *soy* in neat little jars and bottles were finding a sale in Holland, and there is fairly good evidence to indicate that the *soy* was shipped from Ōshima, or from some other part of the Lūchūs. Even in Deshima itself, one interpreter was executed for smuggling, and another committed *hara-kiri* to escape the penalty for the same offence. The old private trade still flourished ; and it was in connexion with this that most of the smuggling took place. Many vain attempts were made to suppress it, even after it had been farmed out at 30,000 gulden annually for the benefit of those interested in it.

Siebold urges—and perhaps rightly—that the Dutch lost a great opportunity in 1814, when the United Provinces became a kingdom and William I ascended the throne of the Netherlands. In his famous instructions to the mission of 1649–50, Caron asserted that the Japanese had no respect for a republic, and the Portuguese and even Cocks were fully conscious of this fact, and took full advantage of it in the early seventeenth century. It might have been advisable to send a special mission to Yedo to make official announcement of the new order of things in the Netherlands, but nothing of the sort was done ; and although the Dutch East India Company had been dissolved in 1798, and all its territories declared national colonies, the missions to Yedo were still in the name of the defunct corporation, and matters in connexion with it remained in much the same condition as they were in the early days of Deshima. No exhibition of the clownish antics Kämpfer and his companions had to provide before the fifth Shōgun was now exacted but, apart from this, Siebold's account of the reception of the mission in 1826, differs but little from the extracts from Kämpfer's narrative cited in a previous chapter. Even the old instructions regarding the Portuguese were given at the audience of leave. In Deshima, too, things continued to move along in the same old traditional grooves, although there had been one innovation. The Director had no longer to return to Batavia and make way for a new man every year. Doeff's involuntary sojourn in Deshima may have had much to do with this change of a time-honoured prescription. The authorities in Nagasaki now professed a preference for the " old " officials in Deshima, that is, for those who were acquainted with, and readily accepted, the established routine, and had no idea of introducing innovations and reforms. Pestilent " reformers " were now and then banished from Japan and told to come no more. Siebold mentions van Sturler, Fisscher, and Nimen as having brought their fate upon themselves by an excess of zeal in the cause of honesty, and it was only by a seasonable change of tactics that the astute and far-seeing Meylan was able to remain in Deshima.

In the seventeenth century, when the Japanese became dissatisfied with the Portuguese, they encouraged their rivals, the Dutch and the English, to establish factories in Japan. In the first half of the nineteenth century they were now and then far from pleased with their prisoners in Deshima, but they cherished no thoughts of adopting the policy of Iyeyasu and his successors. Quite the contrary, indeed. The Russian attacks in the north, and the *Phaeton* episode in Nagasaki, had occasioned the utmost indignation, and the resentment was profound. For the next few years following these so-called outrages, coast-defence was the great problem ; but by the early 'twenties of the nineteenth century, attention to this had begun to relax. However, the whaling industry in neighbouring seas at that period commenced to be prosecuted with considerable vigour, and year after year whalers were to be seen off the Japanese coasts. Sometimes, they sent boats ashore to obtain water or supplies and then the local troops would be mobilized and the whole district thrown into the greatest commotion.

The Yedo Councillors were holding many conferences about this, when a very unpleasant episode was reported by the Satsuma authorities. In 1824 an English vessel appeared at Takara-shima to the south of Kagoshima Gulf and sent men ashore for provisions who acted with a high hand, slaughtering cattle and committing various other depredations. The islanders ran to arms, and in the hard-fought conflict that ensued, several were killed and wounded on both sides. This incident enabled the Bakufu to come to a definite decision, and on 4th April, 1825, the famous " Expulsion Decree " (*Uchi-harai-Rei*) was issued for promulgation throughout the empire. The text of it is as follows :—

" As to the mode of proceeding on the arrival of foreign vessels many proclamations have formerly been issued, and one was expressly issued in 1806 with respect to Russian ships. Also several years ago an English vessel committed outrages at Nagasaki (the *Phaeton*, in 1808) and in later years the English have visited the various ports in boats, demanding fire-wood, water, and provisions. In the past year, they landed forcibly, and seized rice and grain in the junks and cattle on the islands. The continuation of such insolent proceedings, as also the intention of introducing the Christian religion having come to our knowledge, it is impossible to look on with indifference. Not only England, but also the Southern Barbarians and Western Countries are of the Christian religion which is prohibited among us. Therefore, if in future foreign vessels should come near any port whatsoever, the local inhabitants shall conjointly drive them away ; but should they go away (peaceably) it is not necessary to pursue them. Should any foreigners land anywhere, they must be arrested or killed, and if the ship approaches the shore it must be destroyed."

In 1837 the enforcement of this " Expulsion Decree " occasioned some commotion in Japan and provoked considerable unfavourable comment abroad. Six years before, a Japanese junk was blown across to Queen Charlotte Island where the crew were rescued and ultimately sent to London and thence to Macao ; and some American philanthropists interested in mission work now fitted out a small vessel, the *Morrison*, named after the famous missionary, to convey these waifs back to Japan. On reaching Uraga, " the official visitors, discerning she was unarmed, at once showed their contempt and next day she was fired at with shotted guns." She then made for a point in Kagoshima Gulf ; a day or two she remained unmolested, but ultimately preparations were made to open fire, and before she could get under way a battery opened upon her. In both cases, the delay in opening fire had been occasioned by the local officials appealing to their respective headquarters for precise instructions as to how they were to act.[1]

The hesitation of the local authorities to act promptly on the " Expulsion Decree " of 1825, is perhaps not so very remarkable, for any mistake on their part in such a matter might cost them dear,[2] and they generally endeavoured to shirk all onerous responsibilities. What is remarkable is the vigorous protest this action of the authorities elicited from some of the Dutch scholars in Yedo, a topic that will be dealt with in the following chapter. Although these writers suffered for their temerity, their courageous stand was not without its effect.

In the *Yume Monogatari*, a pamphlet then published by Takano Chōei, much was said about the greatness of England and her power in Far-Eastern seas ; and as the pamphlet was read by officials as well as others, some of them began to be impressed with an exaggerated idea of the might of England, and a lively sense of the probable consequences of provoking her wrath. Shortly after this incident came the so-called " Opium War " with China (1840), the Treaty of Nanking, the cession of Hong-Kong, the opening of several Chinese ports to foreign trade, and the payment of an indemnity by China. All these incidents were duly embodied in the yearly reports of foreign occurrences which the Director of the Deshima Factory had to compile and send to the Governor of Nagasaki upon the arrival of the annual Dutch ship. In Yedo, these reports made a great impression upon Mizuno Tadakuni, then at the head of the Great Council, and he came to the conclusion

---

[1] An account of the *Morrison* episode will be found in the *Chinese Repository* for September and December, 1837. Its author was Dr. S. Wells Williams, a very distinguished American missionary and a brilliant Chinese scholar who was afterwards interpreter to the Perry expedition and, in subsequent years, official interpreter to the United States Legation at Peking, who was one of the thirty-seven people on board the *Morrison*. Some of his remarks are interesting : " A people who show the decision of character of the Japanese, silently erecting their batteries to drive away their enemies by force of arms, and bringing their cannon several miles to plant in a favourable position, are not to be lightly despised or to be insulted with impunity. If the immediate aggressor escapes, vengeance usually lights upon some unwary and innocent straggler, and the mutual hatred is thus increased. At Satsuma, a pilot is sent to bring the ship into an anchorage, and the officers are made acquainted with our object, which they apparently approve. It would seem that here too great distrust of the foreigners existed, from the report that the people took us for pirates ; and a rumour of such marauders must have reached their ears." Mr. Williams evidently knew nothing of the Takara-shima incident of 1824 ; and the Satsuma men, no doubt, retained a very lively recollection of it.

[2] A Governor of Nagasaki had been dismissed in 1639 for sending away a Portuguese vessel without having informed the Yedo authorities of her arrival.

that there would be wisdom in mollifying the harshness of the
" Expulsion Decree " of 1825.   Accordingly, in spite of much
opposition, he caused the following important document to be
distributed among the officials and feudatories :—

   " In accordance with the ordinance of 1825, all foreign vessels must
be driven away.   But now that the administration has reverted to the
principles of the Kyōhō-Kwansei periods, it is the Shōgun's gracious
will that all measures should be taken in a humane spirit.

   " It is not thought fitting to drive away all foreign ships irrespective
of their condition, in spite of their lack of supplies, or of their having
stranded, or their suffering from stress of weather.   In accordance with
the ordinance of 1806, after investigating the circumstances of each
case, you should, when necessary, supply them with food and fuel and
advise them to return, but on no account allow foreigners to land.

   " This does not mean that less attention is to be paid to coast defence.
Still greater care must be taken than before, both as regards armament
and men.   Even in case vessels sail along the coast to observe the
situation, you must still act in accordance with the gracious principles
of humanity, not being unreasonably disturbed by their proceedings.
If, however, after receiving supplies and instructions they do not withdraw, you will, of course, drive them away, adopting such measures
as are necessary.

   " As regards coast defence, other instructions will be issued."

   Next year (1843) the Deshima Director sent in a document
of very serious import.   It enlarged upon the power and commercial
prosperity of England, and the recovery of France since Waterloo
and said that these countries were on the point of sending vessels
to the Lūchūs to establish tradal relations there, and that they
might even go on to Japan.   In great anxiety over possible developments, the king of the Netherlands had determined to send a
mission to the Shōgun's Court, and that mission had already been
dispatched on board a national man-of-war.   It was desirable that
the envoy, who stood in quite a different position to the Deshima
Director, and who would be accompanied by a suite and an escort,
should be received with international courtesy, and should tender
his dispatches to the Shōgun in person.   When the purport of this
communication became generally known, there was a terrible
ferment.   Many advocated the repulse of the envoy by arms, and
the probability of a war with the other barbarians was eagerly
discussed.

   In the late summer of the following year (1844) the *Palembang*,
under the command of Captain Koop of the Dutch navy, made her
appearance at Nagasaki, but the envoy was not permitted to
proceed to Yedo and could meet no higher official than the local

Governor who was charged with the duty of receiving and entertaining him. The king's dispatch which he bore was handed to the Governor for transmission to Yedo, where Mizuno had been recalled to the Rōjū for the purpose of dealing with the exigencies of the situation. By this time, the Bakufu had imposed its censorate upon the Dutch books and Dutch scholars, and all communications from the Dutch; but in spite of this the purport of the royal dispatch leaked out among the Daimyō, and became the subject of much heated discussion.[1]

Nearly a year passed before any reply to the dispatch was vouchsafed, it was only on 5th July, 1845, that the Great Councillors put their names and seals to the answer; and before this date Mizuno had already fallen for the second and last time. To the implied suggestion that it would be well to reopen Japan to foreign intercourse, the Rōjū returned a *non possumus*.

"Although the suggestions offered are worthy of adoption, there are reasons why this cannot be. When the founder of the dynasty entered upon his career, intercourse and trade with countries beyond the sea were in an unsettled condition. Later, when the time came for determining with what countries communication should be permitted, intercourse was limited to Korea and Lūchū, and trade to your Excellencies' country and China. Aside from these countries, all communication was strictly disallowed. If now, it were desired to extend these limits, it would be in contravention of the ancestral law. Now, since the ancestral law has been once fixed, posterity must obey. Henceforth, pray cease correspondence. If not, although it should be attempted a second or a third time, communications cannot be received. Pray do not be surprised at this. Letters from your Excellencies will have the same treatment and receive no response . . . Pray communicate this to your Excellencies' Sovereign."

In August, 1609, Iyeyasu made no trouble about entering into personal communication with a " King of Holland " who was no " King " at all, but merely a Count of Nassau. Now, when a real King of the Netherlands goes so far as to send a special envoy with a dispatch to his " Friend, the very noble, most serene, and all-powerful sovereign of the Great Empire of Japan " the *fainéant*, Iyeyoshi, thinks it beneath his dignity to vouchsafe any reply from himself. His ministers, the Great Councillors, address a communication to the " *Oranda Koku-Seifu Shokō Kakka* " which Dr. Greene translates " The Government of Holland ". And in their reply they

---

[1] For the full text of the dispatch, and the Bakufu's reply, see Dr. Greene's paper in *T.A.S.J.*, vol. xxxiv, pt. iv.

assure the Government of Holland that " our Lord in no wise fails in respect towards Your Excellencies' Sovereign, but on the contrary, *deeply appreciates his sincere loyalty* ". One other point has to be noted in this Bakufu dispatch. Christianity had been sternly proscribed by definite enactments in the seventeenth century, and the Spaniards and Portuguese had been banished for ever, as it was supposed, from Japanese soil, but the small officials of the Bakufu would search the Tokugawa statute-books in vain for any decree limiting the intercourse of the empire to Koreans, Lūchūans, Chinese, and Hollanders. As pointed out in a preceding chapter, the " ancestral law " on this point was a figment of the latter-day Bakufu imagination.

Meanwhile the Dutch Factor's warning that French and English warships might be expected in the Lūchūs was soon shown to have been based on substantial grounds. In that very year (1843) the British began surveying operations among the southern islands of the Lūchū chain, and the work was continued during 1844 and 1845. In 1846 a medical missionary, Dr. Bettleheim, was permanently installed at Naha in the main island. Previously to this, one of the survey ships, the *Samarang*, had entered Nagasaki harbour, and had been freely supplied with such provisions as she needed. The Japanese informed the captain that they knew perfectly well of his operations in the Lūchūs, and that they had been apprised of his intended visit by the Dutch. With great difficulty permission to land was obtained to make some astronomical observations, but the Japanese officers earnestly begged that this might not be repeated till they could consult their superiors in Yedo, urging as a reason their own danger of getting into serious trouble. Four years later on (1849) the British surveying ship *Mariner* entered Yedo Bay and charted the anchorage off Uraga. The captain (Matheson) sent his card to the Governor with a note in Chinese, proposing to wait upon him, but the Governor replied that it was contrary to law for foreigners to land, and that he should lose his life if he allowed the captain to come ashore or to proceed any higher up the Bay. Thereupon Matheson went round to the Shimoda coast, off which he spent a week, and actually once went ashore. He was visited on board by Egawa, the Daikwan of Nirayama, then a commissioner for coast defence, who caused the vessel to be supplied with fish, and boats to tow her out. In both cases the British were very courteously treated ; at Nagasaki they had been strongly impressed with the dignified yet respectful behaviour of the Japanese.

Far different was the experience of the officers of the first French war vessel that ever dropped anchor in a Japanese port. When Admiral Cécille, in command of a frigate and two corvettes, arrived in Nagasaki on 29th July, 1846, he was treated with extreme rudeness by the officials who came on board.[1] On the second day he felt constrained to curb their insolence by assuming a rather haughty tone. The reason for the truculent demeanour on the part of the petty officials was that the Japanese were fully aware of what the Admiral had just been doing in Lūchū, and that they regarded him as a dangerous aggressor. Indeed, all unknown to himself, Admiral Cécille had thrown the supreme council of the empire, and even the Shōgun himself, into the greatest perturbation.

Of late years the Roman Catholic missionaries in China and Korea had been revolving many plans for regaining a footing in Japan. Now, the gallant Admiral was a staunch supporter of missionary enterprise, and the missionaries in turn exerted themselves strenuously to find fit and proper interpreters for him. Detained in China by the Lagrené embassy, the Admiral determined to detach a vessel to reconnoitre the Lūchūs. A Roman Catholic priest was left at Naha by this vessel, ostensibly for the purpose of learning the language so as to be able to serve as interpreter for the Admiral when he paid his intended visit later on. This was in April, 1844, but there was no appearance of the Admiral until June, 1846. Meanwhile the missionary, M. Forcade, had had his efforts restricted and impeded by a series of tortuous devices, some of them amusing enough. In 1844 Duplan, the Commander of the *Alcmène*, told the Lūchūan authorities that the French " Emperor " wished to enter into a treaty of commerce with them, and that the Admiral would presently arrive to settle its terms. On reaching Naha, Cécille delivered a rather lengthy document in which it was proposed in the name of the " Emperor " of the French that Lūchū should enter into a treaty similar to the one that had just been concluded between France and China. The French had been made participants in the advantages secured by the treaty of Nanking, and had obtained the free exercise of the Christian religion. Missionaries were to be admitted into China, and the old Churches,

---

[1] See account in Marnas' *La Religion de Jésus ressuscitée au Japon*, vol. i, p. 146. For events in Lūchū see same work, vol. i, pp. 91–188.

which had not been turned into public edifices, were to be restored to them. After a seven weeks' stay at Naha the Admiral, who then took M. Forcade away with him, obtained a guarantee that the two new priests he was to leave behind should not have their personal liberty interfered with in any way. But the islanders had implored him not to force any treaty of commerce upon them. They were poor, and had few surplus products ; such slender outside supplies as they needed came from the isle of Fu-kia-la (?) which belonged to Japan ; and if the Japanese heard that Lūchū had made a treaty with France, they would stop trading, and then how could the Lūchūans find the means of furnishing the tribute to China ? Cécille was not satisfied with this unexpected refusal, which, he said, made it necessary for him to refer the matter to the " Emperor ", and he promised that, within a year, a vessel would arrive to announce His Majesty's decision.

The anomalous position of the " king " of Lūchū has already been adverted to. All real power was in the hands of a Satsuma Resident, who it may be remarked, retired to the depths of the mountains on the rare occasions when a Chinese envoy appeared. It was this Resident who stood behind the Lūchūan authorities in their negotiations with Cécille. Through Kagoshima and the Satsuma *yashiki* in Yedo, the Bakufu was promptly informed of what was occurring, and its instructions were requested. Shimadzu Nariakira (Saihin), the heir to the Satsuma fief, already recognized as one of the ablest men of his day, saw in this conjuncture of affairs a great opportunity. He was convinced that the old seclusion policy would presently have to be abandoned, and he was anxious that the change should be made with as little friction and disturbance as possible. A beginning could readily be made with Lūchū, which, although nominally independent, was really an appanage of the Satsuma fief, and thus indirectly under Bakufu control. Personally he would welcome the conclusion of a treaty between France and Lūchū, for that would mean that Satsuma would furnish all the staples of export, and that she could import European products freely. His views on this point, as well as on a good many others, were not generally acceptable in Kagoshima, for the Conservative faction was very powerful in the Satsuma fiefs, and Nariakira had to beat down a strong opposition there. His Liberal views actually endangered his succession to the headship of the great southern fief : a strong party looked askance at his partiality for foreigners

and foreign science, and wished to have Nariakira set aside in favour
of his younger brother, Hisamitsu. Nariakira was quite aware that
the Bakufu was helpless in this Lūchū question. With the old law
forbidding the construction of warships of more than 500 *koku*
burthen, Japan could do absolutely nothing against the small
French and English squadrons now and then appearing at Naha.
Besides, China was supposed to know nothing about the Japanese
connexion with Lūchū, and it was highly desirable that she should
have no opportunity of learning about it. Nariakira was anxious
that Satsuma, or rather he himself, should be given a free hand to
cope with the exigencies of the situation. The Bakufu submitted
the question to a meeting of the Three Magistracies (Jisha, Machi,
and Kanjō-Bugyō) ; and this assembly proved hostile to Nariakira's
propositions. At the same time, Hayashi, the Rector of the
University, and Tsutsui had been ordered to investigate the matter,
and render an opinion as to what should be done, and they reported
in favour of Nariakira's suggestions. Nariakira meanwhile seems
to have won over Abé Masahiro, the head of the Rōjū, to his views.
At all events, the Shōgun presently took the unusual step of summoning Nariakira and his father, Lord Nariaki, to an audience, and
giving them a free hand to deal with the Lūchūan question, only
they " were to be careful to do nothing that might breed future
trouble ". This incident was supposed to be a State secret, but
like most State secrets of the time, it leaked out, and greatly excited
the wrath of Lord Nariaki of Mito when it reached his ears.
Nariakira, like his ancestor Takahisa in Xavier's time, was eager
for foreign trade, but he wanted nothing to do with foreign religion.
Thus, the two French missionaries (one of them soon died) in Naha
found that they could not make a single convert, and on 27th August,
1848, the last of them left for Manila. Intelligence of this was
promptly transmitted to Yedo. To the Bakufu councillors it was
welcome news indeed, for the incident had caused them the gravest
anxiety.

Although Lūchū entered into no treaty with France, yet in
Nariakira's time (1851–8) a considerable Satsuma foreign trade
was maintained by way of Lūchū. Arms and machinery were the
chief items of import. In 1857, Nariakira, with the sanction of the
Bakufu, had completed preparations for opening Naze in Ōshima
to foreign trade, but his death, in 1858, threw the power into the
hands of the reactionary element in the fief. He had actually

engaged the Dutch to bring a cargo to Naze ; these imports were sent to Kagoshima and thence to Nagasaki ; while the ships and guns sent by the French to Lūchū were disposed of at Foochow through the Lūchūans. It is to be noted that through this inter-course with the outside world through Lūchū, Nariakira and his ministers became fairly well apprised of events abroad, and just before his death, Nariakira had formed the project of secretly dispatching a number of Satsuma youths to prosecute their studies in Europe ; a project that was only realized in 1865.

England so far had shown no inclination to question the right of the Japanese to adhere to their traditional policy of seclusion. Neither had France done so any further than by pressing a treaty of commerce upon the reluctant Lūchūans. Admiral Cécille had really all unwittingly done a great deal to open a new tradal communication with the hermit empire. Holland, as we have just seen, had gone as far as she could possibly go in persuading the Bakufu that the time for the amendment of their " old law " was approaching, and that it would be better for Japan to amend the " old law " of her own free-will, and on her own initiative than to subject herself to the humiliation of having to abrogate it under armed pressure from abroad. The well-meant advice was fruitless ; and within eight years, in 1853, the Bakufu found that it had to deal with a diplomat who had something more than the mere beauties of moral suasion to rely upon in case of need.

CHAPTER XV

DUTCH LEARNING IN JAPAN

THE native accounts of the rise and progress of the study of Dutch, and hence of Western science, in Japan, are in their way no less interesting than the most thrilling romances penned and published during the Yedo period. The unfortunate thing, however, is that they do not always agree in their details with the data which have been incidentally furnished us by the residents of Deshima. Yet this, perhaps is nothing very strange, when we remember certain of the characteristics of the Japanese histories of the events immediately preceding the Revolution of 1868.[1] However, there is no reason to question the good faith of Sugita, the author of *The Beginning of the Study of Dutch.* As regards the immediate events, " quorum magna pars fuit," in the latter half of the eighteenth century, Sugita's testimony may be accepted as unimpeachable. It is in the account of the state of affairs preceding his own days that some of his statements would seem to call, if not for correction, at all events for qualification.

We are told that :—

---

[1] A Dutch writer on the Arima Rebellion (1637–8), adverting to the failure of the Japanese historians to allude to the assistance then rendered by Koeckebacker and the Hollanders, explains it by the jealousy displayed by the Japanese generally when there is any question of acknowledging foreign aid or influence, and adds :—" Thus, for instance, it happens but rarely that the Japanese author of the *Kinsé-shi-riyaku* (translated from the Japanese by Mr. E. M. Satow, Yokohama, 1876) recognizes the influence and aid rendered on many occasions by the Dutch at Nagasaki. The efforts made by the Hollanders before and in 1849 to open the country for the world ; the autographic letter addressed to this effect to the Shōgun by King William II ; the subsequent efforts made by the chiefs at Deshima, Messrs. Levysohn, F. A. Rose, J. H. Donker-Curtius ; the services rendered by the two Dutch naval expeditions, under Pelsrycken in 1855–7, and Huyssen van Kattendyke in 1857-61 ; the introduction at Nagasaki of the first steam-engine, foreign printing presses, the art of photography, telegraphy, foreign medicine and sciences ; and the names of O. Mohnike (1849), J. H. van den Broek (1854), H. Hardes (1857), A. A.s' Grauwen (1855), H. O. Wichers (1857), Pompe van Meerdervdort (1857), and many others are forgotten or ignored by Japanese historians."

Siebold also gives an amusing illustration of this. In 1825, the Netherlands-India Government sent two of their new field-pieces—six-pounders—with all their accessories as a present to the Shōgun. On the part of the Shōgun this present was officially declined, while a certain Takaki, commander of the guard at Nagasaki, contrived to procure them secretly.

" The eighth Shōgun, Yoshimune (1716–44), being much interested in astronomy, and learning that the Dutch were proficient in that science, summoned one Nishikawa, a native of Nagasaki, to be questioned ; that upon this the interpreters Nishi, Yoshio, and others applied to the Government for permission to learn to read and write Dutch, and that on the permission being granted in the period of Kiōhō (1716-35) the Dutch language was then for the first time learned from books."

That the last assertion at all events, is erroneous we learn incidentally from Kämpfer. His statement on this particular matter is a very brief one, but the whole long paragraph in which it occurs throws so much light upon the relations between the Dutch and the Japanese in 1691 and 1692—three to four decades before the alleged beginning of the study of written Dutch in Japan —that it may not be amiss to reproduce it here in full. He tells us that it was his object to get all the knowledge he possibly could of the present state and past history of Japan, and that in achieving it the difficulties he had to encounter were immense. The Japanese officers with whom the Dutch came in contact were all bound by an oath, renewed every year, not to talk with the Dutch, not to make any disclosures to them regarding the domestic affairs of the country, its religion or its politics ; and, furthermore, they were also bound by oath to watch and report each other—which fear of being informed against was indeed their chief dread and restraint. Kämpfer's own description of them is as follows :—

" Naturally the Japanese are, their pride of warlike humour set aside, as civil, as polite and curious a nation as any in the world, naturally inclined to commerce and familiarity with foreigners, and desirous to excess to be informed of their histories, arts, and sciences. But, as we are only merchants, whom they place in the lowest scale of mankind, and as the narrow inspection we are kept under must naturally lead them to some jealousy and mistrust, so there is no other way to gain their friendship and to win them over to our interest but a willing-ness to comply with their desire, a liberality to please their avaricious inclinations, and a submissive conduct to flatter their vanity. 'Twas by this means I worked myself into such a friendship and familiarity with my interpreters and the officers of our island, who daily came over to us, as I believe none before me could boast of, ever since we have been put under such narrow regulations. Liberally assisting them as I did with my advice and medicines, with what information I was able to give them in astronomy and mathematics, and with a cordial and plentiful supply of European liquors, I could also in my turn freely put to them what questions I pleased about the affairs of their country, whether relating to the government in civil or ecclesiastical affairs, to the customs of the natives, to the natural and political history ; *and there was none that ever refused to give me all the information he could when we were alone, even of things which they are strictly charged to keep secret.* The private informations thus procured from those who came to visit me were of great use to me in collecting materials for my intended history of this country ; but yet they fell far short of being entirely satisfactory, and I should not, perhaps, have been able to compass that design if I had not by good luck met with other opportunities. and in particular the assistance of a discreet young man, by whose means I was richly supplied with whatever information I wanted concerning the affairs of Japan. He was about twenty-four years of age, well versed in the Chinese and Japanese languages, and very desirous of improving himself. Upon my arrival he was appointed to wait upon me as my servant, and at the same time to be *by me instructed in physic and surgery.* The Ottona, who is the chief officer of our island (Deshima), having been attended by him under my inspection in a serious illness, suffered him to continue in my service during the whole time of my abode in the country, which was two years, and to attend me in our journeys to Court, consequently four times, almost from one end of the empire to the other—a favour seldom granted to young men of his age, and never for so long a time. As I could not well have attained my end without giving him a competent knowledge of the Dutch language, I instructed him therein with so much success that in a year's time *he could* WRITE *and* READ *it better than any of our interpreters.* I also *gave him all the information I could in anatomy and physic,* and further allowed him a handsome yearly salary to the best of my ability. In return I employed him to procure me as ample accounts as possible of the then state and condition of the country, its government, the Imperial Court, the religions established in the Empire, the history of former ages, and remarkable daily occurrences. There was not a book I desired to see on these and other subjects which he did not bring me, and explain to me out of it whatever I wanted to know. And because he was obliged in several things to inquire or to borrow, or to buy of other people, I never dismissed him without providing him with money for such purposes, besides his yearly allowance. So expensive, so difficult a thing it is to foreigners, ever since the shutting up of the Japanese empire, to procure any information about it." [1]

---

[1] In Kämpfer's time there were eight interpreters employed in Deshima—all living on fees and presents and perquisites from the Dutch. The position of the chief of these was worth about 3,000 taels—say £750 or £800 ; of a subordinate interpreter about half that sum. Then there were also eight *apprentices* or *learning interpreters,* who went to the Dutchmen every day to learn Dutch and *Portuguese,* "as well as the art and mystery of dealing with foreigners." Besides, there were more than 100 so-called *house interpreters* employed by private Dutchmen in their own houses. They were merely spies, for scarcely one in ten of them understood a word of Dutch.

"Two fundamental maxims the interpreters go upon," writes Kämpfer, "to do what lies in their power insensibly to increase the yearly expenses of the Dutch to the advantage of their countrymen as becomes true patriots ; to conceal as much as possible all the tricks and cheats they perpetually play upon us, lest the natives should come to know them. Both these ends they endeavour to obtain by confining us still more and more, looking upon this as the surest means to keep us ignorant of the language of the country, and to prevent all conversation and familiarity with the natives. If there be any of our people that hath made any considerable progress in the Japanese languages, they are sure under some pretext or other to obtain an order from the Governors to expel him from the country."

The last clause italicised in the foregoing extract would seem to invalidate not only the assertion that the study of written Dutch began only between 1716 and 1735 but also the statements that,

"till then medical students in Nagasaki could only take down what the foreign physician imparted to them orally, and that even the interpreters were not allowed to study Dutch, but noted in *kana* what they heard."

The existence of Kämpfer's discreet young man of twenty-four, to whom the worthy doctor gave all the information he could in anatomy and physic, is also not a little awkward for Sugita's contention that down to 1771 no Japanese had had correct ideas on the structure of the human frame. However, this young man seems to have taken such knowledge as he possessed to the grave with him, for in 1775, eighty-three years after Kämpfer had left Japan, Thunberg in Yedo,

"found that the Japanese doctors knew nothing of anatomy or physiology, and were ignorant of the circulation of the blood, feeling the pulse for a quarter of an hour first in one arm and then in the other, not knowing that both beat alike."

This foreign evidence would also appear to tell somewhat against the absolute correctness of some other very important statements in Sugita's book, as will be seen presently.

But, indeed, owing perhaps to a not unnatural desire to appropriate an ample share of the credit that subsequently attached to those that played the *rôle* of pioneers in the introduction of Dutch learning into Japan, we meet with not a few puzzling discrepancies in the various documents examined in connexion with the matter. From one source, for example, we learn that the Shōgun, Yoshimune (1716–44), procured a European almanac and *had it translated by a certain Nakane Genkei*. Then we learn elsewhere that the same Shōgun, having obtained several other Dutch books, was so interested with their engravings that he wished to know the meaning of the explanatory text, and commissioned the Government librarian, Aōki Bunzō, who was continually urging the benefit to be derived from the study of Dutch books, to apply himself to the study of the foreign language. Accompanied by his friend Noro, he went year after year to visit the Dutch when they came to Yedo, but progress was slow. At last, in 1744, or shortly afterwards, they were ordered to Nagasaki to study under the interpreters Nishi and Yoshio, but the results of several years' work there were excessively meagre. By the end of his stay Aōki had acquired a knowledge of about 400 words of daily use, of the various shapes of capitals and of small letters, of the foreign way of spelling monosyllables, together with the method of combining syllables into words. Before his return to Yedo, Yoshimune had died (1751), " and his position was not the same as formerly, for he found himself without a teacher, without fellow-learners, and without books to pursue his studies. He could on this account do no more than publish the books *Dutch Letters*, *Dutch Conversation*, and others.

From what we glean from foreign sources we cannot help suspecting that the Nagasaki interpreters had been somewhat slack in their pedagogic office. Probably they had no desire to see a knowledge of Dutch become general in the empire, for in such a development they no doubt saw a menace to their own importance. The language of Nishi to Mayeno, a later pupil of Aōki's, is certainly very strange, as may be judged from Sugita's account of the matter :—

" I do not remember exactly when it was, but early in the period of Meiwa (1764–7), one spring when the Dutch had come as usual to pay their respects to the Shōgun, Mayeno came to my house, and, on my inquiring whither he was bound, said that he was going to the Dutch quarters to have a talk with the interpreter, and if he favoured it, to begin the study of that language. When we arrived at our destination, we laid our plan before Nishi, the chief interpreter of the year. After hearing what we had to say, he replied discouragingly : ' It is entirely useless for you to try. It is not by any means an easy thing to understand their speech. For instance, if we want to ask what drinking water or wine is, we have no means but to begin by gesture. If it is wine, we first imitate pouring wine into a cup, and then, lifting it up to the mouth, ask what that is. They will say " Drink ". But when we want to know what drinking *much* or *little* is we have no means of asking . . . I was born in a family of interpreters, and have been used to these things all my life. Yet I am fifty years old now, and I understand for the first time the meaning of the word " To like " on this journey. . . . It is by such a tedious process that even we who must see the Dutch every day have to learn. You who live in Yedo must not hope to do much. For this reason two gentlemen, Aōki and Noro, who apply themselves very hard, cannot make any progress. It is by far the best for you not to begin at all.' I do not know what Mayeno thought, but I gave up entirely the idea of undertaking such a troublesome task."

Now there is very strong reason to believe that, to put it mildly, the crafty Nishi was here playing the *rôle* of a diplomat in the interests of that close corporation of which he was the chief. Certainly it is somewhat strange, in view of Nishi's assertion, to find that while in the days of Kämpfer (1691–2) not one in ten of the hundred odd so-called house interpreters in Deshima could understand a word of Dutch, in Thunberg's time (1775–6), only a decade or so after this Yedo episode, the native servants of the Hollanders " had learned to speak the Dutch language ! " At the same time the Dutchmen were strictly prohibited from learning Japanese. We are also told that the interpreters, having adopted the practice of medicine after the European manner, were very inquisitive as to matters of physic and natural history, and very anxious to obtain European books, *which they studied diligently* ! Again, a little later (1779–84), Titsingh was able to make translations of some Japanese books with the aid of the Japanese interpreters. " I found," he says, " among the interpreters belonging to our factory four individuals sufficiently well-informed for my purpose." And from Arai Hakuseki's *Seiyō Kibun*, published in 1712, we learn that the Japanese interpreters in Deshima were then tolerably efficient at least. In view of all these considerations it is somewhat to be feared that in his interview with Mayeno and Sugita, the worthy Nishi, for reasons best known to himself, was a trifle over-modest as regards the extent of his linguistic acquirements. It is certainly suggestive to find that about this time one of the Nishi family of interpreters at Nagasaki contrived to obtain a position as physician to the Shōgun, thanks to his knowledge of Dutch medicine and surgery.

However, Mayeno (1722–1803) was not to be baulked in his project. Like his junior, Sugita, he was a physician in the service of Okudaira, Daimyō of Nakatsu, in Buzen, one of the few Liberal and progressive feudal lords of the time. After some tuition from Aōki, he was sent by this Daimyō to learn Dutch at Nagasaki, whence he returned with a knowledge of some 600 or 700 words. It would appear that the interpreters adopted the same sort of tactics towards him as they had in the case of Aōki, for we are told that " he once more went to Nagasaki, but owing to the fact that the interpreters knew only a few words, and that none were able to read books or to translate, although for several years he sought from them a more perfect knowledge, he failed to acquire anything but the mere elements of the Dutch language ". Finally he *secretly acquired a translated vocabulary* and several medical works, with which he returned to Yedo.

It is at this point that the real thrilling interest of Sugita's

recital begins. One of Mayeno's and Sugita's friends, Nakagawa,
—like themselves a doctor in the service of the Daimyō of Nakatsu—
was keenly interested in the products of different countries, and
was a constant visitor at the quarters of the Dutch whenever they
came to Yedo. One day in 1771 the interpreter exhibited two
Dutch books on anatomy which were for sale, and he took them
home and showed them, among others, to Sugita. The latter, who
could not read a word, was struck by the fact that the illustrations
of bones and organs represented them to be very different from
what he had believed them to be. He wished to buy the book but
was too poor. Fortunately, however, he succeeded in persuading
a *karō* (councillor) of the clan to pay the price from the public
treasury of the fief.[1] Ever after this Sugita longed for an opportunity
to test which of the theories was correct.

He had not long to wait for the *experimentum crucis*, for, as
chance would have it, he was shortly afterwards invited to witness
a dissection which was to take place on the public execution ground
of Kozukappara, near Asakusa. Thither on the appointed day he
repaired with several friends, among them Nakagawa and Mayeno,
the latter of whom brought with him a Dutch book on anatomy
he had purchased while he was in Nagasaki. On examination this
turned out to be another copy of the work the Daimyō had lately
bought for Sugita. When the grisly function performed by the
public executioner (an *eta* who had some experience in such work)
was over, the spectators found that, worthless as may have been
the life of the old crone who furnished the *corpus vile* for the operation, her death had proved of the utmost service to the country.
As Sugita, Nakagawa and Mayeno walked homewards they talked
earnestly.

" Shame that they should have lived all their lives as physicians
and not know till now the construction of the human body on which
the science of medicine was necessarily founded. If they could under-

---

[1] Dr. Mitsukuri, whose synopsis of Sugita's book has been used here, writes
in a footnote : " I have the pleasure of knowing a descendant of Mayeno. He
once showed me a book which belonged to his illustrious ancestor, and which,
I believe, was this very Anatomy mentioned above. It was carefully kept in a box
of *kiri* (name of a kind of wood), wrapped in a purple *fukusa*. It was, I should say,
about 4 inches by 6 in breadth and length and 2 in thickness. My friend told
me that it cost 200 *rios* ; and as Mayeno was too poor to buy it, he had the price
paid at the cost of his *daimyō*, of whom he seems to have been a favourite,
and who seems to have appreciated him fully. The book was yellow with time,
and looked as if it was not worth a quarter of a dollar."   *T.A.S.J.*, vol. v, pt. i.
Dr. Mitsukuri was himself a son of a student of Dutch.—L. H.

stand the true principles of anatomy from the real objects they had just seen, if they could translate this book which they had obtained so luckily, they would do an immense service to the country, and would not have lived in this world in vain. So they went on, and when they separated for the night they had come to the agreement that they would try their best to master the strange language, and that as such things were the better the sooner begun, they would commence the very next day." *T.A.S.J.*, vol. v, pt. i.

When they set about the task they found it " was like managing a ship out on the ocean without a rudder ". Mayeno naturally was chosen the leader, and the other two undertook to learn from him the little he already knew. This was soon done, and they then proceeded to attack the book. In it there was a chart of the exterior of the human body, with the names of the different parts. Now they, knowing the corresponding Japanese names, could compare them together, and thus get at least a foothold which might enable them to proceed from the exterior to the internal construction of the body. Writes Sugita :—

" At that time we did not know anything about such auxiliary words as *de, het, als*, and *welke*, and therefore, though we might occasionally meet with words which we knew, we could not make any connected sense out of them. For instance, such a simple sentence as ' the eyebrow is hair growing a little above the eye ' was all confusing, and we had to spend a long spring day, even till dark, thinking and thinking as hard as we could. One day, when we came to the nose, it said that it was the thing *verheven*. We did not then have any dictionary, but in looking over the list of words which Mayeno had brought from Nagasaki, it said that the tree is *verheven* when a branch is cut off ; and also that when a garden is swept and the dirt put together, it is *verheven*. As usual, we fell to thinking, but could not make it out. A bright thought came to me that when the tree whose branch has been cut off heals, the place is slightly elevated ; and again, that the dirt accumulated will, of course be ' elevated '. Then the word must mean ' elevated '. All agreed that this was quite reasonable, and decided that *verheven* should be translated ' elevated '. The feeling which I experienced then cannot be told. I felt as if I had obtained a whole castle full of precious stones."

It is interesting to observe that in this enterprise " the help of the interpreters was not desired ". That may have been so for one, or some, or all of several reasons. Mayeno may have discovered that these gentlemen always made a point of keeping their knowledge of Dutch to themselves. Or he may really have been deceived by their shamming ignorance so far as to regard them as grossly incompetent. What is more likely, perhaps, is that this company of Yedo scholars wished to have the whole and sole credit of introducing and spreading Dutch scholarship and Dutch science among their countrymen. Thus, unaided, in a little over a year they were able to get over ten lines of coarse print in a day, and four years after beginning the actual work of translation Sugita had a work on anatomy ready for publication. The manuscript of this work had been rewritten ten times! Meanwhile, long before this, other enthusiasts had joined the original trio of pioneers, among them Katsuragawa, the Shōgun's Court-surgeon. The latter, however, was certainly not without assistance from one of the most distinguished European scientists of the time. When Thunberg arrived in Yedo on 28th April, 1776, we are told that "the first who called upon the Dutch were five physicians and two astronomers, prompted especially by Thunberg's scientific reputation which the interpreters had noised abroad. Two of the doctors could speak Dutch—one of them tolerably well." They also had some knowledge of natural history, collected partly from Chinese and Dutch books, and partly from the Dutch physicians who had visited Yedo, but who frequently had not been very well able to instruct them, as they were often, to use Thunberg's expression, "little better than horse-doctors."

"One of the two Japanese, quite a young man, was the Emperor's body-physician; the other, somewhat older and better informed, was physician to one of the chief princes." The former of these was Katsuragawa; the latter Nakagawa. "Both were good-natured, acute, and lively. They attached themselves to Thunberg with great zeal, coming to see him every day and often staying late at night. Though wearied with their questions, yet so insinuating were they in all their manners and so anxious to learn, that the Swedish scholar found much pleasure in their society. They had a number of Dutch works on botany, medicine, and surgery, and Thunberg sold them others. They were particularly struck with the fine set of surgical instruments which he had brought from Amsterdam and Paris."

Just before Thunberg's departure from Yedo, at the request of his two pupils in medicine, he gave them a certificate, in Dutch, of their proficiency, with which they were as highly delighted as ever a young doctor was with his diploma. A warm friendship had sprung up between him and them, and, even after Thunberg's return to Europe, a correspondence was kept up and presents exchanged for some years, down at least to the publication of his travels.[1] From this it would appear that the so-called pioneers

---

[1] Thunberg (1743–1828) had been a pupil of Linnæus, whom he succeeded in the Chair of Botany in Upsala University in 1784. At the date of his death he was an honorary member of no fewer than sixty-six scientific societies.

of Dutch learning in Japan, most diligent and devoted men as they were, were not quite so self-sufficing or so unaided as Sugita would have his readers believe they were.

Be that as it may, however, the fortunes of the original trio are worth following. Nakagawa died in 1781 without achieving anything very remarkable. Sugita's work on anatomy, when published, was not only left untouched by the censor, but copies of it were accepted by the Shōgun and the chief Court nobles of Kyōto; while, later on, the author was appointed head of the new hospital and medical school established in Yonezawa in Northern Japan by the Daimyō, Uyesugi Yōzan, perhaps the greatest reformer and the ablest administrator of his times. As for Mayeno, he devoted himself to Dutch scholarship generally, and before his death in 1803 had published a number of compilations from the Dutch which contributed not a little to intensify the interest of his countrymen in Western science and in the affairs of Europe.

" Intensify " in the last sentence we write purposely, for, in spite of Sugita's assertions, it is a mistake to suppose that the Nakatsu trio of so-called pioneers constituted the only centre from which an interest in foreign affairs was diffused throughout the empire. For example, we know that one Hayashi Shihei (1738–93), a *samurai* of Sendai, went three times—in 1775, 1777, and 1782—to Nagasaki to acquire information about Europe from the Dutchmen at first hand. There he became exceedingly friendly with the occupants of Deshima, and he was sufficiently honest to acknowledge the extent of his obligations to them for information and instruction He was especially impressed by what he learned about the encroachments of Russia in Asia, and early discerning a danger threatening Yezo (Hokkaidō) from that source, he endeavoured to rouse his countrymen to a sense of it in two remarkable publications. The first of these, the *Sangoku Tsuran* (" Exhaustive View of Three Countries "), finished in 1785, and printed in the following year, dealt with the menace itself; in the second, the *Kaikoku Heidan* (" Talks on the Military Affairs of the Sea-Country "), begun in 1777, and printed at Sendai in 1792, Hayashi treated of the fashion in which it should be met, and handled the problem of coast-defence generally. The scurvy reward that attended his patriotic efforts has already been alluded to.

But indeed in the last quarter of the eighteenth century the number of Japanese who knew or at all events, studied, Dutch is much greater than native accounts indicate.

"During my residence in Japan (1779–84)," writes Titsingh, "several persons of quality at Yedo, Kyōto, and Ōsaka applied themselves assiduously to the acquisition of the Dutch language and the reading of our books. The Prince of Satsuma, father-in-law of the present Shōgun, used our alphabet in his letters to express what he wished a third person not to understand. The surprising progress made by the Prince of Tamba, by Katsuragawa Hōshun, physician to the Shōgun, and Nakagawa, physician to the Prince of Wakasa, and several others enabled them to express themselves more clearly than many Portuguese born and bred among us in Batavia. Considering the short period of our residence at Yedo, such proficiency cannot but excite astonishment and admiration. The privilege of corresponding with the Japanese above mentioned, *and of sending them back their answers corrected*, without the letters being opened by the Government, allowed through the special favour of the worthy Governor, Tango-no-Kami, *facilitated to them the learning of Dutch.*" [1]

This and the preceding extracts from European authorities may perhaps serve to indicate how salutary the exercise of caution is in dealing with purely native authorities, and with how great reserve their statements must occasionally be taken. They do not wilfully pervert truth, it may be that they do sometimes handle it so very carelessly that certain of the impressions they convey are substantially misleading. Sugita's book, already alluded to, is certainly not free from errors, while Ōtsuki's sketch of the progress of Dutch learning in Japan is not merely at variance with Sugita's account but is disfigured by several palpable inherent inconsistencies. However, his account of the services rendered by his own grandfather, Ōtsuki Gentaku (1756–1827) of Sendai, is not destitute of interest and value. This Ōtsuki, after some training

---

[1] Among the books Titsingh took home was Hayashi's *O dai ichi-ran*, which, edited by Klaproth, was published at the expense of the Oriental Translation Fund in 1834, under the title of *Annuales des Empereurs du Japon*. It is refreshing to find that Titsingh was by no means inclined to take the early so-called Japanese History on trust, as Kämpfer had done, and as Siebold, Hoffman, and Rein subsequently did. In a letter to the Prince of Tamba, by whom is meant Kuchiki, Daimyō of Fukuchiyama, he writes :—"Must we not suppose that the Japanese, so jealous of their neighbours the Chinese, have, in writing their own history, endeavoured to fill up many gaps in it by prolonging the reigns of their earlier Dairi ? There is in your history a period of one thousand and sixty-one years occupied by the reigns of only sixteen Dairi. The duration of the life of Jimmu, of the reigns of Koan, of Suinin, and the life of Ojin, appear altogether improbable. The first died at the age of one hundred and twenty-seven years. The second reigned one hundred and two years, the third ninety-nine years. The last lived one hundred and ten years. These statements are too extraordinary to be blindly believed. Grant, even, that a chaste and frugal way of living may have secured for these princes a very advanced age, how does it happen that after Nintoku Tennō, the seventeenth Dairi, none exceeded the ordinary limit of human life ? "

first under Sugita and then under Mayeno, proceeded to Nagasaki
to learn Dutch from the Dutchmen, and on returning to Yedo
published his *Steps to the Dutch Language*, in consequence of which
the grandson will have it that " it became possible for all Japanese
to learn, read, and understand Dutch books ". The elder Ōtsuki
had a number of pupils, the most distinguished of whom was
perhaps Udagawa, and the fame he acquired procured him official
employment.

" In 1807, difficulties with the Russians took place in the northern
parts of the empire. In the following year the appearance of the
English on the western coast caused considerable commotion. The
Shōgun's Government decided, therefore, to make itself acquainted
with the condition of these two countries, and Ōtsuki received orders
to compile an account of these two countries from Dutch books.
Accordingly he composed the works in regard to the Russian question.
In 1811, the Shōgun's Government paid Ōtsuki twenty ingots of silver,
and continued this payment yearly, making him translator of Dutch
works. In 1822, he at length received a monthly salary. The above
was the first instance of the Shōgun's Government directly encouraging
Western learning."

It must be added to this that, in consequence of the Russian
aggressions of 1806 and 1807, and the *Phaeton* episode at Nagasaki
in 1808, the Yedo authorities had ordered the college of interpreters
at Nagasaki to take up the study of Russian and English in 1809.
Thus, when Captain Gordon entered Yedo Gulf in June, 1818, his
little craft of sixty-five tons was boarded by two interpreters, one
speaking Dutch, the other *some Russian, and both a little English*.
The English was probably acquired from some of the Dutch in
Nagasaki ; but this is only a surmise. As regards the Japanese
study of Russian at that date, we are on surer ground. The castaways brought back by Laxman in 1792, were the pioneer instructors
in this language ; and some of the Yedo officials, like Takahashi,
the astronomer, made some progress under their tuition. Then in
Golownin's *Narrative of his Captivity* in 1811–13, we meet with
many references to Japanese students of Russian and of European
science.[1]

---

[1] See especially chaps. v, viii, and x, and especially x. The author was
evidently born a grave and serious man ; yet he has penned some rather amusing
passages : " We saw plainly," he writes, " that the Japanese were deceiving us,
and did not intend to set us free, because they wished to make use of us as teachers,
but they had made a great mistake. *We were ready to die, but not to become the
instructors of the Japanese.*" And again, " We have already declared that we would
rather sacrifice our lives than remain in Japan on any conditions, *still less will we*

As a fact, Golownin and his companions spent a good deal of their time in instructing Japanese in Russian and in compiling a grammar for their use. One of the Nagasaki interpreters had been sent for for the purpose of being taught Russian, although he had tried to conceal the fact ; Takahashi had come from Yedo to learn more Russian and mathematics, while Mamiya Rinzō, the explorer of Yezo and of the Amur, whose treatise is translated in Siebold's *Nippon*, tried to utilize the prisoners for his own purposes, and incurred their hearty contempt :—

"We were now daily visited by the Dutch interpreters and the learned man, i.e. Takahashi, the astronomer. The interpreter began to fill up and improve the Russian vocabularies ; he used to refer to a French and Dutch Lexicon for acquiring through the French (*sic*) such Russian words as he did not know ; he then searched for these words in a Russian Lexicon *which he had in his possession*. He was about twenty-seven years of age ; and as he possessed an excellent memory and considerable knowledge of grammar he made rapid progress in the Russian language."

He soon applied himself to translate a *treatise on vaccination*, which one of the returned Japanese had brought from Russia. Later on yet another interpreter arrived from Nagasaki who besides Dutch, spoke some Russian and *had a knowledge of French*.

As regards (Siebold's friend) Takahashi, he busied himself in translating a Russian school treatise on arithmetic, also carried to Japan by one of the returned Japanese in 1792 ; but his object in this was merely to see the Russian methods of dealing with this science and for practice in Russian. Takahashi understood the Copernican system, was acquainted with the orbit and satellites of Uranus, knew the nature and doctrine of sines and tangents, and was familiar with the difference between the old and the new styles. He assured Golownin that Japanese astronomers could calculate eclipses with much exactness ; and he studied with great attention a treatise on physics which with other books had been sent on shore in Golownin's chest. Nor were the Japanese without knowledge of political events in Europe. They informed Golownin of the capture of Moscow by the French, a piece of information

---

suffer the Japanese to make pedagogues of us . . . We were told that one interpreter was not sufficient for the translation of our memorial, the law requiring two ; having consented to teach another, we are now requested to instruct a boy. In this way, a whole school will soon be formed, and that we will never agree to. We are few in number and unarmed, *and our lives may soon be taken, but we are resolved not to be made schoolmasters.*"

which he refused to credit. In fact, the width and accuracy of the knowledge of foreign affairs displayed by some of the Japanese officials Golownin had to deal with must startle any one who peruses the record of his captivity.

Meanwhile work of rare importance for the study of Dutch in Japan was being done at Nagasaki. From 1809 to 1817 there was no Dutch trade there, for Holland had been seized by France and all her colonies by the English. The merchants in Deshima were reduced to such straits that they had to be supported by the Japanese authorities.

" But the Japanese Government, obliged to advance the means for the support of the factory, did not leave the Director (Doeff) entirely idle. He was set to work, with the aid of ten Japanese interpreters, in compiling a Japanese and Dutch dictionary for the use of the Japanese men of science and the Imperial interpreters. A copy of this work was deposited in the Imperial library at Yedo ; another, made by Doeff for his own use, was lost with all his other papers and effects on his return to Europe. The original rough draft of the work was found afterwards, however, at Deshima by Herr Fisscher, and, having made a transcript, though less perfect than the original, he brought it home in 1829, and deposited it in the royal museum at Amsterdam."

In this extract, there is one slight error. It was not a Japanese-Dutch, but a Dutch-Japanese Lexicon that was then compiled by Doeff and his assistants, who used a Dutch-French dictionary as a basis to work from. The Doeff-Halma, as Doeff's Lexicon was generally called, did much to smooth the path for the hundreds of students that directed their energies to the acquisition of Dutch as the key to the mastery of European science, an acquaintance with which was now finding its way into the most unexpected quarters. For instance, in the *Summary of the Ancient Way*, by Hirata, the great apostle of Shintō, we actually meet with a short outline of Kämpfer's *History of Japan*, while the Dutch are there very highly praised for their achievements in natural science and placed far above the Chinese as philosophers.

It seems that the study of Dutch was getting firmly rooted in Japan in the seventh decade of the eighteenth century, about the date of Thunberg's arrival. During Titsingh's three sojourns (amounting in all to about three and a half years) it received a great impetus. It then began to assume the appearance of a fashionable craze, though not so intense, perhaps, as the Portuguese craze at Hideyoshi's Court two centuries before. To the patronage

of Shimadzu Shigehide, the vigorous and accomplished Lord of
Satsuma, it evidently owed a great deal. Shigehide had been
using Dutch letters and words in his correspondence in Titsingh's
time (1780–4); more than forty years later on we find him
frequently calling upon or meeting with Siebold when the latter
visited Yedo in 1826. Between these dates, we hear of Shigehide's
visits to Doeff in 1806, when he solicited the honour of a Dutch name
from the envoy. Then he and several other Daimyō had shown
great attention to Fisscher in 1822. To a party given by the Master
of the Mint and the conductor of the Embassy many of the Japanese
guests came rigged out in Dutch clothes; and as these had been
collected through long intervals and preserved as curiosities, they
presented a very grotesque and antique appearance. Fisscher's
own party were laid under contribution in the same way, their
lady visitors unpacking and rummaging their trunks, and putting
them to the necessity of giving away some of the most valuable
articles.

Four years later (1826) when in Yedo, the Dutch gave a party,
which Siebold described as " das originellste Lustspiel das ich je in
meinem Leben gesehen ". The remark was no ill-humoured one,
for he dwells upon the part the three Dutchmen—or rather the
Swiss and the two Germans—tricked out as if they had walked out
of one of Vandyke's pictures in the costume of the seventeenth
century, contributed to it. At this function the ex-Daimyō of
Satsuma, then in his eighty-fourth year, but looking no more than
sixty or sixty-five, and Okudaira, the Daimyō of Nakatsu, "assisted"
with all the zest of a pair of Burschen.

We have very strong evidence of the high proficiency the Nagasaki
interpreters had meanwhile attained in 1823. In that year Siebold,
then a young man of twenty-seven, arrived from Batavia, ostensibly
in the character of physician to the factory, but really charged
with a mission by Van der Capellen, Governor-General of the Dutch
East Indies, to investigate and report upon the natural history,
the politics and general state of affairs in Japan. Before landing
he was interviewed by some interpreters:—

" who caused me no little perplexity, inasmuch as they spoke Dutch
more fluently than I, and asked some suspicious questions about my
native country. Unfortunately, a few years before, a Belgian doctor
had, by orders of the Japanese, been dismissed from the Factory
because the Japanese could not understand him, while at first they

had made great difficulties about the Swedish naturalist Thunberg.[1] Meanwhile a lucky translation of the word ' Hochdeutscher ' by ' Yama Oranda ', that is ' Dutch mountaineer ', had nationalized me for the Japanese."

Of course, these interpreters owed their command of Dutch not to the tuition of Mayeno or Sugita or Ōtsuki, or to any of the coterie of Yedo scholars, but to their intercourse with the foreigners in Deshima.

Although certain of the native writers who have written on the progress of Dutch learning in Japan have little to say about Siebold [2] —one of them does not even mention his name—there can be no question that the obligations he laid Japanese scholars under were immense. During the greater portion of his six or seven years' stay in Japan (1823–9) his villa at Narutaki near Nagasaki was thronged with eager pupils from almost every quarter of the empire. It was a practice of his to award certificates of proficiency to the most deserving of these, one condition being that they should submit to him satisfactory dissertations on some one or other of the subjects with which he wished to make himself acquainted. As these theses had all to be written in Dutch—mostly after his students had left him and returned to their native provinces —it is plain that a knowledge of this language must, through him, have penetrated to some of the most sequestered nooks of Japan. And from these dissertations, and from his free and unrestrained intercourse with his troops of learned Japanese friends, Siebold found himself in a position to furnish some most interesting details about the previous progress of Western science in the country.

It will have been observed from some of the previous quotations that whenever the Dutch went to Yedo they were sure to be visited by the astronomers. A good deal of attention began to be directed to astronomy in the times of Tsunayoshi (1680–1709) when an

---

[1] One of these difficulties was somewhat amusing. After being six months in Deshima, he obtained liberty to go botanising in the neighbourhood of Nagasaki. A precedent of a similar permission, formerly granted to medical men of the factory, was found, but upon a critical examination of Thunberg's commission he appeared to be a surgeon, while his predecessor who obtained the favour had been a surgeon's mate. It took three months to get over the difficulty and to persuade the Japanese that these two officers were in substance the same. As it was, Thunberg's botanising proved somewhat expensive. Every excursion cost him sixteen or eighteen taels (say £4 to £5), as he was obliged to feast from twenty to thirty Japanese, by whom he was always attended.

[2] On the other hand the centenary of his arrival was celebrated publicly in Nagasaki.—L. H.

Astronomical Bureau was founded in Yedo and placed under the charge of Yasui-Santetsu, one of the two distinguished mathematicians of the time.[1] According to the Japanese accounts, Yasui had been originally a brilliant exponent of " Go " (an intricate game of checkers introduced from China); but, possessing natural talents for mathematics, had discovered upon comparison that the sun's actual position and motion did not always correspond with the place and motions indicated in the almanac, which had been in use for more than eight centuries—since 862. He therefore compiled a new and corrected one, which was distributed throughout the empire under the name of the Jōkiō almanac, and for that service he was made Government Astronomer in 1684. The eighth Shōgun, Yoshimune (1716–44) was keenly interested in astronomy, made some astronomical instruments himself, built a new observatory, in which he placed a large celestial globe constructed to his order by one Katō, an artificer from Kishū, and, as has been said before, he had a European calendar *translated*, and he summoned Nishikawa from Nagasaki to compile a new almanac. This task was completed in 1749, but, before it could be adopted, a farce had to be gone through no less amusing than the one enacted at the same time in connexion with the adoption of the Gregorian calendar in England.[2] From time immemorial all matters in connexion with the stars had to be referred to the head of the Tsuchi-Mikado family of Court nobles in Kyōto for sanction. Hence this new and corrected almanac was subjected to the examination of Abe-no-Yasukuni, and his approval of the corrections requested, upon which Yasukuni went through the ceremony of an astronomical calculation on the winter solstice of the third year of Hōreki (1753), to participate in which the author, Nishikawa, went to Kyōto.

As it was from Nagasaki that he was summoned, it is not at all improbable that Nishikawa was considerably indebted to the Dutch for his astronomical and mathematical erudition. But it might, indeed, have come from another source. Siebold tells us that it was to Ricci, Schaal, and Verbiest that not merely the

---

[1] The other was Seki Shunske (1642–1708). Seki and his immediate successors studied the Binomial Theorem, Theory of Numbers, the Properties of Maxima and Minima, Determinants, and Spherical Trigonometry. Ajima Naomaro in the eighteenth century was acquainted with four series of Pi, and also dealt with the Ellipse; in the early nineteenth century Wada Enzō was acquainted with the Catenary and Cycloid.

[2] Of course we refer to the astronomical *kudos* reaped by Lord Chesterfield on that occasion.

Chinese but also the Japanese owed their knowledge of the higher mathematics. The scientific works of these Jesuits, which had appeared in Chinese in one hundred parts or volumes in Peking, found a ready reception in Japan—provided the monogram of the " Society of Jesus " did not appear upon them. However, it is noteworthy that from the time of Nishikawa the Dutch in Deshima found a constant demand for books, maps, and scientific instruments. Not many years after, at the express request of the Court of Yedo, the " Nautical Almanac " was regularly sent from Batavia, while Japanese artificers were entrusted with the construction of mathematical and astronomical instruments in imitation of those forwarded from time to time by the Hollanders. Siebold tells us :—

" We had an opportunity during our stay in Yedo, of seeing a splendidly made sextant of this description ; and the quadrant in the Kyōto Observatory is also said to have been made by a native artificer."

These and similar data furnished by Siebold may excuse the suspicion that the achievements of Japanese cartographers at the beginning of the last century, undoubtedly great and meritorious, were not after all quite so miraculous as certain modern scholars would have us believe, though the most famous of these carto-graphers, Inō Chukei, was certainly a man of extraordinary ability. Born in 1744, he was adopted into the family of a saké brewer as husband of the daughter and heiress, who thought so little of her spouse as to refuse to allow him to eat with the family, banishing him instead to the servants' mess. When his father-in-law died, his business affairs were found to be at a parlous pass. Inō there-upon came to the rescue, retrieved the situation, and, after amassing considerable wealth, transferred the business to his son, and retired. At this time (1794) he was fifty years of age—somewhat too far on in life, one would say, to begin the study of astronomy. The books at his disposal, we are told, were all in Chinese, and contained many obscure passages which he in vain tried to understand. However, remembering what Siebold has told us about the origin of these Chinese books, we should most likely err if we pitied Inō for having had to waste time over so much mere trash. But Inō availed himself of something better than mere text-books ; he went to Yedo and became a pupil of the Takahashis, father and son, astronomers to the Shōgun. Under the tuition of the Takahashis the elderly student must have made excellent progress for, in 1800, we find him setting out, with the permission of the Government, to survey the island of Yezo at his own expense. In the following year he was commissioned to survey all the coasts and islands of Japan. In this task, his field work, in which he was assisted by thirteen others, four of whom were pupils studying under him, was completed in 1818; and five years later the old man of nearly eighty saw his splendid map of Japan engraved.[1]

Six years after its completion this map of Inō's was the occasion of a tragedy, in which Siebold was involved. In 1826, van Sturler had gone on the quadriennial embassy to Yedo, on which he was accompanied by the illustrious "Dutch mountaineer", whose scientific fame had long preceded him. Eighty miles from Yedo the party was met by an envoy sent by the Daimyō of Nakatsu to escort them to the city, while at Ōmori they had a visit from the Daimyō himself, who was accompanied by the eighty-four years' old ex-Daimyō of Satsuma, all eagerness to make the great doctor's acquaintance. In the city itself Siebold met with a magnificent reception from the scholars of the capital, who exerted themselves heartily to procure permission for him to remain behind after the ambassador had returned. Their device seems to have been to get him engaged as a translator of botanical works, and he had actually been entrusted with the task of translating a Danish edition of Weimann for the Shōgun, when some tradal difficulties, raised by van Sturler, offended the Council and caused the miscarriage of

---

[1] The results of Inō's labours are given in the *Dai Nippon En-Kai-jis-soku-roku*, or, the "Record of the True Survey of the Coasts of Japan" (1821; 14 volumes). This treatise remained in manuscript until 1870 when it was published by the Tokyo University. Three kinds of maps were constructed, the largest consisting of thirty different sheets, the medium sized of two, and the smallest of one. These maps have been the basis of all subsequent ones; and for many places in Japan Inō's measurements of latitude and longitude are the only ones which have yet been made. In Takahashi's preface to Inō's *Table of Latitudes and Longitudes* the following remarks, translated by Professor Nagaoka, are interesting : " The Europeans are of opinion that the magnetic needle generally deviates towards the west, never pointing true north, and that there exist local variations. These statements are to be found in Dutch books. In the coast survey made by Inō the compass needle formed an essential part of his stock of instruments. The best needles are made in Europe, but Inō was under no obligation to Western skill. With needles of his own construction he determined the configuration of the coast line, as well as the positions of mountains and islands . . . He found that the needle always pointed true north and south, and had no westward deviation . . . He says again that in using the needle one must have no steel (" hammered iron ") near. For under the influence of the spirit (or atmosphere) of iron the needle points sometimes east, sometimes west, and cannot then be said to have no deviation. Hence the sword ought not to we worn during survey work, nor should there be any piece of iron allowed near the body." (As Inō was compelled by national etiquette to wear the appearance, at least, of a sword, he filled his scabbard with a wooden one). In Inō's time in Japan the direction of magnetic north really coincided with the direction of geographical north. Now, the magnetic variation has a mean value of about 5° W. for the whole of Japan.

the project. Possibly the intrigues of the physicians who followed the practice of Chinese medicine, against which Siebold fought strenuously, had also something to do with Siebold's abrupt dismissal. To ensure Siebold's prolonged sojourn none had worked harder than Ōtsuki, the official translator, then seventy years of age; the Court physician, Katsuragawa (Wilhelm Botanikus); and the astronomer Takahashi. This, the younger of the two Takahashis (for the father had died in 1804) was the identical " Takarō Sampei " to whom Doeff had given the name of " Globius " in 1806. He had shown Siebold the sheets of Inō's map, and had promised to furnish him with a copy of the smallest edition of it in exchange for a lately issued Russian map of the world which was incomplete or inaccurate only in so far as it regarded Japan and especially Yezo.

Although it was a serious offence for a Japanese to supply a foreigner with maps or plans of the country Kämpfer, Thunberg and Titsingh had all carried off such documents in perfect safety, and Siebold, in December, 1828, was on the very eve of his departure before any attempt was made to check him from doing so. Inasmuch as many erroneous accounts of this important incident are current, it may be excusable to give a condensed translation from Siebold's own diary :—

DEZIMA, 16th December, 1828.

" My learned friend Yoshio Tsujiro, under-interpreter in the Factory, comes to me in the forenoon as usual to assist in translating from Japanese books . . . He was very absent-minded, and appeared to be in a bad humour, which struck me so forcibly that I asked him the reason of his unusual discontent. I had promised to leave him my pocket-chronometer as a souvenir when I left Japan; as my departure was now at hand, and as I had not yet fulfilled my promise, I believed that in that I saw the grounds of his slackness ; and so, opening my desk, I said to him in a friendly tone : ' Look ! There lies your chronometer. But as I have no good watch, you must leave it with me for a few days yet.' My friendly words made a visibly moving impression upon him, and after a mental conflict he threw the book upon the desk and sprang up with the words, ' Now I am the worst Japanese in the Emperor's service.' And I replied quite quietly, ' And I believe you have gone mad ! ' ' No ! ' he replied firmly and earnestly ; and after a pause he said, ' The affair of the map has been betrayed ; I have just come, after taking the Blood-oath—from the Town-house, whither the Governor summoned me. All the details are known, and the part I have taken ; it is known that I am the agent and the friend of the Court astronomer Takahashi. I was arrested and only set free after I had sworn to fetch at least the maps I myself had brought from Yedo and to discover whether and where you kept the other maps and forbidden documents. I had even the commission to bring with me some forbidden books which might serve as incriminating evidence.

"This was a weighty disclosure, and no instant was to be lost in saving my friends and my literary treasures. To gain time we resolved that in the afternoon Tsujiro should hand over to the Governor some maps I had in duplicate, and should promise that possibly the other maps should be forthcoming on the morrow. At the same time I promised that I should also deliver to him on the following day the great map of Yezo and Saghalin, on which they appeared to lay especial stress, and which Tsujiro himself had brought me from Takahashi. He hinted that a further investigation would then be dispensed with. Meanwhile the trusty companion of all my excursions in the neighbourhood of Nagasaki, and my most intimate confidant, Inabe Ishiguro, came into the room. Before him there was no secret. The occurrence surprised him not less than us, and threatened him with a like danger. He was deeply touched—moved to tears, the staunch kindly man. I promised both of them to do everything possible, even to the sacrifice of my own life, to save them, and besought prudence and silence. They went away, and now I was alone; for at the instant I did not venture to communicate the incident, whose consequences were not to be reckoned, to any of my European acquaintances, much less to report it to the Director of the Factory. The most pressing task was now to rescue for science the map of Yezo and the Kuriles, unquestionably the most valuable geographical document I had received from the Court astronomer. In the afternoon I shut myself up in my study, and, working on into and through the night till next morning, completed a true copy of this map, together with the translation of the text . . . On the next day, 17th December, Tsujiro came towards 10 o'clock and said that he had given up the maps and that he was also required to deliver immediately the map of Yezo which he had brought me from Yedo, and that my house would be searched next morning. He advised me to rescue as much as I could. He confided to me that he anticipated being arrested. I handed him the original map, and he left me deeply touched. My friend Ishiguro came not, nor did any of my Japanese acquaintances, and none of my pupils were in the house. In such a dreadful loneliness, I had to consider what in my situation was to be done. My resolution was short; everything that was absolutely necessary for my description of the Empire of Japan, such as manuscripts, maps and books, I would pack into a big tin box, and hide as well as possible, and at the same time I would notify the Director of the Factory (Meylan) of the incident. With the copy of the map of Yezo I repaired to him and informed him of what impended next day. At the same time I handed him the map, sealed in a roll, requesting him to deposit this valuable document in the archives of the Factory, as well to save it as in case of need as to furnish proof that my conduct was excusable on account of the importance of the geographical discovery made."

Siebold's house was frequently searched, as was also the warehouse where he had deposited some of his treasures, and many of these were confiscated, while his servants were arrested and barbarously put to the torture. On 28th January, 1829, he was forbidden to quit the country, and on the following day he had to appear on his knees before the Governor in the first of a series of strict judicial investigations. On these occasions he did everything possible to save Takahashi and his other friends who had meanwhile been arrested, while he spent the greater part of his savings in relieving the needs of the prisoners and their families. His servants were liberated in June, although his pupils and friends were still kept in gaol, and on 22nd October, he was again brought before the Governor, who, in the name of the Great Council, banished him from the country for ever, and told him to leave by the first opportunity. On 30th December, he embarked for Batavia ; on the following day one of his best friends, disguised as a fisherman, approached the vessel to bid him farewell ; on the next he secretly landed at Kosedo, where some of his liberated pupils bade good-bye to him " with heavy hearts ", and on 2nd January, 1830, he left Japan. When he revisited it again in 1859, he found a changed country, and still more remarkable changes in progress.

In certain quarters in Japan voices had been raised in strong protest against the treatment meted out by the Shōgun's Government to the foreigner who had rendered such services to the empire. Some of the Daimyōs showed the greatest eagerness to afford an asylum to Siebold's persecuted pupils. Among these Shimadzu of Satsuma and Daté of Uwajima were prominent, and in these two fiefs European learning made some headway during the following decades. As for the unfortunate Court astronomer, " Globius " himself, he died in prison while his case was pending. According to some Japanese accounts, his body was preserved in salt till the actual trial, the result of which was that Takahashi would have had so pay the death-penalty if he had been living.[1]

This untoward incident had the effect of putting the Dutch into ill-odour with the Tokugawa authorities. Intercourse between the residents of Deshima and their Japanese acquaintances was now carefully and jealously guarded, while the successive quadrennial embassies to Yedo were kept under the strictest surveillance on their route to and from, and during their stay in, the capital. All this proved a great check to the progress of Dutch

---

[1] It is said that the secret of Siebold's possession of the map was betrayed by one of the draughtsmen employed on it to whom Takahashi had given some offence.

learning in the immediate domains of the Shōgun, where the practitioners of Chinese medicine rejoiced at being relieved from a rapidly growing menace. Others of much greater influence than the Chinese physicians had also become embittered against the " Barbarian Company " as they contemptuously termed the votaries of Dutch science. Chinese scholars generally looked with no friendly eye upon the new learning, for they instinctively felt that its spread was threatening to undermine their authority and social prestige. It must not be overlooked, however, that many of the students of Dutch were themselves well versed in Chinese philosophy, and so were in a position to criticize its shortcomings with effect. Watanabe Kwazan, for example, the founder of the " Old Men's Club " for the study of Western science took lessons from a Kangakusha till the age of thirty-four at least. Several of the most prominent Dutch scholars of the time had finished their course in one or other of the Great Provincial schools, a few even in the Tokugawa University of Yedo itself.

It was, however, the alumni of this University of Yedo that organized the opposition to the spread of Dutch learning. Nor is this a circumstance to be wondered at when we recall what has already been said, in a preceding chapter, about the traditions of the *Seidō*, where the tenets of the Teishu school had to be accepted unquestioningly ; any signs of a lapse from orthodoxy, any appearance of a tendency to think for oneself, meant expulsion. And the *Seidō*, it must be remembered, was the nursery of the Bakufu civil service. Naturally enough officials trained in such traditions considered any attempt to question authority—especially to question *their* authority, as a very heinous crime, but even in Yedo, the fortune of Dutch learning showed signs of recovering from the terrible setback it had received from the Siebold-Takahashi episode. A few years thereafter we meet with quite a number of Siebold's former pupils in Yedo, mostly as physicians. These formed the nucleus of an informal association, which from the place of residence of most of the members became known as the " Downtown Club ". This was in contradistinction to another coterie, interested not so much in medicine as in Western science generally, that had its headquarters in the samurai quarter of the city, and was spoken of as the " Up-town Club ". In this latter, Watanabe Kwazan (1794–1840) was perhaps the most prominent figure.[1] He

---

[1] See Miss Ballard's paper in *T.A.S.J.*, vol. xxxii.

was over thirty before he became interested in the new learning, which he absorbed mainly from converse with friends, and from the translations of foreign works (Dutch and a few Russian) that were then becoming rather numerous. To the end of his life he himself could read little, or no, Dutch, but he was a great stimulating force. It was he who founded the " Old Men's Club " already alluded to. Its avowed aim was the study of foreign history and geography, but its members also had the secret purpose of studying with a view to improving the defective maritime defences of the empire. Some of the Daimyō would occasionally submit difficult questions in politics to their consideration, and would place young men under their influence, actions which gave the *Seidō* men in the Civil Service no great satisfaction.

Watanabe's chief source of information, if not of inspiration, was his friend, Takano Chōei.[1] Takano had been a pupil of Siebold's for a short time, and after opening a dispensary in Yedo, he was encouraged by one of the Shōgun's physicians to take up the work of translation. In 1832 he established his reputation by the publication of his *Essentials of Medical Science,* and a work on anatomy. From this date his pen seems to have been seldom at rest; before his death in 1850 he had written or translated no fewer than fifty-two separate works, some of them running to twenty volumes or over. Half of these were on medical subjects, but there were several on military science, and a *History of the Netherlands* in seven volumes was also among them. It is chiefly by the record of his imprisonment, by an essay on the potato and buckwheat, and above all, by his *Story of a Dream* (*Yume Monogatari*) that Takano is best known among his countrymen. The *Story of a Dream* was widely read at the time and several imitations of it were written and published. The circumstances that led to the publication of the little pamphlet were rather peculiar.

It had become customary for the Dutch Director in Deshima to compile an account of all the items of interest as to events in Europe which he had been able to learn from the annual ship, and to send his compilation into the Government office in Nagasaki. Here the report was translated, and the translation forwarded to Yedo for the use of the Great Council. At the close of a meeting of the Dutch scholars on 26th November, 1838, when only fourteen members

---

[1] See Dr. Greene's Essay on Takano Nagahide, *T.A.S.J.*, vol. xli, pt. iii.

remained, Haga, a clerk of the Hyōjōsho, took from his sleeve a document, and said that it seemed to him a matter of importance to the State, and so he had copied it. The document was a resolution which had just been adopted by the Council with regard to the anticipated coming of what was thought to be a British man-of-war, the *Morrison*. Now, as a sober matter of fact, the *Morrison*, as related in the preceding chapter, had already paid her visit to Japan and had been cannonaded, both at Uraga and Kagoshima, in the summer of the previous year, 1837. The Great Council (by a majority of four voices to one) had now decided that the (supposed) man-of-war should be repulsed, and that, if any attempt at a forcible landing was made, the invaders were to meet with no mercy, the ship was to be sunk or burned, and all on board whether crew or passengers, put to death. The seven Japanese castaways said to be on board were not to be received ; they were ordered to be delivered to the Dutch to be brought to Japan on the next Dutch vessel to make the annual voyage. Takano and his friends at once jumped to the conclusion that the authorities had confused Morrison the man, with the ship, and that, as a matter of fact, the British, to emphasize the importance of the mission, had put the vessel in charge of Dr. Morrison as a special envoy. They knew something of Morrison's distinguished work in China, but none of them knew that he had been laid to rest in the terraced cemetery of Macao in 1834, more than four years before. They regarded the supposed confusion of the man with the ship as evidence of the gross ignorance of the Bakufu, and they felt assured that the execution of the resolution of the Great Council could only result in disaster and great discredit to Japan. They also felt that their own knowledge of Western affairs created a special responsibility to make the public aware of the ignorance and incapacity of the Government, and to effect this purpose Takano wrote and published his famous *Story of a Dream*.

The short pamphlet contains several ludicrous misconceptions and two misstatements. For instance, it gives the number of British warships at 25,860 vessels with a complement of about 1,000,000 men, and represents Dr. Morrison as being in command of all the warships in the Southern Seas, where he was training from 20,000 to 30,000 sailors. The writer insists strongly on both the inhumanity and want of policy in repulsing a mission which was one of peace and goodwill.

" Should our authorities drive the British ships away, it may lead to great damage to our own shipping ; for there are many islands relatively near to us under England's control, and her ships are continually passing to and fro. Her enmity would be a great calamity to Japan."

This pamphlet and the popular favour with which it was received, occasioned profound resentment among the *Seidō* men in the Civil Service. Some of them exerted themselves strongly to get the brochure suppressed, and the insolent audacity of its author punished, but Mizuno, Echizen-no Kami, the strongest man in the Great Council, although he had found himself in a minority of one regarding the reception to be accorded to the *Morrison*, ignored the promptings of his rancorous subordinates, the most prominent among whom was a certain Torii, at that time on duty at Uraga. Torii was really the second son of Hayashi, the Rector of the University. He had had a distinguished course in the University, where he had become thoroughly imbued with the despotic, intolerant and narrow-minded traditions of the institution. To him Dutch learning was an utter abomination, and Dutch scholars hateful in the extreme. The former was often at variance with the " Books " and the latter had no regard at all for authority and orthodoxy. Just about this time he found new and more personal grounds for resentment. A coast survey had been ordered, and one of Torii's friends had sent in a map which was found to be very defective, while another, the work of a surveyor recommended by Takano to Egawa, the official in charge, was found to be very satisfactory. This was a great triumph for the new learning, and vastly mortifying to Torii, who had just been made a *metsuke*, or censor, and was eagerly on the outlook for an opportunity to ruin the " Barbarian Company " utterly.

About this time, some men interested in Dutch learning conceived the idea of getting Government permission to colonize the Bonin Islands. By an intrigue, Torii succeeded in inducing one of the new school to bring a serious charge against his associates, and against Dutch scholars generally. Some of them it was alleged were trying to open up communications with the Barbarians under the pretence of colonizing uninhabited islands. The informer sent in a list of persons, high and low, who were infected with the craze for Western science, and he alleged :—

" These are associated together. They respect the Barbarians and are gaining influence by publishing such books as the *Yume Monogatari*.

. . . All this is due to the baneful influence of the Barbarian learning, and it is in danger of bringing untold damage to the state."

Torii at once reported the matter to his patron, Mizuno, and this time Mizuno felt constrained to take action. But the heir to the great Satsuma fief was among those denounced as revolutionaries, and Mizuno was not inclined to proceed against such powerful antagonists as the heir of Satsuma, and one or two others mentioned along with him, smaller fry, such as Takano and Watanabe, could, however, be dealt with promptly. The latter was ultimately sentenced to confinement in his own house, and in 1840, to avoid causing trouble to his Lord, he committed *hara-kiri*. Takano was condemned to imprisonment for life in the common gaol, but on the occasion of a fire in the prison in 1844, he escaped. He was in northern Japan for some time ; for a few weeks at Uwajima, and for some months in Satsuma, but most of the time between 1844 and his death in 1850, he lurked in Yedo, where he earned considerable sums of money by his translations of Dutch works on military science, many of his ventures being commissions from various Daimyō, and some of them even from sympathetic Bakufu officials. His position was a very precarious one, for one thing, he was an escaped convict, and for another, his translations were an infringement of a lately issued Bakufu decree appointing a censor for Dutch books, and forbidding the study of Dutch to all but physicians. The smaller officials were still on the outlook for Takano, and at the end of October, 1850, they finally ran him to earth. He was not taken alive ; he cut down two of the seven officers sent to arrest him, and then committed *hara-kiri*.

His chief foe Torii had already met with condign punishment in 1845, but, in the year before his fall he had contrived to bring undeserved suffering upon another pioneer of Dutch learning in Japan. A certain Takashima Shūhan (1797–1866) had learned a great deal about European military science, especially gunnery, from a former Dutch army officer who had come to Deshima. Takashima soon made a reputation for himself among the Western Daimyō, who consulted him on many matters, and now and then sent some of their retainers to study under him. His fame presently reached Yedo ; and the Bakufu summoned him to the capital and made him instructor in gunnery and cannon-founding. As Takashima and his best pupil, Egawa, were ardent votaries of Western science, Torii very soon came into collision with them, and did everything he could to make them uncomfortable. Presently Takashima went back to Nagasaki. In connexion with the *Morrison* episode, he had expressed himself very freely about Japan's chances in any war with a European power; and he had thereby given grave offence to many of the samurai who maintained that the issue of a war did not depend so much upon armaments as on the spirit of the combatants, and that nothing could stand before their own *Yamato-damashii.* In 1842, a petty officer went up to Yedo and brought a wild charge that Takashima was laying in military stores and had formed a project of seizing the Gotō Islands as a base for operations against the Shōgunate in conjunction with foreigners. The accusation was absurd but, for peculation and other alleged offences disclosed in the course of the trial, Takashima was sentenced to death. Just at this time Torii fell, and Takashima's punishment was commuted to domiciliary confinement for life in the charge of Ichibashi, Shomōsa no Kami. Eight or nine years later, the arrival of Perry in 1853, made Takashima's knowledge and services indispensable, and he once more found himself a very busy man.

This incident again brought Dutch learning into evil odour. The *Seidō* reactionaries had already clamoured for its suppression in connexion with the Siebold-Takahashi case in 1829; they now sent in another petition praying that all further study of Dutch should be strictly prohibited. On the other side, the physicians, Sugita and Katsuragawa, sent in a counter-petition in which it was asserted that the study of Dutch was indispensable for medical men, if their science was to make any progress. The Great Council hesitated to arrive at a decision. Dutch scholars were undoubtedly troublesome; they often supplied the Daimyō with full translations of the Dutch Factor's annual report, and of Dutch treatises on military and political matters; and this was proving very inconvenient. Besides, mainly owing to Dutch scholars, a great commotion was arising about the insufficiency of the coast-defences, for which the Bakufu was held responsible. On the other hand, some of the Councillors, notably Hotta, and perhaps Sanada and Mizuno, had come to have a high regard for the Dutch school of medicine. At this time, the astronomer, Shibukawa Rokuzō, put forward the proposal that the Dutch text of the Deshima Factor's annual reports on foreign events should no longer be translated and retained in Nagasaki, but should be sent on to himself in Yedo, and that physicians alone should be permitted to study Dutch.

The Bakufu at once adopted the memorial, and issued a decree in which its chief points were embodied. The natural result was that henceforth every student of Dutch was professedly a student of European medicine, and a Japanese historian maintains that this is one of the circumstances that go to account for the comparatively advanced state of medical science in modern Japan, although many students attached themselves to physicians of the Dutch school who had no earthly intention of practising medicine at all. In 1838 Dr. Ogata established his school in Ōsaka,[1] and in the twenty-four years of its existence, 3,000 pupils passed through it. Among them, were such men as Ōmura Masujiro, Hashimoto Sanai, Fukuzawa Yukichi, Ōtori Keisuke, Hanabusa, and Sano, all of whom afterwards became prominent figures in modern Japanese history, but not one attained fame through his medical acquirements.

Even before the Shibukawa edict was issued the cause of Dutch medicine had been making great progress in the capital. As the Daimyō, who had all periodically to reside in Yedo for certain terms, were accompanied by their physicians, not a few of the men trained by Siebold thus came to find themselves together in Yedo, and a few years after his departure—before 1843 at all events—we hear of :—

" Itō in the service of the Daimyō of Saga, Totsuka in that of the Daimyō of Satsuma, Ōtsuki in that of the Daimyō of Sendai ; Hayashi, physician to the Lord of Kokura, and Takenouchi from Maruoka, establishing themselves in the metropolis and practising medicine on European principles there. A little later, in the hope of arresting the great mortality among Japanese children, they added vaccination to their other practice.[2] In 1858, these doctors, having formed themselves into a society, established, with the permission of the Government, a private institution for vaccination. During this year the Shōgun

---

[1] An interesting account of Ogata's school is given in Fukuzawa's Autobiography, a précis of which, by W. Dening will be found in the *Transactions of the Japan Society*, vol. xli, 1913.

[2] In Siebold's Diary we meet with several passages referring to his attempts to introduce vaccination into Japan. For example : " April 23rd, 1826.—The Court physicians pass the whole day with me ; they disclose their wish—at first indeed in secret—that I should remain some time in Yedo, and sketch a plan how to accomplish this with the Shōgun. To do this I was invited to give a lecture on children's small-pox and vaccination, and there I took the opportunity of proposing a plan for the introduction of this great benefit into Japan. I declared myself ready, at the order of the Shōgun, to fetch the lymph from Batavia myself and practise vaccination here." " April 27th.—Vaccinated two more children."

In Dr. Whitney's paper in *T.A.S.J.*, vol. xii, pt. 3, will be found some details about the introduction of vaccination into Japan. As early as 1813, Golownin tells us the Dutch interpreter then learning Russian at Matsumaye occupied himself in translating a treatise on vaccination that had been brought from Russia twenty years before.

Iyesada, being sick, sent for Itō, Totsuka and Takenouchi, and made them his Court physicians. This is the first instance in which physicians of the European school who were not also surgeons were appointed to the dignity of Court physicians."

From this sketch it may be apparent that at the time of the arrival of the " black ships " in 1853, the Japanese were by no means so unacquainted with modern science and Western affairs as the Americans anticipated. For such knowledge as they possessed they had to thank the Dutch solely. In fact, it was mainly in order that they might be apprised of what was passing in the outside world that the Yedo authorities maintained their connexion with the Hollanders. The latter, indeed, thought of their profits merely ; but Siebold is very strong in his contention that the Shōgun's advisers set very little store upon the continuance of the foreign trade at Nagasaki for its mere commercial advantages. He points out that limits were placed upon the quantity of copper the Dutch might export chiefly to ensure their prolonged stay in the country, the Japanese being persuaded that on the exhaustion of the mines the Hollanders would be sure to withdraw, and he quotes the remark of one of the councillors (1790) to the effect that :—

" The cause of the friendship with the Netherlanders is trade, and the trade is maintained by the copper. But the copper is diminishing year by year, and if the mines are once exhausted, our friendship with the Netherlanders will also be at an end."

Nor is extraneous evidence lacking to confirm the correctness of Siebold's contention. In the document handed to the Russian captain, Rikord, by the two Japanese commissioners at Hakodate in 1813, the following paragraph occurs :—

" Our countrymen wish to carry on no commerce with foreign lands, for we know no want of necessary things. Though foreigners are permitted to trade to Nagasaki, even to that harbour only those are admitted with whom we have for a long period maintained relations, and we do *not trade with them for the sake of gain, but for other important objects.* From these repeated solicitations which you have hitherto made to us, you evidently imagine that the customs of our country resemble those of your own ; but you are very wrong in thinking so. In future, therefore, it will be better to say no more about a commercial connexion."

The Dutch eagerness for trade, although it disarmed all Japanese suspicion of aggressive territorial designs on their part, and so made them more tolerable in the country than the Spaniards or the Portuguese, had yet at an early date excited displeasure, if not disgust, in certain quarters in Japan. In an interview with Caron in 1637, Suyetsugu Heizō, the Daikwan of Nagasaki, had told him that the

"Hollanders ought to consider it was far more to their interest to please such high statesmen than to think always of their own affairs ; they followed a line in many instances prejudicial to themselves, giving always in the first place their attention to their commerce, and thinking only in the second place of matters of politeness and courtliness. High statesmen had remarked this, their peculiarity, sufficiently, and he deemed it a much wiser plan to give in the first place their attention to the Court and courtly manners, as all their trade and profits accrued from them, and because their interest would be promoted by doing so. He said that it would certainly be disadvantageous to them if those high lords should sometimes hear their unwise answers and proposals. 'Indeed, you talk always of your profits, of your gain, and I don't know what else, as if everybody owed these to you. Consider that no one may earn if he has not sowed and worked for it. One ought to do some service for the profits one enjoys.' "

The service, then, the Tokugawa authorities wished to impose upon the prisoners in Deshima was the discharge of the functions of " Merchants of Light " for Japan.[1] All things considered, the Hollanders discharged these functions not inefficiently. The telescope became of practical use only about 1608 or 1609, and yet, before his death in 1616, Iyeyasu was able to make a present of one to his son Yorinobu, Lord of Kishū, and this was the first of a long succession of European inventions brought to Japan by the Dutch. However, such " light " as they purveyed was far from proving of the general national benefit it might well have done. The Shōgunate was just as anxious to monopolize that, as it was determined to monopolize all foreign trade. Its interests were bound up in the maintenance of the *status quo* as far as possible ; and, exceedingly jealous of the great subject feudatories, it was utterly averse to the diffusion of new practical knowledge in, or the introduction of pestilent inventions into, the fiefs, where they might very well ultimately lead to menacing developments. Hence a partial explanation of the cast-iron restrictions upon all free intercourse with the " Merchants of Light " in Deshima. The Yedo bureaucracy were anxious indeed to have the " light ", but they were no less anxious to retain full and perfect command over

---

[1] " For the several employments and offices of our fellows ; we have twelve that sail into foreign countries, under the name of other nations (for our own we conceal), who bring us the books, and abstracts, and patterns of experiments of all other parts. These we call ' Merchants of light '."—Bacon's *New Atlantis.*

the meter, so that in its distribution and diffusion there might be the strictest economy—and not the slightest risk of explosion.

In 1842, at the date of the repeal of the Expulsion Decree of 1825, Mizuno instructed the Hollanders to supply models of all useful European machines and copies of illustrated books and journals dealing with them, and, ere long, such publications as the *Illustrated London News* began to find their way to the Council room in Yedo Castle. It is not so very strange, therefore, that when the " Governor " of Uraga and his suite were entertained on board Perry's flagship in 12th July, 1853, they should have been found:—

" to be not unacquainted with the general principles of science, and of the facts of geography. Their inquiries in reference to the United States showed them to be not entirely ignorant of the leading facts connected with the material progress of the country. They had heard of roads, probably meaning tunnels, cut through the hearts of mountains and they inquired whether the canal across the isthmus was yet finished, the object of which they knew was to connect two oceans. When invited to inspect the vessel, they never for a moment lost their self-possession, but showed the utmost composure and quiet dignity of manner. They evinced an intelligent interest in all the various arrangements of the vessel, observed the big gun and rightly styled it a ' Paixhan ', and exhibited none of that surprise which would naturally be expected from those who were beholding for the first time the wonderful art and mechanism of a steamship. The engine evidently was an object of great interest to them, but the interpreters showed that they were not unacquainted with its principles. Much of this cool but not unobservant composure may have been affected in accordance with a studied policy ; but yet there can be no doubt that, however backward the Japanese themselves may be in practical science, the best educated among them are tolerably well-informed of its progress among more civilized, or rather cultivated, nations."

CHAPTER XVI

THE REOPENING OF JAPAN

AMERICAN vessels had been occasionally chartered by the Dutch for the annual voyage to Nagasaki towards the end the eighteenth and the beginning of the nineteenth century. At that date the American flag was becoming no rare sight in Far Eastern seas. At Canton, which was in China much what Nagasaki was in contemporary Japan, above half-a-score of American vessels were regularly employed in the Chinese trade. By 1832–3, their number had increased to about sixty, while in 1834, the volume of American exports and imports at Canton was valued at $17,000,000. No wonder, then, that the United States Government should take steps to tap the rich Far Eastern trade at other points. In 1832, Edmund Roberts was named President Jackson's agent for the purpose of examining in the Indian Ocean the means of extending the commerce of the United States by commercial arrangements with the Powers whose dominions border on those seas. Among other instructions he was ordered to be very careful in obtaining information respecting Japan, the means of opening communication with it, and the value of its trade with the Dutch and Chinese. Later on, in the same year, he was told by Livingstone, the Secretary of State, that the United States had it in contemplation to institute a separate mission to Japan. If, however, a favourable opportunity presented, he might fill up a letter and present it to the " Emperor " for the purpose of opening trade. But Roberts died at Macao in 1836.

Shortly afterwards came the " Opium War " and the Treaty of Nanking. The Americans, naturally enough, were desirous of participating in the commercial advantages then conceded by the Chinese ; and in 1844, Caleb Cushing negotiated his treaty of thirty-six clauses, which down till 1860 served as the basis for the settlement of nearly all disputes arising between foreigners and Chinese. In President Tyler's letter to the Emperor of China, it was stated that :—

" On the west we are divided from your dominions only by the sea. Leaving the mouth of one of our great rivers and going constantly towards the setting sun, we sail to Japan and the Yellow Sea."

And in 1845, Congressman Pratt, chairman of the select committee on statistics introduced a resolution recommending :—

" That immediate measures be taken for effecting commercial arrangements with the Empire of Japan and the Kingdom of Korea."

In consequence of this, Commodore Biddle, who was soon after dispatched to the China Seas with a considerable naval force, was instructed among other things to ascertain if the ports of Japan were accessible, to present a letter from President Polk to the Emperor, and to negotiate a treaty of commerce. On 20th July, 1846, Biddle with the *Columbus* and *Vincennes*, arrived off Uraga, where he made a stay of nine days. He tendered copies in Chinese of the English, French, and American Treaties,[1] lately concluded with China ; but the Japanese officers declined to receive them. We are told by Hildreth that :—

" On the 28th an officer with a suite of eight persons came on board with the Emperor's letter, which, as translated by the Dutch interpreter, read thus : ' According to the Japanese laws, the Japanese may not trade except with the Dutch and Chinese. It will not be allowed that America make a treaty with Japan or trade with her, as the same is not allowed with any other nation. Concerning strange lands all things are fixed at Nagasaki, but not here in the bay ; therefore you must depart as quickly as possible, and not come any more to Japan.' "[2]

As to this so-called letter, it has to be remarked that what Biddle received was no letter from the " Emperor ", but a document without any address, seal, signature, or date, and as to its contents, there was, as has already been pointed out, no Japanese statute confining trade to the Dutch and Chinese. Biddle had been requested to go on board a junk to receive the communication, but he insisted that it must be delivered on board his own ship. The officer yielded, but remarked that Biddle's letter, having been delivered on board the American vessel, he thought the " Emperor's "[3] letter should be delivered on board a Japanese one. Biddle, to gratify the officer, thereupon told the interpreter that he would take delivery of the letter on board the junk. An hour afterwards Biddle went alongside

---

[1] The Bakufu, of course, had been duly informed of the concession of these Treaties by the Dutch.

[2] For a full translation see Nitobe's *Intercourse between the United States and Japan*, p. 34.

[3] It is always to be remembered that " the Emperor " signifies the Shōgun.

the junk, in uniform, of course. As he was stepping on board, a Japanese on the deck pushed him back into the boat. Biddle thereupon called to the interpreter to have the man seized, and returned to the *Columbus*. His instructions cautioned him not to do anything " to excite a hostile feeling, or distrust of the United States ", so he readily accepted the apologies tendered. A year later, a shipwrecked American sailor chanced to threaten his Japanese guards with vengeance from some American ships of war ; they told him they had no fears of that, as the year before a common soldier had knocked down an American Commander at Uraga, and no notice had been taken of the matter. In 1849, Dr. Bettleheim in far-off Lūchū informed Commander Glyn of the *Preble* that very exaggerated reports had reached these islands of chastisement inflicted upon an American " chief " who had visited Yedo in a " big " ship. Biddle had of course refused to surrender his powder and armament ; but otherwise he had carried complaisance to an extreme, and had met with but a sorry reward. A week later Admiral Cécille adopted a very different tone at Nagasaki but his visit there was entirely on his own initiative, and had never been sanctioned by his government.

The appearance of these men-of-war with their powerful armaments was an unpleasant revelation, of the strength of Western Powers, to the Japanese authorities. The arrival of the *Columbus* and *Vincennes* at Uraga had excited a great commotion. Two Musashi Daimyō had just before been entrusted with the defence of Yedo Bay ; and one of them (Kawagoye) had now to furnish 516, and the other (Ōshi) 480, guard-boats. Ii of Hikone and Hoshina of Aidzu were soon afterwards ordered to share the responsibility. About this time a Japanese publicist caused much excitement by pointing out that, although Yedo Bay might be made impregnable, yet Yedo could be reduced to starvation if the " barbarian " ships merely confined their operations to interrupting the coastal junk traffic, and cutting off the supplies for the capital. In some quarters there was a strong agitation for the revival of the " Expulsion Edict " of 1825, but clear-headed statesmen, like Abe Masahiro, were convinced that this would be most inadvisable. From Tsushima, and from the sea-board fiefs in northern Japan, he was now getting constant reports about the appearance of foreign ships in their harbours. As things stood, this put the feudatories to much trouble and expense. The duty of initiating actual hostilities when these vessels appeared would be still more onerous, to say nothing of the ulterior consequences that might be involved. The project of embodying a peasant militia to deal with such contingencies he pronounced to be quite impracticable.

The main cause of the rapidly increasing frequency of these uninvited and most unwelcome guests was to be found in the remarkable development of American whaling enterprise in the Northern Pacific. In 1821, Russia had tried to exclude navigators from Behring Straits and the Pacific Coast of her possessions, a step which at once elicited protests from the United States and Great Britain. With the latter the treaty of 1825 placed matters on a satisfactory footing while, in the preceding year (1824), the United States treaty had provided that the navigation and fisheries of the North Pacific should be equally free to Russians and Americans. In 1838, a second convention guaranteed to citizens of the United States freedom to enter all ports, places, and rivers on the Alaskan coast under Russian protection. The citizens of Nantucket, and, later on, of New Bedford were not slow to avail themselves of the advantages of these two Conventions; at the latter town, in 1851, Perry found that American capital to the amount of $17,000,000 was invested in the whaling industry in the Northern Pacific. The whalers found their chief base for necessary repairs at the Sandwich Islands; their temporary supplies were also drawn from these islands, and from the Bonins, where a small colony of English, Americans, and Sandwich Islanders had established itself under the Union Jack. In these circumstances it is but small wonder that necessitous whalers should chafe at being denied the hospitality of Japanese havens. When shipwrecked in northern Japanese seas, as they sometimes were, the whalers had but little good to say of the treatment generally accorded them by their reluctant hosts. They were usually confined in what were rather kennels than prisons, and were ultimately conveyed in *kagos* to Nagasaki, where they were handed over to the Dutch to be sent out of the country.[1] What made this treatment the more galling was the contrast it presented to such acts as those of Captain Cooper of the *Mercator*, who took much pains to repatriate eleven Japanese he rescued from a sinking junk in 1845.[2]

---

[1] For some particulars, see Hildreth's *Japan*, pp. 499–504, and Nitobe's *Intercourse between Japan and the United States*, pp. 35–8.

[2] See Hildreth, pp. 495–6.

In 1849, Captain Geisenger, the American commissioner at Canton, was informed that there were some fifteen foreign seamen in ward at Nagasaki, and that they would probably be kept there till the next annual visit of the Dutch ship. Geisenger, thereupon dispatched Commander Glyn, in the *Preble* (sloop-of-war) to bring the prisoners away. At Naha, Glyn heard from Bettleheim how Biddle had been " chastised " at Uraga in 1846 ; accordingly, on reaching Nagasaki, he assumed a very firm attitude with not unsatisfactory results.[1] On returning to America, Glyn proceeded to Washington and there endeavoured to get sent on a diplomatic mission to Japan with a naval force to support him. Meanwhile the importance of making an attempt to induce, or to force, the Japanese to resume intercourse with the outside world had been kept before the public and the Washington officials by Mr. Palmer, of New York, who was a voluminous writer on the subject of Japan. He sent in memorials to the President and the Secretary of State ; and in this he was backed by some of the principal merchants of New York and Baltimore. By this time, it must be noted, steam navigation had been making remarkable progress, and the question of coaling depots in the Far East—and especially in Japan—had become a pressing one for American naval commanders and steamship owners. In 1851, the year when Glyn went to Washington, the Dutch Minister there assured Daniel Webster, then Secretary of State, that there would be no modification of her exclusive policy by Japan, whereupon Webster resolved to take practical measures. Commodore Aulick, who had just been appointed to the command of the China squadron, suggested to him that it might further the objects of any Japan expedition if some Japanese castaways, picked up by the *Auckland* a few years before,[2] were taken back with it to Japan. Webster approved of his suggestion,[3] and the castaways were ordered to be embarked on the Pacific coast and sent on to Hong-Kong to await the arrival of the warships there. Webster, furthermore, drafted a letter to be signed by the President for presentation to the " Emperor " of Japan, and on

---

[1] See Hildreth, who quotes Senate Documents 1851-2, vol. ix, as his authority.
[2] For details, see Heco's *Narrative of a Japanese*, vol. i. Heco was one of the castaways and was afterwards in the Japanese, as well as the American, service.
[3] See his letter in Lanman's *Leading Men of Japan*, p. 392. For some particulars about the originators of the Japan expedition, see Lanman ; Griffis' *Matthew Galbraith Perry* ; and Nitobe's *Intercourse between Japan and the United States*.

30th May, 1851, Aulick received his commission to negotiate and sign a treaty with Japan. His command was, however, a short one. His commission was cancelled on 18th November, in the same year.[1] On 24th March, in the following year, Perry was formally appointed in his stead, and instructed to assume command of the East India squadron. It was not until 24th November, just seven months later on, that the new Commodore was able to leave Norfolk on his mission ; and even so, all the " squadron " he had with him consisted only of the *Mississippi* steamer, which carried his flag.

It should be said that, at this date, the most important foreign station in the American naval service was the Mediterranean, and that Perry was expecting to be appointed to this command. In his letter to the Secretary of the Navy on 3rd December, 1851, he stated that he considered the relief of Commodore Aulick :—

" a retrograde movement . . . unless indeed, as I have before remarked, the sphere of action of the East India squadron and its force be so much enlarged as to hold out a well-grounded hope of its conferring distinction upon its commander."

It was finally understood that Perry should have an imposing squadron of about twelve ships to support him in his diplomatic mission to Japan. Some of these were on the East India station already ; others were to be sent on as soon as duly equipped. Perry asked, and received, permission to write his own instructions, and Everett, who succeeded Daniel Webster as Secretary of State, made no alteration in the original draft of which Webster expressed his approval. It would perhaps have been well if Everett had changed as little in the letter Webster had drafted for presentation to the "Emperor" of Japan,[2] which was expanded to more than double its original length by Everett, and the expansion can hardly be regarded as an improvement. The months before his start had been employed by Perry in selecting presents for the Japanese, in collecting and mastering the voluminous literature on Japan, and in working out the details of the projected expedition.

" Great interest was naturally excited among literary and scientific circles in the expedition, and numerous applications poured in from all parts of the civilized world for permission to join it ; but all such requests were, for obvious reasons, met with unqualified refusal. The most stringent restrictions, moreover, were imposed upon all those who embarked in the enterprise. They were prohibited from making

---

[1] p. 283 seq.
[2] The original letter will be found in Hildreth and Lanman.

any communications to the public journals touching the movements of the squadron, or the discipline and internal regulations of the vessels composing it ; and even private letters to friends were to avoid these topics. All journals and memoranda kept by members of the expedition were to be considered the property of the government, until permission should be given to publish them. The object of these regulations was to withhold information from other powers, which, if communicated, might imperil the success of the enterprise." [1]

Perry arrived at Hong-Kong on 6th April, 1853, and found the sloops-of-war *Saratoga* and *Plymouth*, and the store-ship *Supply* in the harbour. The steamer *Susquehanna* had gone to Shanghai, where Perry also proceeded, and on his arrival there he transferred his flag to the *Susquehanna* on 17th May, 1853. This vessel was the largest in the squadron ; but she was of no more than 2,450 tons, with an armament of sixteen guns. On 23rd May, the squadron left Shanghai for the Lūchūs, where it arrived on the 26th. Here a stay of thirty-eight days was made, although Perry occupied the fortnight between 9th June and 23rd June on a visit to the Bonins with the *Susquehanna* and *Saratoga*. Something like a base of supplies was established at Naha ; and Americans remained in charge here all the time that Perry was absent on his visits to Japan. Perry was not accurately informed about the real political situation in Lūchū, but from an entry in Wells Williams' Journal (8th June) it is clear that some of the American surmises came very near the truth. Perry believed that any success which might attend his attempts at negotiations in Lūchū would materially facilitate his object in Yedo itself. The most energetic measures of a pacific character were therefore determined on ; while the officers did not neglect to make provision against the possible failure of all such efforts. It was arranged that if the Japanese Government refused to negotiate, or to assign a haven of resort for American merchant and whaling ships, to take under surveillance the island of Great Lūchū, not, however, as a conquered territory, but as a " material guarantee " for the ultimate concession of the American demands. It will be remembered that Admiral Cécille had, seven years before, unwittingly driven the Yedo councillors to their wits' end by much less drastic action than this proposed step.

---

[1] Perry's own official *Narrative* edited by Hawks, and Wells Williams' *Journal of the Perry Expedition to Japan*, are the main foreign " sources ". From the Japanese side, the *Zoku Tokugawa Jikki*, vol. iii, gives many interesting details, while there is much excellent work in Mr. Kobayashi's *Bakumatsu-shi*.

Wells Williams records a visit to some Japanese junks in Naha on 8th June, one of which had just come in from Kagoshima. It may be safely assumed that the Kagoshima authorities were quite well apprised of what was occurring in the Lūchūs at this time, and that they passed on the intelligence to the Bakufu officials. Accordingly the arrival of the American squadron off Uraga on 8th July, 1853, could not possibly have been the staggeringly unexpected event it is sometimes represented to have been. Perry left Naha on the " glorious " fourth of July, with four ships, the *Susquehanna* with the *Saratoga* and the *Mississippi*, with the *Plymouth* in tow. The squadron anchored off Uraga about four o'clock on the afternoon of 8th July " the two steamers being nearest the town ". On this occasion the Commodore's stay was a brief one, between eight and nine days :—

" 17th July : We got under weigh this morning, and each steamer, taking a sloop in tow, passed out of the bay at the rate of nine knots, in a calm, showing most plainly the power of steam to the thousands who watched us. . . . Near Cape Sagami fully a thousand boats were seen, all of them without sails, each containing six to ten people apparently abroad for no other object than to see the ships depart. To a maritime people, the contrast between their weak junks and slight shallops, and these powerful vessels must have made a deep impression."

And on 27th May, 1905, a little more than a brief half-century after Wells Williams jotted this down in his *Diary*, Japan was to fight and win the Battle of the Sea of Japan, the greatest sea-fight since Trafalgar !

In a measure Commodore Perry may be said to have met the Japanese on their own ground. It has always been customary for the Japanese to consider all their plans and projects very carefully and materially before proceeding to execute them, and to arrive at a clear-cut decision as to the manner in which they are to be carried out, and to determine the deportment and conduct of their representatives in all negotiations or public functions. Perry had devoted much thought to what his attitude should be towards the Japanese ; and when he came into contact with them he had the immense advantage of knowing his own mind on this all-important matter. In his own words :—

" In conducting all my business with these very sagacious and deceitful people, I have found it profitable to bring to my aid the experience gained in former, and by no means limited, intercourse with the inhabitants of strange lands, civilized and barbarian ; and this experience has admonished me that, with people of forms, it is necessary either to set all ceremony aside, or to out-Herod Herod in assumed personal consequence and ostentation."

Perry was quite familiar with Langsdorff's account of the Russian mission of 1804, and he was fully resolved to expose himself to none of the mortifications Rezánov had then been subjected to with such elaborate sham courtesy. He knew, furthermore, that Biddle's extremely conciliatory and complacent attitude seven years before had brought him not a jot nearer the accomplishment of his purpose, while the wonderful self-restraint he had exhibited in very trying and aggravating circumstances had been so grossly misinterpreted as to bring the American name into contempt among at least the smaller Japanese officials. Perry was in thorough earnest in his determination to submit to no humiliations, and to be put off with no tergiversations. He came resolved to demand as a right, not to solicit as a favour, those acts of courtesy which are due from one civilized nation to another—not to tolerate those petty annoyances to which his predecessors had been subjected—and to disregard both the acts and the threats of the authorities, if derogatory to the dignity of the American flag. From the very first the Americans now showed the Japanese officials that they meant serious business. The vessels were all prepared for action—ports open, ammunition ready, men at their quarters, while the squadron anchored so as to command with its guns the entire range of forts and batteries around Uraga.[1] Perry had instructed his captains to allow no one to come on board, and none but proper officials were to be admitted to the flagship. Biddle's vessels in 1846, had been freely open to all visitors who had partaken of the officers' hospitality without hesitation, and had made themselves so much at home that when spoken to about going ashore they had answered by signs that it was impossible to do so. Perry decided that there should now be no repetition of this conduct on board his ships. In this he was emphatically right, for few things could lower the prestige of the visitors more among the aristocracy and officials than a readiness to admit all comers to an easy familiarity.

---

[1] The last paragraph of the communication handed to Commodore Biddle in 1846, was as follows : " In conclusion, we have to say that the Emperor positively refuses the permission you desire. He earnestly advises you to depart immediately and to consult your own safety in not appearing again upon our coast." Perry consulted his own safety by appearing on the coast with an armament that was irresistible.

The squadron had been making way against a slight head wind just before anchoring, and the Japanese were rather surprised and startled at the sight. Two guns were discharged from the forts, a rocket went up, and a number of guard boats put off to intercept the intruders. But the Americans paid no heed either to the boats or to the gun that was fired just after they anchored, and when the Japanese began to surround them with the usual cordon of guard-boats, and to clamber unceremoniously aboard the various vessels, the visitors took very vigorous and unexpected action. "When they attempted to get alongside and on board the *Saratoga*, the ropes with which they attached themselves to the ship were unceremoniously cast off. They then attempted to climb up by the chains, but this the crew was ordered to prevent, and the sight of pikes, cutlasses, and pistols, with other indications that the American officers and men were thoroughly in earnest, induced them to desist from the attempt. Several of the commanders in the Japanese boats signified their dissatisfaction at not being permitted to board the ships, but the commander's orders were strictly obeyed throughout the negotiations. One of the boats came alongside the flagship and it was observed that a person on board had a scroll of paper in his hand, which the officer of the *Susquehanna* refused to receive, but the bearer held it up to be read alongside the *Mississippi*, when it was found to be a document in French charging the ships to go away and forbidding them to anchor at their peril. Of course the American squadron had already anchored; and their peril was nothing of consequence. Next day the American survey-boats reported that the "fortifications of Uraga were not very formidable, and that their construction did not exhibit much strength or art. Their position and armament were such as to expose them to an easy assault, the parapets being of earthwork, while many of the buildings, the barracks, and magazines, appeared to be of wood. The few guns mounted were of small calibre, and the embrasures so wide as greatly to expose them". What the Americans could not know, of course, was that, for the only effective pieces in the armament of the forts, the Japanese then did not have so much as ten rounds of ammunition, and that the Governor of Uraga had just written to Yedo that an American assault on his forts would at once expose the utter uselessness of the whole system of coast defence with most disastrous consequences to the Empire! In truth such "peril" as there was in the situation was entirely on the Japanese side, and the Japanese were only too well aware of the fact. The Governor was soon again writing that his uninvited guests were exceedingly calm and collected in their demeanour, and that " these vessels were really not to be easily dealt with ".

The chief functionary, as his boat reached the side of the *Susquehanna*, made signs for the gangway to be let down. This was refused, but the Chinese and Dutch interpreters were directed to inform him that the Commodore would not receive anyone except a dignitary of the highest rank, and that he might return on shore. The interpreter in the Japanese boat (Hori Tatsunosuke) was very pertinacious in urging to be allowed to come on board, but was constantly refused permission, and was told that the commander of the squadron was of the highest rank in the service to which he belonged, in the United States, and could only confer with the highest in rank at Uraga. It was then stated that the Vice-Governor of Uraga was in the boat, and the speaker pointed to one of those in authority at his side, who, he said, held the highest position in the city, and was the proper person to be received. He was now asked why the Governor himself did not come off, to which he replied that he was prevented by the laws from going on board ships in the roads, and proposed that the commodore should appoint an officer of corresponding rank with the Vice-Governor to confer with him, as he was desirous of communicating to the Government the object of the squadron's visit. The Commodore, after some intentional delay, consented to this request, and appointed his aide, Lieutenant Contee, to receive him. The gangway ladder was accordingly lowered, and the " Vice-Governor ", Nakashima Saburosuke, accompanied by his interpreter, who spoke Dutch, came on board and was received in the captain's cabin, where a conference was held, in fact, with the Commodore, who, however, studiously kept himself secluded in his own cabin, and communicated with the Japanese through his aide only.

Nakashima was told that the commodore had come on a friendly mission to Japan, with a letter from the President to the Emperor, and that he desired a suitable officer to be sent to receive a copy in order that a day might be appointed for the envoy to formally deliver the original in person. Nakashima made answer that the squadron must go to Nagasaki—whereupon he was told that the commodore had purposely avoided Nagasaki, and that he *would not go to Nagasaki.* The envoy expected the letter to be duly and properly received where he then was, and that while his intentions were perfectly friendly, he would submit to no indignity. If the guard-boats then collecting around the vessels were not immediately removed *they would be dispersed by force.* Nakashima thereupon went to the gangway and ordered these boats away. A few still remained, however, and an armed boat from the flagship was sent to deal with them. Nothing more of the guard-boats was seen during the stay of the squadron. Nakashima presently took his leave, saying that he had no authority to reply to the commodore's communications, but that next morning an officer of higher rank would probably be sent with definite instructions.

That Perry's attitude was a judicious one will be more readily conceded if we bear in mind that the Japanese had just been playing off a gross fraud upon him. The assertion that Nakashima was Vice-Governor of Uraga was an outrageous lie, for this man was merely a humble *yoriki,* an insignificant officer of police.[1] Next morning the Japanese went on with the farce. At seven o'clock, the arrival of Kayama Yezaimon, who presented himself as the governor and greatest functionary of Uraga, was duly announced to the Commodore, who ordered that this dignitary should be received by Commanders Buchanan and Adams and Lieutenant Contee, the Commodore still refusing to give an interview to anyone but a counsellor of the Empire! The governor was attired as a noble of the third rank! He was duly received by the officers named, and immediately commenced a conference with them, which, however, was in reality with the Commodore, though he still preserved his seclusion. This new functionary had also to be told that it was utterly bootless to mention Nagasaki; the envoy intended to deliver the letter where he was, and moreover, if the Japanese government did not see fit to appoint a suitable person to receive the documents addressed to the Emperor, he, whose duty it was to deliver them, would land with a sufficient force and present them in person. Kayama thereupon hurriedly said that he would send to Yedo for further instructions at once. But, he added, it would take four days to obtain them. As an hour's steaming would have taken the ships in sight of Yedo, the governor was informed that the Commodore would wait three days only for a definite reply.

---

[1] A parallel would be a serjeant of police at Gravesend, an officer just one degree above the constables who were termed dōshin.

Meanwhile, before and during this interview, the American surveying parties had been at work. At one time there seemed to be so lively a prospect of one of these coming into collision with the Japanese that the officer in command ordered his men to rest upon their oars *and fix the caps upon their carbines*. The " Governor " informed the Commodore that it was contrary to the Japanese law to allow such examinations, whereupon he was courteously told that the American laws required them and that the Americans were as much bound to obey the laws of their country as the Japanese were bound to obey those of Japan. The " Governor " was also shown the President's letter, and the Commodore's letter, and the envoy's credentials, and was so evidently impressed with the exquisite workmanship and costliness of the magnificent boxes in which they were enclosed that, for the first time, he offered water and refreshments for the squadron but was told that they were not then required. He was also informed that further discussion would be unnecessary until the time appointed for the delivery of the answer from the Japanese government should arrive.

At this time, the Americans seem not to have had the slightest suspicion of the trick the Japanese were persistently playing. This " Governor " of Uraga, Kayama Yezaimon, was like Nakashima, no more than an insignificant police-officer (*yoriki*). It should be said that there were really two Governors of Uraga, one Toda, Izu no Kami, actually resident in the place ; the other, Ido, Iwami no Kami, then in Yedo, for it was the practice for the Tokugawa Government to have duplicate sets of officials for almost every post. These governors, it should be remembered, stood rather low in the official hierarchy ; between them and the " Councillors of the Empire " with whom alone Perry intended to discuss matters, were more than a score of ranks at least. Next day (10th) was Sunday, and nothing was done. But, early on the morning of the eleventh, the surveying boats protected by the *Mississippi* were ordered to penetrate the bay higher up towards Yedo.

" This step was taken partly for the purpose of ascertaining the navigable capacities of the harbour, and *partly to overawe the Government*, and thereby increase the chances of a favourable answer. The ' Governor ' of Uraga on seeing the advances of the war-steamer, visited the flag-ship with the ostensible object of stating that the letters would be received on the following day (12th), and forwarded to Yedo, but really for the purpose of learning why the *Mississippi* has ascended the bay. The Commodore, anticipating the inquiry, directed that the ' Governor ' should be informed that unless the business which had brought the squadron to the bay of Yedo were arranged during the present visit, he would be *obliged to return in the ensuing spring with a larger force*, and, as the anchorage in front of Uraga was not convenient or safe, he was desirous of seeking a more favourable situation nearer to Yedo, which *would facilitate his communication with that city*."

Next day, the 12th, the " Governor " appeared in great state, and was received by Buchanan and Adams. Perry, through them, now consented to deliver the translations *and* originals of letter and credentials, as also a letter from himself to the " Emperor ", provided the latter should appoint a Japanese officer of the highest rank to receive them directly from his hands. The " Governor " replied that a building would be erected on shore for the reception of the Commodore and his suite, and that a high official personage, specially appointed by the Emperor, would be in attendance to receive the letters ; but, he added, that as no answer could be given in the Bay of Yedo, it would be transmitted to Nagasaki, through the Dutch or Chinese superintendents.

" Thereupon Perry wrote down the following statement for the ' Governor's ' benefit : ' The Commander-in-Chief will not go to Nagasaki, and will receive no communication through the Dutch or Chinese. He has a letter from the President of the United States to deliver to the Emperor of Japan, or to his Secretary of Foreign Affairs, and he will deliver the original to none other ; if this friendly letter of the President to the Emperor is not received and duly replied to, he *will consider his country insulted, and will not hold himself accountable for the consequences. He expects a reply of some sort in a few days, and he will receive such reply nowhere but in this neighbourhood*."

At a second visit to the flagship on the same day the " Governor " intimated that one of the highest dignitaries of the Empire would arrive at Uraga in two days for the purpose of receiving the documents, and that the interview would take place at a house on shore, but that no discussion could take place on the occasion. On the afternoon of the 13th, the " Governor " again went on board the flagship and exhibited the original order of the "Emperor" addressed to the functionary who had been deputed to receive the Commodore. The translation of the order ran as follows :—

Letter of Credence given by the Emperor of Japan to his highness, Toda, Prince of Idzu.

" I send you to Uraga, to receive the letter of the President of the United States to me, which letter has recently been brought to Uraga by the Admiral, upon receiving which you will proceed to Yedo, and bring the same to me."

There was really no great need to send Toda to Uraga, for he was already there and had been there all the time. The Americans were led to believe that he was territorial Prince of Idzu, a province where he owned not a foot of land, and where he exercised no administrative rights whatever. A police officer had been temporarily promoted to the office Toda actually held—the governorship of Uraga. And as promotion seemed to be the order of the day, the Shōgun became Emperor and Commodore Perry an Admiral. Meanwhile the Japanese had been hastily constructing a building for the reception of the envoy at Kuri-ga-hama at the head of a little inlet a short distance from Uraga. Perry had sent a survey party to the inlet, and it was found that the vessels could readily be brought within gunshot of the place. On the following morning, the 14th of July, the two steamers dropped down the bay and anchored off the spot. The "Governor" of Uraga, who was to act as master of ceremonies on this fateful occasion, had already settled all the details of the interview, and he now made his appearance alongside the flagship. Three hundred armed Americans in fifteen boats now put off for the shore, and presently a salvo of thirteen guns indicated that the envoy was stepping into his barge :

"The Americans were for the most part very vigorous, able-bodied men, who contrasted strongly with the smaller and more effeminate-looking Japanese. These latter had mustered in great force to the number the 'Governor' of Uraga stated, of 5,000 ; but this, it was believed, was far below the real number."

In this case, however, the "Governor's" statement seems to have been correct. Some of these 5,000 troops were Bakufu men ; but they mostly came from the four fiefs of Oshi, Kawagoye, Hikone, and Aidzu, which were entrusted with the coast defence of the four provinces round Yedo Bay. Their commanders had been charged to do nothing that might lead to "untoward incidents".

The newly erected structure consisted of an entrance hall and an inner chamber. As the Commodore and his suite ascended to the reception room the two dignitaries who were seated on the left arose and bowed, and the Commodore and suite were conducted to the arm-chairs which had been provided for them on the right. These seats had been hurriedly brought from the local temples, and were really *kyokuroku* or chairs used by Buddhist priests in conducting funeral services ! The interpreters announced the names and titles of the high Japanese functionaries as *Toda, Idzu no Kami*, or Toda, Prince of Idzu, and Ido, Iwami no Kami or Ido, Prince of Iwami. As has been explained, these two men were really the Governors of Uraga ; Ido, who had just come from Yedo, had been acting as a *metsuke* (censor) until a few weeks before.

From the beginning the two " princes " assumed an air of State formality, which they preserved during the whole interview, as *they never spoke a word*, and rose from their seats only at the entrance and exit of the Commodore, when they made a grave and formal bow. For some minutes after the Americans had taken their seats there was absolute silence in the room, not a single word being uttered on either side. At last Hori, the interpreter, inquired whether the letters were ready for delivery ; he announced that " Prince " Toda was prepared to receive them and that the scarlet box at the upper end of the room was the proper receptacle for them. Perry thereupon beckoned to the two pages with the boxes to advance. The two gigantic negroes that escorted the pages followed immediately in the rear of the boys, and marching up to the scarlet receptacle, received the boxes from the bearers, opened them, took out the letters and displaying the writing and seals, laid them upon the Japanese box—all in perfect silence. The envoy instructed his own interpreter (Portman) to indicate to Hori the natures of the various documents, upon which the latter and Kayama, the " Governor " still kneeling both bowed their heads. Kayama now rising approached the " Prince " of Iwami, and prostrating himself on his knees before him, received from him a roll of papers, with which he crossed over to the Commodore, and again falling upon his knees delivered it to him. This was the " Imperial " rescript. The Dutch translation of it thus rendered into English at the time, was fairly correct :—

" The letter of the President of the United States of America, and copy, are hereby received and delivered to the Emperor. Many times it has been communicated that business relating to foreign countries cannot be transacted here in Uraga, but in Nagasaki. Now, it has been observed that the Admiral in his quality of ambassador of the President, would be insulted by it ; the justice of this has been acknowledged ; consequently the above-mentioned letter is hereby received in opposition to the Japanese law. Because the place is not designed to treat of anything from foreigners, so neither can conference nor entertainment take place. The letter being received, you will leave here."

Upon delivery of this " imperial rescript ", the hall again relapsed into profound silence. This was at last broken by the envoy instructing his interpreters to inform the Japanese that the squadron would leave in two or three days for the Lūchūs and Canton, and that he would be pleased to take any dispatches or messages they might wish to send to these places. He also stated that it was his intention to return to Japan in the following spring, and Hori then asked him if he would return with all four vessels. " All of them," was the reply, " and probably more, as these are only a portion of the squadron." At this point it becomes advisable to quote from Wells Williams' *Journal* :—

" Perry then added that there was a revolution in China by insurgents who had taken Nanking and Amoy, and wished to introduce a new religion. ' It will be better not to talk about revolutions at this time,' was the significant reply, and proper one too, for I thought it very mal-apropos to bring in such a topic. Yet one might regard it with interest as ominous of the important changes which might now be coming on the Japanese, and of which this interview was a good commencement."

Rarely indeed has a shaft from a bow drawn thus at a venture hit the mark so shrewdly as in this special case. The writer does not seem to observe that this momentous interview took place on the fateful 14th July—on the sixty-fourth anniversary of the fall of the Bastille and the beginning of the French Revolution. Fifteen years later, on the 4th July, 1868, the ninety-second anniversary of the American Declaration of Independence, the last defenders of the Tokugawa Shōgunate in the Shōgun's own capital were to be hopelessly routed and scattered to the winds in the battle of Uyeno Park !

In so much as even obtaining this interview with the Bakufu commissioners at Uraga, Perry had dealt a serious blow to the supposed Japanese " ancestral law ". Yet the Bakufu tried desperately to save appearances even in this conjuncture. Uraga was no place for the discussion of foreign affairs—Iyeyasu had tried hard to induce both Dutch and English to establish their factories there—and so the commissioners had been instructed not to utter a single word and to make the interview as short as possible. Even with all its long pauses of solemn and profound silence it had not lasted thirty minutes. It may be noted also that the commissioners appeared in their war-hats, and with body armour under their robes. However, on the American side the preparations for the interview had been no less conspicuously strenuous and menacing. Besides the contents of their cartridge boxes, the landing

party carried a full thousand charges of ball, while the two steamers
had been anchored so that they could rake the little bay, with
decks cleared, and everything ready for action. Howitzers were
placed in boats alongside to be dispatched at a moment's notice
at the first appearance of any trouble on land, and the ships' guns
were ready to shower shot and shell on the whole line of Japanese
troops if they opened hostilities.

" Therefore, as the letter has been received, you can leave."
Perry, to show how little store he set upon this intimation, at
once got the whole squadron under way up the gulf towards Yedo,
and in the afternoon the vessels came to anchor fully ten miles
in advance of their previous holding-ground. Presently the very
hard-worked " Governor " of Uraga appeared upon the scene in
great consternation, and he and the interpreters did everything
they could to get the squadron to return and depart. The Americans
paid little heed to his remonstrances ; so the " Governor " consoled
himself with the magnificent feast that was presently set before
him and his companions. On the 15th, the Commodore went on
board the *Mississippi*, and proceeded up the gulf as far as Hommoku,
while a dozen surveying parties were busy at various points. On
the 16th, the " Governor " came on board to renew his assurance
of a favourable reception of the President's letter ; and as nothing
was now said of sending the answer to Nagasaki, it seemed that
the nearer the Commodore approached to Yedo, the more conciliating and friendly the Japanese became. That afternoon when,
after having been generously entertained with abundance of
champagne, the " Governor " was informed that the squadron
was to leave early next morning, his " Excellency " protested
that his affection for his American friends was so great that he
would not be able to restrain his tears on their departure.

Perry was anxious as to the safety of his fellow-countrymen in
Shanghai, which the Taiping rebels were then menacing. He was
also in need of fresh supplies, and he did not wish to be dependent
on the Japanese for anything at this time. Above all he wished to
give the Japanese ample time to reflect on the position, before he
returned with a much stronger force to receive their reply to the
President's letter to the " Emperor ". So far we have told the
story as gathered from American sources ; now let us turn our
attention to what the Japanese were meanwhile doing and thinking.

To judge from the panic and confusion in the Bakufu Councils and in the nation at large, one might naturally suppose that the arrival of the American squadron at Uraga had fallen upon the Japanese like the proverbial bolt from a blue sky. As a matter of fact the authorities had been early apprised of the American preparations for the expedition. The Dutch Minister at Washington had been requested to inform his government of the American intentions, and the Dutch government had promised its moral support. Acting under its instructions, the Governor-General at Batavia had dispatched the astute and able Donker Curtius to Japan to replace the Factor in Deshima, and to watch events. On his arrival at Nagasaki, Donker Curtius at once informed Maki, the Governor, that he carried an important dispatch from the Governor-General to the Bakufu, and that he was anxious that this should be delivered. Maki, who had brought trouble on himself in regard to the Dutch king's letter in 1845, was now very cautious, and he referred the matter to Yedo. Here the affair was referred to the censors, and they reported that, as the Dutch government had been ordered to send no more missions or dispatches to Jápan, it would be impossible to receive any dispatch from the Governor-General of the Dutch East Indies. If, however, the document was placed on the footing of the ordinary annual report from the Deshima Factor, to which no reply was necessary, it might be received. And in this way, the communication ultimately reached Yedo, the greatest precautions being taken to keep its purport secret.

Donker Curtius informed the Governor of Nagasaki about the objects of the projected American expedition, and hinted not obscurely that if the Japanese on this occasion could not see their way to relax the rigours of their " ancestral law " there might be very serious difficulties. He therefore recommended that traders of all nations should be admitted to Nagasaki, where commerce might still be conducted along the traditional lines. On 2nd November, 1852—eight months before Perry's arrival at Uraga—he sent to the Governor the draft of a treaty

" based on the laws, customs, and usages of Japan, which would attain the end (of opening the country) in such a way as no other means can reach, and which, in case the Netherlands succeed, could confer the same advantage upon all other nations."

In his covering letter of the same date explaining the points in the draft submitted Donker Curtius writes :—

" His Majesty the King of the Netherlands hopes and expects that peace will be granted Japan, should it answer the wishes of the U.S. President in this wise."

There is no reason to suppose that Perry ever knew anything of this proposed treaty, but the fact remains that a good many of its provisions coincided with those of his own treaty of March, 1854. However, all knowledge of Donker Curtius' action was confined to the Bakufu officials and on these it made little or no impression. Many of these fancied that the Americans were merely a branch of the English pirates and barbarians, with whom the Dutch were now in collusion for the purpose of breaking through the " ancestral law " of Japan, and reaping more tradal advantages for themselves. They also recalled the fact that the solemn warning from the King of the Netherlands, which had given them so much concern in 1844 and 1845, had remained unjustified by the course of events.

All this being duly considered, we can understand the general consternation that prevailed along the shores of Yedo Bay on the evening of 8th July, 1853. The Americans then saw beacon-fires flaming upon every hill-top, and along the coast as far as the eye could reach, while the men on watch could hear the constant tolling of a great bell all the night through one of the many alarum bells then being set in motion. The nine o'clock gun on the flagship seemed to produce a great commotion on shore ; many of the beacon-fires went out, for their watchers had no desire to be targets for the enemy's cannon.

At Yedo, where messengers by land and water kept constantly arriving, the popular panic was intense, and the officials had no small difficulty in stopping the general exodus that threatened. Indeed the officials themselves at first were at their wits' end ; and to many of them it was a great relief that the Americans had come on a " friendly " mission. Abe and his fellow-councillors were not long in making up their minds that the President's letter must be received, and the Americans sent away peaceably as soon as possible. Uraga was the most strongly fortified point on Yedo Bay ; most of the guns there were obsolete and for the few serviceable pieces there were not more than ten rounds of ammunition. Besides the barbarians could throttle the junk traffic utterly ; and if they chose to do so, Yedo would have to face a famine in a few days. By way of preparing for the worst and of putting as brave a show upon the matter as possible, orders were issued to the seven strong clans of Fukui, Himeji, Chōshū, Kumamoto, Yanagawa, Takamatsu and Tokushima to mobilize their men and protect the sea-board to the south of Yedo. Abe also appealed to Lord Nariaki of Mito for counsel. Nariaki's reply was that as his own warnings had been neglected for years, and the measures he had long advocated had never been adopted, he had nothing to suggest at the moment. However, he did not go so far as to say that the American dispatch should not be received, and hostilities provoked, for although he did not know the very worst, he was quite aware that the Bakufu was helpless for the time being. From the Shōgun, Abe could not expect to receive much inspiration ; indeed Iyeyoshi was so ill that news of the arrival of the Americans could not be communicated to him for some days. The only thing to be done was to get the barbarians away peaceably at any price, and yet to save the " ancestral law " as far as possible. Hence the strange silent interview at Kuri-ga-hama. When, after that, the American ships pushed on up the bay on the following day the consternation in Yedo was extreme. That evening the Great Councillors, the Junior Councillors, the Magistrates, and some other officials repaired to the Castle in war-dress and sat far into the morning in earnest deliberation. Eight days after Perry's departure from Uraga the Shōgun Iyeyoshi died (27th July), after recommending Abe to avail himself of the counsel of Lord Nariaki of Mito, in all matters of importance. As was not unusual, the Shōgun's demise was not made public for a month ; and during this time there was much history in the making.

On the first day of the seventh month (5th August, 1853) when the Daimyōs made their customary visit to the Court, Abe distributed copies of the translation of the President's letter among them, and requested them to express their opinions on the various points in it in written memorials. This was a most extraordinary and totally unprecedented step for any Bakufu Councillor to take. Assemblies of all the Bakufu functionaries for general deliberation were not unknown, indeed they were not unusual. The heads of the three houses of Owari, Kishū and Mito had frequently been convoked to discuss matters of high policy, while great Fudai like Ii of Hikone and Hoshina of Aidzu, had often been consulted on difficult matters of state. It had, however, hitherto been the set policy of the Tokugawa Shōgunate to allow the feudatories at large and especially the great " outside " feudatories no part or voice whatsoever in its councils, while all criticism of Bakufu policy or Bakufu officials was generally sternly repressed. This particular step of Abe (taken with the full approval of Lord Nariaki of Mito) was something more than a mere innovation. It was really the beginning of a revolution. It is true that it was from the Daimyō only that Abe invited an expression of opinion on a special question at this time. But it is easy to see that the discussion of the matter would not be confined to the Daimyō. Some of them indeed were too stupid to be able to express any reasoned opinion at all, and such would be entirely dependent upon the wits of their retainers. Others, perhaps nearly all, submitted the President's letter for discussion to their vassals, and invited them to give their opinions freely, just as they themselves had been requested to do by the Chief of the Great Council. Hitherto the expression of opinion on matters of policy had generally been a costly luxury for the ordinary samurai for the Tokugawa secret service was ubiquitous. Now that a free expression of opinion had been actually invited there was an eager babel of voices in almost every fief in Japan. At present it was only on one topic ; but there was no reason why other and perhaps more dangerous subjects for discussion should not be found when the present was exhausted. The result was that we find the policy, the conduct, and finally the status of the Bakufu discussed and criticized in a fashion that would not have been tolerated for a moment at the beginning of the century, much less in the days of Yoshimune, Tsunayoshi or of Iyemitsu.

By this time Lord Abe must have begun to realize fully that he stood in a very difficult position. To the Daimyō he had affected to speak of the fateful Uraga interview as a mere temporary expedient. But he must have been fully convinced in his heart that, if Perry returned with the increased armament he spoke of it would be no light matter for the Bakufu to refuse the requests in the President's letter. In spite of the utmost efforts of the Bakufu in the meanwhile, Yedo Bay and consequently the fate of Yedo, would be in the foreigner's grip. And Abe knew what perhaps only a dozen or so of the officials knew, that the state of the Bakufu finances made any thought of a determined opposition utterly impracticable. The accumulation of a national debt was still an unknown luxury in Japan, it is true, and there was none. But almost every year there had been a serious deficit in the balance of the Bakufu accounts, and it had only been by frequent issues of a more and more debased coinage that the perennial shortage had been made good. This could not go on for ever ; and there were no fresh sources of revenue to tap. If this fact is henceforth borne carefully in mind, it will serve to explain much that was unavoidable in the Bakufu's action, much that must otherwise seem incomprehensible and even childish. For this reason the Bakufu could never adopt the strong line of policy against the foreigner that was expected by its supporters and demanded by its critics and especially by the Court of Kyōto. But neither Abe nor any other Tokugawa minister dared to make this explanation public, lest some of the great outside feudatories might be only too prompt to take advantage of the Shōgunate's weakness. In the present situation too, the support of the clans was of the utmost consequence to the ministers, now that the empire was menaced with the threat of foreign aggression. To make sure of being able to present a united front to the foreigners Abe laboured unceasingly to conciliate Lord Nariaki of Mito, the leader of the *Joi* or " Expel-the-Barbarian " party, whose enormous latent power was just on the point of being recognized.

When the memorials from the Daimyō presently came pouring in, it was found that almost every one of them was strongly inspired —or infected—with this *Joi* feeling. They nearly all laid it down as axiomatic that the foreigners were coming to Japan with designs upon the independence and territorial integrity of the empire. Nor perhaps was it all so very wonderful that they should be so. Japanese then believed that the Portuguese of old had had territorial designs upon Japan, which they had prosecuted with the two weapons of trade and the propagation of their religion, and that their expulsion had been the natural consequence of the discovery of their real purpose. As for the English, the *Phaeton* incident at Nagasaki in 1808, and the Takarashima episode of 1824, had never been forgotten, while the Dutch accounts of the British conquest of Hindustan, of the " Opium " war and the cession of Hong-Kong, and of the forced opening of Chinese ports to commerce had excited the liveliest apprehension in Japan. Then the Russian aggressions in Saghalin and the Kuriles were still kept fresh in the people's memories—especially by Lord Nariaki of Mito, and his fellow-thinkers. Krusenstern, who had brought Rezánov to Japan in 1804, had published an account of his voyage, and this book had been translated by Siebold's friend Takahashi and a collaborator in 1826. The passage, in which Krusenstern adverted to the extreme weakness of Japan's position in the Northern seas, and the ease with which she could be stripped of Saghalin, Yezo, and the Kuriles, had made a marked impression when the translation appeared, and we find it often referred to at this time. The memorialists were all opposed to any extension of foreign trade. Arai Hakuseki's short tract which has been already quoted expressed the modern doctrine on the subject; and the Daimyō were not minded that the " bones " of the empire—gold, silver, and copper— should be exchanged for mere gewgaws and trifles which the Japanese could very well do without. Some of the Daimyō, notably Saga and Fukui, also dwelt upon the importance of the (supposed) sacred " ancestral law " which forbade any dealings with foreigners save the Dutch and Chinese. But it was among the Bakufu officials— who had also been ordered to send in written opinions—that this point was especially emphasized.

Among the Daimyō there was, on the other hand, a small minority who recognized that the times had changed since Japan had secluded herself two centuries before, and that a rigid and bigoted adherence to the " ancestral " law could not continue much longer. A good deal has been said about Lord Nariakira of Satsuma in a preceding chapter. At this juncture his blood-relations, Kuroda of Chikuzen, Okudaira of Nakatsu, with Date of Uwajima and a few others, expressed themselves in favour of extended foreign intercourse as a temporary measure. But there were two pronouncements still more remarkable than any of these. One was from Hotta, the Daimyō of Sakura, who had been Mizuno's colleague in the Great Council in the earlier forties. The other was from Ii Naosuke, the Lord of Hikone, the chief Fudai in the empire. Hotta as has been already remarked, had for more than a decade been prosecuting a vigorous reform in his fief mainly along modern occidental lines, and as all his councillors were pro-foreign there is perhaps not so much to be surprised at in the tone and tenor of his very enlightened and statesmanlike memorial. But Ii had had to buffet against the stream not merely amongst his fellow-Daimyō but even in his own clan. With one striking exception, all his vassals proved to be orthodox Conservatives of a very pronounced type; yet he boldly adopted the heretical views of Nakagawa and sent in a memorial setting forth strong reasons why a conciliatory reply to the President's letter should be given, for the time at least. Among the Bakufu officials there were also a very few who adopted similar views to those of the two great territorial lords, Koga, the son of the distinguished Dutch scholar, and Toda the Governor of Uraga incurred much odium by implicitly throwing doubts on the possibility of upholding the "ancestral law" any longer. And a very remarkable document came from Takashima, the famous gunnery instructor whom "Viper" Torii worked so hard to ruin.

Long before there was time to read, much less to absorb all these memorials, the Bakufu discovered that the Americans were not the only foreigners with whom it had to deal. Early in August a special report from the Deshima Factor came stating that the Russian Admiral Putiatin was on his way to Japan with several warships, probably for the purpose of watching the operations of Perry's squadron. This warning was very soon followed by reality. On 21st August, 1853, four Russian men-of-war actually entered Nagasaki harbour, but withdrew and anchored for the night outside. That was a night of great confusion in and around Nagasaki. The troops of Kuroda and Nabeshima and the other clans, charged with the port defences, were hastily called out; and the scenes the Americans had witnessed around Uraga Bay were again repeated here. Next morning the vessels again entered the harbour, and came to anchor. When the Japanese officials went out to them, they were readily admitted on board and most hospitably entertained. Putiatin's conduct here was the complete reverse of Perry's at Uraga; the Russians kept open ship and laid themselves out to conciliate the goodwill of all their visitors. The Admiral wrote to the Governor (Ozawa) that he had purposely come to Nagasaki out of respect for the "ancestral law" of Japan, that he was not seeking small trading advantages, but that he was the bearer of an important dispatch from the Russian Foreign Minister, Nesselrode, to the Bakufu, which he desired to deliver to their Excellencies. This communication was sent on to Yedo at once and instructions requested. In a council of all the high Bakufu officials the matter was fully discussed, and no voice was raised against receiving the dispatches, although Rezánov had been told in 1804 that all further intercourse with, or communications from, Russia would be declined. This fact was to be recalled to the Admiral but, if he still insisted on it his dispatches would be received.

There would be no need for him to proceed to Uraga ; a special commission would be sent to Nagasaki to discuss matters with him. Meanwhile the Admiral was to be treated with the greatest courtesy. On 21st September, Putiatin with his suite was received with great ceremony at the Government office ; the Japanese seemed to be convinced that they could no longer afford to treat a Russian envoy in command of four modern warships as they had treated Rezánov half-a-century before. On this occasion, Nesselrode's dispatch and a letter from Putiatin himself were handed over for transmission to Yedo.

The two practical points in the Russian dispatch were a suggestion for the delimitation of the Russian and Japanese territories in the Northern Seas, and a request that Japan should open one or two ports to Russian vessels and trade. Putiatin in his letter said that to carry on negotiations at Nagasaki would waste too much time, and that it would be advisable for him to proceed to Yedo to settle matters personally with the supreme authorities. After some little delay the Bakufu dispatched two commissioners to Nagasaki to treat with Putiatin—Tsuitsui, a Nishimaru official, and Kawaji. The latter was a Kanjō Bugyō, and knowing better than anyone else the deplorable state of the Tokugawa finances, he was strongly in favour of settling matters peaceably with Americans and Russians alike. So was Koga, the son of the famous Dutch scholar, who was attached to the mission. The commissioners were instructed to say that, in consequence of the Shōgun's death and other circumstances, the authorities had such a pressure of business to deal with that they could not discuss the delimitation question. The necessary information, however, would be collected, and in the course of four or five years the question might be discussed and satisfactorily settled. As to the opening of the ports, they had to fall back upon the " ancestral law " of Japan. Meanwhile, Putiatin had become annoyed at the delay, and seeing that his extremely complaisant action was bringing him no real practical advantage he had begun to change his tone towards the two Governors of Nagasaki. There was no need to receive answers through the Dutch, he told them, for Russia had plenty of warships of her own. His threat to leave the port greatly alarmed the Governors, for they fancied he intended to proceed to Yedo Bay. As a matter of fact he did leave Nagasaki in the middle of November —for he had heard of the outbreak of the Crimean War—but his destination was Shanghai. He was back in Nagasaki again by 7th January, 1854, where the commissioners from Yedo arrived five days later. In the course of the next three weeks there were many meetings between the commissioners and Putiatin, with a considerable amount of banqueting and entertaining. Putiatin was exceedingly anxious to get the delimitation question settled, and there was much discussion about Saghalin, which the Japanese claimed up to the fiftieth degree of latitude, and the Kuriles, all of which they insisted had belonged to them for 1,000 years. As views on these points differed widely, and as the commissioners insisted they had come only to explain the Bakufu dispatch and nothing more, no result was reached. About the opening of a port near Yedo and another in the north, all they could say was that Russia would be placed on the same footing as other foreign countries. Putiatin often alluded to the defenceless state of the Japanese sea-board, and urged upon the commissioners the advisability of Japan coming to a good understanding with Russia to secure support against possible aggressors. When he left Nagasaki on 5th February, 1854, the Russian Admiral had so far obtained no material advantage, though in their intercourse with him the Japanese had certainly changed their attitude since the " silent " interview of 14th July, at Uraga. Six days after the Russians left Nagasaki, Perry with a vastly increased squadron entered Yedo Bay on his second visit.

Perry's advance to Hommoku on his previous visit had clearly shown that the coast defences of Yedo Bay were useless and that Yedo itself lay open to attack. The Bakufu felt that the capital must be provided with defences, and a new special commission had at once been constituted to take this and similar projects in hand. The real brain of the body was Egawa, the Daikwan of Nirayama in Idzu. Egawa had been a pupil of Takashima, the famous gunnery instructor, and when the latter had been imprisoned, Egawa had taken up his work. He had established a foundry and a cannon range at Nirayama, and here, during the last few years, pupils not only from Yedo but from various fiefs had placed themselves under his instruction. From the early forties he had acted on commissions for coast defence, but the poverty of the Bakufu made the execution of the projects he proposed, impossible. Even now it was only by a forced contribution of " Thank-money " from the merchants of Yedo and Osaka that funds were found for the

construction and armament of a line of forts extending in the sea
from Shinagawa to Susaki immediately in front of Yedo, and for
the extension of the Nirayama cannon foundry. A still more
important step, although it involved no immediate outlay, was soon
taken by the Bakufu. On 17th October, 1853, Iyemitsu's old
decree forbidding the construction of warships of more than 500
koku was repealed. It will be remembered that Nariaki of Mito
had insistently urged the abrogation of this decree for many years ;
that Shimadzu Nariakira of Satsuma and Dutch scholars like Koga
and Sakuma had condemned it as unsuited to the changed conditions
of Japan and the outside world, while Ii of Hikone, soon to be
Nariaki's dearest foe, in his recent memorial had not merely
advocated its repeal, but had further recommended that Dutch
masters and mariners should be engaged to instruct the Japanese
in the art of navigation.

Meanwhile the question as to how Perry was to be dealt with
on his second visit was being eagerly discussed. At last, on 1st
December, 1853, Abé informed the Daimyō, on their usual visit
to the Castle, that the Shōgun had ordered that no definite reply
should be given to the envoy's demands, and that he should be sent
away without any treaty of amity and commerce. Endeavours
should be made to effect this as pacifically as possible, but in the
event of any appeal to force the Japanese, both high and low, must
see to it that the empire was subjected to no indignity or disgrace.
A week later, the Daimyō and Hatamoto were informed that
careful preparations were necessary, and that they must be ready
for emergencies. In January, 1854, the officials were instructed
that if the Americans did not stop at Uraga, but pushed on further
into Yedo Bay, they must be regarded as coming with hostile
intent, and promptly repelled by force. Abé was thus apparently
assuming a very stalwart attitude, but it is questionable whether he
did so on his own initiative, and was really convinced of the wisdom of
such a course. At this date, Lord Nariaki of Mito was very powerful,
and these decrees and instructions were no doubt largely prompted
by him. He had already been confidentially informed of the
deplorable state of the Bakufu treasury, but he does not seem to
have allowed that consideration to weigh overmuch with him.
Abé was extremely anxious to have no internal dissensions or com-
motions at this fateful conjuncture ; and his bold front was assumed
to secure the support of the Daimyō, especially of Nariaki and his

huge "Repel-the-Barbarian" following. The crisis was rapidly becoming too acute for the wily and cautious Abé ; in spite of all his suppleness, or rather, perhaps, in consequence of it, he was drifting into an irretrievably false position.

Meanwhile Perry's ships were turned towards Japan for a second time. After touching at Naha on his return voyage, where a vessel was left to attend to the depôt, the Commodore went on to the Canton river, and spent the next five months—August to December —at Hong-Kong, Macao, and other Chinese ports. It had been his original intention to remain in that neighbourhood till the spring, but, towards the end of the year (1853) he learned that the French frigate *Constantine* had started on a secret mission to Japan while, a little later on, he received information of Putiatin's presence at Nagasaki. Accordingly he deemed it well to hasten his departure, all the more so, as he had been joined by fresh vessels from America, one of which brought the presents intended for the Shōgun and the Japanese officials. On 20th January, Perry was at Naha for the fourth time. During his short stay there he received a communication from the Governor-General of the Dutch East Indies, conveying information of the death of the Shōgun soon after the reception of the President's letter. The Japanese Government had requested the Dutch Factor at Nagasaki to make this known to the Americans, as this event, according to the laws and customs of Japan, made ceremonies of mourning and arrangements for succession to the "throne" necessary, and consequently all consideration of the President's letter must be postponed for some considerable time. It was therefore most earnestly desired that the American squadron should not return to the Bay of Yedo at the appointed date. Perry suspected that this request was a fabrication, a mere ruse to obstruct the negotiations while, even if true, he saw nothing in the circumstances to delay him. Accordingly he sent on most of his vessels at once ; and on 11th February, 1854, the *Susquehanna* arrived off Kamakura. Here it was found that one of the sailing vessels, the *Macedonian*, had run aground, but she was soon towed off without any damage. On 13th February, the squadron stood into Yedo Bay, and the three steamers each with a sailing vessel in tow, swept on past Uraga and dropped anchor twelve miles above that town. Here a seventh vessel, the *Southampton*, had been lying for the previous three days. On his first visit, Perry had only had two sloops-of-war in addition to the

steamers *Susquehanna* and *Mississippi*. Now he had a third
steamer, the *Powhatan*, which served as his flagship during his
sixty-four days' sojourn in Yedo Bay, while there were presently
four sloops-of-war and two storeships. A tenth vessel, yet another
storeship, came in later. Altogether the squadron now mounted
some 250 guns, and carried about 1,600 men.[1]

Japanese boats had hurriedly put off from Uraga in the vain
hope of getting the squadron to stop there, and presently some
officials appeared alongside the *Susquehanna* whence they were
directed to the *Powhatan*. On board the *Powhatan* they told
Captain Adams their object was to induce the Commodore to return
to Uraga, where they said there were two high officials in waiting,
while more were expected who had been appointed by the
" Emperor " to meet and treat with the Americans.

This statement was correct, although the " high officials " were
by no means of such exalted rank as the underlings from Uraga
represented them. On 8th February, a commission for the reception
of the Americans had been constituted, the chief of which was
Hayashi, Daigaku no Kami, Rector of Yedo University, who was
only a Hatamoto with an annual revenue of 3,000 or 4,000 *koku*.
Along with him acted Ido, a City Magistrate ; Udono a *metsuke*
(censor) ; Izawa, one of the Governors of Uraga, and Matsusaki,
a Chinese scholar.[2]

On the following days Japanese officials frequently visited the
squadron to urge its return to Uraga, but the Americans refused

---

[1] Dr. Wells Williams writes in his Journal: " Three powerful steamers like
the *Susquehanna*, *Powhatan*, and *Mississippi*, each carrying another vessel, the
Vandalia, *Macedonian*, and *Lexington*, showed the Japanese the means we had at
command, and may have inclined them to receive us now we had come, and not
refer to the strong letter they had written Perry through the Dutch requesting
him to stay away for three years."

[2] Matsusaki was regarded as rather an equivocal character by the Americans.
" He was always present at the conferences, but took his seat constantly at a
distance from the other dignitaries, on the further end of the sedan. By him there
continually crouched, upon his knees, a scribe who was employed in taking notes
of what was passing, occasionally under the promptings of his superior. Matsusaki
was a man of sixty years at least, had a long-drawn-out meagre body, a very yellow
bilious face, an uncomfortable dyspeptic expression, which his excessive short-
sightedness did not improve, for it caused him, in his efforts at seeing, to give a
very wry distortion to a countenance, naturally not very handsome. After the
great banquet on board the *Powhatan* on 27th March, " the excited Matsusaki, on
leaving, threw his arms about the Commodore's neck, crushing in his heedless
embrace a pair of new epaulettes, and repeating in Japanese the words, ' Nippon
and America all the same heart.' He then proceeded to his boat supported by
some of his steadier companions."

to do so, on the plea that the anchorage there was unsafe. It was then suggested that they should go to Kamakura, a proposal that was summarily brushed aside. On 18th February, the visitors announced that the " high official " of whom they had spoken had arrived at Uraga, and that they had been sent to request the Commodore to return to meet him there. Perry thereupon wrote saying that he expected to be received at Yedo, agreeably to the customs of all countries ; that so far from returning to Uraga he intended to proceed higher up the Bay towards Yedo where the vessels could be more secure. Meanwhile, Captain Adams was sent to Uraga to see the commissioners, but when he arrived there, the only incident of note that occurred was the reappearance of Kayama Yezaimon, the *soi-disant* " Governor " of Uraga on the previous visit. On 24th February, Perry did actually move his squadron up the Bay, and came to anchor at Kanagawa. Here Captain Adams presently brought the Commodore a letter from Hayashi, Daigaku no Kami, stating that :—

" We desire the Admiral to come to Uraga, there to have the interview in the building aforesaid, and would gratefully acknowledge the friendly meeting of the Lord Admiral in complying with this order of the Emperor and our own wishes."

Presently their old friend the " Governor " of Uraga, arrived to make a final effort to get the Americans to return. On finding Perry immovable and evidently inclined to advance still nearer to Yedo, the " Governor " suddenly withdrew the previous ultimatum of the Japanese commissioners as to the place of meeting, and suggested a spot in the immediate neighbourhood of the village of Yokohama, directly opposite to where the ships were then anchored :—

" Thus after having for ten days interposed all possible objections to the squadron's moving further up the bay, and having used every inducement to prevail upon the commodore to return to Uraga, they relinquished the position from which they so frequently declared they could not possibly be moved. The explanation of this was found in the fact that the Squadron was now only eight (really fourteen) miles off their capital."

As the spot now suggested for the interview was well under the range of the ships' guns, Perry accepted the new proposal at once. A pavilion was to be erected there as had been done at Kuri ga hama on the previous visit, and the 8th March was appointed as the day for the conference. On the 7th, the form of the proceedings for this momentous occasion was arranged through the indispensable and indefatigible " Governor " of Uraga.

On the appointed day the Commodore landed with great parade, with all the pomp and circumstance of glorious war and of diplomatic etiquette. After the purely ceremonial part of the proceedings, the Commodore was invited to enter a smaller room, and here practical work began. A roll of paper was handed to the envoy which proved to be a reply to the President's letter :—

" The return of Your Excellency," it ran, " as the ambassador of the United States to this Empire, has been expected according to the letter of His Majesty, the President, which letter Your Excellency delivered last year to His Majesty the Emperor of this Empire. It is quite impossible to give satisfactory answers at once to all the proposals of your government, as it is most positively forbidden by the laws of our imperial ancestors ; but for us to continue attached to the ancient laws, seems to misunderstand the spirit of the age ; however, we are governed now by imperious necessity.

" At the visit of Your Excellency last year to this Empire, His Majesty, the former Emperor, was ill, and is now dead. Subsequently His Majesty, the present Emperor, ascended the throne ; the many occupations in consequence thereof are not yet finished, and there is no time to settle other business thoroughly.

" Moreover, His Majesty, the new Emperor, at the accession to the throne, promised to the princes and high officers of the Empire, to observe the laws. It is therefore evident that he cannot now bring about any alteration of the ancient laws.

" Last autumn, at the departure of the Dutch ship, the superintendent of the Dutch trade in Japan was requested to inform your government of this event, and a reply in writing has been received.

" At Nagasaki arrived recently the Russian ambassador to communicate a wish of his government. He has since left the said place, because no answer would be given to any nation that might express similar wishes. However, we admit the urgency of, and shall entirely comply with, the proposals of your government concerning coal, wood, water, provisions, and the saving of ships and their crews in distress. After being informed which harbour Your Excellency selects, that harbour shall be prepared, which preparation it is estimated will take about five years. Meanwhile a commencement can be made with the coal at Nagasaki by the next Japanese first month (16th February, 1855).

" Having no precedent with respect to coal, we request Your Excellency to furnish us with an estimate, and upon due consideration this will be complied with, if not in opposition to our laws. What do you understand by ' provisions ' and how much coal ?

" Finally, anything ships may be in want of that can be furnished from the productions of this Empire shall be supplied. The prices of merchandize and articles of barter to be fixed by Kurakawa Kahei and Moriyama Yenosuke. After settling the points before mentioned, the treaty can be concluded and signed at the next interview.

"Seals attached by order of the high gentleman,

MORIYAMA YENOSUKE "[1]

The Commodore having returned the document requesting that it should be signed by the high commissioner and delivered to him next day, entered at once upon the subject which was uppermost in his mind, the negotiation of a treaty. He remarked that it would be better for the two nations that a treaty similar to the one between the United States and China should be made. He had been sent, he continued, by his government to make such a treaty, *and if he did not succeed they would probably send more ships for that purpose*, but he hoped that everything would be soon settled in an amicable manner, and that he would be able to dispatch two of his ships, *as he desired to prevent others from coming.* A copy of the Chinese treaty, written in English, Chinese, and Dutch, accompanied by two notes from the Commodore and a letter in answer to one sent by the high commissioner from Uraga, were now handed to the Japanese, when they asked for time to have the documents translated into their own language.

On 10th March, the reply to the President's letter, duly certified and signed by the Japanese commissioners, was brought on board the *Powhatan*. In his letter the President had stated that the only objects for which Perry had been sent were "friendship, commerce, a supply of coal and provisions, and protection for our shipwrecked people". In the sixth paragraph of the Japanese

---

[1] Dr. Williams tells us (*Journal*, 3rd March) that this Moriyama was a new and superior interpreter "who had recently returned from Nagasaki, whence he arrived in twenty-five days and hurried on at that. He speaks English well enough to render any other interpreter unnecessary, and thus will assist our intercourse greatly. He inquired for the captain and officers of the *Preble* and asked if Ronald McDonald was well, or if we knew him. (This young man, one of the sailors rescued by the *Preble*, had taught Moriyama English during his stay at Nagasaki in 1848-9.) He examined the machinery and at last sat at dinner in the ward room, giving us all a good impression of his education and breeding". But Moriyama soon came to be regarded as a colossal liar by Perry and his people, and Harris was afterwards staggered at his unblushing mendacity. He was very busy in 1858 and in the subsequent years, and in 1863 he accompanied Sir Rutherford Alcock to England. His English was of no very great service on this occasion. Perry spoke to Portman, his Dutch interpreter, the latter spoke in Dutch to Moriyama, and Moriyama then turned the Dutch into Japanese. In an adjoining room, all unknown to the Americans, sat Nakahama Manjirō, to whom all English and Chinese documents were submitted. Nakahama was a Tosa man who had drifted out to sea, been picked up by an American ship and taken to the United States in 1841. In America he got a good common school education, and about 1851 he returned to the Lūchūs viâ Hawai. See Griffis' *Perry*, pp. 351 and 366.

reply it will be seen that the last two points were conceded without any difficulty, while the Japanese authorities were now, or at least now professed to be, in a somewhat different frame of mind from that of eight years before, when they warned Commodore Biddle that he would be consulting his own safety in not appearing again upon their coasts. The only one of the President's requests they actually refused to entertain was the request for commerce. But even in this matter Perry was determined to force their hand. His action at this juncture excited the indignation of his interpreter, Dr. Wells Williams, whose comments on the matter are somewhat noteworthy :—

" The answer to the reply delivered by Hayashi has been translated to-day, and in it, while Perry is pleased that the Japanese Government has granted what Fillimore asked for, which was all that Cabinet at Washington expected to obtain, he says that it is by no means all *he* wants, nor all the President intended, and ' will not satisfy his views '. The letter last year asked for one port ; Perry now wants five. They desired the Japanese to give assurances of good treatment ; now Perry demands them to make a Treaty, and threatens them in no obscure terms with a ' larger force and more stringent terms and instructions ' if they do not. The Japanese may be disposed to comply, but they may not. Yet what an inconsistency is here exhibited, and what conclusion can they draw from it except that we have come on a predatory excursion ? I hardly know just the position in which to place such a document as this, but the estimation of its author is not dubious, Perry cares no more for right, for consistency, for his country than will advance his own aggrandisement and fame, and makes his ambition the test of all his conduct towards the Japanese. Yet if they will, either from fear, from policy, or from inclination to learn and see more of their fellowmen, open their ports and for once do away with the seclusive system, great good to them will result, their people will be benefited, and the stability of the state increased, perhaps. Yet I despise such papers as this drawn up this day, and it may defeat its own object ; it certainly has lowered the opinion I had of its author."[1]

Before the next interview on 17th March, the commissioners sent a note in reply to Perry's communication of the 11th, in which they stated that :—

" as to the opening of a trade such as is now carried on with China by your country, we certainly cannot yet bring it about."

---

[1] In two or three other passages the interpreter criticizes Perry's conduct rather freely. On 11th March, 1854, he writes, " The vexatious manner in which Perry can annoy those under him without himself caring for the perplexity he occasions makes me glad that I was never disciplined to the navy, where undistinguishing obedience is required." 25th February, " I do not at all like the way in which this nation is spoken of by the Commodore and most of the officers, calling them savages, liars, a pack of fools, poor devils ; cursing them and then denying practically all of it by supposing them worth making a treaty with. Truly, what sort of instruments does God work with."

Asserting that Nagasaki was the only Japanese port that could be frequented by American vessels for their supplies. At this second interview, the commissioners interposed, with great pertinacity, all manner of difficulties to the adoption of the American views, strenuously contending that the laws of the Empire positively forbade the grant of the concessions demanded :—

" They insisted, for example, that Nagasaki was the place set apart for strangers ; they stated that the inhabitants and authorities of that city had been trained to enforce the laws with respect to foreigners, and declared that if the Americans were to have another port assigned to them, five years would be required to make similar preparations. The Commodore replied that *the fact of Nagasaki having been appropriated to foreigners was one of the grounds of his objections to it ; that its inhabitants and authorities, having been so long accustomed to the servility of the Dutch, would doubtless exact more from the Americans than they would be inclined to submit to, and serious consequences might follow.* Moreover, the Commodore declared that he desired it to be well understood, that his countrymen visiting Japan must be free from all those oppressive laws which had hitherto been imposed upon foreigners. *In a word, he declared emphatically that he would not think of accepting Nagasaki as one of the ports.*"

The Commodore then informed the commissioners that he should expect five ports to be ultimately opened to the American flag, but would content himself for the present with three—Uraga or Kanagawa in the Main Island, another in Yezo, suggesting Matsumaye, and Naha in the Lūchūs. After innumerable evasions, the commissioners at last made answer that, as the Commodore positively refused to accept Nagasaki, and as they themselves objected to Uraga, Shimoda would be offered. With regard to Lūchū, they declared that, as it was a distant dependency, over which the Emperor had but limited control, they could entertain no proposition, and as for Matsumaye, that also stood in similar relations to the Japanese Government. In spite of all this, Perry persisted in pressing his demands. Finding him thus unbending the commissioners requested to be allowed to retire to another apartment for private consultation. An hour afterwards they said that a longer time would be required before they could give an answer about the opening of Matsumaye ; it was not in the power of the Emperor to grant the use of that port without consulting the hereditary prince by whom it was governed, and to do so would require a year. Perry replied that he could not leave without a reply of some kind, and proposed, if that prince were an independent sovereign, to proceed to Matsumaye and negotiate with him directly. Thereupon the commissioners promised to return a definite answer on the 23rd March. In regard to Shimoda, it was now agreed that the Commodore should dispatch one or more vessels to that port, and the commissioners, a Japanese officer of rank, to meet them, in order that the harbour might be examined and its fitness for the required purposes determined, it being clearly understood that if it did not answer the expectations of the Americans in all respects, another place, somewhere in the south of the main island would be insisted on. The *Vandalia* and the *Southampton* were accordingly dispatched to examine the proposed harbour. On the 23rd March, the answer about the opening of Matsumaye was sent to the *Powhatan*, the purport of it was that American ships, in want of provisions, wood, and water, should be supplied at Hakodate as was desired. As time for preparations would be required, the 17th September, 1855, was fixed for a beginning there. This concession was also accepted on the condition that the harbour, on examination, proved service-able for the purpose intended. Exception, however, was taken to the unreasonable delay.

Meanwhile, on 13th March, several boat-loads of presents for the " Emperor ", his consort, the members of the Great Council, and the five commissioners had been sent ashore, handed over, and the receipt thereof acknowledged in very courteous terms by the Japanese.[1] On 24th March, the Commodore was invited to go ashore to receive some gifts from the Japanese. Meanwhile, the telegraph the Americans brought had been installed, and the rails for the toy locomotive and car laid, and after the collation on shore, these appliances of modern civilization were set in operation for the enlightenment and entertainment of the Japanese. The telegraph had already been worked, but its interest was found to be inexhaustible, and all the beholders were unceasing in their exclamations of wonder and admiration. The Lilliputian loco-motive also was a source of immense delight to the spectators who gathered along the track in great crowds. On the 27th, there was

[1] The " Emperor " and eight of the other recipients were presented with standard literary works. The " Empress " was the only one who received no whisky. The Shōgun received a barrel of it, and the Great Councillors ten gallons each—Abé getting a double allowance of twenty gallons. Hayashi also received twenty gallons, but his four fellow commissioners no more than that quantity between them. Cases of champagne and cherry cordial were also presented, as well as perfumery, rifles, revolvers, clocks, and stores.

a great banquet on board the *Powhatan*, towards the end of which the commissioners, with the exception of the grave and austerely dignified Hayashi, waxed rather hilarious, for they all appreciated the champagne. Next day (25th March) when the conferences were resumed, the Japanese representatives were unusually grave and subdued. They handed over a letter which had just been received from the American officer sent to Shimoda, containing a favourable report on its suitability as a harbour, and Perry at once accepted it as one of his three ports, declaring, however, that it must be opened without delay. Hakodate, he added, would serve for another, and Naha for the third, but in the discussion of the extent of the privileges to be granted to Americans who might visit Shimoda, it became clear that the Japanese meant to prohibit the permanent residence of Americans in Japan. The proposition to have consular agents resident in Japan also occasioned the utmost anxiety, but it was ultimately conceded that one should reside at Shomida, though he was not to be appointed for a year or eighteen months from the date of the Treaty.

At last the Treaty was drawn, and stood ready for signature. Three drafts of it had been prepared, each in four different languages —English, Dutch, Japanese, and Chinese—all of which were duly signed by the accredited representatives of the two nations on 31st March, 1854. The following is a short synopsis of its contents:—

I. Peace and friendship between the two countries.
II. Shimoda and Hakodate open to American ships, and necessary provisions to be supplied.
III. Relief to shipwrecked people.
IV. Americans to be free as in other countries, but amenable to just laws.
V. Americans at Shimoda and Hakodate not to be subject to restrictions ; free to go about within definite limits.
VI. Careful deliberation in transacting business.
VII. Trade in open ports subject to local regulations.
VIII. Wood, water, coal, and provisions to be procured through Japanese officers only.
IX. Most-favoured Nation clause.
X. American ships restricted to Shimoda and Hakodate except when under stress of weather.
XI. U.S. consuls or agents permitted to reside at Shimoda.
XII. Ratifications to be exchanged within eighteen months.

The Most-favoured Nation Clause is said to have been inserted at the suggestion of Dr. Wells Williams, while it was owing to Dr. Williams' representations that Perry did not insist upon extra-

territorial jurisdiction for Americans. On 9th April, notwithstanding a note from the commissioners urgently remonstrating
against the movement, Perry announced his intention of advancing
as near to Yedo as the depth of water would allow. Two interpreters
came off and did everything they could to dissuade him from his
purpose. He paid no heed to them, however ; and although he
ultimately turned round in a hundred feet of water four miles
behind his surveying boats, he came within sight of Shinagawa.
Not wishing to endanger friendly relations by going too far, he
went back to the American anchorage whence he presently proceeded
to inspect the port of Shimoda (18th April). Here he now made
a first stay of twenty-five days, and another twenty-five days were
spent in a trip to Hakodate. Thither the Commodore went mainly
for the purpose of settling the Treaty limits ; but he found no one
empowered to deal with the matter, and it was agreed that it should
be referred to the commissioners at Shimoda. The outcome of
the opening of Hakodate was that the Daimyō of Matsumaye was
expropriated (being assigned an annual stipend) and his fief was
declared Bakufu land. Three Governors of Hakodate were
appointed, one to reside there and another in Yedo, while the third
was to move about wherever his presence might be necessary in
Yezo and the northerly dependencies of the Empire. Bands of
colonists—*rōnin* among the number—were either sent to or induced
to settle in Yezo for the exploitation of its resources and the protection of its coasts, while the two great northern clans of Sendai
and Kubota (Daté and Sataké) were saddled with the responsibility
of the coast defence of the extreme north of the main island, and
the duty of reinforcing the Bakufu troops in Yezo in case of need.

During his second (and final) stay of eighteen days at Shimoda,
Perry settled a number of vexed points with the commissioners—
now seven in number—and the results of the discussions were
embodied in a supplementary convention of twelve articles. Most
of these are unimportant, but one of them—the ninth—was afterwards productive of trouble. Its terms were :—

" Whenever goods are selected in the shops, they should be marked
with the name of the purchaser and the price agreed upon, and then be
sent to the government office, where the money is to be paid to Japanese
officers and the articles delivered by them."

To the official mind, the only way of trading with foreigners
was the immemorial way in vogue at Nagasaki, and all through

the early sixties we shall find the foreign merchants continually protesting against the Bakufu underlings interfering with their transactions.

At last everything was finished, and on 28th June, 1854, after a stay of 135 days, Perry said " good-bye " to Japan. At Naha, in July, he signed a convention with the Lūchū Regent, legalizing commerce with Americans, and making various other arrangements. Naha thus promised to become an open port for the special benefit of the astute and progressive Prince Nariakira of Satsuma.

Perry had already, on 4th April, 1854, dispatched Commander Adams to Washington with a copy of the Treaty of Kanagawa for ratification. In 296 days, on 26th January, 1855, Adams was back in Shimoda to procure the Shōgun's seal and signature. The commissioners had plumed themselves on being able to keep the Shōgun's signature out of the document; now they made difficulties about getting it appended, while they insisted that the ratifications were to be exchanged not *within* but *after* the lapse of eighteen months. After a good deal of discussion they felt constrained to yield on both points, and on 21st February, 1855, the exchange of ratifications was made with all due formality. Perry's Japan Expedition thus turned out to be a brilliant success ; indeed as we have seen the Commodore was able to exact a good deal more than he had been sent to obtain. But to talk of " the moral grandeur of his peaceful triumph ", as has become the fashion in certain quarters, is surely somewhat beside the mark. The Commodore had appeared at Uraga with an irresistible armament, and his attitude and action at once convinced the Japanese that he would not hesitate to employ it in case of need. Later on, he " threatened them in no obscure terms with a larger force ". His own manly and straightforward narrative leaves us in no doubt as to the means and methods by which his brilliant success was achieved.[1] Much was owing to his foresight, his thorough grasp of the exigencies of the situation, his stern determination, and his diplomatic tact. His organization too, although he never had the fleet of twelve vessels for which he had asked, was thoroughly efficient. Although it was to these factors mainly that Perry really owed his good luck, yet " Perry's luck " became proverbial in

---

[1] See some judicious remarks of Professor Chamberlain on Perry in his *Things Japanese*. Dr. Wells Williams says some very sensible and one or two rather amusing things in his *Journal*, pp. 222, 226.

the squadron. The only really bad weather he met, was on his
passage to the Lūchūs after his first visit to Japan, when the two
steamers had to cast adrift the two sloops they were towing.
Curiously enough, at this very time, the Court of Kyōto had sent
solemn missions to the Sun-Goddess in Ise, and to the six other
leading shrines to implore the gods to raise the blasts and disperse
the invaders, even as they had scattered and overwhelmed the
Mongols nearly six centuries before. Another very important point
is adverted to by Dr. Williams :—

" The general good health of the 1,600 persons in the squadron,
destitute as almost all of them have been of fresh provisions since last
January, and the good condition of most of the stores brought on board
calls for particular mention, as the converse might have hampered the
whole enterprise. The Japanese could not easily collect fresh provisions
for so large a body of people, and the extremity of sickness might have
driven us to the extremity of forcibly supplying ourselves with food at
some rate, even if the alternative was instant hostilities and the
attack of Yedo itself. Such a procedure, necessary as we might have
deemed it for our own preservation, and not to be thought of in almost
any position, might have been resorted to by some one less patient, and
(I can conceive) might have removed the peaceful opening of Japan
to an indefinite period. Now, not a shot has been fired, not a man
wounded, not a piece of property destroyed, not a boat sunk, not a
Japanese to be found who is the worse, so far as we know, for the visit
of the American expedition."

It was also fortunate for a peaceful issue to the enterprise
that Perry proceeded to Uraga and persistently kept away from
Nagasaki. For while Uraga was practically defenceless, Nagasaki
was so no longer. Some time before this Nabeshima the Daimyō of
Saga had engaged the famous Egawa to superintend its fortification,
and the harbour was now protected by a number of forts with really
serviceable armaments. In all probability these would have offered
resistance ; and in that case the re-opening of Japan might have
been the reverse of peaceful.

B

Mention has already been made of the Bakufu's announcement,
towards the end of 1853, that it had been decided to avoid
hostilities if possible and yet send the Americans away without
any concessions, or with as few and insignificant concessions as might
be. Abé took this step to allay the rapidly growing commotion

among the Daimyō, and more especially to appease Lord Nariaki
of Mito and his *Jōi* followers. In May, 1855, the Bakufu let it be
known that concessions had been made, unavoidably and under
stress of dire necessity, and attempted to justify its action by pointing
to the incompleteness of the national defences at the time of the
negotiations with Perry, expressing the conviction that a short
interval would suffice for perfecting arrangements to enable the
government to resist any further demands.

Abé soon began to appreciate the consequences of having
taken the most extraordinary and unprecedented step of inviting
free and unrestrained discussion by the territorial magnates of an
all-important question of public policy. To say nothing of Nariaki
of Mito and his party, the outside feudatories were now very free
in the expression of their opinions, and the weak-kneed inconsistency of the Bakufu was sternly denounced in almost every
great *yashiki* in Yedo. Even among the Bakufu officials themselves
there were malcontents and unfriendly critics. Tsutsui and Kawaji
had just succeeded in baffling Putiatin at Nagasaki, and had
contrived to send him away without yielding in one iota to any of
his demands. On their way back to Yedo they learned of what
was happening at Yokohama and, later on, they were not slow to
express the conviction that, if they had been in Hayashi's place,
the negotiations which eventuated in the Treaty of Kanagawa
would have found a very different issue. They failed to appreciate
the fact that Putiatin and Perry were very different men and in
vastly different situations at the time. Putiatin had begun with
blandishments, and with the avowal of a profound respect for the
" ancestral " law of Japan. When all this failed to carry him a
single step towards the attainment of his object, he had had recourse
to threats. Furthermore, in the negotiations he discussed and
argued, and argued and discussed, and now and then changed his
ground, a circumstance of which the astute Kawaji and Tsutsui
were prompt to take advantage. Perry did not condescend to argue
and he never changed his ground. He simply stated his demands
and insisted on getting them, occasionally hinting that he was
anxious to send home intelligence that would make the dispatch
of any more ships unnecessary. This was a hint that could be
disregarded when it was dropped by Putiatin, for at that time the
Russian Admiral, as was well known to the Japanese, had to be
very careful to keep out of the way of the superior French and

British naval forces then on the eager outlook for him in Far Eastern Seas.

Although, however, rebuffed for the time, Putiatin had no intention of abandoning his Japan mission as a hopeless task. Before leaving Nagasaki on 5th February, 1854, he sent in a note to the officials saying that he would return in the spring to have the boundary question definitively settled ; that if the Japanese did not send a commissioner to Sagahlin, the Russian officials would proceed thither independently ; and that originally he had thought of going to Yedo, but had come to Nagasaki out of deference to Japanese susceptibilities, hinting that his next visit would be to the capital. After a short visit to Shanghai he returned to Nagasaki for the third time, on 25th April, 1854, but his stay there this time was a brief one. In June he was known to be in Saghalin, where he instructed Possiet to write to Tsutsui and Kawaji that after with-drawing the Russian garrison from Aniwa Bay he (Putiatin) would proceed to Ōsaka. The Japanese fondly plumed themselves that the evacuation of Aniwa Bay was a tribute to their own national prestige, but in truth the troops were necessary for the defence of Petropavlosk, where a French and British attack had actually to be beaten off in the following autumn. This letter of Possiet's was laid before the Rōjū on 18th November, 1854, but already ten days before (8th November) Putiatin in the frigate *Diana* had made his appearance off Ōsaka. The result was a panic in Kyōto, where an attack upon the Imperial Palace was actually feared by the courtiers. Presently the Ōsaka Commandant received urgent instructions to send Putiatin round to Shimoda, and the *Diana* leaving Ōsaka on 22nd November, arrived at Shimoda twelve days later on, 4th December. Here Putiatin expressed great dis-satisfaction with the harbour—it was so narrow and so unsafe that he said he could not trust his vessel in it, and he spoke of taking her to Yedo. Meanwhile a commission for the reception of the Russian envoy had been constituted, consisting of Tsutsui, Kawaji, and Koga, as before, with the addition of the Governor of Shimoda, a Censor (*Metsuke*), and Muragaki, who had just come back from an exploring trip in Saghalin. These six had their first meeting with Putiatin on 20th December, and after a return visit to the frigate on the following day, negotiations were begun and proceeded with. Two days later, on 23rd December, the great earthquake of 1854 occurred, which shook nearly the whole of the Pacific face of the main island.

In Shimoda harbour the waters rose and fell as if in a boiling cauldron, then they rushed out leaving the bottom nearly bare. After a short pause they poured in with impetuous velocity, piling up into a wave thirty feet above high-water mark, which swept up to the base of the foot-hills carrying everything before it. Then the waters swept furiously out to sea again, once more exposing the bottom of the harbour, and this performance was repeated five several times. The whole of Shimoda with the exception of fourteen houses was carried away, but the loss of life was much less than might have been expected, for out of the 4,000 inhabitants of the town only eighty-five perished—not a single official being among the victims. The Russians on board the *Diana* had a very thrilling experience. The 6 fathoms of water in which they were anchored fell to less than 4 feet, and they could distinctly discern the stock and upper fluke of their anchor. Luckily the anchor held, but the heavy hull of the vessel (with 52 guns and 250 men on board) was carried round and round like a cork in an eddy making forty-three complete revolutions in a space of thirty minutes. The officers and crew became giddy on account of these gyrations, while some of them anticipated that the bed of the harbour might be rent assunder and their vessel swallowed up. The ship was so badly damaged that it was found necessary to send her guns ashore and to overhaul her hull thoroughly. When the Russians asked for a port to be assigned to them for the purpose, the Japanese commissioners found themselves with a fresh anxiety to face, for to open another port in addition to Shimoda or to substitute another port for it would not at all suit the purpose of the Bakufu at this delicate conjuncture. Fortunately the Russians were satisfied with the small fishing village of Heda, 40 miles round the Idzu coast on Suruga Bay. On her way thither under tow, the *Diana* encountered a gale and went to the bottom, her complement escaping with some difficulty.

The Japanese showed no lack of sympathy with the envoy in his unfortunate predicament. His request for shipbuilding materials and facilities was promptly complied with, and henceforth throughout the winter Russian shipwrights and Japanese carpenters were busy with the construction of two schooners. The Japanese freely acknowledge that their earliest instructors in the art of modern shipbuilding were those Russians whom they were to outclass so hopelessly on the blue water just half a century later on.[1]

Meanwhile the *Powhatan* arrived at Shimoda (26th January, 1855) with the ratified American treaty, and from her Putiatin was able to procure supplies. On 15th March, an American trading schooner also came to Shimoda, and the Admiral succeeded in purchasing her cargo of stores and in chartering her to convey part of the *Diana's* complement to Kamchatka. He himself left Japan in the schooner his own men and the Japanese had built, after tendering the Bakufu his written thanks for the kindness he had received. Count Nesselrode, the Russian Foreign Minister, also wrote to express his appreciation of what had been done, and by the Tsar's orders made a gift of the *Diana's* armament of fifty-two guns to the Bakufu.

The negotiations so unexpectedly interrupted by the great tidal wave of 23rd December, were resumed on 11th January, 1855. As regards the boundary question, the Japanese at first refused to budge from the position they had assumed at the Nagasaki conferences ; and finally it was understood that Saghalin for the present should be left equally open for both nations. Muragaki, specially added to the Commission, had just been over the island, and he was convinced that it was next door to worthless. With respect to the Russian demand for commerce the Japanese also stood firm, and no more was granted to Putiatin than had been conceded to Perry. In fact, although the Russian Treaty signed at Shimoda on 7th February, 1855, consisted of but nine articles with four clauses of additional regulations, it was in the main identical with the Treaty of Kanagawa, with the exceptions that in addition to Shimoda and Hakodate, Russian vessels were to be free to visit Nagasaki as well. It was also stipulated that Russia might, in 1856, post agents not only at Shimoda, but at Hakodate as well. To this provision Abé objected most strongly when he received a copy of the agreement three days after it was concluded, so much so that he wrote to the commissioners charging them to get it expunged. In this also we can detect the influence of Lord Nariaki of Mito, with

---

[1] Titsingh's attempts to teach marine architecture about 1780 have been alluded to. The earliest foreign-rigged vessel constructed in Japan seems to have been built in a Satsuma harbour under the direction of two Spanish adventurers ten or twelve years before Will Adams appeared upon the scene. This vessel was afterwards used by the Satsuma men in the Korean war. A year or two before the arrival of Perry, Shimadzu Naiakira had secretly set his clansmen to work on two or three foreign-style craft at Iso near Kagoshima.

whom Abé was in constant communication at this time. The question of Christianity was also brought up, apparently by Nariaki. Neither Putiatin nor the commissioners had alluded to it in any way during the negotiations. Now the commissioners, acting under instructions from Yedo, sent in a note to Putiatin stating that Christianity was strictly proscribed in Japan, and the envoy thereupon wrote in reply that Russian officials never interfered with the religious affairs and beliefs of other peoples.

The Russian treaty of Shimoda was the third and not the second agreement which Japan had so far entered into with foreign countries. In the autumn of 1854, Sir James Sterling, with a squadron of four British ships, arrived in Nagasaki and negotiated a convention with the Governor of the Port and a Censor (*Metsuke*), who acted under instructions from Yedo. Sterling, in his communication to the Governor, explained the state of hostilities between Russia and the Allies, and accused Russia of territorial designs upon Japan. The Bakufu had, however, no wish to offend Russia, and while from apprehension of the consequences of a refusal, they consented to British vessels frequenting Nagasaki and Hakodate for supplies and to refit, it forbade all hostilities in Japanese ports or territorial waters. By his convention of seven articles (14th October, 1854) Sterling obtained nothing more than Perry had just done, and nothing was said about Shimoda. The convention was ratified on 9th October, 1855.

Since Cécille's visit to Nagasaki in 1846, the Japanese had had no dealings with the French, and they were not particularly eager to renew their intercourse with them. While the *Powhatan*, with the ratified treaty, was at Shimoda, a French cruiser appeared there for the purpose of restoring two Japanese castaways. The Governor of Shimoda refused to receive these and maintained that as Japan had no treaty with France, French vessels had no right to come there under any pretext whatsoever. Supplies were refused, and all direct communication with the vessel declined. The castaways were then transferred to the *Powhatan*, and ultimately received from the Americans.

Meanwhile American traders had not been slow to avail themselves of the provisions of the treaty of Kanagawa. Within fifteen days from Perry's departure from Shimoda, the clipper ship *Lady Pierce* arrived at Uraga. This vessel had been fitted out in San Francisco by a Mr. Burrows, who coveted the distinction of taking

the first ship to Japan after the opening of commercial relations.
The castaway he had on board was readily received, and the *Lady
Pierce* was allowed to approach within ten miles of Yedo. Burrows
received many presents and remained on the best of relations
with the Japanese who came on board his vessel in crowds. He was
informed, however, that foreign intercourse with Yedo could not
be permitted, and that all vessels must proceed to Shimoda or
Hakodate. With the next company of Americans that appeared
in Japan relations were by no means so pleasant. It has been
mentioned that Putiatin purchased the stores of an American
vessel and chartered her to take some of his shipwrecked men
to Kamchatka. The owners (Reed and Dougherty) meanwhile
went ashore and passed ten weeks at Shimoda making purchases
of merchandize. This was by no means agreeable to the Japanese
officials ; and their anxiety was not greatly lessened by the circumstance that the Americans were accompanied by three ladies and
some children.[1]   They requested the traders to leave, insisting
that the treaty of Kanagawa gave Americans no right to a permanent
residence in Japan. Commander Rodgers, of the survey ship
Vincennes, just then arrived in Shimoda, and by interpolating some
words in the seventh clause of the treaty of Kanagawa, the Japanese
succeeded in inclining him to adopt their view of the matter,[2]
so that the merchants had to depart. At Hakodate they were also
denied the right of permanent residence, while an American ship
(the *Wilmington*) was not allowed to discharge any part of her
cargo at Shimoda in August, 1855.

Before the close of 1855, the Japanese had entered into yet
another convention, this time with their old acquaintances and
servants, the Dutch. During the last ten years, there had been no
Deshima Mission to Yedo, but the annual presents had continued
to be forwarded, while the Factor had regularly sent in his annual
report on foreign occurrences to the Governor of Nagasaki. We

---

[1] " We do not want any women to come and remain at Shimoda," were the
words of the commissioners.   When Hayashi got so far as to agree to the opening
of Shimoda and Hakodate, he tried to stipulate that *no American women should be
brought to Japan*. When this was interpreted to Perry, the Commodore straightened
up, threw back his boat-cloak and excitedly exclaimed, " Great Heavens ! if I
were to permit any such stipulation as that in the treaty, when I got home *the
women would pull all the hair out of my head !* " The Japanese fairly trembled at
the Commodore's apparent excitement, supposing that they had grossly offended
him.   When, however, the explanation was made by the interpreters, they all
laughed right heartily, and the business continued. Griffis' *Perry*, p. 365.

[2] See Griffis' *Townsend Harris*, p. 133.

have seen that the draft treaty sent from Batavia to be submitted to the Rōjū had been accepted only as an ordinary annual report to which no answer was necessary,[1] for as we have seen, the Yedo authorities rarely, if ever, deigned to take any official recognition of communications from the Deshima Factor. Perry's success must naturally have had an ultimate effect upon the position of the Dutch, but so long as they were represented by an agent who was considered a mere trader in Japan, the Dutch Government was aware that it could not hope to meet with the international courtesies due to it. Accordingly, the Governor-General at Batavia deemed it expedient to raise Dutch prestige by the dispatch of the steam frigate *Soembing* to Nagasaki. The step proved to be a very judicious one, for the Commander and his officers were visited by Japanese officials of high rank, who had just before been treating the Agent with covert disdain, in spite of the substantial services he was rendering to them and the empire.

---

[1] Dr. Nitobe's comparison of this draft with the treaty of Kanagawa is of considerable interest. He writes (*Intercourse between the United States and Japan*, p. 56) " It still remains to be seen how much Perry availed himself of this draft. The first article of Perry's treaty about peace and amity, is but a weaker repetition of the Netherlands' proposal, where the Dutch king assures Japan of his friendship in case the latter should be implicated in war. Perry's demand (Article II) to have Shimoda and Matsumaye as ports for the reception of American ships is expressed in the Dutch treaty, Article IV, section 1, where two coaling stations are asked for, the one in the north, in ' the Bay of Good Hope ', and the other in the south, on one of the islands of the Linschoten Archipelago. What Perry asks for, in articles III and IV, respecting shipwrecked citizens of the United States, is found in substance in the Dutch Article II. In Article IV, though the point conceded is in the main the same as that implied in the Dutch Article VI, section *b*, still the former has included an express phrase to the effect that American citizens should not be confined and restricted as the Dutch and Chinese in Nagasaki. In Article VI Perry would have any business arrangement to be settled by ' careful deliberation between the parties ', and here he deprived the Shōgunal government of the right to have everything its own way, as suggested by the Dutch Article IV, sections *d*, *e*, and *f*; but in Article VIII, Perry conceded that some articles should be obtained only ' through the agency of Japanese officials appointed for the purpose '. The Most-favoured Nation clause, in Perry's Article IX, is equivalent to Article VI of the Dutch treaty. Change the name of Nagasaki in section *a*, Article IV, of the Dutch treaty to Shimoda and Hakodate, and we have Article VII of Perry's treaty. Perry's Article XI, in regard to the residence of United States consuls or agents in the treaty port, corresponds exactly to section *b* of the Dutch Article IV. The twelfth and last Article of Perry's treaty about ratification finds its parallel in the concluding article of the Dutch. ' Thus considered and compared, one finds but little in Perry's treaty that is original. If it is an improvement that he introduced into Articles IV and V, an express demand for freedom for his countrymen, so can it be said on the other hand that he left out what section *j*, Article IV, of the Dutch treaty requires, namely, extra-territorial rights.'

"However, to speak of Perry availing himself of this draft treaty is somewhat beside the mark, for Perry never saw it, never knew of its existence, and so could not possibly owe anything to it. Doubtless it was an intelligent anticipation of what he would be likely to demand, and so far may have been of service in preparing the Bakufu officials. On the other hand, there seems to be no positive evidence of these having studied it minutely, although some of them may very well have done so."

Shortly after Perry left, in 1853, the Bakufu, adopting Lord Nariaki's suggestion, commissioned the Dutch to procure foreign-rigged vessels for them from Holland. The officials had only the vaguest ideas of the cost of a man-of-war, and in giving his order, the Governor of Nagasaki spoke of fifty or sixty vessels, but on account of the great demand for shipping in consequence of the Crimean War, which was in progress at that time, it had been found impossible to furnish even the two steamers which the Bakufu finally ordered. In communicating this intelligence on 7th August, 1854, Donker Curtius, the Dutch agent, said that his Government was about to send one of its steam frigates to Nagasaki, and that her officers and crew would be ready to instruct the Japanese in marine architecture, navigation, and gunnery during the stay of the vessel. The Bakufu expressed its pleasure in accepting the offer, and the *Soembing* was very well received when she arrived soon afterwards. Her officers and the Japanese officials met on equal terms, and this led to the restrictions on the " prisoners " in Deshima being gradually relaxed, so that they could at last visit the town and suburbs of Nagasaki freely. It would seem that the old practice of trampling on the cross (*Fumi-ye*) which had been regularly observed as the years came round for more than two centuries, was also quietly allowed to lapse towards the end of 1853, without anything being said about it officially at that time. When the *Soembing* left she carried a Japanese order for two steam corvettes and, on her return in the following year (1855) she was presented to the Bakufu by the orders of the King of the Netherlands.[1] In the same year the Japanese established a navigation school and shipbuilding yards in Nagasaki, and here, under the instruction of twenty-two Dutch experts, some of the great seamen of modern Japan began their professional careers. Katsu Rintarō, the historian, and in a measure the founder of the Japanese navy, was the most distinguished of the seventy youths then selected by the Bakufu, both from their own domains and various fiefs, to prosecute their studies in the new school. Along with

---

[1] This vessel, which was the first unit of Western construction to be acquired by the Japanese navy, was renamed the *Kanko*, and was used as a training ship, attached to the new naval school which was formed at Tsukiji, Yedo, simultaneously with that at Nagasaki. She is described as a steam paddle-wheel corvette of 6 guns. It is interesting to note that the " Hinomaru ", the Red Sun on a white ground, was at this time adopted as the national flag, and the *Kanko-maru* was possibly the first ship on which it was ever hoisted.

them worked picked men from Satsuma, Saga, Tsu, Fukui, Kake-gawa, and Lord Abé's own fief of Fukuyama. A little later on, Dr. Pompe van Meerdervoort assumed charge of a School of Medicine at Nagasaki, also established by the Bakufu.[1] Shortly afterwards this gentleman was appointed attending physician to the first modern hospital established in Japan.

Meanwhile, the Dutch had been feeling their way towards a formal convention with the Japanese Government, and at last an agreement was signed on 9th November, 1855, and a treaty in the following January. The only difference between these two documents was that the treaty withdrew the right of the Dutch to lease the ground and purchase the buildings at Deshima, which had been affirmed by the convention. It may be worth noting that one article of this treaty provided that "within the buildings at Deshima the Dutch may practice their own or the Christian religion ".[2]

In the following April (1856) official orders were at last formally issued to discontinue the enforcing of the annual *Fumi-ye* (trampling on the cross) ; and in 1857 this was the subject of one of the additional articles then obtained by the Dutch. At the same time, however, the Japanese commissioners declared that it was still strictly forbidden to teach " the pernicious doctrine " (Christianity), or to import books, pictures and images relating to Christianity or to *any other foreign religion*. Before this the Bakufu

---

[1] The Doctor claims that : " The first public instruction in the medical and surgical sciences given by any European in Japan was my inaugural address delivered on the 15th November, 1857." Siebold gave lectures, and in 1649 Dr. Caspar Schambergen, who actually remained some months in Yedo, also seems to have given public instruction in medical and surgical science.

[2] The Japanese regarded Christianity and Roman Catholicism as identical. Although the " Evil Religion " had been strictly proscribed in 1614, Hatch, the English preacher of the *Palsgrove*, discharged his clerical functions in Hirado about 1620 without the slightest objection or interference from the Japanese authorities. In 1662 a Dutch minister married and baptized in Deshima, in the presence of the officials. Kämpfer indignantly repudiates the story that the Dutch, when asked if they were Christians, replied, " What, what, Christians, we are Dutchmen ". But he admits that *one* Hollander actually did make this answer, to wit, Michael Sandtvoort, Will Adams' old shipmate, who afterwards carried on business at Nagasaki down to 1639. Bk. iv, section viii.

This man Sandtvoort seems to have occupied an altogether exceptional position at Nagasaki and to have lived and traded together with another Dutchman in the town quite independently of his fellow countrymen in the factory. He had originally been stranded on the coast (how Kämpfer does not state) and it was afterwards on being challenged by the Japanese officials on the establishment of their inquisition that to save his own and his companion's life he was guilty of the abjuration quoted above. Kämpfer may have been indignant at the application of the charge, for which only one of his countrymen was liable, to the whole Dutch community, but he writes with entire self complacence of their ignoble share in the destruction of many thousands of the native Christians at Shimabara in the fear of being expelled from this golden Ophir.

officials had been instructed to take every precaution to keep the people from being infected by the " pernicious doctrine ", and to restrain them from all intercourse with foreigners so far as possible This goes a long way in enabling us to understand the stiff battle the Americans and, later on, the British and the French had to fight against the persistent attempts made to isolate them from all social intercourse. As we have seen, these tactics had already entirely nullified the efforts of the French missionaries in the Lūchūs, and had occasioned them to abandon their work there as utterly hopeless.

The Dutch were extremely anxious that their treaty (of January, 1856) should be taken as the model for all the commercial treaties which they foresaw Japan would presently have to enter into with the various Western Powers. Shimoda and Hakodate were to be open for the purposes specified in Perry's treaty, but Nagasaki was to remain the sole port for commercial transactions, and commerce there was still to be conducted much along the old lines, with the Geldkammer (*kwaishō*) on the system of tendering by the privileged merchants of the Five Imperial Towns, no contact between individual foreign and Japanese traders, and no export of Japanese money. The Russians, not being very much concerned about commerce, were not averse to these arrangements, and on his fourth visit to Nagasaki in October, 1857, Putiatin signed a new convention of twenty-seven articles embodying most of the stipulations contained in the Dutch convention of forty articles. Before this, it had already become only too plain to the Bakufu that the Americans would not be satisfied with the commercial concessions that had just been made to the Dutch, and promptly accepted by the Russians. So much the new Consul-General, Harris, who had arrived at Shimoda and taken up his post in August, 1856, had given the local Japanese officials clearly to understand. Before dealing with Harris and his achievements, it may be well to have clear and precise ideas of the state of the government he had to negotiate with.

It is often asserted that at this time there was no stability whatever in the Rōjū, and that its personnel was now constantly changing. Between 1841 and 1844, during Mizuno's attempts at Reform, there *had* been a good many changes in the Great Council, but, after 1844, matters in it returned to their normal course. The four Councillors, who signed the answer to the king of the Netherlands in 1845, were Abé, Makino, Aoyama, and Toda. One of the last two had since died and the other had been dismissed in 1848, but Abé and Makino were still in the Rōjū when Harris arrived in Japan in 1856. In 1848, Naitō and two Matsudairas had entered the Great Council, and these, together with Abé and Makino, signed Perry's Treaty of Kanagawa in 1854, and received presents from him. A sixth man also signed that Treaty, Kuze, specially added to the Rōjū in 1853 in consequence of the grave difficulties of the situation. The two Matsudairas must be carefully distinguished. One, Matsudaira, Idzumi no Kami, Daimyō of Nishio in Mikawa, was not of any special consequence. But the other, Matsudaira, Iga no Kami, Daimyō of Uyeda in Shinano, now and then showed the possession of a will of his own, and his stubbornness presently brought him into such conflict with Lord Nariaki of Mito that his retirement from the Rōjū became advisable. This retirement was only temporary, however, in Harris's time, Matsudaira, Iga no Kami, was after Hotta the most influential member of the Council. The two Matsudairas had some little time before being added to the new commission for Coast Defence, originally composed of Abé and Makino only. These commissioners had been making a special study of foreign affairs, and they had already become sufficiently convinced in their own minds that Western powers were much too formidable to be wantonly trifled with or to be set at naught.[1] A good many of the smaller Bakufu officials had also had to devote much attention to foreigners and foreign affairs, and these had nearly all felt themselves driven to adopt the views of Toda, the Governor of Uraga, who had got himself into much trouble by dwelling, in his memorial of 1853, on the helplessness of Japan in any contest with Westerners. Even among the Daimyō there were a few, although only a few, who were modifying their originally uncompromising opposition to foreign intercourse. The most noted instance among these, perhaps, was Matsudaira Yoshinaga (Shungaku) the Lord of Fukui in Echizen, whose conversion was greatly owing to the arguments of the brilliant young Hashimoto Sanai and a few other enlightened and progressive retainers.

---

[1] A small incident may be worth mentioning in this connexion. In addition to twenty gallons of whisky, a box of champagne, perfumery, and other items, Abé had been presented by Perry with copies of Kendall's *War in Mexico*, and Ripley's History of that war. The illustrations to these works were of a rather grim, grisly and realistic nature, and Abé is said to have been very uncomfortably impressed whenever he turned to them.

But although liberal views were surely making headway in
these quarters, the bulk of the nation (by which is meant the
Daimyō and their vassals) was still bitterly opposed to any intercourse with the despised and hated barbarians. At each new concession, the indignation of the great *Jōi* party found still fiercer
expression. Lord Nariaki had been greatly incensed by the Treaty
of Kanagawa, the Stirling Convention of October, 1854, and the
Russian Shimoda Treaty of February, 1855, had added still further
to his wrath. He roundly taxed the Bakufu with its cowardice
and incompetence, laying most of the blame upon the two Matsudairas, especially upon Iga no Kami, whom he accused of
persistently thwarting the counsels he tendered. Abé, fearing that
Nariaki would withdraw his support, at last dismissed both the
Matsudairas in September, 1855, and Nariaki then seemed to be
likely to become all-powerful in the Councils of the Empire. Hitherto
he had gone to the Castle three times a month ; now, he was
requested to favour the Rōjū with his advice on every alternate
day. Abé thus seemed to have succeeded in conciliating the Daimyō,
but it was not long before he discovered that his sacrifice of the two
Matsudairas had not been such a very judicious step as it was
thought at first. The dismissed ministers had many sympathizers
among the lower Bakufu officials, and, furthermore, Abé soon was
made aware that his action had excited strong discontent in another
quarter that had to be seriously reckoned with.

About the Taman-tsume dokoro Daimyō, something has been
said in a previous chapter. At this date there were seven of these
Lords, of whom Hikone (Ii), Aidzu (Hoshina), Kuwana (Matsudaira)
and Takamatsu were the chief. Hotta, Daimyō of Sakura in
Shimosa, who had been dismissed from the Rōjū by Mizuno in
1843, had also been assigned a place in the chamber. These eight
Daimyō were all more or less opposed to Lord Nariaki of Mito,
and the measures he counselled, and Ii of Hikone was also very
strongly opposed to him. We have already spoken of the remarkable
memorial on foreign intercourse Ii had sent in to the Bakufu in
1853, and we have mentioned that Hotta had expressed himself
in favour of limited foreign intercourse for a time as an experiment
on that occasion. Hotta was rather well posted in foreign affairs ;
for the previous fifteen years or so he had greatly encouraged the
study of Dutch and European science among his own vassals, and
had introduced modern weapons and foreign drill among the levies

of his fief.[1] Ii and his fellow Daimyō now insisted that one of the
vacant places in the Great Council should be assigned to Hotta ;
and Abé felt himself constrained to yield to the demand.
Accordingly, on 18th November, 1855, Lord Hotta entered the
Rōjū for the second time, after a seclusion of twelve years. Not
only that, Abé, who had been Chief of the Great Council since 1844,
was beginning to find the responsibility of the position too onerous
for his comfort, and he now vacated the first seat in favour of the
newcomer. Abé, however, still continued to be powerful. His
main efforts continued to be directed towards smoothing over
differences between his colleagues and Lord Nariaki—a task that
became increasingly difficult as events developed themselves. His
health meanwhile had become impaired ; early in 1857 he began
to absent himself from the sittings of the Council, and on 6th August
of that year he passed away. In ordinary circumstances Abé
Masahiro would have ranked high among the long line of statesmen
that administered Tokugawa Japan. But by the date he entered
the Rōjū, the power of that august body had been seriously under-
mined by Iyenari, the eleventh Shōgun, while the desperate and
deplorable weakness of the Bakufu finances made it impossible
for him to deal with the Daimyō as they had been dealt with
hitherto for, in the face of what was considered foreign aggression,
their active support had been indispensable. This consideration
partly accounts for the extraordinary step of formally inviting
their counsels on the question of foreign intercourse, a step which
really heralded the fall of the Bakufu. Abé Masahiro was
intellectually one of the ablest men of his time, but he trusted
overmuch to adroit trimming, and to the conciliation which tries
to conciliate the irreconcilable. It was only a man of steel like Ii
of Hikone that could have saved the Bakufu during the last four
years of Abé's tenure of office.

Even before Abé's death the breach between Lord Nariaki and
the Bakufu had become all but irreparable. Embittered at having
the shrewdest of his counsels over-ridden or ignored, the haughty
and fierce-tempered old man had ceased to attend the meetings
of the Councils early in 1857. At last, on 11th September, 1857,
his appointment as Adviser to the Rōjū was cancelled ; and on
20th October, Abé's vacant place was filled by the re-entry of

---

[1] See Mr. Satoh's *Lord Hotta, the Pioneer Diplomat of Japan.*

Matsudaira, Iga no Kami, who had been previously denounced by
Nariaki for obstructing his plans, and was dismissed by Abé. Lord
Nariaki was now in undoubted opposition; a little later on we shall
find him mining and burrowing in the old capital of Kyōto—(which
suddenly begins to regain something of its ancient importance)—
and there bringing wreck and ruin upon the dearest projects of
the Bakufu, just when they seemed to be on the very verge of
success.   Hotta and Abé were both convinced that foreigners
would not be likely to rest satisfied with such documents as the
Treaty of Kanagawa.   For one thing, that Treaty was in no sense
a Treaty of Commerce ; and the Dutch continuously repeated their
warning that, for her refusal to grant commercial treaties Japan
would be presently menaced as China had been and was being
menaced.   In August, 1856, Donker Curtius wrote to the Governor
of Nagasaki that he had been requested to say that the British
were not satisfied with Stirling's convention, and that Sir John
Bowring, Governor of Hong-Kong, proposed coming to Japan with
a strong squadron for the purpose of negotiating a genuine commercial treaty.   Curtius sent in further letters on the following
days, explaining among other things the recent wonderful development of trade among Western nations and the high importance
placed on it by foreign governments.   In case Japan obstinately
persisted in her present attitude, she would probably find herself
confronted with an irresistible coalition of foreign powers bent on
forcing her hand, and she would be consulting her own safety
as well as her dignity if she made the desired concessions of her
own free will before any menacing force appeared to exact them.
The two censors (*metsuke*) then in Nagasaki, later on transmitted
these recommendations to their superiors in Yedo, and Abé seemed
to discern a gleam of hope of being able to repair the desperate
financial fortunes of the Bakufu from the profits of an extended
foreign trade, believing, of course, that commerce would still
continue to be conducted on the traditional lines as a virtual
government monopoly.   He was very anxious about the threatened
exhaustion of the copper mines, although he was beginning to grasp
the idea that copper supplied at ruinously low rates need not
necessarily constitute the staple of the new and enlarged foreign
trade. To clarify his ideas in the matter, he instructed the officials
to investigate and report on the various methods of trade.

Before this, however, Harris had already established himself at Shimoda and his attitude and demeanour were giving great concern to the Bakufu. To cope with the situation, Lord Hotta was specially commissioned to take charge of all matters concerning foreigners ; in other words, he was practically appointed Minister for Foreign Affairs (14th November, 1856). His first proceeding was to constitute a commission of eight officials for the consideration of foreign commerce and the problems connected with it. From the tenor of the written instructions furnished to this Commission, it seems tolerably clear that while strongly inclined to open the country to commerce, Hotta was more or less imbued with Abé's idea of making it a mere device for replenishing the Bakufu's sadly depleted treasury. The notion still was that all transactions were to be controlled by government officials ; there was no thought of bargaining being a private affair between individual Japanese and foreign traders, the merchant was still to be under the control of the two-sworded man, and to labour for his support. In the discussions that presently followed with the American envoy, we shall do well then to bear in mind that the term " free-trade ", wherever it appears, is not used as the antithesis to protection—it rather means the right for individual merchants to make bargains free from all official interference or control.

It will be remembered that the eleventh article of the Treaty of Kanagawa provided that the United States Government was free to appoint consuls or agents to reside at Shimoda after the expiration of eighteen months from 31st March, 1854, " provided that *either* of the two governments deem such arrangements necessary." This provision had proved especially objectionable to Lord Nariaki ; in it he discerned the first step in an attempt on the territorial integrity of the Empire on the part of the hated barbarians. Abé, it will be recalled, tried when too late to have a similar article in Putiatin's Shimoda treaty expunged. Now, Abé, reading " *both* " for " *either* " in the clause just quoted, fancied it would be possible to escape the danger and so he instructed the Governor of Shimoda to refuse to receive any consular officer. Harris, on arriving with Commodore Armstrong in the *San Jacinto* [1] on 21st August, 1856,

---

[1] It may be interesting to mention that the *San Jacinto* which carried the first consular officer of a Western power to Japan acquired much notoriety a few years later at the beginning of the Civil War in America by arresting on the high seas two Confederate diplomatic agents while travelling to Europe on a British steamer, an incident which very nearly provoked war between Great Britain and the United States.

at once dispatched letters ashore " to the Governor of Shimoda and to the Minister of Foreign Affairs ", sending to the latter a communication from Mr. Secretary Marcy. These documents were promptly transmitted to Yedo ; and from them Abé perceived that his own interpretation of the eleventh article of the Kanagawa Treaty needed reconsideration. On submitting the question to the Great Censors and the Censors, the law-officers of the time, he was told that it was not possible to refuse Harris a landing and a place of residence. Thereupon he dispatched the Censor, Iwase, together with a new Governor (Inouye, Shinano no Kami) to Shimoda with instructions to see to it that the people should not become infected with " the pernicious doctrine " or with the customs of the barbarians, and that Harris's residence at Kakizaki should be closely watched, and Harris himself and his people kept under the closest surveillance.[1] A due appreciation of these instructions will enable us to put the correct interpretations on a good many rather puzzling entries in Harris's *Journal*. At the new Consul-General's first business interview with the local authorities—when no fewer than *seven* scribes were employed to record the proceedings— he was told that they had not expected the arrival of a consul ; that a consul was only to be sent when some difficulty arose, and no such thing had taken place :—

" Shimoda was a poor place, and had recently been destroyed by an earthquake. They had no residence prepared for me, I had better go away, and return in a year, when they hoped to have a house ready. The Treaty said that a consul was to come *if both* nations wished it, that it was not left to the simple will of the United States government."

On the following day the local authorities maintained :—

" that the treaty provide for a consul but not for a Consul-General ; that the additional articles had not been sent out as ratified, that they expected the Government of the United States would send out an ambassador with the ratified articles, and *then* enter on negotiations about sending a consul. They were anxious to know whether I was resolved to go to Yedo, if not received here. I said that would be settled after consultation with the Commodore. They were greatly agitated when I mentioned the going up to Yedo."

At last when the temple at Kakizaki was accepted by Harris as a residence, he was informed that three rooms in it would be required for the Japanese officers who were to be with him night and day " to await his pleasure " Harris at once sent word that

---

[1] See *Townsend Harris,* by Dr. E. W. Griffis.

he needed all the rooms, and that in no circumstances would he permit any Japanese except servants to be in his house, or even to enter it without his permission. That same day the surgeon of the *San Jacinto* had given a Japanese a prescription for a cutaneous affection, and had directed him to go on board the *San Jacinto* for the medicine. An hour later the man returned in great agitation, forced the paper into the doctor's hand, " making significant motions with his finger that his head would be cut off if he took the paper to the ship." On 1st September, Harris and the Commodore met the new Governor.[1] The Commodore was now asked if he would take a letter to the American Government explaining their embarrassed position, and begging for Harris's removal. Next he was asked if he himself would write to his Government—explaining the reasons why the Japanese refused to receive the Consul-General. Harris was then appealed to to write to his Government for his own removal! Later on, the Governor inquired what Harris's powers and privileges were as a consul. After receiving his reply, the Japanese again begged him to write to his Government stating the strong objections they had to receiving a consul at this time, saying that they had opened Shimoda to the Dutch and Russians, and that these too, would send consuls as soon as they knew that he (Harris) was received there. Harris replied that if their Minister of Foreign Affairs wrote on the subject, he might depend on receiving a speedy answer ; but the Japanese replied that their laws forbade this.

On taking up his residence at Kakizaki, the Consul-General had great difficulty in hiring Japanese servants. The authorities strove " hard to have the boys leave at sunset and return at daylight ", but Harris would not hear of that. A guard had been placed in the grounds of the temple, and in spite of protests it was some months before it was withdrawn. At the same time, the Consul's servants were constantly hampered in their marketing. Here also Harris had to take up a firm position. On 26th December, he gave notice that he :--

" would not allow any spies to come into his presence, or even on his premises ; that when the authorities wished to see him he would only receive the principals and interpreters, excluding spies and secretaries."

On 5th June, 1857, he rated the Vice-Governor severely about

---

[1] " I do not like the new Governor. He has a dark sullen look, and I fear I shall have trouble with him ; I much regret the change." But Inouye, the " Prince of Shinano " presently became one of Harris's very best friends.

the marketing, and furthermore demanded the instant removal of the guards, as their presence made him in reality a prisoner, and was a gross outrage and open violation of the treaty.

" The poor Vice-Governor shook in every joint, and the perspiration streamed from his forehead and that of his secretary."

Two days later, at an interview with the two Governors, the Consul-General pressed this matter home ; and after some rather strong language from Harris the Governors gave an assurance that the guards would be removed on the following day.[1] Meanwhile Harris had been asserting the rights of his status, in other directions and other matters, and had entered upon negotiations with the local authorities about the currency ; the right of permanent residence at Shimoda and Hakodate with the privilage of leasing land and owning buildings at either place ; extra-territorial jurisdiction and similar matters. By June, 1857, these negotiations had come to a definite issue, and on the 17th of that month a convention was signed, which, to quote Harris's own words, " contained the following provisions " :—

1. Opens the port of Nagasaki to American ships.

2. Gives the right of *permanent* residence to Americans at Shimoda and Hakodate, and the right to appoint a vice-consul at the latter port.

3. Settles the currency, so that where we paid one hundred, we now pay only thirty-four dollars and a half.

4. Americans to be exclusively under the control of their consuls, and to be tried by American law.[2]

5. Concedes the right of the Consul-General to go where he pleases in Japan, and to be furnished with Japanese money to enable him in

---

[1] "The Russians dealt with the spy nuisance in a more drastic fashion. On 26th November, 1856, Commodore Possiet and Harris's Secretary, Heusken, took a walk south-east from Shimoda and were followed by a Gobangoshi. The Commodore in a decided and stern manner ordered him to go about his business and not to follow him, and the man left them. But soon afterwards he reappeared and pertinaciously kept with them. The Commodore then seized the man and gave him a thorough shaking, and when the Gobangoshi was released he started off running like a deer, and no more appeared."

In 1869, when I first arrived in Japan, and for at least two years later, a special corps of samurai known as the *Betto gumi* was maintained for the protection of Europeans in the capital. A large detachment was posted at the Legation gates and every member of the staff who went outside, whether on foot or on horseback, was invariably attended not by one but by three guards, and their protection was eminently advisable in view of the great numbers of anti foreign samurai who were always on the streets. The unfortunate fellow who received such rough treatment from the overbearing Commodore was perhaps meant as a guard, and in any case was only doing his duty.—J. H. L.

[2] This was the germ of the system of exterritoriality which afterwards became a festering sore in the corporate body of the nation, and was only ended in 1899, after long years of weary diplomatic negotiation. As the Americans were the first to institute the system, so they were the first to *propose* its abolition, but Great Britain was the first power to *accomplish* it.

person, or by his servants, to make purchases without the intervention of any Japanese official.

This is even more than I was instructed to ask by my special instructions dated 4th October, 1855. No classes of Americans are named in the second article so that *missionaries may actually come and reside in Japan.*

Early in October, 1856, the Dutch steam-frigate *Medusa* had called at Shimoda, and from Captain Fabius Harris then received copies of the Dutch Treaty of January of that year, and of the convention of 1855. This helped him greatly in his task, thanks to the Most-favoured Nation Clause in the Treaty of Kanagawa. In denying the existence of these Dutch agreements, the Japanese officials lied most stoutly, the record of deceit in Harris's *Journal* is at once appalling and amusing, and it is therefore no wonder that we meet with the following significant entry in the *Journal* (8th January, 1857) :—

" I am determined to take firm ground with the Japanese. I will cordially meet any real offers of amity, but words will not do. *They are the greatest liars on earth.*" [1]

By some over-zealous admirers of Mr. Harris it has been ostentatiously asserted that in his dealings with the Japanese he never once had recourse to threats or intimidation. There are, however, stray passages in his *Journal* that tell a somewhat different tale. For example, on 3rd March, 1857, he writes :—

" At last I told them I had something of great importance to communicate confidentially and to them alone. To my great surprise the room was at once cleared of all but the two Governors and Moriyama (the interpreter). I then read to them an extract from a letter to me from the Secretary of State, which was to the effect that, if the Japanese sought to evade the Treaty, *The President would not hesitate to ask Congress to give him power to use such arguments as they could not resist.* The fluttering was fearful, the effect strong. They thanked me for the confidence I had placed in them by reading that part of the Secretary's letter, and asked if they might communicate the same to their Government. I told them they could do so."

Seven or eight weeks later on we find this note in the *Journal* :—

" I cannot see what it is that keeps away Commodore Armstrong ; if I had a vessel-of-war here I should have speedy answers to my

---

[1] Sir Rutherford Alcock, writing about five years later, is scarcely less damnatory of the Japanese in this respect than Harris. In both cases, their verdicts were to no small degree founded on ignorance. Where the Japanese were apparently lying they were probably and frequently speaking truths which were quite unintelligible to their hearers. As the result of over thirty years' residence in Japan and association with natives of all degrees, both high and low, from courtiers to coolies, I can assert without hesitation that the standard of truth in Japan is not lower than it is in Christian countries.—J. H. L.

demands on the two points, but I feel sure they will not be settled so long as no ship-of-war comes here."

Shortly after this (5th May, 1857) he jots down :—

" The absence of a man-of-war also tends to weaken my influence with the Japanese. *They have yielded nothing except from fear, and any future ameliorations of our intercourse will only take place after a demonstration of force on our part.*"

If it be objected that all these passages are comparatively early entries in the *Journal* made at Shimoda while Harris was only winning his way into the confidence and goodwill of the Japanese, the following passage needs consideration :—

" To-day the Prince of Shinano visited me for the first time in three days. I determined to bring about a crisis, and therefore began by saying, that it was now twenty-nine days since I had made some very important communications to the Minister of Foreign Affairs, of which no official notice had since been taken ; that they would not even name a period within which I should have a reply. That such treatment could not be submitted to ; that the President had sent me to Yedo on a most friendly mission, having solely the benefit of Japan in view ; that the United States asked nothing for themselves ; that the trade of Japan was no object to us ; that all we cared for was that our ships could make repairs and get supplies in their harbours, and that we had already got that point ; that they must open their eyes and then they would see that I neither asked, nor would I accept, any favours from Japan ; that ten days ago I offered to give them explanations on any points on which they needed information ; and would reply saying *their treatment of me showed that no negotiations could be carried on with them unless the Plenipotentiary was backed by a fleet and offered them cannon-balls for arguments.* I closed by saying that unless something was done, I should return to Shimoda. Poor Shinano listened in evident trepidation . . . This was apparently a bold step on my part, but from my knowledge of this people I felt that I ran no kind of danger of breaking off my negotiations by what I did ; and the more I yielded and acquiesced, the more they would impose on me ; while by taking a bold attitude, and *assuming a threatening tone, I should at once bring them to terms.*"

This passage, be it remarked, was penned in Yedo itself as late as 9th January, 1858 ; by which date Harris had already achieved the seemingly impossible by obtaining an audience with the August Shōgun or Tycoon himself, by having had several long interviews with the Foreign Minister and Chief of the Rōjū, and so being a long way on the road towards the brilliant accomplishment of the main purpose for which he had been dispatched to Japan. Harris had been very careful to say nothing at all about the chief object of his mission to the local authorities at Shimoda. From their query at the meeting of 1st September, 1856, as to what the *secret* object of Harris's government was in sending him to Japan, it would seem that they suspected something, but none of them appear to have divined the actual truth—that Harris had been dispatched to convert the Treaty of Peace and Amity signed at Kanagawa for no specified time into a Treaty of Amity *and Commerce* for a definite term of years.

Two months after his arrival in Shimoda (25th October, 1856) Harris handed the Governor a letter for transmission to the Rōjū. In it he stated that he was commissioned by his government to make representations to the Japanese government regarding a matter of the very highest consequence to Japan, and that he was the bearer of a letter from the President to the Shōgun which could only be delivered to His Highness in person. To discuss and arrange all this it was necessary for him to deal with the very highest officials directly. As soon as arrangements could be made for him to do so, he would proceed to Yedo, and furnish the very highest officials there with further information. He had refrained from going to Yedo in a warship, because he did not wish to excite any commotion among the ignorant people ; and had come accompanied only by a secretary and a few servants. In a postscript to the letter he made reference to Bowring's projected expedition to Japan, of which the Rōjū had just been fully apprised by the Dutch, and he enclosed a Dutch translation of the Treaty he himself had concluded with Siam on his way out to Japan. This letter was submitted to the Commission for Coast Defence. Some of the members of the Commission, such as Tsutsui and Iwase, recommended that Harris should be brought to the capital on the status of the Dutch envoys from Deshima, pointing out that in case his request was not acceded to, *he might ultimately come up the Bay with an American squadron, in which case they would have to yield to force.* The majority of the officials refused to endorse this recommendation, and by this time Japanese public opinion [1] had become a force that the Bakufu could no longer affect to ignore. Accordingly it was resolved that the Governor of Shimoda should be instructed to deal with the

---

[1] " Public Opinion," it is to be borne in mind, here, as always, during the existence of feudalism in Japan, means the opinion of the military classes, i.e. of the territorial nobility and their armed retainers, constituting with their families about one-fifteenth of the whole population. The commoners had neither voice nor part in any political or social reforms. They were never consulted and never thought themselves of obtruding their opinions in discussion of their bodies in fighting.

matter, and that no direct reply should be returned to Harris's communication. On 7th January, 1857, the Governor informed Harris that they had been charged to give an answer to his letter. To quote the *Journal* :—

"I inquired if it was a written answer? They said it was not. I told them I must decline any verbal answer delivered by a third person to a written letter from me. They asked if I objected to their rank. I told them no. They told me that the laws of Japan forbade the writing of letters to foreigners. I told them I knew better ; that letters had been written by the highest officials, and even by the Emperor himself to Commodore Perry, to the Russians, and to the Dutch, that to assert such palpable falsehoods was to treat me like a child, and that if they repeated it, I should feel myself insulted."

On the following day Harris wrote to the Minister of Foreign Affairs, protesting strongly against the attempt to fob him with a mere verbal answer delivered through a third party ; and he notes that one of the Governors is starting for Yedo—"I suppose in consequence of the flare-up of yesterday." What the Rōjū now learned from Inouye, Shinano no Kami, about the resolute front Harris was showing in Shimoda, disquieted them greatly, and the officials were again ordered to deliberate on the question of allowing him to come up to Yedo. Meanwhile the Great Councillors deemed it well to send a written reply to Harris. To quote the *Journal* again :—

"25th February, 1857. (The Governors) brought in, with great ceremony, a box which was reverentially placed before me. Then a vice-governor opened the box, which I found contained five pieces of a very poor satin damask, which I was told was from five members of the Regency at Yedo, one piece from each person. This over, another box was brought in, which, as I was told, contained an answer to my two letters to Yedo, and at last they mustered courage to open it, and unfold a sheet of paper about five feet long by eighteen inches wide, written quite full, and bearing the seals and signatures of the following princes, who are members of the Regency, with a Dutch translation, which they placed in Mr. Heusken's hands :—Hotta, Bitchū no Kami ; Abé, Ise no Kami ; Makino, Bizen no Kami ; Kuze, Yamato no Kami ; Naitō, Kii no Kami. I directed Mr. Heusken to put the letter and the translation into the box and close it. The Governors wished me to have it translated into English at once. This I declined, saying I should prefer having it done at leisure, and that in the meantime I should like to hear their answer on the currency question. On reaching home, Mr. Heusken translated the Dutch copy of the letter, and I found it to be a simple announcement that all business was to be transacted with the Governors of Shimoda, or Hakodate, and not one word in reference to the President's letter to the Emperor of Japan of which I told them I was the bearer."

On the following day (26th February) the Governors told Harris that they had full powers to receive any propositions he had to make, and to treat on all matters referred to in his two letters to the Minister of Foreign Affairs. Harris asked them if they really could give him answers at once on all matters he might propose without waiting to hear from Yedo. On assuring him in the most solemn fashion that they could do so, he then inquired whether they could make a new treaty without such reference. " Their answer soon proved what I before suspected, that in any minor matter they could decide, but on any important matter they could only hear and report." Five days later Harris dropped a bomb-shell by reading the threatening passage from the American Secretary of State's letter already quoted. Then, to cite the *Journal* once more :—

" 1st April, 1857. Dispatch letter, dated 28th March, to Council of State, in reply to their letter received on 25th February. I have delayed writing this letter so long in the hope of bringing things to a quiet close here. 3rd April. Governors wish to see me. Go to Go-yosho at 2 p.m. They wish to know the contents of my letter to the Council of State. Sorry, but it would be improper in me to disclose it."

In that dispatch Harris had told the Rōjū that it was insulting in them to have made not the least reference to the President's letter in their communication of 25th February, and that it was quite impossible for him to discuss the all-important matter he had originally referred to with subordinate officials. The Great Councillors meanwhile were desperately eager to learn what this all-important matter was ; and Harris, surmising as much, began and continued to play on their curiosity with great adroitness.

On 15th April, 1857, Moriyama, the interpreter, told Harris he wished to ask him a question, and that he wanted him to consider it as a dream ! Suppose the Governors of Shimoda should wish to make a commercial treaty with him, what would he do ?

" I replied that I should first ask to see their full powers, and, if those were satisfactory, that I should show them mine ; and after that we would go to work at a treaty at once. He said if that was so they had misunderstood me ; that they supposed that I would only negotiate at Yedo, and with the High Council. I told them that they had confounded two things ; that what I had to say confidentially, as from my government, could only be said at Yedo ; so also the President's letter could only be delivered by me at Yedo, and in the Imperial presence, etc. ; that negotiations were a different thing ; that I was ready to negotiate with any person of proper rank who could show me the requisite full powers."

The party among the Bakufu officials in favour of receiving Harris had meanwhile been making converts among their fellows. It was known, however, that the Daimyō would be sure to interpose strong objections, and so it was determined to exhaust every means to worm Harris's secret out of him and to obtain the President's letter from him without allowing him to leave Shimoda. On 22nd June, the Governor showed Harris :—

" An Imperial mandate, under the seal and signature Royal, commanding them to receive the President's letter and bring it to Yedo, and they are now quite dumbfounded that I refuse to yield to the mandate." On 8th July, 1857, " Shinano no Kami started for Yedo for the purpose of reporting my refusal to deliver the letter of the President anywhere but in Yedo or to anyone but the Emperor. They assure me that it is quite preposterous to even think of an audience of His Majesty, as the laws of Japan forbid it. As it happens, they also told me that the Council of State could not write to any foreigners (the laws forbidding it), and as the Council *has written to me*, I am shrewdly inclined to think that they will be found equally pliable in the matter of the audience." [1]

In this surmise, Harris proved to be correct. But the Councillors after sanctioning his visit to Yedo, fought the audience question to the very last ditch, insisting that the President's letter should be delivered to themselves. However, the following entry in the *Journal* tells the whole story succinctly enough :—

" 25th September, 1857. The Governors informed me that they had received letters from Yedo relating to the President's letter. That after many consultations it was finally settled that I am to go to Yedo in the most honourable manner ; and after my arrival I am to have an audience of the Shōgun, and then present the letter of the President. The manner in which I am to salute the Shōgun is to be the same as in the courts of Europe, i.e. three bows. They made a faint request that I would prostrate myself and ' knockhead ', but I told them the mentioning such a thing was offensive to me. The Governors informed me that Shinano no Kami was ordered to Yedo for the purpose of assisting in the arrangements to be made for my visit. They said a great deal was to be done in the way of preparation, and that it would probably require some two months to complete the arrangements."

---

[1] The reader may be again reminded that the terms "seal and signature Royal", "Emperor", and "His Majesty", all apply not to the Emperor at Kyōto but to the Shōgun, who had not a particle of right to any one of them. This remark applies to these and similar terms wherever they are used throughout this and previous chapters. Harris and all early diplomatists were at the outset of their careers in Japan almost entirely ignorant of the true status of the legitimate Emperor, and of the relative positions of Emperor and Shōgun, as were the Jesuit writers of the seventeenth, and the Dutch writers of the eighteenth and early nineteenth, centuries. An exception may perhaps be made as regards the Dutch in the case of Titsingh, whose *Illustration of Japan* was published in English in 1822, but even he speaks of the "*reigning* dynasty of the Shōguns" as " Sovereigns of Japan ".—J. H. L.

As a matter of fact, the Bakufu deemed the two months' delay necessary for a strenuous attempt at conciliating public opinion and blunting the hostility of the Daimyō. At last, on 28th October, Harris was told that his start was fixed for 23rd November, 1857 ; and at the same time he was informed that :—

" the Shōgun is not the proper appellation of their ruler, but that it is Tai-Kun. *Shōgun* is literally ' generalissimo ', while *Tai-Kun* means ' great ruler '. The genius of the people shines out in this. For more than a year I have spoken and written ' Shōgun ' when referring to their ruler, and they never gave me any explanation ; but now, when I am on the eve of starting for Yedo, they give me the real word."

On the journey up to Yedo Harris threatened to turn back (26th November) if the Japanese persisted in subjecting his palanquin to any inspection by the guard at the Hakone barrier. At Kanagawa, he was :—

" much surprised by the sight of three ships, of European build and rig, which with two schooners were lying about midway between Kanagawa and Yokohama. These ships have been purchased from the Dutch by the Japanese as the beginning of their navy. To the north-east from Kanagawa, I saw the steamer which the Dutch presented to the Japanese. On 30th November, 1857, I could boast that I was the first American who had ever entered Yedo. I calculated the number of persons that lined the street from Shinagawa to my residence at one hundred and eighty-five thousand. On getting near to the site of the present French Embassy, my bearers started on a full run, rushed through a gate-way, across a court and ended by bearing me into the house. This was doing the matter in the most honourable Japanese manner. Mr. Heusken had to leave his *norimono* (palanquin) at the outer gate. As I got out of mine, I was warmly welcomed by *my old friend*, the Prince of Shinano, who conducted me to my rooms and pointed out the arrangements made for my comfort." [1]

Next day, the Prince of Shinano (the " Prince " was really a small Hatamoto with a few hundred *koku* revenue) enlarged on the difficulties he had overcome, and the great labours he had performed to enable Harris to get to Yedo ; he spoke of his anxious days and sleepless nights ; that care and anxiety had taken away his appetite, so that he had become lean in his person ; that his blood had frequently gushed from his nose from his great agitation, " that he had done all this from his friendship for me, etc., etc." Harris took the opportunity of informing Shinano no Kami that he had come

---

[1] " The new Governor was cold and rude ; not even the raw brandy, which he and others drank, seemed to warm his heart or thaw him towards us." *Journal*, 2nd September, 1856. At that date, Inouye Shinano no Kami had just appeared in Shimoda to keep Harris out of Japan if he could.

to Yedo as the Representative of the United States and not in his private capacity ; that the United States did not ask anything from the government of Japan *as a favour* ; that it only demanded its rights, and that nothing would be accepted on the ground of favour ; that :—

" my mission had for its object the good of the Japanese empire ; and that it was no favour to me or to my country that they should listen to my advice, but that it was the Japanese who should feel grateful to the President for the friendship he had shown to Japan, by the messages with which I was entrusted ; that for myself individually I had no wish to come to Yedo and that I only came because my official duty required it ; that I hoped he now fully understood not only my object in visiting Yedo but that he would clearly see that it was not any favour to me, either in my private or in my official capacity, to receive me in Yedo."

The Prince was quite chapfallen at this, and no very great wonder perhaps, that he was so. The " Prince " was considered to be the envoy's host—or rather " keeper ", as Harris suggested—but he was only one of a commission of eight members (*Ōsetsu-gakari*)[1] appointed to look after the American Ambassador. Hayashi, Daigaku no Kami, and Udono, who had treated with Perry at Yokohama in 1854, served on it along with Tsutsui and two or three Censors. On 3rd December, Harris wrote to the Minister of Foreign Affairs (Lord Hotta, who was also chief of the Rōjū) enclosing a copy and a translation of the President's letter to the Taikun (or Shōgun) and stating that he would pay His Excellency a visit of ceremony whenever he should be ready to receive it. Next morning was the time appointed.[2]

At the interview Harris presented Lord Hotta with a copy of his intended address to the Taikun, on the day of the audience ; and after retiring to consider the document, Hotta came back in half an hour to say that this address was quite satisfactory. At

---

[1] Ōsetsu-gakari, interviewing or reception officials.

[2] The *Journal* has a good deal to say about this function. The Dutch used to be objects of great interest to the ladies of Yedo. After telling us that " The buildings on the street have projecting windows like the houses at Cairo and Alexandria ", Harris goes on, " Through the grass screens to these openings we saw plenty of fair faces, and it would appear that Mother Eve's failing is fully inherited by her daughters in Yedo. Every possible part of the window from its sill to the top was plastered with a female face." Next year, while the authorities were considering what course they should adopt towards Lord Elgin's party, then anchored off Shinagawa, " pleasure parties from the city came to look at the ships and their crews. Boat-loads of ladies, with a great deal of white powder on their cheeks, lips painted a brilliant vermillion, and some with teeth dyed hideously black, gazed on the strangers with the utmost interest and delight, making apparently witty remarks, and then laughing immoderately. They were not at all shy like the Chinese ladies, but peeped in at the port-holes with the greatest curiosity and inquisitiveness."

the same time he handed Harris the Taikun's reply, explaining that as the interpreters could not be admitted into the Imperial presence, he thus furnished the envoy with a copy of the answer, so that by having it translated beforehand, the presence of an interpreter would not be necessary.

On the momentous day of the audience with the Shōgun (7th December, 1857) the envoy was taken to the Palace an hour before the time, for the purpose, as it turned out, of rehearsing his part in the audience chamber under the tutelage of Shinano no Kami. Harris gently but firmly refused to do anything of the kind :—

" At last I was informed that the time had arrived for my audience, and I passed down by the poor daimyōs, who were still seated like so many statues in the same place ; but when I had got as far as their front rank, I passed in front of their line and halted on their right flank towards which I faced. Shinano here threw himself on his hands and knees. I stood behind him and Mr. Heusken was just behind me. The audience chamber faced in the same manner as the room in which the great audience was seated, but separated from it by the usual sliding doors, so that although they could see me pass and hear all that was said at the audience, they could not see into the chamber. At length, on a signal being made, the Prince of Shinano began to crawl along on his hands and knees, and when I half turned to the right and entered the audience chamber a chamberlain called out in a loud voice ' Embassador Merican ! ' I halted about six feet from the door and bowed, then proceeded nearly to the middle of the room, where I again halted and bowed. Again proceeding, I stopped about ten feet from the end of the room, exactly opposite to the Prince of Bitchiū (Hotta) on my right hand, where he and the other five members of the Great Council were prostrate on their faces. On my left hand were three brothers of the Tai-Kun[1] prostrate in the same manner, and all of them being nearly ' end on ' towards me. After a pause of a few seconds I addressed the Tai-Kun as follows :—

" ' May it please your Majesty : In presenting my letters of credence from the President of the United States, I am directed to express to Your Majesty, the sincere wishes of the President for your health and happiness, and for the prosperity of your dominions. I consider it a great honour that I have been selected to fill the high and important place of plenipotentiary of the United States at the court of your Majesty, and as my earnest wishes are to unite the two countries in the ties of enduring friendship, my constant exertions shall be directed to the attainment of that happy end.'

" Here I stopped and bowed.

" After a short silence the Tai-Kun began to jerk his head backwards over his left shoulder, at the same time stamping with his right foot. This was repeated three or four times. After this, he spoke audibly and in a pleasant and firm voice what was interpreted as follows :—

---

[1] Really the Go-san-ke.

" ' Pleased with the letter sent with the Ambassador from a far distant country, and likewise pleased with his discourse. Intercourse shall be continued for ever.'

" Mr. Heusken, who had been standing at the door of the audience chamber, now advanced with the President's letter, bowing three times. As he approached, the Minister for Foreign Affairs rose to his feet and stood by me. I removed the silk cover over the box, opened it, and also raised the cover of the letter so that the Minister could see the writing. I then closed the box, replaced the silk covering, and handed the same to the Minister, who received it with both hands, and placed it on a handsome lacquered stand which was placed a little above him. He then knelt down again, and I turned towards the Tai-Kun who gave me to understand my audience was at an end by making me a courteous bow. I bowed and retreated backward, halted, bowed again, retreated again, halted and bowed again, and for the last time. So ended my audience when I was reconducted to the original room where I was served with more tea."

The most interesting, and perhaps the most valuable, part of Kämpfer's *History of Japan* is his narrative of the two missions he accompanied to Yedo in the last decade of the seventeenth century. His account of the reception of the Dutch envoy by the Shōgun has already been reproduced in this work. It is of deliberate purpose that Harris's very own words have now been cited ; for in dealing with such significant incidents as this audience of his was, it is the best course to let the actor or the eyewitness speak for himself. On the following day, Shinano no Kami assured Harris that " all who were present at the audience yesterday were amazed at his ' greatness of soul ', and at his bearing in the presence of the mighty ruler of Japan ; they had looked to see him ' tremble and quake ' and to speak in a faltering voice. He added that the Americans were a very different people from the Dutch." The truth is that the importance of this incident can hardly be over-estimated ; for in a way it marks the beginning of modern Japan. The Japanese had no respect for a republic—in fact they could scarcely grasp the idea of a republic. It is of some consequence to note that Harris with the Deshima envoys down to Doeff's time was a Republican and originally a " mere " merchant.

In an almost equally important matter it is also advisable to reproduce Harris's *ipsissima verba*. On 12th December, 1857, the envoy had his second and most important interview with Lord Hotta, the chief of the Rōjū, and in his *Journal* he gives the following synopsis of his discourse on that occasion :—

" It related to the changed condition of the world by the introduction of steam ; that Japan would be forced to abandon her exclusive policy ;

that she might soon become a great and powerful nation by simply permitting her people to exercise their ingenuity and industry ; that a moderate tax on commerce would soon give her a large revenue by which she might support a respectable navy ; that the resources of Japan, when developed by the action of free trade, would show a vast amount of exchangeable values ; that this production would not in any respect interfere with the production of the necessary food for the people, but would arise from the employment given to the actual surplus labour of Japan, etc., etc. ; that foreign nations would one after another send powerful fleets to Japan to demand the opening of the country ; that Japan must either yield or suffer the miseries of war ; that even if war did not ensue the country would be kept in a constant state of excitement by the presence of these large foreign armaments ; that to make a concession of any value, it must be made in due season ; and that the terms demanded by a fleet would never be as moderate as those asked by a person placed as I was ; and that to yield to a fleet what was refused to an ambassador would humiliate the government in the eyes of all the Japanese people, and thus actually weaken its power. This point was illustrated by the case of China in the war of 1839 to 1841, the events succeeding that war, and the present hostilities.

I told him that by negotiating with me, who had purposely come to Yedo alone and without the presence of even a single man-of-war, the honour of Japan would be saved ; that each point should be carefully discussed ; and that the country should be gradually opened. I added that the three great points would be : first, the reception of foreign ministers to reside at Yedo ; second, the freedom of trade with the Japanese, without the interference of government officers ; and the third, the opening of additional harbours. I added that I did not ask any exclusive rights for the Americans, and that a treaty that would be satisfactory to the President would at once be accepted by all the great Western powers.

" I did not fail to point out the danger to Japan of having opium forced upon her, and said I would be willing to prohibit the bringing of it to Japan. I closed by saying my mission was a friendly one in every respect, that I had no threats to use ; that the President merely informed them of the dangers that threatened the country, and pointed out a way by which not only could those dangers be averted, but Japan made a prosperous, powerful, and happy nation. . . . When I had finished, the minister thanked me for my communication, and said it should be communicated to the Tai-Kun, and have that consideration which it merited, *and that it was the most important matter ever brought before the Government.*"

This summary can scarcely be described as downright inaccurate ; yet, from the Japanese records of the interview, it becomes plain that the astute American made a rather liberal use of the cheap and very convenient British bogey on this occasion. He said :—

" A nation, in order to be aggressive, must have a station in the vicinity of the country where it intends to gain new territory, but the United States had no rendezvous in the Orient, clearly proving the

absence of any aggressive intentions on her part. He strongly condemned the policy of aggression as simply piratical, and said that the
national principle of the United States was prohibitive of such a policy :
never since the United States became a nation had she taken even an
inch of another's territory. All the countries of Europe, especially
England, were placed under the absolute necessity of opening relations
with Japan *even at the risk of war*. In support of this contention, he
referred to the situation then prevailing in the English territory of
India. He said that India, rich and fertile as she was, could never keep
herself free from the menace of Russia from the north. The late
(Crimean) war fought against Russia by the combined armies of England
and France had for its object the checking of the Russian advance.
They knew that Russia wanted to secure Saghalin and Amur from
whence to come down on Manchuria so as to effect the ultimate descent
upon the English territory of India. England would find it no easy
task to arrest this Russian advance. *She might be forced to wrest Yezo
or Hakodate from Japan*, so as to establish a station whereby the
Russians might be checked from the rear. Great Britain could not
adopt better tactics. . . . The envoys of both England and France
had asked the American Government to join in their invasion of China,
but the proposal was flatly rejected on the ground that such was not
in conformity with the principle guiding the policy of the United
States Government, which would not fight against a weak nation
without any cause of provocation. . . . He then spoke of his conversation with Governor Bowring at Hong-Kong, who on learning of his
mission, told him that he also intended soon to enter the Bay of Yedo
with a fleet of ten ships in order to demand the opening of the country,
and that he *was quite prepared to open hostilities should the demand be
refused*. . . . He had reason to believe that France also would appear
on the coasts of Japan. He attributed the delay of both the English
and the French arrival to the situation in China demanding their
attention at that time. . . . Should Japan conclude a treaty with
the United States, he had reason to believe that England and France
would not make any exorbitant demands. Even if they should do so,
he was prepared to say that his Government would exert its influence
to have peace maintained and the safety of Japan assured."

It will be well to keep the purport of these citations carefully in
mind when we come to consider the developments of July, 1858.
On 21st December, the Commissioners called on Harris inquiring
about the object of sending ministers to foreign countries, their
duties, their rights under the laws of nations. On this occasion the
envoy handed them :—

" a written paper containing the basis of a commercial treaty which
I explained to them article by article, and told them I wished that
paper might be taken into serious consideration. I then gave them
champagne which they appeared to understand and to like. I may be
said to be now engaged in teaching the elements of political economy
to the Japanese and in giving them information as to the working of
commercial regulations in the West."

In spite of all these interviews and all the teaching, the American envoy could boast of no practical results, until he was summoned to a third interview with Lord Hotta, on 16th January, 1858, when the Shōgun's answer to the envoy's requests was given. The demand for the residence of a Minister at Yedo was admitted, his place of residence and the rights he was to exercise to be settled by negotiation. The right of " free trade " was also conceded, and commissioners were to be appointed to settle the details. Three harbours having been already opened, and Japan being a small country, the number could not be increased; but as Shimoda had been found unsuitable, another port would be opened in lieu of it. Harris earnestly recommended a reconsideration of the decision about the number of ports, it being impossible for him to make a satisfactory treaty under such restrictions. He was informed that the commissioners to negotiate with him would be appointed immediately, and that the first conference would be held at his own quarters on the next day but one, 18th January, 1858. On that day, he found that he had only two commissioners to deal with; his own " old friend " the formerly dour and sullen-visaged Governor of Shimoda, Inouye, Shinano no Kami, whose coldness had been impervious to raw brandy even, and Iwase, Higo no Kami, a Censor (*metsuke*). Both these men were simple Hatamoto of a rather low rank. Harris shrewdly divined the situation:—

" Although the Commissioners will have full powers, yet in reality I shall be negotiating with the whole Council of State. The Commissioners will hear my arguments and then request time to consider them. They will repeat what I have said to the Council, who will consider the matter and then dictate what the Commissioners shall say. I feel just as sure of this as though I had been told it by themselves."

And on 28th January, when the negotiations were well under way, he puts down:—

" The Commissioners arrive at half-past one p.m. They go to the Castle in the Council of State at nine a.m., and leave at one, eat a hearty meal, and then are ready for business."

But all things considered, the negotiations actually marched much faster than might have been expected, and by 26th February, 1858, after thirteen conferences, Harris was able to hand a clean draft of the treaty to the Japanese. On the next day the commissioners send him word that " they will require until Tuesday next, 2nd March, to examine with the Council of State the final draft of the treaty. If any doubt had existed in my mind that I was in reality negotiating with the Council and that the commissioners had no real full powers, this significant circumstance would remove it.[1]

The name of Harris is a revered one in Modern Japan, and Japanese publicists are ungrudging in their generous recognition of the services he undoubtedly rendered to the Empire. But it is well to bear in mind that he occasionally allowed himself the luxury of some very frank and candid criticism in his *Journal*. On 25th January, 1858, for instance, he writes :—

" In this Journal I shall confine myself to the leading facts of actual transactions, omitting the interminable discourses of the Japanese, where the same proposition may be repeated a dozen times ; nor shall I note their positive refusal of points they subsequently grant, and meant to grant all the while, nor many absurd proposals made by them, without the hope, and scarcely the wish of having them accepted ; for all such proceedings are according to the rule of Japanese diplomacy, and he who shows the greatest absurdity in these matters is most esteemed. *They do not know the value of a straightforward and truthful policy ; at least they do not practise it. They never hesitate at telling a falsehood, even where the truth would serve the purpose.*"

To almost every article in Harris's draft the commissioners made a point of raising some objection or other, with the notable exception of Article VIII, on which he writes :—

" This article I had inserted with scarce a hope that I should obtain it. It provides for the free exercise of their religion by the Americans, with the right to erect suitable places of worship, and that the Japanese would abolish the practice of trampling on the Cross.[2] To my surprise and delight this article was accepted. I am aware that the Dutch have published to the world that the Japanese had signed articles granting freedom of worship and also agreeing to abolish trampling on the Cross. It is true that the Dutch proposed the abolition, but the Japanese refused to sign it."

Neither was there any real difficulty about the grant of extra-territorial jurisdiction over American citizens in Japan, for this had already been conceded in the Shimoda Convention. When Harris brought up the question at Shimoda, his demand had been accepted without the slightest demur as being the most natural thing in the world to ask for. When a Bakufu constable arrested any outside samurai for any cause, the offender was invariably

---

[1] For synopsis of Mr. Harris's treaty see Nitobe's *Intercourse between the United States and Japan*, pp. 66–7.

[2] As we have seen, this had already been done by official order in 1856 ; while in 1853, the practice had been quietly and silently discontinued.

handed over to his own clan authorities for trial and punishment. By Iyeyasu's Charter of Privileges, the English Cape Merchant had full authority over his fellow-subjects in Japan ; and in Hirado the English had hung, and the Dutch beheaded, their murderers and mutineers without the least interference on the part of the Japanese. The simple fact of the matter is that the Bakufu Councillors saw endless difficulties if they assumed judicial control over the " barbarians ", and they had not the smallest wish to do so. Only when the Japanese, later on, became conscious of the fact that in modern states, apart from the rights or privileges of envoys, there was no such thing as extra-territorial jurisdiction, did they become restive about their own concession of extra-territoriality to the Western powers. And then the main objection was not against the injustice or inconvenience of the system ; it was mainly because it was seen to affect the national prestige. As a matter of sober fact, it was a most convenient expedient for the Japanese at the time it was granted, for it undoubtedly saved them from many dangerous quarrels and disputes. Anglo-Saxons, accustomed to the maxim that every accused is to be treated as innocent until proved guilty and to a fair trial by his peers, could not possibly have been subjected to the laws of feudal Japan without producing a tremendous amount of friction. At Shimoda, Harris had inspected the prison and had found nothing much to say against it. But he goes on :—

" There were three prisoners in jail awaiting trial, two for gambling, and one for a small larceny ; they were to be tried to-day, and will go home acquitted or else well whipped to-night. Whipping is inflicted with a small bamboo or rattan over the shoulders or back. The Japanese cannot understand our imprisonment as a punishment. They say for a man to be in a good house and have enough of food and clothing cannot be a punishment for a large portion of men, who only care for their animal wants and have no self-respect, and as they never walk for pleasure they cannot think it hard to be deprived of wandering about."

Prisons were usually for untried suspects ; but at the beginning of the eighteenth century we met with record of several accused detained in Yedo gaols for so many years that none of the oldest officials could say when or for what they had been brought there ! And Japanese prisons generally were far from being as comfortable as Harris found the Shimoda lock-up to be. As regards trial, the accused rarely saw the face of the judge that passed sentence on him, and the confrontation with, or cross-examination of, witnesses was unknown. That is towards the end of the Bakufu; in Yoshi-mune's time it had been otherwise, especially in Ōoka's court. Moreover the application of torture, whether to obtain evidence, or to extort confession, was perfectly legal and of everyday occurrence, while witnesses no less than accused were often treated in a very outrageous fashion. In view of all this—and a good deal more might well be said—the omission of the extra-territorial clause in Perry's treaty can be regarded only as a piece of ill-judged mawkish sentimentality, likely to be productive of an endless crop of difficulties and dangers to Japanese as well as Americans.

The Commissioners fought hard to keep the prospective American Minister out of Yedo, and to make him reside at Kanagawa or Kawasaki. When their hand was forced on this point, they vainly begged that no Minister should be sent to Yedo before 1861. Harris for some time feared that the treaty would be wrecked by the Commissioners' persistent opposition to the article giving diplomatic and consular officers the right to travel freely in any part of the Empire, for they correctly pointed out that the great feudatories claimed the right of excluding for all time from their domains any of their own fellow-countrymen to whom they might think fit to object, and foreigners would certainly be regarded there as uncomparably more unwelcome intruders. On this point the envoy had to make a small compromise; but he had to drop his proposal that every well-conducted American who had resided one year in Japan might travel about as freely as the natives of the Empire. The Shōgun in his reply to Harris's communication had granted "freedom" of trade; yet, at the first conference, the commissioners informed him that it had been determined to open trade with the Americans on the same terms as the Dutch and Russians had just agreed to. Harris appealed to the most favoured nation clause in Perry's treaty; as to the recently concluded Dutch and Russian treaties, he declared that the conditions were disgraceful to all parties engaged in making them; so far as trade was concerned these documents were not worth the paper on which they were written; were he to sign any such stipulations the President would recall him in disgrace. He then demanded that the promise of the Taikun "that freedom of trade should be granted" should be made good. Five days later

"to my great surprise the commissioners added that the American may buy where he can best suit himself as to quality and price, and sell to whom he pleases, *without the intervention of any Government officer*. This is a complete abandonment of the leading principle of the Dutch and Russian treaties, and is one of the chief points I have so long contended for."

It was, however, the question of the new ports to be opened that Harris calls " the Sebastopol of the treaty ". In his draft he had claimed Hakodate, Shinagawa, Ōsaka, Nagasaki, another port in Kyūshū near the coal mines, Hirado, and two ports on the west coast of Nippon, making together eight open ports, and he also claimed that the cities of Yedo and Kyōto should be opened. Hakodate and Nagasaki were already open, Kanagawa was substituted for Shimoda, while Niigata on the Japan Sea was offered and accepted. The Commissioners said that coal had been discovered within a few miles of Nagasaki, and that Hirado was a poor place with no trade ; so Harris dropped his demand for two extra ports in Kyūshū as well as for another besides Niigata on the west coast. After a very stubborn fight, Harris succeeded in getting it arranged that Yedo should be opened on 1st January, 1862, and Ōsaka a year later on. In their attempts to keep the foreigner out of Ōsaka the commissioners had offered Sakai ; but later on Hyōgo was substituted and this harbour was to be opened at the beginning of 1863. As regards Kyōto the commissioners were unyielding and inexorable. At the very first mention of it, they assured Harris that the idea was absolutely impossible, that to attempt to open the city for a permanent residence of foreigners would excite a rebellion. The proposal that the Americans after a year's residence should be free to travel anywhere was also utterly impracticable.

" Many other propositions of the treaty were excessively difficult, but still might be carried into effect, but these two points were absolutely impossible, and here they made a very sensible remark ; they said if foreign nations would go to war with them on account of these two points, they must make the best they could of the calamity ; but under no circumstances was war from abroad so much to be feared as intestine commotion."

By 22nd February, 1858, all the articles of the treaty itself had been agreed to ; and the tariff regulations were then taken up. Harris pronounced the stipulations in the Russian treaty to be at once imperfect and oppressive, and on pointing out the injustice of such regulations to the Commissioners, they admitted the force of his objections, confessing that they really were entirely in the dark on the subject, not having any experience to guide them. They now proposed a tariff of 12½ per cent. on exports and imports alike. The duty was finally fixed at 5 per cent. on exports and also on supplies imported for ships' use ; 20 per cent. on most other imports, and 30 per cent. on all intoxicating liquors. This tariff was to be open to revision after five years.

Early in March the treaty was ready for signature, but Harris had meanwhile to rest content with a written promise from Lord Hotta positively pledging the signatures to the document on or before the 21st of April, 1858. As early as 17th February, the envoy had learned that the signing of the treaty was not likely to be the very easy and simple thing he had expected it to be. On that day the Commissioners told him that :—

" on the eleventh, the treaty as it then stood had been submitted to the Daimios, and instantly the whole Castle had been in an uproar . . . the government could not at once sign such a treaty except at the expense of bloodshed."

For once, at least, there was a good deal of truth in what the Japanese diplomats asserted. To Harris's very presence in Yedo there was an exceedingly strong opposition. Hotta had indeed prepared the officials for the American's visit to the capital, and in two lengthy memoranda he had set forth to them why and wherefore it had become advisable to yield to his demand for an audience with the Shōgun. Even among his own subordinates Hotta met with opposition over this matter, but that he over-rode without much difficulty. As for the Daimyō, he did not consult them, he merely notified them of the arrangements that had been made. Deputations from the most favourably disposed feudatories waited upon him to expostulate with or to caution him, while Lord Nariaki of Mito and his fellow-thinkers were in a ferment of indignation, and, in a memorial which he presented to the Council, Nariaki emphatically declared :—

" Above all to allow a Barbarian to come near the person (of the Shōgun) is very dangerous, and as one of the Go-san-ké duty forbids me to remain silent in the circumstances, even if this memorandum be left unnoticed."

Shortly after he sent his trusted retainer Ajima to concert measures with one of the Councillors of the Echizen fief to prevent Harris from entering Yedo, but on the ground that the matter had been already decided upon, and that it was then too late to do anything, the Echizen man refused to enter into the project. Lord

Nariaki, however, was far from being at the end of his resources. His consort, the mother of the young Daimyō of Mito and of Nariaki's favourite (seventh) son, now adopted into the Hitotsu-bashi family, was a daughter of Arisugawa, one of the Princes of the Blood, while one of his younger sisters was the wife of the Court noble Nijō, and another the wife of the ex-Kwambaku, Takat-sukasa. He thus had ample means of communicating with the Court of Kyōto. In 1856, he had endeavoured to get his views laid before the Emperor through Takatsukasa, but the Kwambaku, Kujō, had early obtained knowledge of the incident. Now Takat-sukasa and Kujō were on notoriously bad terms ; whatever policy the one might favour, the other was certain to oppose out of mere personal rancour to his rival, a circumstance that has to be kept in mind when we come to deal with affairs in Kyōto in the next chapter. Shortly afterwards the Bakufu sent secret instructions to the *Shoshidai* that he was to give the Court nobles to understand that they would do well to pay no heed to communications from Lord Nariaki. Just at this juncture, Nariaki forwarded another memorial to Takatsukasa, in which foreigners were said to be looking at Japan with greedy and gloating eyes, eager to devour the Empire, while the Bakufu was fiercely attacked for its supineness in general, and specially for allowing the American envoy to proceed to Yedo. It was urged that the sovereign should unite the Empire by issuing a decree commanding the "*brushing away of the Barbarians* ". Some authorities maintain that the document which passes current as the text of Nariaki's memorial is a forgery. But it certainly does not misrepresent the sentiments he habitually expressed ; and it is also certain that he had trusted retainers and agents at work propagating these sentiments with great effect among the Court nobles.

It will be remembered that after his interview with Lord Hotta, on 12th December, 1857, Harris could make no progress in his negotiations till after a further interview in the midde of the following January. The reason for this delay was that the Bakufu officials were discussing the envoy's proposals, and trying to come to some definite conclusion regarding them. At the same time, Lord Hotta caused the record of the interview with Harris to be distributed among the Daimyō, requesting them to express their views on the subject in writing. Shimadzu Nariakira of Satsuma frankly declared himself in favour of opening the empire, while the Daimyōs of Fukui, Tokushima and Akashi showed themselves to be well on the way to conversion to Shimadzu's views.   Lord Nariaki now sent in such an extraordinary memorial that the Bakufu quietly returned it to one of his retainers without comment ; a proceeding that greatly enraged the Mito clansmen.[1]   Later on, when visited by Kawaji and Nagai, Gemba no Kami, two of Hotta's best workers, Nariaki declared that Hotta and Matsudaira, Iga no Kami, should be ordered to disembowel themselves, and that Harris should have his head struck off.   In nearly all the memorials the *Jōi* feeling was intense, and from none of them, with the few exceptions mentioned, was it entirely absent.   But the very remarkable thing was that a great majority of the Daimyōs now recommended that the decision of the Court of Kyōto should be invoked.   This seemed to be striking an entirely new note, one of sinister import for the hitherto autocratic Bakufu.   But, it was the fact that, in 1853, after Perry's first visit, one Daimyō had already proposed that the question of how Perry should be received on his second visit should be referred to Kyōto.   And the most remarkable fact of all perhaps is that the Daimyō who made this startling proposition was no other than the chief of the Tokugawa Fudai—Ii Naosuke of Hikone.   The Bakufu Councillors were now greatly impressed with the hold this idea had obtained among the feudatories, and Kawaji had no difficulty in getting them to adopt his proposal to dispatch Hayashi, Daigaku no Kami, and the Censor, Tsuda, to explain the situation to the Court and to obtain its sanction for the opening of the ports.

On 15th February, 1858, Harris :—

"discovered that they wished to delay the signing of the treaty until a member of the Council of State could proceed as Ambassador to the spiritual Emperor at Kyōto and get his approval ; that the moment that approval was received, the Daimios must withdraw their opposition.   On Harris inquiring what they would do if the Mikado refused his consent, they replied in a prompt and decided manner that *the government had determined not to receive any objections from the Mikado*. Previously, on 28th January, the Commissioners spoke almost contemptuously of the Mikado, and roared with laughter when I quoted some remarks concerning the veneration in which he is held by the Japanese.   They say that he has neither money, political power, nor anything that is valued in Japan ; he is a mere cypher."

By 20th February, Harris was getting to be seriously puzzled

---

[1] For some remarks on this document see Mr. Satoh's *Lord Hotta*, p. 66.

about the real power and position of the Mikado ; on that day the commissioners assured him that :—

" even those most violently opposed to the treaty will say, if he decides in favour of the treaty, ' God has spoken, I submit.' This does not agree very well with the almost contemptuous manner in which the Japanese speak of this potentate."

The commissioners were meanwhile beginning to get undeceived about the supposed powerlessness of Kyōto. When it had been resolved to open negotiations with Harris, instructions had been transmitted to Wakizaka, the Kyōto *Shoshidai*, to inform the Court of the exact posture of affairs ; and thus the ground had been prepared for Hayashi and Tsuda, who were dispatched from Yedo on 25th January, 1858. The two *Tensō*, Hirohashi and Higashibojō, were then summoned by the *Shoshidai* ;   and to them Hayashi gave a resumé of what had occurred since the arrival of Perry, explaining that the altered conditions of the outside world, and the weakness of the empire's defences made it impossible for Japan to persist in her traditional policy of seclusion any longer. He set forth all Harris's various demands, and recounted the assiduous efforts of the Bakufu to minimize them, laying the greatest stress upon the Bakufu's determination to allow the foreigners no access to Kyōto or its neighbourhood. Most of the Court nobles confounded the opening of the ports with actual cessions of territory to the Barbarians, who, they were convinced, were bent upon the conquest of the whole Empire. Moreover, they were terribly and grievously offended by Hayashi's accounts of the irresistible superiority of the barbarian armaments. Presently the Court was in a ferment of indignation ; and it soon became only too plain that Hayashi's failure was complete. Among other things, the courtiers professed to consider themselves insulted by the Bakufu sending officials of such low rank on such an important mission. All this was promptly reported to Yedo ; and it was in consequence of this that the Commissioners informed Harris on 17th February that a member of the Council of State was to proceed to Kyōto to procure the sanction of the Mikado for the signing of the treaty. Meanwhile :—

" they proposed that we should go on with the treaty until it was completed and engrossed ; that I should amuse myself by going about, and if I wished to make a trip to Shimoda, the Government would send me down and bring me back in their steamer. In answer I said that what they had told me was unprecedented in the history of negotiations ; that it was much like the acts of children, and unworthy of wise statesmen like those who ruled Japan ; that it was trifling with a serious matter ; that it would be sure to give the President great concern ; that it would have been far better not to have negotiated with me at all than to refuse to sign a treaty which had cost so much labour, for so very trifling a reason, etc. I added that the mere *act* of signing the treaty might be kept as secret as they chose, as I should not divulge it in Japan. They replied that it was impossible to keep anything secret that passed between us (and I have no doubt they spoke truly) ; that they were acting in good faith, and I might rely that the treaty should be executed. I finally told them that I had no power to compel them to execute the treaty ; that I could not give them an answer to their proposition, but I proposed to put that matter aside for the present and proceed to complete the treaty, but they must clearly understand that I did not agree to accept the delay asked for.''

Next day Harris made the following suggestion to Shinano no Kami :—

" Let us proceed and complete the treaty as soon as possible, and have it engrossed and ready for signature. Then let the Council of State, or the Minister of Foreign Affairs, write me a letter saying that the Commissioners appointed to negotiate with me a commercial treaty between the United States and Japan had completed their labours, and that the treaty was now ready for signature ; but for certain important reasons, the signing of the treaty must be postponed for sixty days, on or before the expiration of which time the treaty as it now stood should be signed. Thereupon I would return to Shimoda to prepare my dispatches for my government ; that at the end of fifty days, if not before, the government should send their steamer to Shimoda for bringing me again to Yedo, for the purpose of executing the treaty."

On the following day (19th February) Harris was informed that his proposition had been accepted and

" that the letter pledging the faith of the Government that the treaty should be executed within sixty days from the date would be signed by Hotta, Minister of Foreign Affairs—and that the steamer should be sent to Shimoda ten days before that time to bring him to Yedo."

All these promises were duly implemented. Lord Hotta had determined to undertake the Kyōto mission himself, taking with him the astute Kawaji, and Iwase, one of the two Commissioners negotiating with Harris. Hitherto a word from a member of the Great Council had always proved sufficient to overawe the Kugé, and as the Kugé suffered from chronic impecuniosity, they were notoriously open to the argument of the purse. Harris on 20th February, 1858, notes that large sums of money had already been distributed among the officers of the Mikado, and that larger sums will be applied in the same manner. Hotta was so confident of success that he informed the Daimyō of Echizen that ten days in Kyōto would be ample for the accomplishment of his purpose. He set out on 6th March, and reached the old capital on 19th March. After a stay of ten days there he could easily be back in Yedo again by 12th April; so he was acting in perfect good faith when he promised Harris that he would sign the treaty on or before 21st April, 1858. In the result, he did not get back to Yedo until 1st June, and he then returned an utterly beaten and baffled man.

Five days after his arrival in Kyōto, Hotta had gone to Court when he was kept waiting four long hours for an audience. The Kwambaku, Kujō, made no appearance that day, and nothing could be done, and when Hotta called upon the Kwambaku at his mansion next day he was not received. At Takatsukasa's mansion also he failed to get an interview. However, the long memorial he had sent in had been submitted to the Mikado, who ordered the Court nobles to consider it and to express their views upon it. The document in question was a remarkable one in several ways.[1] Alluding to the calamities that had overtaken China, it went on to say that the condition of international affairs forbade any country to remain secluded, either a war had to be fought or amicable relations established. If Japan persisted in her seclusion, she would presently find herself menaced not by one single nation, but by the whole world; and in any such contest, she would be helpless. Among the rulers of the world, there was then none so noble or illustrious as to command universal vassalage. Let Japan enter the comity of nations, develop her military strength and her resources in every way, and join hands with the powers whose principles were identical with her own. When her national position and prestige became assured, all the peoples of the world would look upon the Mikado as the Great Ruler of all nations, and they would all come to follow Japan's policy and submit themselves to her judgment, for Japan was beyond comparison with other countries where ruling dynasties and national institutions had suffered frequent changes :—

" Now is the opportune moment offered us by the changed condition of the world to abandon the traditional policy of the last two centuries, and make a united national effort to seize the opportunity for realizing the great destiny awaiting our country. For this purpose, speedy permission is respectfully and humbly solicited for opening up intercourse with foreign nations."

---

[1] For a synopsis see Mr. Satoh's Monograph on *Lord Hotta*.

In spite of his assertion of the superiority of the Japanese sovereign to other rulers, and of Japan to the rest of the world, Hotta now gave most deadly offence to many of the courtiers by dwelling upon the might and high civilization of barbarian countries. The *Jōi* feeling in Kyōto had long been strong ; and it was rapidly acquiring a complete ascendancy. Besides Lord Nariaki and his emissaries other formidable underground forces were at work in the old capital, of which Lord Hotta had no idea. In certain quarters the possibilities of utilizing the *Jōi* cry as a means of embarrassing the Bakufu were now beginning to be realized. Kawaji and Iwase had meanwhile been busy explaining and using golden arguments, and had clearly made an impression upon the two *Tensō*, upon Higashibōjō especially. Still more important, the Kwambaku, Kujō, had been won over to the Bakufu side by the devices of Nagano, a secret emissary of Ii of Hikone, who was a connexion of Kujō's by marriage. In spite of this the subterranean forces vigorously at work were proving altogether too powerful for Hotta's representations, and the arguments of his henchmen, Kawaji and Iwase. When, about the middle of April, Hotta was shown a draft of the Imperial reply to his memorial, he was still inclined to be hopeful of ultimate success, although the tone of the document was vague and evasive. It set forth the grave anxiety of the sovereign over the question of foreign relations, and recommended that the opinions of the Go-san-ké and of the Daimyō generally should be obtained, but in its final clause the Yedo government was authorized to use its own discretion in dealing with the question. This draft was never formally delivered to Hotta, who had just received an urgent message from the Rōjū, reminding him that Harris's treaty had to be signed on or before 21st April, and saying that the Councillors would not sign it till they had obtained the express sanction of the Mikado to do so.

On 20th April, Sanjō Sanetsumu and six other high Court officials sent in a memorial strongly denouncing the policy of opening the empire to the hated and despised Barbarians, and five days later, eighty-eight Court nobles memorialized the Kwambaku to expunge the final clause in the draft of the Imperial reply, giving authority to the Yedo Government to " use its own discretion ". Two days later, on 29th April, these eighty-eight nobles, after a tumultuous meeting in one of the chambers of the Palace, assembled after nightfall, all armed with swords, proceeded

to Kujō's mansion and intimidated him into deleting the objectionable final clause from the Imperial reply. A new draft was prepared
by Sanjō, and on 3rd May, this document was formally handed
to Lord Hotta at an assembly of the high Court officials. Its
purport was that the Imperial mind was gravely concerned over
the transactions with the United States, they constituted a dire
menace to the prestige of the Land of the Gods, involving, as they
did, national dangers of the most serious nature ; that any innovation in the fundamental traditional policy instituted by Iyeyasu
would be a rank offence against the spirits of the Imperial Ancestors,
and of the ancestors of the Shōgun ; that any relaxation of that
policy would tend to perturb the national feelings, thereby
jeopardizing the permanent peace of the Empire ; that the Shimoda
convention, which had been signed some time before, was in itself
an outrage, and to add to it a new treaty was considered (by the
Mikado) to be a forfeiture of the national dignity ; that in view of
such momentous questions, it would be imperative to confer first
with the Go-san-ké and the other Daimyō as well, before asking
for the Imperial sanction.

All this came as a most unwelcome surprise to Lord Hotta
and the intensity of his disappointment and chagrin may be readily
imagined. He had fondly counted on being able either to persuade
or to bully the Court into acquiescence within ten days from his
arrival in Kyōto. Down to this date, a stern word, or an angry
frown from a Great Councillor had sufficed so make the boldest
among the Court nobles quail. Now threats and stern looks had
so much lost all their terrors for the courtiers that it was the Bakufu
officials who had to listen to haughty language from the Kugé.
Instead of terrorizing the Kyōto nobles into accepting his views
within ten days, Lord Hotta and his able subordinates, Kawaji and
Iwase, had spent six strenuous weeks in explaining, expostulating,
cajoling, and bribing, and the net result promised to be rank and
utter failure. However, Hotta felt he could not afford to give up
the battle as lost. So he prepared a fresh memorial in which he
most humbly expressed his sorrow for causing uneasiness to the
Imperial mind ; but firmly asserted at the same time that the
urgent nature of the task at issue demanded that the Bakufu should
be at liberty to take special measures regarding the treaty, and he
therefore begged that the Shōgunate should be authorized to
adopt any measure which the exigencies of the situation might

demand. He also stated in another letter that he had sent Iwase to Yedo with the Imperial reply ; and that although he had himself received from the Council strong representations urging him to return to Yedo without further delay, he felt that he could not leave Kyōto until a satisfactory solution had been found for the present crisis.

In due course Hotta received his answer. It was quite impossible to grant his request ; if the foreigners should resort to extreme measures while the matter was under consideration by the Daimyō, the Court was prepared to face the inevitable, and the utmost efforts must be made to carry out the Imperial will. The Bakufu should see to it, (1) that permanent safety should be ensured so that the Imperial anxiety might be removed, (2) that measures should be taken to uphold the national dignity and safeguard the Empire from calamities, and (3) that the national defences should be placed on an efficient footing since the refusal to grant anything beyond the Shimoda treaty might be made a cause of war. In case the conference of Daimyō should find it difficult to arrive at a final decision, the Great Shrine of Ise was to be consulted. On 8th May, Hotta was still more clearly notified of the impossibility of entertaining the proposals of the American envoy and of sanctioning the new treaty, it was also definitely stated in this communication that if the other party should remain obdurate and resort to violence, war should be declared. Although he remained for a few more days in Kyōto, Hotta now saw that the case was hopeless. On 1st June, 1858, he was back in Yedo, a very chastened and humbled man, with a situation of the utmost gravity to face.

Harris, who had gone through a serious illness at Shimoda, reappeared in Yedo on 17th April, to find that nothing could be done, for Hotta was still in Kyōto. Presently, a letter came from Hotta outlining the situation, and requesting a short postponement of the date for the signing of the treaty. Two days after his arrival in Yedo, he invited Harris to his mansion, and entered into a lengthy explanation of the absolute necessity of further delay. *Thereupon Harris threatened to proceed to Kyōto to enter into negotiations with what he now was convinced was the real Sovereign power in Japan.* As we have seen, he had been slowly groping to a sense of the fact that Titsingh had firmly grasped and clearly set forth in his book of Japan seventy years before—that it was the Mikado in Kyōto, and not the Shōgun in Yedo, that was the lawful sovereign of the Empire. The point on which the Court had expressed most concern in its communications to Hotta had been the possible appearance of the Barbarians in Kyōto or its neighbourhood ; both Hayashi and Hotta had had to asseverate over and over again that the Bakufu would never allow foreigners to approach the old capital and that it would exert every effort to cancel the clauses in the new treaty admitting them ultimately to Ōsaka and Hyōgo. Harris's threat to proceed to Kyōto could, of course, never be carried out but it was extremely embarrassing. An attempt to proceed to Kyōto might give rise to the gravest complications, all the more so as the prospect of the speedy arrival of the " English barbarians " with an invincible armament now obsessed the Bakufu officials like a hideous nightmare.

Immediately on his return, Hotta had consulted Matsudaira, Iga no Kami ; and they had resolved to ask Harris for a further delay of two months. On 4th June, only three days after his return to Yedo with the story of his failure, Hotta ceased to be head of the Great Council ; on that day Ii Naosuke, the Lord of the great fief of Hikone, holding also high rank at the Imperial Court, was suddenly and most unexpectedly appointed to the extraordinary office of Tairō (chief minister), and it at once became apparent that he intended to wield dictatorial powers. The new Tairō said that two months were quite insufficient ; six months' delay at least would be necessary. Iwase and Inouye, Shinano no Kami, were entrusted with the unpleasant task of dealing with Harris on this matter ; and on 5th and 7th June, they had long interviews with him. In the end, Harris expressed himself ready to consent to a delay of three months provided no English or French armament appeared in Japanese waters ; *if any such armament did appear the treaty must be signed the day after its arrival.* Inouye and Iwase would not consent to this ; and it was finally agreed that the signature of the treaty was to be postponed until 4th September, 1858, the Japanese to give a written pledge " *not to sign any treaty or convention with a foreign power until the expiration of thirty days after the signing of the American treaty* ". The Council of State was furthermore to write Harris a letter

" in which they would pledge their faith, and that of the Tycoon, that the treaty should positively be signed on the date named above, no matter what might be the state of public feeling at the time."

It should be said that the Dutch had also meanwhile been

moving in the matter of getting a new and more satisfactory treaty with Japan. Donker Curtius came to Yedo on 23rd April, 1858, and had an audience with the Shōgun on 8th May. He had been indiscreet enough to say that he was prepared to make such a commercial treaty as *would* be acceptable to the Daimyō ; and by the stipulation of the thirty days just mentioned, Harris had very adroitly relieved himself from the annoyance of Dutch rivalry. Harris, in transmitting the letter from the Grand Council to the American Secretary of State, writes as follows :—

" The Minister of Foreign Affairs also delivered to me a large box containing a letter from the Tycoon addressed to the President of the United States. I was assured that no letter had been addressed by the Tycoon to any foreign power for more than 240 years, and that the answer to the letter of the King of Holland had been written by the Council of State."

The very first question the Tairō had to deal with was whether the Imperial reply to Hotta should be communicated to the Daimyō or not. Matsudaira, Iga no Kami, who was a staunch and stubborn upholder of the prerogatives and dignity of the Shōgun and the Bakufu, and who loathed the interference of the outside feudatories in State affairs, was strongly of opinion that the text of the reply should not be published, while Hotta maintained that it should. The Tairō at once said that it was to be published, immediately too. Accordingly, on 6th June, copies of it were distributed among the Daimyō in the presence of the Tairō and the Great Councillors. On this occasion Hotta entered into explanations, dwelling especially on the fact that the Mikado really did not wish for war, and that every effort must be made to find a solution that would obviate any recourse to arms. Immediately, the Yedo *yashiki* were again perturbed with heated discussions about the advantages or dis-advantages of the treaty. The Lord of Echizen, who had been co-operating with Lord Nariaki of Mito in the great succession question then pending, tried hard to abate the rancour of the fierce old man's opposition to the opening of the country, but with little success. Some others of the great feudatories, alive to the fact that the Kyōto courtiers were factiously utilizing the situation to embarrass the Bakufu, quite regardless of the probable consequences to the Empire at large, were also working to secure the approval of their fellows to the treaty ; but so far without very much result. Suddenly, on 27th July, 1858, a startling communication was received from Harris, who had gone back to Shimoda on 18th June.

Meanwhile, since Harris's arrival in Japan, events had taken place in China which he was not slow to utilize for the promotion of his own objects. In December, 1857, the British captured Canton, in May, 1858, they reduced the Taku forts at the mouth of the Peiho river, the gateway to Peking, and Lord Elgin had proceeded to Tientsin where he secured the Chinese Emperor's assent to the treaty known by the name of that city. Of course, the Dutch continued to send to the Japanese their annual reports of all foreign occurrences, and so Harris's references to events in China and elsewhere were never without their effect. His biographer tells us :—

" All this time Mr. Harris had used no menace or threats of force, though he had not failed to hint at contemporaneous events in India and China, and at the presence of large British and French fleets in neighbouring waters. He showed how much the Japanese would gain by inaugurating foreign intercourse by a commercial treaty granted reasonably and freely, before they were compelled by force to make disastrous concessions."

Generally speaking when Harris's diplomacy is unprejudicedly reviewed long years afterwards, there are good grounds for this claim on his behalf, and for many others equally honourable to his memory, but on 3rd March, 1857, he certainly did use something analogous to a threat, and two months later on, he notes in his own diary :—

" The absence of a man-of-war also tends to weaken my influence with the Japanese. *They have yielded nothing except from fear, and any future ameliorations of our intercourse will only take place after a demonstration of force on our part.*"

He made good his want of naval support under his own flag by reiterated references to what Japan had to expect from the speedy arrival of the aggressive English with a formidable fleet, statements that the Japanese credited all the more readily, as they had never forgotten the *Phaeton* episode at Nagasaki in 1808, and the Takarashima outrage seventeen years later.

On 3rd July 1858, the U.S. S.S. *Mississippi* suddenly arrived at Shimoda and the " Stars and Stripes " ensign was again displayed in Japanese waters by the ship that was so prominent in Perry's squadron. She brought intelligence of the suppression of the Sepoy mutiny, the capture of the Taku forts, the treaty of Tientsin, and the speedy arrival in Japan of British and French plenipoten-

tiaries with strong squadrons to support them. On the following
day, Harris addressed a letter to Hotta, in which he epitomized the
news and urged " the very great importance of having the treaty
signed without the loss of a single day ". Next day, the *Powhatan*
also arrived ; and Harris proceeded in her to Kanagawa on 27th
July ; and from there he sent on his letter of 24th July.   On
26th July, a Russian vessel, with our old acquaintance Putiatin
in command, also appeared at Shimoda for the express purpose of
notifying the speedy approach of the British squadron.   Putiatin,
in spite of the Governor of Shimoda's attempt to detain him, also
proceeded to Kanagawa. On receipt of Harris's letter, the Bakufu
at once dispatched Iwase and Inouye by steamer to Kanagawa.
They came to anchor alongside the *Powhatan* at midnight on 28th
July, and, despite the rule against salutes after sunset, they were
received with a salvo of seventeen guns. After hearing all particulars
from Harris—it seems he assured them that the English were
coming with " several tens " of warships—they were back in Yedo
again early on the morning of the 29th. Among the Councillors
the great question was whether it was possible to proceed before
the Imperial assent had been formally obtained. Hotta had
not a word to say. Matsudaira, Iga no Kami, was strongly in
favour of signing the treaty at once, and spoke very contemptuously of the Kyōto courtiers. Ii, the Tairō, himself dwelt on the
desirability of waiting for the Imperial assent ; but in this view
he found his sole supporter in the person of Honda, a Junior
Councillor. Iwase and Inouye, who were supposed to know more
about foreigners than any of the others, kept on dilating on the
terrible dangers of delay ; and Ii, after procuring the Shōgun's
assent, finally dispatched them to Kanagawa with full powers.
Harris now wrote a letter to the Council of State asserting

" his belief that the American Treaty would be accepted by the
English and French, and that he was willing to act as a friendly mediator
should any difficulties arise . . . The Commissioners went to their
steamer for the purpose of translating the letter which, being complete,
they returned to the *Powhatan* at three p.m., and the treaty was then
signed. After the signatures had been affixed, Commodore Tatnall
hoisted the Japanese and American flags at his masthead and saluted
them with twenty-one guns."

A Commission of Five, including Iwase and Inouye, had meanwhile been constituted for the reception of the English and French
missions ; and on 16th August, 1858, the new office of *Guwaikoku*

Bugyō, or Commissioners for Foreign Affairs, was instituted, the first appointees being Iwase, Inouye, Hori, and Nagai.

Before this, Putiatin, now on his fifth visit to Japan, had claimed attention. On 12th August, he had gone on to Shinagawa, and had been assigned quarters in the Shimpukuji[1] in the Shiba ward. Next day, he met the Japanese Commissioners, and on 19th August, 1858, a treaty of seventeen articles, with Customs Regulations, based on the American treaty, was signed. On the following day, Putiatin went to the Castle to be received in audience by the Shōgun, but as the Shōgun was alleged to be indisposed, he had to be content with appearing before the youthful heir. The fact was that the Shōgun, Iyesada, the thirteenth of the Tokugawa line, had died six days before, on 14th August, although his death was not announced, nor mourning ordered for him, until the 14th of September. Meanwhile, the indefatigable Iwase, together with Nagai and the Governor of Nagasaki, then resident in Yedo, had been negotiating yet another treaty with Donker Curtius, the Superintendent of Dutch trade, whom Harris had side-tracked so very ingeniously. This last Dutch agreement of ten articles was signed on 18th August, 1858, four days after the death of the Shōgun.

Before this, the much-dreaded English " pirates " whom Harris had so effectively utilized as a bogey[2] to intimidate his Japanese friends into complying with his wishes, had really arrived in Japan. Naturally enough, in using the British to frighten the Japanese into making up their minds promptly about the American treaty, Harris had been incidentally forwarding the purposes of the Earl of Elgin, who was commissioned by Lord Palmerston to open up diplomatic relations with Japan after the accomplishment of his task in China. The treaty of Tientsin had been signed on 26th June, 1858 ; but preliminary to carrying out his Japan instructions,

---

[1] Shimpukuji--a Buddhist temple of the Shingon sect.

[2] " While demonstrating the ' peaceful and friendly policy ' of his own Government, which ' required no material force, and kept no fleets in Eastern seas to make aggressive wars on distant potentates and peoples ', Mr. Harris was really invoking the effective aid of the belligerent resources and prestige which were the objects of his reprobation. This bellicose and aggressive action of England . . . was never brought more decisively to bear ; but this time it was in a new country and by the apostle of peace—the Representative of the United States in person. This was a veritable *tour de maître,* to use and turn to such account the belligerent Allies, holding them *in terrorem* over the Japanese, and to do this in a way that should give the United States all the benefit and the credit without any of the cost of great expeditions ; while to Great Britain was left only the odium of a reputation at once bellicose and exigeant." Alcock's *Capital of the Tycoon,* chap. x.

Lord Elgin "allowed a sufficient time to elapse for the news of his success to reach the authorities in Japan, presuming that it would strengthen his mission there". On 12th August, when he appeared in Yedo Bay, the British plenipotentiary was found to be attended not by twenty or thirty battleships, as Harris had said he would be, but by two steam frigates and a small gunboat only. In addition to these there was, indeed, yet another ship, but this was a magnificently equipped yacht which was to be delivered to the Shōgun as a present from Queen Victoria. At Kanagawa, Lord Elgin steamed past Putiatin's squadron, then anchored there, and pushed straight on up the Bay to Shinagawa. To the request that the vessels should go back to Kanagawa he paid no heed. A letter was at once sent ashore to the " Prime Minister " stating that the Plenipotentiary had come to make a treaty of commerce, and to present a yacht to the " Emperor ", and also requesting that the mission might be lodged in suitable quarters ashore.

From Laurence Oliphant's narrative it would appear that Iwase and Inouye and their three colleagues must have taken infinite pains and trouble to do justice to their position as Commissioners for the reception of the English mission. In the quarters assigned Lord Elgin and his suite

"the apartments were fitted up after the foreign style, and it was quite wonderful how they had forestalled the wants of their European guests. It appears that they were first made acquainted with these requirements of furniture through the American furnishings at Shimoda which they ingeniously copied ; so that the members of the mission were delighted to find not only beds but mattresses and mosquito-curtains, and comfortable dressing-gowns in a city where all such articles had been unknown."

Although Inouye, Shinano no Kami, had known about mosquito-curtains and dressing-gowns from his infancy, he had no doubt contrived to learn a good deal more than mere diplomacy from Mr. Harris, who had also introduced him to raw brandy and champagne, as appears from the *Journal*. Shortly afterwards, Lord Elgin proceeded to have an interview with the " Prime Minister ", but it was Ōta, a new member of the Rōjū and not the Tairō, that he met on that occasion. Next day negotiations began with the ubiquitous, indefatigable, and indispensable Iwase and Inouye, assisted this time by four others. At the luncheon preceding the actual work, the *pièce de résistance* was an English ham, and of this the commissioners partook so freely, and with so much gusto, that one of them expressed the hope that the treaty would not taste of ham and champagne. The negotiations proceeded apace, and on 26th August, the " ham and champagne " treaty of twenty-four articles was ready for the eighty-four signatures that had to be appended to its various editions in Dutch, Japanese, and English. Then came the delivery of the yacht. Lord Elgin proceeded on board, where

" he found the Commissioners awaiting him all dressed in their most gorgeous robes. He then formally addressed them, handing over, on behalf of Her Majesty, the yacht which she had presented to the Tycoon as a token of friendship and good-will. Then down came the English ensign, and up went the red ball on the white ground, the signal for the forts to salute . . . With perfect precision the native gunners fired twenty-one guns, with an interval of ten seconds between each. Then came the sharp ringing response from the 68-pounders of the *Retribution* and *Furious,* and the yacht got slowly under way, commanded by a Japanese captain, manned by Japanese sailors, and her machinery worked by Japanese engineers."

After a sumptuous banquet on board the *Retribution,* the high-contracting parties and their subordinates bade each other farewell in the most friendly manner. In spite of all Harris's vaticinations of dire and impending calamity from them, the English " pirates ", with their insatiable earth-hunger, had proved to be rather hospitable, harmless, easy-going, amiable people on the whole. Harris, however, it should be said, had lent the English mission the invaluable services of Heusken, his very able secretary and interpreter, and had shown the British envoy every possible attention when he had put into Shimoda.

There was still more treaty-making in store for Iwase and Inouye and their colleagues. On 25th September, Baron Gros arrived off Shinagawa as French plenipotentiary. The Shōgun's death had been publicly announced some ten days before; and the Japanese expressed themselves averse to engaging in any negotiations while the mourning lasted. Besides, 300 people were dying of cholera in Yedo every day,[1] so the French had better go away and come another time. From the racy and witty account by the Abbé Mermet, who accompanied the mission as interpreter, it is easy to see that the Japanese scarcely ever expected that their

---

[1] During the months of July and August in this year an epidemic of cholera spread through the country, and in Yedo alone, 30,000 people died. Such a domestic calamity must have added to the embarrassments of the Government, already distracted by their foreign affairs and the difficulty of steering a course between the foreign Legates and the bigotedly conservative courtiers of Kyōto.

objections would be seriously entertained. The Frenchmen were
assigned the quarters the Russians had occupied in the Shimpukuji,
and on 9th October, Baron Gros was able to sign his treaty with
Iwase and Inouye and four other commissioners. With this the
rain of treaties ceased for a space, but Iwase and Inouye had yet
no rest from their labours.

The Tairo, Ii, had taken no part in the negotiations which
eventuated in Harris's treaty ; and he now expressed strong dis-
satisfaction with the opening of Kanagawa as a place of residence
for foreigners. It was a post-station on the Tōkaidō, along which
Daimyō, with their armed trains of vassals, were constantly passing.
Collisions between foreigners and foreign-hating *samurai* were not
merely possible but actually inevitable, and any such collisions
at this time would throw the whole country into such a ferment
that war would be the almost certain result. To change the course
of one of the main high roads of the Empire on account of the
presence of foreigners would also give rise to formidable difficulties,
such a thing would be almost universally regarded as a wound to
the national dignity. Accordingly, Ii determined that the aliens
should not be allowed to settle at Kanagawa, and Inouye and Nagai
were sent to Harris to explain the difficulties and to obtain his
consent to substituting Yokohama for Kanagawa as the seat of the
nascent foreign settlement. Harris discerned in this proposition
a subtle and insidious attempt to convert the new settlement into
a second Deshima, and refused to entertain it. Being pressed
again and again by the Japanese on the question, he finally declared
that he could not give an answer until he had consulted with the
other foreign representatives, none of whom had as yet arrived in
Japan.[1] Inouye and Nagai therefore reconciled themselves to having
to open Kanagawa, and Ōta, the Rōjū in charge of foreign affairs,
thought there was no other course left. But Ii, the Tairō, would
not hear of this for a moment. He at once dismissed three of the
original Commissioners for Foreign Affairs, and appointed new

---

[1] Sir Rutherford Alcock, the first British minister to Japan, had arrived shortly
afterwards, and took up his post on 6th July, 1859. He was entirely in accord
with Mr. Harris in his opposition to this action on the part of the Japanese.
Experience soon proved that both were utterly wrong, and that in this instance,
as in many others, the Tairō showed the practical wisdom of a prudent and far-
seeing statesman. At the Yokohama anchorage, shipping of the usual tonnage
of that period could lie within a quarter of a mile of the shore, with deep water up
to the very verge. At Kanagawa, a couple of miles of shallow mud banks, bare at
low tides, would have intervened between ships and shore.

ones—Mizuno, Muragaki, and Katō, and sent them to reopen the question with Harris. Harris now got very angry for once, and told them he would return no answer until June, 1859. Thereupon the Tairō at once issued orders for a causeway (over two miles along) to be built through the marsh between Kanagawa and Yokohama; to have the ground at Yokohama prepared for building; shops and storehouses erected; stone jetties built; a custom-house and warehouses constructed. He judged that foreigners would find it difficult to argue against accomplished facts, all the more so as the anchorage at Yokohama was far better than that off Kanagawa, and in this forecast he proved to be perfectly correct [1] :—

To quote the author of the *Genji Yume Monogatari* :—
" The Tairō, Ii, Kamon no Kami, assumed more and more authority, and being no longer afraid of anybody or anything opened resolutely at Yokohama in Musashi a port and a town ; erected factories for the Russians, English, Dutch, Americans, and French, and built shops and native houses, and drove a brisk trade. A brothel quarter was also set apart beautified as much as possible, pleasure gardens full of artificial scenery, of fountains, and of the flowers which flourish each season. The vessels of all sizes of the five barbarians came and anchored in numbers in the port ; the sight was most beautiful and incomparable, and the place became the busiest harbour of all the Kwantō ; nay, it was enough to make any one wonder."

In truth, Yokohama very soon became a busy and bustling mart ; in 1860 its imports amounted to £197,023, and its exports to £823,812 in value. In the following year (1861) its foreign community of 126 included 55 British, 38 American, 20 Dutch, 11 French, and 2 Portuguese residents. Mr. Harris removed his consulate from Shimoda to Kanagawa on 1st July, 1859, and six days later he proceeded to Yedo and established the American Legation at the Zempukuji. In Yedo he was no longer to be the solitary figure he had been for nearly three years in Shimoda ; on 26th June, Rutherford Alcock, the British Representative, had already steamed up to the capital and he accepted the Tōzenji as a place of residence. On 6th September, the French *chargé d'Affaires*, Duchesne de Bellecourt, arrived and along with him came the Catholic priest, M. Girard, who was soon appearing at public functions *en soutane* without eliciting the slightest protest from the Japanese. M. Girard was really a missionary in charge of Yedo and Yokohama—a fellow-worker of the brilliant and witty M. Mermet,

[1] See Alcock's *Capital of the Tycoon.*

who established himself at Hakodate before the year was out. At Nagasaki, three Protestant missionaries (among them Mr. Verbeck) were soon quietly at work, while three American missionaries, also Protestants, Dr. Hepburn, Dr. Simmons, and Mr. Brown, settled at Kanagawa in the autumn of 1859. But Christianity was still a proscribed religion for Japanese; the placards offering extravagant rewards for denouncers of *religieux* and Christian believers still stood in all public places, and were still to stand there for yet another decade, though the intimation to the survivors of the Macao Embassy of 1640 was now but a vain threat :—

" So long as the sun warms the earth, let no Christian be so bold as to come to Japan, and let all know that if King Philip himself, or even the very God of the Christians contravene this prohibition, they shall pay for it with their heads."

Every intelligent Japanese must have perceived that the days for holding language of that sort had now gone by. Yet when Harris remonstrated with his Japanese friends about their bigoted intolerance they would make reply :—

" Do not press us on that point. On the article of the Christian religion, our hearts are not of stone—they are of iron. Let time have its course."

It will be noticed that in the foreign census of Yokohama for 1860, two Portuguese were included. The Bakufu concluded a convention with Portugal on 3rd August, 1860, although over 200 years ago the Portuguese had been banished from Japan *for ever* ! Furthermore, the Dutch envoys from Deshima had been solemnly cautioned on each visit to Yedo to see to it that the Dutch should hold no communication with the Portuguese ; that they should notify the Japanese of any Portuguese projects against Japan, and should apprise the Japanese authorities if the Portuguese should conquer any new places or countries, or convert them to the Christian sect. In spite of all this, the hated Portuguese are again securely established in Japan, free, too, to make public profession of that detested Christian religion which had been the main cause for their expulsion in the past. If anything, surely this indicated that the age of seclusion was at an end, and that the main theme of the present volume is exhausted. Meanwhile, since Perry's appearance at Uraga, there were various domestic happenings of the highest interest and importance of which nothing so far has been said, and it is imperative to devote a good deal of space to a full consideration of these momentous developments.

CHAPTER XVII

II, TAIRŌ

IN the preceding chapter it was incidentally remarked that
shortly after the arrival of Perry the old capital of Kyōto began
to assume something of its ancient importance. How rapidly the
Court nobles were regaining power and prestige may be inferred
from the fact that they had been able to thwart all Lord Hotta's
efforts to procure the Imperial sanction for the treaty he had just
negotiated with the American envoy in Yedo. It thus becomes
advisable to look somewhat minutely into the situation at Kyōto
and to follow the course of recent events there with more than
ordinary attention.

It will be remembered that in 1613, and still more fully in
1615, Iyeyasu and Hidetada had subjected the Kyōto Court to
special legislation, and had entrusted the Shōgun's representative,
the *shoshidai*, with special control over it. For the next sixty
years or so this control was very strict indeed. Then came a
change, during the latter years of the fourth Shōgun, relations
between the Bakufu and the Court began to become rather amicable.
In the time of Tsunayoshi, the fifth Shōgun, this tendency became
still more marked ; and in Arai Hakuseki's day, under the sixth
and seventh Shōguns, Kyōto influence, as we have seen, was
actually threatening to become as strong socially in Yedo as it
had been at Kamakura four centuries before. The eighth Shōgun,
Yoshimune, deemed this state of affairs detrimental to his prospects
of achieving the reforms he intended to institute among the military
class ; and so there was somewhat of a reversion to the attitude of
the earliest Shōguns towards the Court. Under the ninth and
tenth Shōguns (1744–86) the Bakufu treated the Imperial Court
not merely with studied neglect but with considerable rigour, and
during the minority of the eleventh Shōgun, Iyenari, there was no
very great improvement in the situation. It was at this time that
the Imperial Title question arose ; and, as has been explained, the
action of Matsudaira Sadanobu in this affair actually lost him the
sympathy and support of the collateral Tokugawa houses who had

been mainly instrumental in raising him to the Regency. About the beginning of the nineteenth century the Bakufu began to put forth great exertions to conciliate Kyōto ; the Shōgun Iyenari's thirst for Court rank and honours was insatiate, and his favourite, Mizuno Tadashige, laid himself out to procure the coveted distinctions for his master. We have already noted that although his official revenue was raised about this time, the *Shoshidai* was constantly falling into debt, for his social duties were getting to be very onerous, and many secret appeals from Court nobles had to be met.

Under the twelfth Shōgun, Iyeyoshi, the good relations between Yedo and Kyōto continued unimpaired. At this time Lord Nariaki of Mito was zealously propagating his doctrine of *Kinnō* ; of loyalty and devotion to the Imperial line. The reforming minister, Mizuno Tadakuni, needed Lord Nariaki's support ; and to ensure that, despite the protests of some of his colleagues, he gave the sovereign and his Court several substantial marks of consideration and respect. After Mizuno's fall came Abé Masahiro ; and Abé was astute enough to appreciate the value of a good understanding with Nariaki of Mito, although removed from the headship of his family and fief and ordered into seclusion, for Nariaki still continued to exercise a potent influence upon the public opinion of the time. Hence, to a certain extent, perhaps, Abé's friendly and deferential attitude towards Kyōto. It must also be borne in mind that the works of Motoori and Hirata had meanwhile been making a profound impression upon outside public opinion no less than upon the courtiers of Kyōto, whose self-esteem was greatly flattered by the tendency of the doctrines therein expounded. It was just shortly before this time, too, in 1851, that the *Dai-nihonshi*, the great national history down to 1413, projected by Lord Mitsukuni of Mito, was first committed to print. The tendency of this huge book was extremely imperialistic, although its cardinal doctrines were rather suggested than categorically emphasized. It is indeed questionable whether it ever had the immense direct influence often attributed to it as a factor in precipitating the revolution of 1868 ; for in the first place it was not printed until 1851 ; in the second place, it was too scholarly to be popular among illiterate samurai, and in the third, it was much too long for the general reader. Doubtless, extracts from it in manuscript had been current, and these could not have been without their effect. Still more effective perhaps, must have been the lectures on it delivered by Mito scholars to the numerous pupils that thronged to learn from them. Far more effectual, as propagandist literature, perhaps, were the works of Rai Sanyō (1780–1832) the *Nihon-gwaishi* and the *Nihon-seiki*. The latter, a posthumous book, sets forth the history of the Empire from Jimmu Tennō down to the abdication of Yōzei II in 1596, and discusses the character and conduct of each sovereign in turn. The late Prince Itō often asserted that he had conned this work over and over again in his youthful days, and that it had made a profound impression upon him, and doubtless others of the great actors in the drama of 1868 had drawn inspiration from it. But the more popular of Rai's two books was the *Nihon-gwaishi*, published in 1827, after two decades of strenuous and incessant toil. It commences with the reasons for the decay of the Imperial power, and the rise of the Taira and Minamoto in the twelfth century, and ends with the establishment of the Tokugawa Shōgunate. Further than this point Rai could not bring the story ; for the writing of a Tokugawa history was forbidden. It was only privileged and official or semi-official authors like Naru-shima, or Arai Hakuseki, or Hayashi that were allowed to deal with events after 1603 ; and even Hayashi found the publication of his work interdicted when it was submitted to the Bakufu and the Go-san-ké. As it was, Rai Sanyō's books were repeatedly purged by the Yedo censors, for he did not hesitate to say in clear, if not emphatic, language what the more cautious and more voluminous *Dai-nihonshi* only implied. To attain his purpose he permitted himself to be extremely unjust to the Hōjō of Kamakura, and did not scruple to stigmatize them as " serpents, fiends, beasts ", for their treatment of the sovereigns and courtiers of Kyōto. In recounting the overthrow of the Mongol invaders he writes that " the repulse of the Tartar barbarians by Hōjō Tokimune, and his preserving the dominions of our Son of Heaven were insufficient to atone for the *crimes* of his ancestors ". And upon some of the Ashikaga Shōguns he is equally severe. In short the *Nihon-gwaishi* was a *Tendenz* history, if ever there was one ; in it, although by implication only, the Tokugawa Bakufu was sternly arraigned at the bar of judgment, and that the author found many of his country-men ready to sit as judges is indisputable. A Tosa samurai, for instance, too poor to buy the book, spent his leisure time in the clan *yashiki* in Yedo copying out the whole work, and carried his

manuscript back with him to Kōchi as one of his most cherished
possessions. Although it consists of as many as twenty-two volumes,
the *Nihon-gwaishi* is really not a very long work, and so it became
very effective as a political propagation which, from its bulk and
its difficult style, the *Dai-nihonshi* could never be.   Much secret
discussion followed the publication of the *Nihon-gwaishi* in 1827 ;
when the Bakufu in a fashion legalized the expression of public
opinion by consulting the Daimyō about Perry's proposals in
1853.   Rai Sanyō's books soon began to be publicly discussed
everywhere, and his doctrines applied to the political situation of
the time.   Here too, the Court nobles found a strong support to
the efforts that they were presently to put forth to regain something
of their ancient prestige and to curb what they characterized as the
arbitrary insolence of the Bakufu.   Just at the time public opinion
was beginning to be dangerous to the Shōgunate, the chief of the
Rōjū had practically removed the chief traditional restraints upon
its free expression.

It may be safely assumed that this public opinion thoroughly
approved the action of the Bakufu when it resolved to notify the
Court of Perry's sudden and embarrassing appearance at Uraga
on 8th July, 1853.   On 14th July, the very day when Perry was
having his remarkable interview with the two silent commissioners
(on which occasion, it will be remembered, he was told it " would be
well not to speak of revolutions "), Wakizaka, the Shoshidai, sent
for the Tensō, and informed them of the portentous event, assuring
them that every precaution would be taken and that the Court
need not allow itself to be perturbed by the wild rumours that would
soon be rife in Kyōto.   Shortly afterwards the Court intimated its
desire that solemn prayers should be offered up in seven temples,
and the seven chief shrines in the Empire for the repulse of the
Barbarians, and this was done on 21st July.   On that day, Perry's
squadron was labouring in the heavy seas that are so often
experienced south of Satsuma, " with yards and topmasts sent down,
guns lashed, and steam reduced."   So that, had the Court but
known of it, the orisons for a wind like that which wrecked the
Mongol armament in 1281 might well have seemed to have been
favourably answered.

In connexion with the installation of the new Shōgun, Iyesada,
on 23rd December, 1853, the Court noble, Sanjō Sanetsumu,
proceeded to Yedo; and in an interview with the Rōjū on 27th

December, he delivered a dispatch from the Kwambaku expressing his opinion about the American affair, while Sanjō verbally set forth the state of feeling in Kyōto. Abé thereupon went into a full explanation of what had been done, dwelling on the fact that the unsatisfactory condition of the coast defences made it necessary for the Bakufu to act with great caution and restraint. He freely acknowledged that it was the duty of the Rōjū to relieve the Imperial anxiety, and he actually requested that the sovereign should favour the Bakufu with an expression of his wishes, whenever he saw occasion to do so. Some authorities even go so far as to maintain that Abé now gave Sanjō to understand that nothing would be finally settled in connexion with this grave affair without the concert and assent of the Imperial Court.

On 2nd May, 1854, the Imperial Palace was burned to the ground and the Bakufu at once set about restoring it, and not only so, but, on the representations of the Lord of Owari, on a more extensive plan and with finer materials than before. The Lord of Owari was connected by marriage with the house of *Konoye*, as was also Shimadzu Nariakira of Satsuma, and it seems that it was really Lord Nariakira who prompted the Lord of Owari to move in the matter. Nariakira was on the best of terms with Abé, and the Satsuma chieftain also expressed his view to Abé on the subject. Furthermore, he presented the Mikado with a large sum of ready money for his personal use, a gift that was acknowledged by an autograph Imperial poem sent to Nariakira. Daimyō were still carefully excluded from Kyōto by the Bakufu, but presently we hear of Nariakira visiting some of the Court nobles like Konoye and Sanjō incognito and discussing national affairs with them. About this time he used rather remarkable language in an address to his vassals :—

" The land of Satsuma and its people have been entrusted to my care by the Emperor at Kyōto, and I do not in any way consider them my own possession or subjects."

Presently we hear of Lord Nariakira receiving secret Imperial instructions to proceed to Kyōto at once in case of a national crisis, and there assume the protection of the Palace. At the same time, however, Nariakira was a staunch supporter of the Bakufu in what he believed to be its legitimate work ; and down to the assumption of power by Ii of Hikone, in June, 1858, he continued to be on the friendliest terms with the Shōgun and Rōjū. For the

few years immediately preceding this event he was perhaps the
most influential man in Japan outside the Rōjū. Lord Nariaki's
rashness and bigotry had begun to discredit him, and Lord Nariakira
had latterly endeavoured to avoid contact with him as much as
possible. But he was intimate with Lord Nariaki's two sons—the
Daimyō of Mito and the young chief of the house of Hitotsubashi.
Over Matsudaira Yoshinaga, the Daimyō of Echizen, and Lord
Daté of Uwajima, two of the four ablest feudal chiefs of the day,
he exercised a strong influence, while among the Daimyō and samurai
at large he had practically succeeded to the position which Lord
Nariaki of Mito held during the preceding twenty years. His
Kinnō doctrines were readily accepted by them; but in his
unreserved advocacy of the reopening of Japan to foreign intercourse
he had a terribly uphill battle to fight. However, even here his
infinite tact was surely making converts; and if he had lived a few
years longer, the subsequent course of events might well have been
very different from what it actually was. Unfortunately this great
Japanese passed away just at the time when his services were most
sorely needed. He was only 49 when he died on 25th August, 1858.

In connexion with the re-erection of the Imperial Palace and
of the mortuary chapels of Shiba and Uyeno, which had been
destroyed by fire shortly before, the following passage from the
Kinse Shiryaku is very instructive :—

" In olden times, whenever any works of the kind were required,
the clans were called upon to contribute towards the expense, but the
rule was departed from on the present occasion, in view of the great
charges they had been put to during the last year or two in maintaining
garrisons at various places. The Bakufu treasury, was, however,
reduced to a very low ebb."

In its dire penury the Bakufu felt that the hearty and uncon-
strained support of the outside feudatories was indispensable now
that irresistible foreign armaments might have to be faced. It
was no longer advisable to saddle the clans with exhausting corvée
work, or to subject them to the humiliations customary during
the preceding 250 years. Security against external aggression was
only to be found in a policy of internal conciliation. Indeed the
Rōjū now laboured to induce the clans to husband their resources
for the development of military power. What Satsuma, Hizen, and
Chōshū were now doing would have been promptly checked a
generation or so before; now the efforts of these energetic clans

met with the high approval of the Bakufu. The Bakufu had meanwhile been issuing fresh *Kenyaku-rei* (Thrift-ordinances), and had discussed a modification, if not a suspension, of the enforced residence of the Daimyō and their families in Yedo. The result was that the feudatories were privately informed that they might send back all superfluous dependents to their provinces, for an open suspension of the old system was felt to be pregnant with danger, even although down to 1858 not a single clan had shown the slightest disposition to question the authority of the Shōgunate.

Putiatin's brief visit to Ōsaka Bay in the autumn of 1854 was a rather costly matter for some of the clans. Ii of Hikone, one of the Daimyō then guarding Yedo Gulf, was ordered to shift his levies to Kyōto, while the troops of two neighbouring fiefs were also mobilized for the protection of the Court on that occasion. Later on, three or four clans held the approaches to Kyōto from the Sea of Japan, and a strong cordon of clan samurai lay around the city itself, while Ōsaka, Sakai, and Hyōgo were put in charge of detachments from Tsu, Okayama, Tottori, Chōshu, and Tosa ; some of these corps having been actually moved down from their former positions in Yedo Bay. Thus, by 1858, the defence of Kyōto must have become a rather serious drain upon the treasuries of several of the Western fiefs. In 1855 the Bakufu proposed to seize the bells of the monasteries throughout Japan and convert them into ordnance, and on the proposal of Lord Nariaki of Mito, it appealed to the Kyōto Dajō-Kwan for a decree sanctioning the measure. The decree was issued, but on account of the opposition of the Princely Abbots of Chion-in and Uyeno, the project had to be abandoned. This was also an unprecedented step on the part of the Bakufu ; and in the opinion of Ii of Hikone, who protested against it, a most ill-judged one ; for it furnished the Court with a precedent for interfering in matters that the Bakufu was entitled to decide for itself. Ii, too, it must be remembered, although the staunchest champion of the Bakufu, had advocated the reference of Perry's proposals to the Imperial Court in 1853. Ii was undoubtedly influenced by the reviving doctrine of *Kinnō* but, like many others, he saw nothing at all in this inconsistent with the strictest loyalty to the Bakufu. In fact, in 1853, many of the feudatories were of the same mind with Ii in this respect ; at that date it is questionable whether a single one of them entertained the slightest idea of opposing, much less of overthrowing, the Bakufu, any more than the average Frenchman dreamed of the abolition of Monarchy in France in the early months of 1789. Furthermore, in 1855, the Court and the Bakufu were still on very amicable relations. In the spring of that year the Court had been informed of the negotiations with Putiatin at Shimoda, and in August, copies of the American, English, and Russian agreements had been forwarded and submitted to the Kwambaku and the Emperor. The Kwambaku, Takatsukasa, was then not only friendly but very friendly to the Bakufu ; and he had no difficulty in obtaining an Imperial decree virtually approving of what had been done, and expressing sympathy with the Bakufu in the difficult and trying circumstances in which it had so unexpectedly found itself. Yet, by the spring of 1858, we have found a complete change in this complaisant and sympathetic attitude of the Court ; it was then actually flouting and humiliating Lord Hotta, the Chief of the Rōjū, who had taken the unprecedented step of proceeding to Kyōto to explain and to implore.

To enable us to understand the important developments that now followed it may be well to cast a brief glance at the general situation in the Court at this particular date. In 1858, the 122nd sovereign of Japan, the Emperor Kōmei, then a young man of twenty-seven, had been on the throne for a dozen years. Next to him came the four princely houses of Fushimi, Arisugawa, Katsura, and Kanin, who could supply an heir to the throne in case the Emperor died without issue. These houses had nominal revenues of 1,016, 1,000, 3,006, and 1,006 *koku* respectively, but they were supposed to be much wealthier than the figures would lead us to expect them to be. With the exception of Arisugawa, none of them makes any great figure in the stirring events of the time. Then there were several princely incumbents of the fourteen abbacies assigned for the support of princes of blood. The chief of these establishments was that of Uyeno in Yedo with a revenue of 13,000 *koku* ; but most of them had only about a tenth of that income. At this date some of them were vacant, while most of the actual incumbents were of very little personal importance. The chief exception was the Abbot of the Shōren-in, a man of many names, for at different times we have to deal with him as Shōren-in Miya, Awata no Miya, In no Miya, Prince Nakagawa, and finally as Prince Kuni. Born in 1824, he was at this time in the full vigour of manhood, able, energetic, and ambitious, with much greater liking for politics than for

religion. He now began to make his influence felt ; and during
the great part of the next stirring decade he was perhaps the most
prominent and powerful personage in the Court.

Around the palace were domiciled 137 *Kugé* families. Some
of these were miserably poor ; indeed, thirty of them had no resources
beyond a small allowance of rice from the Imperial granary. Of
the others, only twenty-one had an income of 500 *koku* or over ;
the total amount devoted to the maintenance of the 137 houses
only amounting to something between 40,000 and 50,000 *koku*.
The wealthiest, as might be expected, were the Go-sekké, the five
families from whom the Kwambaku, the Sesshō, and the Emperor's
chief consort had to be taken. Of these, Konoye's nominal revenue
was 2,860, Kujō's 2,043, Ichijō's 2,044, Nijō's 1,708, and Takatsukasa's 1,500 *koku* ; but some of them had other considerable
sources of income ; Konoye, for example, owning some of the great
saké-brewing establishments between Ōsaka and Hyōgo. Marriages
between Daimyō and Kugé families had been frowned upon by
the early Bakufu, but Mitsukuni of Mito's bride had been a Court
lady, and so had the consort of Tsunayoshi, the fifth Shōgun.
Since that time, marriages between Kugé and members of the
collateral Tokugawa houses had become not uncommon ; we have
already spoken of Lord Nariaki's bonds of affinity with the Court.
The Lord of Owari was now similarly connected with it ; and so
indeed were some of the outside Daimyō, the Lords of Satsuma,
Tosa, Awa, Sendai, and Kaga being among the number. Confidential
communications could thus easily pass between these feudatories,
and the Kugé families with whom they were connected ; and in
permitting such a state of affairs to come about, the Bakufu had
exposed itself to a great future danger.

To a still graver and rapidly growing menace in Kyōto, the
Bakufu remained blissfully unconscious down to this year of 1858.
The Prohibition of Heresies, and the exclusion of all but adherents
of the orthodox Teishu tenets from service under the Shōgunate
and in nearly all the fiefs have already been alluded to. The sturdier
spirits that refused to sacrifice their convictions had to make a
livelihood somehow ; and not a few of them proceeded to Kyōto
to find a meagre subsistence by lecturing to the Court nobles.
Some of these men got taken into the regular service of the more
well-to-do Kugé in various capacities, and many of them, being
men of ability with a knowledge of the outside world, acquired a

great influence over their employers, by whom indeed, some of them came to be regarded as veritable political oracles. Almost to a man, these heterodox scholars detested the Bakufu, and were only too happy to find an opportunity of embarrassing its officials. When the question of foreign intercourse began to be referred to Kyōto and discussed there, the " heretics " were very prompt to avail themselves of the situation. It is quite true that Lord Hotta had had to deal with Lord Nariaki's intrigues, and with his emissaries in Kyōto in 1858, but the ground had been splendidly prepared for both Lord Nariaki and his agents by the scholars serving in various Kugé households. Furthermore, outside samurai, less attached to the Bakufu than their lords were, now began to frequent Kyōto in increasing numbers, while the old capital was becoming a great place of assembly for the *rōnin* lurking or wandering in the various quarters of the Empire. Free discussion, specifically of the Barbarian question, but soon practically of all questions, presently became the order of the day, and the better instructed, keener-witted and bolder among the *rōnin* suddenly found themselves becoming personages. These soon were the loudest in their shouts of " Honour to the Emperor " and " Away with the Barbarian ! " That at present was enough to embarrass the Shōgun's officers ; it was yet a year or two before the third cry of " Down with the Bakufu ! " came to be heard.

In the spring of 1858, the situation at Kyōto was at once very peculiar and very perplexing. Lord Hotta then had to fight a desperate battle against the machinations of Lord Nariaki and his agents, who were resolved to thwart his mission at any price. Yet at the very same time he was in a measure co-operating with these agents, in forwarding a project in which Lord Nariaki was perhaps more keenly interested than he was in the exclusion of these Barbarians, for whose admission into the ports of the Empire, Hotta was then labouring so strenuously to procure the Imperial sanction. The project in question was the nomination of Lord Nariaki's own favourite son as heir to the fainéant and decrepit Shōgun.

The thirteenth Shōgun, Iyesada, was in his 29th year when he succeeded to power in 1853. But his father had known perfectly well that Iyesada would be incompetent for the position, now that the administration had to face difficulties of such exceptional gravity. As a matter of fact, the new Shōgun scarcely ever evinced the possession of any will of his own. Whatever was submitted to him for approval by the Rōjū, he generally approved of without question or discussion; in domestic affairs he was entirely under the control of his mother. This was a state of affairs that caused extreme anxiety to the more intelligent Daimyō and samurai; and there was a growing desire in certain quarters that some strong man should now be appointed to stand by the side of the Shōgun as Hoshina of Aidzu had done in the case of Iyetsuna. By no one perhaps was the necessity of this more deeply felt than by Shimadzu Nariakira of Satsuma. But Satsuma was an outside clan, and outside clans, of course, had no right to interfere in such matters. Lord Nariakira, however, was on very intimate terms with Lord Yoshinaga of Echizen, and Echizen was not only a Tokugawa house, but Lord Yoshinaga had been adopted into the house from the Tayasu family, one of the San-kyō houses that might supply an heir to the Shōgunate in the case of a Shōgun dying without male issue. Thus, Lord Yoshinaga was in a position to move in the matter; and he and Shimadzu Nariakira now agreed to endeavour to place some real statesman by the side of the Shōgun with supreme control of national affairs. Although they felt the advisability of keeping the project secret for the time, Lord Yoshinaga opened his mind to Abé Masahiro. Abé assured him that he was in full agreement with his views, but that precipitate action would be highly injudicious. Lord Yoshinaga presently endeavoured to get the Lord of Owari to pledge his support for Nariaki of Mito, and when Nariaki's collisions with the Bakufu officials made his appointment to the position impossible, Lord Yoshinaga urged the Lord of Owari to accept the office himself. But the Lord of Owari did not receive his overtures favourably. Meanwhile, Nariaki's own favourite son, although still a mere youth, had been giving great promise of ability and force of character; and a party was presently forming in support of him as successor to the Shōgun, Iyesada, who had no son of his own, and, as it was generally known, never could have one. Among the early measures taken by Abé Masahiro to conciliate Lord Nariaki had been his recommendation that Nariaki's seventh son should be made heir of the house of Hitotsubashi, one of the San-kyō, and the house from which the eleventh Shōgun, Iyenari, had actually come. At the time a son of Iyenari's was the head of the Hitotsu-bashi family, and by him Yoshinobu or Keiki, the ten-year-old son of Nariaki, was adopted in 1847. Yoshinobu thus came to have prospects of succession to the Shōgunate in case Iyesada should die without issue. But yet another son of Iyenari had been adopted into the Kishū house which, of course, could also furnish a successor to a childless Shōgun, and a boy born to this son in 1846 was more nearly related by blood to Iyesada than Hitotsubashi Yoshinobu.

About 1856, Yoshinaga of Echizen began to exert himself strongly on behalf of Hitotsubashi Yoshinobu. He still failed to enlist the open support of the Lord of Owari because the latter feared to offend the Bakufu, but Hachisuka of Awa (really another of Iyenari's multitudinous sons), Daté of Uwajima, Tachibana of Yanagawa, and Nabeshima of Hizen, were all now of the same mind as Shimadzu Nariakira, while some of the Fudai Daimyō, like Itakura, were also inclined to co-operate with Yoshinaga of Echizen. In the spring of 1857 Yoshinaga again broached the subject to Abé Masahiro, and the matter then became more or less of a public question. Abé was sympathetic, but he died in the autumn of that year, and later on Matsudaira, Iga no Kami came back into the Rōjū. Iga no Kami had owed his dismissal to Lord Nariaki, Yoshinobu's father, and hence it was presumed that he would now find his opportunity to satisfy the grudge he cherished against Nariaki. However, he assumed the mask of friendliness, and up to the last professed to be well-disposed towards young Hitotsubashi and his supporter, Lord Yoshinaga of Echizen. As regards the exact position of Lord Hotta, the chief of the Rōjū, on this question, the evidence is conflicting. According to some seemingly well-informed authorities he was opposed to Hitotsubashi at first ; he was particularly displeased to find that outside Daimyō had been presuming to meddle in an affair which had always hitherto been considered a purely domestic matter for the Shōgun and his house. But others, perhaps as competent to speak, maintain that Lord Hotta was favourable to Hitotsubashi all along ; for one thing, he wished to placate Lord Nariaki, and thus mitigate the virulence of his opposition to the reopening of the Empire to foreign intercourse. Be that as it may, what seems to be certain is that most of Hotta's trusted subordinates were Hitotsubashi's supporters, among them being Toki, Udino, Nagai, Hori, Kawaji, and Iwase, the latter two of whom accompanied Hotta on his mission to Kyōto.

Lord Nariaki was naturally very eager to see his own favourite in the Shōgun's seat, and in 1855 in his eagerness he compromised himself and his son's prospects very badly by writing to Takatsu-kasa, the Kwambaku, on the subject. The Rōjū soon discovered what he had done, and their knowledge of his manœuvres did much to widen the breach that was already beginning to open between them and him. Besides, Nariaki was very unpopular among the Ladies of the Great Interior, Honjūin, the Shōgun's mother, had an especial dislike for him and his pestilent notions of reform. It was about this time that Shimadzu Nariakira's adopted daughter (Tenshōin) became Iyesada's third consort ; she entered the Great Interior with a mission to counteract the influence of the Shōgun's mother. It was also about this time that Shimadzu gave his friend Yoshinaga of Echizen a friendly hint to drop his intimacy with Lord Nariaki. It should also be noted that the Lords of Echizen and Satsuma were now in full accord on the question of the reopening of the Empire to foreign intercourse as well as on the succession question. Yoshinaga of Echizen had by this time become fully converted to Shimadzu's views, which were strongly advocated by Yoshinaga's own vassal and counsellor, the gifted and brilliant, though very youthful, Hashimoto Sanai. In a remarkable memorial, Hashimoto had demonstrated the impracticability of persisting in the isolation of the Empire any longer. If the national independence was to be maintained, the country must be opened, and not only opened, but reformed. At such a critical juncture, a strong, vigorous, and enlightened Shōgun was indispensable ; it was useless to urge that if a proper Minister were secured, the reforms might be effected.

" That is a grave mistake, and facts prove that it is so. The different ministries of the Bakufu were not lacking in capable men. Such men as Matsudaira, Etchū no Kami, Ōkubo, Kaga no Kami, Mizuno, Echizen no Kami and Abé, Ise no Kami, were all men of no ordinary calibre. But on their removal from office, either from having incurred the Shōgun's displeasure or from loss of popular confidence, their policies also went with them, thus leaving the administration without any firm and definite line of policy. Each Ministry following its own special ideas, the administration of the Bakufu was never free from the evil of lack of unity and continuity in its political principles. The state of uncertainty attending such a system of administration was most embarrassing even in times of national tranquillity. Much more, then, is it to be deprecated at a period like the present when the country is confronted with the grave problem of opening up commercial relations with the other countries of the world. At this crucial moment, it is absolutely necessary to have a wise and full-grown Shōgun at the head of affairs, able to grasp the reins of government with his own hand, and to maintain a consistent and consecutive line of policy after it has been formulated from a careful consideration of the views of the Daimyō on the question of the day. Without firm and fixed principles to guide the administration, apart from all Ministerial changes, the accomplishment of the great national reform of reopening the country to foreign intercourse cannot be hoped for. The urgent necessity at the present moment is the speedy appointment of Hitotsubashi Keiki as the Shōgun's heir, through whom the accomplishment of great reforms in the national policy may be effected."

Long before this, others besides the Lord of Echizen had come to the conclusion that the succession question was of the most urgent importance, although they had vastly different views of how the question was to be settled. The head of this party was the chief of the Fudai Daimyō, that Ii of Hikone whom we have seen advocating the opening of the country in 1853. His views then were in diametrical opposition to those of Lord Nariaki of Mito, although, strange to say, Ii then proposed that this grave problem of foreign policy should be referred to Kyōto for settlement. About the same time Lord Nariaki had urged the construction of the Shinagawa forts on the immediate sea-front of Yedo, and Ii had publicly ridiculed the project, which he pronounced to be worse than useless. While in charge of the defence of Kyōto in 1854, the Bakufu had censured Ii for some falsely reported shortcomings in his conduct on that occasion, and Ii gave Lord Nariaki the credit for this. In 1853, Lord Nariaki's authority in the Mito fief had again become sufficiently strong to enable him to oust Yuki and the other conservative *Karō* who had been in power since 1844, and to get his own right-hand men Fujita and Toda reinstalled in office. These two were among the alleged 104,000 victims of the great earthquake of Yedo in 1855, a loss to Nariaki of the utmost consequence, for upon the death of Fujita Lord Nariaki's counsels began to lose all semblance of sobriety and sanity. Yuki now began to intrigue to get back to power, and actually induced the Daimyō of Takamatsu and Ii of Hikone to interfere on his behalf in the affairs of a fief that belonged to neither of them. When he got to know of this, Lord Nariaki was furious, and Yuki and a good many of his partisans were promptly put to death (1856). Thus it is by no means difficult for us to understand why Lord Nariaki and Ii of Hikone should not love each other.

As early as 1854, Ii had communicated with his friend Matsudaira, Idzumi no Kami, then in the Great Council, about the

succession question, expressing a hope that it would soon be attended
to. He did not then discuss the selection of an heir, but it may be
readily surmised that he had no wish to see the son of his hated foe
in the seat of the Shōgun. Presently a strong party in favour of
the youthful Daimyō of Kishū was being formed ; Mizuno, the Lord
of Shingū, an appanage of Kishū, wishing to establish himself
as an independent Daimyō, was working zealously in the Shōgun's
Court, and spending money lavishly there in the interests of the
boy Daimyō of Kishū. Soon, most of the officials of the Shōgun's
palace had been won over, and—what was most important of all—
Honjūin, the Shōgun's mother, had espoused the cause of the Kishū
candidate. As, according to precedent, the appointment of an
heir was entirely a matter for the Shōgun himself, the Kishū party
now regarded their success as certain, for Iyesada might safely be
expected to do just as his mother told him in this matter, for his
new consort, Tenshōin, had soon perceived that she was no match
for her mother-in-law, who cherished no special love for her.

The Lord of Echizen and his partisans thus saw that they had
but scant hope of success for their candidate, if the succession
question was to be decided in Yedo according to the traditional
custom of the Tokugawa house. So it was resolved to adopt the
very irregular and extraordinary course of carrying the matter to
Kyōto, and there obtaining an Imperial decree in favour of Hitotsubashi's claims. The Lord of Echizen, on the advice of Yamanouchi
of Tosa, who was connected by marriage with the Sanjō family,
now dispatched Hashimoto Sanai to Kyōto to expound his views
to Sanjō in the first place and, through his introduction, to the
Court nobles generally. Hashimoto's mission, however, it should
be said, was a twofold one ; for, besides advocating the necessity
of a " full-grown and enlightened person " as heir to the Shōgun,
he had instructions to exert himself on Lord Hotta's behalf. In
this latter part of his mission he had no success at all ; but in the
promotion of the cause of Hitotsubashi his efforts soon proved
effective. Sanjō was easily convinced, and so was Konoye, who
had just received a letter from the Shōgun's consort, Tenshōin,
setting forth what really were the essential points in the memorial
of Hashimoto, quoted above. Hashimoto, furthermore, soon became
very friendly with Mikuni and Kobayashi, two retainers of the
ex-Kwambaku, Takatsukasa, and through them Takatsukasa was
presently won over to the Hitotsubashi cause. It should be said

that Takatsukasa, who had originally been a strong Bakufu supporter, had been replaced by Kujō as Kwambaku in 1856. Down to that date Kujō had not been well-disposed towards Yedo ; but he now changed his attitude. This meant that Takatsukasa might presently be expected to alter his sentiments, for, as has been said, Kujō and Takatsukasa were on very bad terms. From this date (March, 1858) Takatsukasa and his son began to show a determined opposition to the Bakufu. They exerted themselves strongly to thwart Lord Hotta's mission, and they worked hard to procure an Imperial decree in favour of Hitotsubashi, while Kujō followed a diametrically opposite line of conduct in these matters. Hashimoto, as we have just seen, was supporting both Hotta *and* Hitotsubashi.

Equally peculiar was the fact that at this time Ii of Hikone, who had really placed Hotta in the Yedo Cabinet in 1855, and who had all along been a steady supporter of his nominee, sent a confidential agent to Kyōto to work on Hotta's behalf. This man, Nagano Shūzen by name, was gifted with extraordinary astuteness and infinite resource. In a way he is reminiscent of Fouché, but morally perhaps he was a better man than Fouché, for although utterly unscrupulous and ruthless in his dealings with opponents, he was devoted heart and soul to the interests of his lord and master, Ii of Hikone, in whose service he was always ready to sacrifice his life at any moment. Nagano, on reaching Kyōto, began to work through Shimada, a trusted retainer of Kujō, the Kwambaku, just as Hashimoto was working through Mikuni and Kobayashi in the household of the ex-Kwambaku, Takatsukasa. Thanks to Shimada, Nagano was soon readily admitted into Kujō's presence. One day Kujō casually informed Nagano that Mito and Satsuma men were working on behalf of Hitotsubashi, and that they were actually trying to procure an Imperial decree appointing him heir to the Shōgun, which they hoped would be issued simultaneously with the Imperial reply to Lord Hotta. Sanjō and Konoye had already memorialized the throne on the subject, and incidentally they told him (Kujō) that Satsuma was in favour of the project. Kujō also recapitulated their arguments, which were really those of Hashimoto's famous memorial. He went on to say that Lord Nariaki had several times in the last few months sent letters to Takatsukasa urging the claims of his son, Hitotsubashi. He himself (Kujō) thought all this very strange ; especially strange that an outside clan like Satsuma should presume to meddle in such a matter. He ended by asking Nagano to let him know what views his master, Ii of Hikone, entertained about all this. Now, Nagano held the same position with Ii of Hikone that Hashimoto did with the Lord of Echizen; as Nagano was the man who inspired and often drafted Ii's pronouncements he was in a position to answer Kujō's query on the spot. The reply he now made amounted to a complete and thoroughgoing repudiation of Hashimoto's arguments. The peace of the last quarter of a millennium was entirely owing to the prestige and virtue of the House of Tokugawa. Japan differed from other and less favoured countries in cherishing monarchical principles, and in transmitting the supreme power in an unbroken line of succession according to nearness in blood. The personal ability of the head of the nation or of the house did not enter into the question at all; any defects on the part of the Sovereign or the Shōgun were made good by the devoted support of his relatives and by the selection of faithful and intelligent ministers. So much for the general principle. In the present case the Shōgun was by no means so deficient in ability as the Hitotsubashi faction represented him to be. Furthermore, the attempt to impose an heir upon him was an unpardonable trespass upon the Shōgun's authority. The Shōgun intended to be succeeded by the young Lord of Kishū, who was his nearest blood relation, and who was possessed of abilities and virtues which fully qualified him for the succession, Hitotsubashi, though full-grown and able, was a son of that Lord Nariaki of Mito, who, instead of supporting the Bakufu, as was his duty, had been strenuously opposing and thwarting it, and who at the present moment was trying to bring its authority to naught by his intrigues at the Court of Kyōto.

Nagano lost not a moment in transmitting a full report of all this to Ii of Hikone, who thus became fully apprised of what the Hitotsubashi party were doing in Kyōto. Meanwhile the Rōjū had also got to know of what was really in progress, for the Lord of Echizen had thought it expedient to take Matsudaira, Iga no Kami, into his confidence with the idea of making certain of his powerful support. Although pretending to be sympathetic, Iga no Kami was really furiously indignant, for he had very strong ideas about the prerogatives of the Shōgun, and the authority of the Bakufu; and the attempt to impose an heir upon the Shōgun by Imperial decree he regarded as a most flagrant outrage. He was equally incensed to learn that outside clans like Satsuma and Tosa had presumed to interfere in such a matter. Meanwhile it had been found that Hitotsubashi personally was by no means anxious for the honour his supporters were working so strenuously to thrust upon him, for he dreaded the responsibilities of the position. His reluctance was only over-come when an understanding was reached that the Lord of Echizen should at the same time be entrusted with the supreme direction of the administration. Later on, when the Bakufu got to know of this, the Hitotsubashi partisans, and especially the Lord of Echizen, found themselves in a very dangerous situation; the knowledge that such projects had really been seriously entertained goes a long way to account for the extreme rigour with which the newly appointed Tairō, Ii of Hikone, acted in the summer and autumn of this year (1858).

All this time, the position of Kujō, the Kwambaku in Kyōto, was the reverse of easy or enviable. In his support of Hotta's attempt to obtain the Imperial sanction for the new American treaty, the Kwambaku had to bear up against an almost unanimous Court; and in this matter, as we have seen, his failure was complete. Meanwhile the succession question had become acute, and even here, if not actually Hotta, at all events Hotta's trusted sub-ordinates were exerting themselves strenuously in favour of Hitot-subashi. Now the Rōjū in Yedo, and Ii of Hikone had given Kujō to understand that there must positively be no Imperial decree in favour of Hitotsubashi; but Takatsukasa, Konoye, and Sanjō had meanwhile secured the support of nearly all their fellow nobles, and a note had actually been prepared (3rd May, 1858) approving the appointment of a "full-grown and enlightened" heir to the Shōgun. Three days later formal approval of this by the Throne was to have been issued. This, of course, meant that the young Lord of Kishū's claims had to be abandoned in favour of Hitotsubashi. But Kujō quietly expunged the words "full-grown and enlightened" and thus the appointment of the heir was virtually left to the Shōgun's own discretion after all. It is no great matter for wonder to find that Kujō now enjoyed the distinction of being the best-hated man in Kyōto.

About the same time there were startling developments in train in Yedo. Matsudaira, Iga no Kami, while still retaining the mask of sympathy for the Hitotsubashi factions, and the Lord of Echizen, was using every effort to get Ii of Hikone appointed Tairō. They soon succeeded in convincing the leading personages in the " Great Interior " of the advisability of this step, and were assured of their hearty support and co-operation. Iga no Kami's idea was, to use the expressive Japanese phrase, to " borrow " Ii's name and prestige, and therewith crush both the Mito faction and, more especially, the interfering outside clans. But for once Iga no Kami was reckoning without his host ; like most people around him he had seriously failed to take the real measure of Ii of Hikone. One evening in this May of 1858, Hiraoka, one of the Shōgun's confidential attendants, found his master unusually melancholy and morose. Hiraoka, divining what was troubling him, now ventured to speak the word in season, and remarked that trustworthy help was to be found in the person of Ii, Kamon-no-Kami, and that it might be well to make him Tairō. Iyesada caught at the idea eagerly. A little later (1st June, 1858) Lord Hotta returned from his futile mission to Kyōto, fully convinced that the situation demanded the speedy appointment of Hitotsubashi as the Shōgun's heir. He had also got a hint of the plan to entrust the Lord of Echizen with the supreme direction of affairs, and he was inclined to approve it. At his first audience with the Shōgun after his return, he broached the subject ; but he was then brusquely informed that it had been already decided to instal Ii, Kamon-no-Kami, as Tairō ! On 3rd June, a joint letter from the Rōjū summoned Ii to appear at the Castle on the following day ; and on that very day (4th June) he received his commission as Tairō from the Shōgun himself. On the 5th, the new Tairō appeared in the Council Chamber, entered into argument with the ministers, opposing their views when need was, and settled some very important points of policy in a very downright and autocratic fashion. Thus, Ii was remarkably prompt in indicating that, on this occasion at least, the office of Tairō had to be taken quite seriously.

It is somewhat startling for us at this date to discover that down to June, 1858, Ii of Hikone was held in such scant respect by the general run of his contemporaries. The truth is that, until that time, very few indeed had had any opportunity of learning anything very definite or authentic about him, for his early life had been somewhat peculiar. Born in 1815, the youngest son in a family of fourteen, he had lived as a simple samurai five-and-thirty years, with no prospects before him of ever taking any active part in the affairs of the nation. His time had been chiefly spent in strenuous study in the retirement of the fief. His few friends were mostly selected for their knowledge, ability, and personal character. His condition of life and his discussions with his friends naturally made him better acquainted with practical everyday affairs, both the social conditions of the fief and the political affairs of the nation, than Daimyō or Daimyō's sons generally had the opportunity of making themselves acquainted. With the exception of the heir to the fief, all his elder brothers had been adopted into other families, and thus when his eldest brother died without issue in 1850, Ii Naosuke suddenly and most unexpectedly found himself Lord of the Hikone fief and chief of all the Fudai Daimyō. He at once proceeded to carry out various reforms among his vassals, and to administer the fief in a very vigorous fashion, but as several other clans were trying to reform themselves about that time, Ii Naosuki's innovations do not seem to have attracted any marked measure of public attention. It was not till 1853 that he became prominent in any way, and his sole distinction at that time was that he was one of the two or three Daimyō who took the extremely unpopular course of recommending the reopening of the Empire to foreign intercourse. Ii Naosuke, it should be said, had no real personal liking for foreigners, but he had been convinced by the arguments of Nakagawa, one of his most trusted friends and retainers, that a refusal of Perry's demands would probably precipitate hostilities which could only end in a great national humiliation. As a member of the Tamaritsume Shū he had to express opinions on the various questions of policy submitted to it for consideration by the Bakufu, from time to time ; and on several occasions he had condemned the more extreme measures recommended by Lord Nariaki of Mito. Thus, his few fellow Daimyō of the Tamaritsume Shū soon began to recognize his real calibre, but to the outside world he remained an unknown man. When they heard of his sudden and totally unexpected appointment as Tairō, the Bakufu officials generally were greatly concerned. Some of them declared him to be no more fitted for the position than a child was, while most of them fancied that the Rōjū had just been provided with the luxury of a figurehead, and nothing more. The able men we have found chiefly concerned in the negotiations with foreigners were nearly all strongly opposed to Ii's appointment, Toki, Kawaji, Udono, Nagai, and Iwase all expressed their strong disapproval and lent strong support to the project of placing Lord Yoshinaga of Echizen at the head of affairs instead of the nonentity they considered Ii of Hikone to be. But the malcontents were mostly all transferred to offices of no practical importance, and a little later on dismissed and punished severely. Iwase and Nagai were indeed retained but they were retained merely because their knowledge and experience were felt to be indispensable for the time being.

Within two months of Ii's appointment as Tairō, the composition of the Rōjū had been greatly changed. Lord Hotta seems to have incurred the ill-will of the Ladies of the Great Interior and the Shōgun himself now evinced a wish to be rid of him. The Tairō exerted himself on Hotta's behalf for some time, but it was all to no purpose, and on 2nd August, 1858, Lord Hotta found himself summarily dismissed, ostensibly for his mismanagement of affairs in Kyōto. This was the end of Lord Hotta's public career. In 1859, he retired from the headship of his own fief, and at the beginning of 1863, an official note was sent to the new Lord of Sakura, reprimanding his father for the grave offences committed by him in his dealings with foreigners while in office, and punishing him by perpetual seclusion in his own house. Lord Hotta was undoubtedly an able, honest straightforward man, a true Japanese with the very best interests of Japan closely at heart. It is not without reason that many of his fellow-countrymen now regret the scurvy fashion in which his strenuous labours were rewarded. Along with Hotta, Matsudaira, Iga no Kami was also unceremoniously dismissed. His efforts to " display the power of the Bakufu " had brought so much odium upon him that Ii was convinced his continued presence in the council chamber might compromise his administration. Ii knew, too, that although Iga no Kami had been most strenuous in his efforts to get him (Ii) appointed Tairō, yet Iga no Kami was all along resolved in his own mind to have the real ordering of affairs. Already there had been one or two sharp collisions between the two strong-willed men, and the Tairō was not a man to brook opposition from any subordinate.

One of the vacant places was filled by the return to office of Ii's own personal friend, Matsudaira, Idzumi no Kami, while Manabe, a descendant of Arai Hakuseki's associate of the same name, now entered the Rōjū together with Ōta, whom we have seen according an interview to Lord Elgin. The two great problems the Tairō

had to grapple with were the signing of the new American Treaty,
and the settlement of the succession question. How he disposed
of the former has been recounted in the preceding chapter. As
regards the latter, the Shōgun now decided it by selecting the young
Daimyō of Kishū for his successor, and on 11th July, this fact was
notified to the Go-san-ké and related Daimyō. The appointment,
however, had to be sanctioned by the Emperor, but this was
regarded as a mere formality and a matter of course, and the
date of the public announcement of the adoption was fixed for
29th July. The Tairō, some time before, had summoned the Lord
of Echizen and Daté of Uwajima to his mansion, and had informed
them that, besides other imperative reasons, the previous Shōgun
had left instructions that, in case of need, the heir to the Shōgunate
should be taken from the house of Kishū, and his two visitors then
seemed to be reconciled to the situation. But nevertheless the
Hitotsubashi party had by no means abandoned all hope even now,
for, although vanquished in Yedo, it was still powerful in Kyōto,
and gaining strength there every day. As a result of its intrigues,
the Imperial approval of the selected heir, although dated 19th July
did not arrive in Yedo until 3rd August, five days after the signing
of the American Treaty, and on the very day when the changes in
the Rōjū took place. The 6th of August was then fixed as the date
for the proclamation of the heir apparent. But on 4th August,
a very dramatic incident occurred. On that evening Lord Nariaki
and his son the Daimyō of Mito, the Lord of Owari, and Yoshinaga
of Echizen, suddenly presented themselves, demanding an interview
with the Tairō. Their abrupt appearance was a breach of the
etiquette of Yedo Castle, where Daimyō could only appear on
certain fixed days, or after summons, or at all events after due notice.
Manabe now counselled the Tairō to keep in the background, but Ii
at once gave orders for the three Go-san-ké to be admitted to his
presence. Lord Nariaki began by censuring Ii for signing the
American Treaty before the Imperial sanction to do so had been
received. The Tairō explained why it had been an unavoidable
necessity, and expressed his confidence that his action would meet
with the Imperial approval when the exact circumstances were
known. This subject was dropped, and the visitors now began to
dilate on the need of the times for a " full-grown able " man to be
appointed heir to the Shōgun, and warmly recommended Hitotsubashi. To this the Tairō replied that the appointment of an heir

rested with the Shōgun alone, and that no subject had any right to interfere in the matter ; moreover the question had been already settled, and so it would be improper to enter into any discussion of it. Lord Nariaki thereupon advised the Tairō to postpone the public announcement for a time, and thus manifest a proper sense of respect and deference towards the Imperial cabinet, especially necessary since the Bakufu had signed the American Treaty without the Imperial sanction. Naosuke answered that he had perfect confidence his action would be approved, and that any further delay in the matter of the Shōgun's heir was contrary to the Imperial will. Nariaki next inquired why an envoy had not been sent to Kyōto to explain the circumstances of the signing of the Treaty, and was informed that it had been decided to dispatch Manabe on such a mission, and that he was to receive his official instructions on the following day. Lord Nariaki then made the extraordinary proposal that Yoshinaga of Echizen should be made Tairō. To this Ii made answer that in such a question he was powerless. At this point a small exhibition of wit on the part of Manabe relieved the tension of the situation, and the interview came to a close. The Lord of Echizen had meanwhile been in conference with Kuzé, a member of the Rōjū, for the Tairō objected to his presence on the ground that his official and social standing did not entitle him to a place in the Hall of Audience.

A great object with the Mito faction had been to get the Tairō summoned to Kyōto, where he would find himself as helpless as Hotta had done. If so much could be effected they believed that the prospects of Hitotsubashi need not even yet be a subject of despair. To compass this end, they made full use of the circumstance that the Tairō had concluded the American Treaty without obtaining the Imperial sanction to do so. The so-called exclusion party is often identified with the supporters of Hitotsubashi. But the chief workers on Hitotsubashi's behalf had been Shimadzu of Satsuma, from the very first a strong advocate of the reopening of the country, and Yoshinaga of Echizen, a convert to Shimadzu's views in the field of foreign policy. Then Hotta had latterly been a Hitotsubashi supporter, and so were almost everyone of Hotta's subordinate officers, all of whom were now opposed to the exclusionists. In Kyōto, it is true, the Court nobles were at once anti-foreign and pro-Mito almost to a man. But the strange fact here is that, in winning over the foreign-hating *Kugé* to the support of Hitotsubashi's claims, the chief agent had been that Hashimoto Sanai who had exerted himself so successfully to convince his master, Lord Yoshinaga of Echizen, of the absolute necessity of resuming intercourse with the outside world.

The Shōgun, Iyesada, became dangerously ill early in August, but he learned of the extraordinary visit of Lord Nariaki and his companions to the Castle. He at once gave orders that they should be subjected to condign punishment, and on 13th August, Lord Nariaki was ordered into strict confinement in his own Komagome mansion in Yedo and forbidden to hold communication with any one. On the same day, the Lords of Owari and Echizen were also ordered into close confinement, and were further removed from the headship of their fiefs which were entrusted to junior members of their families. As for the young Lord of Mito, he was cautioned to be more careful in his conduct. These measures occasioned intense surprise among the general public, that the Shōgun should thus deal with what had been hitherto regarded as the main props of his own house struck many critics as an extremely rash and suicidal policy.

Immediately on the signing of the American Treaty, the Rōjū sent (30th July) a joint note to the Kyōto Tensō, stating what had happened, and requesting them to inform the Court. In the enclosure was a full *exposé* of what Harris had just told the Bakufu officials. There was also an apology for transmitting such grave intelligence in such an informal way, and an assurance that an official of proper rank would be presently dispatched to Kyōto to explain everything verbally. Meanwhile it was of the utmost importance that the Imperial sanction for the signing of the treaty should be promptly obtained. The Tensō, however, were able to effect nothing ; while a Court decree was issued summoning a member of the Go-san-ké and the Tairō to Court. This decree reached Yedo on 14th August, the very day on which the Shōgun Iyesada died, and a day after Lord Nariaki and the Lords of Owari and Echizen had been ordered into strict confinement. On the 17th August, the Bakufu replied that it was impossible for the Tairō to leave Yedo at the time, but that later on he would start for Kyōto. Meanwhile Manabe, the Rōjū, together with Sakai, the new Kyōto *Shoshidai*, would be dispatched at once, and they would furnish full particulars of the situation. However, in consequence of the Shōgun's death (which was not announced till 14th

September) and various other matters, Manabe's departure had to be postponed. Meanwhile the Tairō wrote to Kūjō, the Kwambaku, informing him how matters stood, and saying, among other things, that certain unscrupulous persons were factiously trying to thwart the purposes of the Bakufu, and that they must be summarily dealt with. The reference undoubtedly was to the Hitotsubashi party. The Tairō soon received such alarming news from Kujō, the Kwambaku, that it was deemed desirable to hurry off the new *Shoshidai*, Sakai, to Kyōto at once, while that prince of secret service men, Nagano Shūzen, was dispatched along with him. But Nagano hastened on in advance, and entered Kyōto on 8th September, some days before the *Shoshidai* arrived, and while the *Shoshidai* was still several stages distant, Nagano had mastered the intricacies of the situation and hurried back to urge him to drastic action.

Nagano had learned, among other things, that Kujō was tottering to a fall; if he went, Manabe would find no means of getting the Emperor's ear, for Konoye, the new Kwambaku, was one of the three or four leaders of the pro-Mito, anti-foreign, and thus anti-Bakufu faction. Takatsukasa, Konoye and Sanjō had so prejudiced the Mikado against Kujō that he had been constrained to tender his resignation. However, as the appointment of a new Kwambaku had to be sanctioned by the Bakufu, there was still room for hope, "only," wrote Nagano to the Tairō, "let Manabe start on his mission at once." Manabe's original mission had been merely to obtain the Imperial sanction to the Bakufu's action in signing the American Treaty; he was now further commissioned to prevent Kūjō's resignation taking effect. Before reaching Kyōto, he found himself with yet a third commission to execute, and a commission too that brooked of no delay. Bakufu officials had seized a suspicious person at Kusatsu, and found that he was the bearer of a letter from some of the most prominent pro-Mito Court nobles to one of Lord Nariaki's councillors. From this document it appeared that the Court had been consulted as to whether Lord Nariaki's release from confinement could be ordered by an Imperial decree. The answer to this was that if the Tairō were dealt a proper blow there would be no need for any Imperial decree. Nagano had been greatly surprised at the rapidly growing boldness of the pro-Mito Court nobles; and he soon came to the conclusion that they were being used as tools and puppets by obscure men of

considerable ability at least. In a few days he was in possession
of strong evidence that Umeda, the Chinese scholar and lecturer,
was responsible for a great deal of what was going on, indeed, some
of the language of Umeda's memorials to his patrons had been
reproduced in the Imperial decree which had summoned the Tairō
to Kyōto. In some of his letters, Umeda had gone so far as to
denounce the Tairō as a " rebel " for signing the American Treaty
without the Emperor's sanction, and these letters and other equally
compromising documents soon fell into Nagano's hands. In the
numerous assemblies of excited Kugé that were now being held
almost daily, eloquence was mostly expended in assailing the Tairō
for his infraction of the Imperial decree issued to Hotta, and Nagano
had no difficulty in discovering that the selection of this special
line of attack had really been prompted by Umeda and his fellow
Chinese scholars in the service of the chief Kugé houses. In course
of time Nagano got possession of the correspondence of Ajima, one
of Lord Nariaki's chief agents, and from this he was able to unravel
all the intrigues that had gone on, and were indeed still going on in
connexion with the succession question. A little later on Nagano
was in a position to supply his master with full information regarding
an incident that occasioned the Bakufu great perplexity at the
time, and which has often been incorrectly narrated by historians.
Says the *Kinsé Shiryaku*, for example :—

"In September, 1858, secret instructions were sent from Kyōto
to the ex-Prince of Mito which ran thus : ' The Bakufu has shown great
disregard of public opinion in concluding treaties without waiting for
the opinion of the Court, and in disgracing princes so closely allied
by blood to the Shōgun. The Mikado's rest is disturbed by the spectacle
of such misgovernment, when the fierce barbarian is at our very door.
Do you therefore assist the Bakufu with your advice ; expel the
barbarians, content the mind of the people, and restore tranquillity
to His Majesty's bosom.' "

This summary of the document omits all reference to the
complaint that neither the Tairō nor one of the Go-san-ké had
proceeded to Kyōto in compliance with the former decree ; it says
nothing about the necessity of uniting the Court and the camp in a
common effort, and it gives no hint of the important fact that the
decree had to be made known to the Go-san-ké, the Sankyō and all the
Daimyō. The author is also in error in saying that this communication was addressed to the ex-prince of Mito, for it was really sent
to Lord Nariaki's son, the Daimyō of Mito. Lord Nariaki knew how

the decree had been procured, but his son did not. It really had been obtained by Konoye and Sanjō and their fellows, in spite of all that Kujō could do to prevent its being issued. On 14th September a copy of it had been handed by Sanjō to Ukai, Mito's house-steward in Kyōto, and Ukai at once dispatched his own son and a certain Kusakabe with it to Yedo. Two days later, a similar decree was delivered by the Tensō for transmission to the Bakufu by the ordinary routine. This document reached Yedo on 24th September, and on the same day the Lord of Mito sent in a notification that he had been honoured with direct instructions from the Sovereign. Ōta and Manabe were sent to inspect the dispatch, and they were then requested by the Lord of Mito to tell him what he should do. The Tairō presently sent word that the Imperial decree might be shown to the Go-san-ké and the Sankyō, but to none else. As an imperial instruction on political matters to anyone besides the Shōgun had been an unheard of thing hitherto, Konoye, Sanjō, and their fellows had shown great audacity in getting this decree addressed to the young Lord of Mito. At this time, too, the Chinese scholars, the Satsuma, Mito, and Tosa samurai, who had been working in the Hitotsubashi cause, and the *rōnin* were keeping Kyōto in wild commotion by the rumours they fabricated. Shimadzu Nariakira of Satsuma, it was said, was soon to start with 3,000 picked troops to assault Hikone Castle, to crush the Tairō, and free the Imperial Court from its long thraldom, while it was generally credited that Mito, Owari, and Echizen troops would soon appear in force in the old capital. So persistent and so circumstantial were these rumours that Nagano dispatched emissaries to watch all the great highways leading to Kyōto.

Nagano had already urged Sakai, the Shoshidai, to arrest Umeda, but Sakai, afraid lest the arrest should exacerbate the Kugé beyond measure, was inclined to wait for the arrival of Manabe before adopting drastic measures. Nagano, then at Ōtsu, sent word that if Sakai refused to act, he would bring up men from Hikone and act on his own responsibility. Thereupon Umeda was summoned to the City Magistrate's office and placed in ward there, while the seizure of some of Nariaki's agents about the same time placed a great amount of important secret correspondence in Nagano's hands. Manabe, meanwhile, had started from Yedo on 9th October and Nagano now hurried back to meet him on his way in order to report on the situation in Kyōto and urge the prompt arrest of Ukai and the two-sworded men concerned in the issue of the Imperial letters to the Lord of Mito. Manabe's sanction was readily given, and Nagano, at once hurrying back to Kyōto, had all his victims in close ward before Manabe actually entered the city on 23rd October. Manabe at once saw that, before taking up the original object of his mission, Kujō must be restored to office, and that a necessary preliminary was the arrest of all the Chinese scholars, and the other obscure men that were the real prompters of the recalcitrant Court nobles. Sakai, the *Shoshidai*, was averse to interfering with the retainers of the Court nobles, but Nagano succeeded in getting Manabe to over-ride the *Shoshidai*, and several retainers of Takatsukasa, Sanjō, Shōren-in, Konoye, and other magnates were presently seized and imprisoned. To Nagano's mind the " examination " they were subjected to in Kyōto was not sufficiently rigorous ; and in January, 1859, he succeeded in getting them all sent on to Yedo, to be tried there together with about a score of people meanwhile arrested in the Kwantō for intriguing against the Bakufu. In Yedo also, Lord Nariaki was now kept under the strictest surveillance, for it had been discovered that he had been walking abroad in disguise, and under cover of darkness. The authorities could now flatter themselves that they were relieved from all obstruction on the part of Lord Nariaki and his emissaries.

Manabé's, or rather Nagano's, drastic action in Kyōto had a wonderful effect upon the Court nobles, and it soon became apparent that the unwonted courage the Kugé had lately displayed was really nothing so very heroic after all. Sanjō even went so far as to assure the *Shoshidai* that he cherished no hostility to the Bakufu. Konoye alone seemed inclined to persist in public opposition, and even Konoye was constrained to withdraw his objections to the reinstatement of Kujō in his offices of Nairan and Kwambaku. On 28th November, Kujō again made his official appearance at Court, and Manabé, now having a friendly avenue of communication with the sovereign, addressed himself to the task of obtaining the Imperial sanction for the signing of the American Treaty. His first visit to the Court was on 29th November, but he had to attend often, and explain and argue much before he got a formal reply on 2nd February, 1859. The sovereign was bitterly opposed to any intercourse with the barbarians, and their residence in Japan was not to be thought of. But what was especially objectionable was the opening of Hyōgo as a port, and the permission for barbarians to visit Ōsaka. The *Shoshidai* urged that these special clauses in the treaties should be cancelled, in spite of the fact that the Tairō had laid it down that it was impossible to play fast and loose with all-important provisions in a treaty that had once been acceded to. Ii also pointed out that the treaty was not with America alone, but with four other nations as well. Any repudiation of the stipulations that had just been entered into would probably precipitate a joint attack of the barbarians on Japan ; and Japan needed time to develop her resources and organize her forces before she could hope to make any effectual resistance.

At one time Manabé was told that nothing could be conceded beyond what had been accorded to the Russians by the Convention of Shimoda, and the envoy felt so disheartened that he was eager to make the best of a bad business and get back to Yedo as soon as possible. But the Tairō kept sending him imperative instructions to stand firm and press the matter at all costs. At last, on February 2nd, 1859, Manabé was handed a decree, which was supposed to be the sovereign's last word on the subject. The question, it was therein said, had been a constant source of anxiety to His Majesty, inasmuch as it involved a departure from immemorial tradition, and seriously compromised the dignity of the Land of the Gods ; but the unavoidable circumstances and the necessities of the situation having been fully recognized by His Majesty, and the Bakufu having given assurance of its purpose to resume the traditional policy of exclusion, time is granted for the taking of proper measures, and the Shōgun is authorized to adopt the temporary measures suitable for the exigencies of the situation. But it was to be clearly understood that the barbarians were in no case to be allowed to approach Kyōto or to establish themselves at Hyōgo or to visit the neighbouring seas. This, it will be seen, was the reverse of a favourable issue to Manabé's mission. By it the Bakufu was pledged to revert to the old exclusion policy at the earliest opportunity, and it was clearly given to understand that it was to press forward its preparations for a forcible expulsion of the barbarians with the utmost expedition. In the course of the discussions with Manabé it had been suggested that as the foreigners came for the profits of trade, it would be possible to arrange matters in such wise that there should be no profits, and that the unwelcome and avaricious barbarians might thus be brought to withdraw without any need of an appeal to arms. What is exceedingly important to grasp here is that from this date (2nd February, 1859) down to 1865, the Yedo *Government was under a strong Imperial mandate to effect the expulsion of the barbarians at the earliest possible moment.* The Tairō, however, was convinced that it would not be possible to execute the mandate, and he accordingly concentrated his energies upon the task of securing such an ascendancy in Kyōto that he could by and by count upon forcing the Imperial sanction for the opening of the country. Meanwhile the leaders of the faction so hostile to himself and his policy in Kyōto had deemed it advisable to efface themselves for a time ; some of them took the tonsure and nearly all of them retired from office, while about half a score of those who had made themselves particularly conspicuous by their activities, were subsequently sentenced to domiciliary confinement. For the present no more open opposition was to be expected from either Takatsukasa, Konoye, or Sanjō. The Tairō now went on to attempt to negotiate a marriage between the youthful Shōgun and the Emperor's sister, a stroke of policy from which he could have reaped great advantages for the Yedo Government but which actually proved of no great efficacy when it was realized a year or two after his death. Manabé, taking with him some fourteen or fifteen suspected persons for trial, got back to Yedo on 17th April, 1859, and a difference of opinion soon displayed itself between him and the Tairō as to whether the Imperial decree of 2nd February should be made publicly known or not. Manabé argued that, for its promulgation, Kujō's assent was necessary, and for some time the matter was left in abeyance. Meanwhile, other differences between the Tairō and Manabé cropped up, and the usual result speedily followed. In January, 1860, Manabé one morning received a note from the Tairō saying that " he (Manabé) was not now very strong, and that he had better retire from the worries of public office ".

Before this, the fate of the Tairō's opponents arrested in Kyōto and elsewhere had already been determined. Matsudaira, Idzumi no Kami was entrusted with the supervision of their trial which was supposed to be conducted by a full Hyōjōsho, composed of the Three Bugyō, the Ōmetsuke, and the Metsuke. Nagano, the secret service agent, had already cast his net very wide, but he intended that none implicated in the opposition to his master should be allowed to escape. Itakura and another judge showed a disposition to limit the scope of the inquiry, and evinced a spirit of independence which, however creditable to themselves, made them objects of suspicion and dislike to the Tairō. They were forthwith dismissed from office, and their places filled by men who could safely be reckoned on to display proper zeal in the interests of the administration. It seems that one of Lord Nariaki's agents had succeeded in securing an appointment under Ikeda, one of the City Magistrates ; this man now kept the Mito party informed of all the incidents of the trial, and later on assassinated Ikeda for his severity. We get an inkling of how this trial was conducted from some remarks dropped by the biographer of Umeda, that staunch disciple of Yamazaki Anzai, who had done so much to foment opposition among the *Kugé*, and who had been the first of Nagano's captures. His examiners constantly pressed him to acknowledge that he had been instigated by others and to give their names. " The officials examined him many times in a day, sometimes flogging him unmercifully and sometimes compelling him to hold up a heavy stone for hours.[1] The torture which he had undergone made him appear at the point of death, but the attendants took great care to revive him. Umeda, however, died in prison, as did also two or three of his fellows—probably they were simply tortured to death. At length, towards the end of September, 1859, it was known that sentence was soon to be passed upon the accused. Just previous to this the Tairō presented 5,000 *ryō* to the Emperor, made gifts to many of the Court officials, and distributed 20,000 *ryō* among the rank and file of the Court nobles, a tolerably effective device, no doubt, for stifling inconvenient criticism from that quarter. Of the accused fifty, three were punished by transportation to distant islands, banishment from cities, domiciliary confinement, and other penalties. Ajima, Lord Nariaki's councillor and chief agent, was ordered to commit *hara-kiri* ; the two Ukai and one or two other Mito retainers were beheaded. Among the non-Mito men who were immolated on this occasion, Rai Mikisaburō is noteworthy mainly because he was the son of his father, the distinguished historian Rai Sanyō. A more remarkable figure was Yoshida Shōin, or Torajirō, not unknown to English readers on account of R. L. Stevenson's well-known

---

[1] See Mr. John Carey Hall's fourth paper on *Tokugawa Legislation, T.A.S.J.*, vol. xli, pt. v, p. 805.

sketch.   Yoshida had been a pupil of Sakuma Shōzan, whom we
have already mentioned as an early advocate of the reopening of
Japan to foreign intercourse.   He went to Nagasaki early in 1854
with the intention of going on board Putiatin's vessel.   But Putiatin
had left there before he arrived, and in the following summer
Yoshida and a companion vainly endeavoured to get on board one
of Perry's ships then at Shimoda.[1]   For this offence he was handed
over by the Bakufu to his own clan authorities for punishment, and
by them he was condemned to domiciliary confinement at home
in Chōshū.

Yoshida Shoin's aim was to master Western science and apply
it in Japan so as to be able to meet intruders with their own weapons
and ultimately attack them on their own soil.   All along he was
really a bitter anti-foreign fanatic, and from his confinement in
Chōshū he organized a determined opposition to the treaties with
the barbarians.   Emissaries of his were at work in Kyōto, and there
they presented a violent manifesto of Yoshida's to Ōhara, one of
the ablest and most influential of the Court nobles.   A little later,
Yoshida concocted a plot for the assassination of Manabe, whose
arrests of " patriots " had excited his fiercest wrath.   Yoshida had
been handed over by the clan authorities to the Bakufu officers,
who mistakenly suspected him of co-operating with Umeda.   It
was from his own lips that the Yedo officials first heard of the
memorial to Ōhara and the assassination plot.   Some of those who
were destined to be among the greatest statesmen of the Meiji era
were Yoshida's pupils ; after the lapse of half-a-century it was to
be shown that their rancour against Ii, Kamon no Kami, for what
they held to be the judicial murder of their beloved teacher was
still unappeased.   It is sometimes assumed that the severity of
the Tairō on this occasion was in a measure justified by the necessity
of crushing a factious opposition to his comparatively liberal and
advanced notions of foreign policy.   It is to be remembered, however, that Ii looked upon the reopening of Japan as an unfortunate
necessity, a mere tentative temporary measure that might be
revoked when the nation was strong enough to trust to its armaments.   But Hashimoto Sanai was of opinion that the reopening
of the Empire would be quite as advantageous to his own country-

---

[1] See Hawks's *Narrative* and Wells Williams' *Diary*.   Also the *Kinsé Shiriyaku*,
p. 4, p. 13.   For Sakuma Shōzan, see some notes in Nitobe's *Intercourse between the
United States and Japan*, p. 27.

men as it would be to the foreigners then clamouring for a footing in the ports. And yet Hashimoto was among the Tairō's victims on this occasion. It is indeed difficult to pardon Ii of Hikone for the enormity of ending the life of this brilliant young statesman of 25 by the hands of the public executioner.

About the same time the Tairō proceeded to ruin the remnant of the officials who had worked so strenuously under Lord Hotta, all of them, be it remarked, advocates of the reopening of the Empire. Iwase and Nagai had been slightly punished in 1858, but as their services were then still felt to be indispensable they were not dismissed. Now, in September, 1859, they were summarily and ignominiously dismissed. While Kawaji and Toki were stripped of their revenues, and ordered to confine themselves within their own doors. To oppose the Tairō in his foreign policy would thus appear to be no specially heinous offence ; the great crime, the unpardonable sin, was to oppose him and try to thwart him in anything. Another instance was that of Ōta, who was introduced not long previously into the Rōjū by Ii himself. He was found to have been making injudicious remarks and was promptly relegated to private life. It was against the supporters of Hitotsubashi's candidature for the succession to the Shōgun that the Tairō's wrath was chiefly directed. Daté of Uwajima and Yamanouchi of Tosa were now further punished by being ordered to confine themselves to their own mansions, and Hitotsubashi himself was dealt with in a similar fashion. As for Lord Nariaki, the Bakufu had already dealt with him in a very rigorous and drastic fashion. Now, however, it recapitulated all the numerous offences against the administration of which the evidence in the recent trial proved him guilty and sentenced him to be kept in ward in his own castle of Mito for the rest of his natural life. It is scarcely necessary to say that all these sensational developments provoked much secret criticism and great indignation in many quarters of the Empire.

The Tairō was, however, feared even more than he was hated, and men generally felt that they had to be exceedingly careful in the expression of their sentiments. All opposition seemed to be effectually crushed ; as a matter of fact it had only been driven underground to gather force and virulence. Even in Mito itself the Tairō was presently to find that he could not do as he chose, even though the old Yuki party now held the reins of the clan administration, and were unswerving supporters of the Bakufu.

It has already been stated that the Court had been induced to favour the young Lord of Mito with an Imperial decree ; and it has been pointed out that in communicating thus directly with a vassal, the Court had slighted the prestige of the Bakufu greatly. The Tairō was determined to get possession of this document in order to return it to the Court, and Nagano Shūzen was commissioned to see to it that a new Imperial decree should be issued ordering the Lord of Mito to deliver up the dispatch with which he had been favoured. This course became necessary because the Lord of Mito declared himself to be unable to comply with the Bakufu's request that he should hand over the decree : a strong party in Mito would prevent him doing so by force of arms if necessary, and the Bakufu had no wish to precipitate civil strife at this time. However, when Kujō, the Kwanbaku, endeavoured to comply with the Bakufu's request, expressed through Manabe and the Shoshidai, he found the task extremely difficult. The Court nobles who had been parties to the Mito decree naturally enough offered strong opposition to what would be a stultification of their action on that occasion, and so, appreciating the situation, the Bakufu left the matter in abeyance till the fate of the conspirators on trial in Yedo was decided. As the result of this trial, the leaders of the anti-Bakufu party among the Court nobles found it advisable to withdraw into private life ; Kujō was left with a free field for the time being, and on 12th December, 1859, an Imperial decree was addressed to the Lord of Mito instructing him to return the document that had been issued to him in September, 1858. This new decree was to be transmitted to Mito through the Bakufu, and, according to its terms, the 1858 decree was to be returned to the Court not directly, but through the Bakufu. On 28th December, 1859, the Lord of Mito went to the Castle, and on that day the Tairō and the Junior Councillor, Andō, Tsushima no Kami, told him that the 1858 decree had to be returned at once. On the following day, Andō went to the Mito mansion, produced the lately received Imperial decree, and threatened the young Lord with most serious consequences if the document were not handed over within three days. However, as the Imperial paper was then not in Yedo but in Mito Castle, where Lord Nariaki was now in strict confinement, the delivery of the decree was ultimately postponed till 17th January, 1860. Couriers were now repeatedly sent to Mito with letters explaining the situation, and ordering the prompt return of the document, but without the least effect. The old supporters of Lord Nariaki, now out of office, were fully determined that the decree should *not* be returned, and in the face of their opposition the pro-Bakufu fief Councillors, divided in purpose among themselves as they furthermore were, found themselves powerless. The more hot-headed young men, under the leadership of Takahashi Taiichirō, went into camp at Nagaoka, some five miles out of Mito, and there intercepted all correspondence between Yedo and Mito. Moreover they got possession of the decree, and depositing it in the mausoleum of the Mito family, vowed that it never should be taken from there. It was all to no purpose that another month's grace was obtained ; on 17th February, 1860, the decree was still in the Mito mausoleum, and the Nagaoka malcontents still continued to examine all the messengers and correspondence between Mito and the capital. The authority of Lord Nariaki, who now dreaded a confiscation of the fief, had also been invoked, and although sorely against his will, he had at least felt constrained to order an attack upon Nagaoka by the troops of the clan. It was with the utmost difficulty that a small body of these at last got mobilized, and these were doubtless mightily relieved to find that at the very last there was no need for their services. On 17th March, 1860, the Nagaoka samurai and *rōnin* broke up and suddenly disappeared, while at the same time a great many of the discontented opposition party formally severed their connexion with the Lord of Mito and became *rōnin*.

Among the Nagaoka band there had been a sharp division of opinion ; some were for obeying Lord Nariaki's last instructions and crushing those who still opposed them by force. Even among the stalwarts there was a split. Takahashi, with a few companions, dashed off for Kyōto to rouse the Satsuma, Inaba and Chōshū samurai against the Bakufu, a project that ended in speedy destruction to himself. Sano urged the execution of a still more audacious scheme ; and seventeen others joined him in vowing that they would sacrifice their lives in an attempt to take the head of that tyrant and traitor, Ii, Kamon no Kami, the Tairō. The eighteen conspirators were all Mito men with the exception of a certain Arimura, a Satsuma *rōnin*, who did not sign the general manifesto carried by each of his fellows, and who only joined in the plot immediately before its execution. One of the band had already tried to shoot their intended victim three months before, but although the bullet passed through his palanquin, the Tairō had then escaped unscathed.

The Tairō's personal friends were extremely anxious about his safety, and several of his own retainers, as well as of the Bakufu officials, suggested the advisability of his retiring into private life. On 21st March, just three days before Ii, Kamon no Kami met his fate, Lord Matsudaira of Yada had gone to the Hikone mansion and had most earnestly pressed the Tairō to resign his office. "My own safety is nothing when I see the danger threatening the future of the country," was the reply. The Tairō had a way of getting rid of importunate and inconvenient guests by telling them that it was time to go to Court, and then abruptly retiring into another room. On this occasion his friend seized him by the sleeve of his robe and tried to detain him, and part of the garment was left in his clutch. As Lord Matsudaira withdrew he cautioned some of Ii's retainers to be prepared for an emergency at any moment. At this interview the Tairō was advised to strengthen his bodyguard, but he refused to do so; its numbers had been fixed by statute, he said, and he as Tairō could not venture to modify the regulations for the sake of his personal safety. In truth his guard seemed to be quite strong enough to cope with any danger that might be apprehended. His mansion was only a few hundred yards distant from the Sakurada gate of the Castle; from that point up to the Palace everything was perfectly secure. Furthermore, the Tairō trusted greatly to the efficiency of his secret service. Besides the police spies swarming in every nook and corner of Yedo, Ii had his own confidential agents burrowing all over the Empire. Nagano Shūzen was only the most remarkable of a number of sleuth-hounds engaged in similar work. It is stated that one of these agents, operating along the Tōkaido, got to hear of the coming attempt on his master's life; he failed to reach Yedo in time, merely because a sudden flood delayed him for a day at Odawara. The success of Sano's plot was mainly due to the very simplicity and audacity of its conception. The third day of the third month (24th March, 1860) was a stated day for the Shōgun's levee; on that morning all the approaches to the Castle would be thronged by processions of armed men escorting their lords to court. The conspirators determined to await the Tairō's procession at the end of the 400 or 500 yards that separated the Hikone mansion from the Sakurada gate of the Castle, and there see what could be effected by a sudden and determined assault. They had apparently found their way to Yedo some week or so before the attempt, and had been lurking about in twos and threes in various quarters of the city. How some of them had whiled away the time becomes clear from a document found on the person of one of them who committed *hara-kiri* immediately after the accomplishment of their purpose. This was a receipted account from one of the houses in the Yoshiwara itemizing the particulars of a frolic two of the band had indulged in on 18th–19th March.[1] On the night of 23rd March, the whole band met in a house of pleasure at Shinagawa, arranged their final plans, and exchanged the orthodox farewell cups of water. Just as dawn was breaking they passed out and sauntered along the way to Atagoshita in Shiba. Everything seemed to favour the enterprise in the most wonderful way. The morning had begun with a driving sleet and rain, and the sleet had ultimately given way to a thick fall of soft and fleecy snow. There was a cold and cutting blast whistling down from Tsukuba-san, and it whirled the snow-flakes about in such a way that the outlines of objects a few paces distant were all blurred and indistinct. The Tairō's escort would all be cumbered with raincoats ; moreover, they would be sure to have their sword hilts in bags to protect the ornamental work from the wet. Presently, about nine o'clock, the band began to straggle down towards the Sakurada gate in threes and fours, dressed in a variety of fashions, some with clogs and paper umbrellas, others in short drawers with bare legs, others with raincoats, the intention being to simulate a fortuitous and haphazard concourse of peaceful inoffensive merchants, artizans, and peasant folk. Before the gates of the Hikone mansion were thrown open they were all loitering about in the open spaces in front of the Sakurada gate and attracting no particular attention from the guards or any one else, a fact not much to be wondered at as " at the time, so much snow was falling as to make it impossible to see a yard before one." Presently the head of the Tairō's escort of fifty or sixty samurai began to emerge from the Hikone mansion, and the fateful moment for action had arrived.

What now happened was really a matter of seconds rather than of minutes. As the escort approached the gate, some crouching

---

[1] Two *bus* (3s.) for Tamayoshi and two for Chitose, two girls ; one *bu* (1s. 6d.) for a singing-girl, one *bu* for drink, two *bus* for fish, and ten *tempos* (6d.) for rice, with half a *bu* as a present to the servants of the house.

figures assailed its advance-guard from both sides, and cut down the *metsuke* in command and another officer. At the same time others of the band roused the ire of the Hikone men by perpetrating the dire feudal offence of jumping in front of the procession and seizing the spears with tufted tassels always borne upright at the head of the Daimyō's cortège. Naturally the samurai around the palanquin at once rushed forward to inflict condign punishment upon the audacious offenders, and at the same instant others of the conspirators hurled themselves upon the Tairō's rearguard. Taken completely by surprise, hampered by their raingear, and unable to draw their blades from the scabbard, the Hikone men were cut down or mercilessly slashed about and driven furiously back up the hill. A pistol shot was sent into the palanquin, whereupon the bearers threw down their burden and ran. Three or four of the *rōnin* at once thrust their swords fiercely into the palanquin, the door was torn open and the occupant (in all probability already a corpse) pulled out by the right hand. Arimura, the Satsuma man, at once lopped off the head, and uttering a pæan of triumph held it gloatingly aloft for a few seconds and then dashed off with it along the causeway. A badly-wounded Hikone samurai struggled after him and succeeded in maiming him with a blow from behind, but was himself cut down in turn. Meanwhile, when all too late, the rear-guard, reinforced by a swarm of men from the Hikone mansion, came pouring down the slope, and the *rōnin* suddenly disappeared. Four of the Hikone men had been killed on the spot, four others mortally, and fifteen others seriously, wounded. Of the assailants, five either fell or committed *hara-kiri* on the spot, eight delivered themselves up to Hosokawa of Higo and another Daimyō, while five got safely away for the time. Sano, the leader, ultimately died of his wounds in prison ; all the others, including the fugitives with one single exception, suffered the extreme penalty of the law in August, 1861.

The wounded Arimura, with the Tairō's head still in his clutch, had committed suicide in front of the mansion of Endō, the Junior Councillor, and the head had been taken up by some of Endō's retainers. The Bakufu ordered it to be delivered to the Hikone men, not as the head of their master, but of one of the vassals who had fallen in his defence. At the same time, the Hikone Councillors were instructed to keep the death of their Lord a secret ; they were to send in a report that he had been suddenly attacked by a band of ruffians and somewhat seriously wounded in the mêlée. For some weeks formal messengers continued to be sent from the Castle to inquire after the distinguished patient's progress towards recovery. At last on 20th April, 1860, Ii of Hikone was relieved of office as Tairō, and on the following day his death was officially announced. About the same time, the Lord of Mitō was forbidden to appear at the Castle.

During all this time, Naitō, who had now become chief of the Rōjū, was at his wit's end. Cannon had been planted in the grounds of the Hikone mansion, and throngs of vassals came pouring into Yedo from Hikone itself, and from the Hikone appanage of Sano, in Shimotsuke, while the Mito samurai were working strenuously upon the defences of their Yedo *yashiki*. At one time the Mito and Hikone men seemed to be on the point of springing at each other's throats, and an internecine war between two powerful clans, both of which had been the strongest traditional supports of the Bakufu, was at once to be dreaded and deplored. The adroitness of Naitō's diplomacy, however, proved sufficient to avert the disaster that at one time seemed to be imminent, perhaps even unavoidable. A little later on the Rōjū was reorganized. Kuze and Naitō, who had been in the Great Council from Perry's time, and even before, still remained at their posts, and three new men were now called to their assistance. The most important of these was the Junior Councillor Andō, Tsushima no Kami, who was now specially charged with foreign affairs, and who is frequently mentioned with sympathy and respect by the British minister Alcock, in his fascinating book *The Capital of the Tycoon*. It is important to note that Sano and his associates expressly disavowed all hostility to the Shōgunate. They solemnly declared :—

"Our conduct *does not indicate the slightest* enmity to the Bakufu. We swear before Heaven and Earth, gods and men, that our action proceeds entirely from our hope of seeing the Shōgunate resume its proper form, and abide by the holy and wise will of the Emperor. We hope to see our national glory manifested in the expulsion of foreigners from the land."

In truth, at this date, the cry of "Down with the Bakufu" had so far been scarcely heard at all. Individual samurai, like Yoshida Shōin, had actually written against a stray pamphleteer who *had* ventured to assail the Tokugawa Government, and it was only when the Tairō had laid a heavy hand upon Lord Nariaki and the

Lords of Echizen and Owari, thus estranging the fiefs that had been the staunchest supports of the Shōgunate, that Yoshida changed his mind, and declared that the Bakufu could not be saved. But even in 1860, any idea that the Bakufu could be possibly overthrown had occurred only to a few obscure thinkers, who had as yet no influence in the administration of the fiefs. At this time not a single one of the outside Daimyō or of their Councillors had any intention of opposing the Yedo Government by force of arms. Even in Mito the responsible authorities were extremely pliant to the will of the Bakufu, and here we find some of the Nagaoka malcontents even protesting their loyalty to the Shōgun. It was against the person of the Tairō solely that their rancour was directed. To make that much perfectly clear it may be well to cite the gist of the chief manifesto the conspirators carried on their persons :—

" While fully aware of the necessity for some change in policy since the coming of the Americans to Uraga, it is entirely against the interest of the country and a stain on the national honour to open up commercial relations with foreigners, to admit foreigners into the Castle, to conclude treaties with them, to abolish the established practice of trampling on the picture of Christ, to permit foreigners to build places of worship for the evil religion, and to allow the three foreign Ministers to reside in the land. Under the excuse of keeping the peace, too much compromise has been made at the sacrifice of national honour ; too much fear has been shown for foreigners' threats. Not only has the national custom been set aside and the national dignity impaired, but the policy followed by the Bakufu has no Imperial sanction. For all this the Tairō, Ii, Kamon-no-Kami, is responsible. Taking advantage of the youth of the Shōgun he has assumed unbridled power, and to effect his autocratic ends he has gone so far as to confine, under false charges, Daimyō who would be faithful and loyal to the Imperial Court and the Shōgunate. He has proved himself to be an unpardonable national enemy. The power of Government in his hands will be too dangerous for harmonious relations between the Court and the Shōgunate, for he has gone so far as to interfere in the succession. Our sense of patriotism could not brook this abuse of power at the hands of such a wicked rebel. Therefore we have consecrated ourselves to be the instruments of Heaven to punish this wicked man, and we have taken on ourselves the duty of ending a serious evil, by killing this atrocious autocrat."

Yet another document recounted the chief incidents of Hotta's and Manabe's missions to Kyōto, and stated that the signatories were fully resolved to carry out the Emperor's mandate expressed in the decree of 2nd February, 1859, to expel all the hated barbarians from the Empire. It also made mention of as many as sixty Mito men being banded together for this purpose, and what lends countenance to the belief that action was not confined to Sano and his seventeen associates is the fact that on the very day the Tairō was killed an abortive attempt was made upon the life of his friend and coadjutator, the Lord of Takamatsu in Sanuki.

By this time it seemed as if a very epidemic of murder had broken out in Japan. During the preceding course of the Tokugawa Shōgunate there had been occasional cases of political assassination, but on the whole such incidents were of comparatively rare occurrence, often with long intervals of time between them. Indeed, since the murder of the younger Tanuma in 1784, apart from Ōshio Heihachirō's émeute in 1837, there had been scarcely anything of the sort down to the arrival of Perry. More than one hot-headed patriot had thirsted for the portly Commodore's blood, and had concocted ingenious plans for taking his head. Then in Yedo, in January, 1858, Harris had been told that two desperadoes had been arrested and were on trial for a premeditated attempt upon his life. These two *rōnin* we are told, died in prison, probably a euphemistic way of saying that they were tortured to death. A year later came Yoshida's plot against Manabe, and this may be taken as the first instance of the long succession of murderous designs that were constantly being evolved and carried out in Japan during the next decade. The political assassination mania probably reached its culmination in 1862 and 1863. But already, even before the murder of the Tairō, the assassin had begun his horrible work. In the late summer of 1859, three Russians were literally hacked to pieces at Kanagawa, and a little later in the same year a Chinaman in the employ of the French vice-consul had also been cut down. Then in January, 1860, the native linguist at the British legation was assassinated in broad daylight, while on the following 25th February two Dutch merchant-captains were cut to pieces in the main street of Yokohama. Shortly before this, Harris had sent word to the British Minister that it had been reported to him that fifty men had been seized the night before by the police, it having been discovered that they had gone to Yokohama to make an end of all the barbarians there. At first it was the hated barbarians that were the chief victims in this virulent epidemic of assassination. But presently the agents of the Bakufu came to receive their due share of attention in the carnival of political murder. In the autumn of 1862, not a week passed without the head of some alleged official " criminal " being exposed in Kyōto with a placard recounting the crimes that had brought the avenger upon him. On 15th November three constables in the service of the Kyōto City Magistrate were treated in this most summary fashion. The notice placed over their exposed heads stated :—

"Since 1858 these men have assisted Nagano Shūzen and Shimada Sakon in their traitorous schemes and have caused innocent patriots to be condemned unjustly. They are hereby punished for their crimes. A crowd thronged to stare at the sight. In consequence the Bakufu officials concerned with affairs since 1858, were in a great state of alarm ; one of the police, Odera by name, disembowelled himself, while another shaved his head and disappeared no one knew whither. Some abandoned their hereditary appointments, their household goods, and families, and fled far away to hide their shadows from sight. They dreaded the *rōnin* as if they had been tigers or wolves, and remained shrivelled up with fear." [1]

At the great siege of Ōsaka in 1615, Iyeyasu had found an opportunity of clearing the Empire of *rōnin* for the time being, and nearly 100,000 of them were then exterminated. Although another crop of them got effectually dealt with at the date of the Shimabara revolt in 1638, yet the great *rōnin* conspiracy of 1651 had thrown the Bakufu into a panic of fear and dismay. Now, after the lapse of fully two centuries, the *rōnin* is again a sinister figure of dread in the land ; a spectre that ever haunts the dreams of the officials making the weaker-kneed among them sweat the cold sweat of terror. In truth, on probing into the heart of the political situation of the times, it becomes tolerably plain that it was the *rōnin* and their sympathizers that were chiefly responsible for the fall of the Bakufu.

It is noteworthy that the usual ground for their earliest attacks on the Shōgunate was the notorious failure of the authorities to carry out the instructions of the famous Imperial decree of 2nd February, 1859, which ordered the Bakufu to perfect its military preparations and expel the barbarians from the sacred soil of the Land of the Gods at the earliest possible date. It thus becomes necessary to consider how far the Tairō really tried to comply with the Imperial commands, and also how far he sought to give effect to the stipulations of the treaties he had just concluded with the foreign powers, in all good faith, as the foreign plenipotentiaries presumed. In this connexion the memorial transmitted by the Tairō to Kujō the Kwambaku in 1858 is of some considerable importance. The following is the gist of that document :—

---

[1] *Genji Yume Monogatari*, vol. ii.

" The question of foreign intercourse is pregnant with serious consequences. The reason why the treaty with America was concluded was because of the case requiring immediate action. The English and French squadrons, after their Chinese victories, were very soon expected on our coasts, and the necessities of holding conferences with different nations at the same time might cause confusion from which little else than war could be expected. These foreigners are no longer to be despised. The art of navigation, steam-vessels, and naval and military preparations have found full development in their hands. A war with them might result in temporary victories on our part, but when our country should be beset by their combined armaments, the whole land would be involved in consequences which we can divine from China's experience. This question of foreign intercourse has been referred to the Daimyō, and most of them appreciate the disadvantages of war with foreigners. In these circumstances no other recourse was found than to conclude a treaty and open some of the ports to their trade. *Trying this policy for ten or twelve years, and making full preparation for protecting the country during that period, we can then determine whether to close up or to open the country to foreign trade and residence.* To commit the nation to the policy of exclusion before any experiment, appears to be highly inadvisable. If it were only a single nation with which we had to deal, it would be much easier, but several nations coming at the same time with their advanced arts, it is entirely impossible to refuse their requests to open intercourse with our country. The tendency of the times makes exclusion an entire impossibility. Compliance with their requests will tend to bring safety to the whole land, and thus we shall be able to keep His Majesty free from cares and anxieties for his subjects."

From this language it would appear that the writer was inclined to give his experiment of ten years intercourse with foreigners a fair trial; and we have seen that, when Sakai and Manabe wrote to him from Kyōto saying that the objections of the Court to the opening of Hyōgo were insuperable, and suggesting that one or two clauses in the recently-concluded treaties should be cancelled, the Tairō replied that the matter had been already settled, and that important stipulations of treaties solemnly agreed to could not be wantonly trifled with in the manner proposed. Thus there is no room to doubt the Tairō's good faith when he sanctioned the signing of the American treaty. On the other hand, the Imperial decree of 2nd February, 1859, could not fail to place him in an extremely difficult position. Thus, while on the one hand he laboured to obtain Imperial sanction for a permanent opening of the country, it would not be strange that he should meanwhile endeavour to restrict the foreigners to a minimum of the rights actually accorded them by treaty. At Kyōto, it had been suggested to Manabe that, as the barbarians came for the profits of trade, they might be induced to withdraw from the country of their own accord if matters were so ordered that they were allowed no profits to reap, and if their sojourn in the land was made as unpromising and uncomfortable for them as was possible. From what did happen there is ample ground for suspicion that this hint was actually acted upon by the Tairō. It was undoubtedly the Tairō that insisted upon Yokohama and not Kanagawa being made the site for the new foreign settlement ; and we have seen that the British and American representatives were prompt to discern in this an insidious attempt to establish a new Deshima on the shores of Yedo Bay. Ii's new arrangement certainly was found to give the Japanese officials an opportunity of interfering in almost every commercial transaction, if not of controlling the trade as effectually as it had been controlled in Nagasaki from of old. For a year or so, the complaints of the foreign merchants on this score were incessant, and vigorous protests on the part of the Foreign Ministers were necessary before execution was given to the treaty stipulation providing that trade should be perfectly free from the intermeddling of any Japanese official. Harris, as we have seen, had plumed himself greatly upon settling the currency question as he fancied he had done. The ratio of gold to silver in Japan at this time was about one to six, and although the amount of alloy in the Japanese coins was large, the foreigners made immense profits by the purchase and export of Japanese *Kōban* and other pieces. But the Bakufu now promptly minted a new coinage expressly for foreign trade, and the rate of exchange insisted upon for this made nearly all transactions unprofitable, which was no doubt the very object aimed at. Alcock had much trouble in settling this difficulty, and has a good deal to say about it in his dispatches and in his book on *The Capital of the Tycoon*.

The Japanese had entered into the treaties mainly because they had been led to suppose that the British and the French would come with armaments to extort them, and that these armaments would certainly be found irresistible by Japan as they had been by China. Now, in 1859, the French met with disaster in Cochin-China, and at the Taku forts the dreaded British fleet lost three out of nine gunboats and 464 men out of the 1,300 they had had in action to force the boom across the Peiho, and to carry the forts by assault. Shortly after intelligence of these events arrived in Japan, Harris had a second audience with the Shōgun, and his

experience on this occasion was by no means so pleasant as it had
been at his famous reception by Iyesada. No pains were now taken
to keep his passage to the palace free, while his palanquin was
hustled and he himself jostled and incommoded in a most unseemly
way, by the retainers, grooms, and lackeys hanging about the
outer courts as he passed in. It took him the best part of a year to
get any satisfaction for this studied slight. A few weeks after
taking up his residence at Yedo, Harris's secretary Heusken, then
in company with the Dutch consul, got stoned and pelted with mud
near Nihon-bashi, while two-sworded officials looked on with calm
amusement, and about the same time the inmates of the British
legation had to complain of gross rudeness from the populace in
the streets. No doubt, the commoners had got a hint that they
might safely indulge in that sort of thing ; at all events, after a
very vigorous protest from Alcock to the government, the ordinary
street population became uncommonly civil and respectful. Alcock
frequently complains that the Ministers and their suites were kept
in a sort of moral quarantine, allowed to have intercourse with no
Japanese except the armed officials detailed to " protect " them,
who interfered with and hampered their movements on every possible
occasion and in every possible way, while the extortion to which
they were systematically subjected must have been something
colossal. In the summer of 1861 Alcock writes as follows :—

" Life was insecure, trade was being daily restricted, and no
remonstrance, protest, or argument, within the scope of diplomatic
means had hitherto much availed to turn the authorities from a policy
the manifest tendency of which was to nullify the treaties, restrict all
intercourse, and ultimately revert to the former state of isolation
by the expulsion of foreigners. To make trade unprofitable by restrictions, extortions, prohibitions imposed on their own people, with whom
their power is absolute, and render life not only so insecure, but so
intolerable in the conditions of residence that no foreigner would long
submit or find such an existence endurable, seemed really to have been
the chief object kept in view during nearly two years. This was the
summary of their policy ; and if these milder measures failed, the
bravo's sword for assassination was always in reserve, and held *in
terrorem* over the heads of the intruders on their soil, to be resorted to
as occasion might serve without ruth or scruple."

A month before this, Alcock seems to have got something
like an intuition of the real situation. He had steamed down to
Nagasaki, and thence came up to Yedo mainly overland. In Hizen,
the officials of Nabeshima's fief of Saga had insisted on making

him keep strictly to the high-road, and at Uyeno, in the domains of Tōdō of Tsu, he had met with a similar experience. In connexion with these incidents, he writes :—

"It was impossible not to perceive that the 'free right to travel through the Empire' especially stipulated in all the treaties as the privilege of diplomatic agents, was effectually limited by the several Daimyō, with the connivance of the Tycoon's officers, *to the high road*. I think this gave me the first clear insight as to the actual relations established by the treaties entered into on the part of the Tycoon. He had made treaties, but the Mikado had never ratified or sanctioned them, *and the Daimyō could not therefore be compelled to observe them*. Without the Mikado's imprimatur they were binding and obligatory upon no one out of the Tycoon's territories, the ports opened to foreigners and the capital of Yedo, and not upon the Daimyō and their subjects, even at Yedo ! For when these come within the limits of districts wholly under the sway of the Tycoon, they made no scruple in offering insult, or wounding and slaying the treaty-guaranteed foreigner. The Western powers had not made treaties with the Empire or its sovereign, but with the Tycoon, only reigning in five imperial ports with their adjoining districts. Later, when I returned to Yedo, and startling events brought the whole question of the Tycoon's powers under discussion, I found full confirmation of the correctness of this view of the basis of treacherous quicksands on which our actual relations with Japan rest. Notwithstanding the affirmation of the Minister for Foreign Affairs *that the Mikado had ratified the treaties*, I think there can be little doubt that, to this day, they want the sanction of the only recognized sovereign of the Empire ; and this supplies a key to much of the vacillation and weakness of the executive under the Tycoon's authority. They are paralyzed by the want of legality in the treaties, which they are nevertheless constrained to make a show at least of executing in good faith. Hence their confessions of compulsory regard to 'public opinion', of the impossibility of efficient action contrary to it, and their last *petitio ad periculum* as well as *ad misericordiam*, to be released from the clauses which stipulate for the opening of Yedo on 1st January, 1862, and three more ports, Niigata, Hyōgo and Ōsaka. The riddle thus read leaves little further to explain in regard to the jealous obstruction encountered through all the Daimyō's territories."

The Tairō had been killed more than a year before the overland trip from Nagasaki to Yedo which did so much to open Alcock's eyes to the reality of the position. But since his death there had so far been no change in the policy of the Rōjū, and the Court of Kyōto was meanwhile kept assured that the preparations for the expulsion of the barbarians ordered by the Imperial decree of 2nd February, 1859, were being pressed vigorously forward. Alcock came very near indeed to divining the exact purport of what he saw going on around him ; a short extract from his chapter on "The Foreign Relations with Japan" will make that much clear enough :—

" These defences," he says, " have ever since been vigorously advanced. Large numbers of cannon have been cast, new batteries erected, steamships have been bought, and enough powder expended in ball practice and drill to have supplied ammunition for a campaign. These preparations for contingent hostilities were far too obvious and significant to escape the notice of the Foreign Representatives ; and Her Majesty's Government had been more than once advised of the facts and the unavoidable inferences, namely, that the Japanese either regarded a collision with some foreign power and an attack as probable at no distant period, or they had themselves determined on a rupture, and were preparing to resist any attempt on the part of one or all to enforce the treaties. And if the progress of affairs and the succession of events since the opening of the ports be carefully studied, it is difficult to feel any doubt that the latter course was the one really contemplated from the beginning.

" In the meantime there is reason to believe that, in order to gain time, the least violent and reactionary of the party were put in office to maintain relations between the Government and the Foreign Representatives with outward professions of amity and good faith, but secretly under a pledge steadily to pursue a system which should render virtually inoperative all the more important clauses of the treaties in respect to trade, locomotion, and freedom of intercourse ; and more especially to instil a feeling of insecurity and danger into the minds of all foreigners, beginning with the Representatives themselves, as the effect of a strongly excited state of public feeling, increasing and fast becoming intolerable. In support of which, various outrages and assassinations would not be wanting, until one of two things must result—either the Foreign Representatives would be reduced to the state of prisoners in the capital, or they would be driven to abandon the position as wholly untenable. It would not matter very much which ; the desired end would be clearly in view in either case.

" If this were not really the policy and preconcerted line of action among all who exercise a controlling power in the Government of Japan, it would be something marvellous that the whole chain of effects should so perfectly and exactly correspond to the attributed causes. . . . It is not easy to believe in the perfect good-faith of a Government under such circumstances, and how can we trust to their professions of a sincere desire to observe the obligations imposed by treaties with the reservation ' so far as the state of public opinion will permit ', which, by their own showing, is not at all."

Meanwhile, although pledged to effect the " expulsion of the Barbarians " as soon as possible, the Bakufu had been constrained to conclude a new treaty with yet another " barbarian " power. After five months negotiations, Count Eulenberg's Prussian treaty of commerce was signed on 21st January, 1861. In this treaty only Yokohama, Nagasaki, and Hakodate were mentioned, for the Bakufu officials were then exerting themselves to get the stipulated opening of Yedo on 1st January, 1862, and of the city of Ōsaka with the port of Hyōgo, postponed. Already, in the summer of 1860, they had approached the foreign representatives on this matter, and the latter were found to be not unwilling to entertain the proposal. Eventually the Shōgunate dispatched a mission (February, 1862) to Europe to negotiate, which visited all the European Treaty Powers in succession, and returned to Japan at the beginning of 1863, after succesfully accomplishing the main object. This was the second mission sent abroad by the Bakufu ; a previous embassy had been dispatched to America (13th February, 1860) to exchange ratifications of the Harris Treaty and to procure a fresh copy of the Perry Treaty.

Mr. Heusken, the secretary of the American Legation, had put his services at the disposal of the Prussian envoy. On the evening of 14th January, 1861, on his way back from the envoy's quarters, Heusken was assassinated. Mr. Harris claimed and obtained 10,000 dollars as an indemnity for this outrage, but he did not join the other foreign representatives in striking their flags and removing to Yokohama. After a month's negotiations, Harris's colleagues again returned to Yedo upon promises from the Bakufu of satisfactory protection, promises which the Bakufu was powerless to implement. On the night of 4th–5th July, the British Legation was assailed by a band of fourteen Mito *rōnin* ; about a year later on (26th June, 1862) it was again the scene of a murderous attack. On 1st February, 1863, the new British Legation buildings, just approaching completion on Goten-yama, were burned down by some Chōshū clansmen, one of whom was the future Prince Itō. In the May of that year the American Legation was also destroyed by incendiarism, and Pruyn, Harris's successor, was then constrained to join the other foreign representatives in Yokohama, whither all the consular officials at Kanagawa had meanwhile judged it expedient to retire for refuge. Thus, on 25th May, 1863, there was not one single foreigner residing in Yedo or at Kanagawa, while Nagasaki was being literally deserted by Europeans and Americans. The Bakufu might thus not unreasonably consider itself justified in claiming that it was really doing not a little towards the execution of the Imperial instructions given to Manabe on 2nd February, 1859.

CHAPTER XVIII

THE FALL OF THE BAKUFU

A

FROM hundreds of private contemporary letters now available in print, it is easy to realize that the death of the Tairō, Ii, created a tremendous sensation even in the remotest corners of Japan, and that the news of his assassination was received with intense jubilation by many, especially among the younger clan Samurai of inferior rank. The Tairō had been swift to crush all and sundry who presumed to thwart any of his projects ; but it was upon those who had opposed him in the succession question that his hand had fallen most heavily. His signature of the American treaty, without waiting for the Imperial sanction, a few weeks after he assumed office, was a step that augured ill for the popularity of his administration. But that was not the only thing, nor even the chief thing, that concentrated the hate and execration of his enemies upon him. His treatment of opponents was at once arbitrary and merciless, and some of the keenest thinkers of our time in Japan roundly assert that it was the judicial murder of the suspects arrested in 1858 that really brought about the fall of the Bakufu. In their memorial the Mito assassins protested their loyalty to the Bakufu—it was solely against the Tairō, that their animosity was directed. But, even by this time, there were some in the land who drew no such distinction. Already in addition to the cries of " Honour the Emperor " and " Away with the barbarians " a third was beginning to be heard. This was " Down with the Bakufu ! " But so far it had been confined to the *Rōnin*, for in 1861 there was not one single clan administration in Japan that had any thoughts or intentions of a revolt against the Tokugawa Shōgunate.

In the history of the fifteen years between the arrival of Perry and the overthrow of the Shōgunate, four clans played a very important part. In the early days it was Mito that was most prominent on the stage, and about Mito a good deal has been said in the preceding chapters. It has already been pointed out that Mito was distracted by two rival factors contending for place and power since the fourth decade of the nineteenth century, and the course of the strife between them has been roughly sketched down to the death of Nariaki in September, 1860. It remains to be said, however, that shortly after the murder of the Tairō, the order to Mito to return the famous Imperial letter was recalled, and that posthumous honours were bestowed upon Nariaki in 1862. Meanwhile, however, the administration of the clan continued in the hands of the party that had been hostile to Nariaki and his favourite Councillor, Fujita Tōko. Fujita's son, a young man of twenty-five, resented this, and as a way of ultimately getting the better of the " Wicked Party " he raised the cry of " Honour the Emperor " and " Expel the barbarians ", and left the clan with some three hundred armed followers. After extorting requisites from the townspeople in the neighbouring fiefs the band established itself on Mount Tsukuba, where it was presently besieged by Mito levies reinforced by Bakufu troops (1864). At the same time, Ichikawa, the head of the " Wicked Party " in Mito, had been laying a heavy hand upon his opponents that had not gone with young Fujita. They appealed to the Daimyō of Mito in Yedo, and the latter dispatched Takeda Kōunsai, a member of Nariaki's old faction and a friend of Hitotsubashi, to effect a reconciliation between the contending factions, while the Bakufu sent a commissioner for the same purpose. Both were refused admission into Mito, and assailed by an ambuscade of matchlock men. In the fighting that went on for weeks afterwards, Takeda was joined by Fujita and his band from Tsukuba, and Ichikawa was thus presently enabled to obtain the aid of Bakufu troops to crush the " rebels ". The struggle went on for several months, but towards the end of the year (1864) the " Wicked Party " became altogether too strong for the rebels, their opponents. At this date Hitotsubashi was in Kyōto, and Takeda determined to make his way thither and appeal to him. With about a thousand followers, Takeda fought his way along the Nakasendō as far as Mino, when he learned that by Hitotsubashi's orders a strong force had been thrown forward to oppose his further advance. Thereupon the band wheeled to the right over the passes into Echizen, and in January, 1865, at last surrendered to an army from Kaga which it found in front of it at Imago. In March, 1865, Takeda and 350 of his companions were sentenced to death and the rest of the band to exile. For the next three years the " Wicked Party " was supreme in Mito ; but in 1868 the tables were turned completely.   Ichikawa, who had escaped, was captured in 1869, brought to Mito, and " publicly crucified, head downwards, in broad daylight ".

This bitter internecine strife effectually sapped the vigour and vitality of Mito ; and as a clan unit after 1860, it had none of the influence it had wielded in the days of Nariaki.   Down to 1864, the Mito *Rōnin* continued to be formidable, however ; they assaulted a chief of the Rōjū, attacked the British Legation, and kept the foreign community in Yokohama in a state of constant ferment by rumours of impending massacre at their hands.

Tosa was one of the four great clans that played the most prominent parts in the drama of the Imperial Restoration.   About Tosa a good deal has been said in an early chapter of this volume. The Yamanouchi family were established in Tosa by Iyeyasu, who transferred Yamanouchi Kazutoyo from the small fief of Kakegawa (50,000 *koku*) on the Tōkaidō to one of 220,000 *koku* at Kōchi.   Yet Yamanouchi was not one of Iyeyasu's household vassals or Fudai ; from first to last the family was ranked among the Tozama, or outside feudatories.   But its successive heads never forgot the exceptional favour with which their ancestor had been treated by Iyeyasu in 1600, and down to the very last Yamanouchi Yōdō (1827–72) remained loyal to what he considered the true interests of the House of Tokugawa.   We have noted the prominent part played by this Yamanouchi Yōdō in the succession question ; a part for which he was rewarded by the Tairō by deposition from the headship of the fief and strict domiciliary confinement.   From this confinement he was presently released in 1861 ; and from that date he at once began to play an all-important role on the political stage of his time.   Through his marriage connexions with the house of Sanjō, Yamanouchi's intercourse with several of the court nobles became intimate, and in Kyōto he exercised a very considerable personal influence.   In truth, he was one of the four or five feudal chiefs of this time who were distinguished for the possession of any real political insight or ability.   Since the demise of the great Shimadzu Nariakira in 1858, Yamanouchi was perhaps the ablest man among the Daimyō class.   Furthermore, he was served by some vassals of high capacity, and great force of character.

It has already been mentioned that Tosa was one of the few provinces of Japan where the *Gōshi*, or farmer-samurai, continued to linger.   From their practical acquaintance with the actualities

of business these men were usually more intelligent than the average
samurai, and at this date in Tosa there were some first-class intellects
among them. Ever since the days of Yamazaki Anzai there had been
a tradition of *Kinnō* or Devotion to the Imperial House in Tosa, and
the stirring events since 1853 had done much to quicken this sentiment among the lower samurai. Among the Yamanouchi vassals
there was a strong *Kinnō* party by 1862, though none of the party
were in office. The great man in Tosa at this time was Yoshida
Tōyō, who was an out-and-out partisan of the Bakufu. Yoshida's
vigorous administration had greatly advanced the prosperity of the
fief ; in fact critics not at all too well-disposed towards him go so
far as to admit that it was mainly Yoshida who made modern Tosa.
However, the *Kinnō* faction recognized in him an insuperable obstacle
to their plans and projects ; and so it was resolved to remove him.
He was assassinated one dark night in front of his house ; and
although his assassins had to seek safety in flight and become *rōnin*,
the new clan administration did not frown upon the propagation of
Kinnō sentiments as Yoshida had done. The leaders of the *Kinnō*
party had already been coming to the conviction that the Bakufu
was impotent to save Japan from foreign aggression ; the only hope
of national salvation, they held, seemed to lie in restoring the power
of the Court, and entrusting the unified forces and resources of
Japan to a vigorous Imperial Government. The cry " Down with
the Bakufu " was now getting rife among the *rōnin* whose numbers
were increasing every day ; and some among them were beginning
to dream of the possibility of overthrowing the Bakufu by the
efforts of *rōnin*. This matter was discussed by Takechi, the leader
of the Tosa *Kinnō* party, with Kabayama of Satsuma and Kusaka
of Chōshū. Takechi maintained that such a notion was chimerical.
The great object to strain after was the conversion of all the great
clans to *Kinnō* sentiments, to get the administration of the clans
into the hands of loyalists, and so have all the resources of the
respective fiefs available for a united effort. Where possible, Takechi
now argued, *rōnin* should be induced to return to their clans, and
work for this object with heart and soul. From this point onwards,
the loyalists in Tosa and to a less extent in Satsuma and Chōshū
worked along the lines now indicated by Takechi.

In Satsuma also there was now a *Kinnō* party. Just before his
death (25th August, 1858) Shimadzu Nariakira was making preparations to start for Kyōto, with a strong force of vassals behind him,

for the purpose of getting the Bakufu to institute certain reforms, to establish harmonious relations between the Imperial court and the Shōgunate, and to reach an agreement as to how the foreign powers were to be dealt with. For some time before this he had a confidential emissary at work in Kyōto, who was entrusted with a large measure of discretion. This agent was that Saigō Takamori, whose name was subsequently to become one of the very greatest in the history of modern Japan. Saigō had already given ample proof of devotion and ability in the discharge of some weighty and delicate missions where the utmost tact and astuteness were indispensable. He had a great deal to do with the negotiations that led to Naria-kira's adopted daughter becoming the Shōgun's consort. He was also concerned in the dispatch of the secret Imperial letter to the Lord of Mito, and would certainly have caused the project to be dropped if he had returned from his secret mission to Yedo a day earlier than he did. The news of the death of Shimadzu Nariakira was a terrible blow to him, for besides rendering his present work in Kyōto ineffective, he felt sure that there would be a radical change in the policy of the clan administration. Nariakira's successor was his youthful nephew and adopted son, who was to be under the guardianship of his own father, Shimadzu Hisamitsu, a man of a very determined, haughty and autocratic temper. Probably the first result of his accession to power would be the recall to office of the aristocratic conservative councillors and officials whom Nariakira had been constrained to replace by more progressive and abler men of inferior birth. If that were so, the prospects for the Satsuma *Kinnō* party, to which Saigō belonged, would be the reverse of favourable, for all the older Councillors were warm partisans of the Bakufu. At the moment, too, the situation of the loyalists in Kyōto had become critical, for Nagano Shūzen was already at work there and Manabe was on his way. Saigō had contracted an intimate friendship with the loyalist priest Gesshō, who was now secretly harboured in the Konoye establishment, and he was presently requested to convey Gesshō to a place of greater safety. Saigō smuggled the priest out of Kyōto, under the eyes of the emissaries searching for him ; but he soon perceived that there would be no hope of concealing him for long in the neighbourhood of Ōsaka or Kyōto. Accordingly he escorted him to Chikuzen and entrusted him to his friend Hirano, and then passed on to reconnoitre in Satsuma. A week or two later, and the hunt for Gesshō had

become so keen that Hirano deemed the sole hope lay in making for
Satsuma at once, although no messenger from Saigō had so far
arrived.   On applying for shelter in a temple in Satsuma, the
request was declined ; and the clan authorities were furthermore
promptly notified of the incident. From them, Saigō first learned of
the arrival of his friend, and of the fact that Gesshō had been placed
under surveillance.   In a few days the priest was condemned to
" banishment beyond the Western frontier ".   This seemingly
harmless formula, which was frequently made use of when Tokugawa
spies were detected in Satsuma, meant that the exile was to be
summarily cut to pieces by his escort as soon as the party reached
the Hyūga boundary of the clan.   Saigō, on being apprised of the
sentence, hurried to Gesshō's place of detention and conveyed him
and Hirano to a boat ready for them on the Iso strand of the Bay.
A mile or so on their course, Saigō and Gesshō went to the prow of
the boat, and to Hirano they seemed to be admiring the splendour
of the glorious moonlight scenery.   They were really exchanging
the orthodox and inevitable stanzas that Japanese samurai and
scholars were accustomed, and, it may be, still are, to pen before
taking leave of life. Gesshō was drowned ; but there was still life
in Saigō when the boat's crew recovered his body.   The clan
authorities reported his death to the Bakufu, and exiled him to the
island of Ōshima under a change of name.

The incident occasioned intense excitement among the young
samurai of the Satsuma *Kinnō* party—an excitement that went on
increasing as successive reports arrived of the enormities of the
" Swaggering " Tairō, who had meanwhile established a veritable
reign of terror in Yedo and Kyōto.   At last, matters came to such
a pitch that a large party of the clansmen resolved to abandon the
fief and wage war against the tyrant as *rōnin*.   This was serious
enough to make Shimadzu Hisamitsu pause.   Towards the end of
1859 an autograph proclamation over the name of Tadayoshi,
Nariakira's heir, was issued, in which the views of the dead chieftain
were appealingly rehearsed, and his vassals cautioned against rash
and precipitate action.   This had a magical effect, the emotional
samurai now tendered a written oath of devotion attested with the
blood-seal to the ruling Lord of Satsuma.   At this time of stress and
strain only two men left Kagoshima to become *rōnin*, although
several samurai deserted from the clan *yashiki* in Yedo and Ōsaka.
Shortly afterwards, the old aristocratic conservative councillors

were dismissed, and replaced by men of greater mental elasticity. The result of this was that, for the next decade or longer, Satsuma really acted as a unit with individual counsels. At this date, it is to be remarked that Shimadzu Hisamitsu, the real ruler of the fief, cherished no intention of overthrowing the Bakufu. That was to come with lapse of time—about 1866-7—at present all that Hisamitsu aimed at was to induce the Shōgunate to effect certain needful reforms in its conduct of national affairs. For the present, Hisamitsu was anxious to keep away from Yedo and to avoid the necessity of passing the usual alternate year there, which all Daimyō were required to do, he actually caused his Yedo *yashiki* to be " accidentally " burned down. Thus, by one device or another, he was able to defer his journey to Yedo until the beginning of 1862. Before this his Councillors had represented to him that in such trying and troublous times, the sage counsel of Saigō Takamori would be invaluable ; and so Saigō was presently recalled from his three years' exile in the rain- and wind-swept island to which he had been banished. A few weeks later on, Saigō again found himself employed in his old role of secret emissary for his Prince—this time getting but a scurvy reward for the great services he was rendering. But before following him on his mission, it will be well to consider what the Bakufu had been doing during the preceding two years.

On the death of the Tairō (24th March, 1860) the chief responsibilities of the Bakufu seemed to fall upon the shoulders of Naito and Kuzé. These two were veterans who had been in the Great Council in Perry's time, and even before that ; but they were now soon overshadowed by a younger man who had just shortly before been promoted from the Junior Council. This was Andō, Tsushima no Kami, who was more especially concerned with foreign affairs after the death of the Tairō. In other matters, also, his influence soon became preponderant. It was he, for example, who completed the project already set afoot by Ii for the marriage of the Shōgun to an Imperial Princess. The Emperor had a sister (subsequently known as Kadzu Miya) of the same age as the youthful Shōgun, who was born in 1846. This Princess had already been betrothed to a Court noble ; and apart from this initial impediment to Andō's project, there was sure to be a great deal of opposition in the Court to any marriage-alliance between the Imperial line and the house of Tokugawa. A century and a half before, when Arai Hakuseki had proposed that Imperial Princesses should be disposed of in marriage to the Shōgun or his heirs, the idea was well received in Kyōto. But Arai's suggestion had never been acted upon, and now the times had greatly changed. However, by great exertions in Court circles, which were assured that the Barbarians would be expelled in ten years, if the Court and Bakufu were united in counsels, Andō at last succeeded in obtaining the sovereign's sanction to the proposed marriage, and towards the end of 1861, the Princess left Kyōto for Yedo, attended by an escort of some 35,000 men. The nuptials were celebrated in 1862. In overcoming difficulties in Kyōto, the court noble Iwakura had rendered Andō invaluable service. Iwakura was a man who played one of the chief roles in the history of the Restoration ; but the part he had taken in promoting these marriage negotiations presently led to his confinement to his own house for five years or more, and the temporary effacement of one of the two ablest men at the Imperial Court.

Andō fondly fancied that this stroke of his would go far to allay the general unrest among the Samurai. But in this expectation he was utterly mistaken—the marriage-alliance only added fresh fuel to the blazing wrath.

" During this period," according to the *Kinsé Shiryaku*, " the samurai deserted from their clans in daily increasing number. They allied themselves with the *rōnin* in all parts of the country to raise the cry of ' Honour the Mikado and expel the Barbarians ', thus creating a great ferment throughout the empire ".

Before the Shōgun's nuptials were celebrated, Andō disappeared from the political stage. On 14th February, 1862, he was attacked by a band of rōnin (six of them Mito men) and although he escaped with severe wounds, it was judged advisable that he should not reappear at the Council board. At the same time, the Bakufu exerted itself to conciliate the goodwill of the Court nobles by increasing the stipends of some twenty houses and by various other measures. At this juncture, too, it turned to one of the great Outside clans for support—to Chōshū !

Among the Chōshū samurai the *Kinnō* feeling and the *Kinnō* party were exceedingly strong. The moral influence of Yoshida Shōin was of great consequence among the clansmen, and among his pupils were some of the men who have played leading parts in moulding the destinies of modern Japan. By them, what they regarded as the murder of their revered teacher was never forgotten or forgiven, and at this time their resentment against the Bakufu was intense. Chōshū men were hand-in-glove with Mito *rōnin*, weaving intrigue after intrigue against the authorities, and doing everything they could devise to bring these authorities into collision with the hated foreigners. Nowhere was the ardour for the " expulsion of the barbarian " more intense than among the rank and file of Mōri's vassals. They suspected that Satsuma was secretly organizing a great effort for this purpose, and they were greatly disturbed to think that their own clan might be deprived of the honour and glory of " leading the van ", and playing the most prominent part in the work. But, just as had been the case in Satsuma, the clan councillors in Chōshū were conservative and inclined to move in concert with, and in submission to, the Bakufu and its instructions. A very able man, a certain Nagai, Uta no Kami, had the largest share in the confidence of the Lord of Chōshū at this time. As the result of his investigations on a secret mission, he had warned Mōri of the likelihood of the *rōnin* tendering their support to some of the great Daimyō of the west in an attempt to get possession of the Emperor's person, and to utilize the Imperial name possibly for the overthrow of the Bakufu and certainly for the expulsion of the barbarians by force of arms. Mōri, at this time, was on intimate terms with Kuzé, who was now the chief man at the Great Council board ; and Mōri, seems to have spoken to Kuzé about the dangers of the situation in a very frank tone. Kuzé saw that every effort must be exerted to conciliate the court, and to establish harmony and unity of counsels between Yedo and Kyōto. This was the *Kōbu Gattai* (Union of Court and Camp) movement ; and Nagai was dispatched on a mission to Kyōto to promote it. Among other things Nagai tried to convince the court nobles of the impossibility of expelling the barbarians at that time, and had recourse to the arguments that had been used by Lord Hotta four years before. It was this that chiefly occasioned his failure. His fellow-clansmen were so indignant with him that they lay in wait to assassinate him ; and on his return to Yedo, he was condemned to domiciliary confinement. A year later on, he was ordered to commit *hara-kiri*. For the time being, Mōri, his master, lost much in prestige. And yet, in a year from this date, Mōri had all the *rōnin* loyalists at his beck and call, and in yet another year, his clan was able to defy the embattled might of the Bakufu and its supporters ! For the moment the *rōnin* ceased to repose their hopes in Mōri, and turned to Shimadzu of Satsuma, who was now on his way up to Kyōto and Yedo with a thousand picked clansmen behind him.

Here again the ardent hopes of the *rōnin* were doomed to a bitter disappointment, for whatever the sentiments of his vassals, Shimadzu Hisamitsu was exerting himself to bring about an effective unity of counsels between the Court and the Bakufu. Saigo, who had been dispatched to reconnoitre in advance, knew this quite well, of course; but he found it impossible to carry out his orders to have no dealings with the *rōnin*. He had also been instructed to await Shimadzu's arrival at Shimonoseki; but he found the general situation to be much more disturbed than could have been expected, and so he pushed on to Ōsaka for the purpose of repressing the intemperate zeal of the *rōnin* there, and utilizing them instead of allowing them to try to utilize Shimadzu and Satsuma. For this breach of instructions, and for supposed complicity with the *rōnin*, Shimadzu, on his arrival at Hyōgo, ordered Saigō to be placed under arrest and sent back to Satsuma. On reaching Satsuma, he was not allowed to land, he was at once conveyed to Tokunoshima as an exile, whence he was subsequently removed to a smaller and still lonelier islet, where he was subjected to a harsh and rigorous confinement.

Saigō had found the district around and between Ōsaka and Kyōto swarming with *rōnin*, all ready for any venture that might promise advantage to the cause. The chief spirit among them was that Hirano Jirō who assisted Gesshō in his flight to Satsuma and who witnessed his suicide. Ōsaka, Hyōgo, and Sakai he pointed out, had to be opened next year (1863).

" If these three ports were opened the barbarians would erect forts there under the name of factories, and would garrison them strongly. Thus they would get possession of the great strategical points, and cut us off from going to each other's assistance—dividing the Empire into two halves as it were. Then the Imperial residence would be in as precarious a situation as the proverbial pile of eggs. The expulsion of the barbarians would then be hopeless; it was plain that we should have to fold the left lappet over the right, to take to writing across the page, and to have to use their stinking calendar."

A few hundred *rōnin* could not accomplish much by themselves perhaps; but he knew what the sentiments of the Satsuma samurai were.

" Now let Shimadzu Hisamitsu capture Osaka Castle, advance on Kyōto, put the Shōgun's garrison in Nijō Castle to the sword, drive out all the Bakufu officials, set free the Tairō's imprisoned victims, and after issuing the Mikado's orders to all the Daimyō of the seven circuits to carry the phoenix-car (the Mikado's palanquin) over Hakone and punish the crimes of the Bakufu."

Here we are brought fairly face to face with the new aspect in the situation—the cry now is " Down with the Bakufu ! " This cry was unheard till 1859, and few were venturesome enough to mutter it while the Tairō was alive.

Shimadzu Hisamitsu, however, was in no mind to give any heed to it. The points he was going to urge at Court were that an Imperial edict should be sent to Yedo ordering that Kuzé, the chief of the Great Council, should repair to Kyōto, that Andō should be formally dismissed, that all the Tairō's surviving victims should be freed from all pains and penalties, that the ex-Lord of Eichizen (Matsudaira Yoshinaga) should be made *Sōsai* or Director-General of the Administration, and that Hitotsubashi should be appointed the Shōgun's guardian. Shimadzu aimed merely at a rather drastic reform of the Bakufu, not at its destruction. As for Saigō, even at this date he really held that the Bakufu must go down before Japan could be saved ; but he had laboured strenuously to convince Hirano and his followers that the time for its overthrow had not yet ripened. Leaving half his men in the Satsuma yashiki in Ōsaka, Shimadzu pushed on to Kyōto with the others and took up his quarters in the old capital without any disturbance, much to the relief of the Shogun's commandant who had looked forward to an attack. Through the Konoye house, Shimadzu found ready access to Court, where his memorial was well received. When the Rōnin became apprised of its contents, there was a great commotion, the Satsuma men among them being especially disturbed, while some of the young Satsuma samurai left behind in Ōsaka were furiously angry. A band of these started for Kyōto to remonstrate, but Shimadzu, getting timely notice of this, sent some trusty followers to meet them in Fushimi and bring them to reason. The meeting took place in the Teradaya, an inn on the river's bank. When the ringleaders proved recalcitrant to their Lord's commands, the emissaries suddenly fell upon them with the sword. Eight of them were killed on the spot, while nearly all the assailants were wounded and one killed outright. In Satsuma, ideas of discipline were always very strict, and the methods of enforcing it drastic. Shimadzu was now requested to pass some time in Kyōto for the purpose of pacifying the *rōnin*, on whom the object-lesson of the Teradaya had a very salutary effect for the time being, although all *rōnin* sympathy and respect were effectually alienated from Satsuma.

As for Shimadzu's memorial, the Court decided to act upon it in a modified form. Ōhara, a court noble, was appointed Imperial envoy, and Shimadzu was to escort him to Yedo. But the rescript he carried ordered not Kuzé, *but the Shōgun himself* to appear at Kyōto, while in addition to Shimadzu's proposals about appointments, an alternative suggestion was put forward that the Bakufu might now do well to imitate Hideyoshi's device and appoint five of the greater Daimyō whose territories lay on the coast, to be Chief Ministers (*Tairō*). This special suggestion was not adopted, but the others were, and the ex-Lord of Echizen and Hitotsubashi were presently installed in their new offices. And—most important point of all—the Shōgun undertook to repair to Kyōto :—

" In order to come to a complete understanding with the Mikado, and to give expression to his sincere sentiments and intentions, thus laying the foundations of a complete accord and enabling the military prestige of Japan to be developed until she became the most powerful nation in the world."

For two hundred and thirty years or so, not one of eleven successive Shōguns had deigned to honour Kyōto with his presence, and during their government, the Imperial Court would not have dared to summon even a Bakufu Counsellor to appear before it. A few years before, a Tairō found it easy to ignore its mandate to repair to Kyōto. Things were now moving rapidly indeed. Towards the end of the year, yet another imperial mission appeared in Yedo (escorted by Yamanouchi of Tosa) ordering the Bakufu to clear away abuses and reform the administration, and calling upon the Shōgun to repair to Kyōto in the following spring, there to issue his orders to the clans and proceed to achieve the expulsion of the barbarians without delay. In his written reply to this imperial mandate the Shōgun actually signed himself " *Shin* " or vassal ! Such a thing was unprecedented.

Shungaku, as the ex-lord of Echizen was also called, acted as Sōsai or Director-General of the Tokugawa administration for no more than ten months ; yet during that short time there were greater changes in Yedo than there had been during the preceding quarter of a millennium. On the occasion of the Shōgun's marriage with the Emperor's sister there had been a sort of amnesty for some of the Tairō's victims, and Shungaku himself, the ex-Lords of Tosa,

Owari and Uwajima and some court nobles were released from constraint and allowed to appear in public life. Now, there was a general rehabilitation of all those who had suffered in 1858, while drastic punishment was meted out to those who had acted as Ii's tools and satellites. His son and successor in the fief of Hikone was deprived of 100,000 koku of his assessed revenue ; Naitō, Kuzé, and Andō were all dismissed from office, stripped of portions of their domains and ordered into close confinement. Almost every one connected with the negotiation of the foreign treaties was made to suffer, the lesser Bakufu officials being dismissed in tens and dozens. All this was of little consequence in comparison to the mortal wound the Bakufu now dealt itself.

On 17th October, 1862, an edict was issued with reference to official dress and the attendance of the feudatories in Yedo. About the change in dress and similar regulations there is no great need to waste time. But the new provisions about the residence of the feudatories in Yedo were nothing short of revolutionary. Instead of passing every alternate year in Yedo as they had had to do for two centuries and more, the Ōbiroma Daimyō—that is the great " Outside " feudatories like Kaga, Satsuma, Sendai, Tosa—were henceforth expected to remain in Yedo for no longer than one hundred days in three years. The lesser outside Lords and the greater vassals of the Tokugawa house were to spend one year out of three, while the length of residence demanded from the others was also curtailed. Henceforth, also, the Daimyō were no longer obliged to keep their wives and children in their Yedo yashiki. All this simply meant that the system of political hostages —the great sheet-anchor for the security of the Tokugawa Shōgunate —was abandoned ! To quote the Genji Yume Monogatari :—

" In consequence all the Daimyō and Hatamoto who owned lands sent their wives and children to their country residences, and in the twinkling of an eye, the flourishing city of Yedo became like a desert, so that the Daimyō allied to the Tokugawa family and the vassals of the Shōgunate of all ranks, and the townspeople, too, grieved and lamented. They would have liked to see the military glory of the Kwantō shine again, but as the great and small Daimyō, who were not vassals of the Tokugawa, had cut at the root of this forced residence in Yedo, and few of them obeyed the commands of the Bakufu any longer, they also began to distrust it, and gradually the hearts of the people fell away. And so the prestige of the Tokugawa family, which had endured for three hundred years, which had really been more brilliant than Kamakura in the age of Yoritomo on a moonlight night when the stars are shining, which, for more than two hundred and seventy years, had forced the Daimyō to come breathlessly to take their turn of duty in Yedo and had day and night eighty thousand vassals at its beck and call, fell to ruin in the space of one morning."

In the circumstances, as might have been easily foreseen, the political centre of gravity now speedily shifted to Kyōto. The author of the *Genji Yume Monogatari* was a resident of Kyōto, and at various dates he refers to the growing magnificence of the ancient capital. Towards the end of 1862, he notes that the Western Daimyō were beginning to assemble in Kyōto :—

" These were the vanguard of a body of more than forty Daimyō who came up to Kyōto the following spring (1863) and stayed there. All the large temples of the capital were occupied as the headquarters of Daimyō, and those who could not be accommodated within the city got temples in the neighbouring villages. Kyōto had never been so crowded since the visit of Iyemitsu, the third Shōgun in 1634."

It soon became clear that the feudatories were to be no mere birds of passage, roosting in temples for a short season. By the summer of 1863 :—

" The prestige of the court had become so great that every Daimyō tried to obtain an official residence in the capital. The Prince of Satsuma built a residence covering 2,000 or 3,000 *tsubo* in front of the Temple of Sōkokuji. The Princes of Tosa, Chōshū, Kurumé, Yanagawa, Sendai, and Unshū also enlarged the sites of their residences, while the Princes of Chikuzen, Inshū, Higo and others obtained new sites within the city, and the Princes of Owari, Echizen, Kishū, Awa, Aki, Aidzu, Kuwana, obtained sites outside, on which they all built residences. All the other clans, both great and small, and even the Hatamoto, cleared land both within and without the city, to the number of more than a hundred, and erected mansions for themselves. As all these places were filled with troops, the town assumed a very busy and flourishing aspect ; shops were opened everywhere, and the whole population down to the lowest classes began to get rich."

The Bakufu had been careful to keep the feudatories aloof from Kyōto. Even a few years before Shimadzu Nariakira of Satsuma, who was on the best of terms with the Shōgun's ministers, could find no access to the Sovereign ; when actually in Kyōto he would go secretly to the neighbourhood of the Imperial palace to make an obeisance from a distance, while his visits to the various court nobles had to be incognito. Contrast this with the state of things seven or eight years later on, in 1863 :—

" All the Daimyō present in Kyōto went to court to offer their felicitations to the Mikado, in the order of their rank, clad in court dress ; and among them were the court nobles in their court dress also . . . It was truly a beautiful sight. Outside the nine gates were crowds of spear-bearers, matchlock-men, led horse and baggage coolies awaiting the exit of their masters. When the evening came on, hand-lanterns and lanterns on poles were lighted in such numbers that it seemed to be broad daylight in the palace. Such a splendid exhibition of the greatness of the court had not been known since the earliest ages."

One of the earliest of the Daimyō to establish himself in Kyōto was Yamanouchi Yōdō of Tosa. He had received a message from the Court requesting him to join his efforts to those of Satsuma and Chōshū " who had lately been exerting themselves on the Imperial behalf ". Here we have the origin of the compound *Sat-Chō-To—* the combination of Satsuma, Chōshū, and Tosa, which was destined to exercise such a decisive influence upon the march of events during the next generation.

However, as regards Satsuma and Chōshū, there was already a rift in the lute. Iwakura, who was eager for the " Union of Court and Camp " had said that Satsuma and Chōshū were as the two wheels of a carriage or the two wings of a bird, and that their co-operation was indispensable. But there was a good deal of secret jealousy between the two clans ; each dreaded the possibility of having to play a secondary role to the other. Mōri, Lord of Chōshū was at first a strong advocate of a " Union of Court and Camp " but his zeal had cooled, and the clansmen, who wished to settle accounts with the Bakufu, were now dominant in his Councils. When Shimadzu Hisamitsu left Kyōto for Yedo, the younger Mōri was in Kyōto. Shimadzu was requested to co-operate with the elder Mōri when he reached Yedo, but the day before he entered Yedo, Mōri had taken the Nakasendō route for Kyōto, and while Shimadzu was still in Yedo, the younger Mōri arrived with a fresh edict from the Court for presentation to the Shōgun. In one of its clauses reference was made to the Teradaya episode, for which Shimadzu was censured by implication. Until that clause was deleted he refused to meet Mōri. This was one of a number of incidents that made any real co-operation between the two great clans impossible, and led up to the furious combat between them that took place in the streets of Kyōto two years later.

Meanwhile, preparations were being pushed forward for the great event—the Shōgun's visit to Kyōto. Early in February, 1863, Matsudaira Katamori—the Lord of Aidzu, was sent there, not as Shoshidai, but as military Governor, which was a new office ! The Aidzu samurai were among the most warlike men in Japan, and a strong force of them now followed their chieftain to act as a Bakufu garrison for the Castle of Nijō in the old capital. A little later on, Hitotsubashi, the Shōgun's guardian, appeared, while Shungaku of Echizen arrived soon after. The agitation for the speedy expulsion of the barbarian had become intense in Kyōto, and the *rōnin* and the lower class samurai were insistent that the date for the great exploit should be definitely fixed at once. The court noble Sanjō, with some others, acted as their mouthpiece and visited Hitotsubashi to ascertain when operations were to begin. At the same time, Mōri called on the Kwambaku and urged him repeatedly to get the date fixed. Next day Yamanouchi Yōdō of Tosa saw Hitotsubashi and warned him of the seriousness of the position. All that Hitotsubashi, Shungaku and their advisers could do was to put off the evil day by temporisingly asserting that the date might be fixed after the Shōgun's arrival.

This great event took place a fortnight later, on 21st April, 1863. The last occasion on which a Shōgun appeared in Kyōto was in 1634 ; and on that occasion Iyemitsu was accompanied by 307,000 armed men. The Shōgun now brought a retinue of about 3,000 with him ; but among these there were only about a hundred cavalry and some eight hundred musketeers. Just twelve days before, the heads of the wooden statues of the first three Ashikaga Shōguns were found pilloried in the river bed, which was commonly used as an execution-ground, and the contumelious placard attached to them left no room for doubt as to the significance of the incident. In Iyemitsu's time such a thing would have been at once impossible and unthinkable. Aidzu succeeded in arresting some of the perpetrators, but Mōri interceded for them, winning great popularity among the *rōnin* in consequence, and in the end the culprits got off very lightly. Aidzu seems to have divined the danger of Mōri's gaining such an ascendency over the *rōnin*, and he made arrangements to take a certain number of them into the Tokugawa service, a step that was presently adopted on a greater scale in Yedo. Mōri, however, was able to attract the better class of men, and in the subsequent struggle between Chōshū and the Bakufu, the *rōnin* did great work for Chōshū.

At this time it was highly imperative to do something to bring the *rōnin* under control. Since the summer of 1862, they had been guilty of a series of terrible atrocities. The *Genji Yume Monogatari* has a monotonous and melancholy tale to tell of those that fell victims to the political assassin; but even the long list given in its pages is far from complete. In the first place, it was the late Tairō's minions, and those connected with them, who had been especially singled out for attack. Then merchants who raised their prices got summarily cut down. Next, those who had supported the " Union of Court and Camp " were assailed. The Court noble, Chigusa, had supported the Shōgun's marriage suit; the *rōnin* now murdered his trusted retainer and sent one arm of the corpse to his master, and the other to Iwakura, while the head, with a threatening paper attached, was deposited on a charger before Hitotsubashi's door. Freshly severed heads were even cast into the Imperial Palace itself. Iwakura had been ordered to take the tonsure and retire into privacy, while the ladies of his house who had served in the Palace were driven out, much to the grief of the Emperor. The cry of "*Kōbu Gattai*" was now replaced by that of the " Vengeance of Heaven ", and Mōri was the great patron of those *rōnin* who relentlessly " punished " the discredited advocates of the policy which Mōri had at first zealously promoted. He now had a strong party in his favour among the court nobles, who, under the leadership of young Sanjō, pressed for the speedy expulsion of the barbarians with all the vehemence of Hirano Jirō or the most bigoted and bloodthirsty *rōnin* in the land.

The Shōgun had intended to pass no more than ten days in Kyōto; as a matter of fact he was detained there for ninety-four days, and in the end his vassals had almost literally to tear him away. On 24th April (1863) he paid his first visit to the Palace and " worshipped the dragon countenance ". Four days later, he escorted the Mikado on his progress to the Upper and Lower Kamo Shrines, where His Majesty went to worship as a preliminary to beginning the task of " sweeping away the barbarians ". After another audience with the Mikado on 5th June, a notification was issued to the Daimyō that the 25th June, 1863, had been determined as the date for the expulsion of the barbarians, while a subsequent decree ordered each Daimyō to muster a force in proportion to the assessed revenue of his fief, to be placed at the service of the Imperial Court.

On 8th June, the Shōgun again went to Court and begged urgently for permission to set out for the Kwantō where the posture of affairs had become highly critical. Permission to leave *was* accorded; but it was speedily withdrawn, and the Lord of Mito was dispatched to Yedo to deal with emergencies there. A little later, Hitotsubashi followed him for the purpose of accomplishing the closing of the ports, which the Lord of Mito had of course been unable to effect. Presently came word from Hitotsubashi that he had found everything in confusion, and that it was totally impossible to execute the Imperial mandate for the closing of the ports. As for himself, he humbly awaited punishment and begged to be allowed to resign his post of Guardian of the Shōgun. Shungaku of Echizen had already (8th May, 1863) retired from the General Superintendence of the Administration, for he was convinced that the project of the expulsion of the barbarians was impracticable. But the Shōgun was still detained in Kyōto ; the extremists, who were now determined to overthrow the Bakufu, saw the advantage of having him in their power there, while the exponents of the " *Kōbu Gattai* " policy fancied that his presence in Kyōto would strengthen their cause. At last, the Yedo Councillors dispatched an armed force in two chartered steamers to Ōsaka to bring him back by main force ; and this force had got as far as Fushimi (22nd July) when it was learned that the Shōgun was really to leave Kyōto on 24th July. In Yedo, the Shōgun's presence had perhaps never been so absolutely indispensable as it was during the troublous hundred days of Iyemochi's absence. To make that much plain, however, it becomes necessary to hark back to an important incident of the previous year (1862).

On his way back from Yedo, Shimadzu Hisamitsu's retinue was met by a party of four British excursionists (one lady among them) at Namamugi, not far from Kanagawa on the Tokaidō. They did not break through the cortege, as nearly all Japanese accounts say they did, but in the opinion of Shimadzu's attendants they failed to show proper deference for their Lord, for instead of dismounting, they walked their horses along the side of the road past the procession. Narabara, the officer in charge, was an ardent exponent of the " Sonnō Jōi " doctrine, and he at once drew sword to punish this exhibition of foreign insolence. The lady's hat was slashed, but she got off safely ; her three male companions were all wounded, and one so seriously that after fleeing back along the road he fell from his horse. Whether he expired at the moment, or whether he was hacked to pieces a few minutes afterwards is not perfectly clear. The Namamugi affair, as the Japanese call Richardson's murder, created a tremendous excitement at the time, not only

among the little foreign community in Yokohama, but also among
the Japanese, and especially among the Bakufu officials.   For the
murder of two sentries in the last attack on the British Legation,
the Bakufu had been taken sharply to task, and the settlement of
that troublesome question was still pending ; now there was a still
more serious affair to complicate matters.   On 4th December, 1862,
an indemnity of £10,000 was demanded for the death of the sentries,
on 6th April, 1863, Lieut.-Col. Neale, the British Representative,
acting under instructions from the British Foreign office sent in a
long dispatch demanding an apology from the Bakufu for the
Namamugi outrage, and an indemnity of £100,000.   In addition
to this, the assassins were to be brought to justice, and £25,000 more
handed over to be distributed among Richardson's relatives and
his companions who had been assaulted.   To these demands a
categorical answer had to be made within twenty days.

Meanwhile preparations for the Shōgun's visit to Kyōto had
been completed, and Iyemochi had already left Yedo on 3rd April,
taking about half of the Councillors with him, while his Guardian,
Hitotsubashi, and the Director-General, Shungaku of Echizen,
had been in the western capital for some time.   Small wonder then
that the officials left in Yedo professed to be at their wits' end, and
did all they could to evade a settlement.   When they perceived that
further procrastination would surely lead to the opening of hostilities
they signed an agreement to pay the indemnity in instalments on
14th June.   On 17th June they wrote to say that payment was
impossible, and the British representative thereupon broke off all
communication with them, and placed the matter in the hands of
Admiral Kuper who was then in Yokohama with the greater part
of the China squadron.   At one o'clock on the morning of
24th June, the representative was asked at what hour the money
might be brought to the Legation, and four hours later the whole
sum of £110,000 was duly paid over in Mexican dollars ! Less
than three weeks before this, it had been determined in Kyōto that
the expulsion of the barbarians and the closing of the ports should
be undertaken on 25th June ! Now after the money had been
paid over, later on, on the very same day, came a dispatch from
Ogasawara, one of the Great Councillors in Yedo stating that :—

" Orders of the Tycoon had been received from Kyōto to the effect
that the ports were to be closed and the foreigners driven out, because

the people of the country do not desire intercourse with foreign countries."

The foreign representatives, each of whom had received a copy of this extraordinary dispatch, at once returned very vigorous replies. Nine days after, a formal apology for the Namamugi outrage was tendered, one sentence in which was rather strange in the circumstances.

" Thus we hope that affairs likely to break off the intercourse between the two countries may not arise again."

On 18th June, when war seemed to be inevitable, there was a general exodus from Yedo, where many officials absented themselves from duty. The Bakufu officials knew only too well that the closing of the ports and the expulsion of the barbarians were impossibilities, but the orders from Kyōto could not be entirely ignored. The Tycoon's envoys verbally assured the British and French representatives that the :—

" Mikado's edict of expulsion conveyed to representatives of the Treaty Powers as a matter of obligation by the Tycoon was a dead letter with respect to all action in regard to it."

Yet, a few months later, on 26th October, 1863, the Bakufu requested the American and Dutch representatives to :—

" Inform their Governments that the notification of Ogasawara relating to the expulsion of foreigners will be withdrawn, and to ask their consent to have the trade transferred to Nagasaki and Hakodate."

A few days later (12th November, 1863) the astonished representatives received the following communication :—

" As our government has for the present changed its former policy, we request you to return to us the dispatch which Ogasawara Dzusho no Kami addressed to you while he was still in office regarding the closing of the ports."

Of course, the key to what Neale characterized as the "mysterious policy and proceedings of the Shogun's government " at this time, was to be found in Kyōto.

Meanwhile, however, if the Bakufu showed itself so hopelessly lukewarm in the project of expelling the barbarians, the task had been taken vigorously in hand in other quarters. Along the classic strand haunted by the ghosts of the Tairā who had perished in the battle of Dannoura seven centuries before, Chōshū had erected a series of powerful batteries, while the steamer, the brig and the barque, which constituted the nucleus of the navy the clan was forming, were generally kept moored outside the eastern exit of the Straits of Shimonoseki. On 25th June, the very date fixed for the expulsion of the barbarians, an American steamer—the *Pembroke*—passed through the straits and received the fire of two of Chōshū's men-of-war. A few days later the French aviso, *Kien-Chang*, was hulled in seven places, and only escaped destruction by slipping her cable and running out through the Bungo Channel. Again, on 11th July, the Dutch corvette *Medusa* had to fight a vigorous action to get through the straits, she was struck by thirty-one shots, while three 8-inch shells burst on board and four of her crew were killed and five wounded. A few days after this, two French men-of-war appeared to punish the outrage on the *Kien-Chang* ; and on 20th July, a sharp action was fought, when some of the batteries were destroyed. The United States war-steamer *Wyoming* also proceeded to the Straits, and sank Chōshū's steamer, and inflicted other damage at the cost of one man killed and five wounded (16th July). During these encounters, the south side of the Straits remained perfectly quiet, and some time afterwards an Imperial edict reproved the Kokura clan, whose fief lay on that side, by implication for not taking part in the attack on the barbarians. " The neighbouring clans ought to send assistance," it said, " for the peril of Chōshū was the peril of the Empire."

The representatives of Great Britain, France, the United States, and the Netherlands, assembled at Yokohama on 25th July, and determined :—

" To establish a concert of all the disposable military and naval forces, for the purpose of opening the Straits of Shimonoseki, if the Bakufu failed to take prompt action to punish Chōshū for the series of outrages—outrages which were regarded as an attempt to carry out the edicts of the Mikado communicated through the Tycoon for the expulsion of the foreigners."

Six days after this (31st July) the Shōgun at last arrived back in Yedo. One of the first things now done by him was to address a memorial to the Mikado, representing that in the opinion of Mito and Hitotsubashi, with whom he had been directed to consult, the present juncture was an unfavourable one for carrying out the exclusion policy. To attempt it now would merely be playing into the hands of the barbarians. So soon as order was introduced into the administration, and harmony of opinion established, the necessary steps should be taken. He suggested that the fixing of a date should be left entirely to his discretion. This last clause ignored the fact that the date had not only already been fixed, but had expired six weeks before. In the Imperial reply the Shōgun was commended for having come to court and so revived the excellent practice that had remained in abeyance for more than two centuries, thus placing the relations of sovereign and vassal on a proper footing. But the Shōgun was rebuked for failing to keep the Mikado apprised of his doings, for having returned by a steamer instead of overland, and for his unsatisfactory language in regard to the breaking off of foreign intercourse. He deserved to be called to account for his conduct, but out of gracious consideration, proceedings against him would be delayed. Ten short years before this, Kyōto would have quailed at the thought of saying even one tithe of this to a Great Councillor, to say nothing of a Shōgun!

In Kyōto, meanwhile, the advocates of the discredited "*Kōbu Gattai*" policy were gradually pulling themselves together in a supreme effort to wrench the control of affairs from the hands of the extremists. These latter were now represented in the first place by the Chōshū clan, in which that perfervid loyalist Kusaka had become exceedingly influential, by Takechi of Tosa, and by the *rōnin*, while the sympathies of many of the lower class samurai in the various clans went heartily with them. The rank and file of the court nobles, among whom the most influential was Sanjō, were also hostile to the Bakufu as well as to the barbarians. But the higher court nobles were still pledged to the "Union of Court and Camp". Prominent among these were Takatsukasa, Nijō, and the Konoye, father and son, with whom Shimadzu of Satsuma's relations were intimate. But the dominant figure in this coterie was that Shōren-in who had played a prominent part on the political stage four or five years before, and who now, under the title of Prince Nakagawa, and later on of the In no Miya, seems to have been the real power behind the throne at this troublous crisis. At all events this Prince of the Blood had a larger share in the Imperial confidence than any of the court nobles—such at least is the inference from the numerous private notes and letters that passed between him and the Sovereign. From some of these notes it is clear that the Emperor himself wished to proceed with the task of the expulsion of the barbarians with a good deal of circumspection, and that he was greatly concerned over the violent counsels that were then getting the upper hand in Kyōto. He profoundly distrusted the rashness of the extremists. For one thing they aimed at the overthrow of the

Bakufu, while the Emperor, down to the very last, wished to act through the Bakufu. He held the " Union of Court and Camp " to be a prime necessity ; it was only a united Empire that could hope to make head against the insistent menace of foreign aggression. In April, 1863, repeated messages were transmitted to Shimadzu Hisamitsu (now called Shimadzu Saburō), that staunch upholder of the " *Kōbu Gattai* " policy, urging him to come up to Kyōto ; and at last Shimadzu did appear there with a strong following at the beginning of May. In consultation with Prince Nakagawa and his fellow-thinkers, Shimadzu advocated a very strong and drastic way of dealing with the extremists, while Nakabara, the Satsuma samurai, who had distinguished himself in the Teradaya episode and who had cut down the Englishman Richardson on the great eastern highroad, now sought ways and means of making an end of Kusaka of Chōshū, the most active figure among the expulsion zealots. But a few days in Kyōto convinced Shimadzu that the policy of repression he so strenuously advocated could only be enforced by bringing up the whole armed might of Satsuma. Just at this juncture the whole armed might of Satsuma was imperatively needed at home ; and after a brief sojourn in the ancient capital, Shimadzu hurried back to prepare for the British attack presently to be launched against Kagoshima, the capital city of the great fief.

When the British demand for the arrest and trial of Richardson's murderers, and an indemnity of £25,000 was transmitted to the Satsuma authorities by the Bakufu, the Satsuma men determined at all hazards to resist it to the last. On the death of Nariakira in 1858, the conservatives, who had then returned to power in the clan administration, abandoned most of Nariakira's progressive enterprises and projects. Now, under the impending menace of a foreign attack, the Satsuma men were at last in a position to appreciate the dead chieftain's work and foresight, and there was a sudden resumption of his policy. The defences of Kagoshima were rapidly strengthened, and with the completion of nine forts mounting about eighty guns along two miles of the strand in front of the city, and on Sakurajima and one or two other small islands adjacent, the clansmen began to fancy that they had made Kagoshima absolutely impregnable. When announcing the approaching departure of the British China squadron for Kagoshima, the Bakufu informed the Satsuma authorities in Yedo that the English demanded Shimadzu Saburō's head; and this falsehood naturally had the

effect of still further strengthening the determination of the
clansmen to fight to the last.

On 11th August, 1863, the British China squadron appeared at
the mouth of Kagoshima Bay. It consisted of seven vessels ; but
four of these were small craft mounting no more than sixteen guns
between them. The *Perseus* carried 17, the *Pearl* 21, and the flagship,
the *Euryalus*, 35 guns, most of which were Armstrong breach-loading
40-pounder and 100-pounder cannon, a type of gun that was now to
be tested in action for the first time. On this occasion the method
of closing the breach proved to be defective—but, in spite of that,
the destructiveness of the Armstrong gun came as a terrible surprise
to the Satsuma clansmen, " the bravest men in Asia." As soon
as the squadron came up the gulf and anchored close to the southern
end of the city of Kagoshima on the 12th, negotiations began. They
were bound to be abortive, but it is interesting to observe that the
Satsuma minister laid it down that in everything Satsuma had acted
in accordance with the orders of the Yedo Government.

" We have heard something of a treaty having been negotiated in
which a certain limit was assigned to foreigners inside which they might
move about ; but we have not heard of any stipulation by which they
are authorized to impede the passage of a road . . . The insufficiency
of the Yedo Government, who govern and direct everything, is shown
by their neglecting to insert in the treaty (with foreigners) the laws of
the country (in respect to these matters) which have existed from ancient
times."

Here one of the great and venerable institutions of Japan stood
upon its defence behind eighty pieces of modern artillery ; and the
supporters of the Daimyō's right to make every commoner crouch
and knock his head on the ground as the procession swept along the
highway had not the slightest intention of yielding. At this point,
ninety-eight samurai of the clan were drinking farewell cups of
water with their Lord ; they were setting out in the guise of
pedlars to get on board the various barbarian vessels and cut down
the officers, while the batteries were to open fire at the same time.
The largest body of thirty-two did actually get on board the
flagship but the precautions with which they were received precluded
any attempt at the execution of their desperate project. Some of
these desperadoes have since held not merely high office but the
very highest offices in Japan.

On the evening of the 14th, the British representative felt
constrained to place matters in the hands of Admiral Kuper, who

commanded the squadron. Next forenoon (the anniversary of Xavier's landing at Kagoshima) three Satsuma steamers, which were lying further up the Bay at Shigetomi, were seized. These had just cost the clan 305,000 dollars—thrice the amount of the indemnity demanded. As soon as this action was reported to Shimadzu Saburō and his son, orders were given to open fire on the " pirates ". Taken by surprise, the British ships had to cut their cables before they could form in line of column and treat the batteries to their broadsides in succession. Just at this time (noon of 15th August, 1863) a torrential downpour of rain began, which continued till noon of the following day, while the typhoon that accompanied it raged for some hours longer. Nearly all the batteries were silenced, and the chief fort all but demolished ; but the actual Japanese loss of life was wonderfully small, for only ten men were killed, and eleven wounded, against thirteen killed and fifty wounded in the squadron. On the other hand, the loss of property was enormous. The three arrested steamers and some large Lūchū junks were fired and sunk, the arsenal burned, and the greater part of the city of Kagoshima reduced to ashes. The deadly efficiency of modern armaments made a tremendous impression upon the Satsuma men. Although they at once set vigorously to work to repair damages, and to put themselves in a position to meet a second British attack, there was nothing they dreaded more. It would be disastrous to their own fief, and with the chaotic state of affairs in Kyōto and elsewhere, it might well prove disastrous to Japan. Ōkubo, the ablest among the clan councillors, was dispatched to Yedo, there secretly to direct the negotiations which it was determined to open with the British representative. Some of the Satsuma men in Yedo were bitterly opposed to instituting any such negotiations ; on returning to what had been the city of Kagoshima, however, they speedily changed their minds. Four months later on, the indemnity was paid for Satsuma by the branch clan of Sadowara, and an engagement given to search for Richardson's assassins, while Neale undertook to facilitate Satsuma's purpose of purchasing a man-of-war in England. This was really the beginning of the extremely friendly relations that have ever since subsisted between the men of Satsuma and the British diplomatic officials in Japan. Shimadzu Saburō was kept perfectly well-informed of all that then passed in Yokohama ; but the anti-foreign feeling was so strong in Kyōto where he was then strenuously at work that he had to make a pretence of punishing his agents who "had compromised the honour of the clan". The withdrawal of the British squadron from Kagoshima was generally regarded as a glorious victory for Satsuma. Shimadzu was eulogized both by the Court and the Bakufu, and his "brushing away of the barbarians" did much to regain the esteem of the *rōnin* whom he had so sadly disappointed in 1862. But now, as then, Shimadzu wished to have nothing to do with the *rōnin*. In fact, he was sternly resolved to make an end of the *rōnin* nuisance once for all.

Meanwhile, the extremists had met with a serious set-back in Kyōto. One of their leaders, the Court noble Amenokoji, was assassinated, and as some Satsuma men were suspected of the crime, the Satsuma troops were relieved of their ward of the palace gate that had been entrusted to them, and Chōshū became still more powerful in Kyōto. Kusaka, the Chōshū loyalist, and his friends all saw their opportunity in the failure of the Bakufu to close the ports as had been ordered. It was now notified that as an immediate preliminary to "sweeping away the barbarians" the emperor was to go to pray at the tomb of Jimmu Tennō and the Kasuga Temple in Yamato, and afterwards, at the Great Shrines of Ise, while orders were sent to the Daimyō to furnish military contingents in proportion to their assessed revenue. Kusaka's real object seems to have been, if not to obtain control over the person of the Emperor, at all events to obtain Imperial sanction to "Chastise the Bakufu". The Emperor gave Prince Nakagawa to understand that he was really opposed to any such precipitate measures as had been announced. The Prince thereupon took counsel with his friends, summoned Aidzu and Satsuma samurai then in Kyōto secretly on 27th and 29th September, and arranged with them for what was practically a *coup d'état*.

On 30th September, 1863, the Chōshū commandant was informed that henceforth no Chōshū man could be allowed within the precincts of the Palace. At the same time all the nine gates were manned by a strong force of Aidzu and Satsuma samurai, and Inaba, Bizen, Yonezawa, and some others were ordered to send detachments at once, while Sanjō and his friends were stripped of their offices. The result of the terrible commotion that ensued was that the Chōshū men withdrew from Kyōto, taking with them Sanjō and six other court nobles who were soon after put to the ban. The repression of *rōnin* truculence in Kyōto was now taken vigorously in hand, and the city was soon relieved from the unwelcome presence of these blood-thirsty swashbucklers. Some of them, under Nakayama, a court noble, raised a great disturbance in Yamato, where they killed a number of Bakufu officials, seized the government buildings and were only dispersed after the levies of the neighbouring clans had been mobilized to deal with them. Later on, in November, there was another *rōnin* émeute at the mines of Ikuno in Tamba, in which Hirano Jirō and Sawa, one of the seven exiled court nobles were compromised. But Chōshū was now the great refuge for the lordless two-sworded men ; there they were organized in regiments and companies for service against the barbarians, or for any other enterprise that might offer.

Chōshū was presently called upon to explain his action in firing on foreign ships, and in attacking the Kokura clan. His defence was that the 25th June, 1853, was the date fixed for the expulsion of the barbarians, and that it was to be presumed that hostile action was to be immediate, inasmuch as any parleying that might have been contemplated would have already taken place. As the Kokura clan had failed to support the Chōshū efforts, there was surely nothing irregular in sending people to expostulate with it. The Chōshū chieftain also sent in repeated memorials protesting against the events of 30th September, and begging for the restoration of Sanjō and his fellows to office, but without effect. The clans of Inaba, Bizen, Yonezawa, and Tsuyama were all more or less in sympathy with Chōshū, they urged that the Shōgun should be called to task for his failure to close Yokohama, while they warned the Bakufu that " if the offences of the seven nobles and Chōshū were not condoned, calamity would closely follow ". Others, however, were meanwhile getting bold enough to say publicly that the task of expelling the barbarians was an impossible one. The Bakufu had long since realized this much, and Shimadzu and his able councillors now also began to do so. But they could scarcely afford to say as much openly just yet. Shungaku of Echizen was tolerably frank, however. Since his resignation he had kept at home at Fukui, and he now sent up a memorial to the effect that the Court and the Bakufu were both pursuing a mistaken policy. For the Empire to remain isolated was impracticable, and to break off connexions with the Five Western Powers without just reason would amount to a breach of faith. The " pernicious doctrine " so much talked about was quite different from the " Kirishtan " of former times, and as far as he could hear no harm need be anticipated from its toleration. Commerce would enrich Japan, as it had done other countries. Until the Court changed its foreign policy, Shungaku and his son would keep aloof from it.

Before the year (1863) was out, however, Shungaku again found himself in Kyōto. At Otsu he was met by Komatsu, another of Shimadzu's able and trusty Councillors, and Komatsu now said some very remarkable things to him. He said that Japan could not continue to go on as she was doing. To deal with foreign powers a strong government was absolutely necessary. Either the Bakufu must be rehabilitated in its authority, or failing that, *power must be transferred to the Imperial Court.* When a responsible minister of one of the greatest and most powerful fiefs in the Empire began to express views of this sort, matters might be expected soon to get serious for the Bakufu. Meanwhile, Shimadzu Saburō was really exerting himself strenuously for the rehabilitation of its power. For the third time since 1862, he again appeared in Kyōto (13th November, 1863) and at once sent requests to the ex-lords of Tosa, Echizen and Uwajima, to join him there. All of these, it will be observed, were loyal to the Bakufu, and at the same time adverse to the exclusion policy. Shimadzu was also urgent that the Shōgun and Hitotsubashi should pay another visit to Kyōto, to retrieve the mischances of the previous one. Among the Bakufu officials the opposition to this proposal was exceedingly strong ; and after this had been overcome the burning down of Yedo Castle afforded the objectors an excellent excuse for cancelling the arrangements. Shimadzu, however, finally triumphed over all obstacles, and the Shōgun was again in Kyōto from 22nd February to 10th June, 1864. On this occasion, the results were as auspicious for the Shōgun as they had been humiliating on the original visit. He was granted several Imperial audiences, and many addresses and communications passed between him and the Sovereign during the one hundred and thirteen days of his stay. In an early decree the Mikado was made to say that :—

" The subjugation of the ugly barbarians is a fundamental law in our polity, and we must set an army on foot to strike awe into them and chastise them. But we like not, in truth, a reckless attack upon the barbarians. Do you, therefore, ponder an efficient scheme and submit it to Us. We will then discuss its merits with care and come to a firm and irrevocable determination."

In the last Imperial instructions to the Shōgun (3rd June, 1864) a few sentences indicate how thoroughly the good understanding between the Court and the Camp had been established :—

" The duties of the Bakufu are, on the one hand, to govern the Empire in peace, and on the other to subjugate the barbarians . . . His Majesty in the exercise of his wisdom *has seen fit to commit full powers to the Bakufu*, and he desires that the orders of government shall therefore proceed from a single centre so that the suspicions of the popular mind shall not be excited. He therefore orders you to fulfil the duties of your office enumerated above. Further, you must accomplish without fail the exploit of closing the port of Yokohama. With respect to the punishment of Chōshū, His Majesty gives you no special directions as to the runaway nobles and the turbulent retainers of that clan but you are ordered to punish them as you think fit, full powers being entrusted to you for that purpose."

About the closing of Yokohama it should be said that on the very day the Shōgun left Yedo for Kyōto, envoys set out for Europe to negotiate that matter with the various treaty-powers. Their ostensible purpose was to tender an apology to the French Government for the murder of Lieutenant Camus, who had been foully assassinated near Yokohama on 14th October, 1863. Shimadzu Saburō had hotly attacked the project of closing one port and leaving others open ; and he now maintained that this mission of the Bakufu to the various governments would be totally abortive. The reception the envoys met with in Paris sufficed to convince them that the mission was hopeless elsewhere ; in August, 1864, when they returned with a convention engaging the Shōgun to open the Straits of Shimonoseki within three months, they were punished by relegation to private life. Shimadzu was not pleased to find that his views on this point were slighted ; and the Bakufu must have had its misgivings about disregarding them—all the more so, as an Imperial decree had just designated him and the Lord of Aidzu, and the ex-Lords of Echizen, Tosa and Uwajima, as the five most trusty military men in the Empire, and had ordered the Shōgun " to be affectionate to them, and to work with them ".

In all these decrees, the Mikado spoke as the real Sovereign of Japan addressing a subject who had to obey. Ten years before he could have presumed to do no such thing. Furthermore, the Shōgun now really behaved as a respectful and submissive vassal. He sent in a memorial of eighteen articles proposing among other things that all future Shōguns should proceed to Kyōto for their investiture, as should also the Go-san-ké and other Daimyō on succeeding to their fiefs, while all the Western Daimyō were to pay their respects to His Majesty on their way to and from Yedo. We must always remember that for generations all access to the Sovereign had been forbidden to the feudatories by the Bakufu! The Daimyō were also to make annual gifts to the Mikado of the products of their fiefs, while several other new services for the benefit of the Court were imposed upon the Bakufu, the feudatories, and the nation at large. Although the Shōgun had now been reduced to his real status of a vassal, the entrustment of full powers to him was a bitter disappointment to the extreme loyalists whose wrath was gathering apace :—

"The two provinces of Nagato and Suwo (Chōshū) began to get highly excited, and it was soon reported at Kyōto and Ōsaka that the assembled *rōnin* of Chōshū would shortly call upon Lord Mōri and the seven nobles to take command of them and lead them to Kyōto. When this rumour became commonly known men's minds became ill at ease, and all felt as if they were walking on a thin sheet of ice."

Meanwhile the Chōshū men had been giving fresh provocation. In the autumn of 1863, the Bakufu sent a mission to Kyūshū on board one of its own steamers. It was fired upon as it entered the Straits of Shimonoseki, and on word being sent ashore that the vessel belonged to the Bakufu, the Chōshū men replied that any vessel of barbarian construction would be fired at and destroyed. Two censors on board were ordered to land ; they did so and were shortly afterwards assassinated, while the Kokura pilots in the vessel had to commit *hara-kiri*. On 1st February, 1864, a Satsuma steamer was fired on and sunk and the greater part of her crew killed or wounded. The Satsuma men wished to take vengeance, but the Court induced them to leave the settlement of the affair to the Bakufu, whose duties were to *maintain peace in the Empire*, and to subjugate the barbarian. The Chōshū men were now putting forth every effort to have their chieftains reinstated in the favour of the Court, and the seven banished nobles restored to rank and office.

"Numerous petitions were addressed to the Heavenly Court, but the clouds which floated in the air had not yet cleared away, and still continued to obscure the sky. They had alternation of lamentation and wrath, until at last their indignation became so strong that there was nothing left but to go up to Kyōto, with a display of military force, sweep away the traitor, and the wicked man from the Sovereign's side, and force the Heavenly Court to listen to their petitions."

The first expeditionary force of 400 men that set out from Chōshū on 22nd July, consisted largely of *rōnin*. Reaching Ōsaka by sea, on the 24th, it pushed on to Yamazaki between Kyōto and Ōsak$_a$, and established a base on the high grounds of Tennōzan. The commander, Fukubara, advanced to Fushimi with part of the force, and took up his quarters in the clan *yashiki* there (26th July). Meanwhile the Chōshū men who had been permanently staying in their Kyōto *yashiki* had withdrawn to the Tenryūji in Saga to the west of the city. On the last day of the month, a strong body of men were moved up from Yamazaki to Saga, and early in August another Chōshū *Karō*, Kunishi, Shinano no Kami, arrived in Saga with a body of two hundred troops fresh from the fief. Kunishi's ostensible mission was to restrain the impetuosity of the rank and file. A week or so later yet another Chōshū *Karō*, Masuda, was dispatched with another body of troops for a similar purpose. He took up his quarters at Yamazaki on 15th August, 1864. Thus the Chōshū men could operate from the three bases of Yamazaki, Fushimi, and Saga. In the fighting of 20th August, however, it was only the Saga and Yamazaki divisions that appeared in Kyōto, the Fushimi men being effectively held in check by the Bakufu partisans opposed to them. All told, these three bands could not have amounted to as much as 2,000 men. Kyōto at this time was held by some Bakufu troops, and a considerable force of Aidzu samurai under their Lord, Katamori, while there were a good many men in the *yashiki* of the Fudai and outside Daimyō also available for the defence of the palace. Nevertheless, Hitotsubashi, who had resigned his office of Guardian and was now staying in Kyōto as Protector of the Palace and Commander-in-Chief of the Maritime Defences, sent out urgent orders to all the neighbouring clans to hurry up their levies to the capital. Negotiations began by the presentation of a petition from the division at Yamazaki. " They asked that the seven nobles and Mōri and his son might be exonerated from the imputations so unjustly cast upon them, since the two latter had obeyed His Majesty's desire that the barbarians should be expelled. That hoping His Majesty would announce that he had renewed his determination of expelling the barbarians, the clansmen and the servants of the seven nobles had ventured to come and make their tearful prayer." In the council held to discuss this petition, Hitotsubashi and Aidzu—and Aidzu especially—were for stern and rigorous measures. But many of the court nobles and of the outside samurai dwelt on the dangers of the situation and suggested that it might be well to accord the petitioners a patient hearing. Later on, on learning of Masuda's arrival at Yamazaki with fresh troops, Aidzu and the Bakufu men at once memorialized the Mikado to order summary chastisement, and in this they were supported by the all-powerful Prince Nakagawa, now known as the In-no-Miya. On the other hand, no fewer than seventy court nobles signed a petition praying His Majesty to deal with the matter in a spirit of clemency, while a similar document was presented by the outside clansmen. "Thus the counsels of the Court divided between the two courses of action were like the bubbling up of a boiling cauldron." The In-no-Miya and Aidzu stood resolute, however. All the troops in Kyotō, including the samurai of Satsuma, Echizen, Hikone and other clans were ordered to hold themselves in readiness to march, and on 19th August, a document was transmitted to the leaders at Yamazaki and Saga, which indicated that there was absolutely no room for any further parleyings.

"As this attempt to intimidate the Imperial Court is an offence of the highest magnitude, the Imperial Court has decreed the chastisement of the Chōshū clansmen collected in various places. As it is probable that the two provinces of Nagato and Suwo share in the agitation, they will also be chastised severely. Those who have come up to the capital since the rebellion will be dealt with as they deserve, and, if any improper behaviour is manifested in their native country, forces will be continuously poured upon them for their chastisement."

The Chōshū men thereupon at once determined on the wager of battle, and before dawn on the following day (20th August) the Saga band advanced upon Kyōto in two divisions, and succeeded in entering the city, the Saga division in the van. Their great object was to make an end of their arch-foe the Lord of Aidzu, who for the last ten days had been encamped in the grounds of the palace. The fighting that followed was of the most furious description. At first, the Chōshū men forced their way into the palace grounds, and attacked those of Aidzu with such dash that the latter were forced to give way. Satsuma, however, came to the rescue and the Chōshū men were hopelessly overborne by weight of numbers, for in addition to the Shōgun's troops and those of the clans already mentioned, they had to deal with levies from Kuwana, Hikone, Ōgaki, and several smaller clans. The author of the *Genji Yume Minogatari* was a terror-stricken, yet fascinated, eyewitness of the conflict, and in his pamphlet of two-hundred and forty pages he devotes more than seventy to the four hours' fighting that went on around him on the forenoon of 20th August, 1864. There are numerous passages in his narrative that read like a rather poor prose translation of the battle-

scenes in the Iliad. It is startling to reflect that from this Homeric
engagement of 20th August, 1864, to the Yalu and Port Arthur and
the great battles in Manchuria which are now studied [1] as the most
up-to-date practical expositions of the art of war, is only a matter
of forty years. It was in this fierce and furious encounter that
Kusaka, the great Chōshū loyalist, lost his life. Another, who had
been almost as distinguished an exponent of *Kinnō* (Devotion to
the Emperor) as Kusaka, also perished on this occasion. Another
Kinnō apostle, Maki, Idzumi no Kami, escaped with fifty men from
the city and withdrew to Yamazaki and there awaited the pursuing
Aidzu forces. There they were attacked on the following day, and
when, after a desperate resistance to far superior forces, it was seen
to be hopeless, the survivors of the fight died by their own hands.
A Shintō priest of Kurume in Chikugo had been unwearying in the
good cause. For some time he had found a refuge in Chōshū,
where he had been one of the most strenuous advocates of the
dispatch of the ill-fated and disastrous expedition. Now, rather
than return, a baffled and beaten man, he committed *hara-kiri* at
Yamazaki along with Maki's little band. Hirano Jirō had been in
prison since his capture at Ikuno ; he was presently sent with
other prominent samurai to kneel at the blood-pit, and all their heads
were exposed in public, as those of common criminals. And about
the same time, the great Tosa loyalist, Takechi, the coryphaeus
of the movement in modern Japan, was sentenced to death ostensibly
for his share in the murder of Yoshida two years before, but really
because Prince Nakagawa had cautioned the ex-Lord of Tosa about
the possibly serious consequences of his machinations. In Mito, too,
this year the course of events proved disastrous to the loyalists.
Everywhere throughout the Empire, the partisans of the Bakufu
now seemed to have gained the upper hand. In Kyōto the
destruction of property during the fight was very great. The
Takadzukara and many of the Yashiki, both of the Kuge and
Daimyōs, as well as of the dwellings of the ordinary citizens, were
burnt, and both on the streets of the city and the roads leading
from it, the bodies of the slain and wounded were everywhere.
One very significant episode has to be noted. In the rout of the
Chōshū men the Satsuma troops had done yeoman service ; at
more than one crisis of the fight their appearance on the scene

---

[1] This was probably written before the Great War.

served to decide the issue. But when first appealed to for aid by Hitotsubashi, the Satsuma officers, Saigō and Komatsu, refused to stir; they regarded the struggle as one between Aidzu and Chōshū, and they declined to participate in any " private " broil. Only when they got orders from the Court itself to act would they do so, and in this resolution they stood firm. By his action in this incident Satsuma virtually emancipated himself from the control of the Bakufu!

Another incident has also to be noted. Saigō made his reappearance on the political stage. For the last few years Shimadzu Saburō's chief councillors had been Nakayama, Komatsu, and Ōkubo. It was the first of these that was by far the most influential with him; and it was to Nakayama that Saigō mainly owed his exile. Shortly after the British attack on Kagoshima, Nakayama ost all his influence and was relegated to an obscure local administrative office. Saigō's numerous friends in the clan then made a strong effort to get him recalled, as the Chōshū extremists such as Maki, Idzumi no Kami, had strange to say, already done. Ōkubo had incurred Shimadzu's wrath by hinting at the advisability of Saigō's recall, but now that the matter was urged by almost all parties in the clan, it was possible for him to support the proposal with effect. Ōkubo and Komatsū had hitherto been staunch supporters of the " Kōbu Gattai " policy; they now began to ask themselves how far that policy was likely to be of real advantage to the empire at large. The answer depended upon the future action of the Bakufu, and the use it would make of its recently recovered authority. From this point onward, Saigō, Ōkubo, and Komatsu maintained a critical attitude, and the destinies of Satsuma were under the control of that trio rather than of Shimadzu Saburō. For the time being, Satsuma and Aidzu were regarded as the great powers while the Chōshū men spoke of the " Satsuma Brigands " and the " Aidzu rascals " in the same breath.

It was impossible for Chōshū to do anything to retrieve the situation, for the clan was assailed by a combination of four of the Treaty-Powers. Sir Rutherford Alcock had returned to Japan on 2nd March, while the new French representative, Roches, arrived towards the end of April, 1864. Presently, strong squadrons were concentrated in Japanese waters, on board the British vessels being 800 marines from England. On 30th May, Alcock wrote inviting the Bakufu authorities to withdraw the request for the closing of Yokohama, and to see to it that there should be no more obstruction in the Straits of Shimonoseki. The reply of 30th June was deemed so unsatisfactory that a conference of the four foreign representatives determined that a *note identique* should be sent in making a final appeal, and threatening that the settlement of matters would be placed in the hands of the naval authorities at the end of twenty days if no satisfactory redress was meanwhile obtained. Just at this point, the strange intervention of two unknown Japanese youths occasioned a delay in the opening of the threatened hostilities. In the spring of 1863, five Chōshū striplings had been sent to England. As the decree against any Japanese leaving Japan was not cancelled until 1866, their departure had to be in secret. Some of the five had been among the band that had just burned down the British Legation in Goten-yama ; but that did not prevent them taking passage on a British vessel. Their avowed purpose was to master the science of the foreigner, in order to use it to oust the foreigner from Japan. At Shanghai they had already begun to entertain doubts about the feasibility of the project, when they got to London they had no longer any doubts about the matter at all, for the forcible expulsion of the foreigner was, they were convinced, a vain imagining. Chancing to read in *The Times* an account of what had been happening at Shimonoseki, two of the party determined to hurry back to Japan to try to save their Lord and fellow-clansmen from the calamities that were bound to attend the mistaken course that was being followed. On arriving at Yokohama they promptly got in touch with the British representative, and Alcock (21st July) requested the Admiral to afford the two young men the means of returning to their province so that they might lay their views before their feudal lord. A warship at once set out, and the self-constituted envoys were duly landed in Chōshū. As might have been expected, their efforts proved utterly abortive. On 6th August, they returned with a mere verbal message from their Prince to the effect that he could do nothing without the sanction of the Emperor and the Shōgun, which he would try to obtain if a three months' delay were accorded him. In doing as he had done, he was acting on orders which he had received once from the Tycoon, and oftener from the Mikado. The youthful envoys suggested :—

" It as a good measure that the foreign Representatives should throw the Tycoon overboard, and going to Ōsaka, demand an interview with the Mikado's ministers, and conclude a treaty with him. They spoke with great bitterness of the Tycoon's dynasty; that they kept all the trade, not only foreign, but native also, to themselves by seizing all places where trade was likely to develop itself, such as Niigata and Nagasaki, and they told me that those feelings were shared by most of the people of the country."

In the making of modern Japan perhaps no two men have borne a larger share of the burden and heat of the day than Prince Itō and Marquis Inouye. The preceding remarks are consequently of high significance, for it was from the lips of Itō and Inouye that they fell.

The attack on the batteries of Shimonoseki presently followed. The combined fleet consisted of nine British, four Dutch, and three French warships, besides a chartered steamer with a Parrot gun and a crew of fifty Americans on board. A three hours' cannonade on the afternoon of 5th September, 1864, wrecked several of the batteries, and the destruction was virtually completed before noon next day. The landing parties met with no great opposition, although a few casualties were sustained. On the 7th the work of embarking the captured guns was commenced, and the whole sixty-two of them were safely on board the various ships of the fleet by the evening of the tenth. Through Itō on the 8th, and his chief *Karō* on the 10th, Mōri made his submission. Ships passing the Straits were thenceforth to be treated in a friendly manner and were to be allowed to coal and take in provisions. There were to be no more batteries along the strand. And a ransom was to be paid for the town of Shimonoseki. On 22nd October, a convention was signed by the foreign representatives and the Tycoon's plenipotentiary in terms of which the Bakufu was pledged to pay an indemnity of 3,000,000 dollars, in six quarterly instalments of 500,000 dollars each. If it consented to open Shimonoseki or some other port in the Inland Sea, the indemnity would be waived. Of course, the Bakufu was not likely to undertake to open any more ports ; and it would never consent to see a port opened in the territories of an outside feudatory for Itō and Inouye had not libelled it when they spoke of its commercial policy in the bitter terms they used. A sum of about 500,000 dollars was paid to France, Holland, and the United States for specific outrages on their vessels, and the remainder of the 3,000,000 dollars was divided equally among the three powers.

As a result of the encounter of 15th August, 1863, the men of

Satsuma had conceived a deep admiration for the effectiveness of British naval armaments. So far from cherishing any resentment for the attack they were eager to establish a cordial friendship with the British. At the interviews in Yokohama the Satsuma envoys several times hinted that foreign merchants would find a ready welcome at Kagoshima if the port of Yokohama was closed. Now, during the fortnight in which the combined squadrons lay in the Straits of Shimonoseki after the bombardment, the intercourse between the crews and the inhabitants was amicable in the extreme. Two months later, an English gentleman who passed through the Straits was treated with " the utmost kindness and hospitality " by officials and townspeople alike. Henceforth the Chōshū men were as eager for foreign intercourse as they had formerly been averse to it—fully as eager for it as the people of Satsuma already were. Furthermore the great leaders among the Rōnin and the lower samurai, who had been convulsing the Empire with their insistent clamour for the " brushing away of the Barbarians " had just lately perished—Kusaka of Chōshū, Takechi of Tosa, Hirano Jirō, and Maki, Idzumi no Kami, were now all under the sod, while the Mitō extremists were being mercilessly hunted from pillar to post. Yet the old fierce, ferocious, anti-foreign spirit was still in evidence here and there. On 21st November, 1864, Major Baldwin and Lieut. Bird were slashed to pieces at Kamakura by two *rōnin*, one of whom had journeyed from Aomori in the extreme north of Japan to join Chōshū only to find that for the time being Chōshū had no more need of *rōnin*. This time the Bakufu really bestirred itself promptly to secure the culprits and to have justice done upon them. And the fact was remarkable that ever since then, all Japanese who assaulted foreigners with murderous intent got caught and dealt with according to law.

B

In demolishing the Shimonoseki batteries the combined foreign squadron was really doing the work of the Bakufu which had actually sent instructions to the neighbouring clans to leave Chōshū to its fate, and to lend it no help. Two days after the great fight in Kyōto, and a fortnight before the attack on Shimonoseki, the Court had declared Chōshū to be the *Chōteki* (a rebel) and had commissioned the Bakufu to chastise the clan and reduce it to submission. On the following day (24th August, 1864) the Bakufu issued orders to Satsuma and some twenty other fiefs to mobilize troops for the attack.

In the very hour of its triumph, the Bakufu set to work to dig its own grave. To the Rōjū and most of the officials the supreme object was to regain the full plenitude of authority over the clans that had been lost during the preceding four or five years. The abolition of the enforced residence of the Daimyō with their wives and heirs in Yedo in 1862, was seen to have been a fatally disastrous step ; and the Councillors were determined that this fundamental error should be retrieved at all costs, and they now deemed it expedient to speak of restoring the old conditions. But the mere hint of such an intention produced a lively commotion, and vigorous protests and warnings at once proceeded not only from the great outside feudatories but from some of Bakufu's own most loyal supporters, from Owari and Echizen, and even from Aidzu. Dissension thus broke out between the Yedo Councillors and the Bakufu supporters in Kyōto, while the advocates of the " Kōbu Gattai " policy were now forced to reconsider the wisdom of the course they had been following. Furthermore, Yedo now asserted itself in connexion with the selection of the Commander-in-chief of the Chōshū expedition. The clansmen were expecting to serve under Hitotsubashi, but the ex-Lord of Ōwari was appointed, although he had no desire for the post. Parleyings over this question consumed much time, and it was only on 24th November, 1864, that the Commander-in-Chief held his first Council-of-War in the Castle of Ōsaka, and only on 1st December that he left for the headquarters at Hiroshima. By 19th December, however, he had practically achieved all the purposes of the expedition, and on 30th January, 1865, he was able to order the disbandment of the " army of chastisement ". Not a shot had been fired, and not a single man had fallen in battle, for Saigō had meanwhile scored a signal success as a diplomatist.

In Chōshū, as elsewhere, there was an influential conservative party, and the rout of the extremists in Kyōto had enabled its leaders to regain the ascendancy they had lost two or three years before. They had placed the three Karō mainly responsible for the Kyōto expedition under arrest, and were now anxiously casting about for ways and means of arranging terms with the Bakufu. Saigō knew that the Bakufu favoured the harshest measures, and that an accommodation on its terms would be impossible.   With the sanction of the Commander-in-Chief, he started on a mission to Chōshū early in November, and with the help of some Chikuzen men, he was able to induce the Chōshū conservatives now in power to order the three *Karō* to commit *hara-kiri*, and to punish a dozen of their abettors ; to undertake to demolish the new fortifications of Yamaguchi, and to send the banished court nobles out of the territory, on the understanding that the expeditionary force would be disbanded and a reasonable penalty afterwards inflicted upon the clan.   It was only with the utmost difficulty that the extremists could be got to consent to the withdrawal of the Court nobles ; but at last they were removed to Dazaifu in Chikuzen and placed under the guard of troops from Satsuma and several other Kyūshū clans. The Bakufu presently ordered that the Mōri, father and son, should be conveyed to Yedo as prisoners, and the Uwajima clan was instructed to send troops into the Chōshū territory to assume charge of their persons.   This, and other ill-considered steps, called forth a severe rebuke from the Mikado who again summoned the Shōgun to proceed to Kyōto and settle with him what measures should be taken to restore foreign and domestic peace to the country.

The disbandment of the expeditionary force occasioned much anger in Yedo ; and the subsequent course of events in Chōshū seemed to indicate that Ōwari, the Commander-in-Chief, had committed a serious error of judgment in breaking up his army so soon.   At this date there were at least two men in Japan who possessed something uncommonly like military genius.   Takasugi Shinsaku of Chōshū was then only in his twenty-fifth year, of slight figure, sharp ferret-like features, and with a head of close-cropped hair that reminded one cf the burrs of a chestnut rind.   He was already in the grip of that pulmonary consumption to which he was destined presently to succumb (1867).   To quote the *Kinsé Shiryaku :*

" So far back as 1863, Takasugi had arrived at the conclusion that the luxurious samurai class was of no practical value in the field, and he obtained permission to organize troops on a new model.   This consisted in breaking through the prejudice which existed in favour of birth, in selecting strong, able-bodied men from the common people, as well as from the samurai class, and in fixing the pay of the battalions he thus formed at a high figure.   The strictest discipline was enforced, and even the most ruffianly vagabonds cheerfully obeyed him.   His troops were bold and valiant in fight, and went by the name of the Kiheitai or Irregular troops."

The conservatives had tried to arrest Takasugi together with his friends the three *Karō*, but he made good his escape into Chikuzen, while the *Kiheitai* dispersed and went into hiding. Now on the very day of the order for the break-up of the expeditionary force, Takasugi with a small band suddenly captured Shimonoseki and summoned all loyal men to his standard. In a brief space, Hagi, the clan capital, was in his hands. The chiefs of the conservative party now met with short shrift, and their heads soon graced the public pillories. " From this moment dissension ceased, and the whole clan worked strenuously for one common object." The two princes were carried off to Yamaguchi, where the fortifications, instead of being razed, were further strengthened, while every preparation was made to meet the new attack which it was felt the Bakufu was presently bound to level at the clan. Fortunately the Chōshū men were left with plenty of time to organize their defence, for they had no actual fighting to do for eighteen months. The Yedo authorities announced the new expedition against Chōshū in May, 1865, the Shōgun this time was to take the field in person. In July, His Highness arrived in Kyōto for the third time, where he had an audience of the Mikado, and then withdrew to Ōsaka Castle, which was henceforth destined to be his abode until his death on 19th September, 1866.

This second expeditionary force was supposed to attain a total of 120,000 men. Some 50,000 troops were to be furnished by the various Western clans ; the main body of 70,000 men consisted of Tokugawa retainers. Of these about 10,000 were equipped in semi-European fashion ; but as a rule the samurai despised the rifle, and there was no great enthusiasm among the Bakufu vassals for new-fashioned weapons and tactics. Foreign spectators who witnessed the passage of the Tokugawa hosts along the Tōkaidō expressed no very high respect for it or its potentialities. Yet the Bakufu officials assured themselves of success. The quick and easy triumph of the first expeditionary force had deluded them into extravagant expectations and a haughty elation that could scarcely fail to find its nemesis. To equip this motley host was a terrible task for the financial officers ; forced loans had to be exacted from the citizens of Yedo and Ōsaka, and from the towns of Hyōgo and Nishinomiya, as well as from the officials. But everything now seemed to justify a supreme effort to crown the work of restoring the prestige of the Bakufu, which had really been growing steadily since the end of September, 1863. The officials unfortunately overlooked the prominent part that had been played by the great clans, notably by Satsuma, in the rehabilitation of the Shōgunal power. Now these great clans clearly perceived that after Chōshū their own turn would come next. The ex-Lord of Ōwari declined to act as Commander-in-Chief, and the Lord of Kishū had to be appointed in his stead. Inshū (of Tottori, 325,000 *koku*) a brother of Mito by blood, remonstrated against the vagueness of the expression "dangerous schemes" used as a justification for renewed coercion, and warned the Shōgun against the defeat and loss of prestige he foretold. Echizen also protested. And as for Satsuma, she flatly refused to send a single man.

In the West, subterranean forces had been at work, of which the Bakufu, with all its battalions of lynx-eyed spies, never got the slightest hint until the mine was all but ready for the explosion that was to bring the Shōgunate to utter ruin. The eight Chōshū men captured by Satsuma in the Kyōto fight of 20th August, 1864, were royally treated by their captors, and Chōshū felt bound to send a mission to return thanks when the eight were at last sent home to recount their experiences. This was largely Saigō's work; but Saigō felt that it would be hazardous to make any overtures so Chōshū just yet, for the resentment against Satsuma he knew to be strong and rankling. He had learned a lesson from the great Nariakira. One day he had expressed deep sympathy with his Lord in what he supposed to be his anxiety about the death of his young son and the succession to the headship of the house of Shimadzu. Nariakira then assured him that such matters were of small consequence compared to the future of Japan—it was that that chiefly lay heavily on his mind and caused him concern. Saigō had for long been convinced that it was hopeless to expect the Bakufu to settle the question of foreign intercourse satisfactorily, or to maintain the independence, much less the prestige, of the Empire. He had found Katsu Awa, with whom he had had his first interview in the autumn of 1864, to be nearly of the same opinion. Katsu was a loyal servant of the Shōgunate, but he was a strong advocate of keeping faith with the foreign powers, and of putting Japan on a footing to enter into the comity of modern nations. A strongly unified central government was an absolute necessity. Something might be hoped from a concert of the great Daimyō, or rather of their chief retainers, from the men at the Bakufu Council-boards scarcely anything could be expected. At this date, Katsu, as head of the Tokugawa

Admiralty was organizing a dockyard and a naval school at Hyōgo, where he had men from most of the maritime clans among his pupils. Towards the end of 1864, he was suspected of intriguing with Chōshū, and was dismissed from office. To one of his students, a certain Sakamoto Ryūma, he gave a letter of introduction to Saigō asking the latter to find employment for the men in the rapidly growing Satsuma marine. This Sakamoto was a Tosa *Gōshi*, one of the most devoted followers of the loyalist Takechi. In 1862, he became a *rōnin*, one of a batch of ardent spirits that then deserted the clan. Hearing that Katsu was a strenuous advocate of opening the country to foreign intercourse, Sakamoto called upon him with the intention of killing him. Katsu coolly told him he divined the purpose of his visit—only before drawing sword it might be well to listen to what he had to say. The would-be assassin left the house a sincere convert, after begging to be allowed to become a humble pupil. Katsu introduced Sakamoto to Saigō in the autumn of 1864 ; he was considerably amused a few days later when, on his inquiring what he thought of Saigō, Sakamoto coolly said that Saigō was a fool—but whether a great fool or a small one still remained to be seen. On taking up his quarters in Saigō's house in Kagoshima, he had ample opportunity of arriving at an accurate estimate of his host's real mental and moral calibre.

While Saigō was not slow to recognize the fact that his guest was a man of real political genius, Sakamoto was insistent in preaching the imperative necessity of an alliance between Satsuma and Chōshū, and in advocating that very policy which Saigō had been secretly maturing for years. Strangely enough, yet another Tosa man, a certain Nakaoka, had also arrived at the same conclusions. He had connexions both with Chōshū and the banished court nobles ; and on hearing of the second punitive expedition against Chōshū, he had hurried down to Yamaguchi with a friend to obtain the consent of the Chōshū men to his opening up communications with Satsuma on their behalf. Meanwhile Saigō had been holding back for fear of a rebuff, but Sakamoto, as a neutral Tosa man, had at last extorted his permission to go and sound the Chōshū leaders. He had made some progress in his mission when Nakaoka, who had just been to Kagoshima, arrived at Shimonoseki to say that Saigō was on his way and would appear on the spot in a day or two. Saigō, however, had meanwhile received urgent instructions while on the way to Shimonoseki to hurry up to Kyōto

at once ; and his failure to appear roused the wrath of the Chōshū
men, who declared they were being duped and mocked. Sakamoto
and Nakaoka thereupon hurried to Ōsaka and took Saigō severely
to task. Sakamoto now indicated two steps by which the opening
breach might be repaired. In the first place, Chōshū could buy no
arms or ammunition in Nagasaki ; for the Bakufu officials there
were extremely vigilant. In such circumstances it would be of high
moment if Chōshū purchases could be made in the name of Satsuma.
In the next place, Satsuma would presently need rice, if it came to
a contest with the Bakufu. Chōshū had then plenty of rice to sell,
and she needed money for the purchase of arms. With these
projects as guarantees of Satsuma good faith, Sakamoto now
hastened back to Chōshū and readily prevailed upon Kido, the
leading politician in the clan, to make a secret visit to Saigō and
Komatsu in Kyōto. At this juncture everything stood in danger of
being wrecked by some of the fiery Chōshū leaders standing upon
the point of honour. To make a pact with outsiders at this crisis,
and especially with their dearest foe, Satsuma, would be cowardly
and an indelible stain upon their fair fame as *Bushi* (warriors).
Sakamoto hereupon told them very roundly that it might be well
for all if they would put their pride in their pocket. What he
really had been working so assiduously for was neither their interests
nor those of Satsuma particularly, but the interests of the Empire
of Japan. All opposition to Kido's journey was now withdrawn, and
accompanied by a friend of Saigō he left for Ōsaka by sea on 15th
February, 1866. When Sakamoto went up some three weeks later
on, Kido told him that Saigō and Komatsu had been feasting him
like a lord, but so far they had not said a single word about the
projected alliance between the two clans—consequently he had
now as good as resolved to return to Chōshū. Sakamoto at once
went to Saigō and said some very sharp things to him. Saigō had
wished to make absolutely sure of Chōshū's good faith, but he was
in danger of carrying caution and circumspection too far. On
9th March, 1866, the treaty was finally arranged, and next day Kido
sent Sakamoto an outline of its main provisions. The most important
of these were that Satsuma should put forth every exertion to get
Chōshū reinstated in the good graces of the Court. The two clans
were thenceforward to co-operate in all sincerity for the good of the
Empire, pledging themselves to restore the Imperial power and
prestige. Sakamoto's first visit to Shimonoseki was on 23rd June,

1865, the negotiations had thus lasted for nearly eight months. It was not till the beginning of 1868, that the co-operation between the two clans became open and was publicly avowed.

Meanwhile, the Bakufu troops had been assembling at Hiroshima. Here, in January, 1866, two of the Chōshū clan councillors appeared before Tokugawa judges, and in their evidence endeavoured to exculpate the Princes of Chōshū as far as they could, and finally tendered a declaration on their behalf expressing complete submissiveness to the Shōgun, and readiness to accept whatever pains and penalties might be imposed. But the leaders of the new Chōshū army, who were also examined, protested that the Princes, in everything they had done, had merely obeyed the orders of the Shōgun as well as of the Court, and hinted not obscurely that there were no grounds for inflicting penalties at all. The Hiroshima tribunal reported the proceedings to the Great Council, and in March, 1866, a memorial, signed by two Great Councillors, Hitotsubashi and Aidzu, was presented to the Mikado, setting forth that although the Chōshū Princes might have acted with no treasonable intent, yet they ought to be held responsible for their lax exercise of authority over their vassals. In consideration of the loyal conduct of the Mōri family for successive generations, it was recommended as a lenient sentence that 100,000 *koku* of Chōshū land should be confiscated, that the two Princes should be condemned to seclusion for life, the younger prince's son being made head of the clan, while the families of the three *Karō* who had been responsible for the disturbance in Kyōto in 1864, should be attainted. This memorial was at once approved of by the Court, only it was recommended that care should be taken to occasion no popular commotion. The sentence was duly communicated to the Chōshū authorities who were accorded thirty days to decide whether they were to submit to it peaceably or not. As the communication was simply ignored by them, the Bakufu at last applied to the Court for leave to attack.

It was only on 23rd July, 1866, that real hostilities began—nearly two years after Chōshū had been declared a rebel, and eighteen months after the first punitive expedition had been disbanded. Takasugi and his able officers Yamagata (afterwards Prince Yamagata), Inouye (afterwards Marquis Inouye), and Ōmura, had thus ample time to organize their forces and bring their men of the " new model " to a high state of efficiency. The assessed revenue of Chōshū was only 369,000 *koku* and that of the cadet Mōri houses

100,000 *koku* more. But a land survey in the early Tokugawa age had made it clear that the actual annual yield of the two provinces of Suwo and Nagato was over 1,200,000 *koku*. Thus, there was no lack of means for the purchase of breech-loaders and the most efficient modern artillery. Mobility was regarded as of prime importance by Takasugi ; all cumbersome armour was discarded in favour of close-fitting cloth uniforms, and more trust reposed in the rifle than in sword or the spear. Takasugi also had the advantage of holding interior lines, and could shift the 40,000 men at his disposal from any one of the three frontiers attacked to another with great ease and rapidity.

The Chōshū men had already crossed the Strait and formed the league of Kokura, and the Higo and other Kyūshū troops, who mustered to the summons of the Bakufu, were never able to dislodge the besiegers from their lines. On the coast of the Sea of Japan, the invading column met with a speedy repulse, and here the Chōshū men were presently in a position to carry the war into the enemy's country, and reduce the Castle of Hamada and some other strong-holds. On the Hiroshima front, the contest was less one-sided, and the Chōshū troops met with occasional checks from the superior numbers massed against them. But even here, on 16th September, they drove the Bakufu levies back upon Hiroshima, and three days later (19th September, 1866) the young Shōgun died.

On 3rd October, the Court utilized this event as a pretext for ordering a discontinuation of the operations against Chōshū, which orders were at once notified by the Bakufu to all the clans. Later in the same month, Katsu, Awa no Kami, was sent down to Hiro-shima to offer terms to Chōshū and to withdraw the Bakufu troops. He met Inouye and Hirozawa, the Chōshū commissioners, and communicated to them the will of the Mikado and the instructions of the Bakufu. The Chōshū troops were at first disinclined to listen to any terms ; but the two commissioners :—

" Unwilling to disregard the Shōgun's orders, and grateful to Awa no Kami, succeeded in pacifying them, and they returned in great triumph to their native province. The war was now over at last. During its continuance the Bakufu had expended vast sums of money until its treasuries were almost exhausted, and yet it was unable to have its way with Chōshū. From this time onwards the great clans neglected to obey the commands of the Bakufu, and its power eventually decayed."

As has been said, the second expedition against Chōshū had been undertaken mainly with the idea of putting the crown to the

work of restoring the prestige of the Bakufu, which, sadly impaired
between 1860 and 1863, had been growing apace ever since the
coup d'état of 30th September, in the latter year.   And what was the
result ?   Never in its long history of two hundred and sixty years
had any effort of the Tokugawa Shōgunate so miscarried.   The
incompetence and impotence of the Yedo Government now stood
revealed in such a glaring fashion that few could doubt that its
days were numbered.

Two years before this date such a state of affairs would have
been regarded with the gravest anxiety by the foreign representatives
in Japan.   In a dispatch to the Foreign Office written in November,
1864, Sir Rutherford Alcock said :—

" The Tycoon's power with that of the moderate party in the
country has been greatly strengthened, and there is now for the first
time a fair prospect of obtaining the Mikado's formal adhesion to the
existing treaties and thus putting an end to a conflict of authority
between Kyōto and Yedo which has been a constant source of danger.
. . . The dissolution of the Government apart from any immediate
danger would be the destruction of the Treaty-making power. To the
Tycoon and his Government alone could we look for support against
those most hostile to the maintenance of the foreign relations . . .
In the dissolution of his Government and existing relations, we should
lose the only solid foundation for the assertion of Treaty rights.   To
take new ground and go to Kyōto in search of a better basis from the
Mikado would involve a costly expedition to begin with ; and an
explorative voyage of discovery in unknown regions of political difficulty.
*This one danger, above all others, therefore, the disorganization and dis-
appearance of the Tycoon's Government, was, if possible, to be averted.*"

Within a few days over a year from the date of this dispatch,
the following decree was transmitted by the Court to the Shōgun :

" Imperial consent is given to the treaties, and you will therefore
make suitable arrangements."

The very course of taking new ground and going to Kyōto so
greatly deprecated by Alcock was adopted by his successor ; and
the issue of the foregoing Imperial decree on 22nd November, 1865,
relieved the foreign representatives from any further anxiety about
the fate of the Shōgunate, for the dissolution of the Tycoon's Government could no longer be held to be destructive of the Treaty-making
power.

On 18th July, 1865, Sir Harry Parkes, the new British Minister to
Japan, arrived in Yokohama.   This very remarkable man entered
the public service at the age of fourteen, and in the course of three
and twenty years had worked his way up from an apprentice
interpreter to the distinguished position he now filled.

" His energy is untiring, never sparing himself in any way ; personal danger and personal comfort were never thought of when he could in any way advance the public service."

So Sir Charles van Straubenzee had written about him to Lord Elgin six years before. He was before all things a masterful man, with a consuming hate and contempt for all duplicity, sham, and humbug---in short just the sort of man that Carlyle would have selected for one of his heroes. A high Japanese official who had had many years' experience of him and his ways, said of him : " Sir Harry Parkes was the only foreigner in Japan whom we could not twist round our little finger." With such a man who already had twenty years' intimate experience of Chinese diplomacy, the evasions and tergiversations of the Bakufu officials would not be likely to be so efficacious as they had been hitherto. Down to this time, the French and British ministers had almost invariably worked in hearty mutual accord, in fact, if anything broke the concert of the foreign representatives during the years 1861 to 1864, it was the rather peculiar attitude of the American ministers Harris and Pruyn. But with the advent of Léon Roches, a strong chief had come to the French Legation in Yokohama. Roches had earned his spurs as a dragoman in the Algerian campaigns, and he has been well described as a handsome swashbuckler, who always seemed as if he ought to be wrapped in a white burnous astride an Arab charger. Like Parkes, he was a man minded to have his own way, and during the next three years there was a good deal of rivalry between the British and French representatives, marked by some rather lively passages-at-arms from time to time.

It was the Chōshū question, more particularly in relation to the Shimonoseki indemnity, that first occupied Parkes' attention. On this he had a difference of opinion with his colleagues, but by tact and patience, unanimity of counsels was restored. On 21st August, 1865, the first of the six instalments of 500,000 dollars of the indemnity was paid, and the Rōjū then proposed that an interval of twelve months should elapse between the payment of the first and second instalments, and kept silent regarding the discharge of the remaining sums. But Parkes would have no procrastinations or tergiversations ; so much he made clear on his first visit to Yedo, when he incidentally learned that the Shōgun, who was accompanied by no fewer than four of the Councillors, would be likely to remain in Ōsaka for a long time. On a second visit to Yedo, Parkes broached

the subject of the ratification of the treaties by the Mikado, but the
answer he got was evasive. He thereupon induced his colleagues to
agree to proceeding to Ōsaka " with a naval expedition in force,
although with no hostile intent ".   On the Japanese ministers
learning that such a step was contemplated, they came down from
Yedo to Yokohama to dissuade the representatives from undertaking
it. This is noteworthy as the first occasion on which any member of
the Rōjū had called on a foreign minister at his own residence.

On 4th November, 1865, a squadron of six British, two French,
and one Dutch warships appeared in Ōsaka Bay with the representatives of Great Britain, the United States, France, and the
Netherlands on board. The Shōgun was then in Kyōto attended by
the Councillors most conversant with foreign affairs, but it was
arranged that one of these Abé, Bungo no Kami, would meet the
representatives on board ship on the 9th. The interview actually
took place on the 11th. Besides the ratification of the treaties
by the Mikado, the representatives urged the revision of the
customs tariff and the immediate opening of Hyōgo and Ōsaka, in
return for which concessions all further instalments of the indemnity
were to be remitted. Abé admitted that the hostile Daimyō had
abandoned their advocacy of active opposition, and that if the
Mikado's approval of the treaties were once obtained, all obstruction
to foreign intercourse would disappear. Abé was to meet the representatives again on the following day, but on that day he sent to say
that everything had to be submitted to a council, and that this
would prevent his attending till the 14th. But on the 14th, only
subordinate officials appeared to tender excuses, and to ask for delay,
while on the 19th, it was learned that Abé and a colleague who
supported his views had been dismissed by the Mikado !

In Kyōto at this time, Hitotsubashi, Aidzu, and his brother,
Kuwana, who all enjoyed the confidence of the In no Miya and Nijō
the Kwambaku, were exceedingly powerful, and they were especially
occupied in an effort to get the Court to sanction their Chōshū policy.
In opposition to them, Ōkubo of Satsuma insisted that a council of
the great feudatories should be convoked to deal with this matter,
and to settle the national policy generally. As usual, it was through
Konoye that Ōkubo was now operating. On the appearance of the
foreign squadron, Ōkubo also argued that the ratification of the
treaties, the opening of Hyōgo and the whole attitude towards
foreigners should be discussed and decided by his proposed council

of Daimyō. Against Konoye's arguments, Hitotsubashi and his
supporters asserted that matters were so urgent that there was no
time to convoke a council of the territorial magnates. He did not
know that Ōkubo had actually gone to Fukui to urge Shungaku to
proceed to Kyōto, and that he had sent express messengers to
Daté of Uwajima, Yōdō of Tosa, and to his master Shimadzu to
hurry up to the capital. It was the proposal to accelerate the
opening of Hyōgo and Ōsaka that excited most commotion at this
time. Aidzu was especially opposed to the proposal. He roundly
declared that with his own samurai alone he would try conclusions
with the foreigners if they insisted in the matter. Hitotsubashi,
however, declared that the opening of Hyōgo could be deferred,
but the Imperial sanction for the treaties was a different matter.
Abé and his colleague, Matsumaye, had compromised themselves
over the opening of Hyōgo, and Hitotsubashi now hurried down
to Ōsaka on 14th November and ordered them into seclusion. On
his return to Kyōto, he obtained an Imperial decree stripping them
of rank and office. For the Court to presume to punish a Tokugawa
Councillor was unprecedented. The result was that the Shōgun
promptly presented his resignation, recommending Hitotsubashi as
his successor. At the same time he sent in a memorial reviewing
the general situation of affairs and insisting that the opening of the
Empire to foreign intercourse was inevitable. Thereupon, he left
Ōsaka for Yedo, and had got as far as Fushimi when he was met by
Hitotsubashi, all eagerness to capitulate, for the resignation of the
Shōgun had taken him completely by surprise, and had occasioned
the greatest consternation in the capital. Inspired by Ōkubo
Konoye alone had strongly urged that the resignation should be
promptly accepted, that the Court should forthwith assume the
direction of affairs, and at once convoke the projected council of
great feudatories. It was in such circumstances that the famous
decree of 22nd November, 1865, sanctioning the treaties, was
issued. This was communicated to the foreign representatives on
24th November, but the second of its three clauses was suppressed.
This set forth that there were several stipulations in the existing
treaties that did not harmonize with the Mikado's views, that a
report must be made on these points after careful examination,
and that the Imperial decision would be given after discussion by
the clans. The third clause was that " the question of opening
Hyōgo must be dropped ". The Bakufu officials now merely

informed the representatives they were unable to discuss that point
at the moment ; they would continue to pay the indemnity, and
instructions would be sent to Yedo to negotiate the amendment of
the tariff.

"The appearance off Ōsaka of an imposing naval force, though not
employed for coercion, or to support a menace, would at least serve to
remind the faction that had hitherto placed itself in opposition to the
treaties that the Powers, with whom these engagements have been
concluded, possess the means of insisting upon the fulfilment of them
when they see fit to do so, and speaking after the event, I can assert
with confidence that had it not been for the presence of the allied fleet
on this occasion, the Tycoon would not have been persuaded to make
to the Mikado those energetic remonstrances and representations
without which union between these rulers on the subject of the Treaties
and the foreign policy they render necessary, would not have been
effected."

In this dispatch to Earl Russell, who was then Minister of Foreign
affairs, it is all very well for Parkes to speak of the naval force not
being employed for coercion or to support a menace. Hitotsubashi
firmly believed that in case the Imperial sanction for the treaties
were withheld, the squadron would certainly proceed to hostilities,
and he had little difficulty in convincing the Court nobles of this.
From first to last, from Perry in 1853 and 1854 down to Parkes in
1865, the "gun-boat" policy was the determining factor in foreign
relations with Japan. Harris was really no exception; at an early
stage he had recourse to mysterious threats, and had sighed for the
presence of a man-of-war; later on he had most adroitly terrorized
the Bakufu officials with his lurid accounts of the aggressive British
and the prospect of their speedy appearance to press things in
Japan at the mouth of the cannon.

The treaties of 1858 were finally amended or supplemented by
the new tariff convention of 25th June, 1866, an instrument which
in conception and execution was practically the work of the indefatigible Parkes. The tariff was generally reduced to a five per
cent. ad valorem rate ; the convention abolished many customs-
house abuses and provided against interior customs duties being
levied either on exports (as had been the case) or imports. The
creation of a free mint was contemplated, and an efficient bonded
warehouse system was established. And finally what Harris had to
fight for so strenuously was now guaranteed. The freest commercial
and social intercourse with foreign countries and with foreigners at
the open ports was now granted to all classes and conditions of

Japanese people without any government interference or supervision whatever.

Towards the end of 1865, Parkes got into touch with Chōshū officials at Shimonoseki, who expressed satisfaction on being shown a copy of the Mikado's decree sanctioning the treaties. At Nagasaki, the agents of the great Kyūshū Daimyō also assured Parkes of their approval of the step just taken by the court of Kyōto. In 1866, the envoy was invited by Shimadzu Saburō and his son to visit Kagoshima.[1] Nothing could possibly have been more hearty than the reception accorded to the Minister and his party, while the Satsuma men could not fail to be highly pleased with the salutes from the warship and the other marks of respect tendered the Prince and his father on that occasion. Intercourse on this footing between a Daimyō and a foreign representative was something entirely new ; the very notion of such a thing would have been inconceivable three short years before. Ōkubo was now pressing on his reforms with feverish activity. Cannon were being cast, breech-loaders manufactured, and steamers purchased—as many as six were acquired in Nagasaki in 1865, in addition to some in 1864. Two or three Satsuma men accompanied the first Bakufu mission to Europe ; some of these now took charge of a batch of Satsuma youths who were quietly smuggled on board ship from a sequestered islet of the fief for a course of instruction in England. The leaders of the party were able to communicate their views to Lord Clarendon, the British Foreign Secretary ; a fact that was in due official course communicated to Parkes. In 1865, the customs dues of Yokohama alone amounted to 452,000 dollars, and the whole of this amount together with the revenues of Nagasaki and Hakodate went into the Bakufu's coffers. Satsuma, and those who thought with him, regarded this as unfair.

" They have no objection to the Tycoon drawing a profit from foreign trade, but they do object to his drawing the whole, and to this feeling is to be traced . . . the difficulty made lately in admitting foreigners to trade at Ōsaka, so long as the Tycoon would alone profit from it. This difficulty is not likely to be removed even when the appointed time for opening the port arrives unless the cause of it is removed . . . The Tycoon's government now stands between two dangers—hostility on the part of the foreigners, if they evade the fulfilment of their engagements, and hostility on the part of the Daimyō if they attempt to fulfil them according to the system acted upon at present."

---

[1] An account of this episode will be found in Black's *Young Japan,* and fuller details in the files of the *Japan Herald.*

Ōkubo was resolved that the Bakufu should never open Hyōgo and Ōsaka to foreign trade ; this was to be done by Imperial decree after a council of the great feudatories sanctioned the step.   At present this was the ground on which he fancied he could best mass the attack on the Bakufu which he was meditating, and great was his disappointment when he ultimately perceived that he would have to seek another base of operations.

From Kagoshima, Parkes proceeded to Uwajima and met with an equally warm reception there from that most astute politician, Daté Muneki, the Hatamoto's son.   Later on, a similar visit was paid to Lord Hachisuka of Awa, while a letter was sent to Yaman-ouchi Yōdō of Tosa to say that it was only because the harbour was too shallow to admit the vessel that the British Minister did not then call at Kōchi.   From the very first the officials attached to the British Legation were noted for their ability ; under Parkes, the Japan diplomatic and consular service was brought to the highest possible efficiency.   Some of the members of his staff attained a perfect command over the spoken, and a considerable mastery of the exceedingly difficult written, language of the country, and the energetic minister saw to it that none of his subordinates kept his talents wrapped up in a napkin.   Of the various currents and undercurrents of opinion Parkes was kept wonderfully well apprised, and he had no great difficulty in coming to the conclusion that a revolution was imminent.   At the earliest possible opportunity he gave it to be clearly understood that, in the case of an internal commotion, the government he represented would observe a strict neutrality.

Parkes' rival, the French representative, M. Léon Roches, adopted a different course. He laid himself out to gain the confidence and goodwill of the Shōgunate, and there is reason to believe that he gave the Bakufu to understand that in certain contingencies it might count upon French support in a contest with the feudatories. Shortly after the opening of the Chōshū campaign in July, 1866, a French warship is said to have notified the Chōshū authorities at Shimonoseki that :—

" France had entered into an alliance with the Japanese Government. and that if Chōshū refused to obey the order of the latter, they, the French, would be compelled to assist their allies . . . It is said the French had been to Nagasaki on a secret errand for the Bakufu."

At this time Roches was exerting himself to obtain for a French firm in Yokohama extensive Bakufu contracts for the construction of docks and arsenals, and the supply of arms, uniforms, and stores for the Tokugawa army and fleet. One day, it is said, Roches in a rather aggressive mood informed Parkes that he was going to bring over a *mission militaire* to drill the Shōgun's troops. This roused Parkes to say: "Then I shall get my Government to send over a *mission navale*," and he did. The French mission was headed by Colonel Chamoine, who was many years later on to earn some notoriety in connexion with the Dreyfus affair; the naval mission was led by Captain Tracy. These two men, Chamoine and Tracy, with their staff officers, had much to do with laying the foundation of that modern Japanese army and navy whose achievements have startled the world. In February, 1868, Roches addressed a memorial to his colleagues advocating the extension of the support of the Treaty Powers to the Shōgun in his contest with the "loyal" clans that had just then begun. Saigō was obsessed with the dread of such a French intervention ; his biographers enter into long accounts of the artful fashion in which he had sounded Parkes and Satow on the subject some months before he threw off the mask.

When the fourteenth Tokugawa Shōgun died, childless, in September, 1866, Hitotsubashi became the head of the house of Tokugawa, and the deceased Shōgun had designated him as his successor ; but Hitotsubashi, who had only been a reluctant candidate for the office in 1858, was now even less enamoured of the post. Since 1862, as Guardian of the Shōgun, and later as Protector of the Palace, he had had ample opportunities of appreciating the extraordinary difficulties of the position, and the failure of the second Chōshū expedition, which he had pressed upon the Emperor, did much to weaken his own influence with the Sovereign. The Chōshū men were still in arms, for they urged that there was no guarantee that the war would not be renewed immediately after the mourning for the Shōgun was over. To control the great feudatories was now getting to be an exceedingly difficult task, while even in the domestic councils of the Bakufu, union was sadly lacking. Shungaku of Echizen tried to dissuade Hitotsubashi from accepting the dangerous office; but the clamour of Aidzu, Kuwana, and the Bakufu's own vassals finally determined him to assume the responsibility. However, he made it a condition of his doing so that the Mikado should listen to his counsels, and the Daimyō should not only approve of his appointment, but

promise him their loyal support in the execution of the domestic
and foreign policy he might deem it necessary to pursue. It was
not until 10th January, 1867, that he was formally invested as
Shōgun. The ceremony took place not in Yedo, as had been the
custom for more than two centuries, but in the Castle of Nijō in
Kyōto, and during the last year of the existence of the Tokugawa
Bakufu, the Shōgun was never in Yedo at all.

Three weeks after the Shōgun's investiture, the Emperor Kōmei
died of small-pox on 3rd February, 1867. The Court thereupon ordered
the troops on both sides in the Chōshū struggle to be disbanded, and
this order was at once promulgated by the Shōgun. During the
fifty days of mourning, no national business could be transacted,
while, after that, some time was consumed in connexion with the
accession ceremonies of the new Sovereign. This means that on the
surface there was a lull in public affairs down to the beginning of
April, 1867. The death of the Emperor Kōmei was a severe blow
for the new Shōgun, Keiki, as we must henceforth call Hitotsubashi.
The new Sovereign, a boy of fifteen years, was the son of the Lady
Nakayama, and, as was usual, the relatives of the Emperor's mother
now became powerful at Court. Lord Nakayama, a bitter foreign-
hater, was not a man of any commanding ability, but he had the
Emperor's ear, and so he found himself courted by everyone opposed
to the Bakufu, to the In no Miya, and the Kwambaku, Nijō, the
sturdy supporters of the Bakufu at court. The two Konoye were
on intimate terms with Lord Nakayama, and it was through the
Konoye that Ōkubo of Satsuma had constantly worked in his
efforts to influence the counsels of the court. Many, perhaps the
great majority of the courtiers, were still hostile to the Bakufu, but
with the degradation and enforced seclusion of some twenty of its
leaders in 1863 and 1864, this faction had ceased to be formidable.
Now it began to group itself around Nakayama, while behind
Nakayama, the Bakufu, although it was blissfully unconscious of
the fact, had presently to deal with a much more redoubtable
antagonist.

It will be remembered that Iwakura had a great deal to do with
arranging the marriage of the Emperor's sister and the Shōgun. For
this he was afterwards degraded and sentenced to perpetual seclusion.
Recently, the clan leaders had been paying surreptitious visits to his
suburban retreat, and even the very ablest of them was impressed by
his grasp, originality and fertility of resource in political discussion.

It was easy for Saigō and Ōkubo to perceive that Iwakura was quite as much on their side as were Sanjō and his companions at Dazaifu. Hitherto, Sanjō had been able to effect nothing in Kyōto on account of the lack of any man of ability among the anti-Bakufu court faction; it was now desired to bring Sanjō in Dazaifu and Iwakura in his suburban Kyōto retreat into touch with each other. But Sanjō cherished a bitter detestation for Iwakura, and this was a difficult obstacle that it was necessary to overcome. Nakaoka, the Tosa samurai who co-operated with Sakamoto in forming the Chōshū-Satsuma secret alliance, now undertook the task of inducing Sanjō to consent to work with Iwakura, and by using the same tact and perseverance that he had done in the first case, he was once more successful, and a most formidable underground combination was the result—a numerically strong party of courtiers with two of the subtlest intellects in the land to direct it. If Sanjō did not possess the full measure of the In no Miya's ability, Iwakura certainly did, and on him fell the chief share in the elaboration of the special scheme of Imperial government that was lying ready for use the moment the Shōgun should tender his resignation.

During the period of national mourning, when the Bakufu could do nothing, the conspirators were very busy. In Kyōto, Saigō took the clansmen of Aki and Uwajima into his confidence to a certain extent, and disclosed some of his projects to them, and then, leaving Ōkubo behind, he hastened down to Kagoshima to urge Shimadzu Saburō's presence in Kyōto. On this occasion he ensured the support of Ōmura, Hirado, and various other Kyūshū clans, and then crossed to Shikoku where Daté Muneki and Yamanouchi Yōdō both promised to proceed to Kyōto at once. On 15th May, 1867, Saigō himself reappeared there, together with Shimadzu Saburō and 700 picked Satsuma troops. Shungaku of Echizen had already arrived, and on 7th June, 1867, Shungaku, Daté, Yamanouchi Yōdō, and Shimadzu Saburō, attended by their chief retainers, met in conference in the Echizen *yashiki*. Before this date, however, the Shōgun had begun to appreciate the fact that there were new forces at work in the court at Kyōto. The real brain of the Bakufu was now a certain Hara Ichi-no-shin; and Hara divined correctly enough that it was really Ōkubo that was organizing the opposition. From this point onwards some writers regarded the struggle of the next few months as a duel between the wits of Ōkubo and the wits of Hara.

The new Shōgun invited the foreign representatives to wait upon
him at Ōsaka early in April, when he received them in public and
private audience and entertained them at his own table in accordance
with French etiquette.   The main business was to discuss the
opening of Hyōgo, Ōsaka, and Yedō to foreign trade, which in 1862
was deferred with the consent of the Treaty-Powers until 1st January,
1868.   On 9th April, the Shōgun memorialized the Court about
the opening of Hyōgo.   The orders to give up the question of
opening Hyōgo, he pointed out, was not communicated to the
Foreign Representatives in 1865, on account of the complications
that might have resulted.   The treaties were sanctioned in general
terms by the Imperial decree of 22nd November, 1865, and nothing
was then said about Hyōgo to the foreign ministers.   However, the
latter were constantly urging that the matter should be definitely
settled as the stipulated date was fast approaching.   The Shōgun
himself was convinced that the only safe course to pursue was to
carry out the treaties in all good faith, for any other policy would
interfere with the most urgent need of the moment, viz., that
Japan should acquire the ships and arms in which the foreigners
were superior, and that she should develop her national resources.
He dwelt on the value of international treaties as guaranteeing the
weak against the strong, and declared that in the present state of
the world it was no longer practicable to maintain a policy of
seclusion.   The reply to this memorial said that it was impossible,
out of respect to the late Emperor's memory, and in view of the
opinions expressed by the various clans, to sanction the opening
of Hyōgo.   On 26th April the Shōgun begged for a reconsideration of
the matter, as it was of such vital importance to the interests and
safety of the country.   But Ōkubo was determined that this
question should not be settled till a council of the feudatories had
debated it, and it, together with the question of an amnesty for
Chōshū, was what mainly occupied the attention of the conference
of feudatories in the Echizen *yashiki* on 6th June, 1867.

Another point then urged was that men of real ability should be
selected for service in the Court, and the names of several anti-
Bakufu Court nobles were submitted to the Kwambaku as suitable
for various offices.   Hara countered this by presenting another list
of pro-Bakufu Kugé for the posts indicated, while he also succeeded
in getting the Court convinced that the opening of Hyōgo was a more
pressing question than the pardon of Chōshū.   An edict was

accordingly issued on 26th June, 1867, annulling the second and
third clauses of the decree of 22nd November, 1865, which had
ordered the treaties to be amended and the question of the opening
of Hyōgo to be dropped. At the same time, another decree recommended a lenient settlement of Chōshū's case.

It was only after repeated urging that the four Daimyō consented
to wait on the Shōgun at his castle of Nijō ; indeed Shimadzu
Saburō was at the time acting as if there was no Shōgun, while
Yamanouchi Yōdō began to divine that it was the purpose of
Satsuma to overthrow the Shōgunate at all costs, by an appeal to
arms if need be, and that the necessity of such an appeal would be
rather welcomed than regretted. Some very lively passages-at-arms
took place between Shimadzu Saburō and Yōdō ; and all the efforts
of Daté and Shungaku were required 'to keep the peace between
them.   The conference presently broke up, and the four Daimyō
left Kyōto without having effected anything of consequence.
Ōkubo and Saigō were fully convinced that the Bakufu was only
to be got rid of by an appeal to the last argument of armed force.
While the conference of the four Daimyō was still in progress, secret
emissaries from Chōshū were lurking in the Satsuma *yashiki*,
and they, now fully persuaded of Satsuma's good faith, returned
home to have everything made ready for emergencies. Satsuma
was very insistent in its advocacy of a speedy pardon for Chōshū,
mainly because that would allow Chōshū troops again to appear
openly in the capital. At the same time, an influential party in the
Tosa clan, led by Itagaki and Tani, had pledged themselves to
co-operate with Saigō, and to endeavour to induce their lord,
Yōdō, to abandon his support of the Bakufu.

After Yōdō's departure from the capital, Gōtō was sent to
assume direction of the Tosa *yashiki* in Kyōto. Gōtō was rapidly
coming to the front in the politics of the clan, and his abilities now
made an impression upon Saigō, who at once saw that Gōtō was
a man who would have to be seriously considered. The two soon
came to an agreement to have the national affairs put on such a
basis that the territorial integrity and the honour of Japan could be
effectually safeguarded. The rule of the Mikado was to be restored,
and the Shōgun was to revert to his constitutional position as one
among the vassals of the crown. But Saigō was careful to tell
Gōtō nothing about his intention of effectively clipping the wings
of the Tokugawa clan and of appealing to arms if need be to effect

his purpose. Gōtō, however, speedily got to know of it from other sources. In conversation with Sakamoto, he expressed his great anxiety about the situation and its impending developments, and Sakamoto then threw out the suggestion that the danger of hostilities might be averted and Tokugawa prestige saved if the Shōgun could be induced to tender his resignation voluntarily. The best way to bring this about would be to get Lord Yōdō to memorialize him to do so. Gōtō thereupon set to work to draft such a memorial ; he then submitted the paper to some of his own clansmen in Kyōto, to some Aki retainers, and to Saigō and Ōkubo. Various slight amendments in the wording were proposed, but none of these came from Satsuma. Saigō and Ōkubo, however, expressed their approval of the project, and got Shimadzu Saburō to write to Lord Yōdō urging him to fall in with the views of Gōtō, who presently arrived at Kōchi, the capital of the fief, to submit them. To Yōdō the suggestion came as a most welcome way of exit from his troubles ; he had seen that a continuance of the dual system of government was an impossibility, but, on the other hand, he was sincerely devoted to the best interests of the House of Tokugawa.

On 18th October, 1867, Gōtō set out for Kyōto to submit the following all-important document for the Shōgun's consideration :—

" It appears to me that although the government and the penal laws have been administered by the military class ever since the middle ages, yet from the arrival of the foreigners we have been wrangling among ourselves, and much public discussion has been excited. The East and the West have risen in arms against each other, and civil war has never ceased, the effect being to expose us to insult from foreign nations. The cause of this lies in the fact that the administration proceeds from two centres, causing the Empire's eyes and ears to be turned in two different directions. The march of events has brought about a revolution, and the old system can no longer be obstinately persevered in. Your Highness should restore the governing powers into the hands of the Sovereign, and so lay a foundation on which Japan may take her stand as the equal of all other countries. This is the most imperative duty of the present moment, and is the heartfelt prayer of Yōdō. Your Highness is wise enough to take this advice into consideration."

Appended to this document was a brief outline draft of a national constitution in which the anti-foreign policy was definitively discarded. This was really the work of Sakamoto who had accompanied Gōtō to Kōchi, but who had not been accorded an interview by Yōdō. The paper was signed by Yōdō, Gōtō and two other

Tosa samurai ; it was sent in as an enclosure along with the actual memorial, which was signed by Yōdō alone.

It was no easy matter for Gōtō to ensure that these documents should reach the hands of the Shōgun. On 12th September, Hara was assassinated by three anti-foreign fanatics who had heard that he was chiefly responsible for the opening of Hyōgo, and who came from Yedo for the express purpose of taking his head. The loss of what a Japanese writer calls his " wisdom-bag " was a signal misfortune for the Shōgun, Keiki. Gōtō, now that Hara was no longer available to forward his purpose, had recourse to the good services of the Junior Councillor, Nagai, who could read the signs of the times better than any one else in the Bakufu service, with the single exception of Katsu, Awa no Kami. Itakura, the chief of the Rōjū, was a stubborn upholder of the Bakufu authority ; and if Yōdō's memorial were tendered through him he would be likely to pigeon-hole, if not to destroy, it. At last, after due preparations, Gōtō did present the memorial on 27th October, 1867, to Itakura, who found that matters had been so arranged that he could not venture to keep it back from the Shōgun. Nagai had no difficulty in convincing Keiki of the wisdom of Yōdō's advice, for the recommendation to surrender the administrative power jumped very closely with his own natural inclination. On 8th November, the representatives of some forty clans were summoned to Nijō Castle to express their opinion on the Shōgun's purpose. The cardinal passage in the two documents then laid before them ran as follows :

" I confess with shame that the present unsatisfactory condition of affairs is due to my shortcomings and incompetence. Now that foreign intercourse is becoming more extensive, unless the administration is directed from a single central authority, the foundations of the state will be imperilled. If, however, the old evils be amended, and the administrative authority restored to the Imperial Court, if national deliberations be conducted on a broad basis and the Imperial decision secured, and if the Empire be sustained by the harmonious efforts of the whole people, then our country will be able to maintain its rank and dignity among the nations of the earth. Such is my view, but you will express your opinions without the slightest reserve."

As a matter of fact there was no discussion. Nagai produced a sort of note-book and requested those who approved to sign their names in it. Komatsu of Satsuma first wrote his own name and then those of Tsuji of Aki and of Gōtō and Fukuoka of Tosa, as it had been previously arranged he should do, and all the others present thereafter signed in succession. The Shōgun then summoned

Komatsu and the three others who had signed into another room, and Komatsu, Tsuji, and Gōtō all dwelt upon the absolute necessity of the step he was taking—Fukuoka merely saying that he agreed with Gōtō. Next day was a ceremonial day at Court, and so the memorial could not be presented then. But the four men saw the Kwambaku at once, and insisted that Court usage should for once be broken through on such a momentous occasion; and on 9th November, the Shōgun's surrender of administrative authority was duly presented. In the last clause it was stated that the step had been communicated to the clans.

On the very next day, 10th November, Keiki was notified that his surrender of the administrative power was accepted. He was instructed to exert himself in harmony with the empire, and still to defend and protect the realm so as to ensure the tranquillity of the Imperial mind. A special paper of instructions directed him to deal with foreign affairs in conference with the Daimyō, and to continue to use the Gisō and the Tensō as the medium of communication with the Court for routine business. All other matters were to be settled after the arrival of the Daimyō in Kyōto. Some other paragraphs were so ambiguous that Keiki had to write to the Kwambaku for a definite interpretation of their purport. Convinced at last that the object was to place him in a false position, he sent in his resignation of the office of Shōgun on 19th November. Before this, some fifty Daimyō, each with revenues of more than 100,000 *koku*, had been summoned to Kyōto and on 16th November, it was resolved to order all feudatories of not less than 10,000 *koku* to assemble in the capital.

Many of the Bakufu officials, such as Itakura, were exceedingly mortified at the course events had taken. They expected that the Shōgun's surrender of administrative power would not be accepted by the Court. As for the clans more intimately connected with the Bakufu, Aidzu, Kuwana, and Kishū, they were greatly excited, while many of the Fudai were profoundly dissatisfied with the new aspect of affairs. Even in Tosa, when there were no fewer than four factions besides Gōtō's party, there was a group of conservatives pledged to maintain the Bakufu in all the plenitude of its powers. Itagaki and his followers, on the other hand, were for extreme measures against it, in spite of the Shōgun's surrender of authority, for Itagaki had already committed himself to co-operation with Saigō, Ōkubo, and Iwakura. That trio had brought their schemes to a head early in November, and on the very day on which the Shōgun sent in his memorial to the Court, an Imperial Decree was issued to Satsuma and Chōshū instructing them to chastise the Bakufu, Aidzu and Kuwana by force of arms.   The Kwambaku knew nothing about this decree, nor did the In no Miya, nor the Gisō, nor the Tensō.   It had been surreptitiously obtained by Lord Nakayama, who at once took it to Iwakura's suburban cottage, and by Iwakura it was at once handed to Saigō of Satsuma and Hirosawa of Chōshū.

The surrender of his powers by the Shōgun at first threatened to interfere with the plans of the conspirators.   Tsuji of Aki, and even Komatsu of Satsuma thought there would be no occasion to appeal to arms, and that a new government could be organized without any serious disturbance.   Saigō, however, was of a different opinion.   The resources of the House of Tokugawa were immense, and so long as the Tokugawa chieftain had these resources at his disposal, it would be possible for him to overawe the other clans and to impose his will upon the Empire.   Besides surrendering the administrative power, Tokugawa Keiki must also *surrender his lands and his revenues, the private property of his house, to the Sovereign.* Saigō contended that an Imperial Decree should be issued instructing him to do so.   In case of any hesitation to comply on his part, let him forthwith be declared a rebel, and a commander appointed to direct the " army of chastisement " against him.   Thus, Gōtō was premature in congratulating himself that he had out-generalled Saigō by inducing the Shōgun to make a voluntary surrender of his administrative powers, for the sacrifice Saigō was bent on exacting from Keiki went far beyond that—a fact which Gōtō had not suspected.   The sacrifice involved not only the abolition of the Shōgunate under which the nation had been governed for 700 years, and for the last 250 years of that period in absolute peace, and the surrender by the head of the Tokugawa House of their hereditary office of royal dignity and of more than royal authority but the financial ruin of that great and nobly descended House.   Saigō's project commended itself to both Ōkubo and Iwakura, while, of course, the Chōshū men would have been satisfied with no other course of action.

Three days later, Komatsu, Saigō, and Ōkubo left for Satsuma, accompanied by the Chōshū men who had been lurking in Kyōto. At Yamaguchi the three Satsuma councillors had an interview with the Chōshū princes and made arrangements for concerted military action between the two clans and Aki which had adhered to the secret alliance some time before. Komatsu remained in Satsuma, and Ōkubo presently returned to Kyōto while Saigō was to come up with the young Lord of Satsuma, and a strong body of troops a week or so later.

Satsuma troops were soon disembarked at Mitajiri in Chōshū, and here, on 12th December, Saigō arranged the details of the ensuing campaign with the Chōshū and Aki commanders. Five days later Saigō entered Kyōto with his troops, while the Chōshū vanguard advanced and occupied Nishinomiya on 23rd December, the main force being then at Ōnomichi waiting for instructions from Kyōto. On 28th December, Saigō and Ōkubo called on Gōtō and informed him of the full scope of their plans and asked for the co-operation of Tosa in their execution. Gōtō was astounded ; he merely said that no definitive reply could be given until Yōdō's arrival which was expected a day or two later. Ōkubo had already given Shungaku of Echizen a hint of what was designed, and after immediate communication with Gōtō, Shungaku immediately sent an outline of the plot to the ex-Shōgun. Keiki kept his own counsel ; he remained the only one in Nijō Castle who was aware of the great crisis that was impending. As for the Kwambaku, the In no Miya, and most of the Court functionaries, they had not the faintest inkling of what was really in train.

Lords Nakayama, Saga, and Nakamikado, were the agents through whom Iwakura, Saigō, and Ōkubo were mining and moling. On 2nd January, 1868, there was some very important business dealt with at Court. The nobles who had been in enforced seclusion since 1863 were restored to rank and office as were the five banished Kugé at Dazaifu, while the Chōshū princes were pardoned, and their presence in the capital sanctioned. Of course, this meant that Chōshū troops were once more free to appear in Kyōto, and on the preceding evening Saigō actually sent a messenger with a copy of the decree to be issued to the Chōshū commander at Nishinomiya and—perhaps most important of all—Iwakura was restored to rank and office. For six long years he had been unable to pass the doors of his cottage. Now, on the following day, he was to appear at Court once more. On this fateful occasion he was to bring with him the box which contained the decrees and documents which made an end of the Shōgunate, and re-established the personal rule of the Mikado !

Everything was now ready for the great *coup d'état*. Saigō, who assumed command of the " loyal " troops, assigned to the contingents from the five clans of Satsuma, Aki, Tosa, Echizen, and Ōwari, their positions at the various gates of the palace. There they were found in possession when the ordinary guards from Aidzu and Kuwana appeared only to be told that they were relieved of their duties by Imperial Decree. They sullenly withdrew to the Castle of Nijō, which was presently humming like an angry hive. Among the various instructions given to the new guards was one to the effect that only those indicated to them as being summoned to court were to be admitted into the palace. By three or four o'clock on the afternoon of 3rd January, 1868, three Princes of the Blood, eight court nobles, and five Daimyō, with fifteen of their clansmen, had been admitted. It presently appeared that these were the personnel of the new government that was just about to be promulgated as replacing the Shōgunate.

When all had been marshalled to their places, the youthful sovereign appeared and charged " the nobles and the others to exert themselves on behalf of the country ". Then the great decree restoring the old and original rule of the Emperor was solemnly read out. Imperial sanction for this had been obtained by Nakayama, Saga, Nakamikado, and Iwakura. Among other points it declared that the offices of Kwambaku and Shōgun were abolished, as were also those of the Gisō and Tensō, together with the Protectorship of Kyōto (now held by Aidzu) and the Shoshidai (filled by Kuwana). The new provisional government was to be in the hands of a *Sōsai*, or President, of Ten Gijō or Ministers, and twenty Sanyō or Councillors, Prince Arisugawa, the head of the Princely House that was next in seniority to the Emperor and heir presumptive to the throne, was designated as Sōsai. The Gijō comprised two princes of the blood, three court nobles (Nakayama and his two confederates) and the five Daimyō of Satsuma, Aki, Tosa, Echizen, and Ōwari. The Sanyō included five court nobles, the most important personage among them being Iwakura—and three retainers from each of the five clans. Among these latter, Gōtō of Tosa, and Saigō and Ōkubo of Satsuma, were the leading figures. On this occasion, Saigō did not sit in the assembly ; his hands were fully occupied with the direction of the guards outside, for an assault from Nijō Castle might be expected at any moment.

The first question the newly-born government had to settle was its attitude towards the former Shōgun and the house of Tokugawa. Yōdō of Tosa began by asking why Tokugawa Keiki had been excluded from the administration. Why was he not present with them ? Iwakura now disclosed what the real aims of the conspirators were. Keiki, he said, might be admitted to a seat in the Council, when he had given a pledge of his good faith by resigning his Court offices, and by *surrendering his lands and revenues*. Hot words were exchanged between Yōdō and Iwakura, while Gōtō twitted Ōkubo with what he called the baseness of Satsuma intrigue. In the midst of this the Emperor ordered a recess. Saigō, on hearing for the first time how things were going, sent word to Iwakura that it was a dirk that was wanted, and Iwakura then indirectly gave Yōdō to understand that if he persisted in his attitude he would be invited to an ante-chamber where he and Iwakura would poniard each other. On the discussion being resumed, it appeared that Aki sided with Satsuma, while Echizen and Ōwari, though siding with Yōdō, were working for a compromise. The ultimate result of the debate, which was protracted till past midnight, was that Echizen and Ōwari were deputed to wait upon Tokugawa Keiki on the following day and inform him that his resignation of the office of Shōgun was accepted, at the same time suggesting that he should further resign his Court offices and surrender his lands and revenues.

Next morning the Kwambaku Nijō, the In no Miya and some twenty Court nobles, who had supported the Bakufu cause, found themselves stripped of rank and office and ordered into seclusion, while Echizen and Ōwari as they set out for Nijō Castle met Chōshū's vanguard defiling through the streets of the capital. In the court-yard of Nijō the two Daimyō were welcomed with angry scowls and muttered maledictions. Each of them had done his part in the work that had brought the Shōgunate to the dust. Ōwari had misconducted the first expedition against Chōshū, and it was Echizen who had been mainly responsible for the ruin of Yedo when he abolished the immemorial forced residence of the Daimyō, their wives and their heirs, as hostages in the Tokugawa metropolis. If the samurai had been conversant with the full purport of their present mission, the two Lords would probably have never lived to discharge it. The acceptance of his resignation was quite in order, Keiki remarked ; as for speaking about the other two points, it was out of the question at present, for the samurai in Nijō were in too ugly a mood as the Princes could readily see for themselves. On the following day,

Keiki sent for Echizen and informed him that the purport of his previous visit had leaked out, and that the situation was getting too serious for his control. Keiki's last wish at this time was to precipitate a conflict and to get promptly branded as a rebel. He had a lively recollection of the terrors and horrors of the strife in Kyōto on 20th August, 1864, when the greater part of Kyōto was reduced to ashes, and he had no desire for a repetition of that baneful experience. Under cover of darkness, he slipped out of Nijō Castle on the night of 6th January, and proceeded to Ōsaka, where he was presently joined by the garrison of Nijō and all the Bakufu troops in Kyōto. Just before leaving he sent in a document to the Court explaining his reasons for doing so.

" I trust that the Emperor will understand that I am taking this action solely in the interests of the Throne, being anxious that order should be preserved and tranquillity maintained within the precincts of the palace. I ought to have begged for leave from the Throne before quitting Kyōto, but it would have taken time to obtain permission, and I was apprehensive lest in the interval, through some inconsiderate incident, a grave national crisis might be precipitated."

Keiki signed this merely as head of the Tokugawa house, for the Tokugawa Shōgunate was now a thing of the past. The destinies of Japan were henceforth in the hands of the newly-born, or—as the patriots maintained—restored Imperial government. The most urgent question that first confronted that Government was the treatment to be accorded to the House of Tokugawa. Events showed that this problem could only be solved by an appeal to the sharp arbitrament of the sword, as Ōkubo and Saigō had foreseen it would have to be. Tokugawa vassals or partisans remained in arms against the new government for a period of eighteen months, albeit entirely against the will of Tokugawa Keiki. The history of that period really belongs to the history of the Meiji era, and is in fact only a part of the larger question of the transition from the hoary feudal system to modern national institutions, and will be more conveniently dealt with in a possible future volume.

CHAPTER XIX

IMPERIAL GOVERNMENT RE-ESTABLISHED

THE author of this volume concluded his task with his description of Yoshinobu's resignation, as he considered that event to mark the close of the Tokugawa epoch of Japanese history. His story must, however, be carried a step further, until the time when the last expiring struggles of the Tokugawa partisans came to an end. It was only then that the dual system of government, which had continued without a break since its foundation at the close of the twelfth century by Yoritomo, the first Sei-i-Tai-Shogun, the Barbarian-subduing-great-General, came to an end, and the legitimate Emperor, the descendant of the gods of Heaven and their vicegerent on earth, was once more vested with the national executive which had theoretically belonged to him ever since the foundation of the Empire. For a brief space after Yoshinobu's formal resignation it seemed as if all would be well and that the head of the Tokugawa house having bowed to the times and surrendered his office, peace would be established and the Restoration accomplished without further bloodshed. But this was not to be, and many events, some of a very gruesome nature, with much shedding of blood, were yet to take place before the great change was completed and Japan was able to enter safely on her new career which was destined to convert her from an Oriental Empire, scarcely known to the world otherwise than as a geographical entity, into one of the great military and commercial powers of the world.

Now the great Taikun had resigned and was practically a fugitive from the Imperial capital, which until now had shivered under his control. Slighted at every turn by the Court party, and unable to bear the repeated humiliations cast upon him, he withdrew to Osaka, the great commercial city, twenty-seven miles from Kyoto, where he owned another lordly castle and palace even more imposing than his home in Yedo. His faithful followers there gathered around him, his own loyal vassals and the clansmen of Aidzu and Kuwana, all hot with anger at the injustice and treachery of which they considered he and they had been made the victims. The Lords of Owari and Echizen, both great Daimyo, both of Tokugawa blood and closely related to the Taikun, were sent as Imperial messengers from Kyoto to Osaka, to urge him to stifle his resentment and return with a small escort to Kyoto, where he would be admitted to the presence of the Emperor, and where his personal safety would be guaranteed by his own relatives who were around the Emperor. These inducements were placed before him as the commands of the Emperor, and at first he was inclined to obey them, but the same night the two lords of Aidzu and Kuwana and his own councillors gathered around him and urgently impressed upon him :—

"No faith can be placed in the declaration of the two lords. If your Highness determines to go your servants will follow, even at the risk of their own lives. On this expedition we will remove from the Emperor his bad counsellors and try the issue with them by the sword."

The Taikun yielded and determined to enter Kyoto at the head of his forces. The Foreign Diplomatic representatives were in Osaka at the time, whither they had all temporarily moved from Yokohama in expectation of the opening of the city of Osaka and the port of Hiogo to foreign trade and residence. This event, against which the late Emperor had continued to protest with all his strength, till his death, had actually occurred on the 1st January : but the Foreign Representatives were between the devil and the deep sea. They had hitherto been accustomed to deal with the officials of the Shogunate, though they were by this time well aware of the true position of the Taikun *vis-à-vis* the Emperor. Now the Shogunate was at an end, but no new government was as yet visible, and political chaos seemed to reign both in Kyoto and Osaka, while news came of serious disturbances in the eastern capital. They were received in formal audience by the Taikun, and in answer to their inquiry, voiced by the Minister of France as the *doyen* of the diplomatic corps, he explained to them clearly enough how he had been ousted from the Government, with which he had been charged when his resignation of the Shogunate was accepted by the Court Guardians of the young Emperor, yet his sole objects were to preserve the unity of the Empire, and to prevent the outbreak of hostilities. With those objects in view, he had left the capital, and come down to Osaka, but he could not view with indifference those now possessed of the person of the young

Emperor giving rein to their own selfish desires under the name of the Emperor's wishes and distressing the people by the political unrest which they provoked. He therefore proposed to ask the opinion of the majority of a general council of the nation, and, until the form of Government was settled in accordance with those opinions, by a majority of the whole country, it was his office to observe the Treaties and conduct Foreign affairs generally.

This audience took place on 10th January. His good intentions lasted only a fortnight. It was on the night of the 25th that he received the exhortations already described of his own principal and trusted retainers ; and on that night he made up his mind and determined to enter Kyoto with the clans of Aidzu and Kuwana in the front of his following.

The die was cast, and news of the Taikun's decision reached Kyoto almost as soon as it was taken. Two roads, each about twenty-seven miles in length, lead from Osaka to the capital, one on each side of the river Yodo ; one passing round Fushimi, a town seven miles from Kyoto on the left bank of the river, and the other through Toba, a smaller town on the right bank, somewhat nearer. Troops from the Satsuma and Chōshu clans, the latter especially animated with a bitter hatred engendered by what they had suffered during the previous four years, were hastily dispatched to block the roads both at Fushimi and Toba, with orders to prevent at any cost, the Taikun continuing on his march to Kyoto, if accompanied by a large force, while the Aidzu and Kuwana clans were to be absolutely forbidden to pass under any circumstances.

On the 27th Tokugawa messengers came to the barrier and announced the intention of the Taikun to force his way through if obstructed. They were soon followed by the van of their army, and a battle, which lasted for three days, was begun. It was fought with intense determination and heavy loss on both sides. The numbers engaged on both sides have been very variously stated, but the nearest correct estimate may be taken as that of Sir E. Satow: 10,000 of the Tokugawa followers, and 1,500 of the Kwangun, the Imperial army, mostly Satsuma and Chōshu clansmen. With such a disparity in numbers it seems strange that victory should have been on the side of the smaller force. But the larger had to advance across exposed rice-fields that lay in front of Fushimi, and by narrow paths through open fields in front of Toba, both exposed to the fire of strongly entrenched artillery.

There was a still stronger explanation ; treachery, which has
so often played its part in the great events of Japanese history,
here decided the day as it had done in the great sea-fight of Dan-
no-Ura five centuries before, and at Sekigahara, Iyeyasu's crowning
triumph, in 1600. The samurai of the Tsu clan, who were implicitly
trusted by the Tokugawa, were posted on the left flank of their
army and the safeguarding of that position was left entirely in
their charge. On the night of the second day of the battle they
went over to the Kyoto army, and admitted its artillery to their
position. On the following day fire was at once opened on the
unsuspecting Tokugawa, and a general attack in strength soon
followed. A panic ensued, and the whole army was soon in full
retreat to Osaka where their lord the Taikun and some of his
chief officers had been waiting events. He had not led the van of
his own army. All was now over. His army, utterly broken
and disorganized, was pouring into Osaka with the pursuing
enemies on its heels, and on the spot he could do nothing more.
Yedo was still his own home, and all his influence and authority
in the Gokinai, the five Home Provinces that lay around Kyoto,
even in his own family town of Osaka, was gone. He gave a hasty
warning to one of the foreign representatives, who were all still
there, that he could no longer guarantee their safety, and then
fled himself, proceeding down the river by boat, getting safely
across the dangerous bar, on which a few weeks before the American
Admiral and his whole boat's crew had perished, and the English
Admiral, the redoubtable old sea-dog, Sir Harry Keppel, and his
staff, together with Lord Redesdale who was with him, had only
escaped by a miracle ; and taking refuge on the U.S.S. *Iroquois*,
that was with other foreign ships of war lying in the roadstead.
There he was not recognized nor did he announce his own identity,
but after a short stay he was able to transfer himself to one of his
own ships, the *Kayo Maru*, and in her he proceeded at once to Yedo.

Osaka was still in disorder. There was no government and the
excited troops of both armies were pouring into it in confusion, and
no one knew what was going to happen. The great and splendid
palace within the castle walls was set on fire and, with all its art
treasures, burnt to ashes. The temporary Legations of the Dutch
and French Ministers were plundered and burnt. The ministers
and their staffs, having previously packed their archives, followed
the Taikun's example, and escaped as he did, by boat down the

river, but only proceeding as far as Hiogo (Kobe of the present day) there to await events, and finding such accommodation as they could in the few buildings that had as yet been erected in the newly opened port, thankful that they had roofs over their heads, fresh food and a bottle of curaçoa over which the diplomatic body made merry.

We may now turn aside from the fortunes of the beaten and fugitive Taikun, and tell what took place at Hiogo, where the Foreign Ministers continued their temporary residence. Many gruesome incidents were destined to occur before peace and good order were firmly established, and the new port fairly started on its career, which was ultimately to make it one of the greatest seats of foreign trade and shipping in the East. On the downfall of their lord, the Tokugawa officials, who had now over ten years' experience of European intercourse, and who had been sent from Yokohama to make the necessary arrangements that were incidental to the opening of the port, all abandoned their posts and, following the example of their master, fled to Yedo. There was no administrative or governing authority left on the spot, and the Representatives of the Powers had to take into their own hands the arrangements that were pressingly necessary for the establishment of Europeans at the port, and indeed generally to maintain order until the officials of the new Imperial Government should come upon the scene. Foreign traders of several nationalities were already arriving, in not inconsiderable numbers, the majority, as was almost invariably the case in those days throughout the Far East, being of British nationality, and these were impatient to initiate their business, from which great things were expected. The first step was to provide them with land on which warehouses and residences suitable to their present and prospective requirements could be erected.

For this purpose the site had already been marked out for a foreign settlement, that is a place where foreigners could acquire land on perpetual leases for purposes of trade and residence, which was to a certain extent exempt from the jurisdiction of the native authorities, and from which native subjects were entirely excluded as residents. Such settlements existed, and in China still exist, under slightly varying local conditions at all the open ports both of Japan and China. That chosen in this case was a piece of ground on the sea front, measuring 600 by 400 yards, and lying on the north-east of Hiogo. Kobe was the name of the little fishing village that was formerly on this site, and the name was given, at the beginning, to the new settlement, and it was subsequently extended to the great town that has since grown up around it.

On the afternoon of the 2nd February, about two o'clock, some of the Ministers were busily engaged in supervising the partitioning of this site into suitable lots, and many of their country-men, interested in the proceedings, were also present, when a party consisting of several hundred samurai of the Bizen fief made its appearance, marching in regular military order, and debouching from the main street of Hiogo which led directly on the north side of the proposed new settlement. They were all *kerai* of Matsudaira Ikeda, Bizen no kami, a daimyo of 310,000 *koku*, whose capital was Okayama, a town on the Inland Sea, about 90 miles from Kobe, with a population of 32,000 people. They had come from Okayama, and had just landed at Hiogo, on their way to Kyoto, whither they had been summoned by their lord to join the Imperial forces already in that city. The foreigners on the settlement site were fully exposed to their view as they passed along its northern boundary. Various conflicting versions are given, even by those who were actually on the spot at the time, and at this date it is difficult to describe with complete confidence what actually occurred.

It was said that a member of the military escort which attended the French Minister, but who was not on duty at the time, broke the line of the Bizen procession, a most serious offence in feudal Japan, and received a slight lance prick from one of the angered men. The officer in command thereupon suddenly dismounted from his horse and gave an order to fire. The whole party, newly armed with modern American rifles, thereupon opened a rapid fire on the European ministers and their staffs, naval officers and expectant merchants. All the latter, who were entirely unarmed, very naturally sought with all speed such shelter as could be found, and when the men of Bizen had no more to fire at, they continued on the march towards Kyoto. Fortunately they had just recently received their new rifles, and had not yet learned the proper use of the sights, which were fixed at too high an elevation, so that the bullets passed high over the heads of the foreigners, and the only casualty that occurred, apart from the lance-pricked Frenchman, was a sailor boy of the U.S.S. *Oneida*, slightly wounded by gunshot.

An incident of this nature had not been entirely unanticipated by the Europeans, though it was not expected from the direction from which it came, and arrangements had been made to meet it, so the Bizen men were not allowed to proceed in peace. Large forces of seamen and marines with field guns were promptly landed from the ships of war in harbour, and with both the mounted guard of the British Minister and a small detachment of the 9th regiment of the line, now the Norfolk regiment, which also attended him, at their head, all lead by the Minister in person, they were soon in hot pursuit. The Japanese, who were greatly outnumbered, did not wait for them, but abandoning their baggage, broke and fled to the hills near at hand where they were soon lost to sight. An examination of the abandoned baggage subsequently showed that they were well equipped with every requisite for taking the field, including medical and surgical appliances. The pursuit was then abandoned, and the whole international force of British, French, and United States sailors and marines returned to the settlement, which was at once placed in a state of siege, breastworks thrown up, Armstrong and other field guns posted, full directions given to the civilian residents as to their conduct in case of a night attack, and all proper preparations made to resist an attack in force. The whole place was also, it is to be remembered, well under the guns of the powerful fleet anchored in the harbour. The latter played its part by taking immediate possession of all the Japanese merchant steamers that chanced to be in the adjoining harbour of Hiogo.

The only casualty in this affair, in addition to the lance-pricked Frenchman and the American sailor boy, was one very old woman of the *eta* class, who received a slight gunshot wound during the cavalry charge of the mounted guard of the British Minister. The whole affair, with all its panoply of war—it may be added that both sailors and marines, when the danger was over, indulged in extensive looting at the expense of both Western and Japanese traders—may well appear to have partaken largely of the character of a burlesque, but it had both its serious side and its tragic after-math. It was serious in that it testified to the hatred of Europeans cherished by the clansmen of wealthy and powerful feudatories, who were the most ardent supporters of the restoration of the Emperor, whose policy was summed up in three words, " *Sonnō Joi Sakko.*" "Honour the Emperor, expel the Barbarians, close

the ports," who, in the faith that the restoration was a prelude to
the enforcement of their policy in its fullest details, had given their
whole-hearted support to the forcible deposal of the traitorous
Taikun who had betrayed his country in assenting to its pollution
by " savage beasts " and who were now influential parties in the
new Government. If this incident was a fair index of the spirit
of the majority of the clansmen and their officers throughout the
Empire, there were still stormy times in store before trade and
intercourse could start on their fair way, before foreigners could
reside in Japan with any confident sense of personal safety. It was
possible that none of these men of Bizen, all samurai of gentle birth,
had until now ever set eyes on Europeans, for whom equal hatred
and contempt had been instilled into them from their earliest
years.

They had displayed the natural results of this training by a very
offensive demeanour to the few foreigners whom they met on their
march through the narrow streets of Hiogo prior to the main incident,
and in some cases their offensiveness threatened to turn into actual
physical violence. Some excuse may, however, be made for them
in that they had been accustomed to see their own fellow-countrymen
kneel and bow their heads to the very ground whenever a high officer
passed by, while here were mere despicable foreigners meeting and
passing their officer, a man of high degree in their own fief, not
only without outward simulation of deference, but with an apparent
and arrogant sense of equality, of having the right to the streets
which, in accordance with all feudal tradition, was for the moment
the sole prerogative of the samurai marching on service in formal
array. Indignation had no doubt already reached the boiling
point, when the Frenchman unwittingly added the final insult.
There were not only scores of other clans in the Empire in the same
position and cherishing the same spirit, but hundreds of *rōnin*
who were responsible to no one but themselves, and who were
roaming all over the country singly and in bands, all ready at any
moment to cut down foreigners to gratify their own hatred, confident
that in doing so they were rendering the highest service to the
gods, their Emperor, and their country. Their attitude in the
future, whenever either clansmen or *rōnin* were brought into
contact with foreigners, became a serious problem, and its possible
dangers had to be guarded against by every legitimate expedient
that could be taken.

The first expedient that naturally commended itself was the punishment of the chief offender in this case. There could of course, be no question as to his identity, and here came the most tragic part of the whole incident. The officer primarily responsible for it " was a Karo of the clan, named Taki Zensaburo, a stalwart man, thirty-two years of age, with a noble air." He was surrendered by the Lord of Bizen to the Government without demur, and after the completion of the proper formalities was condemned to death by hara-kiri, the punishment provided by law for a samurai guilty of grave offences. The penalty was duly paid on the evening of the 2nd March, in the temple of Seifukuji in Hiogo. It had been arranged that one representative of each of the Treaty Powers, seven in all, should be present, and Lord Redesdale was the one who appeared on behalf of Great Britain. He has described in his *Tales of Old Japan*, the whole of the imposing and solemn scene in impressive and eloquent language. " It was horrible." No more need be said here, either of the incident itself, or of its last gruesome episode, beyond that a full apology was demanded from, and readily given with all proper formality, by the new Government. Fortunately no European had been sufficiently injured to justify the demand for a pecuniary indemnity that in those days seemed to attend every controversy that arose in our relations with the countries of the Far East, and elementary decency forbade any idea of imposing on the Japanese any responsibility for the looting of the stores by the allied sailors and marines.

During the month which elapsed between the outrage (2nd February) and the payment of the last dread penalty for it much had been done.

Two proclamations were issued to the Japanese public at the time when the foreign settlement in Kobe was put into a state of siege, one by the Foreign Ministers to assure all peaceable Japanese that they need be under no apprehensions, and that all unarmed persons were at perfect liberty to proceed about their business, the other, similar in effect, by some of the Chōshu officials. These and the Satsuma officials who were in the port, tried to bring about a settlement of the difficulty ; but the foreign representatives declined to listen to anyone who was not empowered to treat with them by the Emperor. Accordingly Higashi Kuze, an important member of the Court nobility, was sent to Hiogo as an envoy from the Emperor, and assured the foreign representatives that it was the sincere desire of His Majesty to uphold and carry out the engagements entered into by the Shōgun, and that foreigners would be protected from any assault and disturbers of the peace punished. A proclamation to this effect was issued on the following day. The foreign representatives thereupon put an end to the state of siege, the Japanese ships were released, and the guards of blue-jackets and marines were sent back to their ships.

On the 10th the Imperial envoy returned to Kobe, and formally announced that Ito Shunské was appointed Governor of Hiogo. Under this name the future Prince Ito was then known. His part in making arrangements for the residence of foreigners in the newly opened port may be counted as not the least of his many achievements.

On 8th March, another attack on foreigners by a party of samurai occurred. The French Vice-Consul at Kobe and Commandant Roy, of the French corvette *Venus*, set off from Osaka to see the town of Sakai and its neighbourhood, and asked that a boat from the *Dupleix* should be sent to meet them. Arrived at a bridge, they were turned back by a band of armed men who were guarding it. These armed men, samurai of Tosa, then went to the landing-place at Sakai to await the French boat. After the crew had landed, and most of them had returned to the boat, the Tosa men opened their surprise attack, seized the two Frenchmen who were ashore and fired on the boat till they had accounted for all the others except an engineer, who had remained hidden in the water between the launch and a Japanese boat. He was the only one of the crew who returned to his ship alive, some of his mortally wounded comrades helping him to hoist a sail and turn the boat round. On hearing of this occurrence the French Minister immediately demanded an apology from the New Government, an indemnity of 150,000 dollars, and the decapitation of the assassins. All these demands were accepted, and on the 16th March, eighteen of the Tosa men and two officers were led to execution in the presence of many French officers and seamen. When eleven of these had been executed, M. Roches, the French Minister, requested that the rest should be spared, as the boat's crew which had suffered their attack was only eleven in number.

On the 22nd March, the British Minister was on his way to present his credentials to the Emperor, at Kyoto, when a sudden attack was made upon him and his mounted escort. The Minister's life was saved by Gōtō Shōjiro (afterwards known as General Gōtō) who promptly dismounted from his horse and cut off the head of the nearest assassin. Gōtō was at that time in command of the Tosa forces.

It will be seen that the New Government, as soon as it felt its power secure, quite abandoned the anti-foreign sentiment which it had used to help it attain its commanding position, and proceeded to show much moderation both in dealing with the West and with its own opponents, who were still making an unsuccessful resistance, pursued by the Imperial army, of which Prince Arisugawa Takehito was appointed Commander-in-Chief on the 9th February. By the 5th March he had entered Shizuoka, sacred to the memory of Iyeyasu, who had spent the last eleven years of his life there. Proceeding northward, he was about to attack Yedo when the ex-Shōgun sent a deputation headed by Ōkubo and Katsu Awa to negotiate for peace with the Emperor through Saigo Takamori, who, though years afterwards prominent as a rebel, was at that time a mainstay of the Imperial army. Saigo personally submitted the terms proposed by the deputies to the Emperor, for his assent, and the matter was arranged. The Imperial army occupied Yedo, the last of the Shōguns retired to Mito, his original home, and a revenue of 700,000 *koku* was apportioned for the maintenance of the Tokugawa family.

Some of the Tokugawa partizans, however, could not feel reconciled to these conditions, so they entrenched themselves at Uyēno, a northern suburb of Yedo, in the grounds of To-ei-san, the temples enshrining the tombs of many of their lord's predecessors, and prepared to defend themselves. They were driven out on 4th July, 1868, and Ōtori Keisuke, their leader, retreated with them towards the north, but his little band was routed by the Imperial troops at Utsunomiya, and again at Nikko.

On the following 6th November, the castle of Wakamatsu, the stronghold of the Aidzu clan, fell to the Imperial army. Matsudaira (Hoshina) Katamori, the Daimyō of Aidzu, with the Daimyō of Sendai, Morioka, and Tsurugaoka, who made their submission as soon as the castle, the last hope of their side, was taken, were condemned to detention. Hoshina was afterwards allowed an honourable retirement as guardian of the Tōshōgu temple at Nikko, the fane built to hallow the tomb of Iyeyasu. His descendants to-day enjoy the title of viscount. Ōtori escaped to Hakodate, and the war on the main island of Japan was ended.

Meanwhile the Emperor had been formally enthroned at Kyoto on the 12th October, and on the 9th February following his marriage was celebrated, the Empress being a daughter of the *kugé* family of Ichijo. In April the Court was transferred to Yedo, henceforth to be known as Tokyo, the Eastern Capital, in distinction to Saikyo (Kyoto) the Western Capital. At this time, and for some years afterwards, the foreign settlement at Yokohama was guarded from possible violence of *rōnin* and other lawless characters by a portion of a British regiment. When the Imperial *cortège* was due to pass, the regimental band was led to the point where the Tokaido, the great main road from Kyoto to Yedo, came nearest to Yokohama and, as the palanquin containing His Majesty came into view, it was saluted with music, the band playing " The British Grenadiers " in default of a more suitable tune, as at that time no Japanese National Anthem had been established.

The last of the pro-Tokugawa party were still holding out at Hakodate in Yezo (Hokkaido) where they were strongly fortified and under the able leadership of Enomoto Takeaki, an officer in the Shōgun's navy, who had spent six years in Holland from 1860 to 1866. On the deposition of the Shōgun, he had gone to Hakodate with several warships, with the intention of establishing a separate State on the Northern Island. Ōtori Keisuke joined him there after the fall of Wakamatsu castle. Hakodate town is situated on a small peninsula and looks towards the southernmost mountains of Yezo across a fine large harbour, which is bounded on the side opposite the entrance by a long narrow sandy strip connecting the little range of high hills which constitute the peninsula with the mainland. A strong fort of massive stone masonry half-way across the sandy isthmus and another at the mouth of the harbour, made the defences apparently complete. It was not till 27th June, 1869, that the rebel garrison was finally captured. The Imperial forces were brought unobserved to the back of the peninsula, which only measures a few miles in any direction, and landed quietly by night in small boats at the foot of the range of hills, rising to just over 1,000 feet at its highest peak, which on that side slopes down steeply to the water's edge. These slopes, though far too rugged to be used on ordinary occasions, were not inaccessible to resolute climbers, so the defenders of Hakodate were surprised from the rear, and were forced to surrender to Kuroda Kiyotaka, a Satsuma samurai, who afterwards, as General Kuroda, took a prominent part in suppressing the Satsuma rebellion, headed by Saigo Takamori.

Thus ended the last struggle against the unification of the country under its ancient dynasty of rulers, an unification which has since been made extremely thorough.

The formerly paramount House of Tokugawa is now only one among the many noble houses of Japan, loyal to its Sovereign, and contributing its share of members to the public services, but without the least territorial jurisdiction in any part of the Empire. So, on a peaceful note, ends the record of the Tokugawa epoch in Japanese history.

As a postscript it may be added that

Enomoto was kept prisoner in Tokio for three years, which time he devoted largely to study. He was liberated on the petition of his vanquisher, General Kuroda. Shortly after his liberation he was given an appointment by the Imperial Government as Secretary General of the Department for the Colonization of Yezo, and in this post did valuable work. He subsequently was appointed Vice-Admiral in the Imperial Navy, was Ambassador to Russia and to China, and held various positions from time to time in the Ministry under Japan's modern constitution. Ōtori, like Enomoto, was imprisoned for a relatively short time, only two years, and then pardoned. He was also given a post in the administration of Yezo, and afterwards occupied various high positions under the Imperial Government. He is principally remembered as the Japanese Minister to Korea, just previous to the outbreak of the war between Japan and China.

The rank and file of the rebel army were set to work on the task of erecting, at Hakodate, the raised terrace surrounded by a stone embankment, which forms a forecourt to the shrine dedicated to the spirits of those who lost their lives on the Imperial side. Samurai did the work of navvies, overseen by their conquerors, who never reprimanded a man twice for slackness; the first time it was a word, the second time the offender was cut down—so says local tradition. This suitable pennance accomplished, they were set free, and like their chiefs, became loyal subjects of the Emperor, and took their places among the makers of modern Japan in the Meiji era.

APPENDICES

I.—LIST OF EMPERORS.

Posthumous Name	Birth	Accession	Abdication	Death
	B.C.	B.C.	B.C.	B.C.
1. Jimmu	711	660		585
2. Suisei	632	581		549
3. Annei	567	548		511
4. Itoku	553	510		477
5. Kōshō	506	475		393
6. Kōan	427	392		291
7. Kōrei	342	290		215
8. Kōgen	273	214		158
9. Kaikwa	208	157		98
10. Sujin	148	97		30
				A.D.
11. Suinin	70	31		70
		A.D.	A.D.	
12. Keikō	12	71		130
	J.-C.			
13. Seimu	83	131		190
14. Chūai	149	192		200
Jingō (Regent)	170	201		269
15. Ōjin	201	201		310
16. Nintoku	290	313		399
17. Richū	336	400		405
18. Hanshō	352	406		411
19. Inkyō	374	412		453
20. Ankō	401	454		456
21. Yūryaku	418	457		479
22. Seinei	444	480		484
23. Kensō	440	485		487
24. Ninken	448	488		498
25. Buretsu	489	499		506
26. Keitai	450	507	531	531
27. Ankan	467	536		539
28. Senkwa	466	534		535
29. Kimmei	510	540		571
30. Bitatsu	538	572		585
31. Yōmei	540	586		587
32. Sushun	523	588		592
33. Suiko *	554	593		628
34. Jomei	593	629		641
35. Kōgyoku *	594	642	645	
36. Kōtoku	596	646		654
37. Saimei *		655		661
38. Tenchi	626	662		671
39. Kōbun	648	672		672
40. Temmu	622	673		686
41. Jitō *	646	687		703
42. Mommu	683	697	695	707
43. Gemmei *	662	708		722
44. Genshō *	681	715	714	748
45. Shōmu	699	724	723	756

Posthumous Name	Birth	Accession	Abdication	Death
46. Kōken *	718	749	748	
47. Junnin	733	759	758	765
48. Shōtoku *		765	764	769
49. Kōnin	719	770		781
50. Kwammu	736	782		805
51. Heijō	774	806		824
52. Saga	785	810	809	842
53. Junwa	786	824	823	840
54. Nimmyō	810	834	833	850
55. Montoku	827	851		858
56. Seiwa	851	859	876	881
57. Yōzei	868	877	884	949
58. Kōkō	830	885		887
59. Uda	867	888	897	931
60. Daigo	885	898		930
61. Shujaku	923	931	946	952
62. Murakami	926	947		967
63. Reizei	950	968	969	1011
64. En-yū	959	970	984	991
65. Kwazan	980	987		1011
66. Ichijō	968	985	986	1008
67. Sanjō	976	1012	1016	1017
68. Go-Ichijō	1008	1017		1036
69. Go-Shujaku	1009	1037		1045
70. Go-Reizei	1025	1046		1068
71. Go-Sanjō	1034	1069	1072	1073
72. Shirakawa	1053	1073	1086	1129
73. Horikawa	1078	1087		1107
74. Toba	1103	1108	1123	1156
75. Sutoku	1119	1124	1141	1164
76. Konoe	1139	1142		1155
77. Go-Shirakawa	1127	1156	1158	1192
78. Nijō	1143	1159		1165
79. Rokujō	1164	1166	1168	1176
80. Takakura	1161	1169	1180	1181
81. Antoku	1178	1181	1183	1185
82. Go-Toba	1179	1184	1198	1239
83. Tsuchimakado	1195	1199	1210	1231
84. Juntoku	1197	1211	1221	1242
85. Chūkyō	1218	1221	1221	1234
86. Go-Horikawa	1212	1222	1232	1234
87. Shijō	1231	1233		1242
88. Go-Saga	1220	1243	1246	1272
89. Go-Fukakusa	1243	1247	1259	1304
90. Kameyama	1259	1260	1274	1305
91. Go-Uda	1267	1275	1287	1324
92. Fushimi	1265	1288	1298	1317
93. Go-Fushimi	1288	1299	1301	1336
94. Go-Nijō	1285	1302		1308
95. Hanazono	1297	1309	1318	1348

* Empress

Posthumous Name	Birth	Accession	Abdication	Death	Posthumous Name	Birth	Accession	Abdication	Death
96. Go-Daigo	1287	1319		1338	109. Myōshō *	1623	1630	1643	1696
97. Go-Murakami	1328	1339		1368	110. Go-Kōmyō	1633	1644		1654
98. Chōkei	?	1369	1372	?	111. Go-Saiin	1637	1655	1662	1685
99. Go-Kameyama	1347	1373	1392	1424	112. Reigen	1654	1663	1686	1732
100. Go-Komatsu		1392	1412	1433	113. Higashi-yama	1675	1687	1709	1709
101. Shōkō	1401	1413		1428	114. Nakamikado	1702	1710	1735	1737
102. Go-Hanazono	1419	1429	1464	1471	115. Sakuramachi	1720	1736	1746	1750
103. Go-Tsuchi mikado	1442	1465		1500	116. Momozono	1741	1746		1762
104. Go-Kashiwabara	1464	1501		1526	117. Go-Sakuramachi*	1740	1763	1770	1813
105. Go-Nara	1497	1527		1557	118. Go-Momozono	1758	1771		1779
106. Ōgimachi	1517	1558	1586	1593	119. Kōkaku	1771	1780	1816	1840
107. Go-Yōzei	1571	1587	1611	1617	120. Ninkō	1800	1817		1846
108. Go-Mi-no-o	1596	1612	1629	1680	121. Kōmei	1831	1847		1867
					122. Meiji-tenno	1852	1868		1912

Northern Dynasty

Posthumous Name	Birth	Accession	Abdication	Death
(1) Kōgon	1313	1331	1333	1364
(2) Kōmyō	1322	1336	1348	1380
(3) Sūkō	1334	1349	1352	1398
(4) Go-Kōgon	1338	1353	1371	1374
(5) Go-En-yū	1359	1372	1382	1393
(6) Go-Komatsu	1377	1383	1392	

The 123rd Emperor,
His Majesty now reigning

* Empress.

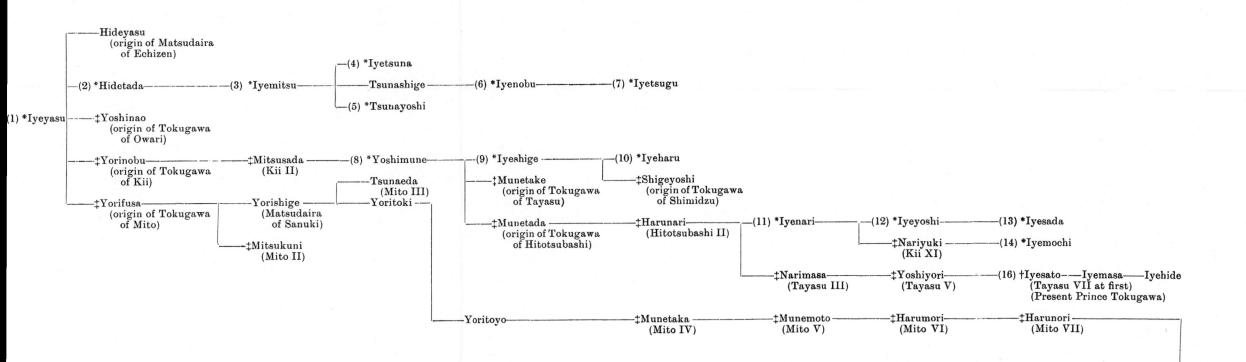

Hideyasu
(origin of Matsudaira
of Echizen)

(1) *Iyeyasu

(2) *Hidetada —————— (3) *Iyemitsu

‡Yoshinao
(origin of Tokugawa
of Owari)

‡Yorinobu
(origin of Tokugawa
of Kii)

‡Yorifusa
(origin of Tokugawa
of Mito)

—(4) *Iyetsuna

Tsunashige —————— (6) *Iyenobu —————— (7) *Iyetsugu

—(5) *Tsunayoshi

‡Mitsusada —————— (8) *Yoshimune
(Kii II)

Yorishige
(Matsudaira
of Sanuki)

‡Mitsukuni
(Mito II)

Tsunaeda
(Mito III)

Yoritoki —

Yoritoyo

—(9) *Iyeshige —————— (10) *Iyeharu

‡Munetake
(origin of Tokugawa
of Tayasu)

‡Shigeyoshi
(origin of Tokugawa
of Shimidzu)

‡Munetada —————— ‡Harunari —————— (11) *Iyenari —————— (12) *Iyeyoshi —————— (13) *Iyesada
(origin of Tokugawa   (Hitotsubashi II)
of Hitotsubashi)

‡Nariyuki —————— (14) *Iyemochi
(Kii XI)

‡Narimasa —————— ‡Yoshiyori —————— (16) †Iyesato——Iyemasa——Iyehide
(Tayasu III)   (Tayasu V)   (Tayasu VII at first)
(Present Prince Tokugawa)

‡Munetaka —————— ‡Munemoto —————— ‡Harumori —————— ‡Harunori
(Mito IV)   (Mito V)   (Mito VI)   (Mito VII)

‡Narinaga
(Mito VIII)

‡Nariaki —————— (15) *Yoshinobu
(Mito IX)   [commonly pronounced
                  Keiki]
                  (Hitotsubashi IX, at
                  first)

—Yoshihisa —————— Yoshimitsu

* Indicates Shogun.   † Indicates next in order of succession, but never reigned.   ‡ Indicates head of branch House.

To face p. 791.]

II.—LIST OF SHŌGUNS.

Minamoto (Kamakura)

Name	Born	Nominated	Abdicated	Died
1. Yoritomo	1147	1192		1199
2. Yoriie	1182	1202	1203	1204
3. Sanetomo	1192	1203		1219

Fujiwara (Kamakura)

Name	Born	Nominated	Abdicated	Died
1. Yoritsune	1218	1226	1244	1256
2. Yoritsugu	1239	1244	1252	1256

Imperial Princes (Kamakura)

Name	Born	Nominated	Abdicated	Died
1. Munetaka	1242	1252	1266	1274
2. Koreyasu	1264	1266	1289	1326
3. Hisa-akira	1274	1289	1308	1328
4. Morikuni	1302	1308		1333
5. Morinaga	1308	1333	1334	1335
6. Narinaga	1325	1334	1338	1338

Ashikaga (Kyōto)

Name	Born	Nominated	Abdicated	Died
1. Takauji	1308	1338		1358
2. Yoshiakira	1330	1358	1367	1368
3. Yoshimitsu	1358	1367	1395	1408
4. Yoshimochi	1386	1395	1423	1428
5. Yoshikazu	1407	1423		1425
6. Yoshinori	1394	1428		1441
7. Yoshikatsu	1433	1441		1443
8. Yoshimasa	1435	1449	1474	1490
9. Yoshihisa	1465	1474		1489
10. Yoshitane (1)	1465	1490	1493	
11. Yoshizumi	1478	1493	1508	1511
Yoshitane (2)		1508	1521	1522
12. Yoshiharu	1510	1521	1545	1550
13. Yoshiteru	1535	1545		1565
14. Yoshihide	1564	1568		1568
15. Yoshiaki	1537	1568	1573	1597

Tokugawa (Yedo)

Name	Born	Nominated	Abdicated	Died
1. Ieyasu	1542	1603	1605	1616
2. Hidetada	1579	1605	1623	1632
3. Iemitsu	1604	1623		1651
4. Ietsuna	1641	1651		1680
5. Tsunayoshi	1646	1680		1709
6. Ienobu	1662	1709		1712
7. Ietsugu	1709	1712		1716
8. Yoshimune	1684	1716	1745	1751
9. Ieshige	1711	1745	1760	1761
10. Ieharu	1737	1760		1786
11. Ienari	1773	1786	1837	1841
12. Ieyoshi	1793	1837		1853
13. Iesada	1824	1853		1858
14. Iemochi	1846	1858		1866
15. Keiki	1837	1866	1868	

III.—LIST OF YEAR-NAMES OR NENGO.

Taikwa	645–650	Chōgen	1028–1037	Kempo	1213–1219
Hakuchi	650–655	Chōryaku	1037–1040	Shōkyō	1219–1222
....	....	Chōkyū	1040–1044	Tei-ō	1222–1224
Sujaku	672	Kwantoku	1044–1046	Gennin	1224–1225
Hakuhō	673–686	Eishō	1046–1053	Karoku	1225–1227
Shuchō	686–701	Tenki	1053–1058	Antei	1227–1229
Taihō	701–704	Kōhei	1058–1065	Kwanki	1229–1232
Keiun	704–708	Chiryaku	1065–1069	Tei-i	1232–1233
Wadō	708–715	Enkyū	1069–1074	Tempuku	1232–1234
Reiki	715–717	Shōhō	1074–1077	Bunryaku	1234–1235
Yōrō	717–724	Shōryaku	1077–1081	Katei	1235–1238
Shinki	724–729	Eihō	1081–1084	Ryakunin	1238–1239
Tempyō	729–749	Ōtoku	1084–1087	En-ō	1239–1240
Tempyō-shōhō	749–757	Kwanji	1087–1094	Ninji	1240–1243
Tempyō-hōji	757–765	Kahō	1094–1096	Kwangen	1243–1247
Tempyō-jingo	765–767	Eichō	1096–1097	Hōji	1247–1249
Jingo-keiun	767–770	Shōtoku	1097–1099	Kenchō	1249–1256
Hoki	770–781	Kōwa	1099–1104	Kōgen	1256–1257
Ten-ō	781–782	Choji	1104–1106	Shōka	1257–1259
Enryaku	782–806	Kashō	1106–1108	Shōgen	1259–1260
Daidō	806–810	Tennin	1108–1110	Bun-ō	1260–1261
Kōnin	810–824	Ten-ei	1110–1113	Kōchō	1261–1264
Tenchō	824–834	Eikyū	1113–1118	Bun-ei	1264–1275
Shōwa	834–848	Gwan-ei	1118–1120	Kenji	1275–1278
Kashō	848–851	Hōan	1120–1124	Kōan	1278–1288
Ninju	851–854	Tenji	1124–1126	Shōō	1288–1293
Seikō	854–857	Taiji	1126–1131	Einin	1293–1299
Ten-an	857–859	Tenshō	1131–1132	Shōan	1299–1302
Jōkwan	859–877	Chōshō	1132–1135	Kengen	1302–1303
Genkei	877–885	Hōen	1135–1141	Kagen	1303–1306
Ninwa	885–889	Eiji	1141–1142	Tokuji	1306–1309
Kwampyō	889–898	Kōji	1142–1144	Enkei	1309–1311
Shōtai	898–901	Ten-yō	1144–1145	Ōchō	1311–1312
Engi	901–923	Kyūan	1145–1151	Shōwa	1312–1317
Enchō	923–931	Nimpyō	1151–1154	Bumpō	1317–1319
Shohyo	931–938	Kyūju	1154–1156	Gen-ō	1319–1321
Tenkei	938–947	Hōgen	1156–1159	Genkyō	1321–1324
Tenryaku	947–957	Heiji	1159–1160	Shōchū	1324–1326
Tentoku	957–961	Eiryaku	1160–1161	Kareki	1326–1329
Ōwa	961–964	Ōhō	1161–1163	Gentoku	1329–1331
Kōhō	964–968	Chōkwan	1163–1165	Genkō	1331–1334
Anwa	968–970	Eiman	1165–1166	Kemmu	1334–1336
Tenroku	970–973	Nin-an	1166–1169	Engen	1336–1340
Ten-en	973–976	Kaō	1169–1171	Kōkoku	1340–1346
Teigen	976–978	Shōan	1171–1175	Shōhei	1346–1370
Tengen	978–983	Angen	1175–1177	Kentoku	1370–1372
Eikwan	983–985	Jishō	1177–1181	Bunchō	1372–1375
Kwanwa	985–987	Yōwa	1181–1182	Tenju	1375–1381
Eien	987–989	Juei	1181–1184	Kōwa	1381–1384
Eiso	989–990	Gwanryaku	1184–1185	Genchū	1384–1393
Shōryaku	990–995	Bunji	1185–1190		
Chōtoku	995–999	Kenkyū	1190–1199	**Northern Dynasty**	
Chōhō	999–1004	Shōji	1199–1201		
Kwankō	1004–1012	Kennin	1201–1104		
Chōwa	1012–1017	Genkyū	1204–1206	Ryaku-ō	1338–1342
Kwannin	1017–1021	Ken-ei	1206–1207	Kōei	1342–1345
Chian	1021–1024	Shōgen	1207–1211	Teiwa	1345–1350
Manju	1024–1028	Kenryaku	1211–1213	Kwan-ō	1350–1352

Bunwa	1352–1356	Ōnin	1467–1469	Genroku	1688–1704
Embun	1356–1361	Bummei	1469–1487	Hōei	1704–1711
Kōan	1361–1362	Chōkyō	1487–1489	Shōtoku	1711–1716
Jōji	1362–1368	Entoku	1489–1492	Kōhō	1716–1736
Ō-an	1368–1375	Meiō	1492–1501	Gembun	1736–1741
Eiwa	1375–1379	Bunki	1501–1504	Kwampō	1741–1744
Kōryaku	1379–1381	Eishō	1504–1521	Eikyō	1744–1748
Eitoku	1381–1384	Tai-ei	1521–1528	Kwan-en	1748–1751
Shitoku	1384–1387	Kyōroku	1528–1532	Hōreki	1751–1764
Kakei	1387–1389	Tembun	1532–1555	Meiwa	1764–1772
Kōō	1389–1390	Kōji	1555–1558	An-ei	1772–1781
Meitoku	1390–1393	Eiroku	1558–1570	Temmei	1781–1789
		Genki	1570–1573	Kwansei	1789–1801
		Tenshō	1573–1592	Kyōwa	1801–1804
		Bunroku	1592–1596	Bunkwa	1804–1818
Meitoku	1393–1394	Keichō	1596–1615	Bunsei	1818–1830
Ō-ei	1394–1428	Genwa	1615–1624	Tempū	1830–1844
Shōchō	1428–1429	Kwan-ei	1624–1644	Kōkwa	1844–1848
Eikyō	1429–1441	Shōhō	1644–1648	Kaei	1848–1854
Kakitsu	1441–1444	Keian	1648–1652	Ansei	1854–1860
Bun-an	1444–1449	Shōō	1652–1655	Men-en	1860–1861
Hōtoku	1449–1452	Meireki	1655–1658	Bunkyū	1861–1864
Kyōtoku	1452–1455	Manji	1658–1661	Gwanji	1864–1865
Kōshō	1455–1457	Kwambun	1661–1673	Keiō	1865–1868
Chōroku	1457–1460	Empō	1663–1681	Meiji	1868–1912
Kwanshō	1460–1466	Tenwa	1681–1684	Taisho	1912
Bunshō	1466–1467	Teikyō	1684–1688		

IV.—LIST OF PROVINCES

AND THE CORRESPONDING MODERN PREFECTURES

PROVINCES	CHINESE NAMES	PREFECTURES OR *ken*	PROVINCES	CHINESE NAMES	PREFECTURES OR *ken*
Go-Kinai			**Hokurokudō**		
1. Yamashiro	*Jōshū*	Kyōto	1. Wakasa	*Jakushū*	Fukui
2. Yamato	*Washū*	Nara	2. Kaga	*Kashū*	Ishikawa
3. Kawachi	*Kashū*	Ōsaka	3. Noto	*Nōshū*	,,
4. Izumi	*Senshū*	,,	4. Echizen	*Esshū*	Fukui
5. Settsu	*Sesshū*	,, , Hyōgo	5. Etchū	,,	Toyama
			6. Echigo	,,	Niigata
			7. Sado	*Sashū*	,,
Tōkaidō			**San-in-dō**		
1. Iga	*Ishū*	Mie			
2. Ise	*Seishū*	,,	1. Tamba	*Tanshū*	Kyōto, Hyōgo
3. Shima	*Shishū*	,,	2. Tango	,,	,,
4. Owari	*Bishū*	Aichi	3. Tajima	,,	Hyōgo
5. Mikawa	*Sanshū*	,,	4. Inaba	*Inshū*	Tottori
6. Tōtōmi	*Enshū*	Shizuoka	5. Hōki	*Hakushū*	,,
7. Suruga	*Sunshū*	,,	6. Izumo	*Unshū*	Shimane
8. Kai	*Kōshū*	Yamanashi	7. Iwami	*Sekishū*	,,
9. Izu	*Zushū*	Shizuoka	8. Oki	*Inshū*	,,
10. Sagami	*Sōshū*	Kanagawa			
11. Musashi	*Bushū*	Tōkyō, Kanagawa, Saitama	**San-yō-dō**		
12. Awa	*Bōshū*	Chiba			
13. Kazusa	*Sōshū*	,,	1. Harima	*Banshū*	Hyōgo
14. Shimōsa	,,	,, , Ibaraki	2. Mimasaka	*Sakushū*	Okayama
15. Hitachi	*Jōshū*	Ibaraki	3. Bizen	*Bishū*	,,
			4. Bitchū	,,	,,
			5. Bingo	,,	Hiroshima
Tōsandō			6. Aki	*Geishū*	Hiroshima
			7. Suwō	*Bōshū*	Yamaguchi
			8. Nagato	*Chōshū*	,,
1. Ōmi	*Gōshū*	Shiga			
2. Mino	*Nōshū*	Gifu	**Nankaidō**		
3. Hida	*Hishū*	,,			
4. Shinano	*Shinshū*	Nagano			
5. Kōzuke	*Jōshū*	Gumma			
6. Shimotsuke	*Yashū*	Tochigi	1. Kii	*Kishū*	Wakayama, Mie
7. Iwaki	*Ōshū*	Fukushima, Miyagi			
8. Iwashiro	,,	,,	2. Awaji	*Tanshū*	Hyōgo
9. Rikuzen	*Ōshū*	Miyagi, Iwate	3. Awa	*Ashū*	Tokushima
10. Rikuchū	,,	Iwate, Akita	4. Sanuki	*Sanshū*	Kagawa
11. Mutsu	,,	Aomori	5. Iyo	*Yoshū*	Ehime
12. Uzen	*Ushū*	Yamagata	6. Tosa	*Toshū*	Kōchi
13. Ugo	,,	Akita, Yamagata			

Provinces	Chinese Names	Prefectures or *ken*	Provinces	Chinese Names	Prefectures or *ken*
Saikaidō			**Hokkaidō**		
1. Chikuzen	*Chikushū*	Fukuoku	1. Oshima		Hokkaidō-chō
2. Chikugo	,,	,,	2. Shiribeshi		,,
3. Buzen	*Hōshū*	,, Ōita	3. Ishikari		,,
4. Bungo	,,	Ōita	4. Teshio		,,
5. Hizen	*Hishū*	Nagasaki, Saga	5. Kitami		,,
6. Higo	*Hishū*	Kumamoto	6. Iburi		,,
7. Hyūga	*Nisshū*	Miyazaki, Kagoshima	7. Hidaka		,,
8. Ōsumi	*Gūshū*	Kagoshima	8. Tokachi		,,
9. Satsuma	*Sasshū*	,,	9. Kushiro		,,
10. Iki	*Ishū*	Nagasaki	10. Nemuro		,,
11. Tsushima	*Taishū*	,,	11. Chishima		,,
12. Ryūkyū		Okinawa			

V.—THE LEGACY OF IYEYASU

[The following translation of the Legacy of Iyeyasu was made by the late Mr. J. F. Lowder, formerly H.M. Consul at Yokohama, and published at Yokohama in pamphlet form in 1874. It has never been published in England, and as the original edition has been long out of print, it is here reprinted,[1] with the consent of the widow of the translator, leaving out some chapters which deal only with items of administrative detail. The explanatory notes are by the present writer.]

THIS manuscript, consisting of one hundred chapters, was written by Toshōgu of Kunō, in the province of Suruga. It is contained in the Imperial depository, and may not be seen by any but the Gorōjiu, who profoundly secreting it even when within the precincts of the official residence in order to conceal it from the sight of others, shall reflect upon, and record it in their hearts.[2]

CHAPT. I.—It is necessary before all to apply the undivided attention of the mind to that which is naturally distasteful, setting aside one's own inclinations.

CHAPT. II.—Show special commiseration for the widower, the widow, the orphan, and the lone ; for this is the foundation of charitable government.

CHAPT. III.—Keep your heart pure ; and as long as your body shall exist, be diligent in paying honour and veneration to the gods.

CHAPT. IV.—In future ages, in the event of there being no direct successor to a dynasty, the Chief Councillors of Ii, Honda, Sakakibara, and Sakai,[3] will assemble in conference ; and after mutual deliberation and consultation, unbiassed by considerations of consanguinity or affinity, choose a fit and proper person, and duly insure the succession.

CHAPT. V.—The etiquette to be observed upon being installed as Sei-Shōgun, is to be patterned after the example of the Lord of Kamakura (Yorimoto).

The whole amount of the revenue of the Empire of Japan is 28,190,000 koku [of rice]. Of this, 20,000,000 is to be divided among the Daimiō and Shomiō, who render faithful service, and the remaining 8,190,000 koku form the public revenue, which should provide for the effectual protection of the Emperor, and for keeping in subjection the barbarians of the four coasts.[4]

---

[1] In "The Story of Old Japan", by J. H. Longford.

[2] This heading, which is that of the copy preserved in the Court of the Shōgun, is not part of the original manuscript. Toshōgu is the posthumous name of Iyeyasu, the name that is bestowed after death by the Buddhist priests. Kunō is the name of the temple near Shidzuoka in which Iyeyasu was first buried, prior to the erection of the great mausoleum at Nikkō, in which many people say that his remains still rest, only a hair of his head having been carried to Nikkō.

[3] The four leading Fudai Daimios ; Ii, the first named, was the ancestor of Ii Kamon no Kami, in whose family the office of Tairō or regent for the Shōgun was hereditary.

[4] Public revenue means the revenue of the Shōgun's Government, the chief duties of which were to guard the Emperor from danger, and to preserve peace in every quarter of the Empire. Rice was the standard of value, and one koku at that period was worth about fifteen shillings.

CHAPT. VI.—Although it has been said that ancient customs are to be preserved as laid down in the several articles of the laws framed for the military classes, these may be modified or supplemented as it becomes beneficial.

CHAPT. VII.—The Fudai are those samurai who followed me, and proffered me their fealty before the overthrow of the castle of Osaka, in the province of Sesshiu.

The Tozama are those samurai who returned and submitted to me after its downfall, of whom there are 86.

There are 8,023 Fudai cavalry-lancers. Besides these there are eighteen samurai of my own house, and five Guests of honour.

This division is recorded, that they be not regarded as all holding the same position.

CHAPT. VIII (Omitted).—Describes the castle at Yedo and its guards.

CHAPT. IX (Omitted).—Names the Fudai samurai who accompanied Iyeyasu from his ancestral seat at Mikawa, and directs that the members of the Gorōjiu shall be chosen from them.

CHAPT. X.—The Fudai Samurai, great and small, all have shown the utmost fidelity, even suffering their bones to be ground to powder, and their flesh to be chopped up for me. In what way soever their posterity may offend—for anything less than actual treason, their estate may not be confiscated.

CHAPT. XI.—If there be any one, be he Kokushi, Riōshiu, or Jōshiu, Tozama or Fudai—none are excepted—who shall disobey the laws, to the injury of the people, his territory or castle shall immediately be confiscated, that martial severity may be reverenced. This is a part of the Shōgun's duty.

CHAPT. XII.—In order to prevent any misunderstanding as to precedence among officers, of the higher grades of the same seniority, it is decreed that they take order according to the amount of their revenue. [This does not apply to the Gorōjiu and Wakadoshiyori.]

CHAPT. XIII.—The magistrates of the Civil and Criminal Courts are reflectors of the mode of Government. The persons invested with this office should be chosen from a class of men who are upright and pure, distinguished for charity and benevolence. Once every month one of the Gorōjiu should be sent unexpectedly, to inquire into their mode of administration ; or the Shōgun should himself go unexpectedly, and investigate and decide the case on hand.

CHAPT. XIV (Omitted).—Table of precedence among the officials of the Shōgun's Government.

CHAPT. XV.—In my youth, my sole aim was to conquer and sub-jugate inimical provinces, and to take revenge upon the enemies of my ancestors. Yuyō teaches, however, that " to assist the people is to give peace to the Empire ", and since I have come to understand that the precept is founded on sound principle, I have undeviatingly followed it. Let my posterity hold fast this principle. Any one turning his back upon it is no descendant of mine.

The People are the foundation of the Empire.

CHAPT. XVI.—The reclamation and filling in of new ground was originated in the time of Yoritomo ; and there are doubtless ancient regulations extant, bearing upon this subject. Petitions having in view the recovery of land should be taken into consideration, and no opposition should be made to them ; but if there exists the slightest objection, according to ancient usages, it is strictly prohibited to entertain them.

CHAPT. XVII.—In the absence of precedent, forbid the making of new ground, new water courses, and so forth, and framing of any new measures of what kind soever. Know that disturbances always rise from such innovations.

CHAPT. XVIII.—It is forbidden to alter a faulty regulation if, through inadvertency, it has been allowed to remain in force during fifty years.

CHAPT. XIX.—There will always be some individual of ancient lineage to be found living among the lower classes of district towns and hamlets. Such a one as this should be selected for appointment to minor official situations ; but care should be taken not to choose refugees and the like.

The import of this should be notified to the Tax-Collectorates particularly ; and also to Kokushi, Riōshu, Jitō,[1] and downwards.

CHAPT. XX.—The Daimiō and Shomiō of the Fudai and Tozama classes who do not hold official appointments, are divided into two halves. One of these is to reside in Yedo, until relieved by the other.

When relieved, they are to employ their period of rest in making a tour of inspection into the prosperity or adversity of the population of their territories.

Those on service should be entrusted with the various duties connected with the castle, and the protection of the outer enclosures. They should lend assistance in repairing rents and damages, in the erection of new buildings, and in extinguishing fires, and so on.

These duties are not exacted solely for myself or my house ; but for the Shōgun, whose duty it is to protect and defend the Emperor.

CHAPT. XXI.—The modes of commending virtue and rewarding merit are :

1st—Grant of name or title [often bestowed after death].
2nd—Spoken commendation.
3rd—Rank and Revenue.
4th—Official situation.
5th—Minor superintendencies.
The modes for punishing crime for the repression of vice are :—
1st—Branding (or tattooing).
2nd—Splitting the nose.
3rd—Banishment.
4th—Transportation.
5th—Imprisonment.
6th—Decapitation and exposition of the head.

---

[1] Jitō=lord of a district.

7th—Crucifixion and transfixion.

8th—Burning.

9th—Decapitation, and so on.

These rewards are to be bestowed and punishments to be inflicted only after a strict investigation into the merits of commendable or criminal conduct ; and although a notification to the above effect has been issued to the Courts of Law, particular pains should be taken to impress it upon their strict observance.

The infliction of the severe punishments of tying a criminal's legs to two oxen, and driving them in different directions, and of boiling in oil, is not within the power of the Shōgun.

CHAPT. XXII.—You should not hastily attach to your person officers of the higher grades who are ever ready and obedient ; nor should you precipitately dismiss the lukewarm. They should be attached or dismissed in a quiet way, after due consideration of the behaviour of each, and consultation with the Gorōjiu. Neither should be done in a hurried or inconsiderate manner.

CHAPT. XXIII.—It has been said of old, " Although advised on all sides to put to death, put not to death : but when all the people of the country advise capital punishment, inflict it only after reiterated investigation into the merits of the case in question.

" Though advised on all sides to confer reward, confer not reward ; but when all the people of the country advise the bestowal of reward, concede only after reiterated inquiry into the merits of the case in question."

The art of governing a country consists in the manifestation of due deference on the part of a suzerain towards his vassals. Know that if you turn your back upon this, you will be assassinated, and the Empire will be lost.

CHAPT. XXIV.—Although a person of former days deprecates the custom of fishing with divers, and of hawking, such sauntering for amusement does not entail a needless destruction of life. " The tribute offering, by noblemen, of the spoil of the hunt and of the chase to the Emperor " is an ancient custom among the military class of other countries as well as of Japan. It tends to render soldiers expert in the use of the bow, and in horsemanship ; and in times of great peace is beneficially remindful of the excitement of war. It is a custom which should not be discontinued.

CHAPT. XXV.—Although singing and instrumental music are not the calling of the military class, at times they expand the spirits, and relieve depression, and are delightful recreations in the joyfulness of great peace. In the first festivals of the years and months, these also should not be discontinued.

CHAPT. XXVI.—The successive generations of military chiefs of the family of Gen,[1] from Sadazumi Shin-no downwards, are enshrined

---

[1] The Minamoto family. Seiwa was the fifty-sixth Emperor (859–877) and Prince Sadazumi was his sixth son, from whom the Minamoto claimed to be descended. One of the Minamoto founded a branch family which took the surname of Nitta from its estate in the province of Hitachi. The branch again subdivided in later years into new families which bore the surnames, all of

at Momijiyama, in the Western Inclosure, for the repression of evil
influences, and for the protection of the shrines dedicated to ancestors
within the boundaries of the castle. Future generations shall pay them
the highest respect and veneration, and shall be diligent in sacrificing
to, and worshipping them.

CHAPT. XXVII.—I, although the offspring of Seiwa, and born in
the family of Matsudaira of Mikawa, was overcome by inimical provinces
and for a long time depressed and confined among the common people.
Now, I am thankful to say, being engirdled with the favour of Heaven,
the ancestral estates of Serata, Nitta, Tokugawa, and Matsudaira have
returned to me. Henceforth let succeeding generations venerate these
four families, and not depart from the teaching :—" Let there be a
careful attention to parents, and let them be followed when long gone."

CHAPT. XXVIII.—Reverting to the scenes of battle at which I have
been present during my career, there must have occurred eighty or
ninety hand to hand encounters. Eighteen times have I escaped with
my life from ten thousand deaths.

On this account I have founded eighteen " Danrin " (lit., sandal
groves, or temples) [1] at Yedo as a thank-offering. Let my posterity
ever be of the honoured sect of Jōdo (Buddhist sect).

CHAPT. XXIX.—With respect to the temple of Yeizan on the East
of the Castle in the Military capital (Yedo) I have received much and
repeated instruction from the late Daishi. Is it well that I should
not demonstrate my gratitude ? I have reverentially begged for him
the office of Preceptor of the first degree, and Chief Priest of Tendai
and have offered up prayers and supplications that wicked resentment
may entirely cease, and that the country and its households may enjoy
undisturbed peace and harmony.[2]

---

geographical origin, of Serata, Tokugawa and Matsudaira, and Iyeyasu was
entitled not only to use any one of the four surnames, but that also of Minamoto.
All the Kamon daimio (the daimio of the house and blood of the Tokugawas),
exclusive of the San Kei, bore the name of Matsudaira, and the name is largely
represented in the new peerage of the present day. There is an omission in the
translation here. The chapter concludes with the instruction that Tokugawa
should thenceforward be the distinguishing name of Iyeyasu's own family.
Momijiyama (Maple Hill) is part of the gardens of the castle at Yedo, now the
Imperial palace.

[1] These temples include not only those at Shiba and Uyeno in Yedo, but
others in other parts of the Empire.

[2] Yeizan is the temple of Toyeizan at Uyeno, destroyed in the last fight of the
war of the Restoration (vide p. 786). Daishi is the highest honorary title that
can be given to a Buddhist priest. Tendai is one of the great Buddhist sects.
This and the following chapter illustrate the far-seeing policy of Iyeyasu. The
legality of his office depended on the Emperor, who, living at Kioto, might,
though he was always closely guarded by Iyeyasu's own adherents, and though
all the territorial princes were forbidden access to him or even to visit Kioto,
sometimes fall into the power of, or, like Go Daigo, join enemies to the Shōgunate.
A prince of the Imperial family was therefore always installed as Chief Abbot
(or Preceptor) of Toyeizan, where he was always under the direct eye of the
Shōgun, so that, in either of the above eventualities, the deposition of the Emperor
and the installation of the Princely Abbot on the throne might be proclaimed
at once. When the adherents of the last of the Shōguns were finally driven from
Yedo in 1868, they endeavoured to put this policy in force, and carrying the Princely
Abbot at that time with them to the North, they proclaimed him as Emperor.

CHAPT. XXX.—The Preceptor will be a sufficient provision for the defence of the royal castle ; and in the event of the Imperial residence being assailed by inimical barbarians, he shall be elevated to the " Throne of divine blessings ", and the Shōgun shall aid and assist him in subjugating and exterminating them.

CHAPT. XXXI.—High and low alike may follow their own inclinations with respect to religious tenets which have obtained down to the present time, except as regards " the false and corrupt school " [Roman Catholic]. Religious disputes have ever proved the bane and misfortune of the Empire, and should determinedly be put a stop to.

CHAPT. XXXII.—The familes of Gen, Pei, Tō, Kitsu, the two families of Kan and Ki-Ariwara and Kiowara,[1] derive their names from the Supreme Ruler (Emperor). It would be no shameless thing if one among these, attaining to the military command-in-chief, although apparently possessing the necessary capability, were nevertheless a man void of knowledge and erudition to whom the path of wisdom and virtue is dark, all whose deliberations proceed from his own mind, ignorant of the military accomplishments necessary in a military man.

From time to time colleges should be instituted, where by self-exertion others may be stimulated and encouraged to enter, and receive virtuous instruction.

CHAPT. XXXIII.—The way to govern a country and to keep an Empire tranquil originally proceeds from the " Gate of Perfection of Wisdom " (Confucian teachings).

To endeavour to attain to literary or military perfection in any other path is like " climbing a tree in search of fish, or plunging into the water to look for fire ".

Reflect that this is the height of shallow-brained stupidity.

CHAPT. XXXIV.—There is always a certain amount of sickness among the population of the Empire. A sage of old, being grieved at this, established a medical code ; and although there may be proof, in the effectual cure of disease, that others have drawn from this stream, such should not be endowed with large territory, lest being in possession of landed estate they straightway become indolent in the exercise of their profession. A suitable reward should be bestowed upon them, adequate to the shallowness or depth of the cure effected.

CHAPT. XXXV.—By an ancient custom of the Empire, Niidono, the Spiritual Chief,[2] has the entire control of every particular connected with the physical study of the Heavens, and the management of the Spirits of the five grains. Should any one, however, set himself in opposition to the examples and precepts of the Military Chief of the Empire, there should be no hesitation or delay in punishing him severely.

Their subsequent defeat rendered the policy useless. The Abbot was subsequently known as Prince Kita Shirakawa. He forsook the priesthood for the army, became a distinguished general, and died while in command of the army engaged in the subjugation of Formosa after its cession by China.

[1] The families of Minamoto, Taira, Fujiwara, Sugiwara, etc., all claiming divine descent through the Emperor, or directly as in the case of the Fujiwara.

[2] The chief Shintō priest.

CHAPT. XXXVI.—All wandering mendicants, such as male sorcerers, female diviners, hermits, blind people, beggars, and tanners, have had from of old their respective rulers. Be not disinclined, however, to punish any such who give rise to disputes, or who overstep the boundaries of their own classes, and are disobedient to existing laws.

CHAPT. XXXVII.—A girded sword is the living soul of a samurai. In the case of a samurai forgetting his sword, act as is appointed; it may not be overlooked.

CHAPTS. XXXVIII and XXXIX (Omitted).—Regulate the number of Cavalry soldiers to be furnished by each Daimio in proportion to the value of his domains as assessed in the survey of 1592.

CHAPT. XL.—By a fortunate choice on my part, Ii Manchio-maru is created Commander-in-chief, and holds the " Golden Baton ". Honda Hehachiro is created second commander, and holds the " Silver Baton ". Murakami Hikotaro is created third commander, and is authorized to bear the " Paper Baton ". It is necessary that every samurai should know these particulars.

CHAPT. XLI.—The boundary lines of possessions held by samurai may not be varied or trespassed upon so much as a hair's breadth. In the event of disputes of this nature being referred for decision, the plan in the Civil Court should be compared with the Register, and the boundary line fixed. But if there should be any difficulty in determining the matter, an Inspector, a Chief Supervisor, and a Judge should repair to the place in dispute, and in the usual manner give their decision in accordance with the Register. In the event of such decision not being accepted, and one of the disputants making still further complaint, the place in dispute shall be confiscated, and the amount of the possessions of the appellant reduced.

CHAPT. XLII.—There is a difference in the ceremonies to be observed by direct retainers and secondary retainers of rank.

CHAPT. XLIII.—Parties fighting and wounding each other with sharp instruments are equally culpable, but should be judged according to the severity of the wounds inflicted. The rule of procedure on such occasions is to arrest the criminal party ; but at times it may not be expedient to trace him.

CHAPT. XLIV.—The strictest and most careful search shall be made for persons guilty of murder by stratagem, or with malice prepense— of poisoning for selfish purposes, and of wounding others while robbing a house—who, when found, shall be executed.

CHAPT. XLV.—The samurai are the masters of the four classes. Agriculturists, artizans, and merchants may not behave in a rude manner towards samurai. The term for a rude man is " other than expected fellow " ; and a samurai is not to be interfered with in cutting down a fellow who has behaved to him in a manner other than is expected.

The Samurai are grouped into direct retainers, secondary retainers and nobles, and retainers of high and low grade ; but the same line of conduct is equally allowable to them all towards an " other than expected fellow ".

CHAPT. XLVI.—The married state is the great relation of mankind. One should not live alone after sixteen years of age, but should procure a mediator, and perform the ceremony of matrimonial alliance. The same kindred, however, may not intermarry.

A family of good descent should be chosen to marry into; for when a line of descendants is prolonged, the foreheads of ancestors expand. All mankind recognizes marriage as the first law of nature.

This subject should be circulated, that it be not lost sight of.

CHAPT. XLVII.—A childless man should make provision, by the adoption of a child, to ensure the succession of the family estate; but it is not customary for a person under fifteen years of age to adopt a child.

An adopted son of the Emperor is called " Hom-miya "; of the Shōgun is termed Shōkun (heir apparent); of a Lord of a province is designated Seishi; of Hatamoto [1] and downwards is called Yōshi (adopted child).

The family estate of a person dying without male issue and without having adopted a son, is forfeited without any regard to his relations or connexions.

Nevertheless, as it is taught by the sages and worthies that the Empire is the Empire of its people and does not appertain to one man alone, in the event of an Infant on the point of death wishing to adopt a child, there is no objection to his being allowed to prolong his race in the person of one who is of age.

CHAPT. XLVIII.—In lieu of the practice which has hitherto obtained, viz., that of the Emperor in person making a tour of investigation to the several provinces for the purpose of hearing verbally from the Princes an account of their several administrations, let an Inspector be sent every five or seven years to the different provinces to examine into the traces of the behaviour of the Kokushiu and Riōshiu during their absence from Yedo. The inspection into the well-being or dissatisfaction of the peasantry, the increase or decrease of the produce, the repairs and alterations effected in the castles, and so on, are not to be discontinued.

CHAPT. XLIX.—The territories entrusted to the Daimiō, with the exception of the Kokushiu, shall not be perpetuated to successive generations. They should be interchanged every year, the territories being apportioned relatively. Should the territory entrusted to one Daimiō remain in his possession for too long a time, he is certain to become ungovernable and oppress the people.

CHAPT. L.—If a married woman of the agricultural, artizan, or commercial class shall secretly have illicit intercourse with another man, it is not necessary for the husband to enter a complaint against the persons thus confusing the great relation of mankind, but he may put them both to death. Nevertheless should he slay one of them and spare the other, his guilt is the same as that of the unrighteous persons.

---

[1] Hatamoto were a class of territorial gentry created by Iyeyasu, who occupied a position inferior to that of the daimio, but as landowners higher to that of the squires or retainers of the daimio.

In the event, however, of advice being sought, the parties not having been slain, accede to the wishes of the complainant with regard to putting them to death or not.

Mankind, in whose bodies the male and female elements induce a natural desire towards the same object, do not look upon such practices with aversion ; and the adjudication of such cases is a matter of special deliberation and consultation.

CHAPT. LI.—Men and women of the military class are expected to know better than to occasion disturbance by violating existing regulations, and such a one breaking the regulations by lewd trifling or illicit intercourse, shall at once be punished without deliberation or consultation. It is not the same in this case as in that of agriculturists, artizans and traders.

CHAPT. LII.—In respect to revenging injury done to master or father it is granted by the wise and virtuous (Confucius) that you and the injurer cannot live together under the canopy of heaven.

A person harbouring such vengeance shall notify the same in writing to the criminal court ; and although no check or hindrance may be offered to his carrying out his desire within the period allowed for that purpose, it is forbidden that the chastisement of an enemy be attended with riot.

Fellows who neglect to give notice of their intended revenge are like wolves of pretext ; and their punishment or pardon should depend upon the circumstances of the case.

CHAPT. LIII.—The guilt of a vassal murdering his suzerain is the same in principle as that of an archtraitor to the Emperor. His immediate companions, his relations, and all even to his most distant connexions, shall be cut off (and mowed to atoms) root and fibre. The guilt of a vassal only lifting his hand against his master, even though he does not assassinate him, is the same.

CHAPT. LIV.—The position a wife holds towards a concubine is the same as that of a lord towards his vassal.

The Emperor has twelve Imperial concubines. The Princes may have eight concubines. Officers of the higher class may have five mistresses. A samurai may have two handmaids. All below this are ordinary married men.

A sage of old makes this known in his Book of Rites, and it has been a constant law from of old to the present day.

Silly and ignorant men neglect their true wives for the sake of a loved mistress, and thus disturb the most important relation. In olden times the downfall of castles and the overthrow of kingdoms all proceeded from this alone. Why is not the indulgence of passion guarded against ? Men so far sunk as this may always be known as samurai without fidelity or sincerity.

CHAPT. LV.—It is a righteous and world-recognized rule that a true husband takes care of outside business, while a true wife manages the affairs of the house. When a wife occupies herself with outside affairs, her husband loses his business, and it is a pre-evidence of ruin to the house ; it is as when a hen is afflicted with a propensity to crow at morn, and an affliction of which every samurai should beware. This again is an assistance in the knowledge of mankind.

CHAPT. LVI.—The nine Castles, viz., those of Iwatsuki, Kawagoi, and Oshi in the province of Musashi, of Sakura, Sekiyado and Kogawa, in the province of Shimo-osa, of Takazaki in Kōzuke, of Utsunomiya in Shimōdzuke, and of Odawara in Sagami, are all branch-castles of the chief Castle at Yedo.

They may not be entrusted to the charges of any one but a samurai of the Fudai class specially appointed to the trust. They are outworks for the protection of the chief Castle.

CHAPT. LVII.—The two castles of Fuchiu and Kunō in the province of Suruga shall be intrusted to the guardianship of the Chief of the " Private Guards ". They are accessory to the principal castle.

CHAPT. LVIII.—The Warden of the two castles of Osaka in the province of Setsu, and of Fushimi in the province of Yamashiro should be a vassal of ancient lineage, and above the " Fourth Grade ". Certain of the " Guards " should be stationed there as resident guards. When war is made, one of these Castles should be the head-quarters of the Main Army.

CHAPT. LIX.—There are sixteen guard-houses established on the main roads and by-roads of the districts and provinces, some on the seashore, some inland, in order to prevent man or woman disturbing the public peace, and for defences of the boundaries of the state. The superintendence of these should be entrusted to a samurai of the Fudai class of ancient lineage, without regard, however, to his wealth. He shall see that the rules written for their regulation are properly carried out. Under certain circumstances not even a needle should be permitted to pass ; but on ordinary occasions horses and vehicles may go through.[1]

CHAPT. LX.—The protection of the Castle of Nijo [2] shall be entrusted to some reliable and trustworthy Fudai of good lineage, instead of to that of the Commander-in-Chief ; he shall be called " The Kiōto Representative ", and on all occasions of disturbance the Thirty Western States shall take their orders from him.

CHAPT. LXI.—The office of Prefect of Kiushiu has for a long time, since the time of Odono, been temporarily discontinued. This office

---

[1] From a very early period it was the custom to maintain barriers guarded by troops at certain mountain passes and other strategic points. Their original object was to guard against incursions by the savage Ainu into the Japanese colonies, but from the time of Yorimoto onwards, their sole object was to prevent treacherous communications between the Shōgun's Court in the Eastern provinces (Kuantō) and the Imperial Court of Kioto. The best known were Auzaka near Kioto (page 96) and Hakone (page 104). The latter was only abolished in 1871, and its remains still exist. A watch was kept here to prevent the wives of Daimios escaping from Yedo (page 213), and women proceeding to Yedo were also subjected to a strict search, lest they should be the medium of carrying treasonable documents. One curious result of this was a large number of barbers' shops in the town of Odawara, at the foot of the Hakone Pass, who drove a prosperous trade in re-dressing the locks of the ladies, dishevelled in the search to which they were subjected at the barrier.

[2] The castle used as a residence by the Shōgun when he visited Kioto—still existing.

should be entrusted on alternate years to the two houses of Shimadzu (Satsuma) and Nabeshima (Hizen).[1]

It is forbidden to give this trust to any other house for ever.

CHAPT. LXII.—In the inner enclosure, beneath the Castle at Yedo, there are twenty-eight curtained guard-houses ; and there are also twenty-eight in the outer inclosure.

The superintendence of the Inner Inclosure shall be entrusted to a Fudai, for the time being resident in Yedo ; that of the Outer Inclosure to a Hatamoto on duty at the time.

They shall be directed as a matter of course to attend to the guard-house regulations, and to see that the military weapons, swords, insignia, and all the implements of war are kept clean and in proper order.

CHAPT. LXIII.—The several duties about the castle to be performed by the samurai on duty, and the work to be done in connexion therewith should be well considered, and allotted in proportion to their revenues ; but they should not be appointed to high offices of state. Some three, four, or five of them should be set apart for the transaction of contingent official business.

CHAPT. LXIV.—Nagasaki, in the province of Hizen, being a port at which vessels of other countries touch, has dominion over three nationalities.[2] The administration of this place should be entrusted to the chief member of the Gorōjiu.

The resident guard shall consist of four chiefs from among the Fudai samurai, each in receipt of 3,000 koku upwards. They shall each be provided with a riding horse and foot soldiers, and are salaried officers.

CHAPT. LXV.—In the revolution of nature, lands, houses, mountains, rivers, and ferries become damaged and ruined, and considerable outlay is requisite to put them in repair.

A part of such expenses is to be borne by the neighbouring province in proportion to the number of koku it produces. This tax is called " Provincial thank-tribute ".

Yorimoto introduced this custom, taking example from the period of the sages ; the principle is by no means a selfish idea of my own. It is a custom which shall be observed by future generations for ever.

CHAPT. LXVI.—Regarding thoroughfares, both in Government territory and throughout the Empire, 36 feet is the proper width of the " great sea road " ; but including the trees on either side, it should have a uniform width of 120 feet ; 18 feet is the proper width of the

---

[1] Odono—more properly Ōtomo—was the family name of the Territorial Princes of Bungo, who were the greatest feudatories in Kiushiu, until their power was destroyed by Satsuma early in the last quarter of the sixteenth century. From the time of Yorimoto until then, they had continuously held an office which might be described as the Vice-Royalty of Kiushiu. Both Otomo and Satsuma were said to be direct descendants of illegitimate sons of Yorimoto. Nabeshima was the territorial prince of Hizen, one of the Kokushiu daimios, whose direct descendant is now the Marquis Nabeshima, and was some years ago Japanese minister at Rome.

[2] Japanese, Chinese and Dutch, the two latter the only foreigners permitted to reside in Japan.

" small sea road " ; but including the margins on either side it should be of a uniform width of 60 feet.

Twelve feet is the proper width of cross-roads and horse roads ; inclusive of the side-walks 30 feet should be the uniform width.

Six feet is the proper uniform width of foot-paths, inclusive of margins on either side.

Three feet is the proper uniform width of by-paths, and paths through the fields, inclusive of margins on either side.

On either bank of a river, where crossed by a ferry, there should be an open space of 360 feet or thereabouts.

Post houses have been established at intervals for the dispatch of public business, and are also of manifest assistance to foot passengers.

This is an ancient regulation, handed down from Oinos'ke, an ancestor of the Tokugawa.

CHAPT. LXVII.—The several taxes leviable on hills, rivers, seas and ports, should not be exacted irregularly. They should suffice for the current expenses of the Imperial household.

CHAPT. LXVIII.—Dwellings shall not be erected on ground under cultivation by husbandmen, as the growth of bamboos and trees round the walls is prejudicial to the crops.

When disputes arising from a question of new and old plantations is referred for decision, the test is in the height of the trees forming the enclosure of such plantation.

If they are seen to be three feet high, the plantation may be known to be an old one ; if they are not three feet high, the plantation is a new one, and the trees should be cut down, and the party in the wrong confined to his house for one hundred days.

CHAPT. LXIX.—If the boughs of large trees, in the immediate neighbourhood of villages in which the houses are built consecutively, become so large as to interfere with the drying of grain, or to interrupt the payment of annual tribute, in the first place the branches shall be cut off ; and if that is not sufficient the whole tree shall be cut down.

Overshadowing branches should be lopped off annually.

CHAPT. LXX.—Although there are many bad roads and bridges in the frontier villages of the different provinces, there is a great deal of carelessness and neglect evinced, and the consequence is great inconvenience to travellers.

The care of aqueducts for water in case of fire also is neglected, and water is allowed to stagnate in the drains, because it is not the business of any particular individual to look after them. And the deepening or filling in of the beds of rivers is overlooked as entailing trouble.

Circular instructions should be issued in the customary years from the Inspectorate, that such neglect cease to exist.

CHAPT. LXXI.—From of old the harmony between lord and vassal has been likened to that existing between water and fish. Ought it not to be so ? It is, indeed, no difficult thing ! If the golden rule, " Do not unto others that which you would not have others do to you " be so firmly grasped in the heart as not to be lost sight of for a moment, the force of example will induce inferiors to conform to this virtuous teaching ; and not only immediate attendants, but the population at large, will naturally flow smoothly along as water to its outlet.

CHAPT. LXXII.—My body, and the bodies of others, being born in the " Empire of the Gods ", to adopt the teachings of other countries *in toto*, such as Confucian, Buddhist, and Tauist doctrines, and to apply one's whole and undivided attention to them, would in short be to desert one's own master, and transfer one's fidelity to another. Is not this to forget the origin of one's being ?

Judging from a medium and unprejudiced point of view, a clear decision should be arrived at as to what is proper to adopt, what to reject. The delusions of witchcraft and superstitious arts should on no account be unquestionably accepted ; but on the other hand they should not be forcibly and obstinately rejected.

CHAPT. LXXIII.—Virtuous men have said both in poetry and standard works that houses of debauch for women of pleasure, and for street-walkers, are the worm-eaten spots of cities and towns. But they are necessary evils, which if forcibly abolished, men of unrighteous principles would become like ravelled thread, and there would be no end to daily punishment and flogging.

These separate characters are intended to suffice as a general basis to the law of the Empire ; but with regard to minute details affecting the inferior classes individually, learn the wide benevolence of Kōso, of the Kan dynasty.

CHAPT. LXXIV.—As a pattern for the house of Tokugawa, adjust your line by that of the Lord of Kamakura (Yoritomo) ; you may not adopt the fashions of other houses. Nevertheless, the tendencies of the Lord of Kōmatsu should not be entirely rejected.[1]

CHAPT. LXXV.—Although it is undoubtedly an ancient custom for a vassal to follow his Lord in death, there is not the slightest reason in the practice. Confucius has ridiculed the making of Yo. These practices are strictly forbidden, more especially to primary retainers, and also to secondary retainers even to the lowest.

He is the opposite of a faithful servant who disregards this prohibition ; his posterity shall be impoverished by the confiscation of his property as a warning to those who disobey the laws.[2]

CHAPT. LXXVI.—A knowledge of military tactics, and the art of managing an army, are nothing but necessary accomplishments in a leader.

---

[1] Kōmatsu, the posthumous name of Higemori, Kiyomori's eldest son, who died before his father, whose virtues and mercy were as prominent as his father's vices and cruelty.

[2] The compulsory observation of this practice was forbidden by the Emperor Suinin, and its voluntary observation was several times forbidden by edicts of subsequent Emperors. It still continued, however, and there were frequent occasions not only in Iyeyasu's lifetime, but afterwards, notwithstanding his drastic prohibition, in which vassals killed themselves on their lord's death. Daté Masamune, one of the most celebrated of the territorial princes, both during Iyeyasu's lifetime and in his son's, when on his deathbed, honoured his retainers by selecting those who were to follow him in death, all of whom committed *hara-kiri* when he died. On the death of Iyemitsu, the third of the Tokugawa Shōguns, two of the daimios, who must have been well acquainted with the legacy of Iyeyasu, also committed *hara-kiri*.

An ordinary man is like a manufactured article, he is not composed of many bodies. Every manufactured article has its own separate use, and a hammer will not answer the purpose of a chisel, nor can a gimlet be used for the purpose of a saw.

In precisely the same manner, every individual man has a special use. Make use of a wise man's wisdom ; of a brave man's courage ; of a strong man's strength ; of a weak man's weakness ; of each, in short, according to his individual capability ; for just as a gimlet will not answer the purpose of a saw, neither will an ignorant nor a weak man answer the purpose of a strong man, and should therefore not be employed in his stead. The substance of this in inculcated as an incipient principle by the five virtues ; and the adoption or disregard of this principle tests the ability or inability of a chief.

In looking at the principle again as applied to men who are employed for purposes of war, unity of feeling among one another and mutual regard between high and low, will ensure peace and tranquillity in the Empire without having recourse to arms. This does not apply exclusively to times of war, but is equally applicable to all occasions.

CHAPT. LXXVII.—When military power becomes full to overflowing, even in the absence of all ambition, the proper veneration for the " Throne of Divine blessings " is apt to become blunted ; and there arrives a tendency, as has been demonstrated in the persons of so many of old, to remissness in respect, and oblivion of the origin of the " Kingdom of the Gods "—the source of self-desire is apt to overflow. Such a sin is not a light one, and will be undoubtedly followed by annihilation from Heaven.

CHAPT. LXXVIII.—The Shinnō and the several Miya, being related to the son of Heaven, should be treated with the highest respect. This immediately concerns the Shōshō. You should not set yourself in opposition to the Kugé, who by ancient custom come next in order. Impolite behaviour and a rough and indifferent manner are to be avoided.[1]

CHAPT. LXXIX.—There are five families whose heads are by custom Guests of honour ; and mindful of the circumstances on record from which this custom originated, your intercourse with them should resemble the mutual friendship of neighbouring states. The manners, customs and fashions of their houses are not under the care of the Tokugawa family ; nevertheless, if any one among them evince contempt towards superiors, or injure the people by tyrannical oppression, he should be immediately reprimanded. This is a duty of the " Barbarian destroying Shōgun ", and one which should not be delayed for a moment.[2]

CHAPT. LXXX.—With regard to the posterity of Owari, Kishiu, and Mito and the fifteen Kamon immediately following them, the

---

[1] Shinnō is the Prince Imperial and Miya are the other princes of the Imperial family. Shōshō (properly Sho-shi-dai) was the Shōgun's representative at Kioto.
[2] The five families were those of the five greatest territorial princes, who on their annual arrival in Yedo were entitled to the courtesy of being met and escorted to their palaces in the capital by a high officer of the Shōgun.

fortune descends to the eldest male child, and the revenue of their possessions shall not be divided among the remaining children. These last should choose some family of good pedigree and great wealth, and marry into it. The family thus allied shall rank only with the Kamon, who should receive them with amity. The thirteen families, however, may not become thus united.

CHAPT. LXXXI.—Daimiō with an annual revenue of 100,000 koku and upwards—the Gorōjiu, public officers, of the higher grades, and all Generals though in receipt of small incomes, are entitled to the same distinguishing insignia, etc., as the Lord of a province or a castle.

CHAPT. LXXXII.—The travelling *suites* of Fudai and Tozama, and likewise higher grades of officers, who may be on their way to assume their duties at Yedo, or returning from Yedo after being relieved, shall strictly observe the established rules. They shall not carry their flowery manifestations beyond the adjusted limits, neither shall they in aught detract from the regulations. They shall not disturb or harass the people at the post-houses, being puffed up with military pomp.

This subject should be impressed upon their attention by the Gorōjiu at the time of leave taking.

CHAPT. LXXXIII.—Regarding the charges for boats and rafts—men and horses, horse-hire, boat-hire, porterage, and so on should be regulated by the distance to be travelled, and weight by scale. This regulation should be made generally known to prevent misunderstanding.

The Horse-express, and Government Carriers, however, are not included in this regulation ; particular care should be taken to afford them every facility for speedy locomotion.

CHAPT. LXXXIV (Omitted).—Regulates the complimentary presents to be made by Daimio to the Gorōjiu.

CHAPT. LXXXV.—Among the many employés there will be some who flatter, adulate, and endeavour to bribe influential men having authority ; again there will be others, true men, who evince a grave and decorous respect towards their superiors.

The faithful and unfaithful are clearly apparent among these, and ignorance in distinguishing between them tends to degeneracy in the Government. Much reflection and grave consideration is requisite ; and a liberality in punishment and reward.

CHAPT. LXXXVI.—Regarding the erection of (temples called) " Ji-in " and " Sam-mon ".[1] At the time I established the " Sandal

---

[1] " Ji-in " means simply a Buddhist Temple or Monastery. Sandal Grove is the literal translation of the word Danrin, which is a fanciful term also for Buddhist Temples or Monasteries. Sam-mon means the front gate of a Buddhist Temple, but it is specifically used to denote Enriaku, the Temple of the Tendai Sect of Buddhists in Japan on Mount Hiyei, founded by the Emperor Kwammu (782–806), the first Emperor to establish his capital at Kioto, destroyed by Nobunaga in 1591 (p. 174), and restored, though with very diminished splendour, by Iyeyasu. The Tendai sect took their name from Mount Tien-tai in China, where their doctrine was first preached, and where the welfare of the Emperor of China was specially prayed for. Kwammu erected an exact replica of the Chinese Temple on Mount Hiyei, intending that the welfare of the Kioto Court should be specially prayed for as was that of China in the original Temple at Tien-tai. It was known as *the* Sam-mon, and the Abbot's grievance was, that Iyeyasu had extended the honourable term to the other Temples which he built in Yedo and elsewhere.

Grove ", an embarrassing remonstrance was made by the Chief Priest of the Sect of Tendai (Buddhist). He argued thus :

" My mountain is situated immediately under the Three felicitous stars exactly in the centre of the heavens, by permission of a former Emperor, who intended that it should give adequate protection to the Imperial Palace of the Empire. The idea was taken from the Tendai Sam-mon, instituted for the defence and protection of the Imperial Capital of another Empire [China] ; and for this reason the term Sam-mon can be properly applied to my mountain alone throughout the Empire of the Rising Sun. By what right does the Shōgun raise another Sam-mon ? "

On this occasion I was dumb before him ! But at last I found words, and replied that I had established it in perpetuity in order that the omniscient Being of Kinjo [Emperor at the time] might attain eternal longevity ! I at the same time made a reform in the nomination of the " Ji-in " throughout the Sixty-six provinces and seventy-three different temples came to be termed " Sam-mon ". A memorandum was drawn up, setting forth their number and situation, and sent to the chief temple of Tendai on the eleventh day of the fourth moon of the second year of Bunroku (A.D. 1593).

From the first, though cognizant of the law, I yet wilfully made an innovation. This should not be done.

CHAPT. LXXXVII.—The title of Sei-Tai-Shōgun originated in the person of Yoritomo, and the ceremonies observed on appointment are the bestowal of the " Sancho-no-Fuyétsu " and " Chingo-no-In ", and the grant of the " Sambo-no-Gōréi " by the Emperor.

This office is similar to that of " Shingi-K'wan ",[1] inasmuch as samurai employed under it to fill official situations, high and low alike, are required, upon the death of a blood relation, to retire into solitary confinement to purify themselves from contaminating uncleanness, in accordance with ancient custom. This custom should be carefully and circumspectly maintained.

CHAPT. LXXXVIII.—To neglect one's daily occupation in gambling and excess in wine to stupefaction, is to rob the clear day light ; and although to yield to this can hardly be pronounced an insubordination, it is a practice eminently calculated to have an evil effect upon the lower classes, eventually resulting in the destruction of their families and the extermination of their lives.

It has been well said that " To be a teacher and not to teach, is the

---

[1] Shingi Kwan—more accurately Jingi Kwan—was in former ages, the department of the Imperial Government which administered all matters connected with the Shintō religion, both Temples and ceremonies. The writer has consulted several Japanese friends in London, as to the other terms in this chapter, but in the absence of reference books and of the original Japanese version of the Legacy, none are able to explain or even translate them any more than the writer. Sanchō-no-Fuyétsu probably refers to a sword bestowed by the Emperor on the Shōgun at his investiture, though Fuyetsu strictly means battle-axe. Sambo-no-Gōréi probably means the orders or commands of the three precious things—Buddha, the Law, and the Priesthood ; and Chingo-no-In, the protecting palace, perhaps the castle of Nijō. The two last explanations are in the circumstances little better than guess-work as Sambō and In both have many meanings, varying according to the original Chinese characters with which they are written.

fault of the teacher ; but to neglect his teaching is the fault of the pupil." By this rule the severity or leniency of the punishment should depend upon circumstances.

CHAPT. LXXXIX.—When the four classes neglect their several avocations, they are reduced to hunger and cold, and eventually commence to break the laws, and vex and disturb mankind. These are serious crimes, and should be distinguished as capitally punishable.

Incendiaries, forgers of seals, poisoners, forgers of coin, all these ruffians are liable to the severe punishments of burning, exposition of the head after decapitation, and crucifixion and transfixion.

CHAPT. XC.—In cases of investigation, if public and martial intimidating power is properly directed, there is nothing between Heaven and Earth, in the distant abodes of the Barbarians throughout the four quarters of the globe, at the roots of the grass, or even under the earth, which cannot be brought to light. The only thing which is difficult to discover is the thread of the heart of man. Yoritomo adopted an ingenious plan of Sokutaku of the Daito dynasty,[1] and caused the Sotsu-hearts of the lower orders to be reflected by suspending gold and silver, or advertising rewards, on notice boards which were exhibited in the thoroughfares and streets of the capitals.

This custom is still kept up ; but it is to be feared that there is an indisposition on the part of samurai to respond to the spirit of this principle of reflection.

CHAPT. XCI.—When the Imperial mode of government is unclear the five grains do not ripen.

When punishments and executions abound in the Empire, it may be shown that the Shōgun is without the virtue of benevolence, and degenerate. Such crises should induce reflection upon past conduct and concern not to act remissly or carelessly.[2]

CHAPT. XCII.—When laws are made by the eminent and issued to the people, a nonconformity to the provisions of such laws on the part of the eminent engenders ridicule and opposition on the part of the lower orders.

It is no easy matter to make one's practice conform to what one preaches ; so that it is incumbent to face one's own self, and investigate each particle of conduct with grinding torture.

CHAPT. XCIII.—When a Kokushiu or Riōshiu of great wealth shall unwittingly commit a fault against the Shōgun, or in the event of a difference of opinion between them, it hardly amounts to a punishable crime ; but when it is of such a nature as not to admit of its being lightly passed over, instead of criminating the offender, appoint him some arduous duty, incommensurate with the amount of his revenue.[3]

CHAPT. CXIV.—The departure from life of the Emperor, the Imperial Sire, the Imperial spouse or the Imperial mistresses, or any

---

[1] Daito, an Imperial dynasty of China.

[2] The five grains are rice, barley, millet, sorghum and beans. Wheat is included in barley.

[3] This was the method employed by Iyeyasu, when he advised Hideyori to rebuild the Temple of Daibutsu at Osaka.

of the Imperial blood relations, are occasions of profound darkness, and great and ominous calamity for the whole Empire. In high antiquity on such occasions the eight sounds [1] were suppressed within the four seas ; and holidays and festivals on the 1st day of the year and months, the " Gosek'ku ", the feast of the first appearance of the Boar, and all kinds of festivals were observed in silence.

When an occasion of public mourning arises, a fixed term of mourning should be appointed for observance by the Ministers of State, the " Sanko ",[2] the Shōgun in office at the time, and by all Government officers ; during which every instrument that emits a sound, of what kind soever, shall cease.

CHAPT. XCV.—It is the duty of the Shōgun to provide the necessary expenses upon the accession of the Emperor to the throne, and for the " Daijoyé ". They should not be parsimoniously diminished in an infinity of ways.

CHAPT. XCVI.—On those occasions when foreigners come to offer presents, they should be entertained with proper abundance and uniform politeness. The beauty and elegance of the military accoutrements and the caparisons of the horses should be made to appear to the utmost advantage. From the port at which the ship arrives, as far as the Yedo capital, whether the road lie through Government or other territory, the castles and moats, and all the houses on the way should be in a thorough and complete state of repair, that the broad and extensive affluence, and the intrepidity of the military power of the Empire may shine forth. The whole management should be undertaken by the Ministers of the Shōgun.

CHAPT. XCVII.—When foreign vessels arrive by chance at our shores information of the fact shall immediately be given, and by means of written communication through an interpreter their business shall be learned. According to circumstances, they shall be treated with commiseration and benevolence, or with dignified reserve. In all cases a guard shall be placed on board for their restraint.

CHAPT. XCVIII.—The accessor to the imperial throne should look upon the people as one who nourishes an infant. How much more should the Shōgun to whom the Empire is entrusted cherish this feeling. The term applied to this feeling is " benevolence " ; and benevolence includes the whole of the five relations. Further through its practice the noble and ignoble become apparent.

I, having learnt this, distinguish between the attachment of the Fudai and the reserve of the Tozama ; nor is this discrimination at all at variance with Heavenly principles ; it is by no means a partial and one-sided idea of my own.

---

[1] The eight sounds included music, dramatic performances, street cries, etc. The Go Sekku were the five principal annual festivals. The last occasion of great public mourning was on the death of the Dowager Empress in 1897. All music, etc., was then strictly forbidden throughout the Empire for one month.

[2] The Sankō were the three principal ministers of state at the Imperial Court at Kioto, the Daijo Daijin, the Prime Minister, and the Sa Daijin and U Daijin— the ministers of the Left and Right. In Japan, the left takes precedence of the right.

I cannot particularly accord this for transmission to posterity by tongue or pen ; but it is a subject which will naturally develop itself if viewed with deep attention from a medium point between the two extremes.

CHAPT. XCIX.—When rewards and punishments are not properly administered, faithful servants are hidden, and not made manifest ; when they are properly regulated all mankind esteem the one and dread the other.

There should not be the difference of the slightest particle of dust either in excess or insufficiency ; but they should be administered with self-possession, and after deep reflection.

Confucius has exemplified my meaning in his " Comments on the Law of the Mind ".

CHAPT. C.—Since I have attained to my present office, I have increased and diminished the ancient examples of successive generations of the house of Gen ; and although I have drawn up these several heads of rules of conduct, my object has been to be a transmitter, not a framer. I have not allowed myself to be in the slightest degree influenced by selfish motives ; but have rather embodied the foregoing Chapters as an example, which, although it may not hit the mark, will not be very far wide.

In all questions of policy cherish precedents and do not give exclusive attention to small or large matters ; let this be the rule of your conduct.

There are further subjects I would bring under notice, but I have no leisure.

Let my posterity thoroughly practise with their bodies the particulars I have above declared. They are not permitted to be looked upon save by the Fudai-Gorōjiu. In them I have exposed and laid bare the limited reflections of my breast. Let no future generation be induced to ridicule me as having the heart of a venerable old grandmother.

I bequeath this record to my posterity.

LIST OF AUTHORITIES CONSULTED

Kaempfer . . .	History of Japan.
Griffis . . .	The Mikado's Empire.
Longford . . .	The Story of Old Japan.
Mitford . . .	Tales of Old Japan.
Walter Denning .	Wounded Pride and How it was Healed. (English Readers, book 5.)
Valentyn . . .	Deshima Diary.
Titsingh . . .	Illustrations of Japan.
Inouye . . .	Sketches of Tokio Life.
Zacharias Waegenaer	
Murray's . . .	Handbook of Japan.
Asakawa . . .	Early Institutional Life of Japan.
Aston . . .	Handbook on Japanese Literature.
Père S. le Gall .	Le Philosophe Tchou-Hi, sa doctrine son influence.
B. H. Chamberlain	Things Japanese.
Aston	Japanese Literature.
Brinkley . .	Japan. Vol. IV.
Dr. N. G. Munro .	The Coins of Japan.
F. V. Dickens .	The Chushingura or the Loyal League. A Japanese Romance.
Sir Rutherford Alcock	The Capital of the Tycoon.
Hulbert . . .	History of Korea.
Cocks . . .	Diary.
Dr. Nachod . .	Die Beziehungen der Nederlandischen Ostindischen Kompagnie zu Japan im siezehnten Jahrhundert.
Dr. Rein . . .	Allerlei aus Japan. Vol. II.
de Harlez . . .	Ecole Philosophique de la Chine.
Klaproth . . .	Translation of *Honcho Tsuyo Jiryaku* by Arai Hakuseki.
L. Deplace, S.J. .	Le Catholicisme au Japon.
Rev. W. Campbell	Formosa under the Dutch.

VALENTYN . . .	Oud en Niew Oist-Indien.	
MARNAS . . .	La religion de Jesus ressuscitée au Japon. Tome I.	
ASAKAWA . . .	Journal of the American Oriental Society. Vol. XXXI, part 2.	
UCHIMURA KANZO .	Japan and the Japanese.	
IKEDA	Life of Uyesugi Harunori. 1906.	
SIEBOLD . . .	Nippon.	
OYANGUSEN . .	Arte de la Lingua Japonica. 1738.	
ALVAREZ, S.J. .	De Institutiones Grammatica libri iii cum versione Japonica. 1593.	
RODRIGUEZ . .	Arte du Lingua de Japon. 1604.	
COLLADO . . .	Ars Grammatica Japonicæ Linguæ. 1632.	
ASTON . . .	Nihongi.	
MIHARU . . .	Biography of the Regent Matsudaira Sadanobu.	
E. PAPINOT . .	Dictionaire d'Histoire et de Geographie du Japon.	
HILDREDTH . .	Japan as it Was and Is.	
T. YOSHIMOTO .	Translation of Tomita's Hotoku-ki.	
THUNBERG . . .		
KLAPROTH . .	Annuales des Empereurs du Japon. 1806.	
Miss ATHERTON .	North American Review. May, 1909.	
GOLOWNIN . .	Narrative of his Captivity.	
RIKORD . . .	Account.	
S. WELLS WILLIAMS	Chinese Repository. Sept., Dec., 1837.	
E. SATOW . .	Translation of Kinsei Shiryaku. 1876.	
NAGAOKA . .	Translation from Takahashi.	
SIEBOLD . . .	Diary.	
NITOBE . . .	Intercourse between the United States and Japan.	
J. HECO . . .	Narrative of a Japanese.	
LANMAN . . .	Leading Men of Japan.	
GRIFFIS . . .	Matthew Galbraith Perry.	
,, . . .	Townsend Harris.	
WELLS WILLIAMS .	Journal of the Perry Expedition to Japan.	
BLACK . . .	Young Japan.	
. . .	Japan Herald.	
. . .	Japan Gazette. Jubilee Number, 1903.	
R. YOUNG . .	Japan Chronicle. Jubilee Number, 1918.	

TRANSACTIONS OF THE ASIATIC SOCIETY OF JAPAN

WIGMORE . . . . Vol. XX
McCLATCHIE . . . . . . Vols. II, VI, VII
MILNE . . . . Vol. VIII
SIMMONS and WIGMORE . . . . . Vol. XIX, Pt. I
J. C. HALL . . . . . . Vols. XXIX, XXXV, XLI
CLEMENT . . . . Vol. XXVI
E. SATOW . . . . . Vols. I, Pt. IV; III, appendix
Dr. KNOX and Mr. HAGA . . . Vol. XX, Pt. II
GALEN M. FISHER . . . . . Vol. XXXIV, Pt. II
Rev. ARTHUR LLOYD . . . . . Vol. XXXIV, Pt. IV
WALTER DENING . . . Vols. XXXVI, Pt. II; XLI
Rev. T. LINDSAY and J. KARN . . . . Vol. XVI, Pt. II
C. W. KNOX . . . . Vols. XX, Pt. I; XXIV, XXX
VAN DER POLDER . . . . . Vol. XII, Pt. II
WRIGHT . . . . Vol. IX, Pt. II
B. H. CHAMBERLAIN . . . . . . Vol. XVI
LONGFORD . . . . Vol. V, Pt. II
GARRETT DROPPERS . . . . . . Vol. XXII
Rev. R. C. ARMSTRONG . . . . Vol. XXVII, Pt. II
W. G. ASTON . . . . Vol. I, Pt. I
D. C. GREENE . . . Vols. XXXIV, Pt. IV; XLI, Pt. III
Dr. MITSUKURI . . . . . . Vol. V, Pt. I
Miss BALLARD . . . . . . Vol. XXXII
Dr. WHITNEY . . . . Vol. XLI

MITHEILUNGEN DER DEUTSCHEN GESELLSCHAFT FÜR NATUR UND VOLKER KUNDE OSTASIENS

Dr. SCRIBA . . . . Vol. XXIX
Dr. LÖNHOLM . . . . Vol. LIV

BOOKS IN JAPANESE

Azuma Kagami.
Tokugawa Jikki.
Oshiroboshu.
Taiheki.

Nihon Shiryo.
Kujikata Osadamegaki.
Ooka Seidan.
Yume Monogatari.
Genji Yume Monogatari.
Tao Teh King (Chinese).

WORKS OF

Hayashi Shunsai.
Rai Sanyo.
Kuranari.
Bakin.
Shirakawa Rakuo.
Rin Shi-hei.
Ikheda.
Otsuki.
Moto-ori.
Hirata.
Takano Choei.
Arai Hakuseki.
Ino Chukei.

SELECTED BIBLIOGRAPHY

BEASLEY, William J.: *The Modern History of Japan.* London, Weidenfeld and Nicolson, 1963

BENEDICT, Ruth: *The Chrysanthemum and the Sword.* Boston, Houghton Mifflin, 1946

BOXER, Charles R.: *The Christian Century in Japan, 1549-1650.* Berkeley, University of California Press, 1951

BORTON, Hugh: *Japan's Modern Century.* New York, Ronald Press, 1955

BRINKLEY, Frank: *Japan, Described and Illustrated by the Japanese.* Boston, J. B Millet Co., 1904

ELIOT, Sir Charles: *Japanese Buddhism.* London, E. Arnold, 1935

FEIS, Herbert: *The Road to Pearl Harbor.* Princeton University Press, 1950

GOWEN, Herbert H.: *An Outline History of Japan.* New York and London, D. Appleton Co., 1927

GROUSSET, René: *The Civilization of the East;* volume IV: Japan. New York, A. Knopf, 1931

HARA, Katsuo: *An Introduction to the History of Japan.* New York and London, G. P. Putnam's Sons, 1920

IKE, Nobutake: *The Beginnings of Political Democracy in Japan.* Baltimore, Johns Hopkins Press, 1950

JAMES, David H.: *The Rise and Fall of the Japanese Empire.* London, G. Allen and Unwin, 1951

KAWAI, Kazuo: *Japan's American Interlude.* Chicago University Press, 1960

KENNEDY, Malcolm D.: *A History of Japan.* London, Weidenfeld and Nicolson, 1963

LATOURETTE, Kenneth S.: *The History of Japan.* New York, Macmillan Co., 1957

LATOURETTE, Kenneth S.: *The Development of Japan.* New York, Macmillan Co., 1938

REISCHAUER, Robert: *Early Japanese History.* Princeton University Press, 1937

REISCHAUER, Edwin O.: *Japan, Past and Present.* New York, A. Knopf, 1953

ROGERS, Philip G.: *The First Englishman in Japan.* London, Harvill Press, 1956

SADLER, Arthur L.: *A Short History of Japan.* Sydney, Angus and Robertson, 1963

SADLER, Arthur L.: *The Maker of Modern Japan; the Life of Tokugawa Ieyasu.* London, Allen and Unwin, 1937

SANSOM, Sir George B.: *A History of Japan.* Stanford University Press, 1958-1963

SANSOM, Sir George B.: *Japan, a Short Cultural History.* New York, D. Appleton Century Co., 1943

SANSOM, Sir George B.: *Japan in World History.* London, G. Allen and Unwin, 1952

SATOW, Sir Ernest: *A Diplomat in Japan.* London, Seeley, Service 1921

STORRY, Richard: *The Double Patriots.* London, Chatto and Windus, 1957

STORRY, Richard: *A History of Modern Japan.* A Pelican book, 1960

TSUNODA, Ryûsaku: *Japan in the Chinese Dynastic Histories.* Editor: Luther C. Goodrich. South Pasadena, P. D. and I. Perkins, 1951

TSUNODA, Ryûsaku; DE BARY, William T.; and KEENE, Donald: *Sources of the Japanese Tradition.* New York, Columbia University Press, 1958

WALWORTH, Arthur: *Black Ships off Japan.* New York, A. Knopf, 1941

YANAGA, Chitoshi: *Japan since Perry.* New York, McGraw Hill, 1949

INDEX.